Theodoret of Cyrus: *Commentary on Daniel*

Society of Biblical Literature

Writings from the Greco-Roman World

John T. Fitzgerald, General Editor

Editorial Board

Number 7

Theodoret of Cyrus: *Commentary on Daniel*

Volume Editor
Richard Price

Theodoret of Cyrus:
Commentary on Daniel

Translated with an Introduction and Notes by
Robert C. Hill

Society of Biblical Literature
Atlanta

THEODORET OF CYRUS: *COMMENTARY ON DANIEL*

Library of Congress Cataloging-in-Publication Data

Theodoret of Cyrus, Bishop of Cyrrhus.
[Commentary on Daniel. English]
Commentary on Daniel / Theodoret of Cyrus ; translated with an introduction and notes by Robert C. Hill.
p. cm. — (Writings from the Greco-Roman world ; no. 7)
Includes bibliographical references and index.
ISBN-13: 978-1-58983-104-9 (paper binding : alk. paper)
ISBN-10: 1-58983-104-7 (paper binding : alk. paper)
1. Bible. O.T. Daniel—Commentaries—Early works to 1800. I. Hill, Robert C. II. Title. III. Series.

BR65.T753C6613 2005
224'.507–dc22

2005016905

06 07 08 09 10 11 12 13 — 5 4 3 2 1

The book is printed in the United States of America on recycled, acid-free paper.

For

Pauline Allen

President, International Association of Patristic Studies

Table of Contents

Acknowledgments

This volume on Theodoret of Cyrus appearing now in the series Writings from the Greco-Roman World, and others on Diodore of Tarsus and Theodore of Mopsuestia, will hopefully contribute to a greater appreciation of the way the Old Testament was read in Antioch. That, at least, is my intention and hope.

I am grateful to the General Editor of the series, John T. Fitzgerald, and to the Editorial Director of the Society of Biblical Literature, Bob Buller, for acceptance of this work. My appreciation is due also to Richard Price of Heythrop College, the University of London, for kindly acting as editor of the volume.

Robert C. Hill

Abbreviations

Aug	*Augustinianum*
BAC	Bible in Ancient Christianity
CCSG	Corpus Christianorum: Series graeca
CCSL	Corpus Christianorum: Series latina
CPG	*Clavis patrum graecorum*
DBSup	*Dictionnaire de la Bible. Supplément*
DTC	*Dictionnaire de théologie catholique*
FC	Fathers of the Church
GO	Göttinger Orientforschungen
ITQ	*Irish Theological Quarterly*
LXX	Septuagint
MSU	Mitteilungen des Septuaginta-Unternehmens
NJBC	*The New Jerome Biblical Commentary*
NS	new series
OCP	*Orientalia christiana periodica*
PG	Patrologia graeca
PL	Patrologia latina
RB	*Revue biblique*
SBLWGRW	Society of Biblical Literature Writings from the Greco-Roman World
SC	Sources chrétiennes
StPatr	Studia patristica
ThH	Théologie historique
TRE	*Theologische Realenzyklopädie*
WBC	Word Biblical Commentary

Introduction

1. THEODORET: HIS LIFE AND WORKS

Born about 393 in Antioch, Theodoret owed his name to grateful parents, who also had a hand in his entering monastic life at an early age. Since his famous predecessors in that school, if we may use the term,[1] John Chrysostom and Theodore of Mopsuestia—both pupils of Diodore of Tarsus—had been appointed to episcopal responsibilities, respectively, in Constantinople in 397 and in Mopsuestia in Cilicia in 392, they cannot have exercised much direct influence on Theodoret's formation. In 423 he was elected bishop of Cyrus (so named after the Persian emperor of that name), a city about 100 kilometers northeast of Antioch, perhaps "a little backwater"[2] yet a see with responsibility for eight hundred parishes, Theodoret tells us in his letters. Caught up in the theological turmoil of the time in the wake of the council of Constantinople of 381, he took an active part in representing the positions of the oriental bishops against those supporting Cyril of Alexandria on christological questions. His episcopal and civic duties, not to mention these theological concerns, did not prevent his writing many works of a dogmatic, apologetic and historical nature as well as commentaries on Paul's letters and most of the Old Testament, beginning with the Song of Songs about the time of the council of Ephesus in 431. He could make the claim to have produced works on "all the prophets, the

[1] Although we do find Johannes Quasten, *Patrology* (3 vols.; Westminster, Md.: Newman, 1950–1960), 2:121–23, speaking in a local and physical sense of "the school of Antioch founded by Lucian of Samosata" in opposition to the "school of Caesarea," Origen's refuge after his exile from Egypt, we prefer to use the term only of a fellowship of like-minded scholars joined by birth, geography, and scholarly principles, even if some members did exercise a magisterial role in regard to others.

[2] The term of Frances M. Young, *From Nicaea to Chalcedon. A Guide to the Literature and Its Background* (Philadelphia: Fortress, 1983), 267, who also concedes (268) the extent of Theodoret's pastoral responsibilities on the evidence of *Ep.* 113.

psalter and the apostle" in a letter written in 448[3] shortly before being deposed at the "Robber Council" of Ephesus, soon to be reinstated by Pope Leo and play a leading role in having the council of Chalcedon convened in 451. He died about 460.[4]

It is a moot point whether Theodoret's commentary on the book of Daniel should be listed among his works on Old Testament prophecy; his own principal assertion in the work, contesting the contemporary Jewish position, was robustly in the affirmative, and helped account for the book's continuing location in the Christian Bible among the (Latter) Prophets instead of being placed—more correctly—as a piece of apocalyptic among the Writings, as in the Hebrew Bible. For Christians, Daniel has historically been ranked among the "four (major) prophets," and it is the σκοπός of Theodoret's commentary to vindicate this placement by proving the book's prophetic character—a task for which he comes inadequately prepared by the ignorance of apocalyptic which he shares with his fellow Antiochenes. Instead, he claims the authority of Jesus, the other prophets and the Jewish historian Flavius Josephus as guarantee of the status of "Daniel the prophet."

2. CIRCUMSTANCES OF COMPOSITION OF THE COMMENTARY

It is an index both of the significance of Daniel and of the urgency of need to dispute the contrary, Jewish position on the character of the work that he comes to comment on it very early in his exegetical career (using this word loosely).[5] He turns to it directly after his initial commentary, on the Song of Songs, probably within a year or so, in response (he claims in introducing his later Psalms commentary) to those of his flock who "were anxious to have a

---

[3] *Ep.* 82 (Yvan Azéma, trans., *Théodoret de Cyr, Correspondance* [4 vols.; SC 40, 98, 111, 429; Paris: Cerf, 1955–1998], 2:202), written to Eusebius of Ancyra.

[4] For a somewhat more lengthy summary of Theodoret's life and works, see Jean-Nöel Guinot, "Theodoret von Kyros," *TRE* 33:250–54.

[5] Cf. the caution of John N. D. Kelly, *Golden Mouth: The Story of John Chrysostom: Ascetic, Preacher, Bishop* (Ithaca, N.Y.: Cornell University Press, 1995), 94: "Neither John, nor any Christian teacher for centuries to come, was properly equipped to carry out exegesis as we have come to understand it. He could not be expected to understand the nature of Old Testament writings."

close knowledge of the man of desires"[6] (the sobriquet for Daniel he finds in his version by Theodotion at 9:23; 10:11,23), though it is a commonplace of his—and doubtless many other authors—to cite an imaginary public clamoring for satisfaction. He begins by saying he has a double obligation to undertake the work, not only this popular demand but also the biblical injunction to teach the ignorant:[7] "It is not only the divine law that prompts us: many illustrious acquaintances also have made earnest supplication to us and obliged us to summon up courage for this contest."[8]

The precise date of composition is a matter of conjecture, depending on the Song commentary, which can be placed about a year before or after the council of Ephesus in 431,[9] at which he and John of Antioch represented the oriental churches. Some interval must have elapsed between these works, one would presume on psychological grounds, considering the utter contrast in the two styles of commentary—the earlier a remarkably spiritual interpretation in the manner of Origen of a unique opus in heated opposition to the historical approach of (it seems) Theodore,[10] the later by contrast a vigorous effort to force the haggadic and apocalyptic material of Daniel into just such an historical mould Theodoret had eschewed in the Song commentary. No author, no matter how flexible and "modéré,"[11] could easily and quickly pass from one to the other. A significant clue, it seems, is to be found

---

[6] PG 80:860.

[7] Theodoret cites Deut 4:9.

[8] PG 81:1257.

[9] I have discussed the likely date of the Song commentary in the introduction to my *Theodoret of Cyrus: Commentary on the Song of Songs* (Early Christian Studies 2; Brisbane: Australian Catholic University, 2001), 3–4, 15–16.

[10] The evidence for Theodore's having composed a commentary on the Song is not conclusive. His arch critic Leontius of Byzantium later informs us of his view that the Song should be excluded from the canon (*Contra Nestor. et Eutych.* 16 [PG 86:1365]), and according to Quasten, *Patrology* 3:406, the Acts of the fifth ecumenical council quote a passage from Theodore giving the historical interpretation that Theodoret explicitly rejects in his work (PG 81:29). But no such work is included in the catalogues of the Nestorian Syriac writers of the thirteenth and fourteenth centuries to whom we are indebted for sympathetic commentary on Theodore's works.

[11] The term used of Theodoret by Gustave Bardy, "Interprétation chez les pères," *DBSup* 4:582.

in the commentator's repeated remarks about the *pax Romana*, the Roman Empire being in his (misguided) view the last of the four empires of which the book speaks. He associates it with "submission, good order and the rule of law," and sees it continuing from its inception under Augustus until the second coming: "The Roman kingdom remained in power under him, and has lasted even to this day."[12] By the time of his Psalms commentary in the mid 440s, on the contrary, he has had reason for doubts as to its untroubled continuance, following invasions in 434 by the Huns and in 441 by the Persians.[13] A date like 433 therefore suggests itself for Theodoret's Daniel commentary.

Never forthcoming on the readership for whom he is writing in his commentaries, Theodoret does not specify it in this case, either. At one place he betrays the fact that his readers may be literate enough to access the works of Flavius Josephus which, in his historical approach to this work, he cites at some length; after quoting those works yet again on chapter eleven, he demurs: "In case I prolong the account excessively by narrating other events as well, I refer an interested reader to them." An intriguing feature of his opening commentary on chapter four of Daniel is its length, moral character and degree of scriptural documentation; after protracted development of the arrogance of Nebuchadnezzar, Theodoret concludes, "Lest in citing all the prophecies of him I prove obnoxious by their length, I shall, after referring the present listeners (ἀκούοντας) and later readers (ἐντευξομένους) to them if they want to learn of his conceit and cruelty, return to the matter in hand."[14] Is there an implication here that some of his flock in 433 are hearing this commentary directly from their bishop, while later ages will have the possibility of reading the text, as with his commentaries generally? Today's reader certainly finds this section atypically prolix and moralistic, as would be more appropriate if it appeared first in a homily.

[12] PG 81:1304, 1308.
[13] Cf. PG 80:978. Even in the Ezekiel commentary, which followed Daniel, he reminds readers of the invasion of the Huns, which allows us to date the work to perhaps late 434.
[14] PG 81:1352.

Theodoret's overall approach to his readers, however, does not parallel that of Chrysostom in his homilies to his congregations, with whom he engages in living intercourse.[15] He is scrupulous in respecting the limits of his role, being reluctant even as a pastor (we shall see) to apply the biblical text to his readers' lives; and he is likewise reluctant to comment on the society of his day. Such observations in this work, therefore, strike us as relatively more frequent: he remarks on the behavior of deranged people of his day in comment on 4:33, on taxation and widespread poverty as effects of imperial government (7:23), on titles in use in correspondence (5:10), and on the likelihood that the τακτι-κοί mentioned in his text at 6:2 for "supervisors" of the Persian satraps corresponds to the ὕπαρχοι more familiar to his readers.

It may also be of significance that, though the work begins with a lengthy preface, stating the commentator's principal σκο-πός as vindication of Daniel's prophetic status and acknowledging the work of predecessors, it concludes only with a brief peroration and doxology such as closed the other eight τόμοι into which it was divided (for reasons of length). There is thus none of the familiar appeals to the readers to make allowances for his shortcomings and reward him with their prayers, such as we find closing his works on the Twelve and the Psalms. We did not find such a conclusion in his previous work on the Song, either, though there his significant "preface" was clearly a postscript; and this may be the case here, or he may yet have to develop the rather stylized form of conclusion.

3. TEXT OF THE COMMENTARY AND THEODORET'S BIBLICAL TEXT

As is the case with most of Theodoret's biblical commentaries, while grateful for its survival in direct manuscript tradition, we are not yet in the position of being able to read the text in a modern critical edition. The editors of Sources chrétiennes, to whom we are indebted for producing such an edition of his Isaiah commentary, are currently occupied with the *Commentary on the Twelve*. For the immediate future, then, the text to hand is that

---

[15] Photius, *Bibliotheca* 172 (R. Henry, ed., *Photius: Bibliothèque* [9 vols.; Paris: Belles Lettres, 1959–91], 2:168), speaks of people interjecting during Chrysostom's homilies on Genesis, so that they should (he suggests) be called ὁμιλίαι rather than λόγοι.

of J. P. Migne's *Patrologia graeca* deriving from the seventeenth-
and eighteenth-century editions of available manuscripts. The
eighteenth-century edition of J. L. Schulze reproduced in PG
81:1256–1546 details the characteristics of manuscripts from
Augsburg and from Paris in particular, one of the former recom-
mending itself to him.[16]

In Theodoret's Bible the book of Daniel occurs, as previously noted, among the prophets and following Ezekiel, a
placement he vigorously defends. (His canon of the Old Testament, incidentally, seems to include 1–2 Esdras and 3 Maccabees,
but—as with his fellow Antiochenes—not Esther.)[17] The text of
Daniel in front of him comprises chapters 1–12, plus verse 1 of the
deuterocanonical story of Bel and the Dragon (but not Susanna).
Whereas he and his fellows at Antioch are reading the Old Testament in their local Greek version, which is normally that form of
the Septuagint known (Jerome tells us) as κοινή or "Lucianic,"[18]

---

[16] PG 81:9–14. Cf. *CPG* 6207.

[17] It is in dealing again at the beginning of chapter 9, as at the end of
chapter 5, with the nonhistorical "Darius the Mede" that Theodoret will quote
1 Esdras in the same breath as Jeremiah and Zechariah on the length of the exile.
Second Esdras had been invoked by him in the preface to the Song commentary
in acquitting the work of the charge on licentiousness on the grounds that Ezra
had recomposed it and the other Scriptures burnt by Manasseh or lost in the
Babylonian sacking of Jerusalem—a fact "the blessed Fathers were aware of in
ranking it with the divine Scriptures" (PG 81:32). Third Maccabees is quoted
in connection with the doings of Antiochus II (the Great) in comment on 11:7.
The appearance in chapter 5 of the queen, whom Theodoret takes as Belshazzar's mother, would have been likely to evoke a reference to Queen Vashti, who
played a similar part in Esther, had the book been canonical for Theodoret, just
as Theodore in commentary on Ps 66:2 would not have needed to cite from Josephus the text of Esther 8:14–17 if his Bible had contained the book.

[18] *Ep.* 106.2 (PL 22:838). Paul Kahle, *The Cairo Geniza* (2nd ed.; Oxford: Blackwell, 1959), 256–57, argues that a translation distinct from that of
Alexandria called the Septuagint was earlier developed in Antioch and was
revised by Lucian in the third century. In the view of Sidney Jellicoe, *The Septuagint and Modern Study* (Oxford: Clarendon, 1968), 160–61, Lucian's lack
of Hebrew relegated him to the role of reviser. Natalio Fernández Marcos, on
the other hand, *The Septuagint in Context: Introduction to the Greek Versions of
the Bible* (trans. Wilfred G. E. Watson; Leiden: Brill, 2001), 54, does not accept Kahle's proposal of a number of Greek translations like the many Aramaic
targums, though he refers to the LXX as a "collection of translations" (xi, 22).
Kahle, *The Cairo Geniza*, 257, cites T. W. Manson, agreeing (on the basis of
Irenaeus) that the text associated with the name Theodotion rested on an early

after the scholar-priest of Antioch who acted as translator or—
more likely—reviser, in the case of the book of Daniel it is the
version associated with the name of the earlier Jewish translator
Theodotion that they find as their biblical text in preference to
the LXX. At one place, 2:28, the text adopts a phrase found in the
LXX. At another, 8:2, where Theodoret finds Theodotion retain-
ing a transliterated Hebrew form (for "river") in its version, "I was
at the Οὐβαλ," he offers as a paraphrase "I seemed to be standing
at the gate (some translators rendering it this way)," thus revealing he is aware of the LXX's πύλη—but unaware that it is rather
Hebrew *abul*, "gate," that the Seventy are reading, his ignorance
of Hebrew being another exegetical limitation he shares with his
Antiochene fellows (and, in fact, all the Fathers but Jerome and
perhaps Origen).[19] He is thus not in a position to remark on the
unique feature of the book's survival partly in Aramaic (despite
his native familiarity with Syriac, a dialect of Aramaic),[20] partly
in Hebrew, or to note that the Greek alone includes the prayer of
Azariah and the hymn of the three (young) men as 3:24–90 not
found in the Aramaic section of our Masoretic text.

There are a half-dozen individual features of this local text
of his (noted below where they occur), but they are of no particular significance. In this work Theodoret is not concerned often
to question the accuracy of his version; beyond checking the LXX
in the above cases and at 9:24, he seeks clarification on rare occasions from other manuscripts, ἀντίγραφα.[21] Unlike his earlier work
on the Song, and later on the Psalms, here he does not look for
light from the alternative versions of Aquila and Symmachus, the
latter cited once only, on 1:3, where Theodotion had settled for
transliterating a Persian word (though in a similar case, on 11:16,

version made in Ephesus.

[19] Cf. Henri Crouzel, *Origen* (trans. A. S. Worrell; San Francisco:
Harper & Row, 1989), 12: "Certainly it would be wrong to credit Origen with a
knowledge of Hebrew like Jerome's, but he must have had enough to direct the
compilation of the *Hexapla*, even if the actual work was done by some assistant."
John N. D. Kelly, *Jerome: His Life, Writings and Controversies* (London: Duckworth, 1975), 50, traces Jerome's fluency to his time in Chalcis with a Jewish
convert.

[20] Cf. Pierre Canivet, *Histoire d'une entreprise apologétique au Vᵉ siècle*
(Paris: Bloud & Gay, 1957), 26–27.

[21] The verses in question are 6:3; 7:5, 25; 8:5.

he cites a version that we know from Jerome to be that of Symmachus).[22] His focus is clearly not so much on textual criticism as on the "historical" references in the text and their New Testament "fulfillment" that will endorse the prophetic status of the "man of desires." He is not inclined, either, to take refuge in textual inconsistencies or other evidence of interference with the text that suggest to modern commentators the hand of redactors. He does not consider the possibility that the prayer in 9:4–20 has been inserted, nor that the book closes with the stylized ending at 12:4, even when later editors' additions introduce different time spans that he is in some difficulty accommodating to his factual approach.

4. THEODORET'S σκοπός: TO ACCREDIT DANIEL AS PROPHET

Theodoret is instead clearly preoccupied with the status of this book, found in the Hebrew Bible but relegated there to the Writings, not having been listed among Torah or Prophets in the catalogue of Ben Sira 48:22–49:12 in the early second century (probably not composed by then, in fact).[23] Hence the urgency of his treating Daniel before coming next to Ezekiel, and well before his treatment of Isaiah and Jeremiah that concludes his exegetical career (apart from Paul and the *Quaestiones*). He is aware from the outset of the anomaly of the priority he gives to this book, addressing the matter early in the preface by citing again popular demand for commentary while also betraying that underlying concern, Jewish rejection of its prophetic status.

> Firstly, it is because our friends required of us commentary
> on this author, and we consider it a duty to give the petition-
> ers the favor they request. But furthermore it is the Jews'
> folly and shamelessness that causes us to pass over the oth-
> ers for the moment and expound this author's prophecies

[22] Jerome, *Commentariorum in Danielem* [CCSL 75A; S. Hieronymi Presbyteri Opera pars 1, opera exegetica 5; Turnhout: Brepols, 1964], 910).

[23] Cf. Otto Eissfeldt, *The Old Testament: An Introduction* (trans. Peter R. Ackroyd; Oxford: Blackwell, 1965), 520: "It can be clearly proved that the book derives from the period between the return of Antiochus IV from his second campaign against Egypt (167) and his death in April 163." The late date, of course, is a further reason for the book's failure to be included in the corpus of Prophets in the Hebrew Bible.

and make them clear, embarking as they did on such brazen
behavior as to cordon off this author from the band of the
prophets and strip him of the prophetic title itself.[24]

Theodoret honestly cannot understand how Jews can deny what
should be obvious to them of all people, how they "presumed
to place this divine prophet outside the prophetic corpus, despite learning by experience the truth of the prophecy."[25] The
other prophets cede pride of place to Daniel, he claims without documentation, "the Jews of old used call blessed Daniel the
greatest prophet," and Josephus can be quoted to the same effect;
and, for a Christian, Jesus personally clinches the matter by citing "Daniel the prophet" in Matt 24:15 in reference to the end
times. In fact, as we shall see, the citation in apocalyptic passages in the Gospels, the Pastorals and Revelation (mistakenly
read as confirmation of Old Testament prophecy) of the apocalyptic material in Daniel (mistakenly read as prophecy) is critical
to Theodoret's defense of the book's prophetic status. While the
promotion of Daniel ahead of, say, Isaiah—"the most articulate of
all the prophets," in Chrysostom's widely supported view[26]—is
testimony to Theodoret's (and perhaps his peers') sensitivity to
contemporary Jewish hermeneutical positions, his failure to recognize the haggadic and apocalyptic character of this book and of
similar material in the New Testament is symptomatic of flaws in
their exegetical formation, which will affect their commentary on
other biblical books as well.

If there is truth, then, in Theodoret's claim that he is responding to popular demand for explication in taking on the task
of commenting on Daniel, the urgent question he has to address is,
What is biblical prophecy? How is one to interpret it? He begins
at once by endorsing people's experience, that the prophets do not
yield to superficial reading, citing implicitly the sentiments of the
familiar saw from 2 Cor 3:6, "The letter kills,"[27] and he makes

---

[24] PG 81:1260.

[25] PG 81:1544.

[26] *Homily 2 In Oziam* (PG 56:108).

[27] Theodoret had already cited the maxim in justifying his departing
from Antioch's preference for the obvious sense of a text in his Song commentary (PG 81:37): "We do not take the text in the way that we read it, nor do we
rely on the letter that kills; instead, by getting within it, we search for the Spirit's meaning, and enlightened by him we take spiritually the Spirit's meaning."

a claim to a share for himself in the gift of interpretation, thanks to his betters. He proceeds straightway to pose the key question, putting it to Jewish opponents.

> For us to establish their brazen behavior convincingly, let us pose this question to them: what do you claim is typical of a prophet? Perhaps your reply would be, Foreseeing and foretelling the future. Let us see, therefore, whether blessed Daniel had a foreknowledge of it and foretold it.[28]

Theodoret has thus, as we would expect of an Antiochene exegete, adopted the concept of prospective prophecy, of the prophet as seer, of a tight relationship between prophecy and historical fulfillment, whether within the bounds of the Old Testament (a perspective Diodore and especially Theodore would prefer)[29] or extending to the New and beyond. And Daniel does not disappoint: the book begins by citing the "historical" data of Nebuchadnezzar's assault on Jehoiakim's Jerusalem: "This very feature, his mentioning the kings of the time and the dates, betrays his prophetic character, it being possible to find the other prophets doing likewise."[30] The case is as good as closed.

This, then, is what prophecy is about, this is what prophets do; and the book of Daniel, with its (apocalyptic) preoccupation with empires and "times" and obscure rulers, is the prime analogue of prophecy in the view of an Antiochene.[31] For all his

This is not quite the approach he adopts to Daniel, however.

[28] PG 81:1260.

[29] Cf. Christoph Schäublin, *Untersuchungen zu Methode und Herkunft der antiochenischen Exegese* (Theophaneia: Beiträge zur Religions- und Kirchengeschichte des Altertums 23; Köln: Hanstein, 1974), 84: "Jedes Buch soll aus einer bestimmten, vom Exegeten zu erkennenden geschichtlichen Situation heraus verstanden und gedeutet werden; diese Situation hat innerhalb der Grenzen des Zeitraums zu liegen, den die Schriften des Alten Testaments selber noch erfassen" ("Each book should be understood and interpreted on the basis of an individual historical situation that the exegete must discern; this situation must lie within the parameters that the Scriptures of the Old Testament themselves span" [my trans.]).

[30] PG 81:1260.

[31] Obviously not having been drilled in these matters, Theodoret (like Theodore) does not highlight for his readers a significant literary difference between prophecy and apocalyptic, as Eissfeldt explains it, *The Old Testament*, 150: "It is immediately noticeable that in the apocalypses the saying, the genre which takes up the bulk of space in the prophetic books, is entirely or almost

own warning that the "the letter kills," Theodoret proceeds to read the references off the page in historical mode, thus becoming embroiled like them in the hazards of such a literalist interpretation. By way of some acknowledgement of the alternative role of prophet as *nabi'* and not just seer, he will briefly concede that a prophet differs from a chronicler in not including all historical details—"only those things of which mention was required with a view to bringing benefit"[32]—and hence he explains the movement in the text directly from Nebuchadnezzar to "Belshazzar" in 5:1 without inclusion of Evil-merodach (in his foreshortened catalogue of Babylonian kings). Samuel, too, is cited in the preface as one who, "instead of exercising the style of prophecy of the other prophets," was still "the greatest of the prophets"[33] despite not reeling off kings and empires and battles and dates. And by the time Theodoret comes to Isaiah fifteen years later, under the influence of predecessors of another school he will accept that quite another dimension can be given to prophecy.[34]

In this first foray of his into biblical prophecy, however, the prophets are primarily concerned to give a precise forecast of the future (and precision, ἀκρίβεια, is vital to an Antiochene). If chapter 1 closes with the statement (in the way Theodoret takes it), "Daniel was there for one year of King Cyrus,"[35] the prophet meant to convey information as precisely as did the author of 2 Chr 36:22–23 (whom the commentator quotes in support) in speaking of Cyrus's reign. "It was not without purpose," he comments on this 1:21, "that he added this detail: he wanted to make clear the time of the whole prophecy. This was the reason he conveyed the beginning of the prophetic work and added the end of it, for us to reckon the years between the kingdoms and come to realize the whole period of the prophetic work"[36]—even if this makes Daniel

entirely lacking. The apocalyptists thus do not set forth divine utterances ultimately received in a state of ecstatic possession, and are no longer speakers, but simply authors. It follows that no saying of theirs could be collected."

[32] PG 81:1377.

[33] PG 81:1261.

[34] See Jean-Nöel Guinot, ed. and trans., *Théodoret de Cyr: Commentaire sur Isaïe* (3 vols.; SC 276, 295, 315; Paris: Cerf: 1980–1984). An English translation of Theodoret's *Commentary on Isaiah* will be published in the SBLWGRW series in the near future.

[35] PG 81:1281.

[36] PG 81:1281.

about ninety at the time and involves a contradiction with the time reference in 10:1.

Prophecy, then, has to square with history; the book of Daniel will therefore be supported in its "historical" statements by other biblical works and secular historians like Flavius Josephus. When at the close of chapter 5 the nonhistorical personage "Darius the Mede" comes on stage, Theodoret commences the following chapter with a very lengthy investigation into his origins (Mede or Persian?) in which he inevitably finds himself involved in errors and contradictions, finally insisting that he has got it right but is prepared for his readers to differ.

> This we found, then, by looking for the truth in each of the inspired works; let each person take a position on it as choice dictates: no harm will flow from uncertainty about race.

Truth, factual accuracy, ἀλήθεια, is vital to prophecy; biblical statement cannot contradict itself, prophetic "coherence" is a first principle.[37] What the commentator has to do is to show prophecy achieving fulfillment in πράγματα, τέλος, ἔκβασις. When 11:27–28 speaks of the campaigns of Antiochus IV in Egypt and their outcome, and of what Theodoret takes to be his religious persecution in Judea, he is pleased to be able to cite confirmation: "Both the book of the Maccabees and the account of Josephus report this."[38] He insists at the same time that, even though the other authors reported this activity of Antiochus as a past event, Daniel is speaking "in advance,"[39] a phrase recurring frequently;[40] prophecy *ex eventu* is not a possibility if Scripture is to be taken at face value. The plight of the young men recounted in chapter 3, their long

[37] Frances M. Young, *Biblical Exegesis and the Formation of Christian Culture* (Cambridge: Cambridge University Press, 1997), 182, sees Antioch rejecting the word "allegory" because it was associated with a tradition of exegesis "which shattered the narrative coherence of particular texts, and the Bible as a whole.... What we do have is an important stress on the 'reality' of the overarching narrative." Cf. Schäublin, *Untersuchungen*, 170: "Der Bezug auf die 'Realität', die ἀλήθεια, stellt aber die wohl entscheidende Komponente der antiochenischen 'historischen' Auslegung dar" ("Reference to the reality, *alētheia*, forms the firmly established basis of the Antiochene historical hermeneutic" [my trans.]).

[38] PG 81:1520.
[39] PG 81:1520.
[40] See, for example, PG 81:1445, 1448, 1513, 1520, 1521.

hymn and the prayer of Azariah (in the text of Theodotion) he pointedly declines to apply to those suffering persecution under Antiochus.

5. THE CHALLENGE OF APOCALYPTIC

What prevents Theodoret thinking of this text in other terms than prospective prophecy is that he (and his fellow Antiochenes) finds in haggadic tales and apocalyptic material something inimical to their understanding of Scripture. If all the Old Testament authors—with the exception of the sages and a mere chronicler, but including the psalmist—are προφῆται because inspired by the Spirit, then they are capable of more than mere reflection on the past or vague prognostications of a future still to be revealed. (Hence debate even among modern scholars as to whether biblical apocalyptic finds its roots in prophecy—the more widely held view—or in wisdom, with Gerhard von Rad.)[41] We find Theodore also having problems with the apocalyptic material he finds in the Twelve, such as in sections of Joel and Zechariah, and with recognizing apocalyptic motifs like the Day of the Lord. Theodoret will do little better when he reaches the Twelve and before that the apocalyptic account of Gog and Magog in chapters 38–39 in Ezekiel; here he fails to recognize the character of Daniel as a collection of haggadic tales in its first half assembled and retold by the author, and apocalyptic revelations in the second,[42] the overall purpose being to encourage Jews suffering persecution under Antiochus IV Epiphanes in the mid-second century—just as paleo-Christian and medieval art will adopt the motifs (in the Roman catacombs and on the Irish high crosses, e.g.) to the same

[41] *Old Testament Theology* (trans. D. M. G. Stalker; 2 vols.; Edinburgh: Oliver & Boyd, 1962–1965), 2:305–6.

[42] John E. Goldingay, *Daniel* (WBC 40; Dallas: Word, 1989), 322, in writing of the genre of the book classes it (on the basis of its second part) as "an apocalypse," explaining this decision thus: "Apocalypse as a genre of writing is now usefully distinguished from apocalyptic eschatology, a particular form of eschatological belief that can appear in writings of various literary forms, and from apocalypticism, a form of religious faith that can arise in particular social contexts and in which apocalyptic eschatology has a prominent place." Alexander A. Di Lella, "Daniel," *NJBC*, 408, identifies two literary genres in the book, "the haggadic genre and the apocalyptic genre."

end.

The sweeping scenario of the book, especially its reference to a range of epochs and empires and rulers, does not register with Theodoret as the stuff of apocalyptic. In fact, in his preface he appeals to it to validate Daniel's claim to prophetic status by comparison with Obadiah, Jonah, and Nahum, who trod a much smaller stage and are yet classed as prophets by Jews. Daniel's skill as an interpreter of dreams only qualifies him as a successor to the prophet Samuel (he says in the preface), not an apocalyptic seer. The temptation to take the variation in names from Daniel to Belteshazzar in the early tales as an index of a recycled miscellany is resisted. In particular, Theodoret has extreme difficulty with the numbers, a feature of apocalyptic; try as he may, he cannot get the "seventy years" and "seventy weeks" and "a time, and times, and half a time," to add up, one problem being that he does not see in the numeral seven a symbol of completeness. In chapter 9 he is at his wits' end, despite constant efforts to get the numbers to compute; but on first principles he cannot capitulate.

> Whereas some commentators suffering from unbelief think the holy prophets are at odds, those nourished on the sacred words and enlightened by divine grace find consistency in the holy prophets.[43]

For an Antiochene, prophetic "coherence" is at risk.

The result of this inability of Theodoret and his peers to grasp the nature of apocalyptic and recognize the material before them in the book of Daniel, preferring to see it as prophecy with a factual basis, ἱστορία, is that much time is spent by the commentator reconciling contradictory details and establishing historical accuracy—hence all the effort spent at the beginning of chapter 6 on identifying "Darius the Mede."[44] Unfortunately, the failure to identify genre affects interpretation of the New Testament as well. Daniel is extensively cited there, explicitly and implicitly, especially in equally apocalyptic passages, such as Jesus' eschatological

---

[43] PG 81:1457.

[44] Likewise in regard to the vision in chapter 10, Theodoret could never accept what Di Lella, "Daniel," 418, says of it: "The apocalypse has the usual purpose of guaranteeing the truth of the prediction of ultimate salvation by recounting in the form of prophecies what are actually past events."

discourse in Matt 24, the treatment of the antichrist (lit., "the law-less one") in the deutero-Pauline 2 Thessalonians, and the book of Revelation. The authors' purpose in these places, as always with apocalyptic, is to substitute for unavailable factual preci-sion the imaginative imagery and furniture of the end-times, like cataclysms, figures of good and evil, angelic messengers, final bat-tles, cosmic struggles, judgment scenes, divine triumph—usually to encourage the virtuous to endure under trial. It is critical, if these New Testament passages are to be properly understood, that historical realism is not presumed, and that borrowings of Old Testament motifs are not taken as confirmation of outcomes fore-known and foretold.

Theodoret, approaching Daniel as he does, is unwilling or unable to achieve this when acknowledging New Testament cita-tion of parts of the book. Doubtless influenced by his predecessors in Antioch and beyond, he sees the four empires that continue to figure throughout the book (today recognized as Babylonian, Mede, Persian, and Greek) as Babylonian, Medo-Persian, Greco-Seleucid and Roman. Daniel is thus thought to be looking forward to New Testament times, Jesus in his eschatological statements is taken to be confirming the prophet's forecasts ("With the Lord's prophecy corresponding to this prophecy, we shall be able to un-derstand the verses before us," Theodoret tells the readers of 11:40–45[45]), and the figure of Antiochus IV whom the author retrospectively meditates on becomes the future antichrist of 2 Thess 2.[46] Interpretation of Old and New Testament texts is thus clouded—a pity in one who always aspires "to bring obscurity to clarity," and who labors tirelessly to achieve it. In the view of one commentator on writers of this period, we are witnessing "a 'tam-ing' of apocalyptic in order to integrate it into a larger picture of a Christian world order, a 'history of salvation' culminating in the redeemed life of the disciples of the risen Christ."[47]

[45] PG 81:1529.

[46] PG 81:1533.

[47] Brian E. Daley, "Apocalypticism in Early Christian Theology," in *The Encyclopedia of Apocalypticism* (ed. Bernard McGinn, John J. Collins, and Stephen J. Stein; 3 vols.; New York: Continuum, 1998), 2:6.

6. THEODORET'S APPROACH TO COMMENTARY

Greater clarity was Theodoret's exegetical aim. This goal was conspicuously achieved in the case of the Song of Songs[48] for the reason that there he explicitly abjured an attachment to ἱστορία in dealing with lyricism. He repeats this goal here in the preface to Daniel, stating that he writes to "make clear to those in ignorance the inspired composition of the most divine Daniel."[49] His failure, we have seen, arises predictably from his unwillingness in this case to divorce apocalyptic from ἱστορία. It is not the result of perversity; rather, his Antiochene formation imposed hermeneutical blinkers on him, and in this case his predecessors had less to offer him than did Origen on the Song. He did, however, find grist for his mill in commenting on the prophets in the work of Cyril of Alexandria on the Twelve,[50] and he admits his indebtedness to predecessors in accepting the interpretation of the fourth beast enumerated in chapter 2 as the Roman Empire, which had been espoused by Hippolytus, Irenaeus, Origen, Eusebius, and Jerome:[51] "While we for our part have thus understood the meaning of the divinely inspired Daniel, therefore, we ought also give attention to the views of some commentators before us, which is the way for the truth to be demonstrated more obviously"[52]—a characteristic attitude of his in approaching the task of commentary. In adopting that more widely supported interpretation he rejects the view that his fellow Antiochene Theodore (it seems—if Theodore did

---

[48] Theodoret had set himself this aim, in obedience to his fellow bishop John of Antioch, in the Song commentary (cf. PG 81:212).

[49] PG 81:1257.

[50] Philip E. Pusey, ed. *Sancti Patris Nostri Cyrilli Archiepiscopi Alexandrini in XII Prophetas* (2 vols.; Sancti patris nostri Cyrilli archiepiscopi Alexandrini 1–2; Oxford: Clarendon, 1868; repr., Brussels: Culture et Civilisation, 1965). For Cyril's concern as a commentator with the historical context of composition and for the fulfillment of biblical prophecy in subsequent history, especially that of the Roman Empire, see Alexander Kerrigan, *St. Cyril of Alexandria: Interpreter of the Old Testament* (AnBib 2; Rome: Pontifical Biblical Institute, 1952), 294–345.

[51] So Guinot informs us, *L'Exégèse de Théodoret de Cyr* (ThH 100; Paris: Beauchesne, 1995), 715, also suggesting (747–48) that it is by way of Eusebius that Theodoret taps into the thought of Origen and even cites Josephus.

[52] PG 81:1305.

in fact compose such a commentary)[53] received from his brother Polychronius of Apamea, which would have proved more helpful: "I for my part am quite surprised at some teachers of religion referring to the Macedonian Empire as the fourth beast."[54]

As always, Theodoret comes to the sacred text with a conviction of the divine inspiration of its authors: "We know they are all instruments of the divine Spirit,"[55] he says at the opening. Not so ready as Chrysostom to comment on the divine considerateness, συγκατάβασις, manifested in the mundane language of the text, he is sensitive instead to the risk the readers run of infringing divine transcendence by misinterpreting its anthropomorphisms. He resonates with the warning of the heavenly messenger at the close of the work (an editorial embellishment, in fact) that the words are to be kept sealed and secret, paraphrasing it thus: "It was not without purpose that I said this obscurely and have imposed obscurity on the words like seals, nor should divine things be presented to everyone indiscriminately."[56] Like Chrysostom, he is happy to concede the relative obscurity of the Old Testament generally, and this work in particular, for the reason of the riddles, αἰνίγματα, contained there by comparison with the New Testament.[57] The implication is that the commentator/reader should bring precision, ἀκρίβεια, to bear while respecting the elevated character of the revelation—a lesson he sees Gabriel imparting to Daniel in 9:22–23:

> For your part, give precise attention to what is said; what will
> be said is too profound for a human being (the meaning of

[53] Cf. Jacques M. Vosté, "La Chronologie de l'activité littéraire de Théodore de Mopsueste," *RB* 34 (1925): 69–70, who on the grounds of the silence on the matter by Greek historians and council anathemas disputes the claim of Theodore's later Syriac champions to this effect.

[54] PG 81:1436.

[55] PG 81:1257.

[56] PG 81:1540.

[57] Cf. Chrysostom's two homilies on the obscurity of the Old Testament, critically edited by Sergio Zincone, *Omelie sull'oscurità delle profezie* (Verba Seniorum NS 12; Rome: Edizioni Studium, 1998), 74: " The Old Testament, in fact, resembles riddles; there is much difficulty in it, and its books are hard to grasp, whereas the New is clearer and easier" (my trans.). See also Robert C. Hill, "Chrysostom on the Obscurity of the Old Testament," *OCP* 67 (2001) 371–83; and *St. John Chrysostom: Old Testament Homilies* (3 vols.; Brookline, Mass.: Holy Cross Orthodox Press, 2003), 3:1–51.

xxviii THEODORET: *COMMENTARY ON DANIEL*

understand what is in the vision), that is, what will be said is
in riddles, and requires of you precise attention for grasping
it. Now, riddles occur when divine realities are spoken and
written, the purpose being to prevent what is revealed to the
holy ones becoming clear to everyone; after all, familiarity
breeds contempt.[58]

That is Antioch's first rule of commentary, "Give precise attention
to what is said," and Theodoret obeys it faithfully—overly so, in
light of the genre. All the details of an apocalyptic composition are
seized upon; he notes, for instance, that Nebuchadnezzar's dream
comes in the second year of his reign (2:1), the author "adding this
further detail not without purpose, but for us to get a precise grasp
of the time as well."[59] Likewise, when Daniel in his text of 10:3
claims to be fasting from "desirable bread" before the vision on
the banks of the Tigris, Theodoret seeks the reason why bread is
called desirable, namely, "its being nourishment for everyone alike
and more sought after than any other food"[60] by comparison with
the meat and wine also mentioned, the fare of the affluent.

If these are habitual features of Theodoret's commentary on
a biblical text, this book invites him to develop also a distinctive
approach. We have noted that he accepts it as a single, continuous, original work by one author; collection of previously existing
haggadic tales is not an admissible view, nor is editorial insertion.
The most he is prepared to admit is the difference in style after
chapter 6 between those tales and the ἀποκαλύψεις of the remain-
der; he comments at that halfway point, "Having recounted those
things as a historian (συγγραφεύς), as it were, he now begins to convey the predictions he learned about through the revelations."[61]
The language of the prayer inserted as 9:4–20 must have reminded
commentator and readers of the cultic credos of Deuteronomy, but
Theodoret does not allude to the possibility of different author-
ship. So, as will be the case when he comes to the book of Jonah,
he is faced with the anomaly of author being also central character.
It is not an issue he raises in the preface, but he is forced to address
it when the text immediately presents Daniel and the young men
in a favorable light: "He mentions their self-control and sound

[58] PG 81:1468–69.
[59] PG 81:1285.
[60] PG 81:1492.
[61] PG 81:1412.

values, not indulging in self-glorification but proposing a beneficial lesson to those prepared to accept benefit"[62]—so there is no
problem. We might have expected also from a commentator some
initial remarks on structure and the unique linguistic character of
the text Theodotion is translating, but these are not forthcoming.
The most he aspires to offer in the preface is, as usual for an Antiochene, "to make clear the theme (ὑπόθεσις) of the inspired work,
and then in this fashion come to the textual (κατὰ λέξιν) commentary."[63]

Comment on the language underlying the version before
him, we noted, is beyond him, though as elsewhere he is loath to
admit his lack of familiarity with Hebrew. When the "holy one"
in 8:14 indicates in obscure fashion the length of the persecution
as three and a half years, Theodoret claims that "calculated by the
Hebrew system" it amounts to six and a half years, thus losing the
significance contained in half of seven (which, however, he fails
to appreciate elsewhere, in any case).[64] He is put on his mettle in
particular in cases where Theodotion settles for transliterating a
Hebrew term, and the commentator is forced to look elsewhere for
enlightenment as to the term's meaning, as at 11:16.

> *He will make a stand in the land of Sabeir.* Some of the
> manuscripts have "in the land of Sabeim," while some of
> those turning the Hebrew term into Greek refer to the *land
> of Sabeir* as the "land of choice" (θέλησις), the meaning being
> the land of promise, which is a matter of choice, and Mount
> Sion, which God loved and chose to dwell on it. "Sabeim,"
> on the other hand, means "power." In any case, whether
> Judea is called land of choice or land of power (in fact, he
> called it *power* above, and here Sabeim or *Sabeir*), the king
> of the north will come into this land as well.[65]

At a loss before the Hebrew, he first checks a LXX version, finding
a Greek rendering θέλησις (correctly translating the Hebrew *sebiy*,
"choice"); but aware that another version (that of Symmachus, in
fact, Jerome tells us) offers "power," he boldly—without reference to the Hebrew—claims the meaning is "power," whereas this

---

[62] PG 81:1276.
[63] PG 81:1264.
[64] PG 81:1448.
[65] PG 81:1512.

XXX   THEODORET: *COMMENTARY ON DANIEL*

probably derives from a similar but different Hebrew form *saba'*, neither Hebrew form occurring in 11:7, as he claims. He is clearly not equipped for the task of exegesis strictly so-called, though his native Syriac helps him with another transliteration in 8:13 and a case of Semitic usage in 11:13.

Where Theodoret does excel as a biblical commentator is in his readiness (by comparison, e.g., with Theodore) to provide the background of his text for the benefit of his readers. And this work offers him ample occasion for assisting them: right from the preface he begins distinguishing kings of Judah that bear similar and alternative names that could prove confusing. In comment on chapter 7 he finds it helpful to outline for the readers the extent of the Persian Empire in biblical times as compared with his own day, and the divisions of Alexander's empire after his death; on 11:4 he informs them that, while the Persian rulers they are familiar with belong to the Arsacid dynasty, Cyrus came from the Achaemenids. As he will reveal in his work on the Psalms, an author's imagery is not lost on him, either, and he takes pains to unpack images for the readers, as he does at length with the *Benedicite* hymn of the (young) men in chapter 3. Though not recognizing the haggadic tales in the first half of the work for what they are, he responds to them as their original author would have intended, warming to their moral character. He gets so carried away with the trial of the three men by Nebuchadnezzar as to forget that, if time cues are to be respected, the "young men" must have matured somewhat after a couple of decades at the king's court. "Against him, by contrast, God sent in vengeance not an angel, as he did in the case of that fellow Sennacherib, but three young captives forced to live in a foreign land, pressed into service at this early age, in the very springtime of their lives."[66] Theodoret is not for spoiling a good story with the facts, for all his commitment to ἱστορία.

In his enthusiasm for providing background for the text, and despite his aspiration to ἀκρίβεια (a term meaning "precision," of course, not "accuracy"—though often so translated), he can blot his copy at times. The Bible has not helped him by telescoping the succession in the Babylonian monarchy, and by coming up with the mythical "Darius the Mede," a real thorn in his side. He has recourse half-a-dozen times to Josephus (through Eusebius,

[66] PG 81:1320.

Guinot suggests[67]) when the Bible, especially Maccabees, needs supplementing.

The Antiochenes in their biblical commentaries are not given to spending time applying the sacred text to the lives of their readers, even in the case of the Psalms; we need only refer to the treatment of a moving hymn like Ps 42 by Diodore, Theodore, Chrysostom and Theodoret, respectively.[68] Though the psalmists, like Daniel and his companions, find themselves in situations of trial and tribulation, and give vent to expressions that have appealed to the religious sentiments of people through the ages, Antioch is prepared to let them speak for themselves, the commentator being content with clarification. Theodoret will warm to the narrative of the plight of the (young) men, even embellishing it; but when it comes to their long hymn *Benedicite*, he is content to analyze the imagery, not to play spiritual director (perhaps presuming the hymn is familiar to them from the liturgy). As has been remarked, theirs is an "asceticism without mysticism."[69]

7. THEOLOGICAL ACCENTS

If Daniel is seen as a prophetic work by the commentator, its prophecy is not generally seen as christological in reference, even to the extent of the prophecies of the Twelve soon to undergo commentary at Theodoret's hands. It is as though only Jewish exegesis to the contrary elicits any christological elaboration here. The commentator does not, of course, bypass the figure of the Son of Man at 7:13, where he sees (in typically Antiochene dyophysite terms) Daniel "prophesying the second coming of the Savior, clearly calling him *Son of Man* on account of the nature he had assumed, *coming on the clouds* in keeping with his own promise to bring out his authority, and receiving as man *honor and rule and kingship* from the Ancient of Days."[70] But he does not elaborate

[67] See PG 81:1393, 1396, 1477, 1505, 1508, 1513, 1520 (2x), 1544 (Guinot, *L'Exégèse*, 748).

[68] Cf. Robert C. Hill, "Psalm 41 (42): A Classic Text for Antiochene Spirituality," *ITQ* 68 (2003): 25–33.

[69] A phrase of Louis Bouyer, *The Spirituality of the New Testament and the Fathers* (trans. Mary Perkins Ryan; New York: Desclee, 1963), 446.

[70] PG 81:1425.

on this identification. Likewise, when he comes to 9:24, "Seventy weeks have been determined for your people and your holy city for the fault to grow old and the sin finished," he cites a battery of evidently well-rehearsed texts to show that the reference is to the Jews' crime of crucifixion and to the forgiveness of believers by Christ the Lord.[71] The text to which most lengthy christological attention is paid is 2:34–35 mentioning "the stone hewn out of a mountain without hands being used"; after again rehearsing an arsenal of texts to confute Jewish interpretation, and borrowing the detail of the virgin birth from another source, Theodoret concludes, "So we learn from Old and New Testaments that our Lord Jesus Christ was called *stone*: it was cut from a mountain without hands being used, being born of a virgin independently of marital intercourse."[72] For Theodoret, Jesus' principal role in connection with Daniel is in citing the book in his eschatological discourses in the Gospels, as though this established its ἀλήθεια and Daniel's status as a prophet.

If Theodoret did not appreciate the purpose of the book of Daniel as encouragement of the Jews under persecution in the second century by the tyrant Antiochus, he relished its happy ending in the three (young) men's survival and Daniel's rise to prominence and esteem—an outcome in keeping with Antiochene morality. That Daniel should enjoy the confidence of the palace master on arrival in Babylon was only fitting: "Divine care is a consequence of our free will," comments Theodoret, "and once it opts for the divine commands, it enjoys divine assistance."[73] This priority given to human initiative over divine grace appears also in Theodoret's comment on the opening to Daniel's prayer that has been inserted into the text as 9:4–20: "He spoke of his *keeping covenant and mercy with those who love him* in recalling the promises to Abraham, Isaac and Jacob. Being very precise in his prayer, he mentions that he does not keep it with anyone, but with *those who love him and keep his commandments*: if someone transgresses your commands, he renders himself unworthy of the promises."[74] On the other hand, the commentator closes his

---

[71] PG 81:1472.

[72] PG 81:1301.

[73] PG 81:1277.

[74] PG 81:1458.

preface by begging for divine assistance in beginning his commentary.[75] Antioch can be ambiguous on the respective roles of grace and human effort in the moral life.[76]

8. THE SIGNIFICANCE OF THEODORET'S
COMMENTARY ON DANIEL

We would relish the opportunity to read commentaries on the book of the "man of desires" by all the major Antiochenes. Unfortunately, we have no guarantee that any but Theodoret completed such a work (Theodore's claim resting on uncertain grounds)—and this fact alone gives his *Commentary on Daniel* particular significance in the history of exegesis. Would all his peers have adopted the same tack that makes his so intriguing and annoying at the same time, and have allowed us to see them directly addressing that basic issue we find him proposing, What constitutes prophecy? What does a prophet do? Although there is evidence that Theodore's brother Polychronius thought differently, we are encouraged to see in this uniquely extant work from the school of Antioch features that are typical. The very aspects of Daniel that led Jewish and more recent commentators to class it as apocalyptic—times and numbers and a sweeping geographical and chronological scenario—lent its author in the Antiochene view a supposed basis in ἰστορία beyond the great figures normally classed (by today's readers) as major prophets, thus making the work irresistible. In its uniqueness, therefore, this commentary from Theodoret, conceded to be Antioch's most mature and "modéré" representative, is valuable in exemplifying its understanding of the nature and role of biblical prophecy, as do to a less extent his work and Theodore's on the Twelve (Minor) Prophets, where the basic issue does not arise in such a challenging way.

As to Theodoret's success in his task of commentary on this book, he brings the same abilities and commitment as elsewhere in responding to the author's thought and poetic expression with typical precision, if subjecting his biblical text to even less rigorous paleographical scrutiny than his linguistic limitations allow.

---

[75] PG 81:1268.

[76] Cf. Robert C. Hill, "A Pelagian Commentator on the Psalms?" *ITQ* 63 (1998): 263–71.

His dedication to clarity and conciseness is as patent here as in his other exegetical works. What hinders him in particular in doing justice to such a challenging text for his readers, however, is his inability to recognize the haggadic and apocalyptic material before him, which undermines his attempt to convince them of the book's claim to a place in the Bible's prophetic corpus—the aim he set himself from the very outset. That ignorance of genres common to all the Antiochenes prevents his distinguishing apocalyptic from prophecy: Daniel must be a prophet (Jesus said so, and "the Jews of old" admitted as much), prophecy has to square with history, and can only be prospective. Hence the book is about "the kings of the time and the dates," and it is only a matter of deciphering the former and getting the latter to compute; the author is contemporary with Babylon's greatness, as he claims, and the real plight of Jews under Antiochus Epiphanes is beyond his ken. The harder Theodoret works at backgrounding this oblique material for his readers—and none of his peers works harder—the less justice he does to the author's purpose, which is at variance with the commentator's.

His fellow Antiochenes (Polychronius aside) would probably have fared no better; Daniel, like the New Testament apocalyptic Theodoret cites in support, does not yield its secrets to that approach. By contrast, his previous work on the Song of Songs had opened up for him a different way to respond to Old Testament material, as would the Psalms later. But predecessors of a different school were not so helpful in this case; and in any event the "man of desires" could not be taken at a spiritual level: his status as a prophet was under question by Jewish savants of the commentator's time, and he had to be firmly attached to the fabric of history. Predictably, the effort to reconstruct an historical context, doubtless convincing for Theodoret's contemporaries, does not work for modern readers. He will not feel the need to repeat the exercise when he comes to commenting on Ezekiel and Isaiah,[77] whose place among the Latter Prophets was never under question as was Daniel's, and whose recourse to apocalyptic is limited.

---

[77] While it is his *Commentary on Jeremiah* that concludes Theodoret's treatment of the Bible's prophetic corpus, the form in which that work has come down to us (PG 81:496–806, including Baruch and Lamentations, showing signs of derivation from the catenae) leaves us less certain of his approach to that prophetic text.

Theodoret:

Commentary on Daniel

ΤΟΥ ΜΑΚΑΡΙΟΥ ΘΕΟΔΩΡΗΤΟΥ ΕΠΙΣΚΟΠΟΥ ΚΥΡΟΥ ΥΠΟΜΝΗΜΑ ΕΙΣ ΤΑΣ ΟΡΑΣΕΙΣ ΤΟΥ ΠΡΟΦΗΤΟΥ ΔΑΝΙΗΛ.

1256

ΠΡΟΘΕΩΡΙΑ

Εἰ πᾶσι ῥάδιον ἦν τὰ τῶν θείων προφητῶν ἀναπτύσσειν θεσπίσματα, καὶ τοῦ μὲν γράμματος ὑπερβαίνειν τὴν ἐπιφάνειαν, εἰς δὲ τὸ βάθος καταδύνειν, καὶ τὸν ἐκεῖ κρυπτόμενον τοῦ νοήματος μαργαρίτην θηρεύειν, ἴσως ἂν εἰκότως ἐνομίσθη παρέλκον ἀνάγραπτον τούτων ποιεῖσθαι τὴν ἑρμηνείαν, πάντων εὐπετῶς παρ' αὐτὴν τὴν ἀνάγνωσιν τῆς
1257 προφη|τικῆς διανοίας ἐφικνουμένων· ἐπειδὴ δέ, μίαν μὲν ἅπαντες φύσιν ἐλάχομεν, οὐκ ἴσην δὲ ἅπαντες γνῶσιν ἐλάβομεν (« Ἑκάστῳ γὰρ δίδοται, φησίν, ἡ φανέρωσις τοῦ Πνεύματος πρὸς τὸ συμφέρον, καὶ ἄλλῳ μὲν δίδοται διὰ τοῦ Πνεύματος λόγος σοφίας, ἄλλῳ δὲ λόγος γνώσεως κατὰ τὸ αὐτὸ Πνεῦμα, ἑτέρῳ δὲ πίστις ἐν τῷ αὐτῷ Πνεύματι· » καὶ τὰ ἑξῆς δὲ ὡσαύτως κατὰ διαίρεσιν ἅπαντα διανέμεται)· οὐδὲν ἀπεικὸς οἶμαι ποιεῖν, εἰ τοῖς ἀγνοοῦσι τὰ θεῖα τούτων συγγράμματα ἔγγραφον παραδώην διδασκαλίαν, παιδόθεν μὲν αὐτοῖς ἐντραφείς, παρὰ πολλῶν δὲ συγγραφέων εὐσεβῶν σμικράν τινα γνῶσιν ἐρανισάμενος· καὶ γὰρ ὁ θεῖος παρακελεύεται νόμος, ἃ παρὰ τῶν πατέρων μεμαθήκαμεν, τοὺς ἐγγόνους διδάσκειν. « Διδάξεις γὰρ αὐτά, φησί, τοὺς υἱούς σου, καὶ τοὺς υἱοὺς τῶν υἱῶν σου· » οὗ χάριν καὶ ὁ μέγας διδάσκαλος Δαβίδ, « Προσέχετε, λαός μου, φησί, τὸν νόμον μου, κλίνατε τὸ οὖς ὑμῶν εἰς τὰ ῥήματα τοῦ στόματός μου· ἀνοίξω ἐν παραβολαῖς τὸ στόμα μου, φθέγξομαι προβλήματα ἀπ' ἀρχῆς. » Εἶτα δεικνὺς πόθεν ταῦτα μεμάθηκεν, « Ὅσα ἠκούσαμεν,

COMMENTARY ON DANIEL

If it were easy for everyone to explicate the utterances of the divine prophets, to get beyond the surface of the letter and penetrate to the depths,[2] and to light upon the pearl of the contents hidden there, perhaps it would rightfully be thought an idle endeavor to produce a commentary on them in writing if everyone easily arrived at the prophetic message simply by reading. | But though we all share in the one nature, we do not all enjoy equal knowledge: "To each is given the manifestation of the Spirit for the common good; to one is given the utterance of wisdom through the Spirit, to another the utterance of knowledge according to the same Spirit, to another faith by the same Spirit,"[3] and so on in similar fashion, everything being distributed differently. Hence I think it in no way improper for me to put into writing their teaching for those ignorant of their divine written works, raised on them as I have been from my youth and the beneficiary of some little knowledge from many pious writers.[4]

After all, the divine law bids us teach our offspring what we have learned from our parents: "Teach it to your children and your children's children."[5] This is the reason the great teacher David also says, "Heed my law, my people, incline your ear to the words of my mouth. I shall open my mouth in proverbs, I shall utter riddles from of old." Then to make clear from what source he learned

---

[1] The numbers given in the margin throughout the translation refer to the column numbers in PG 81.

[2] Cf. Matt 13:45–46; 2 Cor 3:6.

[3] 1 Cor 12:7–9.

[4] Theodoret admits to being a beneficiary or borrower (ἐρανισάμενος; cf. his dogmatic work *Eranistes*) of pious writers—not so much teachers, among whom Theodore may have figured.

[5] Deut 4:9, a text Theodoret will cite again when he comes to comment upon the following psalm in his later *Commentary on the Psalms*. For the latter, see Robert C. Hill, trans., *Theodoret of Cyrus: Commentary on the Psalms* (2 vols.; FC 101–102; Washington, D.C.: Catholic University of America Press, 2000–2001).

φησί, καὶ ἔγνωμεν αὐτά, καὶ οἱ πατέρες ἡμῶν διηγήσαντο ἡμῖν, οὐκ ἐκρύβη ἀπὸ τῶν τέκνων αὐτῶν, εἰς γενεὰν ἑτέραν.» Καὶ τῆς γνώσεως τὴν αἰτίαν διδάσκων, «Νόμον γὰρ, φησίν, ἔθετο ἐν Ἰσραήλ· ὅσα ἐνετείλατο τοῖς πατράσιν ἡμῶν, τοῦ γνωρίσαι αὐτὰ τοῖς υἱοῖς αὐτῶν, ὅπως ἂν γνῷ γενεὰ ἑτέρα, υἱοὶ τεχθησόμενοι· καὶ ἀναστήσονται, καὶ ἀναγγελοῦσιν αὐτὰ τοῖς υἱοῖς αὐτῶν.» Καὶ τὴν ἐκ τῆς διδασκαλίας ὠφέλειαν δεικνὺς ἐπάγει· «Ἵνα θῶνται ἐπὶ τὸν Θεὸν τὴν ἐλπίδα αὐτῶν, καὶ μὴ ἐπιλάθωνται τῶν ἔργων τοῦ Θεοῦ, καὶ τὰς ἐντολὰς αὐτοῦ ἐκζητήσωσι.» Ταύτην τοίνυν τὴν διδασκαλίαν παρὰ τῶν πατέρων δεχόμενοι, χρέος δίκαιον τοῖς μεθ' ὑμᾶς γενομένοις τε καὶ ἐσομένοις ὀφείλομεν, καὶ προσήκει τούτου τὴν ἔκτισιν εὐγνωμόνως ποιήσασθαι. Οὐ μόνον δὲ ἡμᾶς ὁ θεῖος διεγείρει νόμος, ἀλλὰ καὶ πολλοὶ τῶν ἐπισήμων συνήθων, θερμῶς ἡμᾶς λιπαρήσαντες, θαρρῆσαι τὸν ἀγῶνα τοῦτον ἠνάγκασαν. Φέρε τοίνυν, τοῦ θειοτάτου Δανιὴλ τὴν προφητείαν, ὡς ἔνι μάλιστα, σαφῆ τοῖς ἀγνοοῦσι ποιήσωμεν. Ἴσως δέ, οὐδὲ τοῖς γνώσεως ἠξιωμένοις ἄχρηστος οὗτος ὁ πόνος γενήσεται· ἢ γὰρ πλείονα εὑρήσουσιν ὧν νενομίκασιν, ἢ τὰ αὐτῶν ἐν τοῖς ἡμετέροις εὑρίσκοντες, βεβαιώσουσι τῇ κοινωνίᾳ τὸ ὑπὸ σφῶν αὐτῶν θηρευθέν· φιλεῖ γάρ πως ἡ τῶν πλειόνων συγκατάθεσις κρατύνειν τὰ νοηθέντα. Τοῦτον δὲ τὸν προφήτην ἐπὶ τοῦ παρόντος ἑρμηνεύειν πειρώμεθα, οὐχ ὡς τῶν ἄλλων καταφρονοῦντες, μὴ γένοιτο·

ἅπαντας γὰρ ἴσμεν τοῦ θείου Πνεύματος ὄργανα· ἀλλὰ πρῶτον | μέν, ὅτι τούτου τὴν ἑρμηνείαν ἡμᾶς οἱ συνήθεις ἐπήγγειλαν, καὶ προσῆκον ἡγούμεθα ἣν ᾐτήθημεν χάριν, ταύτην δοῦναι τοῖς ᾐτηκόσιν. Ἔπειτα δὲ ἡμᾶς ἡ Ἰουδαίων ἄνοιά τε καὶ ἀναίδεια παρασκευάζει τοὺς μὲν ἄλλους ἐν τῷ παρόντι καταλιπεῖν, τὰς δὲ τούτου προρρήσεις γυμνοῦν, καὶ δήλας ποιεῖν· εἰς γὰρ τοσαύτην ἀναισχυντίαν ἤλασαν, ὡς καὶ τοῦ χοροῦ τῶν προφητῶν τοῦτον ἀποσχοινίζειν, καὶ αὐτῆς αὐτὸν τῆς προφητικῆς

these things, he says, "All that we heard and came to know, and that
our fathers recounted to us, was not hidden from their children for
another generation." And to bring out the source of the knowledge, he says, "He gave a law in Israel, everything he commanded
our ancestors to convey to their children so that another generation may know them, children yet to be born to them; they will
rise up and announce them to their children." And to bring out
the value of the teaching he goes on, "That they may place their
hope in God, and not forget his works but seek out his commandments."[6] Having received this teaching from our parents, then, we
owe a due debt to those who come after you and are yet to be, and
must discharge this obligation gratefully. Now, it is not only the
divine law that prompts us: many illustrious acquaintances also
have made earnest supplication to us and obliged us to summon
up courage for this contest.

   So come now, let us to the best of our ability make clear to
those in ignorance the inspired composition of the most divine
Daniel. Perhaps this labor of ours, however, will not prove without benefit even to those already enjoying knowledge: they will
either discover more than they thought, or by discovering their
ideas in ours they will confirm by the commonality what they came
upon through their own efforts, the consensus of a greater number normally strengthening our convictions. Now, for the moment
let us endeavor to comment on this prophet without scorning the
others—perish the thought: we know they are all instruments of
the divine Spirit. Firstly, however, | it is because our friends re-   1260
quired of us commentary on this author, and we consider it a duty
to give the petitioners the favor they request. But furthermore it
is the Jews' folly and shamelessness that causes us to pass over the
others for the moment and expound this author's prophecies and
make them clear, embarking as they did on such brazen behavior
as to cordon off this author from the band of the prophets and strip
him of the prophetic title itself.[7]

   [6] Ps 78:1–7.
   [7] It is clear from Ben Sira (cf. Sir 48:22–49:12) in the early second century B.C.E. that Daniel (probably composed later than that) was not numbered
among the (Latter—a still later term) Prophets with Isaiah, Jeremiah, Ezekiel,
and The Twelve ("minor" or shorter, Augustine's term) Prophets. Hence in the
Hebrew Bible the book is included instead among the Writings, whereas the LXX
and Vulgate place it after Ezekiel. Theodoret, in fact, is treating of it before the

προσηγορίας ἀποστερεῖν. Ἔστι δὲ αὐτῶν ἀναιδὲς μέν, οὐκ ἀπὸ σκοποῦ δὲ τὸ τέχνασμα· ἐπειδὴ γὰρ τῶν ἄλλων ἀπάντων πολλῷ σαφέστερον τὴν τοῦ μεγάλου Θεοῦ καὶ Σωτῆρος ἡμῶν Ἰησοῦ Χριστοῦ προεθέσπισε παρουσίαν, οὐ μόνον ἃ ποιήσει προαγορεύσας, ἀλλὰ καὶ τὸν χρόνον προειρηκώς, καὶ τὸν μέχρι τῆς αὐτοῦ παρουσίας τῶν ἐτῶν ἐντεθεικὼς ἀριθμόν, καὶ ἅπαντα σαφῶς καταλέξας τὰ τούτους αὐτοὺς μετὰ τὴν ἀπιστίαν καταληψόμενα λυπηρά, εἰκότως, ἅτε δὴ θεομισεῖς καὶ τῆς ἀληθείας ἐχθροί, τολμῶσιν ἀναιδῶς λέγειν ὡς οὐκ ἔστι προφήτης ὁ ταῦτα καὶ μυρία ἕτερα χρησμολογήσας, ἀποχρῆν ἡγούμενοι τὴν οἰκείαν ἀπόφασιν εἰς τὴν τοῦ ψεύδους βεβαίωσιν. Θαυμαστὸν δὲ οὐδέν, εἰ κατὰ τοῦ Μονογενοῦς λυττήσαντες, τοὺς εὔνους τοῦ Δεσπότου συκοφαντοῦσι θεράποντας· συμβαίνει γὰρ τοῖς προτέροις τὰ δεύτερα. Διὸ καὶ ὁ Κύριός φησιν· «Εἰ ἐμὲ ἐδίωξαν, καὶ ὑμᾶς διώξουσι.» Καὶ πάλιν· «Εἰ τὸν οἰκοδεσπότην Βεελζεβοὺβ ἀπεκάλεσαν, πόσῳ μᾶλλον τοὺς οἰκιακοὺς αὐτοῦ;» Ἵνα δὲ ἐκ πολλοῦ τοῦ περιόντος τὴν ἀναίδειαν αὐτῶν διελέγξωμεν, πυθώμεθα αὐτῶν οὕτως· Τί προφήτου ἴδιον εἶναί φατε; Ἀλλὰ γὰρ ἴσως ἂν εἴποιεν, τὸ τὰ μέλλοντα προειδέναι τε καὶ προλέγειν. Ἴδωμεν τοίνυν, εἰ μὴ ταῦτα καὶ προμεμάθηκε, καὶ προείρηκεν ὁ μακάριος Δανιήλ. Καὶ τὸν μὲν περὶ τοῦ Δεσπότου Χριστοῦ λόγον τέως ἐπισχῶμεν, τὰς δὲ ἄλλας αὐτοῦ προφητείας εἰς μέσον ἀγάγωμεν. Εὑρίσκομεν τοίνυν αὐτὸν πολλὰ μὲν περὶ τῆς Βαβυλωνίων βασιλείας, πολλὰ δὲ περὶ τῆς Περσῶν καὶ Μακεδόνων, πολλὰ δὲ καὶ περὶ τῆς τῶν Ῥωμαίων προαγορεύσαντα· καὶ τίνα μὲν πείσεται ὁ Βαβυλωνίων βασιλεύς, ὅπως δὲ Πέρσαι τὴν ἐκείνου παραλήψονται βασιλείαν, ἔπειτα ὅτι τούτους καταλύσας ὁ Μακεδὼν τελευτήσει μὲν αὐτὸς ὡς τάχιστα, τέτταρες δὲ ἀνθ᾽ ἑνὸς κληρονομήσουσι τὴν βασιλείαν· καὶ ὅτι ἐξ ἑνὸς τούτων βλαστήσας τις μυρία ὅσα ἐργάσεται τοῖς Ἰουδαίοις δεινά, καὶ ὅτι θείας ἀπολαύσαντες βοηθείας τῆς ἐκείνου θηριότητος ἀπαλλαγήσονται. Εἶτα μεταβὰς ἐκεῖθεν προλέγει τὴν Ῥωμαίων ἰσχύν, καὶ ὅτι πάσας καταγωνισάμενοι τὰς βασιλείας, τὸν παρὰ πάντων κομιοῦνται δασμόν. Τί δεῖ λέγειν, ὅσα περὶ τοῦ τῶν Αἰγυπτίων, καὶ τοῦ

1261 | τῶν Σύρων προηγόρευσε βασιλέων, καὶ ὅσα ἀλλήλοις ἐργάσονται δεινά,

Yet while this contrivance of theirs is brazen, it is not without significance. After all, he prophesied much more clearly than
all the others the coming of our great God and Savior Jesus Christ,
not only foretelling what he would do but also foretelling the time,
stipulating the number of years until his coming and clearly listing
all the disasters that would befall them personally in consequence
of their unbelief. So it is not surprising that as haters of God and
enemies of the truth they would shamelessly presume to claim that
the one who gave utterance to these and countless other oracles is
no prophet, confident that their own judgment was sufficient to
confirm this falsehood. Now, it is not surprising if after inveighing
against the Only Begotten they malign the Lord's devoted ministers, this latter behavior being in accord with the former. Hence
the Lord, too, says, "If they persecuted me, they will also per-
secute you," and again, "If they called the master of the house
Beelzebul, how much more will they abuse his household."[8]

For us to refute their brazen claims in abundance, however,
let us pose this question to them: what do you claim is typical of a
prophet? Perhaps their reply would be, Foreseeing and foretelling
the future. Let us see, therefore, whether blessed Daniel had a
foreknowledge of it and foretold it. For the time being let us pass
over the account of Christ the Lord, and concentrate on his other
prophecies. We find him, then, making many prophecies about
the kingdom of the Babylonians, many about that of the Persians
and the Macedonians, and many also about that of the Romans,
what the king of the Babylonians will suffer, how Persians will take
over his kingdom, then the fact that the Macedonian will destroy
them and will himself meet a rapid end, and four people will succeed to the kingdom in place of one, and the fact that from one of
these someone will spring up and wreak havoc on the Jews, and
they will receive divine help and be freed from his ferocity. From
that point he then moves to foretell the power of the Romans, and
the fact that they will conquer all the kingdoms and exact tribute
from them all. What should be said of all his prophecies of the
kings of the Egyptians and | the Syrians, all the troubles they will   1261

others, leaving Ezekiel for his next work, and Isaiah and Jeremiah until the end
of his exegetical career; the reason for its priority seems to be a polemical one,
the question raised by the Jews about its place in the prophetic corpus (which
modern readers would also raise), as well as those appeals from curious readers.

[8] John 15:20; Matt 10:25.

καὶ τὰς μετὰ ταῦτα τῆς εἰρήνης σπονδάς, καὶ τὰς ἐπιγαμίας καὶ συγγενείας, εἶτα πάλιν τοὺς ἀκηρύκτους πολέμους μετὰ τὴν γεγενημένην
καταλλαγήν; Τὸν τοίνυν ταῦτα πάντα προεγνωκότα καὶ προειρηκότα,
καὶ ἀνάγραπτον τὴν μνήμην αὐτῶν καταλιπόντα, πῶς οὐ δυσσεβὲς καὶ
ἀνόσιον τοῦ τῶν προφητῶν ἐξορίζειν χοροῦ; Εἰ γὰρ ταῦτα προφητείας
ἀλλότρια, τίνα προφητείας τὰ ἴδια; Εἰ δὲ ὅτι τῶν οἰκείων οὐ προτίθησι λόγων τό, Τάδε λέγει Κύριος, καὶ τούτου χάριν τῆς προφητικῆς
αὐτὸν ἀποστεροῦσι συμμορίας, εἰπάτωσαν ἡμῖν, τί τοιοῦτον Ἀβραὰμ ὁ
πατριάρχης εἰρηκὼς προφήτης ὑπὸ τοῦ τῶν ὅλων προσηγορεύθη Θεοῦ.
Περὶ τοῦ γὰρ Ἀβραὰμ ἐλέχθη· «Καὶ νῦν ἀπόδος τὴν γυναῖκα τῷ ἀνδρί,
ὅτι προφήτης ἐστί, καὶ προσεύξεται περὶ σοῦ, καὶ σωθήσῃ σὺ καὶ πᾶς ὁ
οἶκός σου.» Καὶ ὁ μακάριος δὲ Δαβὶδ περί τε αὐτοῦ, καὶ τοῦ υἱέως, καὶ
τοῦ ἐκγόνου φησίν, ὅτι «Ἤλεγξεν ὑπὲρ αὐτῶν ὁ Θεὸς βασιλεῖς, λέγων·
Μὴ ἅπτεσθε τῶν χριστῶν μου, καὶ ἐν τοῖς προφήταις μου μὴ πονηρεύε-
σθε.» Καὶ ὁ μέγιστος δὲ προφήτης Σαμουήλ, ὁ παιδόθεν νεωκόρος, οὐ
κατὰ τοὺς ἄλλους ἔχει προφήτας τῆς προφητείας τὸ εἶδος, ἀλλὰ καὶ αὐτὸς ἢ δι' ὀνείρων, ἢ διὰ μεθημερινῶν τινων ἀποκαλύψεων προγνώσεις,
ἐννοίας, καὶ προρρήσεις ἐδέξατο. Πολεμεῖτε τοίνυν καὶ ἐκείνοις ἀναφαν-
δόν, καὶ τοῦ συλλόγου τῶν προφητῶν αὐτοὺς ἐκβάλλετε προφανῶς. Εἰ
δὲ τὴν εἰς ἐκείνους παραιτεῖσθε παροινίαν, φεύγετε καὶ τὴν κατ' αὐτοῦ συκοφαντίαν· προφήτης γάρ, καὶ προφήτης ἐπιθυμίᾳ καὶ πόθῳ τῶν
μελλόντων τὴν γνῶσιν δεξάμενος, ἱδρῶσι καὶ πόνοις, νηστείᾳ καὶ κα-
κουχίᾳ τὰ ἐσόμενα διδαχθείς, οὐχ ἃ μόνοις Ἰουδαίοις συμβήσεται, ἀλλὰ
τῶν κοινῶν τῆς οἰκουμένης πραγμάτων τὴν οἰκονομίαν καὶ προμαθὼν
καὶ προδιδάξας. Σκοπήσατε τοίνυν, εἰ μὴ λίαν ἄδικον, Ἀβδιοῦ μὲν τὰ

bring on one another, the later peace treaties through marriage and kinship, then in turn the implacable wars after reconciliation had been achieved?

How, therefore, would it not be impious and sacrilegious to exclude from the band of the prophets the one who foreknew and foretold all this, and left a record of it in writing? I mean, if this does not belong to prophecy, what is typical of prophecy? If, on the other hand, they eliminate him from the company of prophets for the reason that he does not prefix to his own words the phrase, Thus says the Lord, let them tell us what expression of this kind the patriarch Abraham uttered to be called prophet by the God of all. It was said of Abraham, remember, "Return the wife to her husband now, because he is a prophet, and he will pray for you, and you and all your household will live." Blessed David said of himself, his son and his descendants, "God charged kings on their behalf, Lay no hand on my anointed, do no harm to my prophets."[9] And Samuel, the greatest prophet, a temple minister from his youth, instead of exercising the style of prophecy of the other prophets was given foreknowledge, understanding, and prophecy either in dreams or in revelations by day.[10] So take issue openly also with them, and expel them publicly from the group of the prophets. If, on the other hand, you decline to exhibit madness toward them, be careful not to slander him as well: he is a prophet, and a prophet who received knowledge of the future by desire and longing,[11] was instructed in future events by sweat and tears, fasting and ill-treatment, and who learned and taught ahead of time not only what would happen to the Jews but the divine plan for the common affairs of the whole world.

Consider, then, whether it would not be highly unfair to include among the prophets Obadiah, who forecast only the troubles

[9] Gen 20:7 (loosely cited); Ps 105:14–15.

[10] Theodoret accords this title "greatest of the prophets" not to Moses (unlike the New Testament) but to Samuel, possibly on the basis of the communications to him as a child recorded in 1 Sam 3 (though interpretation of dreams is another feature of apocalyptic), whereas that book (cf. ch. 12) shows him claiming prophetic status not as a seer but as one who transmits God's will to the people.

[11] In Theodotion's version of Dan 9:23; 10:11, 23 the prophet is called a "man of desires," the term by which Theodoret will refer to him in his preface to the Psalms commentary.

τοὺς Ἰδουμαίους μόνον καταληψόμενα κακὰ προαγορεύσαντα, καὶ Ἰωνᾶν δέ, καὶ Ναοὺμ, περὶ μιᾶς πόλεως προθεσπίσαντας τῆς Νινευῒ τοῖς προφήταις ἐγκαταλέγειν, τὸν δὲ μακάριον Δανιὴλ οὐ περὶ πόλεως μιᾶς, οὐδὲ περὶ ἔθνους βραχέος, ἀλλὰ περὶ τῶν μεγίστων βασιλειῶν προειρηκότα, Χαλδαϊκῆς, Περσικῆς, Μακεδονικῆς, Ῥωμαϊκῆς, καὶ τῶν κατὰ μέρος ὑπὸ τούτων γεγενημένων, τῆς προφητικῆς προσηγορίας ἀποστερεῖν, καὶ τῆς πνευματικῆς χάριτος ἀλλότριον εἶναι λέγειν. Καὶ μὴν ἔδει

1264 καὶ λίαν ὑμᾶς ὄντας ἀγνώμονας τὸν Ναβουχοδονόσορ αἰδεσθῆναι τὸν | δυσσεβῆ, τὸν θηριώδη, τὸν βάρβαρον, τὸν τῶν θείων ἀμύητον, βοῶντα περὶ τοῦ Δανιὴλ, καὶ λέγοντα· «Ὅτι Πνεῦμα Θεοῦ ἅγιόν ἐστιν ἐν αὐτῷ.» Καὶ γὰρ τῷ ὄντι τοῦ θείου Πνεύματος ἔργον ἦν, καὶ τὸ ἐνύπνιον εἰπεῖν, ὃ ἕτερος θεασάμενος ἐπελήσθη, καὶ τούτου δηλῶσαι τὴν ἑρμηνείαν ἀκριβῶς τε καὶ ἀληθῶς. Ὑμᾶς δὲ οὐδὲ τοῦτο πείθει τὴν κατὰ τοῦ προφήτου καταλῦσαι μανίαν, ἀλλὰ διὰ τοῦ προφήτου τῷ τοῦ προφήτου πολεμεῖτε Δεσπότῃ. Ἀλλ' ὁ μὲν προφήτης οὐδὲν ἐκ τῶν ὑμετέρων βλαβήσεται τεχνασμάτων· προφήτην γὰρ αὐτὸν δείκνυσι τὰ θεῖα συγγράμματα, βεβαιοῖ δὲ τὴν πρόγνωσιν καὶ τὸ τῆς προρρήσεως τέλος. Ἀλλὰ γὰρ νῦν ὁρῶντες τὰ πράγματα νοοῦμεν ἐκεῖνα τὰ παλαιὰ θεσπίσματα, καὶ ὑπ' αὐτῶν ποδηγούμενοι τῶν πραγμάτων ῥᾳδίως λαμβάνομεν τὴν τῶν πραγμάτων κατάληψιν· ὑμεῖς δὲ τὴν οἰκείαν παροινίαν καὶ διὰ τούτων δηλοῦτε. Ἀλλὰ νῦν μὲν ἐν κεφαλαίῳ τῆς ὑμετέρας ἀναιδείας τοὺς ἐλέγχους ἐποιησάμεθα· ἡ δὲ κατὰ μέρος ἑρμηνεία ἐναργέστερον ὑμῶν ἐλέγξει τὴν ἄνοιαν. Φέρε τοίνυν, τήν τε ὑπὲρ ἡμῶν αὐτῶν ἀπολογίαν, καὶ τὴν Ἰουδαίων κατηγορίαν ἀποχρώντως ποιησάμενοι, τὴν τῆς προφητείας ὑπόθεσιν δήλην πρότερον καταστήσωμεν, εἶθ' οὕτως τῆς κατὰ λέξιν ἑρμηνείας ἁψώμεθα. Μετὰ τὸν Ἰωσίαν (εὐσεβὴς δὲ οὗτος γεγένηται βασιλεύς) ἐβασίλευσε τῆς Ἰουδαίας Ἰωάχαζ, ὁ υἱὸς αὐτοῦ, τρεῖς μῆνας ὅλους καὶ ὀλίγας ἡμέρας· διώνυμος δὲ οὗτος ἦν· ἐν μὲν γὰρ ταῖς Βασιλείαις, καὶ τοῖς Παραλειπομένοις, Ἰωάχαζ ὀνομάζεται· ὁ δὲ μακάριος Ἱερεμίας αὐτὸν ὁ προφήτης Σελεὶμ προσαγορεύει. Τοῦτον δορυάλωτον ὁ τῆς Αἰγύπτου βασιλεὺς Φαραὼ Νεχαὼ λαβών, αἰχμάλωτον εἰς τὴν Αἴγυπτον ἀπήγαγεν· ἐχειροτόνησε δὲ ἀντ' αὐτοῦ βασιλέα Ἐλιακεὶμ τὸν ἀδελφὸν αὐτοῦ, καὶ Ἰωακεὶμ αὐτὸν προσηγόρευσεν. Ἐβασίλευσε δὲ οὗτος ἓν καὶ δέκα ἔτη πρὸς ὀλίγοις μησίν. Ἐν δὲ τῷ τρίτῳ ἔτει τῆς τούτου βασιλείας ἐπιστρατεύσας Ναβουχοδονόσορ, ὁ τῶν Βαβυλωνίων βασιλεύς, ἔλαβε μὲν οὐκ ὀλίγους δορυαλώτους τῶν ἐπ' εὐγενείᾳ λαμπρυνομένων· ἔλαβε δὲ καὶ ἔνια τῶν ἱερῶν σκευῶν τῶν ταῖς θείαις λειτουργίαις

befalling the Idumeans, and Jonah and Nahum, who prophesied about a single city, Nineveh, but to strip blessed Daniel of the title of prophet, though he made prophecies not of a single city or of a tiny nation but of the greatest kingdoms—Chaldean, Persian, Macedonian, Roman—and what was done by them individually, and to say he has no claim to the spiritual charism. Indeed, in your gross ingratitude you should even respect Nebuchadnezzar, that | 1264 irreligious, cruel, savage man, a stranger to the divine mysteries, who cried aloud about Daniel in the words, "The holy Spirit of God is in him."[12] It was, in fact, an effect of the truly divine Spirit both to describe the dream another person had seen and forgotten and to give a precise and correct explanation of it. Yet not even this convinces you to cease your frenzy against the prophet; instead, in the prophet you contend with the Lord of the prophet. The prophet, however, will suffer no harm from your machinations: the divine writings show him to be a prophet, and the fulfillment of the prophecy confirms the foreknowledge: witnessing the events in our time, we understand those ancient prophecies, and with guidance from them we easily appreciate the occurrence of the events, whereas you display your peculiar frenzy even in this. While for the time being, however, we have in summary fashion refuted your brazen claims, the verse-by-verse commentary will provide a yet clearer refutation of your folly.

So come now, having given an adequate defense of ourselves and sufficient accusation of Jews, let us first make clear the theme of the inspired work, and then in this fashion come to the textual commentary. After Josiah, the king who proved to be pious, Jehoahaz his son ruled Judah for three whole months and a few days. He had two names, being called Jehoahaz in Kings and Chronicles, whereas the blessed prophet Jeremiah calls him Shallum.[13] Pharaoh Neco king of Egypt took him prisoner and led him off as a captive to Egypt, in his place appointing his brother Eliakim king and calling him Jehoiakim; he reigned eleven years and a few months. In the third year of his reign Nebuchadnezzar king of the Babylonians invaded, taking prisoner not a few of the nobility, seizing also some of the sacred vessels dedicated to divine worship,

---

[12] Cf. Dan 4:8–9.
[13] Cf. 2 Kgs 23–24; 2 Chr 36; Jer 22:11 (Jehoahaz perhaps his coronation name, as his brother Eliakim became Jehoiakim).

ἀφιερωμένων· δασμὸν δέ τινα ἐπιθεὶς τῷ Ἰωακεὶμ ἀπῆρεν εἰς τὴν Βαβυλῶνα. Εἶτα, τούτου τὸν ὁρισθέντα φόρον ἐκτῖσαι μὴ βουλομένου, πάλιν
ἐπεστράτευσε τοῖς Ἱεροσολύμοις, καὶ τὴν πόλιν ἑλών, καὶ τοῦτον ἀν-
ελών, καθίστησιν ἀντ' αὐτοῦ βασιλέα τὸν ἐξ αὐτοῦ, Ἰωακεὶμ μὲν ὑπὸ
1265   τῶν Ἰουδαίων ὀνομασθέντα, Ἐλιακεὶμ δὲ πάλιν | μετονομασθέντα. Καὶ
τοῦτον δὲ ὁ μακάριος Ἱερεμίας ὁ προφήτης Ἰεχονίαν ὀνομάζει. «Ζῶ
γὰρ, φησί, λέγει Κύριος, ἐὰν γενόμενος γένηται Ἰεχονίας, υἱὸς Ἰωακεὶμ
βασιλέως Ἰούδα, ἀποσφράγισμα ἐπὶ τῆς χειρός μου τῆς δεξιᾶς, ἐκεῖθεν
ἐκσπάσω σε, καὶ παραδώσω σε εἰς χεῖρας ζητούντων τὴν ψυχήν σου, ὧν
σὺ εὐλαβῇ ἀπὸ προσώπου αὐτῶν, εἰς χεῖρας τῶν Χαλδαίων.» Καὶ τούτου
τοίνυν τρεῖς μῆνας πρὸς ὀλίγαις ἡμέραις τὴν βασιλείαν πρυτανεύσαντος,
τότε πάλιν ὁ Ναβουχοδονόσορ, ὁ τῶν Βαβυλωνίων βασιλεύς, στρατιὰν
ἀποστείλας καὶ στρατηγόν, τοῦτον μὲν αἰχμάλωτον ἀπήγαγεν εἰς τὴν
Βαβυλῶνα, τῷ δὲ Σεδεκίᾳ θείῳ πρὸς πατρὸς αὐτοῦ ὄντι τὴν βασιλείαν
ἐνεχείρισε· καὶ τούτου δὲ ἐνιαυτὸν ἕνα πρὸς τοῖς δέκα βασιλεύσαντος,
εἶτα τὸν ἐγκείμενον οὐ δεδωκότος φόρον, μετὰ πολλῆς μὲν δυνάμεως
ἐπιστρατεύει τοῖς Ἱεροσολύμοις τῶν Βαβυλωνίων ὁ βασιλεύς, ἔπειτα
πολιορκήσας, καὶ τῷ λιμῷ κατ' αὐτῶν συμμάχῳ χρησάμενος, καὶ μηχα-
νήματα τοῖς περιβόλοις προσενεγκών, ῥήγνυσι μὲν τὸ τεῖχος, ἀναιρεῖ δὲ
τοὺς πλείστους, τοὺς δὲ λοιποὺς ἐξανδραποδίσας ἀπάγει δορυαλώτους,
πυρὶ τήν τε πόλιν καὶ τὸ ἱερὸν παραδούς. Ἀλλ' ὁ τῶν ὅλων Θεός, ὁ ταῦτα
παθεῖν Ἰουδαίους διὰ τὴν πολλὴν αὐτῶν συγχωρήσας παρανομίαν, οὔτε κολάζων παντελῶς αὐτοὺς τῆς οἰκείας κηδεμονίας ἐγύμνωσεν· ἀλλὰ
τοῖς μὲν ἐν τῇ Ἰουδαίᾳ οἷόν τινας παιδονόμους ἐδεδώκει, τόν τε Οὐρίαν
τὸν Σαμαίου, καὶ Ἱερεμίαν τὸν τοῦ Χελκίου, ἄνδρα ἱερωσύνῃ καὶ προφητείᾳ λάμποντα· τοῖς δὲ κατὰ τὴν πρώτην αἰχμαλωσίαν δορυαλώτοις
ἀπαχθεῖσιν εἰς Βαβυλῶνα, τοὺς περὶ τὸν μακάριον Δανιὴλ συναπέστειλεν,
Ἐζεκιὴλ, καὶ Ἀνανίαν, καὶ Ἀζαρίαν, καὶ Μισαήλ· ἵν' ἔχοντες τῆς νομι-
κῆς πολιτείας ἀκριβεῖς διδασκάλους, μὴ πολλὴν ἐκ τῆς τῶν βαρβάρων

imposing a tribute on Jehoiakim and departing to Babylon. Then, when he refused to pay the tribute, he attacked Jerusalem again, captured the city, slew him and in his place appointed as king his son, called Jehoiachin by the Jews but once more given a different name Eliakim,[14] | the prophet Jeremiah calling him Jeconiah: "As 1265 I live, says the Lord, if Jeconiah, son of Jehoiakim king of Judah, were to be the signet ring on my right hand, I would tear you from there and give you into the hands of those who seek your life, of whose presence you are afraid, into the hands of the Chaldeans."[15] So when he had governed the kingdom for three months and a few days, Nebuchadnezzar king of the Babylonians then sent his army and a general once again, and took him off in captivity to Babylon, entrusting the kingdom to his uncle Zedekiah; he reigned eleven years. Next, when he did not pay the tribute that had been imposed, the king of the Babylonians marched against Jerusalem with great might, then besieged it, used famine as an ally against them, brought siege machines to the ramparts, breached the wall, slew most of them, captured the rest and took them off in chains, consigning both city and temple to the flames.

The God of all, however, who allowed Jews to suffer this on account of their grave lawlessness, did not deprive them of his characteristic care with the purpose of punishing them absolutely: he gave those in Judea as pedagogues Uriah son of Shemaiah[16] and Jeremiah son of Hilkiah, a man conspicuous for priesthood and prophecy.[17] In the company of those taken off as prisoners to Babylon in the first captivity, he sent with Daniel also Ezekiel, Hananiah, Azariah and Mishael so that they might have diligent teachers in the way of life according to the law and incur no se-

[14] It is thought, rather, that Jehoiakim died of natural causes (though Dan 1:2 could encourage Theodoret's idea of his execution), leaving the throne to Jehoiachin (a name not different in form in Greek from Jehoiakim—hence Theodoret's gratuitous remark that he also bore the name of Eliakim, Jehoiakim's original name).

[15] Jer 22:24–25.

[16] Cf. Jer 26:20–23.

[17] As in his commentary on Jer 1:1, Theodoret seems to presume Jeremiah is himself a priest rather than simply from a priestly family (Hebrew and Greek of that verse being ambiguous, and modern commentators also undecided). He proceeds to conflate, as he has done with 1–2 Kings, 1–2 Chronicles, and Jeremiah, the evidence from Daniel and Ezekiel as though prophetical books of equal status and historical value.

ἐπιμιξίας δέξωνται λώβην, ἀλλ' ἔχωσιν ἀρχέτυπα τῆς προγονικῆς αὐτοὺς ἀρετῆς καὶ φιλοσοφίας ἀναμιμνήσκοντα. Τοσαύτην ὁ τῶν ὅλων Θεὸς τῶν ἁμαρτωλῶν ποιεῖται προμήθειαν, ὅτι τοὺς εὐνοϊκῶς αὐτῷ δουλεύοντας, καὶ θεραπεύειν αὐτὸν διαπαντὸς προθυμουμένους, τῆς ἐκείνων ἕνεκεν ὠφελείας αἰχμαλώτους συνεχώρησεν ἀπαχθῆναι, καὶ δουλείαν χαλεπὴν ὑπομεῖναι, καὶ πολλοῖς κινδύνοις περιπεσεῖν, καὶ διὰ κυμάτων καὶ κλύδωνος ὁδεῦσαι τὸν βίον. Οὕτω γὰρ καὶ διὰ 'Ωσῆε τοῦ προφήτου φησίν, ὅτι «'Απέκτεινα δι' ὑμᾶς τοὺς προφήτας ἐν ῥήματι στόματός μου.» Οὕτω τὴν τῆς οἰκουμένης πραγματευόμενος σωτηρίαν, τοὺς ἁγίους συνεχώρησεν ἀποστόλους ἐκεῖνα παθεῖν τὰ ἀνάγραπτα πάθη. Ταύτην τῶν 'Ιουδαίων ποιούμενος πρόνοιαν, καὶ τοὺς περὶ τὸν μακάριον Δανιὴλ ᾠκο-

νόμησε σὺν αὐτοῖς τὴν Βαβυλῶνα καταλαβεῖν, ὃς ὡς νέος ὢν | καὶ τῇ ὥρᾳ λάμπων, σὺν τοῖς φιλοθέοις ἐκείνοις μειρακίοις ἐν τοῖς βασιλείοις ἀνατραφείς, καὶ παιδόθεν τὴν θείαν χάριν ἐσχηκὼς ἐπανθοῦσαν, σοφίας παντοδαπῆς καὶ συνέσεως ἔμπλεως γεγονώς, πολλὴν μὲν ἐκτήσατο παρὰ τῷ κρατοῦντι τὴν παρρησίαν, τὸν δὲ τῆς εὐσεβείας κηρύξας λόγον, ὠφελείας κἀκείνῳ γεγένηται πρόξενος· οὐκ ἐκείνῳ δὲ μόνῳ, ἀλλὰ καὶ πᾶσι τοῖς ὑπηκόοις· ἃ γὰρ ἔμαθεν ἐκεῖνος διὰ τῆς τούτου διδασκαλίας, εἰς τοὺς ὑπηκόους παρέπεμψε, νόμον τεθεικὼς τὸν διαρρήδην παρεγγυῶντα ἅπαντας τοὺς ἀρχομένους τὸν ὑπὸ τούτου πρεσβευόμενον προσκυνεῖν Θεόν. Ὅτε μὲν οὖν εἰς τὴν Βαβυλῶνα ὁ θεσπέσιος οὗτος ἀπήχθη προφήτης, καὶ τίνος ἕνεκεν, καὶ ὅσων ἀγαθῶν γεγένηται πρόξενος, οὐ τοῖς ὁμοφύλοις μόνον, ἀλλὰ καὶ τοῖς Βαρβάροις, συντόμως εἰρήκαμεν· τῆς δὲ προφητείας τὴν δύναμιν ἐκ τῆς κατὰ μέρος ἑρμηνείας ἀκριβέστερον θησόμεθα. Τὴν θείαν τοίνυν χάριν καλέσαντες συνεργὸν σαφηνείας ἀρξώμεθα.

rious harm from association with savages, having them instead as
a model to remind them of their forbears' virtue and sound values. The God of all displays such great care of sinners in allowing
those devoted to his service and ever zealous in attending on him
to be taken captive for their benefit, to endure harsh slavery and
incur grave dangers, and to pass their life in storms and billows.
This is why, in fact, he says in the prophet Hosea, "For your sake
I killed the prophets with a word of my mouth";[18] this is why
to procure the salvation of the world he allowed the holy apostles to endure the sufferings that are on record. To display this
providence for the Jews, he also arranged for those in the company of blessed Daniel to reach Babylon with them; he was young
| and in the bloom of youth, was reared in the palace with those   1268
God-loving youngsters, enjoyed from his youth the blossoming
of divine grace, was filled with wisdom and understanding of every kind, and on the one hand won great favor with the potentate,
and on the other was a source of benefit to him by proclaiming the
message of true religion.[19] And not only to him but also to all his
subjects: what he learned from this man's teaching he transmitted
to his subjects by publicly proclaiming a law bidding all the citizens to serve the God of which he was the mediator.

When it was that this divinely inspired prophet was taken off
to Babylon, therefore, why he was, and for what great benefits he
was responsible, not only to his kinsmen but also to the foreigners,[20] we have told concisely.[21] The force of his prophecy, on the
other hand, we shall give more precise attention to in the detailed
commentary. So, after calling upon divine grace in support, let us
begin the clarification.

---

[18] Hos 6:5.

[19] As with the book of Jonah, it is not an issue for Theodoret that the
name Daniel applies to the book's central character, not necessarily the author;
he does not address the question whether the two are one.

[20] Theodoret frequently uses the term Βάρβαροι, which indicates those
who speak a foreign language (esp. non-Hellenes) to refer to the Babylonians.

[21] Helpfully as a teacher, Theodoret sums up his introduction, which
typically he claims—rightfully—was done with conciseness, συντομία, a virtue
with which Photius will credit him. Precision, ἀκρίβεια, is also an Antiochene
characteristic, as is the view that divine grace acts in a supportive (συνεργόν) role,
not initiating the author's work.

ΤΟΜΟΣ Α' — ΚΕΦΑΛΑΙΟΝ Α'

α'. «Ἐν ἔτει τρίτῳ τῆς βασιλείας Ἰωακεὶμ, βασιλέως Ἰούδα, ἦλθε Ναβουχοδονόσορ, βασιλεὺς Βαβυλῶνος, εἰς Ἱερουσαλήμ, καὶ ἐπολιόρκει αὐτήν.» Ἀναγκαίως πρὸ τῶν ἄλλων ἁπάντων, καὶ τοῦ τηνικάδε βασιλέως ἐμνημόνευσε, καὶ τὸν χρόνον ἡμᾶς ἐδίδαξεν, ἵνα ἔχωμεν εἰδέναι σαφῶς τὸν τῆς πρώτης αἰχμαλωσίας καιρόν. Ἐν γὰρ τῷ τρίτῳ ἔτει τῆς βασιλείας Ἰωακεὶμ, τοῦ καὶ Ἐλιακεὶμ, ὃς ἐβασίλευσε μετὰ τὸν Ἰωάχαζ, πατὴρ δὲ ἐγένετο τοῦ Ἰωάχαζ, ὃς καὶ Ἰωακεὶμ καὶ Ἰεχονίας ὠνομάζετο, ἡ πρώτη ἅλωσις τῶν Ἱεροσολύμων ἐγένετο. Καὶ αὐτὸ δὲ τοῦτο, τῶν τότε βασιλέων μεμνῆσθαι, καὶ τῶν χρόνων, τὸν προφητικὸν ὑποδείκνυσι χαρακτῆρα. Οὕτω γὰρ καὶ τοὺς ἄλλους προφήτας ἔστι ποιοῦντας εὑρεῖν. «Ὅρασις γάρ, φησίν, ἣν εἶδεν Ἡσαΐας, υἱὸς Ἀμώς, ἐν ἡμέραις Ὀζίου, καὶ Ἰωάθαμ, καὶ Ἄχαζ, καὶ Ἐζεκίου, οἳ ἐβασίλευσαν τῆς Ἰουδαίας.» Καί· «Ἐγενήθη λόγος Κυρίου πρὸς Ἱερεμίαν ἐν ἡμέραις Ἰωσίου, υἱοῦ Ἀμώς, βασιλέως Ἰούδα, ἔτους τρισκαιδεκάτου ἐν τῇ βασιλείᾳ αὐτοῦ.» Καὶ Ἐζε|κιὴλ δέ, καὶ τῶν ἄλλων προφητῶν ἕκαστος, ὡς τὰ πολλὰ τούτῳ τῷ προοιμίῳ τῆς προφητείας κέχρηται. Ἀπόχρη τοιγαροῦν καὶ τοῦτο τὴν Ἰουδαίων ἐλέγξαι παρανομίαν, καὶ διδάξαι προφήτην τὸν τῷ ὄντι προφήτην.

β'. «Καὶ ἔδωκε Κύριος ἐν χειρὶ αὐτοῦ τὸν Ἰωακεὶμ, βασιλέα Ἰούδα, καὶ ἀπὸ μέρους τῶν σκευῶν οἴκου τοῦ Θεοῦ.» Καὶ τοῦτο δὲ τὴν πνευματικὴν αὐτοῦ δείκνυσι χάριν. Οὔτε γὰρ πάντων ἐστὶ τὰς θείας οἰκονομίας εἰδέναι· οὗτος δὲ τοῦ θείου Πνεύματος ἠξιωμένος, καὶ ἔγνω σαφῶς, καὶ τοὺς ἄλλους διδάσκει, ὅτι τοῦ Θεοῦ τῶν ὅλων συγχωρήσαντος, διά τε τὴν τοῦ λαοῦ καὶ τοῦ βασιλέως παρανομίαν, καὶ τὴν πολλὴν ἀσέβειαν, καὶ ἡ πόλις ἑάλω, καὶ τῶν ἱερῶν σκευῶν ἔνια ὑπὸ τὴν τῶν πολεμίων ἐξουσίαν ἐγένετο. Καὶ λίαν δὲ ἀναγκαίως τέθεικε τό· «Ἔδωκε Κύριος ἐν χειρὶ αὐτοῦ τὸν Ἰωακεὶμ, βασιλέα Ἰούδα,» ἵνα μή τις ὑπολάβῃ οἰκείᾳ δυνάμει τὸν Ναβουχοδονόσορ χρησάμενον τῆς τῷ Θεῷ ἀνακειμένης περιγενέσθαι πόλεως· μάθωσιν ἅπαντες καὶ ἀκριβῶς, ὅτι

CHAPTER I

In the third year of the reign of Jehoiakim king of Judah, Nebuchad-
nezzar king of Babylon came to Jerusalem and besieged it (v. 1). Of
necessity he made mention before everything else of the king of the
time and informed us of the period so that we might know clearly
the time of the first captivity: it was in the third year of the reign
of Jehoiakim, known also as Eliakim, who reigned after Jehoahaz
but was the father of the Jehoahaz who was called both Jehoiachin
and Jeconiah, that the first capture of Jerusalem occurred.[22] Now,
this very feature, his mentioning the kings of the time and the
dates, betrays his prophetic character, it being possible to find the
other prophets doing likewise. Scripture says, remember, "A vision which Isaiah son of Amoz saw in the days of Uzziah, Jotham,
Ahaz and Hezekiah, kings of Judah"; and "A word of the Lord
came to Jeremiah in the days of King Josiah son of Amon of Ju-
dah in the thirteenth year of his reign."[23] And Ezekiel | and in   1269
most cases each of the other prophets employed this introduction
to their prophecy. So it suffices also to convict Jews of frenzy and
establish the prophet as truly a prophet.

    The Lord gave Jehoiakim king of Judah into his hand, and some
of the vessels of the house of God (v. 2). This also shows the spiritual grace in him: while it is not possible for everyone to know the
divine dispensations, he had been accorded the divine Spirit and
knew them clearly, and he informs the others that with the permission of the God of all it was due to the lawless behavior and
grave impiety of the people and the king that the city was taken
and some of the sacred vessels fell into the power of the enemy. It
was quite inevitable that he should make the statement *The Lord*
gave Jehoiakim king of Judah into his hand, lest anyone form the impression that it was by using his own power that Nebuchadnezzar
prevailed over the city dedicated to God; and it was for everyone

---

    [22] Is Theodoret confused here (perhaps by the fact that Jehoiakim and
Jehoiachin appear identically in Greek) in adding the detail that Jehoiachin's father was also a Jehoahaz—or is the translator misrepresenting him? What he
does not advert to is that "the third year" of Jehoiakim's reign, 606, is in fact
a year before Nebuchadnezzar's becoming king and nine years before his first
siege of Jerusalem; ἀκρίβεια does not necessarily denote accuracy.
    [23] Isa 1:1; cf. Jer 1:2–3.

τοῦ Θεοῦ προδεδωκότος, καὶ τὴν πάλαι φρουροῦσαν τὴν πόλιν ἀποστήσαντος χάριν, ὑπὸ τοὺς πολεμίους ἐγένετο. Τοῦτο καὶ διὰ Ἡσαΐου τοῦ προφήτου σαφὲς ποιῶν αὐτὸς ὁ τῶν ὅλων Θεὸς οὕτω φησί· «Μὴ δοξασθήσεται ἀξίνη ἄνευ τοῦ κόπτοντος ἐν αὐτῇ; ἢ ὑψωθήσεται πρίων ἄνευ τοῦ ἕλκοντος αὐτόν;» Διδάσκει δὲ διὰ τούτων, ὡς αὐτὸς τοῖς ἀνθρώποις ἐπιφέρει τὰς τιμωρίας, κέχρηται δὲ ὀργάνοις τοῖς εἰς τοῦτο ἐπιτηδείοις. «Καὶ ἤνεγκεν αὐτά, φησίν, εἰς γῆν Σενναὰρ, εἰς οἶκον θεοῦ αὐτοῦ, καὶ τὰ σκεύη εἰσήνεγκεν εἰς οἶκον τοῦ θησαυροῦ τοῦ θεοῦ αὐτοῦ.» Καὶ ἴσως ἄν τις εἴποι· Τί δήποτε τῶν ἀνθρώπων ἡμαρτηκότων, τὰ ἅγια σκεύη, τὰ τῷ Θεῷ ἀνακείμενα, παρεδόθη δυσσεβέσιν ἀνθρώποις; Φασὶ δὲ ταῦτα οἱ τῶν θείων οἰκονομιῶν τὸν σκοπὸν ἀγνοοῦντες. «Ψυχικὸς γὰρ ἄνθρωπος οὐ δέχεται τὰ τοῦ Πνεύματος τοῦ Θεοῦ· μωρία γὰρ αὐτῷ ἐστιν· ὁ δὲ πνευματικὸς ἀνακρίνει πάντα,» κατὰ τὸν θεῖον Ἀπόστολον· καὶ πέπεισται μὲν ὅτι μάτην οὐδὲν ὑπὸ τῆς θείας προμηθείας οἰκονομεῖται, φωτιζόμενος δὲ ὑπὸ τοῦ θείου Πνεύματος, καὶ τὰς αἰτίας μανθάνει· ὥσπερ ἀμέλει καὶ τὸ νῦν ζητούμενον ἔστι καταμαθεῖν τὸν πνευματικῶς νοεῖν προαιρούμενον. Πολλὴ γὰρ ἐντεῦθεν οὐχὶ Ἰουδαίοις μόνον, ἀλλὰ καὶ αὐτοῖς τοῖς βαρβάροις ὠφέλεια γεγένηται. Πρῶτον μὲν γὰρ ἐδιδάχθησαν Ἰουδαῖοι τὸ τῆς θείας φύσεως ἀνενδεές· οὐ γὰρ ὡς δεόμενος τῶν ὅλων Θεὸς τὰ παρὰ τῶν ἀνθρώπων προσφερόμενα δέχεται, ἀλλ' ἐκείνους εὐγνωμοσύνην διδάσκων, καὶ διδοὺς θεραπείαν τε καὶ ἀντιδόσεως ἀφορμήν. Πῶς γὰρ ἂν ἑτέρως ἠδυνήθημεν, ὑπὲρ ὧν εὐεργετήθημεν, ὡς δυνατὸν ἀμείψασθαι τὸν εὐεργέτην Θεόν, εἰ μὴ τὰ | βραχέα ταῦτα καὶ εὐτελῆ παρὰ τῶν προσφερόντων ἐδέχετο; Πεῖσαι τοίνυν βουλόμενος Ἰουδαίους, ὡς οὐ τὴν οἰκείαν χρείαν ἀναπληρῶν, ἀλλὰ πρὸς τὴν ἐκείνων ἀσθένειαν συγκατιών, τὰς παρ' αὐτῶν προσφερομένας θυσίας ἐδέχετο, εἰκότως ἀποστραφεὶς αὐτοὺς καὶ αἰχμαλωσίᾳ παραδούς, καὶ τὰ ὑπ' αὐτῶν προσενεχθέντα σκεύη, δι' ὧν αὐτὸν θεραπεύειν ἐνόμιζον, σὺν αὐτοῖς αἰχμάλωτα δέδωκεν. Ὁ γὰρ τοὺς λογικοὺς παραδοὺς τιμωρίᾳ, τί δήποτε τῶν ἀψύχων ἐφείδετο; Διδάσκει δὲ αὐτοὺς καὶ δι' αὐτῶν τῶν πραγμάτων, ὅτι Βαβυλωνίων, τῶν βαρβάρων, τῶν δυσσεβῶν, κατ' οὐδὲν διαφέρουσιν· ἀσεβοῦσι γὰρ ὥσπερ

1272

to learn precisely that it fell into the hands of the enemy when God surrendered it and withdrew the grace that formerly protected the city. To make this clear the God of all speaks in these terms also through the prophet Isaiah, "Surely an axe will not be glorified without the one wielding it, or a saw be exalted without the one using it?"[24] In this he brings out that he personally will inflict retribution on people and use instruments suited to that end.

He brought them to the land of Shinar, to the house of his god, and introduced the vessels into the house of the treasury of his god. Perhaps you may ask,[25] Why on earth was it that, with people sinning, the holy vessels dedicated to God were surrendered to impious people? Those who say this are ignorant of the purpose of the divine dispensations. "Unspiritual persons do not receive the gifts of God's Spirit, being foolishness to them, whereas spiritual persons discern everything,"[26] according to the divine apostle, and, being illuminated by the divine spirit, are convinced that nothing planned by divine providence is without purpose, and come to learn the reason, just as of course the person who opts to understand in a spiritual fashion is able to grasp what is our present object of enquiry. You see, great benefit accrued from this not only to Jews but also to the foreigners themselves: Jews first were instructed in the immunity from need in the divine nature, God accepting what is offered by human beings not out of need but to teach them gratitude and supply them with attention and grounds for response. I mean, how would we otherwise be able to repay a beneficent God for his benefits to us unless | he accepted these trifling and insignificant things from the offerers? In his wish to convince Jews, therefore, that it was not to satisfy his own need but to make allowance for their weakness that he accepted offerings from them, he was right to turn away from them and hand them over to captivity, and allowed to be captured with them the vessels offered by them through which they thought to serve him. After all, if he handed over rational beings to retribution, why did he spare inanimate things?

He teaches them even through events themselves that they are no different from Babylonians, barbaric and godless though

1272

---

[24] Isa 10:15.

[25] One question the readers might legitimately ask is the meaning of "Shinar," the ancient name for Babylonia (cf. Gen 10:10; Isa 11:11).

[26] Cf. 1 Cor 2:14–15.

ἐκεῖνοι, μᾶλλον δὲ πλέον ἤπερ ἐκεῖνοι. Οἱ μὲν γὰρ οὔτε νόμον δεξάμενοι, οὔτε προφητῶν ποδηγῶν ἀπολαύσαντες, ἀγνοίᾳ κατείχοντο· οἱ δὲ ὑπὸ μυρίων παλαιῶν τε καὶ νέων φωτιζόμενοι προφητῶν, καὶ μυρίων ὅσων θαυμάτων αὐτόπται γενόμενοι, κατεφρόνουν μὲν τοῦ τῶν ὅλων Θεοῦ, τὰ δὲ ἄψυχα εἴδωλα θεραπεύοντες διετέλουν. Παρέδωκε τοίνυν τοῖς βαρβάροις τὰ σκεύη, μονονουχὶ λέγων δι' αὐτῶν τῶν πραγμάτων, ὅτι Κατ' οὐδὲν τῶν βαρβάρων διαφέρετε· ὁμοίως γὰρ αὐτὰ καὶ ὑμεῖς ταῖς παρανομίαις μολύνετε, καὶ ἴσον ἐστὶν ὑμᾶς τε ταῦτα ἔχειν, καὶ Βαβυλωνίους· ἀσέβεια γὰρ καὶ ὑμῶν κἀκείνων κρατεῖ. Τοὺς μὲν οὖν Ἰουδαίους ἱκανὸν ἦν τοῦτο καὶ ἐλέγξαι, καὶ παιδεῦσαι, καὶ ὠφέλειαν αὐτοῖς οὐ μικρὰν πραγματεύσασθαι· οἱ δὲ Βαβυλώνιοι, ἡνίκα μὲν ἐτίμησαν, ὡς ἐνόμισαν, τὰ σκεύη, ἀνθρωπείας μὲν αὐτὰ χρήσεως ἔξω πεποιηκότες, τοῖς ὑπ' αὐτῶν δὲ προσκυνουμένοις ἀνατεθεικότες θεοῖς, τῶν λυπηρῶν οὐδαμῶς ἐπειράσθησαν. Ἐπειδὴ δὲ Βαλτάζαρ ὁ βασιλεὺς χρήσασθαι τούτοις ἐτόλμησεν ἑστιώμενος, ἐκολάσθη μὲν παραυτίκα καὶ τὴν ἀξίαν ἔτισε δίκην, ἐδίδαξε δὲ ἅπαντας διὰ τῆς τιμωρίας, πόση τοῦ Θεοῦ ἡ δύναμις τῶν σκευῶν ἐκείνων, καὶ ὅτι οὐκ ἄκων ἀπεστερήθη τῶν ἑαυτοῦ, ἀλλ' ἑκὼν αὐτὰ προὔδωκε διὰ τὴν πολλὴν τοῦ λαοῦ παρανομίαν. Τοῦτο δὲ καὶ ἐπὶ τῆς κιβωτοῦ πάλαι πεποίηκεν. Ἐπειδὴ γὰρ Ὠφνὶ καὶ Φινεές, οἱ Ἡλὶ τοῦ ἱερέως παῖδες παράνομοι καὶ βδελυροί, ταύτην λαβόντες εἰς ἐπικουρίαν τῶν ὁμοφύλων ἐξῆλθον, ἐλέγχει μὲν αὐτῶν τὴν ἀσέβειαν ὁ Θεός, οὐδεμιᾶς ἀξιώσας προνοίας, ἀξίᾳ δὲ σφαγῇ παραδούς, τὴν δὲ κιβωτὸν τοῖς ἀλλοφύλοις· πάλιν τὸν Ἰσραὴλ παιδεύων, καὶ διδάσκων, ὡς οὐκ αὐτῷ χρεία τῆς κιβωτοῦ, ἀλλ' αὐτῶν ἕνεκεν αὐτὴν κατεσκεύασε, περιττὴ δὲ αὐτοῖς ἡ ταύτης χρεία, ἀδεῶς τὸν θεῖον νόμον παραβαίνουσι, καὶ ἀσεβείᾳ συζῆν προαιρουμένοις. Ἵνα δὲ μὴ μέγα φρονήσαντες οἱ ἀλλόφυλοι, ὡς αὐτοὶ περιγενόμενοι τοῦ Θεοῦ (ἐνόμιζον γὰρ τὴν κιβωτὸν αὐτὸν εἶναι τὸν τῶν Ἰουδαίων Θεόν, τεκμηρίῳ χρώμενοι τῇ τῶν οἰκείων εἰδώλων κατασκευῇ), καὶ ἵνα μὴ πολλὴν ἐν|τεῦθεν ἐπισπάσωνται βλάβην, ὡς αἰχμάλωτον λαβόντες τὸν τῶν Ἰουδαίων Θεόν, καὶ οἷόν τι ἀριστεῖον τοῖς οἰκείοις ἀνατεθεικότες θεοῖς· παρασκευάζει μὲν τὸν Δαγών, τὸ ὑπ' αὐτῶν προσκυνούμενον εἴδωλον, πεσεῖν τε καὶ πρὸ τῆς κιβωτοῦ συντριβῆναι, καὶ τὸ τῆς προσκυνήσεως ὑποδεῖξαι σχῆμα, καὶ ὁμολογῆσαι διὰ

1273

they are; for they are as impious as the latter—or, rather, even more than the latter: without being in receipt of a law or enjoying guidance of prophets, these people were in the grip of ignorance, whereas the former had been enlightened by both ancient and recent prophets and were witnesses of countless marvels, yet scorned the God of all and kept serving lifeless idols. So he handed the vessels over to the foreigners as if to say through the events themselves, You are no different from the foreigners, defiling these things in similar fashion in your case with your transgressions, and it is the same thing for you to have them as for the Babylonians, since godlessness has control of both you and them. This sufficed, therefore, to censure and chastise also the Jews, and to bring them no little benefit, while the Babylonians, in showing respect for the vessels in their fashion by keeping them from human usage and devoting them to the gods worshiped by them, came to no harm. But when King Belshazzar presumed to use them at a banquet, he was immediately punished and paid the due penalty, on the one hand, and on the other he provided a lesson to everyone through the punishment of the great power of the God of those vessels and of the fact that, far from being deprived of his own things against his will, he had willingly handed them over as a result of the people's grave lawlessness.[27]

He had also done this of old in the case of the ark: when Ophni and Phineas, lawless and loathsome sons of the priest Eli, took it in support of their kinsmen and went off, God charged them with impiety, according them no providence, and consigning them deservedly to slaughter and the ark to the Philistines.[28] His purpose again was to chastise Israel and convey the fact that instead of his needing the ark, he had made it for them; but use of it was lost on them when they transgressed the divine law and opted for a life of impiety. Lest the Philistines boast, however, of prevailing over God, thinking the ark was the Jews' god by analogy with the manufacture of their own idols, and in case | they incur great   1273 harm from taking the Jews' god captive and devoting it to their own gods as a kind of trophy, he caused the idol Dagon worshiped by them to fall and break in pieces in front of the ark so as to give an idea of worship, to admit its defeat by the event and demon-

[27] Dan 5.
[28] 1 Sam 4.

τῶν πραγμάτων τὴν ἧτταν, καὶ τὴν τοῦ ἐνοικοῦντος δαίμονος ὑποδεῖξαι δουλείαν· καὶ τοῦτο οὐχ ἅπαξ, ἀλλὰ καὶ δὶς καὶ πολλάκις. Ἐπιφέρει δὲ καὶ αὐτοῖς διαφόρους πληγάς, ἕως οὗ τὴν κιβωτὸν ἀπέδοσαν, καὶ ἀναθέματα δηλοῦντα τὴν τιμωρίαν ἀνέθεσαν. Διπλῆ τοίνυν καὶ τηνικαῦτα, καὶ ἐπὶ τοῦ Ναβουχοδονόσορ ἡ ὠφέλεια γεγένηται· οὐ γὰρ μόνον Ἰουδαίους, ἀλλὰ καὶ τοὺς βαρβάρους ὠφέλησεν ἡ πρὸς βραχὺ παρὰ τοῦ Θεοῦ γενομένη συγχώρησις.

γ΄, δ΄. «Καὶ εἶπεν ὁ βασιλεὺς Ἀσφανὲζ τῷ ἀρχιευνούχῳ αὐτοῦ, εἰσαγαγεῖν ἀπὸ τῶν υἱῶν τῆς αἰχμαλωσίας τῶν υἱῶν Ἰσραήλ, καὶ ἀπὸ τοῦ σπέρματος τῆς βασιλείας, καὶ ἀπὸ τῶν φορθομμίν· νεανίσκους, ἐν οἷς οὐκ ἔστιν ἐν αὐτοῖς μῶμος, καλοὺς τῇ ὄψει, καὶ συνιέντας ἐν πάσῃ σοφίᾳ, καὶ γινώσκοντας γνῶσιν καὶ σοφίαν, καὶ διανοουμένους φρόνησιν, ἐν οἷς ἐστιν ἰσχὺς ἐν αὐτοῖς, τοῦ ἑστάναι ἐν τῷ οἴκῳ τοῦ βασιλέως, καὶ τοῦ διδάξαι αὐτοὺς γράμματα καὶ γλώσσας Χαλδαίων.» Ὁ μὲν οὖν ὅλων Θεὸς ἐξελέξατο τὰ μωρὰ τοῦ κόσμου, καὶ τὰ ἀσθενῆ, καὶ τὰ ἐξουθενημένα, ἵνα διὰ τούτων καταισχύνῃ τοὺς σοφοὺς καὶ δυνατούς· ἄνθρωποι δὲ σωμάτων ὥραν, καὶ μέγεθος, καὶ ῥώμην ἐπιζητοῦσι, καὶ σοφίαν, οὐ τὴν τὰ θεῖα γινώσκουσαν, ἀλλὰ τὴν εὐγλωττίᾳ κεκομψευμένην. Ἔστι τοίνυν καὶ ἐντεῦθεν μαθεῖν, ὁπόσον τῶν θείων καὶ ἀνθρωπίνων τὸ μέσον. Δηλοῖ δὲ τοῦ βασιλέως τὴν ἀλαζονείαν, τὸ μὴ μόνον τοὺς ἄλλους αἰχμαλώτους ὑπηρέτας ἐθελῆσαι λαβεῖν, ἀλλὰ καὶ τοὺς ἐκ τοῦ βασιλικοῦ γένους ὑπάρχοντας. Πληροῦται δὲ ὅμως ἐνταῦθα ἡ Ἡσαΐου πρόρρησις, ἣν Ἐζεκίᾳ βασιλεῖ προεῖπεν. «Ἄκουσον, φησί, τὸν λόγον Κυρίου Σαβαώθ, ὃν ἐλάλησε πρός με· Ἰδοὺ ἡμέραι ἔρχονται, καὶ λήψονται πάντα τὰ ἐν τῷ οἴκῳ σου, καὶ ὅσα συνήγαγον οἱ πατέρες σου ἕως τῆς ἡμέρας ταύτης εἰς Βαβυλῶνα ἥξει, καὶ οὐδὲν οὐ μὴ καταλίπωσιν, εἶπεν ὁ Θεός· ὅτι καὶ ἀπὸ τῶν τέκνων σου ὧν γεννήσεις λήψονται, καὶ ποιήσουσι σπάδοντας ἐν τῷ οἴκῳ βασιλέως τῶν Βαβυλωνίων.» Ταύτης ἡμᾶς τῆς προφητείας ἀναμιμνήσκων ὁ μακάριος Δανιήλ, φησὶ προστάξαι τὸν βασιλέα εἰσαγαγεῖν ἀπὸ τῆς αἰχμαλωσίας τῶν υἱῶν Ἰσραήλ, καὶ ἀπὸ τοῦ σπέρματος τῆς βασιλείας, καὶ ἀπὸ τῶν φορθομμίν. Φορθομμὶν δὲ τὰς παρθένους ἐκάλεσε τῇ Ἑβραίων φωνῇ· ὁ δὲ Σύμμαχος τὸ πόρθμιν ἐπιλέκτους ἡρμήνευσε. |

strate the subjection of the demon inside it. This happened not only once but many times; he inflicted different disasters on them until they gave back the ark and made many offerings suggesting retribution.[29] At that time, too, in the case of Nebuchadnezzar, therefore, the benefit proved to be twofold: the license given by God for a short time was of benefit not only to Jews but also to the foreigners.

The king told Ashpenaz his chief eunuch to bring in some of the captive children of the people of Israel of royal birth and from the partemim, young men of no deformity, comely to behold, versed in all wisdom, endowed with knowledge and insight, grounded in good manners, gifted with strength, to take their place in the house of the king and be taught the literature and language of the Chaldeans (vv. 3–4). Whereas the God of all, then, chose the world's lame, weak, and despised so as to shame the wise and powerful,[30] human beings look for bodily charm, stature, and good health, not the wisdom acquainted with divine things but the wisdom adorned with fine speech. From this you can also learn, therefore, the gap between divine and human criteria. It betrays the king's arrogance in wanting to take as attendants not only the other captives but also those of royal blood. Yet here is fulfilled the prophecy of Isaiah spoken to King Hezekiah, "Listen to the word of the Lord of hosts which he spoke to me, Lo, days are coming when they will take everything in your house, and everything your fathers have amassed to this day will come to Babylon, and they will leave nothing, God said, because they will even take some of the children you have begotten and will make them eunuchs in the house of the king of the Babylonians."[31] To remind us of this prophecy, blessed Daniel says the king ordered *some of the captive children of Israel of royal birth and some of the partemim be brought in,* by the Hebrew term *partemim* referring to the maidens, though *partemim* Symmachus rendered as "chosen."[32] |

---

[29] 1 Sam 5–6.

[30] Cf. 1 Cor 1:27–28.

[31] Isa 39:5–7.

[32] Theodoret finds in his Greek text (known as Theodotion-Daniel) a transliterated form of the Hebrew term, itself deriving from Persian, meaning "nobility"; but despite the (rare) reference to the version of Symmachus to suggest otherwise, he hazards a version of his own—unwise in view of his lack of Hebrew.

ε', ς'. «Καὶ ἔταξεν αὐτοῖς ὁ βασιλεὺς τὸ τῆς ἡμέρας καθ' ἡμέραν ἀπὸ τῆς τραπέζης τοῦ βασιλέως, καὶ ἀπὸ τοῦ οἴνου τοῦ πότου τοῦ
αὐτοῦ, καὶ ἐκθρέψαι αὐτοὺς ἔτη τρία, καὶ μετὰ ταῦτα στῆναι αὐτοὺς
ἐνώπιον τοῦ βασιλέως. Καὶ ἐγένετο ἐν αὐτοῖς ἐκ τῶν υἱῶν Ἰούδα, Δανιήλ, καὶ Ἀνανίας, καὶ Ἀζαρίας, καὶ Μισαήλ.» Ἐνταῦθα μὲν οὖν τὴν
τοῦ βασιλέως ἡμᾶς διδάσκει φιλοτιμίαν, ὅτι οὐχ ὡς δορυαλώτοις εὐ-
τελῆ τινα καὶ δουλοπρεπῆ παρεῖχε τροφήν, ἀλλὰ τῆς βασιλικῆς αὐτοὺς
τραπέζης ἀπολαύειν ἐκέλευσε. Μετὰ βραχέα δὲ τὴν σφῶν αὐτῶν ἐγκρά-
τειαν καὶ φιλοσοφίαν διδάσκει, οὐ φιλοτιμίᾳ χρώμενος, ἀλλ' ὠφελείας
διδασκαλίαν τοῖς ὠφελεῖσθαι προαιρουμένοις προτεθεικώς. Ἔστι δὲ αὐτοῦ ἰδεῖν καὶ τὸ μέτριον τοῦ φρονήματος· εἰρηκὼς γὰρ ἄνω, ὅτι ἀπὸ
τοῦ τῆς βασιλείας σπέρματος προσέταξεν ὁ βασιλεὺς ἐκλεγῆναι νεανίας,
κάλλει λάμποντας, καὶ μεγέθει διαπρέποντας, καὶ τεθεικὼς ἐνταῦθα τὰ
τῶν προσώπων ὀνόματα, τῆς Ἰούδα φυλῆς ἁπλῶς ἐμνημόνευσε, καὶ τὴν
τῆς βασιλείας συγγένειαν ἔκρυψε.

ζ'. «Καὶ ἐπέθηκεν αὐτοῖς ὁ ἀρχιευνοῦχος ὀνόματα· τῷ Δανιὴλ
Βαλτάσαρ, καὶ τῷ Ἀνανίᾳ Σιδράχ, καὶ τῷ Μισαὴλ Μισάχ, καὶ τῷ Ἀζαρίᾳ Ἀβδεναγώ.» Καὶ τοῦτο δὲ παρά τισι δεσποτείας νενόμισται δίκαιον·
ὠνούμενοι γὰρ οἰκέτας τὰς προσηγορίας ἀμείβουσιν, ἵνα καὶ τῇ τῆς προσηγορίας ἐναλλαγῇ τὴν δουλείαν γνωρίζωσι. Καὶ τοῦτο καὶ ἐνταῦθα ὁ
ἀρχιευνοῦχος ἐποίησε, καὶ τὰς Ἑβραϊκὰς ἀφελὼν προσηγορίας, Χαλδα-
ικὰς ἐπιτέθεικεν, ἐπειδὴ καὶ τὴν Χαλδαίων γλῶσσαν μαθεῖν τοὺς νεανίας
ὁ βασιλεὺς παρενεγγύησε.

η'. «Καὶ ἔθετο Δανιὴλ ἐπὶ τὴν καρδίαν αὐτοῦ, τοῦ μὴ ἀλισγη-
θῆναι ἐν τῇ τραπέζῃ τοῦ βασιλέως, καὶ ἐν τῷ οἴνῳ τοῦ πότου αὐτοῦ,
καὶ ἠξίωσε τὸν ἀρχιευνοῦχον, ὅπως μὴ ἀλισγηθῇ.» Οἱ γὰρ φιλόθεοι οὐκ
ἐν τόπῳ ζητοῦσι τὸν ἐπὶ πάντων Θεόν, ἀλλ' ἔνθα ἂν ἀφίκωνται τὴν
αὐτὴν αὐτῷ θεραπείαν προσφέρουσι, καὶ ἐν κακοπραγίαις ὄντες ὡσαύτως τὸν οἰκεῖον προσκυνοῦσι Δημιουργόν. Ἐνταῦθα δὲ πολλὴν ἔστιν
εὑρεῖν θαύματος ὑπερβολήν· παῖδες γὰρ παρὰ Ἰουδαίοις τεθραμμένοι,
καὶ τὴν τοπικὴν τοῦ Θεοῦ λατρείαν μεμαθηκότες, εἶτα τὴν ξένην οἰ-
κοῦντες, καὶ δουλεύειν ἠναγκασμένοι νέαν ἄγοντες κομιδῇ τὴν ἡλικίαν,
ὑπὸ νόμοις ἑτέροις ἀναγκαζόμενοι ζῆν, τὴν πατρῴαν εὐσέβειαν φυλάττειν
σπουδάζουσι· καὶ ἐπειδὴ τοὺς Βαβυλωνίους ἑώρων ταῖς μὲν τῶν εἰδώλων ἐπικλήσεσι τὰ ὄψα μολύναντας, σπονδαῖς δὲ τὸν οἶκον μιαίνοντας,
τῆς ὁρωμένης καταφρονήσαντες σωτηρίας, καὶ τῆς βασιλικῆς πανδαι-
σίας τὴν ἡδονὴν πατήσαντες, τὸν ἀρχιευνοῦχον ἱκετεύουσι παραχωρῆσαι

The king ordered them daily portions of food from the king's table and wine from his supply. They were to be educated for three years, and after that to take their place before the king. Among them were Daniel, Hananiah, Mishael, and Azariah from the children of Judah (vv. 5–6). So here he informs us of the king's generosity in providing them with nourishment that was not of an ordinary kind fit for captives and slaves; instead, he gave orders for them to share in the king's table. Shortly afterwards he mentions their self-control and sound values, not indulging in self-glorification but proposing a beneficial lesson to those prepared to accept benefit. It is possible to see also the moderation in his thinking: after mentioning above that the king ordered young men of royal birth to be chosen, fair to behold and of becoming stature, and citing at this point the persons' names, he simply referred to the tribe of Judah and concealed their royal connections. *The chief eunuch gave them names, to Daniel Belteshazzar, to Hananiah Shadrach, to Mishael Meshach, and to Azariah Abednego* (v. 7). This was considered by some the right of masters, in buying slaves to change their names so that also by the change in name they would recognize their servitude. The chief eunuch did it in this case, too, taking away their Hebrew names and giving Chaldean ones, also for the reason that the king had ordered the young men to learn the Chaldean language.

Daniel's heartfelt resolve was that he not be defiled by eating the king's food and drinking his wine, and he made a request to the chief eunuch not to be defiled (v. 8). Those who love God, you see, take no account of place in seeking God in everything: wherever they go, they offer him the same worship, and when in misfortune they likewise adore their creator. In this case you can find an extraordinary example of this marvel: reared by Jews and versed in the local requirements for worship of God, then inhabiting a foreign land, forced into slavery at a very young age and obliged to live under other laws, they were anxious to preserve their ancestral religion. Since they saw the Babylonians defiling their food with invocation of the idols and polluting their drink[33] with libations, they showed scorn for their material welfare, spurned the delights of the king's voluptuous fare, and begged the chief eunuch to al-

---

[33] Although the text in PG 81 reads οἶκον here, it is probably a (rare) misprint for οἶνον. In fact, food from a king's table as such was not a problem for Jews until the second century (cf. Jehoiachin's similar diet in exile in 2 Kgs 25:29–30), when abstinence from any Gentile food became a Jewish touchstone.

1277 σφίσιν αὐτοῖς τῶν βασιλικῶν σιτίων παραιτουμένοις μεταλαβεῖν. |

θ'. «Καὶ ἔδωκεν ὁ Θεὸς τὸν Δανιὴλ εἰς ἔλεον καὶ οἰκτιρμὸν ἐνώπιον τοῦ ἀρχιευνούχου.» Ἀκολουθεῖ γὰρ ταῖς γνώμαις ἡ θεία κηδεμονία, καὶ ἅμα τὰ θεῖα προείλοντο, καὶ τῆς θείας ἐπικουρίας ἀπήλαυσαν. Τοῦτο καὶ ἐπὶ τοῦ Ἰωσὴφ γεγενημένον ἔστιν εὑρεῖν· «Ἦν γὰρ, φησί, Κύριος μετὰ Ἰωσὴφ, καὶ ἦν ἀνὴρ ἐπιτυγχάνων, καὶ κατέχεεν αὐτῷ ἔλεον, καὶ χάριν ἐναντίον τοῦ δεσμοφύλακος.» Διδασκόμεθα τοίνυν κἀντεῦθεν, ὡς οὐδένα τῶν εἰς αὐτὸν πεπιστευκότων ἀτημέλητόν πώς ποτε καταλέλοιπεν ὁ Θεός. Διὸ καὶ ἕτερος προφήτης βοᾷ· «Ἐρωτήσατε γενεὰς τὰς γενομένας προτέρας ὑμῶν, τίς ἐνεπίστευσε Κυρίῳ, καὶ κατησχύνθη;»

ι'. «Καὶ εἶπεν ὁ ἀρχιευνοῦχος τῷ Δανιήλ· Φοβοῦμαι ἐγὼ τὸν κύριόν μου τὸν βασιλέα, τὸν ἐκτάξαντα τὴν βρῶσιν καὶ τὴν πόσιν ὑμῶν, μή ποτε ἴδῃ τὰ πρόσωπα ὑμῶν σκυθρωπὰ παρὰ τὰ παιδάρια τὰ συνήλικα ὑμῶν, καὶ καταδικάσητε τὴν κεφαλήν μου τῷ βασιλεῖ.» Οὐκ ἄλογον τοῦ ἀρχιευνούχου τὸ δέος· ἄνθρωπος γὰρ ἦν πνευματικῆς χάριτος οὐ γεγευμένος, ἀνθρωπίνως δὲ σκοπῶν τὰ ἀνθρώπεια, καὶ ἡγούμενος ἐκ μόνης δύνασθαι τῆς τῶν ἐδεσμάτων πολυτελείας τρέφεσθαί τε καὶ ἀνθεῖν τὰ σώματα, δέδοικε μὴ τῶν μὲν πολυτελῶς τρεφομένων, τούτων δὲ ἀσκητικῶς βιοτευόντων, διαφορά τις ἐν τοῖς προσώποις φανῇ, καὶ τιμωρίαν ἐσχάτην ὑπομείνῃ παρὰ τοῦ τἀναντία προστεταχότος βασιλέως. Ἀλλ' ἐπειδὴ τοῦτον εἶδε δειμαίνοντα ὁ μακάριος Δανιὴλ, μεταφέρει πρὸς τὸν Ἀμελάσαρ τὴν παράκλησιν, ὃν κατέστησεν ὁ ἀρχιευνοῦχος κηδεμόνα αὐτοῦ τε καὶ Ἀνανία, καὶ Ἀζαρία, καὶ Μισαὴλ, καί φησι·

ιβ', ιγ'. «Πείρασον δὴ τοὺς παῖδάς σου ἡμέρας δέκα, καὶ δότωσαν ἡμῖν ἀπὸ τῶν σπερμάτων, καὶ φαγώμεθα, καὶ ὕδωρ πιώμεθα. Καὶ ὀφθήτωσαν ἐνώπιόν σου αἱ ἰδέαι ἡμῶν, καὶ αἱ ἰδέαι τῶν παιδαρίων τῶν ἐσθιόντων τὴν τράπεζαν τοῦ βασιλέως· καὶ καθὼς ἐὰν ἴδῃς, ποίησον μετὰ τῶν παίδων σου.» Οὐδὲν τῆς εἰς Θεὸν πίστεως ἰσχυρότερον, καὶ δὴ τοῦτο πολλαχόθεν καὶ ἄλλοθεν ἔστι μαθεῖν, οὐχ ἥκιστα δὲ καὶ ἐκ τῶν τοῦ θεσπεσίου Δανιὴλ ῥημάτων. Τὸ γὰρ πιστεῦσαί τε καὶ θαρρῆσαι, ὡς τῆς θείας ῥοπῆς ἀπολαύσεται, καὶ μὴ ἐσθίων τῶν ἐσθιόντων καὶ τρυφώντων, καὶ τῆς βασιλικῆς ἀπολαυόντων χλιδῆς, εὐπρεπέστερός τε καὶ περικαλλέστερος φανήσεται καὶ μείζων, ποίαν εὐσεβείας ὑπερβολὴν καταλείπει;

low them to decline a share in the royal victuals. | *God granted* 1277
Daniel to find mercy and compassion with the chief eunuch (v. 9). Divine care is a consequence of our free will, and once it opts for
the divine commands, it enjoys divine assistance. You can see this
happening also in the case of Joseph: "The Lord was with Joseph;
he was a successful man, and the Lord poured mercy on him and
favor with the jailer."[34] So we learn from this that God never left
to their own devices any of those who believe in him. Hence another inspired author also cries aloud, "Ask the generations before
you, Who trusted in the Lord and was disappointed?"[35]

   The chief eunuch said to Daniel, I am afraid that my lord the
king, who has prescribed your food and drink, may chance to no-
tice that your appearance is wan by comparison with the youngsters
of your age, and you would cause the king to have my head (v. 10).
The chief eunuch's apprehension was not without reason: he was
a person without experience of spiritual grace, considering human things in a human fashion, and believing that bodies could
be nourished and developed only with rich and varied foods. So
he was afraid that a difference in appearance would emerge between those richly nourished and those living austerely, and he
would receive the ultimate penalty at the hands of the king, who
had given orders to the contrary. When blessed Daniel saw his apprehension, however, he directed his appeal to Amelasar,[36] whom
the chief eunuch put in charge of him, Hananiah, Azariah, and
Mishael, saying, *Please test your servants for ten days, give us veg-*
etables to eat and water to drink. Compare our appearance with the
appearance of the youngsters eating the king's fare, and deal with your
servants as you observe (vv. 12–13). Nothing is stronger than faith
in God; you can learn this also from many other places, but especially from the words of the divinely inspired Daniel. I mean,
what greater degree of piety is left to match believing and trusting that he would enjoy divine favor and appear more comely and
charming and stronger by not eating when the others were eating and being fed and enjoying the royal delicacies? Now, he did

---

[34] Gen 39:21, the second clause not occurring in other forms of the LXX,
including Chrysostom's text of Genesis.

[35] Sir 2:10 loosely cited, Theodoret perhaps thinking of another author,
as the sages normally are not referred to as προφῆται.

[36] In his Greek text "the guard," Hebrew *ha melsar*, becomes a proper
name.

Καλῶς δὲ καὶ τῷ πιθανῷ τὴν ἱκετείαν ἐκέρασε· «Πείρασον γάρ, φησί,
1280 τοὺς παῖδάς σου ἡμέρας δέκα, | καὶ δότωσαν ἡμῖν ἀπὸ τῶν σπερμάτων,
καὶ φαγώμεθα, καὶ ὕδωρ πιώμεθα·» καὶ γενοῦ σὺ τῶν προσώπων κριτής·
κἂν εὕρῃς βλάβην τινὰ γινομένην τοῖς σώμασιν ἐκ τῆς τοιαύτης τροφῆς,
τὸ μὲν δοκοῦν σοι κελεύσεις, ἡμεῖς δὲ οὐκ ἀντιλέξομεν. Τοσαύτην εἶχε
παιδόθεν ὁ θεῖος οὗτος ἀνήρ, καὶ τῶν θείων νόμων φροντίδα, καὶ πίστιν
περὶ τὸν νομοθέτην· καὶ ὁ μὲν ταῦτα ἔλεγεν, ὁ δὲ τὴν ἱκετείαν ἐδέχετο.
   ιδ′, ιε′. «Καὶ εἰσήκουσε γὰρ αὐτῶν, φησίν, εἰς τὸ ῥῆμα τοῦτο,
καὶ ἐπείρασεν αὐτοὺς ἡμέρας δέκα. Καὶ μετὰ τὸ τέλος τῶν δέκα ἡμερῶν
ἐωράθησαν αἱ ἰδέαι αὐτῶν ἀγαθαί, καὶ αὐτοὶ ἰσχυροὶ ταῖς σαρξὶν ὑπὲρ
τὰ παιδάρια τὰ ἐσθίοντα τὴν τράπεζαν τοῦ βασιλέως.» Ἔτυχε γὰρ ὧν
ἠθέλησεν ὁ θεῖος οὗτος προφήτης, καὶ τὰς ὑποσχέσεις ὑπέδειξεν ἀληθεῖς
τῷ τὴν ἐπιμέλειαν αὐτῶν ἐγκεχειρισμένῳ· τῆς γὰρ θείας χάριτος ἀπολαύσαντες ὤφθησαν ἀμείνους πολλῷ τῶν τῆς βασιλικῆς ἀπολαυόντων
τραπέζης.
   ιϛ′. «Καὶ ἐγένετο Ἀμελάσαρ ἀναιρούμενος τὸ δεῖπνον αὐτῶν, καὶ
τὸν οἶνον τοῦ πόματος αὐτῶν, καὶ ἐδίδου αὐτοῖς σπέρματα.» Καὶ δι-
πλοῦν ἐκαρπώσατο κέρδος· πρῶτον μὲν γὰρ μεμάθηκεν, ὡς δυνατὸν καὶ
νηστείᾳ χρώμενον σωματικὴν ῥώμην καὶ εὐπρέπειαν κτήσασθαι· ἔπειτα
δὲ καὶ τὴν ἐκείνοις χορηγουμένην αὐτὸς λαμβάνων τροφήν, προθυμότε-
ρον αὐτοῖς ἐχορήγει τὰ ποθούμενα σπέρματα· εἶτα, ἐπειδὴ περὶ ἑαυτοῦ
μόνου διηγήσατο, ἀναγκαίως καὶ τοὺς κοινωνοὺς τῆς εὐσεβείας εἰς μέσον
καλεῖ, καί φησι·
   ιζ′. «Καὶ τοῖς παιδαρίοις τοῖς τέσσαρσιν ἔδωκεν αὐτοῖς ὁ Θεὸς
σύνεσιν καὶ φρόνησιν ἐν πάσῃ γραμματικῇ σοφίᾳ.» Οὐ γὰρ ἡ Χαλδαίων,
φησί, παιδεία συνετοὺς αὐτοὺς ἀπέφηνε, καὶ σοφίας ἁπάσης ἐνέπλησεν,
ἀλλ’ ἐκ θείας χάριτος καὶ συνέσεως καὶ σοφίας καὶ πάσης ἐπιστήμης
ἀξιωθέντες, κρείττους ἁπάντων ἐδείχθησαν. «Καὶ Δανιήλ, φησί, συνῆκεν ἐν πάσῃ ὁράσει, καὶ ἐνυπνίοις.» Παιδόθεν γὰρ θείας ἀποκαλύψεις
ἑώρα, οὐκ ὄναρ μόνον, ἀλλὰ καὶ ὕπαρ· καὶ ἑρμηνεύειν δὲ ἠδύνατο τὰ τοῖς
ἄλλοις ἀποκαλυπτόμενα· τὸ γὰρ συνῆκε τοῦτο παραδηλοῖ. Διδασκόμεθα δὲ κἀντεῦθεν, ὡς οὐκ οἶδεν ἡλικίας διαφορὰν ὁ τῶν ὅλων Θεός, ἀλλ’
εὐσέβειαν μόνον καὶ φιλοθεΐαν ζητεῖ· κἂν εὕρῃ ταύτην ἐν νέῳ, πολλῶν
τοῦτον προτίθησι πρεσβυτέρων. Τὸ αὐτὸ δὲ καὶ ἐπὶ τοῦ Ἰωσὴφ ἔστιν
αὐτὸν εὑρεῖν πεποιηκότα, καὶ ἐπὶ Σαμουὴλ τοῦ προφήτου· παιδίῳ γὰρ
ὄντι κομιδῇ νέῳ, καὶ ἐπεφάνη, καὶ τὰς κατὰ τοῦ πρεσβύτου τιμωρίας

well to combine petition with persuasion, *Test your servants for ten days,* | *give us vegetables to eat and water to drink,* and become the 1280
judge of our appearance: if you find harm coming to our bodies
from such a diet, do what you think best, and we shall not object.
Such concern for the divine laws and faith in the lawgiver did this
divine man have from his youth.[37]

What one man asked the other accepted. *He heard this pe-*
tition of theirs, and tested them for ten days. At the end of the ten
days their appearance was good, and they were strong in body by com-
parison with the youngsters who had been eating the king's fare (vv.
14–15). In other words, the divine prophet gained what he wished,
and proved the promises to be true that he had made to the man
entrusted with their care: by receipt of divine grace they appeared
much better than those in receipt of the royal fare. *Amelasar with-*
drew their food and the wine for drinking, and gave them vegetables
(v. 16). The benefit gained was twofold: firstly, he learned that it is
possible for the person fasting to acquire bodily health and charm,
and next, by taking the food provided for them he was more eager
to supply them with the vegetables they wanted.

Then, though he had spoken only of himself, he inevitably
brought attention to his fellows in piety in the words, *To these four*
young men God gave understanding and judgment in all matters of
letters and wisdom (v. 17): it was not Chaldean education that made
them knowledgeable and filled them will all wisdom; rather, by divine grace they were vouchsafed wisdom and understanding and
all knowledge, and were shown to be better than anyone. *Daniel*
had understanding of all visions and dreams: from his youth he had
divine revelations, not only in dreams but also while awake, and
was also able to interpret those revealed to others, as is indicated by
he had understanding. Now, we learn from this that the God of all
is not in the habit of respecting differences of age, looking instead
only for piety and love of God: even if he finds it in the young, he
prefers them to many of their elders. You can find him doing the
same also in the case of Joseph, and of Samuel the prophet: though
very young, he appeared to him and bade him forecast retribution

---

[37] Theodoret is astray in implying the law's dietary requirements forbade
consumption of such foods (cf. Exod 21–23; Lev 17–26).

προαγορεύειν ἐκέλευσεν, εἰς κατηγορίαν μὲν τοῦ γεγηρακότος, ἀπόδειξιν
1281 δὲ τῆς ἐπανθούσης τῷ μειρακίῳ χάριτος. |

ιη' κ'. «Καὶ μετὰ τὸ τέλος τῶν ἡμερῶν, ὧν εἶπεν ὁ βασιλεὺς
εἰσαγαγεῖν αὐτούς, εἰσήγαγεν αὐτοὺς ὁ ἀρχιευνοῦχος ἐνώπιον Ναβουχοδονόσορ. Καὶ ἐλάλησε μετ' αὐτῶν ὁ βασιλεύς, καὶ οὐχ ηὑρέθησαν ἐκ
πάντων αὐτῶν ὅμοιοι Δανιήλ, Ἀνανία, Ἀζαρίᾳ καὶ Μισαήλ· καὶ ἔστησαν ἐνώπιον τοῦ βασιλέως. Καὶ ἐν παντὶ ῥήματι σοφίας καὶ ἐπιστήμης,
ὑπὲρ ὧν ἐζήτησε παρ' αὐτῶν ὁ βασιλεύς, ηὗρεν αὐτοὺς δεκαπλασίονας
ὑπὲρ πάντας τοὺς ἐπαοιδοὺς καὶ μάγους, τοὺς ὄντας ἐν τῇ βασιλείᾳ αὐτοῦ.» Ἀλλ' ὁ μὲν Ἀμελάσαρ ᾔδει τὴν τῶν ἐδεσμάτων διαφοράν, καὶ
ἔμαθε πάντως τῆς θείας χάριτος τὴν ἰσχύν· ὁ δὲ βασιλεὺς ἴσως ἐγνώκει τούτων οὐδέν. Πῶς γὰρ ἔμαθε, τῆς μὲν τροφῆς ὁμοίως παρ' αὐτοῦ
χορηγουμένης, ὑπὸ δὲ τοῦ Ἀμελάσαρ ἀναλισκομένης; Ἀλλ' ὅμως οὐ
σμικρὰν καὶ οὗτος ὠφέλειαν ἐδέξατο, πάντων αὐτοὺς τῶν ἐξ ἑτέρων
ἐθνῶν ἐκλεγέντων ἀμείνους εὑρών, κάλλει τε καὶ μεγέθει σώματος, σοφίᾳ τε καὶ συνέσει ψυχῆς, ῥυθμῷ τε λόγων καὶ πάσῃ λογικῇ ἐπιστήμῃ.
Τὰς δὲ συγκρίσεις οὐχ ἁπλῶς ἐποιήσατο, ἀλλ' ἐρωτήσεις τινὰς προσα-
γαγών, τὴν πεῖραν ἔλαβε τῆς ἀληθείας διδάσκαλον, καὶ ηὗρεν αὐτοὺς οὐχ
ἁπλῶς ὑπερκειμένους, ἀλλὰ δέκα μοίραις ἀμείνους ὑπάρχοντας· καὶ τέως
μεμάθηκεν, ὅτι τῶν ἄλλων πάντων ἐθνῶν Ἰουδαῖοι σοφώτεροι. Ταῦτα
εἰρηκὼς ἐπήγαγε

κα'. «Καὶ ἐγένετο Δανιὴλ ἕως ἔτους ἑνὸς Κύρου τοῦ βασιλέως.»
Οὐχ ἁπλῶς δὲ τοῦτο προστέθεικεν, ἀλλὰ τῆς προφητείας ἁπάσης τὸν
χρόνον δῆλον ποιῆσαι θελήσας. Τούτου χάριν καὶ τὴν ἀρχὴν ἡμᾶς τῆς
προφητείας ἐδίδαξε, καὶ τὸ τέλος προστέθεικεν, ἵνα τῶν μεταξὺ βασιλέων
ἀριθμοῦντες τὰ ἔτη, μάθωμεν ἅπαντα τῆς προφητείας τὸν χρόνον. Πρὸς
δὲ τούτοις ἡμᾶς διδάσκει, ὅτι καὶ τὸν ποιησάμενον τῆς αἰχμαλωσίας
τὴν ἄφεσιν ἐθεάσατο Κῦρον, καὶ τῷ παρόντι βίῳ παραψυχῆς ἀπήλαυ-
σε τὴν τῶν ὁμοφύλων ἐλευθερίαν ἰδών· ἐν αὐτῷ γὰρ τῷ πρώτῳ ἔτει τῆς
βασιλείας ἐπανελθεῖν ὁ Κῦρος εἰς τὴν Ἰουδαίαν τοὺς βουλομένους Ἰουδαίους προσέταξε, καὶ τὸν θεῖον ἀνήγειρε νεών, παρ' αὐτοῦ τοῦ μακαρίου
Δανιὴλ τὴν Ἡσαΐου τοῦ προφήτου πρόρρησιν διδαχθείς· ἐκεῖνος γὰρ
διαρρήδην ἐβόα· «Λέγων Ἱερουσαλήμ, Οἰκοδομηθήσῃ· καὶ ταῖς πόλεσι

against his elder by way of accusation of the greybeard and proof of the youngster's blossoming grace.[38] |

At the end of the time the king had mentioned for bringing them in, the chief eunuch brought them into the presence of Nebuchadnezzar. The king spoke with them, and none of them was found equal to Daniel, Hananiah, Azariah, and Mishael, and they took their place in the king's presence. In every matter of wisdom and understanding on which the king questioned them, he found them ten times better than all the magicians and soothsayers in his kingdom (vv. 18–20). Whereas Amelasar knew of the difference in diet, and was completely aware of the power of divine grace, however, the king was probably unaware of it all; after all, how could he have known, when the food was supplied in the usual manner but consumed by Amelasar? Nevertheless, he too gained no little benefit, finding them better than all those chosen from other nations in beauty and bodily stature, wisdom and understanding of soul, fluency in language and all rational understanding. He did not simply make comparisons, however: he put questions to them and used experience to teach him the truth, finding them not simply superior but ten times better; and for the time being he came to realize that Jews were wiser than all other nations.

After saying this, he went on, *Daniel was there for one year of King Cyrus* (v. 21). It was not without purpose that he added this detail: he wanted to make clear the time of the whole prophecy. This was the reason he conveyed the beginning of the prophetic work and added the end of it, for us to reckon the years between the kingdoms and come to realize the whole period of the prophetic work.[39] In addition to this he informs us that he witnessed Cyrus bringing the captivity to an end, and in the present life enjoyed consolation from seeing the release of his kin; it was, you see, in the first year of his reign that Cyrus ordered those Jews who were interested to return to Judah, and restored the divine temple, after being informed by blessed Daniel himself of the prophecy of Isaiah the prophet, who cried out boldly, "He who says to Jerusalem, You will be rebuilt, and to the cities of Judah, You will be in-

---

[38] Cf. 1 Sam 3.

[39] The year specified is 539–538, which makes Daniel about ninety years of age if he were a young man at the beginning in 606 as mentioned in verse 1. There is also an apparent contradiction involved with "the third year of King Cyrus" in 10:1.

τῆς Ἰουδαίας, Κατοικισθήσεσθε· ὁ λέγων Κύρῳ φρονεῖν, καὶ πάντα τὰ θελήματά μου ποιήσειν.» «Τάδε λέγει Κύριος τῷ χριστῷ μου Κύρῳ, οὗ ἐκράτησα τῆς χειρὸς αὐτοῦ, ὑπακοῦσαι ἔμπροσθεν αὐτοῦ ἔθνη, καὶ πόλεις οὐ συγκλεισθήσονται· ἐγὼ γὰρ προπορεύσομαι πρὸ προσώπου σου, καὶ ὄρη ὁμαλιῶ· πύλας χαλκᾶς συντρίψω, καὶ μοχλοὺς σιδηροῦς

1284 συν|θλάσω, θησαυροὺς σκοτεινοὺς ἀποκρύφους ἀοράτους ἀνοίξω σοι.» Ταῦτα μαθὼν ὁ Κῦρος τοῖς βουλομένοις τῶν Ἰουδαίων τὴν εἰς τὴν ἐνεγκοῦσαν ἐπάνοδον ἐχαρίσατο· καὶ ἡ βίβλος δὲ τῶν Παραλειπομένων τὸν χρόνον ἡμᾶς διδάσκει. «Ἔτους γὰρ, φησί, πρώτου Κύρου, τοῦ βασιλέως Περσῶν, μετὰ τὸ πληρωθῆναι ῥῆμα Κυρίου διὰ στόματος Ἱερεμίου, ἐξήγειρε Κύριος τὸ πνεῦμα Κύρου, τοῦ βασιλέως Περσῶν, καὶ παρήγγειλε Κῦρος κηρύξαι ἐν πάσῃ τῇ βασιλείᾳ αὐτοῦ ἐν λόγοις Γραφῆς, λέγων· Τάδε λέγει Κῦρος ὁ βασιλεὺς Περσῶν· Πάσας τὰς βασιλείας τῆς γῆς ἔδωκέ μοι Κύριος ὁ Θεὸς τοῦ οὐρανοῦ, καὶ αὐτὸς ἐνετείλατό μοι οἰκοδομῆσαι αὐτῷ οἶκον ἐν Ἱερουσαλήμ, τῇ ἐν τῇ Ἰουδαίᾳ· τίς ἐν ὑμῖν ἐκ παντὸς τοῦ λαοῦ αὐτοῦ; Κύριος ὁ Θεὸς ἔσται μετ' αὐτοῦ, καὶ ἀναβήτω.» Τούτου χάριν καὶ ὁ μακάριος Δανιὴλ τὸν τῆς προφητείας διδάσκων χρόνον, ἐντέθεικε τοῖς Ἰουδαίων συγγράμμασι τό· «Ἐγένετο Δανιὴλ ἕως ἔτους ἑνὸς Κύρου τοῦ βασιλέως.» Ἡμεῖς δὲ ἐνταῦθα τὸν ἀκροατὴν διαναπαύσαντες, τὸν ἀγαθὸν Δεσπότην ὑμνήσωμεν, τὸν πατάσσοντα καὶ ἰώμενον, μαστιγοῦντα καὶ ἰατρεύοντα, τιμωρίᾳ καὶ φιλανθρωπίᾳ χρώμενον· αὐτῷ ἡ δόξα εἰς τοὺς αἰῶνας τῶν αἰώνων. Ἀμήν.

TOMOΣ Β′ — ΚΕΦΑΛΑΙΟΝ Β′

α′. «Ἐν τῷ ἔτει τῷ δευτέρῳ τῆς βασιλείας Ναβουχοδονόσορ ἐνυπνιάσθη ἐνύπνιον, καὶ ἐξέστη τὸ πνεῦμα αὐτοῦ, καὶ ὁ ὕπνος αὐτοῦ ἀπεγένετο ἀπ' αὐτοῦ.» Ἐντεῦθεν μανθάνομεν, ὡς εὐθὺς καὶ παραχρῆμα τῆς βασιλείας ἀρξάμενος ἐπεστράτευσε τῇ Ἰουδαίᾳ ἐν τῷ τρίτῳ ἔτει τῆς βασιλείας Ἰωακεὶμ, καὶ τὸν μὲν ἐκέλευσε φέρειν δασμόν, τοὺς δὲ λαβὼν αἰχμαλώτους εἰς τὴν τῶν Ἀσσυρίων ἀπήγαγε χώραν. Μαρτυρεῖ

habited; he who tells Cyrus to have good sense, and carry out all
my wishes." "The Lord says this to my anointed Cyrus, whose
right hand I have taken, for nations to be obedient before him, and
cities will not be shut. For I shall go before you and level moun-
tains; I shall smash doors of bronze and shatter iron bars; | I shall   1284
open to you treasures that are in darkness, hidden and unseen."⁴⁰
When Cyrus learned of this, he granted to those of the Jews who
were willing to return to their homeland. The book of Chronicles also informs us of the time: "In the first year of Cyrus king of
the Persians, after the fulfillment of the word of the Lord through
the mouth of Jeremiah, the Lord stirred up the spirit of Cyrus
king of the Persians. Cyrus ordered a proclamation in his whole
kingdom in the words of Scripture, Thus says Cyrus king of the
Persians: The Lord the God of heaven has given me all the kingdoms of the earth, and he has commanded me to build him a house
in Jerusalem, which is in Judah. Whoever is among you of all his
people, may the Lord God be with him, and let him go up."⁴¹

This is the reason blessed Daniel also conveyed the time of
the prophecy, recording in the Jews' writings the statement *Daniel
was there for one year of King Cyrus*. Let us for our part at this
point give our reader a rest,⁴² and sing the praises of the good
Lord, who strikes and heals, scourges and cures, applies punishment and lovingkindness. To him be glory for ages of ages. Amen.

CHAPTER 2

*In the second year of his reign Nebuchadnezzar had a dream, his spirit
was perturbed and his sleep left him* (v. 1). From this we learn that
it was at the very beginning of his reign that he invaded Judah in
the third year of the reign of Jehoiakim, ordered tribute to be paid,
made prisoners and took them to the country of the Assyrians.⁴³

⁴⁰ Isa 44:26; 45:1–3.

⁴¹ 2 Chr 36:22–23.

⁴² Thus closes the first of Theodoret's τόμοι, for reasons of length. So a
brief doxology is in order.

⁴³ The Antiochenes tend to speak interchangeably of Babylonians and
Assyrians (cf. note 51 below). Theodoret is having some difficulty in reconciling dates here; he is not prepared, like modern commentators, to treat as a gloss
the chronological details in Jer 25:1 that he quotes, which also take some ratio-
nalizing. Nor does he at this point account for the fact that Dan 1:5 spoke of

δὲ καὶ Ἱερεμίας ὁ προφήτης τοῖς χρόνοις, οὑτωσὶ λέγων· «Ὁ λόγος ὁ γενόμενος ἐπὶ Ἱερεμίαν τὸν προφήτην, ἐπὶ πάντα τὸν λαὸν Ἰούδα, ἐν τῷ ἔτει τῷ τετάρτῳ Ἰωακεὶμ υἱοῦ Ἰωσίου βασιλέως Ἰούδα, οὗτος ἐνιαυτὸς πρῶτος τῷ Ναβουχοδονόσορ, βασιλεῖ Βαβυλῶνος.» Εὑρίσκομεν

1285 τοίνυν | ἐνταῦθα, ὡς τοῦ τρίτου ἔτους τῆς βασιλείας πληρουμένου τῷ Ἰωακεὶμ βασιλεύσας ὁ Ναβουχοδονόσορ τὴν κατὰ τῶν Ἰουδαίων στρατείαν ἐποιήσατο· ἐν ἀρχῇ δὲ τοῦ τετάρτου ἔτους ὁ προφήτης Ἱερεμίας παραίνεσιν τῷ λαῷ προσφέρων, ἔφη πρῶτον εἶναι τοῦτον τὸν ἐνιαυτὸν τῷ βασιλεῖ Ναβουχοδονόσορ. Καὶ ὁ μακάριος δὲ Δανιὴλ τὴν πρώτην αἰχμαλωσίαν εἰρηκὼς γεγενῆσθαι ἐν ἔτει τρίτῳ τῆς βασιλείας Ἰωακεὶμ βασιλέως Ἰούδα, ἐπήγαγε νῦν· «Ἐν τῷ ἔτει τῷ δευτέρῳ τῆς βασιλείας Ναβουχοδονόσορ ἐνυπνιάσθη ἐνύπνιον.» Ταῦτα δὲ οὐχ ἁπλῶς προστέθεικε, ἀλλ᾽ ἵνα καὶ τὸν χρόνον ἀκριβῶς καταμάθωμεν. Τούτου χάριν καὶ οἱ θεῖοι προφῆται, μεμνημένοι τῶν βασιλέων, καὶ τὸν ἀριθμὸν τῶν ἐτῶν ἀναγράφουσιν.

«Ἐν τῷ ἔτει τοίνυν τῷ δευτέρῳ τῆς βασιλείας Ναβουχοδονόσορ ἐνυπνιάσθη ἐνύπνιον, καὶ ἐξέστη τὸ πνεῦμα αὐτοῦ, καὶ ὁ ὕπνος ἀπέστη ἀπ᾽ αὐτοῦ. (β΄.) Καὶ εἶπεν ὁ βασιλεὺς τοῦ καλέσαι τοὺς ἐπαοιδούς, καὶ τοὺς μάγους, καὶ τοὺς φαρμακούς, καὶ τοὺς Χαλδαίους, τοῦ ἀναγγεῖλαι τῷ βασιλεῖ τὸ ἐνύπνιον αὐτοῦ.» Ἡ μὲν οὖν τοῦ Θεοῦ οἰκονομία τοῖς ἐχέφροσι δήλη· γνώριμον γὰρ αὐτοῦ τὸ ἐνύπνιον ποιῆσαι βουλόμενος τὸν οἰκεῖον προφήτην, ἵνα τὰς ἀγαθὰς καὶ σωτηρίους ἐντεῦθεν δέξηται παραινέσεις, δεδίττεται μὲν αὐτὸν τῷ ἐνυπνίῳ, ἀφαιρεῖται δὲ τοῦ ἐνυπνίου τὴν μνήμην. Ἀλλ᾽ ὥσπερ δήλη τοῦ Θεοῦ τῶν ὅλων ἡ προμήθεια, οὕτω γνώριμος ἅπασι τοῖς εὐσεβέσι καὶ ἡ τοῦ βασιλέως παράνοια. Πῶς γὰρ οὐκ ἄκρας παραπληξίας τὸ παρ᾽ ἑτέρων ζητεῖν τοῦ ἐνυπνίου τὴν μνήμην; Ἀλλ᾽ ὅμως, κληθέντες, φησίν, «ἦλθον, καὶ ἔστησαν ἐνώπιον τοῦ βασιλέως.»

γ΄, δ΄. «Καὶ εἶπεν αὐτοῖς ὁ βασιλεύς· Ἐνυπνιάσθην ἐνύπνιον, καὶ ἐξέστη τὸ πνεῦμά μου τοῦ γνῶναι τὸ ἐνύπνιον. Καὶ ἐλάλησαν οἱ Χαλδαῖοι τῷ βασιλεῖ Συριστί, καὶ εἶπον· Βασιλεῦ, εἰς τὸν αἰῶνα ζῆθι· σὺ εἰπὲ τὸ ἐνύπνιον τοῖς παισί σου, καὶ τὴν σύγκρισιν αὐτοῦ ἀπαγγελοῦμεν.» Καὶ τὴν μὲν αἴτησιν τῷ ὄντι ἀκόλουθον ἐποιήσαντο· ἀλαζονικὴν δὲ τὴν ὑπόσχεσιν· οὔτε γὰρ ἀνθρωπίνης ἦν διανοίας θείας ἑρμηνεύειν ἀποκαλύψεις δίχα τῆς ἄνωθεν συνεργείας. Συριστὶ δὲ τὴν διάλεξιν οἱ Χαλδαῖοι

The prophet Jeremiah also confirms the date in speaking in these terms, "The word came to Jeremiah the prophet, to all the people of Judah, in the fourth year of Jehoiakim son of Josiah king of Judah, the first year of Nebuchadnezzar king of Babylon." So we find | here that after the completion of the third year of the reign   1285 of Jehoiakim Nebuchadnezzar came to the throne and launched a campaign against the Jews, whereas it was in the beginning of the fourth year that the prophet Jeremiah in delivering his exhortation to the people said it was King Nebuchadnezzar's first year. Blessed Daniel, after saying the first captivity happened in the third year of the reign of Jehoiakim king of Judah, then went on, *In the second year of his reign Nebuchadnezzar had a dream*, adding this further detail not without purpose, but for us to get a precise grasp of the time as well. This is the reason the divine prophets in mentioning the kings also record the number of years.

So *in the second year of his reign Nebuchadnezzar had a dream, his spirit was perturbed and his sleep left him. The king gave orders to summon the magicians, the soothsayers, the sorcerers, and the astrologers*[44] *to tell the king his dream* (vv. 1–2). God's designs, then, are clear to people of good sense, his wish being that his own prophet explain his dream so that he might receive sound and salutary advice from it; so on the one hand he alarmed him with the dream, and on the other made him lose remembrance of the dream. But just as the providence of the God of all was obvious, so too the king's frenzy was clear to all religious people; after all, how could it not be a mark of utter insanity to look from others for a recollection of one's dream? Yet once called, the text says, *they came and stood in the king's presence. The king said to them, I had a dream, and my spirit is perturbed by the desire to understand it. The astrologers spoke to the king in Aramaic, O king, live forever! Tell your servants the dream, and we shall give its interpretation* (vv. 2–4). While the request they made was quite logical, the promise was arrogant: human intuition is incapable of interpreting divine revelations without assistance from on high. Now, the astrologers conducted the dialogue in Aramaic, assembled as they were from

---

a lapse of three years before Daniel gained entrance to the royal court. Inconsistency in biblical authors' dating is unpalatable to an Antiochene, as is textual emendation.

[44] Lit., "Chaldeans," who were renowned in astrology—and is thus rendered "astrologers" whenever it bears this sense.

πεποίηνται, ὡς ἐκ διαφόρων συνειλεγμένοι ἐθνῶν, καὶ ἰδίαν μὲν γλῶτταν ἐχόντων ἐκάστου, κοινῇ δὲ πάντων τῇ Σύρων χρωμένων, διδάξαι βουλόμενοι τὸ τῆς ἀποκρίσεως ἀκόλουθον. Ἀλλ' οὐδὲ οὕτως ἔπεισαν τὸν ἀλαζόνα βασιλέα μὴ ἀπαιτεῖν παρ' ἀνθρώπων τὰ παρὰ τὴν φύσιν.

ε', ς'. «Ἀπεκρίθη γὰρ εὐθὺς ὁ βασιλεύς, καὶ εἶπε τοῖς Χαλδαίοις· Ὁ λόγος ἀπέστη μου· ἐὰν οὖν μὴ γνωρίσητέ μοι τὸ ἐνύπνιον, καὶ τὴν 1288 σύγκρισιν αὐτοῦ, εἰς ἀπώλειαν ἔσεσθε, καὶ οἱ οἶκοι | ὑμῶν διαρπαγήσονται. Ἐὰν δὲ τὸ ἐνύπνιον καὶ τὴν σύγκρισιν αὐτοῦ γνωρίσητέ μοι, δόματα καὶ δωρεάς, καὶ τιμὴν πολλὴν λήψεσθε παρ' ἐμοῦ· πλὴν τὸ ἐνύπνιον καὶ τὴν σύγκρισιν αὐτοῦ ἀπαγγείλατέ μοι.» Ταῦτα δὲ οὐ μόνον αὐτοῦ τὸ θρασὺ καὶ θηριῶδες, ἀλλὰ καὶ τὸ λίαν ἀνόητον ὑποδείκνυσιν· ἀνοίας γὰρ ἐσχάτης τὸ νομίσαι, ἢ τῇ ἀπειλῇ τῶν κακῶν, ἢ τῇ ὑποσχέσει τῶν ἀγαθῶν, πλείονα τοῖς Χαλδαίοις ἐγγενήσεσθαι γνῶσιν. (ζ'.) Αὐτίκα τοίνυν ἐκεῖνοι πρὸς αὐτὸν ἔφησαν· «Εἰπὲ τὸ ἐνύπνιόν σου τοῖς παισί σου, καὶ τὴν σύγκρισιν αὐτοῦ ἀπαγγελοῦμεν.» Τὴν μὲν γὰρ δουλείαν, φησίν, ὁμολογοῦμεν, ἀλλὰ καὶ τὴν φύσιν γινώσκομεν· καὶ ἑρμηνεῦσαι μέν, εἰ μάθοιμεν, τὸ ἐνύπνιον δυνησόμεθα, ἐρεῖν δὲ αὐτό, σοὶ μὲν γνωρισθέν, εἶτα λήθῃ παραδοθέν, οὐ δυνάμεθα. Ἀλλ' οὐδὲν ἧττον ὁ μάταιος ἐπέκειτο τοῦ ἐνυπνίου ζητῶν τὴν ἀνάμνησιν. Ἀπεκρίθη γάρ, φησίν, ὁ βασιλεύς, καὶ εἶπεν·

η'. «Ἐπ' ἀληθείας οἶδα, ὅτι καιρὸν ὑμεῖς ἐξαγοράζετε, καθότι εἴδετε ὅτι ἀπέστη ἀπ' ἐμοῦ τὸ ῥῆμα. (θ'.) Ἐὰν οὖν τὸ ἐνύπνιον μὴ ἐπαγγείλητέ μοι, ἕν ἐστι τὸ δόγμα ὑμῶν, καὶ οἶδα ὅτι ῥῆμα ψευδὲς καὶ διεφθαρμένον συνέθεσθε εἰπεῖν ἐνώπιόν μου, ἕως οὗ ὁ καιρὸς παρέλθῃ· τὸ ἐνύπνιόν μου εἴπατέ μοι, καὶ γνώσομαι ὅτι τὴν σύγκρισιν αὐτοῦ ἀναγγελεῖτέ μοι.» Τούτων δὲ τῶν λόγων ἡ μὲν ἀπαίτησις αὐθάδης καὶ μανική, ἡ δὲ κατηγορία λίαν ἀληθής· Βούλεσθε γάρ, φησί, μαθεῖν τὸ ἐνύπνιον, ἵνα κοινῇ τινα πλασάμενοι ἑρμηνείαν ψευδῆ, φενακίσητέ με συνήθως, συνεργὸν λαμβάνοντες τοῦ χρόνου τὸ μῆκος, καὶ τῆς ἐκβάσεως τὸν καιρὸν ἀναμένοντες. Τούτων ἀκούσαντες οἱ Χαλδαῖοι (ὡς γὰρ ἔοικεν, οὗτοι πλείονα τῶν ἄλλων εἶχον παρ' αὐτῷ παρρησίαν), ἀποφαντικῶς λοιπὸν διαλέγονται, καὶ παντελῶς ἀπαγορεύουσι τοῦ ἐνυπνίου τὴν ἀνάμνησιν.

ι'. «Οὐκ ἔστι γάρ, ἔλεγον, ἄνθρωπος ἐπὶ τῆς ξηρᾶς, ὅστις δυνήσεται γνωρίσαι τὸ ῥῆμα τῷ βασιλεῖ, καθότι πᾶς βασιλεὺς μέγας καὶ ἄρχων ῥῆμα τοιοῦτον οὐκ ἐπερωτᾷ ἐπαοιδὸν καὶ Χαλδαῖον. (ια'.) Ὅτι ὁ λόγος,

different nations, and though having their own language in each case, they all used Aramaic in common in their wish to convey a unanimous reply.[45]

Even so, however, they did not dissuade the proud king from seeking help from human beings with things beyond human nature. *Immediately the king replied, saying to the astrologers, My decree is this: Unless you tell me of the dream and its interpretation, You will perish, and your houses | will be seized. But if you do tell me of the dream and its interpretation, you will receive presents and gifts and great honor from me. But tell me the dream and its interpretation* (vv. 5–6). This demonstrates not only his audacity and ferocity, but also his extreme derangement, it being a mark of utter madness to think that by threats of sanctions or promises of rewards the astrologers would acquire greater knowledge. At once they replied to him, *Tell your dream to us all, and we shall let you know its interpretation* (v. 7): though we profess obedience, we also recognize the limits of nature; we would be able to interpret the dream if we knew it, but we cannot tell it if it was known to you and then lost in oblivion.

Yet the effort to prevent his seeking a recollection of the dream proved fruitless, the king replying in the words, *I know with certainty that you are trying to gain time because you see the decree has been issued by me; so if you do not tell me the dream, there is one verdict for you. I know you have agreed to utter a false and corrupt statement in my presence until opportunity presents itself. Describe the dream to me, and I shall know that you will tell me its interpretation* (vv. 8–9). While the demand in these words was high-handed and insane, the accusation was very true: You want to learn what the dream was, he is saying, so as to hatch in common some false interpretation and trick me as usual, using the lapse of time as an advantage and waiting for the moment of fulfillment. On hearing this the astrologers (probably exercising greater forthrightness than the others) then spoke with some force, and completely denied the possibility of a recall of the dream. *There is no one on earth,* they said, *who could explain the matter to the king, because no king, mighty and influential though he be, ever put such a question to ma-*

1288

---

[45] Speaker of Syriac (i.e., a dialect of Aramaic) though he is, Theodoret is not aware that the mention of Aramaic here is a gloss to let the reader know the text is in Aramaic from this point to 7:28. (See the introduction for the languages in which the text occurs.)

ὃν ὁ βασιλεὺς ἐπερωτᾷ, βαρύς· καὶ ἕτερος οὐκ ἔστιν, ὃς ἀπαγγελεῖ αὐτὸν ἐνώπιον τοῦ βασιλέως, ἀλλ᾽ ἢ θεοί, ὧν οὐκ ἔστιν ἡ κατοικία μετὰ πάσης σαρκός.» Ὅθεν οὐκ ἐνδέχεται γενέσθαι καθάπερ οἴει. Ἀνθρώπινα, φασί, παρ᾽ ἡμῶν ἐπιζήτησον, μὴ τὰ παρὰ τὴν φύσιν· πάντων γὰρ μάλιστα βασιλεῦσιν ἁρμόττει δικαίως τὴν βασιλείαν ἰθύνειν, καὶ τὰ δυνατὰ παρὰ τῶν ὑπηκόων αἰτεῖν· ἃ δὲ νῦν ἀπαιτεῖς, οὐ δικαίως ἀπαιτεῖς· οὐ γάρ ἐστιν ἀνθρώπων τῶν σάρκα περικειμένων ἡ | τοιαύτη γνῶσις, ἀλλὰ τῆς ἀσωμάτου φύσεως τῆς ἀκριβῶς ἅπαντα γινωσκούσης. Ταῦτα μὲν οὖν παρὰ τῶν Χαλδαίων ἐρρέθη, προῳκονομεῖτο δὲ ἡ τοῦ Δανιὴλ ἀνάρρησις. Τούτων γὰρ εἰρηκότων, Οὐκ ἔστιν ἀνθρώπων, ἀλλ᾽ ἢ θεῶν, τὸ ταῦτα γινώσκειν, ὁ θεσπέσιος Δανιὴλ ἀναμιμνήσκει μὲν τοῦ ἐνυπνίου τὸν βασιλέα, ἀκριβῶς δὲ λίαν καὶ σαφῶς ἑρμηνεύει· διδάσκει δὲ τὸν βασιλέα, ὅτι ἡ τοιαύτη γνῶσις οὐκ ἀνθρώπων ἐστί, τῶν ἐπὶ τῆς γῆς ἑρπόντων, οὔτε μὴν θεῶν τῶν οὐκ ὄντων, ἀλλὰ τοῦ τὰ σύμπαντα πεποιηκότος Θεοῦ. Ἀλλὰ τούτων μὲν ἕκαστον ἐν τῷ οἰκείῳ χωρίῳ τὴν ἁρμόττουσαν ἑρμηνείαν δέξεται.

ιβ′, ιγ′. «Τότε, φησίν, ὁ βασιλεὺς ἐν θυμῷ πολλῷ καὶ ὀργῇ εἶπεν ἀπολέσαι πάντας τοὺς σοφοὺς Βαβυλῶνος. Καὶ τὸ δόγμα ἐξῆλθε, καὶ οἱ σοφοὶ ἀπεκτείνοντο, καὶ ἐζήτησαν τὸν Δανιὴλ καὶ τοὺς φίλους αὐτοῦ ἀνελεῖν.» Τυραννικόν, ἀλλ᾽ οὐ βασιλικὸν τὸ ἐγχείρημα, ἄδικον προφανῶς, καὶ δικαιοσύνης ἔρημον· ἀλαζονεία γὰρ καὶ τῦφος προσλαβὼν ἐξουσίαν, ὄλεθρον μηχανᾶται τοῖς ὑπηκόοις Ἰουδαίοις. Ἀλλ᾽ ὁ θειότατος Δανιὴλ τὴν ἄδικον ταύτην σφαγὴν θεασάμενος, πυνθάνεται τοῦ Ἀριώχ, ὃς τὸν ὠμότατον τοῦτον ἐνεχειρίσθη φόνον, λέγων· «Ἄρχων τοῦ βασιλέως, περὶ τίνος ἐξῆλθεν ἡ γνώμη ἡ ἀναιδὴς ἐκ προσώπου τοῦ βασιλέως;» Ἠγνόει γάρ, ὡς ἔοικεν, ἅτε μὴ κληθεὶς εἰς τὸν σύλλογον τῶν σοφῶν Βαβυλῶνος· οὐδέπω γὰρ τὰ τρία παρεληλύθει ἔτη, ἐν οἷς αὐτοὺς τῇ βασιλικῇ τραφέντας τροφῇ μετὰ τὸν ῥητὸν τοῦτον χρόνον εἰσαχθῆναι προσέταξεν αὐτῷ τῶν Βαβυλωνίων ὁ βασιλεύς. Εἰ δὲ πρὸ τούτων διηγήσατο τὸν λόγον, ὅτι καὶ εἰσῆλθον, καὶ τῶν ἄλλων προεκρίθησαν ἀμείνους ὀφθέντες, θαυμαζέτω μηδείς· ἐκεῖνο γὰρ τὸ διήγημα συμπερᾶναι βουληθείς, ἅπαντα σαφῶς ἐδίδαξε τὰ τηνικαῦτα συμβάντα· εἶτα μεταβαίνει λοιπὸν ἐφ᾽ ἕτερον διήγημα τῶν ἐν τῷ μεταξὺ χρόνῳ

*gician or astrologer. The demand the king makes is exorbitant, and
there is no one who can explain it in the king's presence except gods,
whose dwelling is not with all flesh* (vv. 10–11): hence it is not possible for it to happen as you think; look for human things from us,
not for what is beyond human nature. After all, to kings it belongs
most of all to govern their kingdom fairly, and to ask of their subjects what is possible; but in this case it is not fair of you to ask
what you are asking, such knowledge belonging not to human be-
ings clad in flesh | but to the incorporeal nature that has a precise   1289
knowledge of everything.

With this statement by the astrologers, then, Daniel's dec-
laration was providentially prepared for: when they claimed,
Knowing this is possible not to human beings but to gods, the divinely inspired Daniel recalls the dream to the king and interprets
it very precisely and clearly; but he informs the king that such
knowledge belongs not to human beings, who crawl on the earth,
or even to gods wrongly so-called, but to the God who made everything. Each of these things, however, will have its due comment in
its proper place.

At that point, the text says, *in a great rage and anger the king
gave orders for all the wise men of Babylon to be killed. The decree
was issued, and the wise men were on the point of being slain, and
they looked for Daniel and his friends to kill them* (vv. 12–13).[46] It
was the exploit of a tyrant, not a king, manifestly unjust, and devoid of righteousness: arrogance and conceit outstripped authority
and plotted the downfall of the Jewish subjects. On observing this
unjust slaughter, however, the most divine Daniel enquired of Arioch, who was entrusted with this cruel slaughter, *Lieutenant of
the king, why has the shameful policy issued from the king's presence?*
(v. 15) The reason for his ignorance, in fact, was probably that he
had not been invited to the assembly of Babylon's sages, the three
years not having passed in which, by the king's order, they were
to be nourished on the king's fare and after the specified time be
introduced to him. If, on the other hand, his version of the story
was that they had been introduced before this and were judged to
be better in appearance than the others, let no one be surprised:
wanting to bring that story to a conclusion, he conveyed clearly ev-

---

[46] Modern commentators often suggest that vv. 13–23 are a later insertion.

γεγενημένων. Ὅτι γὰρ οὐδέπω τῶν παρρησίαν ἐχόντων ἦν πρὸς τὸν βασιλέα, ἡνίκα τοὺς σοφοὺς συνήγαγε Βαβυλῶνος, ἡ τῆς ἀδίκου σφαγῆς ἄγνοια μαρτυρεῖ· ταύτην γὰρ ἀγνοῶν τὴν αἰτίαν τὸν Ἀριὼχ ἠρώτα. Καὶ ἐπειδὴ ἔμαθε, θαρρεῖ μὲν τὴν πρὸς τὸν βασιλέα διάλεξιν, ἀξιοῖ δὲ αὐτὸν ὀλίγον αὐτῷ χρόνον ἐνδοῦναι εἰς τὴν τοῦ ἐνυπνίου ζήτησιν, καὶ τῆς ἑρμηνείας τὴν εὕρεσιν· εἶτα διδάσκει ἡμᾶς τὸν τῆς εὑρέσεως τρόπον, οὐκ αὐτὸς φιλοτιμούμενος, ἀλλ' ἡμᾶς ἐπὶ τὴν ὁμοίαν σπουδὴν ἐκκαλούμενος.

ιζ', ιη'. «Εἰσῆλθε γὰρ, φησί, Δανιὴλ εἰς τὸν οἶκον αὐτοῦ, καὶ τῷ Ἀνανίᾳ, καὶ τῷ Ἀζαρίᾳ, καὶ τῷ Μισαὴλ, τοῖς φίλοις αὐτοῦ ἐγνώρισε τὸ ῥῆμα. Καὶ οἰκτιρμοὺς ἐζήτουν παρὰ τοῦ Θεοῦ τοῦ οὐρανοῦ ὑπὲρ τοῦ μυστηρίου τούτου, ὅπως μὴ ἀπόλωνται Δανιὴλ καὶ οἱ φίλοι αὐτοῦ, μετὰ τῶν ἐπιλοίπων | σοφῶν Βαβυλῶνος.» Ἀληθῶς πολὺ τῆς ἀληθείας καὶ τοῦ ψεύδους τὸ μέσον· οἱ μὲν γὰρ τοῦ ψεύδους ἐργάται τῆς θείας εἰσὶν ἔρημοι συμμαχίας, καὶ λογισμοῖς μόνοις ἀνθρωπίνοις εὐσεβείας γεγυμνωμένοις χρώμενοι, πάντα καὶ λέγουσι καὶ πράττουσιν εἰς ἀπάτην ἀνθρώπων· οἱ δὲ τρόφιμοι τῆς ἀληθείας λέγειν ἢ πράττειν ἀνέχονται οὐδὲν δίχα τῆς ἄνωθεν βοηθείας· τὰ δὲ σφῶν αὐτῶν αἰτήματα τῆς πάντα ἐφορώσης προμηθείας ἐξάπτοντες, ἱστᾶσιν ἀκίνητοι, μὴ κλονούμενοι, μηδὲ τῇδε κἀκεῖσε περιφερόμενοι, ἀλλὰ τῆς ζάλης τῶν ἀνθρωπίνων λογισμῶν ἀπηλλαγμένοι. Καὶ τούτου μάρτυς ὁ θεσπέσιος Δανιὴλ, ὀλίγον μὲν χρόνον αἰτήσας εἰς τὴν τοῦ ἐνυπνίου εὕρεσιν, οὐκ εἰς λογισμοὺς δὲ ἁπλῶς τὸν καιρὸν δαπανήσας, ἀλλ' εἰς ἱκετείαν καὶ προσευχὴν, καὶ οὐδὲ ἑαυτῷ μόνῳ θαρρήσας, ἀλλὰ καὶ τοὺς ὁμοτρόπους εἰς κοινωνίαν τῆς ἱκετείας λαβών· καὶ οὐκ ἐψεύσθη τῆς ἐλπίδος.

ιθ' κβ'. «Τότε γὰρ, φησί, τῷ Δανιὴλ ἐν ὁράματι τῆς νυκτὸς τὸ μυστήριον ἀπεκαλύφθη, καὶ ηὐλόγησε Δανιὴλ τὸν Θεὸν τοῦ οὐρανοῦ. Καὶ εἶπεν· Εἴη τὸ ὄνομα Κυρίου τοῦ Θεοῦ εὐλογημένον ἀπὸ τοῦ αἰῶνος καὶ ἕως τοῦ αἰῶνος, ὅτι ἡ σοφία καὶ ἡ σύνεσις αὐτοῦ ἐστι. Καὶ αὐτὸς ἀλλοιοῖ καιροὺς καὶ χρόνους, καθιστᾷ βασιλεῖς καὶ μεθιστᾷ, διδοὺς σοφίαν τοῖς σοφοῖς, καὶ φρόνησιν τοῖς εἰδόσι σύνεσιν. Αὐτὸς ἀποκαλύπτει βαθέα καὶ ἀπόκρυφα, γινώσκων τὰ ἐν τῷ σκότει, καὶ φῶς μετ' αὐτοῦ ἐστιν.» Διὰ πάντων τὴν οἰκείαν εὐγνωμοσύνην δείκνυσι, καὶ πλέκει τὸν ὕμνον οὐχ ἁπλῶς, ἀλλὰ τῆς πλοκῆς ὕλην ποιούμενος τοῦ ἐνυπνίου τὴν εὕρεσιν. Προσήκει γὰρ, φησί, τὸν ἀΐδιον καὶ αἰώνιον διηνεκῶς ἀνυμνεῖν Θεόν, σοφίας ὄντα καὶ συνέσεως πηγήν, ὀρθῶς ἅπαντα καὶ ἀγαθῶς πρυτανεύοντα, καὶ ταῖς τῶν πραγμάτων μεταβολαῖς ἐλέγχοντα μὲν τὸ τῆς ἀνθρωπίνης

erything that happened at that time, then shifted to another story
about what happened in the intervening time. His ignorance of
the unjust slaughter actually confirms the fact that to that point
he was not part of those who had free access to the king when he
assembled the wise men of Babylon, his enquiry to Arioch being
made in ignorance of the reason. When he found it out, he was
forthright in speaking with the king, and he asked for a little time
to be given him for an investigation of the dream and discovery of
its interpretation.

He then informs us of the way he discovered it, not out of
ambition, but to invite us to a like zeal. *Daniel went into his house,
and told his friends Hananiah, Azariah and Mishael of this decree.
They sought pity from the God of heaven in regard to this mystery
lest Daniel and his friends perish along with the rest of | Babylon's* 1292
sages (vv. 17–18). There is truly a great gap between truth and
falsehood: whereas the agents of falsehood are bereft of divine assistance, have recourse only to human ways of thought that are
devoid of piety, and say and do everything to deceive people, the
disciples of truth cannot bring themselves to say or do anything
without help from above; by directing their own petitions under
the watchful eye of providence, they stand firm and unruffled, not
tossed this way and that, but free of the tempest of human reasoning. As proof of this, the divinely inspired Daniel, though begging
for a short time for a way into the dream, did not spend his time
simply on human reasoning but on prayer and supplication; and
instead of trusting in himself alone, he got his like-minded friends
to join him in supplication.

His hope was not disappointed. *At that point the mystery was
revealed to Daniel in a vision of the night, and Daniel blessed the
God of heaven in the words, May the name of the Lord God be blessed
from age to age because wisdom and understanding are from him. He
changes times and seasons, enthrones kings and dethrones them, giving wisdom to the wise and insight to those with understanding. He
it is who reveals deep and hidden things, knowing what is in darkness, and light is with him* (vv. 19–22). In everything he reveals his
gratitude, not only composing the hymn but making the discovery of the dream the theme of the composition. It is proper, he is
saying, constantly to sing the praises of God, who is eternal and
everlasting, fount of wisdom and understanding as he is, governing everything correctly and beneficently, proving the instability

εὐημερίας ἀβέβαιον, δεικνύντα δὲ ἅπασιν ἐναργῶς τὴν οἰκείαν ἰσχύν· χει-
ροτονῶν γὰρ βασιλέας, πάλιν αὐτοὺς ἀποχειροτονεῖ ῥαδίως, καὶ διδοὺς
ἐξουσίαν ἀφαιρεῖται ταύτην, ὅταν ἐθέλῃ· καὶ σοφίας δὲ καὶ φρονήσεως
οὗτός ἐστι χορηγός· δίδωσι δὲ ταύτην οὐχ ἁπλῶς, ἀλλὰ τοῖς συνιέναι
αὐτὸν βουλομένοις· ἀποκαλύπτει δὲ ὡς ἐθέλει τὰ μηδαμῶς φαινόμενα,
ἀλλ' οἷόν τινι βυθῷ κρυπτόμενα τῷ μηδέπω γενέσθαι· καὶ φῶς ὑπάρχων νοερόν, φῶς οἰκῶν ἀπρόσιτον, ἀκριβῶς ἅπαντα γινώσκει τὰ ἐν τῷ
σκότει γινόμενα.

κγ'. «Διό σοι, ὁ Θεὸς τῶν πατέρων μου, ἐξομολογοῦμαι καὶ αἰνῶ,
ὅτι σοφίαν καὶ δύναμιν ἔδωκάς μοι, καὶ νῦν ἐγνώρισάς μοι ἃ ἠξιώσαμεν
1293   παρὰ σοῦ, ὅτι τὸ ὅραμα τοῦ βασιλέως ἐγνώρισάς μοι | τοῦ γνωρίσαι τῷ
βασιλεῖ.» Τοιαῦται τῶν εὐσεβῶν αἱ ψυχαί, καὶ ἐν ταῖς χρείαις τὸν Θεὸν
ἐπιστάμεναι χορηγόν, καὶ τοῖς αὐτοῦ λιμέσι προστρέχουσαι, καὶ μετὰ
τὴν τῶν ἀγαθῶν χορηγίαν οὐκ ἀνεχόμεναι λήθῃ παραδιδόναι τῶν δωρεῶν τὴν μνήμην, ἀλλ' ὕμνοις ἀμειβόμεναι τὸν εὐεργέτην Θεόν. Ἄξιον
δὲ ἐπισημήνασθαι τοῦ θείου τούτου ἀνδρὸς καὶ τὸ μέτριον φρόνημα· καὶ
γὰρ καὶ τὴν αἴτησιν ποιούμενος, κοινωνοὺς ἔλαβε τοὺς ὁμοτρόπους τῆς
προσευχῆς, καὶ τὸν ὕμνον ὑφαίνων ὑπὲρ ὧν ἔλαβε, πάλιν αὐτῶν ἐμνημόνευσεν. Οὐ γὰρ εἶπεν, Ἐγνώρισάς μοι ἃ ἠξίωσά σε, ἀλλ', «ἃ ἠξιώσαμεν
παρὰ σοῦ.» Οὕτω τὸν θεῖον συμπεράνας ὕμνον·

κδ'. «Καὶ εὐθὺς ἦλθε, φησί, Δανιὴλ πρὸς Ἀριὼχ, ὃν κατέστησεν
ὁ βασιλεὺς ἀπολέσαι τοὺς σοφοὺς Βαβυλῶνος, καὶ εἶπεν αὐτῷ· Τοὺς σοφοὺς Βαβυλῶνος μὴ ἀπολέσῃς, εἰσάγαγε δέ με ἐνώπιον τοῦ βασιλέως,
καὶ τὴν σύγκρισιν τοῦ ὁράματος ἀναγγελῶ τῷ βασιλεῖ.» Πρέπων καὶ
οὗτος τῷ προφήτῃ ἔλεος· οὐ γὰρ ἠνέσχετο μόνος μετὰ τῶν φίλων τῆς
ἀδίκου ἀπαλλαγῆναι σφαγῆς, ἀλλὰ καὶ τοῖς Χαλδαίοις πραγματεύεται
σωτηρίαν, ἐλπίζων διὰ τοῦδε τοῦ θαύματος, καὶ τῆς ἀσεβείας αὐτοὺς
ἀπαλλάξειν, καὶ τῷ τῶν ὅλων προσάξειν Θεῷ

κε'. «Ὁ δὲ Ἀριώχ, τούτων ἀκούσας τῶν λόγων, σπουδῇ τὸν Δανιὴλ εἰσήγαγεν ἐνώπιον τοῦ βασιλέως, καὶ εἶπεν αὐτῷ· Εὕρηκα ἄνδρα
ἐκ τῶν υἱῶν τῆς αἰχμαλωσίας τῆς Ἰουδαίας, ὅστις τὸ σύγκριμα τῷ βασιλεῖ ἀναγγελεῖ.» Πάλιν ἐντεῦθεν σαφὲς ἡμῖν γέγονεν, ὅτι οὐδέπω τῆς
τοῦ Δανιὴλ ἀρετῆς πεῖραν ὁ βασιλεὺς εἰλήφει. Οὐ γάρ, εἴπερ ἐγινώσκετο,
ἀορίστως εἶπεν ὁ Ἀριώχ· «Εὕρηκα ἄνδρα ἐκ τῶν υἱῶν τῆς αἰχμαλωσίας
τῆς Ἰουδαίας, ὅστις τὸ σύγκριμα τῷ βασιλεῖ ἀναγγελεῖ.»

κς'. «Ὁ δὲ βασιλεὺς περιχαρὴς γενόμενος εἶπε τῷ Δανιήλ, οὗ τὸ
ὄνομα Βαλτάσαρ· Εἰ δύνασαι ἀναγγεῖλαι τὸ ἐνύπνιον, ὃ εἶδον, καὶ τὴν
σύγκρισιν αὐτοῦ;» Ἐπισημήνασθαι δεῖ καὶ τοῦτο, ὅτι Βαλτάσαρ αὐτὸν

of human prosperity with the change in circumstances while making very clear to everyone his peculiar power, appointing kings and
in turn easily removing them, giving authority and taking it away
as he wishes, source of wisdom and insight, giving it not indiscriminately but to those intent on understanding him, revealing
as he wishes what has yet to come to light and is still hidden in
the depths, as it were, because it has not yet occurred, a light to
the mind's eye, dwelling in inaccessible light, knowing precisely
everything that occurs in darkness.

Hence to you, O God of my ancestors, I confess and give praise
for granting me wisdom and power, and for now making known to me
what we asked of you, for making known to me the king's vision | *to*   1293
make known to the king (v. 23). This is what devout souls are like,
realizing God is their resource in time of need and taking refuge
in him as their haven, refusing after the bestowal of good things to
consign to oblivion the memory of his gifts and instead repaying
the beneficent God with hymns of praise. Now, it is worth noting
this divine man's modesty as well: in making his request he joined
with him his like-minded friends in prayer, and in composing the
hymn of thanks for what he had received he once more referred to
them: he did not say, You made known to me what I asked of you,
but what we asked of you.

After thus concluding the hymn to God, *Daniel immediately*
went to Arioch, whom the king had commanded to kill the wise men of
Babylon, and said to him, Do not kill the wise men of Babylon; take
me into the king's presence, and I shall tell the king the interpretation
of the vision (v. 24). It was becoming for the prophet to make this
gesture of mercy: far from being interested solely in being spared
from unjust slaughter along with his friends, he involves himself
also in the safety of the astrologers, hoping through this miracle
both to rid them of impiety and to bring them to the God of all. *On*
hearing these words, Arioch eagerly brought Daniel into the presence
of the king, and said to him, I have found a man among the captive
people of Israel who will tell the king the interpretation (v. 25). Again
at this point it becomes clear to us that to this point the king had
no experience of Daniel's virtue: had he known him, Arioch would
not have spoken in vague terms, *I have found a man among the cap-*
tive people of Israel who will tell the king the interpretation. The king
was overjoyed, and said to Daniel, whose name was Belteshazzar, Are
you able to tell me the dream I had and its interpretation? (v. 26).

οὐκ ἀεὶ προσαγορεύει, ἀλλ' ὅτε τῷ βασιλεῖ διαλέγεται, ταύτην αὐτῷ τὴν προσηγορίαν ἐπιτεθεικότι. Ἐρωτηθεὶς δὲ ὅμως, εἰ δύναιτο καὶ τὸ ἐνύπνιον, καὶ τὴν ἑρμηνείαν ἐπαγγεῖλαι τῷ βασιλεῖ, ἀπεκρίνατο λέγων·

κζ'. «Τὸ μυστήριον ὃ ὁ βασιλεὺς ἐπερωτᾷ, οὐκ ἔστι σοφῶν, μάγων, ἐπαοιδῶν, Γαζαρηνῶν ἀναγγεῖλαι τῷ βασιλεῖ. (κη'.) Ἀλλ' ἔστι Θεὸς ἐν οὐρανῷ ἀποκαλύπτων μυστήρια.» Θαυμαστῶς τῆς διδασκαλίας ἤρξατο· ἐκβαλὼν γὰρ τὸν τῶν ἀφρόνων ἐκείνων χορόν, καὶ γυμνώσας αὐτῶν τὴν ἀσθένειαν, τὸν Θεὸν εἶναι ἔφη τῆς τῶν μυστηρίων ἀποκαλύψεως διδάσκαλον· προστέθεικε δέ, ἐν οὐρανῷ, τοὺς κάτω γινομένους καὶ προσκυνουμένους ἐκβαλὼν θεούς. | Καὶ τῷ μὲν ἑνικῷ ὀνόματι τὸ πλῆθος ἐκβάλλει τῶν οὐκ ὄντων θεῶν, τῇ δὲ ἐν οὐρανῷ διαγωγῇ τοὺς κάτω φαινομένους δείκνυσιν οὐ θεούς, ἀλλ' ἀπάτην ἀφορμὴν ἔχουσαν τῶν ἀνθρώπων τὴν τέχνην. «Οὗτος ἐγνώρισεν ὁ Θεὸς τῷ βασιλεῖ Ναβουχοδονόσορ ἃ δεῖ γενέσθαι ἐπ' ἐσχάτων τῶν ἡμερῶν.» Οὕτω προοιμιασάμενος, πάλιν ἐπισπᾶται τῇ εὐλογίᾳ εἰς εὔνοιαν τοῦ βασιλέως τὴν ἀκοήν. «Βασιλεῦ, γάρ, φησίν, εἰς τοὺς αἰῶνας ζῆθι.» Ἐπειδὴ γὰρ μέλλει καὶ τὸ ἐνύπνιον λέγειν, καὶ τὴν ἑρμηνείαν ἐπάγειν, καὶ προλέγειν αὐτῷ τὴν τῆς βασιλείας κατάλυσιν, προοιμιαζόμενος· Εὐχή, φησίν, ἐστὶν ἐμοί, ζῆν σε διηνεκῶς· μὴ τοίνυν ἐμοὶ ἐπιγράψῃς τὸ ὑπὸ τοῦ ἐνυπνίου δηλούμενον. Εἶτά φησι· «Τὸ ἐνύπνιόν σου, καὶ αἱ ὁράσεις τῆς κεφαλῆς σου, ἐπὶ τῆς κοίτης σου, τοῦτό ἐστι, βασιλεῦ.» Ἀντὶ τοῦ· Ἃ νύκτωρ ἐθεάσω, ταῦτά ἐστιν·

κθ'. «Οἱ διαλογισμοί σου ἐπὶ τῆς κοίτης σου ἀνέβησαν, ἃ δεῖ γενέσθαι μετὰ ταῦτα.» Ἐλογίζου, φησί, κατακείμενος ἐπὶ τῆς κλίνης, εἴτε εἰς ἀεὶ ζήσῃ, εἴτε τῷ νόμῳ τῶν ἀνθρώπων ὑπὸ τὸν θάνατον γενήσῃ· ἐπεθύμεις δὲ μαθεῖν καὶ τὰ μήπω γεγενημένα. Καὶ ὁ ἀποκαλύπτων μυστήρια ἐγνώρισέ σοι ἃ δεῖ γενέσθαι. Πανταχοῦ δὲ τὸν ἕνα κηρύττει Θεόν, τῆς πολυθεΐας ἐκβαλὼν τὴν πλάνην· εἶτα καὶ τοῦ οἰκείου φρονήματος τὴν μετριότητα δείκνυσιν.

λ'. «Ἐμοὶ γάρ, φησίν, οὐκ ἐν σοφίᾳ τῇ οὔσῃ ἐν ἐμοὶ παρὰ πάντας τοὺς ζῶντας, τὸ μυστήριον τοῦτο ἀπεκαλύφθη, ἀλλ' ἕνεκεν τοῦ τὴν σύγκρισιν τῷ βασιλεῖ γνωρίσαι, καὶ ἵνα γνῷς τοὺς διαλογισμοὺς τῆς καρδίας σου.» Ταύτης γάρ, φησί, τῆς ἀποκαλύψεως ἔτυχον, οὐκ ἐπειδὴ πάντων εἰμὶ τῶν ἀνθρώπων σοφώτερος, ἀλλ' ἵνα σὺ μάθῃς ἃ μαθεῖν

This, too, should be noted, that he does not always call him Belteshazzar, only when he is speaking to the king, who was the one who gave him the name.

Nevertheless, on being asked if he could tell the king both the dream and its interpretation, he replied as follows, *It is not possible for wise men, soothsayers, magicians, diviners to tell the king the mystery of which he asks—only for God in heaven, who reveals mysteries* (vv. 27–28). He made a remarkable beginning to his teaching: eliminating the band of those foolish people and laying bare their limitations, he said that God is the instructor in the revelation of mysteries, adding *in heaven* to eliminate gods made and worshiped here below. | On the one hand, by the use of the singular he eliminates the plurality of the false gods, and on the other by mention of a dwelling in heaven he shows those appearing to be gods here below not to be so but only a deceit that has its basis in human artifice. *This is the God who has made known to King Nebuchadnezzar what must happen at the end of time.* After making this beginning, he further wins the king's attention in his favor with a blessing: *King, live forever!*[47] You see, since he was about to tell the dream and go on to mention its interpretation, and foretold to him the destruction of the kingdom, after the beginning he says, My prayer is for you to live always; so do not ascribe to me what is indicated by the dream.

He then says, *This, O King, is the dream and the visions in your head on your bed*, meaning, This is what you saw at night. *Your thoughts of what must happen later came down on your bed* (v. 29): you were thinking as you lay on your bed whether you would live forever or fall under death's power by the law for human beings; and you longed to know as well what had not yet happened. *The one who reveals mysteries made known to you what must happen.* At all points he proclaims the one God so as to eliminate the error of polytheism. He then makes clear also the modesty of his own attitude. *It is not through any wisdom in me beyond all living people that this mystery has been revealed to me, but for the purpose of making known the interpretation to the king, and for you to know the reasonings of your heart* (v. 30): I was granted this revelation, not that I am wiser than all human beings, but for you to learn what you de-

margin: 1296

---

47 In fact, this brief remark appears only in the LXX version, not that of Theodotion that Theodoret has been using.

ἐπεθύμησας· ἐμοὶ δὲ διακόνῳ ταύτης ἐχρήσατο τῆς γνώσεως, ὡς οἰκείῳ θεράποντι. Ἄρχεται τοίνυν τῆς ἐξηγήσεως, καὶ λέγει πρῶτον αὐτὸ τὸ ἐνύπνιον.

λα' λγ'. «Σύ, βασιλεῦ, ἐθεώρεις, καὶ ἰδοὺ εἰκὼν μία, πολλὴ, ἡ εἰκὼν μεγάλη, καὶ ἡ ὄψις αὐτῆς, ὑπερφερὴς ἑστῶσα πρὸ προσώπου σου, καὶ ἡ ὅρασις αὐτῆς φοβερά. Εἰκών, ἧς ἡ κεφαλὴ χρυσίου καθαροῦ, αἱ χεῖρες, καὶ τὸ στῆθος, καὶ οἱ βραχίονες αὐτῆς ἀργυροῖ, καὶ κοιλία καὶ οἱ μηροὶ χαλκοῖ. Αἱ κνῆμαι σιδηραῖ, οἱ πόδες μέρος μέν τι σιδήρου, καὶ μέρος δέ τι ὀστράκινον.» Τέτταρας μὲν ὕλας διὰ τῶν προειρημένων ἐσήμανε, τὸν χρυσόν, τὸν ἄργυρον, τὸν χαλκόν, τὸν σίδηρον· ὄστρακον γὰρ οὐ κατ' αὐτὸ εἶπεν, ἀλλὰ τῷ σιδήρῳ συμμεμιγμένον. Δηλοῖ δὲ διὰ τούτων τὰς μεγίστας τε καὶ καθολικωτάτας βασιλείας, αἳ τοῦ πλείστου τῆς οἰκουμένης ἐκράτησαν ἀλλήλας διαδεξάμεναι. Ὅτι μὲν γὰρ καὶ ἄλλαι βασιλεῖαι συνέστησαν, καὶ ἐπὶ τοῦ παρόντος δὲ συνεστᾶσι, δῆλόν ἐστι·
1297 οὐ μὴν τῶν πάντων ἢ τῶν πλειόνων | ἔστιν αὐτὰς κρατούσας ἰδεῖν, ἀλλ' ἢ ἑνός, ἢ δύο μόνον ἐθνῶν. Λέγει τοίνυν πρώτην ἁπάντων γεγενῆσθαι τὴν τῶν Ἀσσυρίων ἡγεμονίαν, ἥτις αὕτη ἐστὶν ἡ τῶν Βαβυλωνίων· Ἀσσύριοι γὰρ οὗτοι κἀκεῖνοι· ἀλλὰ ποτὲ μὲν ἐν τῇ Νίνῳ, τῇ παρ' Ἑβραίοις Νινευὴ καλουμένῃ, τὰ βασίλεια ἐσχήκασι, ποτὲ δὲ ἐν Βαβυλῶνι. Ὅτι δὲ μία ἐστὶν ἡ βασιλεία τούτων κἀκείνων, καὶ αὐτὸς ὁ προφήτης μαρτυρεῖ· ἑρμηνεύων γὰρ τὸ ἐνύπνιον, φησίν· «Ἡ κεφαλὴ ἡ χρυσῆ σὺ εἶ, βασιλεῦ.» Καὶ ὁ μακάριος δὲ Ἱερεμίας ὁ προφήτης φησί· «Ποτήριον χρυσοῦν Βαβυλὼν ἐν χειρὶ Κυρίου, μεθύσκον πᾶσαν τὴν γῆν· ἀπὸ οἴνου αὐτῆς ἐπίοσαν ἔθνη· διὰ τοῦτο ἐσαλεύθησαν, καὶ ἄφνω ἔπεσε Βαβυλών, καὶ συνετρίβη.» Εἰ δὲ ἑτέρα ἦν παρὰ ταύτην ἡ τῶν Ἀσσυρίων βασιλεία ταύτης πρεσβυτέρα, ποίαν ἄν τις ὕλην αὐτὴν καλέσειεν; Μαρτυρεῖ δὲ καὶ ὁ θειότατος Μωσῆς ταῦθ' οὕτως ἔχειν· ἐν γὰρ τῇ κοσμογενείᾳ περὶ τοῦ Νεβρώδους εἰρηκώς, ὅτι γίγας κυνηγὸς ἔναντι Κυρίου, ἐπήγαγε· «Καὶ ἐγένετο ἡ ἀρχὴ τῆς βασιλείας αὐτοῦ Βαβυλών, Ὀρὲχ καὶ Χαλάνη.» Καὶ οἱ ἔξω δὲ συγγραφεῖς τοὺς Βαβυλωνίους Ἀσσυρίους προσαγορεύουσι, καὶ

sired to learn; he employed me, his servant as I am, as minister of this knowledge.

He begins the explanation, therefore, and speaks first of the dream itself. *You were gazing, O King, and lo, a single image, mighty, a huge image of marvelous appearance, standing tall before you, its impact fearsome. The image had a head of pure gold, its hands, breast and arms of silver, its belly and thighs of bronze, its legs of iron, feet partly of iron and partly of clay* (vv. 31–33). In the foregoing he indicated four kinds of material—gold, silver, bronze and iron—clay being mentioned not by itself but mixed with iron. Now, in these things he is referring to the great and far-flung kingdoms which succeeded one another in controlling most of the world. While obviously other kingdoms existed, and exist to this day, they cannot actually be seen to control all or most people |, only one or two   1297 nations. So he means that the rule of the Assyrians was the first of them all to come into being, which is the same as the Babylonians, both one and the other being Assyrians; at one time they had their palace in Nin, which is called Nineveh in Hebrew, at another time in Babylon. The fact that the kingdom of both former and latter is one the prophet also actually confirms by saying in interpreting the dream *You are the head of gold, O King* (v. 38). The blessed prophet Jeremiah also says, "Babylon was a golden cup in the Lord's hand, intoxicating all the earth, nations drank of her wine; hence they tottered, and Babylon suddenly fell and was smashed to pieces."[48] If, on the other hand, the kingdom of the Assyrians was another one than this and older than it, what sort of material would he have assigned to it? The most divine Moses also confirms that this is the way things are: when in Genesis [49] he refers to Nimrod to the effect that "he was a mighty hunter before the Lord," he went on, "The beginning of his kingdom was Babylon, Erech, and Calneh."[50] Profane historians call the Babylonians

---

[48] Jer 51:7–8, cited doubtless because of the mention of a golden cup, though in Jeremiah's case the gold suggests not priority but luxury.

[49] Theodoret here calls Genesis Κοσμογένεια, with Diodore calling it Κοσμοποιΐα and Theodore Κτίσις.

[50] Gen 10:9–10 (the final city usually being amended to Accad), with Nineveh also occurring in the list of cities but suppressed by Theodoret. As he goes on to imply, despite the evidence of secular historians for the separate identity of the two cities and kingdoms (Assyria being the older), Jewish historians of the Hellenistic age (and with them the biblical author) combined them and

μέχρι δὲ τοῦ παρόντος Ἀσσυρίαν αὐτὴν ὀνομάζουσι Πέρσαι. Οὐκοῦν ἡ μὲν πρώτη ὕλη, ἥτις ἐστὶν ὁ χρυσός, τὴν Ἀσσυρίων καὶ Βαβυλωνίων σημαίνει βασιλείαν· κεφαλὴν δὲ αὐτὴν ὀνομάζει, ὡς πρώτην γεγενημένην· ἡ δευτέρα δέ, ἥτις ἐστὶν ὁ ἄργυρος, ἡ Περσῶν ἐστι καὶ Μήδων. Κῦρος γὰρ ἑκατέρωθεν ὁρμώμενος, μητρόθεν μὲν ἐκ Μήδων, πατρόθεν δὲ ἐκ Περσῶν, κατέλυσε μὲν Ἀσσυρίων, εἴτουν Βαβυλωνίων, τὴν βασιλείαν, μετατέθεικε δὲ τὴν βασιλείαν εἰς Πέρσας. Στῆθος δὲ αὐτὸν προσηγόρευσε καὶ *βραχίονας*, ἵνα δείξῃ τὴν πρὸς δύο ἔθνη συγγένειαν· διὰ μὲν γὰρ τῆς δεξιᾶς τὸ πατρῷον αὐτοῦ σημαίνει γένος, μητρῷον δὲ διὰ τῆς εὐωνύμου, ὦν τὴν συνάφειαν τὸ στῆθος πεπίστευται, τὴν καρδίαν ἔχον τῶν λογισμῶν τὸ ταμεῖον, λογισμῷ δὲ καὶ τὰ γαμικὰ τελεῖται συμβόλαια. Τὸν δὲ χαλκὸν προσηγόρευσε τὴν Μακεδονικὴν βασιλείαν μετὰ τὴν Περσικὴν ἀναφανεῖσαν, καὶ αὐτὴν ὁμοίως ἁπάντων κρατήσασαν. *Κοιλίαν* δὲ αὐτῇ καὶ τοὺς *μηροὺς* ἀπένειμε, τήν τε μοναρχίαν τοῦ Ἀλεξάνδρου διὰ τῆς κοιλίας μηνύων, καὶ διὰ τῶν μηρῶν τὴν μετὰ τὴν ἐκείνου τελευτὴν γεγενημένην τῆς βασιλείας διαίρεσιν. *Σίδηρον* δὲ τὴν Ῥωμαϊκὴν προσηγόρευσε βασιλείαν· αὕτη δὲ τὴν Μακεδονικὴν διεδέξατο· ἀπένειμε δὲ αὐτῇ τὰς *κνήμας*, ἅτε δὴ περὶ τὸ τέλος οὔσας τοῦ παντὸς σώματος, καὶ φέρειν ἅπαν δυναμένας τὸ σῶμα· τὰς δὲ τῶν ποδῶν βάσεις, σιδηρᾶς μὲν καὶ αὐτάς, ὀστράκῳ δὲ ἀναμεμιγμένας. Διὰ δὲ τούτου οὐχ ἑτέραν αἰνίττεται βασιλείαν, ἀλλὰ τὴν αὐτὴν ἀσθενεστέραν ἑαυτῆς ἐσομένην, καὶ τῇ τοῦ | ὀστράκου ἀσθενείᾳ συμμεμιγμένην. Τὴν δὲ τῶν ὑλῶν διαφορὰν ἀνέθηκεν, οὐ τῆς τιμῆς, ἀλλὰ τῆς ἰσχύος δεικνὺς τὸ διάφορον· τοῦ μὲν γὰρ χρυσοῦ ὁ ἄργυρος στεγανώτερος· τοῦ δὲ ἀργύρου στερρότερος ὁ χαλκός· ὁ δὲ σίδηρος καὶ αὐτοῦ τοῦ χαλκοῦ πολλῷ τῷ μέτρῳ στερεμνιώτερος. Ἡ διαφορὰ τοίνυν οὐκ ἐν τῇ τιμῇ, ἀλλ' ἐν τῇ ἰσχύϊ τε καὶ δυνάμει. Ἀναγκαῖον δὲ ζητῆσαι, τί δήποτε ἐν εἰκόνι τῶν ὑλῶν τούτων ἐθεάσατο τὴν συνθήκην· οὐδὲν γὰρ ἁπλῶς, οὐδὲ μάτην ὑπὸ τοῦ Θεοῦ τῶν ὅλων ἀποκαλύπτεται. Ἡ εἰκὼν σχήματα, ἀλλ' οὐ πράγματα, ἔχει. Τοιοῦτος δὲ ὁ παρὼν βίος, οὐδὲν ἔχων διαρκές, οὐδὲ μόνιμον· διὸ καὶ ὁ μακάριος Παῦλος ἐβόα, ὅτι «Παράγει τὸ σχῆμα τοῦ κόσμου τούτου.» Καὶ

Assyrians, and up to the present time Persians call it Assyria.

The first material, gold, therefore refers to the kingdom of the Assyrians and Babylonians; he calls it *head* as being the first. The second, silver, is that of the Persians and Medes, Cyrus stemming from both, on his mother's side from the Medes, on his father's side from the Persians, and destroying the kingdom of the Assyrians, or Babylonians, and transferring the kingdom to the Persians. He called him *breast* and *arms* to bring out the relationship to two nations, by the right arm suggesting the paternal race, by the left the maternal, which the breast is given the task of connecting, containing as it does the heart, the seat of thought, while by thought marriage agreements are arranged.[51] *Bronze* is the name he gave the Macedonian kingdom, which likewise controlled them all after the disappearance of the Persian; he ascribed to it a *belly* and *thighs*, referring to the monarchy of Alexander by mention of *belly*, and by *thighs* the division of the kingdom that happened after his death. By *iron* he referred to the Roman kingdom; it succeeded to the Macedonian, and he ascribes to it *legs* as being extremities of the whole body and capable of carrying the whole body. The soles of the feet are also of iron, but mixed with *clay*. Now, in this he is not referring to another kingdom but to the same one, that would be weaker than itself | and mixed with the   1300 weakness of clay.

Now, he cited the different kinds of materials to bring out a difference, not in esteem but in strength, silver being denser than gold, bronze more solid than silver, and iron to a far greater degree being firmer than bronze. So the difference is not in esteem but in strength and power. Now, the question must be asked, why did he see in an image a combination of these materials? Nothing is revealed by the God of all idly and to no purpose. An image has form, not substance; the present life is like that, having nothing permanent about it, nothing lasting—hence the cry of blessed Paul, too, "The form of this world is passing away," and elsewhere

gave pride of place to Babylon, a notion he and his peers adopted.

[51] We saw Theodoret inheriting the Hellenistic amalgamation of Assyria and Babylonia; and for this interpretation he also accepts the traditional combination of Medes and Persians as the second member of the series of four empires, the Macedonian and Roman being the remaining two. It is clear, however, from Daniel's interpretation of the four beasts in chapter 7 that the four kingdoms are rather those of the Babylonians, Medes, Persians, and Greeks.

ἀλλαχοῦ παραινῶν λέγει· «Μὴ συσχηματίζεσθε τῷ αἰῶνι τούτῳ.» Καὶ
ὁ μακάριος Δαβὶδ τῆς ἀνθρωπίνης εὐημερίας διελέγχων τὸ μάταιον, φη-
σί· «Πλὴν τὰ σύμπαντα ματαιότης, πᾶς ἄνθρωπος ζῶν.» Μέντοι γε ἐν
εἰκόνι διαπορεύεται ἄνθρωπος, θησαυρίζει, καὶ οὐ γινώσκει τίνι συνάξει
αὐτά. Ἐπειδὴ τοίνυν καὶ ὁ παρὼν βίος ὀξυρρόπους ἔχει τὰς μεταβολὰς
(θνητὰ γὰρ ἅπαντα τὰ ὁρώμενα, καὶ πρόσκαιρα, καὶ ἐπίκηρα), καὶ ἡ
εἰκὼν δὲ τῶν μὲν πραγμάτων τὴν ἐνέργειαν οὐκ ἔχει, μόνα δὲ τὰ σχήματα δείκνυσι βασιλέων, καὶ ἀρχόντων, καὶ ὑπηκόων, πρὸς δὲ τούτοις
καὶ αὐτὸ τὸ σχῆμα εὐδιάλυτον ἔχει· εἰκότως ὁ τῶν ὅλων Θεὸς τὸν ἀλαζόνα ἐκεῖνον παιδεῦσαι βουληθεὶς βασιλέα τῆς ἀνθρωπίνης ὀφρύος τὸ
μάταιον, καὶ διδάξαι, ὅτι ῥάστην ἔχει τὰ ἀνθρώπινα τὴν μεταβολήν, εἰκόνα μὲν αὐτῷ ὄναρ προτίθησι, τὰ δὲ ταύτης μόρια μερίζει ταῖς ὕλαις,
τὰς συχνὰς καὶ ἐπαλλήλους διδάσκων τῶν βασιλέων διαδοχάς, καὶ πείθων ἅπαντας, ὡς αὐτὸς μόνος διηνεκὲς ἔχει τὸ κράτος, ἄναρχόν τε καὶ
ἀτελεύτητον, καὶ ἀπαξαπλῶς αἰώνιον τὴν βασιλείαν. Τούτοις ἐπάγει ὁ
μακάριος Δανιὴλ τὰ λοιπὰ τοῦ ἐνυπνίου διδάσκων.

λδ΄, λε΄. «Ἐθεώρεις, ἕως ὅτου ἀπεσχίσθη λίθος ἀπὸ ὄρους ἄνευ
χειρῶν, καὶ ἐπάταξε τὴν εἰκόνα ἐπὶ τοὺς πόδας τοὺς σιδηροῦς καὶ ὀστρακίνους, καὶ ἐλέπτυνεν αὐτοὺς εἰς τέλος. Τότε ἐλεπτύνθησαν εἰσάπαξ ὁ
σίδηρος, τὸ ὄστρακον, ὁ χαλκός, ὁ ἄργυρος, ὁ χρυσός, καὶ ἐγένοντο
ὡσεὶ κονιορτὸς ἀπὸ ἅλωνος θερινῆς, καὶ ἐξῆρεν αὐτὰ τὸ πλῆθος τοῦ
πνεύματος, καὶ πᾶς τόπος οὐχ ηὑρέθη ἐν αὐτοῖς, καὶ ὁ λίθος ὁ πατάξας τὴν εἰκόνα ἐγένετο εἰς ὄρος μέγα, καὶ ἐπλήρωσε πᾶσαν τὴν γῆν.»
Τοιοῦτον τοῦ ἐνυπνίου τὸ τέλος· προσήκει δὲ κάτωθεν ἡμᾶς ἄρξασθαι
τῆς ἑρμηνείας. Ζητήσωμεν τοίνυν πρότερον, τίς λίθος προσαγορευόμενος, καὶ βραχὺς πρότερον φαινόμενος, ὕστερον ἐδείχθη μέγιστος, καὶ τὴν
οἰκουμένην ἐκάλυψεν. Οὐκοῦν ἀκούσωμεν αὐτοῦ τοῦ Θεοῦ διὰ Ἡσαΐου
τοῦ προφήτου λέγοντος· «Ἰδοὺ τίθημι ἐν Σιὼν λίθον πολυτελῆ, ἀκρογω-
νιαῖον, ἔντιμον, ἐκλεκτόν, εἰς τὰ θεμέλια αὐτῆς, καὶ πᾶς ὁ | πιστεύων ἐπ᾽
αὐτῷ οὐ μὴ καταισχυνθῇ.» Ἀκούσωμεν δὲ καὶ τοῦ μακαρίου Δαβὶδ προ-
θεσπίζοντος, καὶ βοῶντος· «Λίθον ὃν ἀπεδοκίμασαν οἱ οἰκοδομοῦντες,
οὗτος ἐγενήθη εἰς κεφαλὴν γωνίας.» Ταύτην δὲ τὴν μαρτυρίαν καὶ αὐτὸς
ὁ Δεσπότης Χριστὸς ἐν τοῖς ἱεροῖς Εὐαγγελίοις Ἰουδαίοις προσήνεγκεν,
«Οὐκ ἀνέγνωτε, λέγων· Λίθον ὃν ἀπεδοκίμασαν οἱ οἰκοδομοῦντες, οὗτος ἐγενήθη εἰς κεφαλὴν γωνίας. Παρὰ Κυρίου ἐγένετο αὕτη, καὶ ἔστι

1301

he says by way of exhortation, "Do not be conformed to this age." And blessed David says to prove the futility of human prosperity, "Yet everything is futility, every living person."[52] Of course, in an image a person goes his way, stores things up, without knowing for whom he is amassing them. So, since the present life also experiences rapid changes (all visible things being mortal, impermanent, passing), and an image does not enjoy the operation of substance, but brings out only the forms of kingdoms, rulers and subjects, and in addition to this it has a form that easily dissolves, the God of all in his wish to instruct that arrogant king in the futility of human conceit and teach him that human affairs are easily subject to change was justified in bringing that image to him in a dream and itemizing its parts in the materials. He wanted to convey succession of kings and to persuade everyone that he alone has unceasing control, without beginning and without end, and a kingdom that is absolutely eternal.

After this blessed Daniel proceeds to convey the rest of the dream. *You kept gazing and saw how a stone was hewn out of a mountain without hands being used, and it struck the image on its iron and clay feet, and smashed them to pieces. Then the iron, the clay, the bronze, the silver, the gold were crushed in one go and became like dust from a threshing floor in summer. The wind carried them away, and no trace of them was found. The stone that struck the mountain became a huge mountain, and filled the whole earth* (vv. 34–35). Such was the end of the dream; we must begin the interpretation starting at the end. So let us enquire first who is given the name *stone*, seeming first to be small, later shown to be immense and covering the whole world. Let us listen, then, to God himself speaking through the prophet Isaiah, "Lo, I put in Sion a precious stone, a corner stone, honorable, special, as its foundation; anyone | believing in it will not be ashamed."[53] Let us listen also to blessed David prophesying in a loud cry, "The stone which the builders rejected has become the cornerstone."[54] Christ the Lord himself in the sacred Gospels also cited this text to Jews, "Did you not read the text, The stone which the builders rejected has become the cornerstone. It was done by the Lord, and is a marvel in our

1301

[52] I Cor 7:31; Rom 12:2; Ps 39:5.
[53] Isa 28:16.
[54] Ps 118:22.

θαυμαστή ἐν ὀφθαλμοῖς ἡμῶν;» Καὶ ὁ μακάριος δὲ Πέτρος ἐν Ἰουδαίοις δημηγορῶν, καὶ τοῦ Κυρίου τὴν προφητείαν εἰς μέσον παραγαγών, φησίν· «Οὗτός ἐστιν ὁ λίθος ὁ ἐξουθενηθεὶς παρ' ὑμῶν τῶν οἰκοδομούντων, ὃς ἐγένετο εἰς κεφαλὴν γωνίας.» Καὶ ὁ μακάριος δὲ Παῦλός φησιν· «Ἐποικοδομηθέντες ἐπὶ τῷ θεμελίῳ τῶν ἀποστόλων καὶ προφητῶν, ὄντος ἀκρογωνιαίου αὐτοῦ Ἰησοῦ Χριστοῦ.» Καὶ ἀλλαχοῦ φησι· «Θεμέλιον οὐδεὶς δύναται θεῖναι παρὰ τὸν κείμενον, ὅς ἐστιν Ἰησοῦς Χριστός.» Καὶ πάλιν· «Ἔπινον, φησίν, ἐκ πνευματικῆς ἀκολουθούσης πέτρας, ἡ δὲ πέτρα ἦν ὁ Χριστός.» Οὐκοῦν ὑπὸ Παλαιᾶς καὶ Νέας Διαθήκης διδασκόμεθα τὸν Κύριον ἡμῶν Ἰησοῦν Χριστὸν προσηγορεῦ[ς]θαι λίθον. Οὗτος γὰρ ἐτμήθη ἀπὸ ὄρους ἄνευ χειρῶν, γεννηθεὶς ἐκ Παρθένου γαμικῆς κοινωνίας χωρίς· οἶδε δὲ πολλάκις καὶ τὴν παρὰ φύσιν γέννησιν λατομίαν ἡ θεία προσαγορεύειν Γραφή. Ἰουδαίους γὰρ Ἡσαΐας, τῆς παρὰ φύσιν γενομένης τῷ Ἀβραὰμ παιδογονίας ἀναμιμνήσκων, «Ἐμβλέψατε, ἔλεγεν, εἰς τὴν στερεὰν πέτραν, ἐξ ἧς ἐλατομήθητε.» Οὐκοῦν ὄρος μὲν ἡ Δαβιδικὴ φυλή, λίθος δὲ ὁ Χριστὸς κατὰ τὸ ἀνθρώπινον, οὐ κατὰ τὸν νόμον τῆς φύσεως τμηθείς· οὗτος δὲ πάλαι σμικρὸς φαινόμενος, δι' ἣν περιέκειτο φύσιν, ἀθρόον ἐδείχθη ὄρος μέγιστον, πᾶσαν πληρώσας τὴν οἰκουμένην. «Ἐπληρώθη γὰρ ἡ σύμπασα γῆ τοῦ γνῶναι τὸν Κύριον, ὡς ὕδωρ πολὺ κατακαλύψαι θαλάσσας» Οὗτος πατάξει τὴν εἰκόνα ἐπὶ τοὺς πόδας τοὺς ὀστρακίνους καὶ σιδηροῦς, τουτέστι, καὶ τὴν ἐσχάτην καταπαύσει βασιλείαν, φροῦδόν τε καὶ ἀφανῆ ποιήσει. Οὐ γὰρ ἑτέρα ταύτην διαδέξεται βασιλεία, ἀλλὰ τὴν οἰκείαν γυμνώσει, καὶ πᾶσι

eyes?"⁵⁵ Blessed Peter preaching among the Jews and focusing on the prophecy of the Lord says, "He is the stone despised by you the builders, which has become the cornerstone."⁵⁶ Blessed Paul says, "Built on the foundation of the apostles and prophets, with Jesus Christ himself as a cornerstone;" and elsewhere he says, "No one can lay any foundation stone other than the one laid, which is Jesus Christ"; and again, "They drank from the spiritual rock that followed them, and the rock was Christ."⁵⁷

So we learn from Old and New Testament that our Lord Jesus Christ was called *stone*: it was cut from a mountain without hands being used, being born of a virgin independently of marital intercourse.⁵⁸ Now, the divine Scripture is in the habit of calling preternatural birth "quarrying": in reminding Jews of the begetting of children that happened preternaturally in Abraham's case, Isaiah said, "Look to the solid rock from which you were quarried."⁵⁹ So *mountain* means the Davidic tribe, and *stone* Christ in his humanity, not hewn according to the law of nature: formerly insignificant in appearance on account of the nature with which he was invested, he was suddenly shown to be a mighty mountain, filling the whole world. "The whole world was filled with the knowledge of God," Scripture says, remember, "like a great volume of water covering the seas."⁶⁰ He it is who will strike the image in its feet of clay and iron, that is, he will bring the last kingdom to an end, and make it futile and evanescent: far from any other kingdom succeeding it, he will reveal his own one and make

---

⁵⁵ Matt 21:42. (The citation of the psalm verse in Luke 20:17 is followed by an implicit reference to "the stone that crushes anyone on whom it falls," and so would have been a more pertinent reference.)

⁵⁶ Acts 4:14.

⁵⁷ Eph 2:20; 1 Cor 3:11; 10:4.

⁵⁸ The symbolism of the stone Theodoret takes in the light of many Old Testament and New Testament references, as he will do in a similar exercise when he comes to comment on Ps 118:22 in his Psalms commentary. For Daniel the stone is the kingdom that God will establish, that will outlast all other kingdoms; the Old Testament elsewhere uses a similar image, as in Isa and Ps 118, for God's people. In the New Testament the sense of the stone passes from the theocratic kingdom to the king himself, Jesus. The reference to the virgin birth, made here and in commentary on the verse in Psalms, Theodoret doubtless gets from another source (none so far acknowledged; cf. note 65 below).

⁵⁹ Isa 51:1.

⁶⁰ Isa 11.9.

ταύτην ὑποδείξει· ἐκείνων δὲ τῶν βασιλειῶν ἁπασῶν καὶ αὐτὴν ἀφανιεῖ τὴν μνήμην κονιορτοῦ δίκην, ἐξ ἅλωνος μὲν τικτομένου, ὑπὸ δὲ πνεύματος σκεδαννυμένου. Οὕτω τὸ ἐνύπνιον ἅπαν εἰρηκὼς τῷ βασιλεῖ, ἐπήγαγε·

λζ', λζ'. «Τοῦτό ἐστι τὸ ἐνύπνιον, καὶ τὴν σύγκρισιν αὐτοῦ ἐροῦμεν ἐνώπιον τοῦ βασιλέως. Σὺ βασιλεῦ, βασιλεὺς βασιλέων.» Οὐ κολακεύων τοῦτο | εἴρηκεν, ἀλλὰ τῇ συνήθει προσηγορίᾳ χρησάμενος· κατὰ γὰρ πάντων τῶν ἐθναρχούντων, βασιλέων ὀνομαζομένων, εἶχε τὸ κράτος. «Σύ, φησί, βασιλεῦ, βασιλεὺς βασιλέων, ᾧ ὁ Θεὸς τοῦ οὐρανοῦ βασιλείαν κραταιὰν καὶ ἰσχυρὰν καὶ ἔντιμον ἔδωκεν ἐν παντὶ τόπῳ.» Οὐ γὰρ ἀπὸ ἰσχύος, φησίν, ἀνθρωπίνης πάντων περιγεγένησαι, ἀλλὰ τοῦ Θεοῦ, τοῦ τὴν ἐπουράνιον ἔχοντος βασιλείαν, ταύτην σοι δεδωκότος τὴν ἐξουσίαν, ὥστε τῶν ἐν παντὶ τόπῳ ὄντων ἀνθρώπων ἡγεμονεύειν τε καὶ βασιλεύειν, ὅπου κατοικοῦσιν υἱοὶ τῶν ἀνθρώπων. Θηρία τε ἀγροῦ καὶ πετεινὰ οὐρανοῦ δέδωκεν ἐν τῇ χειρί σου, καὶ κατέστησέ σε κύριον πάντων. Καὶ θηρία μὲν καλεῖ τοὺς θηριωδέστερον ζῶντας βαρβάρους, πετεινὰ δὲ τοὺς συνέσει κεκοσμημένους, καὶ τῶν ἄλλων ἀνθρώπων ὑπερτέρους, καὶ πτηνοὺς τὴν διάνοιαν. Τούτων, φησίν, ἁπάντων ἀπέφηνέ σε βασιλέα. «Σὺ τοίνυν εἶ ἡ κεφαλὴ ἡ χρυσῆ·» τουτέστιν, ἡ σὴ βασιλεία. Οὔτε γὰρ περὶ τοῦ προσώπου λέγει, ἀλλὰ περὶ αὐτῆς τῆς βασιλείας. Καὶ γὰρ μετὰ τὴν τελευτὴν αὐτοῦ, Εὐϊλὰδ Μαρωδὰχ ἐβασίλευσε τῶν Βαβυλωνίων, καὶ μετ' ἐκεῖνον Βαλτάσαρ. Εἰ δὲ περὶ αὐτοῦ τοῦ προσώπου ἔφη, ὅτι «Σὺ εἶ ἡ κεφαλὴ ἡ χρυσῆ,» πῶς νοήσομεν τό· «Ὀπίσω σου ἀναστήσεται βασιλεία ἑτέρα ἥττων σου;» Οὔτε γὰρ τὴν τῶν υἱέων αὐτοῦ βασιλείαν μηνύει, ἀλλὰ τὴν Περσικήν. Οὐκοῦν κεφαλὴ ἡ χρυσῆ οὐκ αὐτὸς ὁ Ναβουχοδονόσορ, ἀλλὰ πᾶσα ἡ τῶν Ἀσσυρίων, εἴτουν Βαβυλωνίων βασιλεία.

λθ'. «Καὶ ὀπίσω σου ἀναστήσεται βασιλεία ἑτέρα ἥττων σου.» Ἡ Περσική· ἥττονα δὲ αὐτὴν καλεῖ, οὐχ ὡς ἀσθενεστέραν, ἀλλ' ὡς δευτέραν. «Καὶ βασιλεία τρίτη, ἥτις ἐστὶν ὁ χαλκός, ἣ κυριεύσει πάσης τῆς γῆς.» Τὴν Μακεδονικὴν λέγει· ἐκυρίευσε δὲ πάσης τῆς γῆς Ἀλέξανδρος ὁ Φιλίππου, ἐν δώδεκα ἔτεσι τῆς βασιλείας πάντας ὑποτάξας ἀνθρώπους.

μ'. «Καὶ βασιλεία τετάρτη ἔσται ἰσχυρά, ὡς ὁ σίδηρος· ὃν τρόπον

it obvious to everyone, and will even wipe out the very memory of all those kingdoms like dust stirred up from the threshing floor and scattered by the wind.

Having thus described the whole dream to the king, he went on, *This is the dream and we shall give its interpretation in the presence of the king. You, O King, king of kings* (vv. 36–37). He said this, not by way of flattery, | but employing a customary title; after all, he had power over all rulers of nations, all who were called king. *You, O King, king of kings, to whom the God of heaven has given a kingdom mighty and powerful and honorable in every place*: it is not from human power that you have prevailed over all, but from the God who has the heavenly kingdom, who gave you this authority for you to lead and reign over people living in every place wherever humankind dwells; he gave the beasts of the field and the birds of the sky into your hand, and set you as lord of all. He refers to the barbarians who live in the wildest fashion as *wild beasts* (v. 28), and as *birds* to those endowed with understanding, more elevated than other people and uplifted in mind. He means that he made you king of everything. So *you are the head of gold*, that is, your kingdom (referring not to the person but to the kingdom: after his death Evil-merodach reigned over the Babylonians, and after him Belshazzar).[61] If, on the other hand, he referred to him in person in saying *You are the head of gold*, how are we to take the statement *After you will arise a kingdom inferior to yours* (v. 39)? He does not mean the kingdom of his sons, only the Persian one. So *the head of gold* is not Nebuchadnezzar personally, but the whole kingdom of the Assyrians (or Babylonians).

And after you will arise a kingdom inferior to yours, that is, the Persian; he calls it inferior, not in the sense of weaker, but as coming second. *And a third kingdom, of bronze, which will dominate the whole earth.* He means the Macedonian: Alexander son of Philip gained control the whole earth, subjecting all people in his reign of twelve years. *And there will be fourth kingdom, strong as iron:*

---

[61] Perhaps influenced by the story in chapter 5, where a king appears with the name Belshazzar, which is meant to refer to the son of Nabonidus, the last ruler of Babylon, Theodoret comes up with a royal line which proceeds from Nebuchadnezar to Evil-merodach (Hebrew form of Amel-marduk; cf. 2 Kgs 25:27; Jer 52:31) to Belshazzar, omitting (as does the Bible) Neriglissar, Labashi-marduk, and Nabonidus, succession admittedly taking only a few years as Babylonian rule rapidly declined.

1304

γὰρ ὁ σίδηρος λεπτύνει καὶ δαμάζει πάντα, οὕτως λεπτυνεῖ πάντα καὶ δαμάσει.» Τὴν Ῥωμαϊκὴν λέγει βασιλείαν, ἰσχυροτάτην μὲν γενομένην, καὶ πάντων, ὡς ἔπος εἰπεῖν, τῶν ἐθνῶν περιγενομένην, δασμὸν δὲ καὶ φόρον παρὰ πάντων κομισαμένην. Τὸ γὰρ λεπτυνεῖ ἐπὶ τούτου τέθεικε, τὸ δὲ δαμάσει ἐπὶ τῆς ὑπακοῆς τε καὶ εὐταξίας, καὶ τῆς ἐννόμου πολιτείας.

μαʹ. «Καὶ ὅτι εἶδες τοὺς πόδας, καὶ τοὺς δακτύλους, μέρος μέν τι σιδήρου, μέρος δέ τι ὀστράκου, βασιλεία ἄλλη διῃρημένη ἔσται, καὶ ἀπὸ τῆς ῥίζης τοῦ σιδήρου ἔσται ἐν αὐτῇ, ὃν τρόπον εἶδες τὸν σίδηρον ἀναμεμιγμένον τῷ ὀστράκῳ τῷ πηλίνῳ.» Ἄλλην οὐ κατὰ τὸ γένος εἶπεν, ἀλλὰ κατὰ | τὴν ποιότητα τῆς δυνάμεως. Εἰ γὰρ κατὰ τὸ γένος ἔλεγεν, ἄλλην εἶπεν ἂν αὐτὴν πέμπτην, ὥσπερ αὖ εἴρηκε τρίτην τε καὶ τετάρτην. Ἐπειδὴ δὲ ἀσθενέστερα οἶδε τῆς σιδηρᾶς βασιλείας τὰ τέλη, ἄλλην τέθεικε διὰ τὴν ἀσθένειαν, καὶ μάλα εἰκότως. Σφόδρα γὰρ αὐτὴν ἰσχυροτάτην ἔδειξεν ἄνω· τοιαῦτα γὰρ αὐτῆς τὰ πρῶτα. Ἀλλ᾽ ὅμως οὐδὲ τὰ τελευταῖα αὐτῆς παντελῶς ἀσθενῆ ἔσεσθαι λέγει.

«Ἀπὸ γὰρ τῆς ῥίζης, φησί, τοῦ σιδήρου ἔσται ἐν αὐτῇ, ὃν τρόπον εἶδες τὸν σίδηρον ἀναμεμιγμένον τῷ ὀστράκῳ τῷ πηλίνῳ. (μβʹ.) Καὶ οἱ δάκτυλοι τῶν ποδῶν, μέρος μέν τι σιδήρου, μέρος δέ τι ὀστράκου.» Τοῦτο δὲ οὐδὲ τῆς ἡμετέρας ἑρμηνείας προσδεῖται· αὐτὸς γὰρ ὁ Προφήτης ἑρμηνεύων, φησί· «Μέρος τι τῆς βασιλείας ἔσται ἰσχυρόν, καὶ ἀπ᾽ αὐτῆς ἔσται συντριβόμενον.» Τούτοις ἐπάγει·

μγʹ. «Καὶ ὅτι εἶδες τὸν σίδηρον ἀναμεμιγμένον τῷ ὀστράκῳ τῷ πηλίνῳ, συμμιγεῖς ἔσονται ἐν σπέρματι ἀνθρώπων.» Τοῦτο δὲ μάλιστα δείκνυσιν, ὡς οὐχ ἑτέρα ἐστὶν αὕτη ἡ βασιλεία παρὰ τὸν σίδηρον, ἀλλ᾽ ἡ αὐτὴ ἀσθενέστερον διακειμένη, καὶ μέρος μέν τι αὐτῆς ἰσχυρόν, μέρος δὲ ἀσθενές· συγγενείας δὲ ὅμως θεσμὸς συνάψει τὴν ἀσθενῆ μοῖραν τῇ ἰσχυρᾷ. Τὸ γὰρ, «Συμμιγεῖς ἔσονται ἐν σπέρματι ἀνθρώπων,» τοῦτο δηλοῖ. Ἐπιμιξία, φησί, τις ἔσται καὶ ἐπιγαμία τούτων κἀκείνων, ἀλλ᾽ ὅμως ἡ διχόνοια τὰ τῆς συγγενείας δίκαια διαφθερεῖ. Οὐκ ἔσονται γάρ, φησί, προσκολλώμενοι οὗτος μετὰ τούτου, καθὼς ὁ σίδηρος οὐκ ἀναμίγνυται τῷ ὀστράκῳ. Ἡμεῖς μὲν οὖν οὕτω τὴν ἑρμηνείαν τοῦ θεσπεσίου Δανιὴλ νενοήκαμεν· προσήκει δὲ καὶ ἐνίων τῶν πρὸ ἡμῶν ἡρμηνευκότων

just as iron crushes and tames everything, so it will crush and tame everything (v. 40). He refers to the Roman Empire, which was the strongest and, so to say, prevailed over all the nations, taking tribute and taxes from all; he used *crush and tame* of it in reference to the submission, good order, and the rule of law.[62] *And as you saw its feet and toes were partly iron and partly clay; it will be another, divided kingdom, and some of the strength of iron will be in it in the way you saw the iron mixed with potter's clay* (v. 41). He used *other* not in respect of quantity but in respect of | the quality of power: 1305 if he had meant in respect of quantity, *other* would have meant it was a fifth kingdom, as he had already referred to a third and a fourth. Since, however, he knew the final stages of the iron kingdom would be weaker, he used *other* on account of the weakness, and rightly so: he had shown it to be by far the strongest initially, its early stages being like that, whereas (he means) not even its final stages will be completely weak.[63] *Some of the strength of the iron will be in it in the way you saw the iron mixed with potting clay. And the toes of the feet were partly iron and partly clay* (vv. 41–42). This does not call for comment from us: the prophet himself gives the interpretation in saying *A part of the kingdom will be strong, and will be crushed by it.*

After this he proceeds, *As you saw the iron mixed with potter's clay, they will be mixed in human offspring* (v. 43). This it is in particular that brings out that this is no different kingdom from the iron one, only the same one in a weaker condition, part of it being strong and part of it weak; a bond of kinship will connect the weak part with the strong, suggested by the phrase *they will be mixed in human offspring.* He is saying, There will be a mingling and intermarriage of the one and the other, but discord will spoil the rights of kinship: the one will not be attached to the other (he is saying), just as iron does not mix with clay.

While we for our part have thus understood the meaning of the divinely inspired Daniel, therefore, we ought also give attention to the views of some commentators before us, which is the

---

[62] Theodoret later, in commenting on Ps 46:9 and Isa 2:4, will show appreciation for the stability of the *pax Romana.*

[63] Division of a kingdom would apply more closely to the Greco-Seleucid kingdom (Theodoret's "Macedonian") than to the Romans, had he opted for that listing of kingdoms.

τὰς δόξας εἰς μέσον παραγαγεῖν· οὕτω γὰρ ἐναργέστερον ἡ ἀλήθεια δειχθήσεται. Τινὲς τοίνυν τῶν συγγραφέων τὴν τετάρτην βασιλείαν, τουτέστι τὸν σίδηρον, Ἀλέξανδρον ἔφασαν εἶναι τὸν Μακεδόνα· τοὺς δὲ πόδας καὶ τοὺς δακτύλους τῶν ποδῶν ἐκ σιδήρου καὶ ὀστράκου συγκειμένους, τοὺς μετ' αὐτὸν βασιλεύσαντας Μακεδόνας, Πτολεμαίους, καὶ Σελεύκους, καὶ Ἀντιόχους, καὶ Δημητρίους, τοὺς μὲν ἀσθενῶς, τοὺς δὲ λίαν ἀνδρικῶς κρατήσαντας, καὶ ἐπιγαμίαν δὲ ποιησαμένους καὶ τὴν ἀλλήλων ἀσπασαμένους συγγένειαν. Ἔδει δὲ αὐτοὺς συνιδεῖν, πρῶτον μὲν ὅτι τὴν κεφαλὴν τὴν χρυσῆν αὐτὸν ἔφη εἶναι τὸν Ναβουχοδονόσορ, τουτέστι, τὴν τῶν Βαβυλωνίων, εἴτουν Ἀσσυρίων, βασιλείαν· διεδέξατο δὲ αὐτὴν ἡ Περσῶν καὶ Μήδων βασιλεία κατὰ ταυτόν· ὁ γὰρ Κῦρος ἐξ ἑκατέρου ἔθνους ἦν ὁρμώμενος, καὶ τούτων κἀκείνων κρατῶν, τῶν Βαβυλωνίων καταλύσας τὴν βασιλείαν ἐκράτησε τῶν Περσῶν· τὴν δὲ Περσῶν δευτέραν οὖσαν Ἀλέξανδρος ὁ Μακεδὼν καταλύει, καὶ αὐτὸν ἔφη ὁ μακάριος Δανιὴλ κυριεῦσαι πάσης τῆς γῆς. Ταύτην τὴν βασιλείαν τρίτην ὠνόμασεν· οὐδεμία δὲ αὐτὴν ἑτέρα, ἀλλ' ἡ τῶν Ῥωμαίων διεδέξατο. Ἔδει | τοιγαροῦν αὐτοὺς πρῶτον μὲν ἐκ τοῦ ἀριθμοῦ, καὶ τῶν παραδηλωθέντων πραγμάτων συνιέναι, καὶ μαθεῖν, ὡς τρίτη ἐστὶν ἡ τῶν Μακεδόνων βασιλεία, τουτέστιν ὁ χαλκός· τετάρτη δὲ ἡ Ῥωμαίων, τουτέστιν ὁ σίδηρος Εἰ δὲ καὶ ὅλως ἀσαφέστερα αὐτοῖς ἔδοξεν εἶναι ἐκεῖνα, ἀπὸ γοῦν τοῦ τέλους ἔδει πᾶσαν διαγνῶναι τὴν πρόρρησιν· εὐθὺς γὰρ μετὰ τὸ δεῖξαι τῆς σιδηρᾶς βασιλείας τὸ ἀσθενὲς καὶ ὀστράκινον τέλος, ἐπήγαγε·

μδ'. «Καὶ ἐν ταῖς ἡμέραις τῶν βασιλέων ἐκείνων.» Τουτέστι, τοῦ ὀστρακίνου καὶ τοῦ σιδηροῦ τὴν ἐπιμιξίαν ἐχόντων, καὶ τὴν μετ' ἀλλήλων συγγένειαν ἀσπασαμένων, ὁμόνοιαν δὲ μηδὲ ἐκ τῆς συγγενείας ἐσχηκότων.

«Ἀναστήσει ὁ Θεὸς τοῦ οὐρανοῦ βασιλείαν, ἥτις εἰς τοὺς αἰῶνας οὐ διαφθαρήσεται, καὶ ἡ βασιλεία αὐτοῦ λαῷ ἑτέρῳ οὐχ ὑπολειφθήσεται. Λεπτυνεῖ καὶ λικμήσει πάσας τὰς βασιλείας, καὶ αὐτὴ στήσεται εἰς τοὺς αἰῶνας. (με'.) Ὃν τρόπον εἶδες, ὅτι ἐτμήθη ἀπὸ ὄρους λίθος ἄνευ χειρῶν, καὶ ἐλέπτυνε τὸ ὄστρακον, καὶ τὸν σίδηρον, τὸν χαλκόν, τὸν ἄργυρον, τὸν χρυσόν.» Ταῦτα δὲ ἀντικρὺς δείκνυσι τῶν μὲν παρόντων πραγμάτων

τὸ

way for the truth to be demonstrated more obviously.[64] Some historians, then, claim that the fourth kingdom—namely, the iron one—is Alexander the Macedonian; its feet and the toes of the feet were a mixture of iron and clay—namely, the Macedonians ruling after him, successors of Ptolemy, Seleucus, Antiochus, and Demetrius, some holding a weak grasp on power, others a very vigorous grasp, contracting intermarriage and being involved in relationships with one another. Now, they should understand, firstly, that he said *the head of gold* was Nebuchadnezzar, that is, the kingdom of the Babylonians (or, if you like, Assyrians). The kingdom of the Persians and Medes together succeeded to that, Cyrus being from both races, and while ruling the one and the other he destroyed the kingdom of the Babylonians and gained control of the Persians. The Persians' kingdom, the second, Alexander the Macedonian destroyed, and blessed Daniel declared he dominated the whole earth, calling it *the third kingdom.* There was no other than that of the Romans to succeed to it. They need, | therefore,   1308 to understand and grasp from the numbering and from the factors outlined that the third kingdom, of bronze, is that of the Macedonians, and the fourth, of iron, is that of the Romans.

If, on the other hand, they even judged this to be definitely more obscure, they should at least have discerned the prediction from the conclusion: as soon as he pointed out the weakness of the iron kingdom's clay extremity, he went on, *And in the days of those kingdoms,* namely, the clay and iron ones that intermingled and contracted a relationship with each other without this resulting in harmony. *The God of heaven will raise up a kingdom that will never be destroyed, and this kingdom will not be left to another people. It will smash and scatter all the kingdoms, and it will stand forever, in the way you saw that a stone was hewn from a mountain without hands being used, and it smashed the clay, the iron, the bronze, the silver and the gold* (vv. 44–45). Now, this clearly demonstrates the

---

[64] In his previous work on the Song of Songs, Theodoret had been much under the influence of Origen's work. Here, for the first of a dozen times in this work, he acknowledges a wider range of predecessors (to whom Eusebius helped introduce him), whose views he typically treats seriously, if unable to accept them. Guinot (*L'Exégèse*, 715) suggests that in this case the view he is rejecting of the four kingdoms is that of Polychronius of Apamea, brother of Theodore, not a similar Jewish interpretation from Porphyry; he prefers the view found in Josephus, Hippolytus, Irenaeus, Origen, Eusebius, and Jerome.

τέλος, τῆς δὲ τῶν οὐρανῶν βασιλείας τὸ ἀτελεύτητον. Τῆς γὰρ σιδηρᾶς βασιλείας ἀσθενῶς διατεθείσης, καὶ τοῦ ὀστράκου τὴν ἐπιμιξίαν λαβούσης, φανήσεται μὲν «ὁ λίθος ὁ τμηθεὶς ἄνευ χειρῶν, καὶ λεπτυνεῖ τὸ ὄστρακον, τὸν σίδηρον καὶ τὸν χαλκόν, τὸν ἄργυρον, τὸν χρυσόν,» καὶ φροῦδα ποιήσει παντελῶς, καὶ ἀδιάδοχον, καὶ αἰώνιον, καὶ ἀπέραντον βασιλείαν τοῖς ἀξίοις παρέξει. «Εἰς γὰρ τοὺς αἰῶνας, φησίν, οὐ διαφθαρήσεται, καὶ λαῷ ἑτέρῳ οὐχ ὑπολειφθήσεται· καὶ λεπτυνεῖ, καὶ δαμάσει πάσας τὰς βασιλείας, καὶ αὐτὴ στήσεται εἰς τοὺς αἰῶνας.» Εἰ δέ τις ζυγομαχεῖ, καὶ ταῦθ' οὕτως ἔχειν οὐ βούλεται, δειξάτω τί τῶν ἀνθρωπίνων αἰώνιον, ποία δὲ τῶν ἀνθρώπων βασιλεία τέλος οὐ λήψεται. Εὔηθες γὰρ καὶ λίαν ἀνόητον, συντέλειαν μὲν ἀναμένειν τοῦ παρόντος αἰῶνος, βασιλείαν δέ τινα λέγειν κατὰ τὸν παρόντα βίον ἀτελεύτητον ἔσεσθαι. Εἰ δὲ καὶ αὐτοῖς συνδοκεῖ διὰ τούτων τῶν λόγων τὴν δοθησομένην ὑπὸ τοῦ Θεοῦ βασιλείαν τοῖς ἀξίοις σημαίνεσθαι, οὐκ ἄρα τὴν Μακεδονικὴν βασιλείαν ὠνόμασε σίδηρον· οὐδὲ γὰρ ἐκείνης κρατούσης ὁ παρὼν βίος ἐδέξατο τέλος, ἀλλ' ἡ Ῥωμαϊκὴ τὴν Μακεδονικὴν καταλύσασα κατέχει τῆς οἰκουμένης τοὺς οἴακας. Εἰ δέ φασι τὴν προτέραν τοῦ Κυρίου παρουσίαν διὰ τούτων τῶν λόγων σημαίνεσθαι, δειξάτωσαν καταλυθεῖσαν τὴν τῶν Ῥωμαίων ἡγεμονίαν εὐθὺς μετὰ τὴν τοῦ Σωτῆρος ἡμῶν ἐπιφάνειαν. Πᾶν γὰρ τοὐναντίον ἔστιν εὑρεῖν, κρατυνθεῖσαν αὐτήν, ἀλλ' οὐ καταλυθεῖσαν ἅμα τῇ τοῦ Σωτῆρος γεννήσει. Αὐγούστου γὰρ βασιλεύοντος ὁ Δεσποτικὸς ἐγένετο τόκος. Ὃς δεύτερος μὲν ἐβα|σίλευσε, πάντας δὲ ὡς ἔπος εἰπεῖν. ἀνθρώπους ὑπηκόους ἐποιήσατο, ἀπεγράψατό τε πᾶσαν τὴν οἰκουμένην κατὰ τὴν τῶν Εὐαγγελίων φωνήν, καὶ δασμὸν φέρειν ἐνομοθέτησεν. Ὑπ' ἐκείνου δὲ ἡ Ῥωμαίων κρατυνθεῖσα βασιλεία μέχρι καὶ νῦν διήρκεσεν. Οὐκοῦν εἰ ἡ προτέρα γέννησις τοῦ Κυρίου τὴν Ῥωμαίων ἡγεμονίαν οὐ κατέλυσε, λείπεται τοίνυν αὐτοῦ τὴν δευτέραν νοεῖν ἐπιφάνειαν. Ὁ γὰρ ἤδη πρότερον τμηθεὶς λίθος ἄνευ χειρῶν, καὶ γενόμενος εἰς ὄρος μέγα, καὶ τὴν οἰκουμένην καλύψας, οὗτος ἐν τῇ δευτέρᾳ παρουσίᾳ πατάξει τὴν εἰκόνα ἐπὶ τοὺς πόδας τοὺς ὀστρακίνους, τουτέστιν, ἐν αὐτῷ τῷ τέλει τῆς σιδηρᾶς φανήσεται βασιλείας, ἀσθενοῦς ἤδη γεγενημένης·

end of present realities, and the unending character of the heavenly kingdom: with the iron kingdom being in a weak condition and the clay one being intermingled, there will appear a stone hewn without hands being used, and it will smash the clay, the iron, the bronze, the silver, and the gold, will bring them to naught; it will be without successors, eternal, and will provide to those worthy an unending kingdom. *It will never be destroyed,* the text says, *and it will not be left to another people; it will smash and tame all the kingdoms, and will itself stand forever.*

If, on the other hand, there are those who are uncomfortable with this and prefer not to have it this way, they need to prove what human exploit is eternal and what human kingdom has no end: it is silly and quite absurd, on the one hand, to be awaiting a consummation of the present age and, on the other, to claim that some kingdom in the present life is unending. Now, if it is agreed even by them that in these words an indication is given of a kingdom that will be given by God to the worthy, then it was not the Macedonian kingdom he called iron: the present life did not come to an end when that was in power—instead, the Roman one destroyed the Macedonian and took over the helm of the whole world. If, on the other hand, they claim that the first coming of the Lord is suggested in these words, let them show that the governance of the Romans was terminated immediately after the appearance of our Savior; on the contrary, in fact, it is easy to find that quite the opposite is the case, that it held power and was not terminated at the very moment of the birth of the Savior. Augustus, in fact, was reigning when the Lord's birth occurred, the second to come | to the throne, and so to say he made subjects of all people and "had the whole world registered,"[65] in the words of the Gospels, and required tribute to be given. The Roman kingdom remained in power under him, and has lasted even to this day. If, then, the first coming of the Lord did not overturn the governance of the Romans, it therefore follows that we see a reference to his second coming: he is the stone already first hewn without use of hands, turning into a huge mountain and covering the world, and at his second coming he will strike the image on its clay feet—that is, he will appear at the very end of the iron kingdom, already ren-

1309

---

[65] Luke 2:1. Augustus, in Theodoret's view (as expressed in his comment on 9:25), is the second Roman emperor, Julius Caesar being the first.

καὶ πάσας μὲν καταλύσει τὰς ἡγεμονίας, καὶ λήθῃ τινὶ παραδώσει, τὴν δὲ αἰώνιον αὐτοῦ βασιλείαν τοῖς ἀξίοις παρέξει. Ταῦθ᾽ οὕτως ἑρμηνεύσας ὁ Δανιὴλ ἀναγκαίως ἐπήγαγεν· «Ὁ Θεὸς ὁ μέγας ἐγνώρισε τῷ βασιλεῖ, ἃ δεῖ γενέσθαι μετὰ ταῦτα. Καὶ ἀληθινὸν τὸ ἐνύπνιον, καὶ πιστὴ ἡ σύγκρισις αὐτοῦ.» Ἄξιον δὲ θαυμάσαι τὴν τοῦ Θεοῦ τῶν ὅλων περὶ πάντας ἀνθρώπους κηδεμονίαν. Οὐδὲ γὰρ τοὺς δυσσεβείᾳ συζῶντας τῆς οἰκείας προμηθείας γυμνοῖ, ἀλλὰ καὶ τούτους πάσης ἐπιμελείας ἀξιοῖ, ὥσπερ ἀμέλει τοῦτον τὸν βάρβαρον, καὶ θηριώδη, καὶ δυσσεβῆ οὐ καταλέλοιπεν ἀτημέλητον, ἀλλὰ πρῶτον μὲν διὰ τῶν ἀποκαλύψεων τῆς εὐκληρίας τοῦ παρόντος βίου δείκνυσιν αὐτῷ τὸ ἐπίκηρον, καὶ τῆς βασιλείας αὐτῆς τὸ ὀξύρροπον, καὶ ὅτι οὐδὲν μόνιμον τῆς ἀνθρωπίνης εὐημερίας, ἀλλὰ δίκην ἀνθῶν ἢ κρίνων μαραίνεται ἢ σβέννυται. Καὶ ἱκανὰ ταῦτα ἦν τὴν ἀλαζονικὴν αὐτοῦ καὶ τετυφωμένην ὀφρὺν καταλῦσαι, καὶ πεῖσαι φρονεῖν ἀνθρώπινα, καὶ ἀναμένειν καὶ τῆς ζωῆς καὶ βασιλείας τὸ τέλος. Πρῶτον μὲν οὖν διὰ τούτων αὐτοῦ ποιεῖται τὴν ἐπιμέλειαν, ἔπειτα τῇ λήθῃ τοῦ ἐνυπνίου ἐλέγχει τὴν τῶν μάγων καὶ Χαλδαίων ψευδολογίαν· δείκνυσι δὲ τὴν τῶν οἰκείων θεραπόντων ἀλήθειαν, καὶ διὰ τῆς τῶν θεραπόντων σοφίας τὴν θείαν αὐτοῦ δύναμιν παραδηλοῖ, καὶ εἰς προσκύνησιν ἕλκει τὴν ἑαυτοῦ τοὺς ἀγνοοῦντας, μᾶλλον δὲ τοὺς τὴν παρὰ πάντων ἀπαιτοῦντας προσκύνησιν τοὺς ἁγίους αὐτοῦ θεράποντας προσκυνεῖν ἀναγκάζει. Καὶ τοῦτο ἡμᾶς ἡ ἱστορία διδάσκει.

μς΄. «Τότε γάρ, φησίν, ὁ βασιλεὺς Ναβουχοδονόσορ ἐπὶ πρόσωπον ἔπεσε, καὶ τῷ Δανιὴλ προσεκύνησε, καὶ μαναὰ καὶ εὐωδίαν εἶπε σπεῖσαι αὐτῷ.» Ἐνθυμήθητι δέ, ἡλίκον ἐκεῖνον τὸν ἀλαζόνα, τὸν μεμηνότα, τὸν καὶ Θεὸν εἶναι νομίσαντα (δι᾽ ἑτέρου γὰρ προφήτου φησὶν ὁ Θεὸς πρὸς αὐτόν· «Σὺ δὲ εἶ ἄνθρωπος, καὶ οὐ Θεὸς»), τὸν πάντας ἀνθρώπους ὑπηκόους ποιησάμενον, τὸν αἰχμάλωτον προσκυνεῖν τὸν Ἰουδαῖον, τὸν ἀνδραπόδου τάξιν ἀποπληροῦντα, καὶ ἡγεῖσθαι διὰ τούτου τὸν τού-
1312 του προσκυνεῖν Θεόν. Τούτου γὰρ χάριν «μαναὰ καὶ | εὐωδίαν σπεῖσαι αὐτῷ,» τουτέστι, λιβανωτὸν καὶ θυμίαμα προσενεχθῆναι αὐτῷ ἐνετείλατο. Αἰνίττεται δὲ διὰ τούτων ἡ ἱστορία, ὡς τοῖς δοκοῦσιν ἱερεῦσι τοῦτο ποιῆσαι παρεγγύησεν. Ὁ γὰρ προσκυνήσας πάντως ἂν καὶ τὴν εὐωδίαν προσενηνόχει, εἴπερ ἱερατεύειν εἰώθει. Ἐπειδὴ δὲ τοῦτο ἄλλοις πάντως ἁρμόττον ἦν, αὐτὸς μὲν οὐκ ἐπεχείρει ποιεῖν, ἃ μὴ προσῆκον ἦν, τοῖς δὲ

dered weak. He will destroy all governing powers, consign them to a kind of oblivion, and provide his eternal kingdom for the worthy.

Having given this interpretation of these things, Daniel naturally proceeded, *The mighty God made known to the king what must happen after this. The dream is true, and its interpretation trustworthy.* Now, it is worth admiring the care of the God of all for all people: he does not deprive of his providence even those living in godlessness. Instead, he grants them every attention as well, just as of course he did not leave neglected this cruel and godless foreigner: firstly, by means of the revelations he shows him the impermanence of the prosperity of the present life and the rapid decline of the kingdom itself, and the fact that human felicity, far from being lasting, fades and disappears like flowers and lilies. This was sufficient to repress his arrogant and conceited attitude, and to persuade him to think in human terms and expect the end of life and reign. Firstly, then, in this he shows his care; then by his forgetting the dream he proves the falsity of the soothsayers and astrologers, shows the truth of his own servants, revealing his divine power in the wisdom of his servants, and draws the ignorant to worship of him—or, rather, he obliges those who require worship from everyone to worship his holy servants.

The story informs us of this. *Then King Nebuchadnezzar fell on his face and worshiped Daniel, and he gave orders for a grain offering and incense to be offered to him* (v. 46). Think how great a thing this was for that proud and demented man, who considered himself even to be God (God telling him through another prophet, remember, "You are man, not God")[66] and made all people his subjects, to worship this Jewish prisoner, serving in the role of a slave, and to think that in him he was worshiping his God—hence his | offering him a grain offering and incense, that is, he gave instructions for him to be offered a censer with frankincense. Now, in this the story suggests that he gave orders to those thought to be priests to do this: the person worshiping would always offer incense as well if he normally served as priest. But since it was quite appropriate for others, he personally would not venture to do what

1312

[66] Ezek 28:2, 9—though the rebuke is addressed to the king of Tyre; a rebuke addressed to Nebuchadnezzar might have been cited more suitably from Isa 14:12–14.

ποιεῖν εἰωθόσι τοῦτο ποιῆσαι παρακελεύεται. Καὶ ἵνα μὴ δόξῃ, μάτην ἄνθρωπον προσκυνεῖν, λέγει τῷ Δανιήλ· «Ἐπ' ἀληθείας ὁ Θεὸς ὑμῶν οὗτός ἐστι Θεὸς θεῶν, καὶ Κύριος τῶν βασιλέων, καὶ ὁ ἀποκαλύπτων μυστήρια, ὅτι ἠδυνήθης ἀποκαλύψαι τὸ μυστήριον τοῦτο.» Τοσαύτην ἔκ τε τοῦ ἐνυπνίου, καὶ τῆς τοῦ ἐνυπνίου λήθης ὠφέλειαν αὐτῷ τῶν ὅλων ὁ πρύτανις προσενήνοχε. Πρῶτον μὲν γὰρ ἔγων τὴν οἰκείαν εὐτέλειαν, ἔπειτα μεμάθηκε τῶν ὑπ' αὐτοῦ προσκυνουμένων θεῶν τὴν ἀσθένειαν, πρὸς τούτοις ἐδιδάχθη τὴν ἐνέργειαν τοῦ ὄντως Θεοῦ. Οὗ χάριν βοᾷ· «Ἐπ' ἀληθείας ὁ Θεὸς ὑμῶν, οὗτός ἐστι Θεὸς τῶν θεῶν, καὶ Κύριος τῶν βασιλέων, καὶ ἀποκαλύπτων μυστήρια.» *Θεὸν δὲ θεῶν* προσαγορεύει, οὐ κατὰ τὴν διάνοιαν τῆς θείας Γραφῆς· ἡ μὲν γὰρ θεία Γραφὴ τοὺς ἠξιωμένους ἱερωσύνης ὀνομάζει *θεούς·* «Θεοὺς γὰρ, φησίν, οὐ κακολογήσεις, καὶ ἄρχοντα τοῦ λαοῦ σου οὐκ ἐρεῖς κακῶς·» οὗτος δὲ θεοὺς τὰ εἴδωλα προσηγόρευσεν· οὐδέπω γὰρ ἠδυνήθη τὸ παντελῶς αὐτῶν ἀσθενὲς συνιδεῖν. Μεμάθηκε δὲ ὅμως τὸ διάφορον, διὸ καὶ *Θεὸν τῶν θεῶν* τὸν τῶν ὅλων προσαγορεύει Θεόν, καὶ *Κύριον βασιλέων.* Ταῦθ' οὕτως ὁμολογήσας,

μη'. «Ἐμεγάλυνε τὸν Δανιὴλ, καὶ δόματα πολλὰ ἔδωκεν αὐτῷ, καὶ κατέστησεν αὐτὸν ἐπὶ πάσης τῆς χώρας Βαβυλῶνος, καὶ ἄρχοντα σατραπῶν, καὶ ἐπὶ πάντας τοὺς σοφοὺς Βαβυλῶνος.» Καὶ τοῦτο δὲ τῆς θείας κηδεμονίας ἴδιον. Μεγίστην φέρει τοῖς ὑπηκόοις τὴν ὠφέλειαν τοῦ ἄρχοντος ἡ εὐσέβεια· τοῦτο δὲ καὶ ἐπὶ τοῦ Ἰωσὴφ πεποίηκεν ὁ Δεσπότης. Καὶ συντομώτερον ὁ μακάριος Δαβὶδ τὰ κατ' αὐτὸν διηγούμενος, καὶ τὴν θείαν πρόνοιαν ὑμῶν, φησίν· «Ἐξαπέστειλεν ἔμπροσθεν αὐτῶν ἄνθρωπον, εἰς δοῦλον ἐπράθη ὁ Ἰωσήφ.» Εἶτα τὰ συμβεβηκότα αὐτῷ δυσχερήματα λέξας, καὶ τῆς εἰρκτῆς, καὶ τῶν δεσμῶν μνημονεύσας, ἐπήγαγεν· «Ἀπέστειλε βασιλεύς, καὶ ἔλυσεν αὐτὸν ἄρχων λαοῦ, καὶ ἀφῆκεν αὐτόν, καὶ κατέστησεν αὐτὸν κύριον τοῦ οἴκου αὐτοῦ, καὶ ἄρχοντα πάσης τῆς κτήσεως αὐτοῦ· παιδεῦσαι τοὺς ἄρχοντας αὐτοῦ, ὡς ἑαυτόν, καὶ τοὺς πρεσβυτέρους αὐτοῦ σοφίσαι.» Οὕτω κἀντεῦθεν πεποίηκε τῶν ὅλων ὁ Πρύτανις. Ἄρχοντα γὰρ σατραπῶν καὶ τῶν | σοφῶν Βαβυλῶνος τὸν τρισμακάριον Δανιὴλ καταστήσας, ἀρχέτυπον αὐτὸν εὐσεβείας καὶ τῆς ἄλλης προὔθηκεν ἀρετῆς· ἀλλ' ὅμως οὐκ ἠνέσχετο μόνος ταύτης ἀπολαῦσαι τῆς τιμῆς ὁ προφήτης, ἀλλὰ τοὺς κοινωνοὺς τῆς εὐχῆς κοινωνοὺς ἔλαβε καὶ τῆς τιμῆς.

μθ'. «Ἠτήσατο γὰρ, φησί, παρὰ τοῦ βασιλέως, καὶ κατέστησεν ἐπὶ πάντα τὰ ἔργα τῆς χώρας Βαβυλῶνος τὸν Σιδράχ, Μισάχ, καὶ Ἀβδε-

should not to be done, instead giving orders to those accustomed to do it. And lest he seem to be worshiping a human being to no purpose, he says to Daniel, *In truth this God of yours is God of gods and Lord of kings, the one who reveals mysteries, because you were able to reveal this mystery* (v. 47). The governor of all things brought him so much benefit both from the dream and from the forgetting of the dream: firstly, he discovered his own worthlessness; next, he came to know the weakness of the gods worshiped by him, and as well he was instructed in the operations of the true God—hence his cry, *In truth this God of yours is God of gods and Lord of kings, the one who reveals mysteries.* Now, he does not call him *God of gods* according to the thinking of the divine Scripture: while the divine Scripture gives the name gods to those thought worthy of priesthood ("You shall not revile gods, or speak evil of the leader of your people," Scripture says, remember),[67] he called the idols *gods*, not yet completely able to grasp their weakness. Yet he had come to appreciate the difference; hence he called the God of all *God of Gods and Lord of kings.*

After making this profession, *he extolled Daniel, gave him many gifts, and set him over the whole country of Babylon, chief of satraps and over all the wise men of Babylon* (v. 48). This, too, is a mark of divine care: the godliness of the ruler brings very great benefit to his subjects, as the Lord did also in the case of Joseph. Blessed David, in treating more concisely of him and singing the praises of divine providence, says, "He sent someone ahead of them, Joseph was sold as a slave"; then, after listing the adversities that befell him and mentioning his imprisonment and bondage, he went on, "The king sent, the leader of the people released him and let him go, and appointed him lord of his house and ruler of his possessions to train his rulers like himself and make his elders wise."[68] Here, too, the governor of all things acted likewise: after appointing thrice-blessed Daniel chief of satraps | and Babylon's wise men, he proposed him as a model of piety and other virtues.   1313

Nevertheless the prophet could not bring himself to enjoy this prominence on his own: he made his fellows in prayer sharers also in prominence. *He petitioned the king, and he set Shadrach,*

---

[67] Exod 22:28 LXX, which here gives *ᵓelohim* a plural rendering with θεούς, Theodoret also in comment on Ps 50 applying it to "priests and others to whom judgment is entrusted."

[68] Ps 105:17, 20–22.

ναγώ, καὶ Δανιὴλ ἦν ἐν τῇ αὐλῇ τοῦ βασιλέως.» Συμβαίνει καὶ ταῦτα τῇ τοῦ Ἀποστόλου διδασκαλίᾳ· «Νῦν γὰρ, φησί, μένει πίστις, ἐλπίς, ἀγάπη· τὰ τρία ταῦτα, μείζων δὲ πάντων ἡ ἀγάπη.» Καὶ γὰρ καὶ οὗτος ὁ θεῖος προφήτης ἠγάπησε μὲν τὸν Θεὸν ἐξ ὅλης καρδίας, καὶ ἐξ ὅλης ψυχῆς, καὶ ἐξ ὅλης ἰσχύος, καὶ ἐξ ὅλης δυνάμεως· ἀγαπήσας δὲ θερμῶς ἐπίστευσεν εἰλικρινῶς, εἰλικρινῶς δὲ πιστεύσας ἤλπισε τῆς παρ᾽ αὐτοῦ τεύξεσθαι βοηθείας· τυχὼν δὲ ὧν ἤλπισεν, ἔδειξε τὴν περὶ τὸν πέλας ἀγάπην, καὶ κοινωνοὺς τοὺς ὁμοφύλους, ὧν ἔλαβεν, ἐποιήσατο. Ὅσα δὲ προεγράφη, εἰς τὴν ἡμετέραν διδασκαλίαν προεγράφη, ἵνα διὰ τῆς ὑπομονῆς, καὶ διὰ τῆς παρακλήσεως τῶν Γραφῶν τὴν ἐλπίδα ἔχωμεν, ἐν Χριστῷ Ἰησοῦ, μεθ᾽ οὗ τῷ Πατρὶ δόξα, σὺν τῷ ἁγίῳ Πνεύματι, εἰς τοὺς αἰῶνας τῶν αἰώνων, Ἀμήν.

ΤΟΜΟΣ Γ΄ — ΚΕΦΑΛΑΙΟΝ Γ΄

α΄. «Ἔτους ὀκτωκαιδεκάτου Ναβουχοδονόσορ ὁ βασιλεὺς ἐποίησεν εἰκόνα χρυσῆν, καὶ ἔστησεν αὐτὴν ἐν πεδίῳ Δεηρᾷ ἐν χώρᾳ Βαβυλῶνος.» Ὁ μὲν ἀγαθὸς ἡμῶν καὶ φιλάνθρωπος Δεσπότης, ἅτε δὴ ποιητὴς καὶ δημιουργός, βούλεται «πάντας ἀνθρώπους σωθῆναι, καὶ εἰς ἐπίγνωσιν ἀληθείας ἐλθεῖν·» καί, «Οὐ θέλει τὸν θάνατον τοῦ ἁμαρτωλοῦ, ὡς τὸ ἐπιστρέψαι αὐτὸν καὶ ζῆν.» Οὗ χάριν ἅπαντα ὑπὲρ τῆς ἡμετέρας πραγματεύεται σωτηρίας. Οἱ δὲ ἀναλγησίᾳ νοσοῦντες, καὶ τῷ ἀνηκέστῳ πάθει τῆς ἀλα|ζονείας δουλεύοντες, οὐδεμίαν ἐκ τῶν θείων φαρμάκων ὠφέλειαν καρποῦνται, ἀλλ᾽ ἐοίκασί τισιν ἀρρώστοις, ἀποστρεφομένοις μὲν τὴν παρὰ τῆς ἰατρικῆς τέχνης προσαγομένην αὐτοῖς θεραπείαν, ἀκρασίᾳ δὲ καὶ ἀταξίᾳ πολλῇ χρωμένοις, καὶ τὴν ἐπικειμένην αὐτοῖς αὔξουσιν ὁσημέραι νόσον. Τοιοῦτος ἦν οὗτος ὁ ἀλαζὼν βασιλεύς, ὃς τοῦ Θεοῦ τῶν ὅλων ἀμέτρῳ φιλανθρωπίᾳ χρησαμένου, καὶ μετὰ τὰς μυρίας παρανομίας τε καὶ δυσσεβείας θεραπείαν αὐτῷ προσενηνοχότος, καὶ ὑποδείξαντος τῆς

Meshach, and Abednego over all the works of the country of Babylon,
and Daniel was in the king's court (v. 49). This accords also with the
teaching of the apostle, "There now remain faith, hope, love, these
three, but the greatest of all is love."[69] In other words, this divine
prophet loved God with his whole heart, his whole soul, his whole
strength, and his whole power;[70] and since he loved ardently, he
believed sincerely; and since he believed sincerely, he hoped to
gain help from him; and on attaining what he hoped for, he manifested love for his neighbor and made his fellows sharers in what
he had received. Now, "all that was recorded was recorded for our
instruction, so that by perseverance and the encouragement of the
Scriptures we might have hope,"[71] in Christ Jesus, to whom with
the Father and the Holy Spirit be glory, for ages of ages. Amen.

CHAPTER 3

In the eighteenth year of his reign King Nebuchadnezzar made a
golden statue, and set it up on the plain of Dura in the country of
Babylon (v. 1). Our good and loving Lord, being maker and creator, wants "all people to be saved and come to the knowledge of
the truth," and "wishes not the death of sinners so much as their
being converted and living."[72] For this reason he brings about everything for the sake of our salvation. On the other hand, those
suffering from insensitivity and in thrall to the incurable ailment
| of arrogance reap no benefit from the divine remedies, resem-   1316
bling instead sick people resisting the treatment offered them by
medical science, addicted to severe licentiousness and intemperance, and daily aggravating the ailment afflicting them.

This was what the proud king was like. The God of all
had exercised lovingkindness without limit, had proposed to him
treatment for his countless acts of lawlessness and impiety, and

---

[69] 1 Cor 13:13.

[70] Cf. Matt 22:37.

[71] Rom 15:4. The closure of the second chapter is marked by a brief doxology that emerged after fierce debate in the preceding century. It reads literally,
"... in Christ Jesus, with whom to the Father be glory together with the Holy
Spirit, for ages of ages. Amen." The same doxology concludes chapters 3, 4, 5,
6, 7, 9, and 12.

[72] 1 Tim 2:4; Ezek 18:23. The time reference does not occur in the Hebrew.

τε παρούσης εὐημερίας τὸ ἐπίκηρόν τε καὶ μάταιον, καὶ τῆς ἀρετῆς τὸ
ὑψηλὸν καὶ περίβλεπτον, ἢ καὶ τοὺς δορυαλώτους, καὶ τὸν τῆς δουλείας
ζυγὸν φέρειν ἠναγκασμένους, ἀποφαίνει λαμπρούς, εὐθὺς μὲν ἐθαύμασε
τὴν τοῦ προφήτου σοφίαν, καὶ τὸν τούτου Θεὸν τῶν ὅλων εἶναι Θεὸν
ὡμολόγησεν· ὀλίγου δὲ χρόνου διελθόντος, εἰς ἑαυτὸν ἐπανῆλθεν, ὥσπερ
κύων εἰς τὸν ἴδιον ἔμετον, ἦ φησιν ἡ θεία Γραφή, καὶ κατασκευάζει μὲν
εἰκόνα χρυσῆν, τὸ μὲν ὕψος ἔχουσαν πήχεις ἑξήκοντα, τὸ δὲ εὖρος πήχεις
ἕξ, καὶ ταύτην ἐν ἰσοπέδῳ στήσας χωρίῳ, ὥστε ἴσως ἁπάντων ὑπερέχειν
καὶ ὑπὸ πάντων ὁμοίως ὁρᾶσθαι, παρὰ πάντων αὐτὴν κελεύει προσκυνεῖσθαι τῶν ὑπηκόων. Οὐχ ἁπλοῦς δὲ οὗτος τῆς ἀλαζονείας ὁ τρόπος, ἀλλ'
ἀντίθεος ἀντικρὺς καὶ θεομισής. Ἐπειδὴ γὰρ ὁ Θεὸς ὄναρ αὐτῷ μεγίστην
ὑπέδειξεν εἰκόνα ἐκ τεττάρων ὑλῶν πεποιημένην, καὶ διὰ τούτων αὐτῷ
τὰς τῶν τεττάρων βασιλειῶν διαδοχὰς παρεδήλωσεν, ἀντιστρατευόμενος
τῷ Θεῷ τὸν οἰκεῖον τῦφον, κατασκευάζει δὴ καὶ αὐτὸς εἰκόνα μέγεθος
αὐτῇ δεδωκώς, ὅσον ἡ τῶν ἀνθρώπων παρασχεῖν ἠδύνατο τέχνη. Οὐκέτι
δὲ καὶ ταύτην ἐκ χρυσίου, καὶ ἀργύρου, καὶ χαλκοῦ, καὶ σιδήρου ποιεῖ,
ἀλλ' ἐκ μιᾶς ὕλης τῆς τοῦ χρυσοῦ κατασκευάζει, οἰόμενος ὁ δείλαιος
οὗτος ψευδεῖς ἀποδείξειν τοῦ Θεοῦ τὰς προρρήσεις. Καὶ ἐπειδὴ ὁ μακάριος Δανιὴλ τὸ ἐνύπνιον ἑρμηνεύων, αὐτὸν εἶναι ἔφη τὴν κεφαλὴν τὴν
χρυσῆν, τουτέστι τῶν Βαβυλωνίων, εἴτουν Ἀσσυρίων βασιλείαν, τὰ δὲ
ἄλλα μόρια τῆς εἰκόνος ἐκ τῶν ἄλλων ὑλῶν, αἳ τὴν κεφαλὴν διεδέξαντο,
αὐτὸς πᾶσαν ἐκ τοῦ χρυσίου τὴν εἰκόνα κατασκευάζει.

β'. «Συνήγαγε, φησί, πάντας τοὺς σατράπας, ὑπάρχους τε καὶ
στρατηγούς, καὶ τοπάρχας, ἡγουμένους τε καὶ τυράννους, καὶ τοὺς ἐπ'
ἐξουσιῶν, καὶ πάντας τοὺς ἄρχοντας τῶν χωρῶν, ἐλθεῖν εἰς τὰ ἐγκαίνια
τῆς εἰκόνος, ἧς ἔστησε Ναβουχοδονόσορ ὁ βασιλεύς.» Καὶ τούτων δὲ
ἕκαστον τὴν ἄκραν ὑπερηφανίαν παραδηλοῖ. Οὐ γὰρ ἁπλῶς τοὺς τυχόν-
τας τῶν ὑπηκόων εἰς τὴν τῆς εἰκόνος συνεκάλεσεν ἑορτήν, ἀλλὰ τούς
τε τοπάρχας, καὶ τοὺς στρατηγούς, τοὺς τῶν σατραπειῶν τὴν ἡγεμονίαν
1317 πεπιστευμένους, καὶ εἴ τι ἕτερον εἶδος ἀρχῆς παρ' | ἐκείνοις ἐνενόμι-
στο. Καὶ εὐθὺς μὲν ἡ κλῆσις ἁπλῆ τις ἐνομίζετο, ὕστερον δὲ τὸ διὰ τῆς
κλήσεως τυραννευόμενον ἐφωράθη. Ἐπειδὴ γὰρ συνῆλθον ἅπαντες,

«Ὁ κήρυξ, φησίν, ἐβόα ἐν ἰσχύι (τουτέστι, μεγίστη χρώμενος τῇ
φωνῇ)· Ὑμῖν λέγεται, ἔθνη, λαοί, φυλαί, γλῶσσαι· (ε', ς'.) Ἦ ἂν ὥρα
ἀκούσητε τῆς φωνῆς τῆς σάλπιγγος, σύριγγός τε καὶ κιθάρας, σαμβύ-
κης τε καὶ ψαλτηρίου, καὶ συμφωνίας, καὶ παντὸς γένους μουσικῶν,

had shown him evidence of the impermanence and futility of present prosperity and the exaltation and fame coming from virtue in rendering illustrious the captives obliged to carry the yoke of slavery. At the outset the king admired the prophet's wisdom, and professed belief that his God is the God of all; but with the passage of a brief space of time he returned to his former self, like a dog to his vomit, as the divine Scripture says.[73] He made a golden statue, sixty cubits high and six cubits wide, set it up on level ground so that it reared above all alike and similarly was visible to all, and bade it be worshiped by all his subjects. Now, this form of arrogance, far from being without implication, was openly hostile and hateful to God: since God had revealed to him in a dream a mighty image made of four materials, and in this had indicated to him the succession of four kingdoms, he set his own conceit in opposition to God and made a statue, personally giving it dimensions as huge as human skill could attain. Instead of making it this time of gold, silver, bronze and iron, he made it of a single material, gold, this wretch thinking to prove God's prophecies false. Since blessed Daniel in interpreting the dream had said he was the head of gold—that is, the kingdom of the Babylonians (or, if you like, Assyrians)—whereas the other parts of the image succeeding to the head were of other materials, he for his part made the statue completely of gold.

He assembled all the satraps, prefects, generals, local officials, leaders, tyrants, those in authority and all the rulers of the land to the dedication of the statue which King Nebuchadnezzar had set up (v. 2). Each of these suggests his extreme arrogance: far from gathering together to the festival for the statue some chance members of his subjects, he assembled local officials and generals, those entrusted with government of the satrapies and any other kind of control | 1317 in use among them.[74] Although at the outset the invitation was thought to be without implication, later the imperious nature of the invitation was detected: when all were assembled, the text goes on, *the herald cried out with force* (that is, in a loud voice), *You are told, nations, peoples, tribes, tongues, that when you hear the sound of the trumpet, pipe, lyre, sambuca, harp, bagpipe, and every kind*

[73] Prov 26:11.
[74] A comment is due on the disparate collection of titles in the Greek text, arising from an array in the Hebrew of terms of Akkadian and Persian origin (unbeknown to Theodoret).

πίπτοντες προσκυνεῖτε τῇ εἰκόνι τῇ χρυσῇ ᾗ ἔστησε Ναβουχοδονόσορ ὁ βασιλεύς. Καὶ ὃς ἂν μὴ πεσὼν προσκυνήσῃ, αὐτῇ τῇ ὥρᾳ ἐμβληθήσεται εἰς τὴν κάμινον τοῦ πυρὸς τὴν καιομένην.» Οὕτως ἥρπασεν ὁ δείλαιος, ὡς ἐνόμισε, τὴν θείαν τιμήν, καὶ οὐκ ἀπέχρησεν αὐτῷ τὸ προσκυνεῖσθαι παρὰ τῶν ὑπηκόων, ἀλλὰ καὶ τῇ εἰκόνι προσφέρεσθαι τὴν προσκύνησιν ταύτην ἐνομοθέτησε, καὶ καταπλήττει μὲν ἅπαντας τῇ τε ὕλῃ, καὶ τῇ τέχνῃ, καὶ τῷ μεγέθει τῆς εἰκόνος· κατακηλεῖ δὲ καὶ καταθέλγει τῇ παντοδαπῇ τῶν μουσικῶν ὀργάνων ἠχῇ· τοὺς δὲ μηδὲ τὸ μέγεθος τῆς εἰκόνος ἐκπληττομένους, μηδὲ ὑπὸ τῆς τῶν ὀργάνων ᾠδῆς τε καὶ ἡδονῆς καταθελγομένους, τῇ ἀπειλῇ τοῦ καμίνου δεδίττεται. Καὶ ἐπὶ μὲν τῶν ἄλλων ἁπάντων οὐ διήμαρτε τοῦ σκοποῦ· ἑώρα γὰρ ἅπαντας τὸ κελευόμενον ποιοῦντας, καὶ φόβῳ καὶ ἡδονῇ δουλεύειν εἰθισμένους· μόνοι δὲ οἱ τρισμακάριοι παῖδες ἐκεῖνοι τὴν πατρῴαν εὐγένειαν ἀκήρατον καὶ ἐν δουλείᾳ φυλάξαντες, Ἀνανίας, καὶ Ἀζαρίας, καὶ Μισαὴλ, ἠρνήθησαν μὲν τὴν προσκύνησιν, οὐκ ἔλαθον δὲ τοὺς δυσσεβείᾳ συζῶντας Χαλδαίους, οἳ κοινωνοὺς ἅπαντας ἔχειν τῆς ἀσεβείας ἠβούλοντο. Αὐτίκα τοίνυν προσίασι μὲν τῷ βασιλεῖ, ἀναμιμνήσκουσι δὲ αὐτὸν τοῦ τεθέντος νόμου διαρρήδην διαγορεύοντος ἅπασι τοῖς ὑπηκόοις προσκυνεῖν τὴν εἰκόνα, καὶ τοῖς τοῦτο ποιεῖν παραιτουμένοις ἀπειλοῦντος τὴν κάμινον· εἰσαγγέλλουσι δὲ τοὺς ἱεροὺς ἄνδρας ἐκείνους λέγοντες, ὅτι

ιβ΄. «Εἰσὶν ἄνδρες Ἰουδαῖοι, οὓς κατέστησας ἐπὶ τὰ ἔργα τῆς χώρας Βαβυλῶνος, Σιδράχ, Μισάχ, καὶ Ἀβδεναγώ· οἱ ἄνδρες ἐκεῖνοι οὐχ ὑπήκουσαν τῷ δόγματί σου, βασιλεῦ.» Καὶ τόν τε οἰκεῖον φθόνον διὰ τούτων παραδηλοῦσι, τοῦ τε βασιλέως ἐξάπτουσι τὴν ὀργήν, αἰνιττόμενοι διὰ τούτων, καὶ μονονουχὶ λέγοντες· Ὅρα τίνας ἡμῶν προτετίμηκας, τίσι τῶν Βαβυλωνίων ἡγεμονίαν ἐπίστευσας· οὐδὲ τῆς τιμῆς τὸ μέγεθος εἰς νοῦν λαβεῖν ἠβουλήθησαν, καὶ εὐγνώμονες περὶ τὸν τετιμηκότα γενέσθαι, ἀλλὰ τῆς τιμῆς τὸ μέγεθος ἀτιμίας ἀφορμὴν ἐποιήσαντο, ἀντικρὺς τοῖς σοῖς ἀντιλέγοντες νόμοις, καὶ τὰ σὰ πληροῦν οὐκ ἀνεχόμενοι δόγματα. Οὐκ ἐντεῦθεν δὲ μόνον ἔστι θεωρῆσαι τὸ τυραννικόν τε καὶ ἄγνωμον· ἀλλὰ καὶ ἑτέρωθεν καταμαθεῖν δυνατόν, ὡς οὐδὲν δρῶσιν ὑπηκόοις ἁρμόττον· οὓς γὰρ νομίζεις θεούς, οὐ νομίζουσι, καὶ τὴν προσ|ήκουσαν λατρείαν τοῖς ὑπὸ σοῦ προσκυνουμένοις θεοῖς οὐ προσφέρουσι· καὶ τῆς

of musical instrument, fall down and worship the golden statue that King Nebuchadnezzar set up. Whoever does not fall down and worship will at that very hour will be cast into the furnace blazing with fire (vv. 4–5). In this way the wretch, as he thought, arrogated to himself divine honor: far from it being sufficient for him to be worshiped by his subjects, he legislated for this worship to be offered also to the statue. While he astonished everyone with the material, the skill, and the size of the statue, and charmed and seduced them with the varied sound of the musical instruments,[75] he terrified with the threat of the furnace those not impressed even by the size of the statue or won over by the pleasant sound of the instruments. In all these requirements he did not fail in his purpose: he observed everyone doing his bidding, accustomed as they were to serving fearfully and gladly. Only those thrice-blessed young men Hananiah, Azariah and Mishael kept unalloyed their ancestral nobility even in slavery, refusing to pay worship.

They did not, however, escape the notice of the astrologers in their addiction to godlessness, who wanted to make everyone partners in their impiety. So immediately they approached the king and reminded him of the law passed publicly, ordering all the subjects to worship the statue and threatening with the furnace those who declined to do so. They informed on those sacred men in these terms, *There are Jewish men whom you appointed over the works of the country of Babylon, Shadrach, Meshach, and Abednego; those men did not obey your decree, O King* (v. 12). In this they both betrayed their own envy and inflamed the anger of the king by such suggestions, as if to say, Observe who it is you preferred to us, who it is to whom you entrusted governance of the Babylonians. They refused to take account of the greatness of the honor or be grateful to one who honored them, instead making the greatness of the honor an occasion for dishonor by publicly opposing your laws and refusing to discharge your decree. Their overbearing and ungrateful attitude can be perceived not only from this, however: it can be learned also from other indications that they do nothing befitting subjects. In fact, what you believe to be gods they do not, nor | do   1320 they offer due adoration to the gods worshiped by you; and they

---

[75] Modern commentators observe that the terms for some of the musical instruments in the Hebrew text derive from Greek terms that could not have been introduced before the Hellenistic period.

εἰκόνος δὲ τὴν προσκύνησιν, ἣν ἅπαντες οἱ ἀρχόμενοι προσενηνόχασιν, ἠρνήθησαν προφανῶς. Τούτων ἀκούσας ὁ φρενοβλαβὴς ἐκεῖνος βασιλεύς, καὶ ἐπιλαθόμενος τῶν ὑπ' αὐτοῦ πρὸς τὸν Δανιὴλ εἰρημένων, «'Επ' ἀληθείας ὁ Θεὸς ὑμῶν οὗτός ἐστι Θεὸς τῶν θεῶν, καὶ Κύριος τῶν βασιλέων,» ἄγει τοὺς ἄνδρας εἰς μέσον· πυνθάνεται δέ, εἰ τῷ ὄντι κοινωνεῖν αὐτῷ τῆς τῶν θεῶν οὐκ ἐθέλουσι θεραπείας, καὶ τῆς εἰκόνος φεύγουσι τὴν προσκύνησιν. Εἶτα παραινεῖ καὶ συμβουλεύει τοῦτο ποιεῖν, τῇ τοῦ πυρὸς ἀπειλῇ δεδιττόμενος. «'Εὰν γὰρ μὴ προσκυνήσητε, αὐτῇ τῇ ὥρᾳ ἐμβληθήσεσθε εἰς τὴν κάμινον τοῦ πυρὸς τὴν καιομένην.» Ἔπειτα τὴν ἄρρητον ἐκείνην καὶ θηριώδη βλασφημίαν τολμᾷ· «Καὶ τίς ἐστιν ὁ Θεός, ὃς ἐξελεῖται ὑμᾶς ἐκ τῶν χειρῶν μου;» Οὕτω ταχέως ὃν ὡμολόγησεν ἐβλασφήμησε· καὶ ὃν Θεὸν θεῶν ἀπεκάλεσε, καὶ ἀνθρώπου ἀσθενέστερον ὑπέλαβεν εἶναι· ὃν Κύριον βασιλέων προσηγόρευσε, νικᾶν ὁ δείλαιος ἐνεανιεύσατο. Προγονικὰ δὲ αὐτῷ τὰ τοιαῦτα τολμήματα· καὶ γὰρ ὁ Σενναχηρεὶμ ἐκεῖνος στρατείᾳ μεγίστῃ κατὰ τῆς 'Ιερουσαλὴμ χρησάμενος, ἐπιστέλλων τῷ 'Εζεκίᾳ τοιαῦτα ἐφθέγξατο· «Μή σε ἀπατάτω ὁ Θεός σου, ἐφ' ᾧ σὺ πέποιθας ἐπ' αὐτῷ, ὅτι ῥύσεται 'Ιερουσαλὴμ ἐκ τῶν χειρῶν μου. Μὴ ἐρρύσαντο θεοὶ τῶν ἐθνῶν ἕκαστος τὴν ἑαυτοῦ χώραν ἐκ χειρός μου; ποῦ ὁ θεὸς 'Εμάθ, καὶ ποῦ ὁ θεὸς 'Αρφάθ, καὶ ποῦ ὁ θεὸς τῆς πόλεως Σεπφαρίμ; μὴ ἠδυνήθησαν ῥύσασθαι Σαμάρειαν ἐκ χειρός μου, ὅτι ῥύσεται Κύριος τὴν 'Ιερουσαλὴμ ἐκ χειρός μου;» 'Αλλ' εὐθὺς καὶ παραχρῆμα ἔλαβε τῆς βλασφημίας τὰ ἐπίχειρα, καὶ αἱ πολλαὶ μὲν ἐκεῖναι μυριάδες ὑφ' ἑνὸς ἀνῃρέθησαν ἀγγέλου· αὐτὸς δὲ φυγών, καὶ τὴν ἐνεγκοῦσαν καταλαβών, σφαγέας οὓς ἐγέννησεν, ἔσχηκεν. 'Επειδὴ γὰρ κατὰ τοῦ Ποιητοῦ τὴν γλῶτταν ἐκίνησε, δέχεται τὴν σφαγὴν παρὰ ἀνθρώπων οὓς ἐγέννησεν. 'Αλλ' οὐδὲ τούτου τὸ παράδειγμα τοῦ Ναβουχοδονόσορ ἐχαλίνωσε τὴν γλῶτταν, οὔτε τὸ ἐνύπνιον ἐκεῖνο τὰς τῶν βασιλέων ὑποδεῖξαν διαδοχὰς ἐδίδαξε σωφρονεῖν, ἀλλ' ἔμεινε κατὰ τοῦ πεποιηκότος λυττῶν· ἀντιστρατεύει δὲ αὐτῷ ὁ Θεὸς οὐκ ἄγγελον (ὅπερ ἐπὶ τοῦ Σενναχηρεὶμ ἐκείνου πεποίηκεν), ἀλλὰ τρία παιδάρια αἰχμάλωτα, τὴν ξένην οἰκεῖν ἠναγκασμένα, τὸν τῆς δουλείας ἕλκοντα ζυγόν, νέαν ἄγοντα τὴν ἡλικίαν, ἐν αὐτῷ ὄντα ἔαρι τοῦ χρόνου· οὗτοι γὰρ παραυτί-

openly refuse worship to the statue which all the subjects have offered.

On hearing this, that deranged king forgot what had been
said by him to Daniel, "In truth your God is God of gods and
Lord of kings." He brought the men into the open and enquired
whether they really refused to give him a share in the worship of
the gods and shunned worshiping the statue. Then he urged and
advised them to do, instilling terror with the threat of fire: *If you do
not worship, at this very hour you will be cast into the furnace blazing
with fire* (v. 15). Then he committed that unspeakably wild blasphemy, *Who is the god who will deliver you out of my hands?* So
rapidly did he blaspheme against the one in whom had professed
belief, the one he had called God of gods he presumed was weaker
even than a human being, and the one he had named Lord of kings
the wretch was hot-headed enough to think he had vanquished.

Now, such awful presumption was hereditary: the infamous
Sennacherib directed a mighty army against Jerusalem, and sent
an ambassador to Hezekiah to utter such things: "Do not let your
God in whom you trust deceive you into supposing that he will
save Jerusalem from my hand. Surely gods of the nations in each
case did not save their country from my hand? Where is the god
of Hamath, the god of Arpad, the god of Sepharvaim? Surely they
were not able to save Samaria from my hand to give you grounds
for thinking the Lord will save Jerusalem from my hand?"[76] As
soon as he embarked on his blasphemous exploit, however, those
countless hordes were immediately slain by a single angel, while
he fled, reached his own country, and had for executioners those
whom he had begotten:[77] the words he directed against the creator
were fulfilled in his execution by people he had begotten.

Not even the example of this man kept in check the tongue of
Nebuchadnezzar, however, nor did the dream indicating the succession of kingdoms teach him restraint; instead, he continued to
rage against his maker. Against him, by contrast, God sent in
vengeance not an angel, as he did in the case of that fellow Sennacherib, but three young captives forced to live in a foreign land,
pressed into service at this early age, in the very springtime of their

[76] Cf. Isa 37:10–13. To one who confuses Assyrians and Babylonians,
Nebuchadnezzar is in the blood line of Sennacherib.
[77] Cf. 2 Kgs 19:35–37.

κα τῆς λύττης ἐκείνης καὶ μανικῆς βλασφημίας ἀκούσαντες, θυμοῦ καὶ ζήλου πλήρεις ἐγένοντο, καὶ ἀπεκρίθησαν, καὶ εἶπον τῷ βασιλεῖ· «Οὐ χρείαν ἔχομεν ἡμεῖς περὶ τοῦ ῥήματος τούτου ἀποκριθῆναί σοι.» Περιττὴ, φησίν, ἡ πεῦσις ἡ παρὰ σοῦ ἡμῖν προσαγομένη· ἃ γὰρ ἐφρονοῦμεν, καὶ νῦν φρονοῦμεν, καὶ οὐδεμίαν μεταβολὴν ἐκ τῶν σῶν ἀπειλῶν δεξό-

1321 μεθα. |

ιζ'. «Ἔστι γὰρ ὁ Θεὸς ἡμῶν ἐν οὐρανοῖς, ᾧ ἡμεῖς λατρεύομεν, δυνατὸς ἐξελέσθαι ἡμᾶς ἐκ τῆς καμίνου τοῦ πυρὸς τῆς καιομένης, καὶ ἐκ τῶν χειρῶν σου, βασιλεῦ, ῥύσεται ἡμᾶς.» Τίς οὐκ ἂν εἰκότως ἐκπλαγείη τῶν μακαρίων τούτων νέων τὴν ἀνδρείαν, τὴν σοφίαν, τὴν εὐσέβειαν, τὴν περὶ τοὺς νόμους δικαιοσύνην, τὴν περὶ πάντα σωφροσύνην; Τὸ μὲν γὰρ μὴ καταπλαγῆναι τὸν τοσοῦτον ἐκεῖνον τύραννον, μετὰ πάντων, ὡς ἔπος εἰπεῖν, ἀνθρώπων ἀντιτεταγμένον, καὶ τὴν μεγίστην ἐκείνην πυράν, οὐ λόγοις μόνον ἀπειλουμένην, ἀλλὰ καὶ ὁρωμένην, τὴν ἀδάμαντος στερροτέραν αὐτοῖς ἀνδρείαν μαρτυρεῖ. Τὸ δὲ τοὺς θείους νόμους τῆς παρούσης προτιμῆσαι ζωῆς, ποίας δικαιοσύνης ὑπερβολὴν καταλείπει; Τὴν δὲ σωφροσύνην αὐτῶν κηρύττει, τὸ μήτε θρασέσι κατὰ τοῦ βασιλέως χρήσασθαι λόγοις, μήτε δειλίᾳ πάλιν καταισχῦναι τὸ γένος· τὴν δὲ φρόνησιν καὶ σοφίαν ἡ τοῖς δυσσεβέσι καὶ βλασφήμοις λόγοις ἀντιτεθεῖσα εὐσέβεια. Ὁ μὲν γὰρ ἔλεγε· «Τίς ἐστι Θεός, ὃς ἐξελεῖται ὑμᾶς ἐκ τῶν χειρῶν μου;» Οἱ δὲ ἐβόων· «Ἔστιν ὁ Θεὸς ἡμῶν ἐν οὐρανοῖς, ᾧ ἡμεῖς λατρεύομεν, δυνατὸς ἐξελέσθαι ἡμᾶς ἐκ τῆς καμίνου τοῦ πυρὸς τῆς καιομένης, καὶ ἐκ τῶν χειρῶν σου, βασιλεῦ, ῥύσεται ἡμᾶς.» Μὴ γὰρ νομίσῃς τὸν ἡμέτερον Θεὸν τοῖς σοῖς ἐοικέναι θεοῖς. Ἐκείνων γὰρ εἰκότως καταφρονεῖς, ἐξ ὕλης τε καὶ τέχνης ἐσχηκότων τὸ εἶναι· ὁ δὲ ἡμέτερος Θεός, οὐρανοῦ τε καὶ γῆς, καὶ τῶν ἁπάντων Δημιουργός, δύναμιν ἔχων, ἣν δείκνυσι τὰ ὁρώμενα. Τὴν γὰρ ὑπὲρ ταῦτα τοῖς τῶν θείων ἀμυήτοις οὐ ῥᾴδιον κατιδεῖν· τοῦτον πρεσβεύοντες τὴν παρ' αὐτοῦ βοήθειαν ἀναμένομεν. Ἱκανὸς γὰρ ἡμᾶς καὶ τῶν σῶν ἀπαλλάξαι χειρῶν, καὶ τῆς καμίνου τοῦ πυρός, ἣν σὺ κατεσκεύασας. Τὰ δὲ μετὰ ταῦτα ῥηθέντα οὐδεμίαν ἀνδρείας καὶ φιλοθεΐας ὑπερβολὴν καταλείπει. Εἰρηκότες γάρ· «Ἔστιν ὁ Θεὸς ἡμῶν ἐν οὐρανοῖς, ᾧ ἡμεῖς λατρεύομεν, δυνατὸς ἐξελέσθαι ἡμᾶς ἐκ τῆς καμίνου τοῦ πυρὸς τῆς καιομένης, καὶ ἐκ τῶν χειρῶν σου, βασιλεῦ, ῥύσεται ἡμᾶς,» εὐθὺς ἐπήγαγον·

ιη'. «Καὶ ἐὰν μὴ, γνωστὸν ἔστω σοι, βασιλεῦ, ὅτι τοῖς θεοῖς σου οὐ λατρεύομεν, καὶ τῇ εἰκόνι τῇ χρυσῇ, ᾗ ἔστησας, οὐ προσκυνοῦμεν.» Οὐ γὰρ ἐπὶ μισθῷ τῷ ἡμετέρῳ Δεσπότῃ δουλεύομεν, ἀλλὰ φίλτρῳ καὶ πόθῳ νυττόμενοι, πάντων ὁμοῦ τὴν τοῦ Θεοῦ ἡμῶν προαιρούμεθα θεραπείαν. Οὗ χάριν οὐδὲ τὴν ἀπαλλαγὴν τῶν κακῶν ἀορίστως αἰτοῦμεν, ἀλλὰ τοῦ

lives. Immediately on hearing of this insane rage and blasphemy, in fact, they were filled with anger and zeal, and replied by saying to the king, *We have no need to make a reply to you on this matter* (v. 16): it is unnecessary for an enquiry on your part to be brought against us; the attitude we had before is still our attitude now, and we have undergone no change as a result of your threats. | *Our*
God in heaven, whom we serve, is able to deliver us from the furnace blazing with fire, and will rescue us from your hands, O King (v. 17) Who in their right minds would not be struck by the courage of these blessed young people, their wisdom, their piety, their righteous attitude to the laws, their good sense in every respect? I mean, their not being daunted by that awful tyrant, who was at odds with all people, so to say, or by that mighty pyre, which was not only presented to them as a threat in word but also set before their eyes, confirms their courage to have been more unbending than steel. What a marvelous degree of righteousness emerges from their placing more importance on the divine laws than on the present life! Their directing no insolent words to the king or shaming their race in fear proclaims their self-control, while their piety in contrast to the impious and blasphemous words proclaims their good sense and wisdom: when he said *Who is the god who will deliver you out of my hands?* they cried aloud *Our God in heaven, whom we serve, is able to deliver us from the furnace blazing with fire, and will rescue us from your hands, O King.* Do not think our God is like your gods: you are right to despise them, owing their existence to materials and artistry, whereas ours, God of heaven and earth, and creator of everything, has power which is revealed in visible things, a power over them which by the uninitiated in divine things is not easily observed. He it is we serve, and look to him for help, capable as he is of freeing us both from your hands and from the furnace of fire you have prepared.

What is said after this surpasses the bounds of courage and love of God: after saying *Our God in heaven, whom we serve, is able to deliver us from the furnace blazing with fire and to rescue us from your hands, O King*, they immediately went on, *If not, let it be known to you, O King, that we will not serve your gods and worship the golden statue that you set up* (v. 18): far from serving our Lord for payment, we are motivated by affection and longing, and at the same time prefer the service of our God to everything. Hence, instead of asking for relief from the troubles unconditionally, we

Δεσπότου τὴν οἰκονομίαν καὶ προμήθειαν στέργομεν· καὶ τὸ συνοίσειν μέλλον οὐκ εἰδότες, τῷ κυβερνήτῃ παραχωροῦμεν ἰθύνειν, ὡς ἂν ἐθέλῃ. Ὅτι μὲν γὰρ ἀπαλλάττειν ἡμᾶς τῶν ἠπειλημένων κακῶν ἰσχύει, σαφῶς ἐπιστάμεθα. Εἰ δὲ καὶ βούλεται τοῦτο ποιεῖν, ἀγνοοῦμεν· σοφῷ δὲ ὄντι παραχωροῦμεν πρυτανεύοντι, καὶ δεχόμεθα τὴν ψῆφον, ταύτην ἡμῖν συμφέρειν πιστεύοντες. Εἴτε οὖν ῥύεται, εἴτε καὶ μὴ, τῆς εἰκόνος σου καὶ τῶν θεῶν σου φεύγομεν | τὴν προσκύνησιν. Πρὸς τοιαύτας σοι ψυχὰς ἡ παράταξις· ὃν ἂν ἐθέλῃς τρόπον ἀνταγωνίζου, οὔτε καταθέλξεις τιμῶν, οὔτε καταπλήξεις ἀπειλῶν· πάντων γὰρ ἡμῖν ὁ Θεὸς ἐρασμιώτατός τε καὶ φοβερώτατος. Τί τούτων ὑψηλότερον τῶν ῥημάτων; Τούτοις τὴν ἀποστολικὴν ἐκείνην ἐφαρμόσαι προσήκει φωνήν· «Τὸ γὰρ τί προσευξώμεθα καθ᾽ ὃ δεῖ, οὐκ οἴδαμεν.» Ἀλλ᾽ ὁ θηριώδης καὶ μανικώτατος τύραννος, ἔμπλεως θυμοῦ γενόμενος, ὡς καὶ δηλῶσαι τῷ προσώπῳ τὴν τῆς ψυχῆς ταραχήν, ἐπιπλεῖστον μὲν ἐκκαυθῆναι τὴν κάμινον παρενεγγύησε· πεδηθῆναι δὲ τοὺς ἁγίους ἄνδρας παρεκελεύσατο, καὶ ὥστε μηδεμίαν γενέσθαι τῆς τιμωρίας ἀναβολήν, τῆς ἐσθῆτος καὶ τῶν ὑποδημάτων ἀφαιρουμένων, σὺν αὐτοῖς τούτοις τῇ πυρᾷ παραδοθῆναι προσέταξε· τουτέστι, σὺν τοῖς σαραβάροις αὐτῶν, καὶ τιάραις, καὶ περικνημῖσι. Σαράβαρα δέ ἐστι Περσικῶν περιβολαίων εἴδη· τιάραι δὲ τῶν κεφαλῶν τὰ καλύμματα· περικνημῖδας δὲ τὰς καλουμένας ἀναξυρίδας λέγει, ἢ τὰς σκυτίνας τὰς ἔξωθεν, ἢ τὰ σκύτινα ὑποδήματα. Οὕτω πεδηθέντες οἱ ἅγιοι ἄνδρες παρεδόθησαν τῷ πυρί· καὶ ὁ μὲν τάχους χάριν καὶ συντομίας οὕτως αὐτοὺς κατακαυθῆναι προσέταξεν· ἡ δὲ θεία χάρις ἕτερον ἐντεῦθεν ᾠκονόμει μυστήριον. Τὰ μὲν γὰρ ἐπιβληθέντα αὐτοῖς ἐκ σιδήρου δεσμὰ συνήθως ἡ τοῦ πυρὸς διέλυσε φύσις· εὔπρηστα δὲ ὄντα λίαν τὰ περιβόλαια ἀκήρατα διεφύλαξε· καὶ τοὺς μὲν τῶν ἁγίων ἀνδρῶν κατηγόρους, καὶ τοῦ δυσσεβοῦς προστάγματος διακόνους, ἐκτὸς ἑστῶτας ἡ φλὸξ κατηνάλωσεν· αὐτοῖς δὲ τοῖς ἁγίοις προσπελάζειν οὐκ ἴσχυσεν, ἀλλὰ τοῖς ἔνδον τὰ νῶτα παρέχουσα, κατὰ τῶν οἰκείων ἐχώρει προσκυνητῶν, ὥσπερ δίκας αὐτοὺς ὑπὲρ τῶν τοῦ Δεσπότου θεραπόντων εἰσπραττομένη. Τοσαύτης δὲ ἔνδον οἱ τῆς εὐσεβείας κήρυκες ἀδείας καὶ θεραπείας ἀπήλαυον, ὅτι τῶν ἀνθράκων οἷόν τινων ἐπιβαίνοντες ῥόδων.

embrace the Lord's planning and providence; and without knowledge of what will be of benefit, we leave the helm to the pilot, no
matter what he wishes, understanding clearly that he is able to free
us from the threatened evils. Whether he wishes to do so, we do
not know; but we leave it to him, wise governor as he is, and accept
his verdict, confident that it is to our benefit. Whether he rescues us or not, therefore, we shun worship of your statue and your
gods. | Your contest is with souls of such caliber: whatever way   1324
you choose to engage us, you will neither win us over with com-
pliments nor deter us with threats; our God is the most loved and
the most fearsome of all. What could be more elevated than these
words? To them it is appropriate to apply that apostolic dictum,
"We do not know how to pray as we ought."[78]

That savage and most insane tyrant, however, was so filled
with rage as to betray his soul's dismay on his face. He bade
the furnace be heated more than usual, ordered the holy men be
bound, and to prevent there being any delay in their punishment
by removal of clothing and footwear, he commanded they be consigned to the fire with these as well, namely, *with their sarabaras,
tiaras, and leggings* (v. 21). Now, *sarabara* is a kind of Persian gar-
ment, *tiaras* coverings for the head, and *leggings* refers to what
are called trousers, or leathers worn outside, or leather sandals.[79]
Thus bound, the holy men were consigned to the fire; for his
part he ordered them to be incinerated for the sake of rapidity
and speed. But divine grace arranged for a further mystery to
ensue from this: whereas as usual the fire naturally dissolved the
iron bonds restraining them, the garments that would normally be
easily burned it kept intact; and while the flames consumed the
holy men's accusers, ministers of the impious command, standing outside, it was unable to get near the holy ones themselves,
instead turning its back on those inside and advancing on its own
worshipers, as though calling them to account on behalf of those
serving the Lord.

The spokesmen of godliness inside enjoyed such security
and attention that they walked on the coals as though on roses of a

---

[78] Rom 8:26.

[79] Whereas modern commentators, also noting the Persian origin of the
obscure terms in the Hebrew text, suggest trousers, shirts and hats for these
terms, the Theodotion version in front of Theodoret retains two Persian terms
(the LXX reading "sandals" for *sarabara*).

κγ'. «Περιεπάτουν, φησίν, ἐν μέσῳ τῆς φλογὸς ὑμνοῦντες τὸν Θεόν, καὶ εὐλογοῦντες τὸν Κύριον.» Καὶ ταῦτα δὲ ἔμφασιν τῆς ἄκρας αὐτῶν ἔχει φιλοσοφίας· οὔτε γὰρ ἤτουν, φησί, τῶν δεινῶν ἀπαλλαγὴν, ἀλλ' ὕμνουν τὸν οὕτω τὰ κατ' αὐτοὺς πρυτανεύσαντα, καὶ τῆς καλῆς ταύτης αὐτοὺς ὁμολογίας ἀξιώσαντα. Ἔστι δὲ ἰδεῖν ἐοικότα τοῖς νέοις τὰ παλαιά· καὶ γὰρ οἱ μακάριοι ἀπόστολοι Πέτρος καὶ Ἰωάννης, ὑπὸ τῆς τῶν Φαρισαίων αἰκισθέντες συμμορίας, ἐξῆλθον χαίροντες, ὅτι κατηξιώθησαν ὑπὲρ τοῦ ὀνόματος Ἰησοῦ ἀτιμασθῆναι· καὶ ὁ θειότατος δὲ Παῦλος σὺν τῷ Σίλᾳ, μετὰ τὰς αἰκίας ἐκείνας τὰς ἐν Φιλίπποις ὑπὸ τῶν στρατηγῶν αὐτοῖς προσενεχθείσας, δεσμωτήριον οἰκοῦντες, καὶ ποδοκάκη προσδεδεμένοι, κατὰ τὸ μεσονύκτιον, φησί, «Προσευχόμενοι ὕμνουν τὸν Θεόν.» Οὕτω καὶ οἱ μακάριοι | παῖδες οὗτοι ἐν καμίνῳ χορεύοντες τὸν θεῖον ὕμνον διετέλουν ὑφαίνοντες. Καὶ πρῶτον μὲν ὁ Ἀζαρίας στόμα κοινὸν γενόμενος, καὶ ὑπὸ τῶν τῆς φλογὸς κυμάτων περικλυζόμενος,

«Ἀνοίξας, φησί, τὸ στόμα αὐτοῦ ἐν μέσῳ τοῦ πυρός, εἶπεν· (κς'.) Εὐλογητὸς εἶ, Κύριε ὁ Θεὸς τῶν πατέρων ἡμῶν, καὶ αἰνετόν, καὶ δεδοξασμένον τὸ ὄνομά σου εἰς τοὺς αἰῶνας.» Τίς ἂν πρὸς ἀξίαν τοῦ προοιμίου τὴν σοφίαν θαυμάσειεν; Οὐδὲ γὰρ ἐν εὐημερίᾳ ὢν καὶ εὐκληρίᾳ, οὐδὲ κατὰ ῥοῦν τοῦ βίου φερομένου, ἀλλ' ἐν καμίνῳ τοσαύτῃ τὸν τῶν ὅλων ὕμνει Θεόν, καὶ ἐκάλει αὐτὸν τὸν πατέρων Θεόν, καὶ τὴν τοῦ φρονήματος δεικνὺς μετριότητα, καὶ τῶν πατέρων ἀνακηρύττων τὴν ἀρετήν. Ὑμνοῦμεν γάρ σε, φησίν, ὦ Δέσποτα, ἡμεῖς οἱ πατέρας ἔχοντες ἐκείνους, ὧν ἠθέλησας κληθῆναι Θεός. Σὺ γὰρ εἶπας τῷ θεράποντί σου Μωσῇ· «Ἐγὼ ὁ Θεὸς Ἀβραάμ, καὶ ὁ Θεὸς Ἰσαάκ, καὶ ὁ Θεὸς Ἰακώβ·» τοῦτό σου τὸ ὄνομα αἰνετόν ἐστι, καὶ δεδοξασμένον, οὐκ ἐν καιρῷ τινι καὶ χρόνῳ ῥητῷ, ἀλλ' εἰς πάντας τοὺς αἰῶνας.

κζ'. «Ὅτι δίκαιος εἶ ἐπὶ πᾶσιν, οἷς ἐποίησας ἡμῖν.» Ὑμνοῦμεν δέ σε, φησί, τὸ δίκαιον τῆς σῆς ἐπιστάμενοι κρίσεως· ὀρθῇ γὰρ καὶ δι-

kind. *They walked about in the middle of the fire singing God's praises and blessing the Lord* (v. 24). This highlights the eminence of their sound values: far from asking for release from their fate, they sang the praises of the one who had thus controlled their situation and allowed them this excellent confession. Now, it is possible to see the old resembling the new: when the blessed apostles Peter and John had been ill-treated by the party of the Pharisees, they went out rejoicing that they had been thought worthy to be dishonored for the name of Jesus.[80] The most divine Paul along with Silas, after that ill-treatment inflicted on them by the officials in Philippi, were confined to prison and bound in shackles, but at midnight (the text says) "they prayed and sang God's praises."[81] Likewise these blessed | young people moving to and fro in the furnace, too, celebrated by continuing to compose the divine hymn. 1325

Firstly, Azariah became their spokesman, and surrounded by the billowing flames, he opened his mouth in the midst of the fire and said, *Blessed are you, Lord, God of our fathers, your name is to be praised and glorified for ever* (v. 26).[82] Who could worthily admire the wisdom of the introduction! It is not in good fortune and prosperity, nor in life's steady progress, that he sings the praises of the God of all, but in such an awful furnace. He called him *God of the fathers*, bringing out his modest attitude and proclaiming the virtue of the fathers: We sing your praises, Lord, he is saying, we who have as our fathers those whose God you wished to be called, saying to your servant Moses, "I am the God of Abraham, the God of Isaac and the God of Jacob."[83] This name of yours is to be praised and glorified, not in one instance and at a specified time, but for all ages. *Because you are righteous in all you have done for us* (v. 27): we sing your praises, knowing as we do the righteousness of your judgment; you exercised a right and proper verdict in

[80] Cf. Acts 5:17–42, where John does not rate special mention.
[81] Acts 16:25.
[82] The Antioch text has the name as being the object of praise, not the Lord. Theodoret gives no indication of being aware that vv. 24–90, comprising principally the hymn of the three men, was not always part of the text or story. Whereas modern commentators presume they are translated from a Hebrew or Aramaic original (possibly of liturgical origin), Theodoret's silence on such matters does not, of course, suggest they were part of any Hebrew text known to him, as they are not part of our Masoretic text.
[83] Exod 3:6.

καία χρησάμενος ψήφῳ ἐξανδραποδισθῆναι ἡμᾶς, καὶ πόρρω τῶν οἰκείων γενέσθαι προσέταξας.

«Καὶ πάντα σου, φησί, τὰ ἔργα ἀληθινά, καὶ εὐθεῖαι αἱ ὁδοί σου. (κη΄.) Καὶ πᾶσαι αἱ κρίσεις σου ἀληθιναί, καὶ κρίματα ἀληθείας ἐποίησας, κατὰ πάντα ἃ ἐπήγαγες ἡμῖν, καὶ ἐπὶ τὴν πόλιν τὴν ἁγίαν τὴν τῶν πατέρων ἡμῶν Ἱερουσαλήμ, ὅτι ἐν ἀληθείᾳ καὶ κρίσει ἐπήγαγες ταῦτα πάντα ἐφ᾽ ἡμᾶς διὰ τὰς ἁμαρτίας ἡμῶν.» Τὴν αὐτὴν μὲν διάνοιαν ἅπαντα ἔχει τὰ εἰρημένα· διαφόρως δὲ αὐτὰ εἴρηκε, τὴν δικαίαν τοῦ Θεοῦ κρίσιν ὑμνῶν, καὶ χώραν οὐδεμίαν τῇ ἀχαριστίᾳ διδούς. Διὰ τοῦτο καὶ τῆς Ἱερουσαλὴμ μνημονεύσας, καὶ *ἁγίαν* αὐτὴν ὀνομάσας, καὶ *τῶν πατέρων ἐκείνων τῶν ἐκλεκτῶν πόλιν* προσαγορεύσας, εὐθὺς τὴν τῆς τιμωρίας αἰτίαν ἐπήγαγε·

«Ταῦτα πάντα, φησίν, ἐπήγαγες ἐφ᾽ ἡμᾶς διὰ τὰς ἁμαρτίας ἡμῶν. (κθ΄.) Ὅτι ἡμάρτομεν καὶ ἠνομήσαμεν ἀποστάντες ἀπὸ σοῦ.» Οὐ γὰρ μάτην, φησί, καὶ ἣν ἀφιέρωσας παρέδωκας πόλιν τοῖς πολεμίοις, καὶ ἡμᾶς εἴασας δορυαλώτους γενέσθαι, ἀλλ᾽ «ὅτι ἡμάρτομεν, καὶ ἠνομήσαμεν ἀποστάντες ἀπὸ σοῦ.» Πολλὴν δὲ ἔμφασιν ἔχει τὸ ἀπὸ σοῦ, ἀντὶ τοῦ, Τοῦ Ποιητοῦ καὶ Δημιουργοῦ, τοῦ ἀγαθοῦ Δεσπότου, τοῦ τροφέως, καὶ φύλακος, τοῦ τῆς Αἰγυπτίων δουλείας ἀπαλλάξαντος, τοῦ θάλατταν τεμόντος, τοῦ δι᾽ ἀβύσσου ποδηγήσαντος, τοῦ πέτραν ξηρὰν | ὠδῖσι πληγῶν κατακλύσαντος, τοῦ τ᾽ ἄλλα πάντα ἀνάγραπτα ἀγαθὰ χορηγήσαντος. Ἡμάρτομεν τοίνυν ἀποστάντες ἀπὸ σοῦ· «Καὶ ἐξημάρτομεν ἐν πᾶσιν.» Οὐ γὰρ τόδε, ἢ τόδε παρέβημεν, ἀλλὰ πάντα σου τὸ προστάγματα.

λ΄. «Καὶ τῶν ἐντολῶν τοῦ νόμου σου οὐκ ἠκούσαμεν, οὐδὲ ἐφυλάξαμεν αὐτάς, οὐδὲ ἐποιήσαμεν, καθὼς ἐνετείλω ἡμῖν, ἵνα εὖ ἡμῖν γένηται.» Κἀνταῦθα πάλιν τὴν τῆς εὐσεβείας καὶ σοφίας ἔδειξεν ὑπερβολήν. Ἡ γὰρ τῶν νόμων, φησί, καὶ τῶν ἐντολῶν φυλακή, σοὶ μὲν τῷ νομοθέτῃ παρεῖχεν οὐδέν, ἡμῖν δὲ ἀγαθῶν ἀφθονίαν προεξένει· τούτου τοίνυν χάριν καὶ τοὺς νόμους ἐτεθείκεις ἐκείνους, ἀφορμὰς ἡμῖν χορηγῶν σωτηρίας. Ἐπειδὴ τοίνυν, φησί, παρέβημεν,

λα΄. «Πάντα ὅσα ἡμῖν ἐπήγαγες, καὶ πάντα ὅσα ἐποίησας ἡμῖν, ἐν ἀληθινῇ κρίσει ἐποίησας.» Ἀξία γὰρ τῆς ἁμαρτίας ἡ τιμωρία. Εἶτα ταύτην δεικνὺς ἐπάγει·

λβ΄. «Καὶ παρέδωκας ἡμᾶς εἰς χεῖρας ἀνόμων, ἐχθίστων, ἀποστατῶν, καὶ βασιλεῖ ἀδίκῳ καὶ πονηροτάτῳ παρὰ πᾶσαν τὴν γῆν παρέδωκας ἡμᾶς.» Ἐπειδὴ γάρ σε τὸν ἡμέτερον οὐκ ἐθεραπεύσαμεν βασιλέα, ἀλλὰ τῆς σῆς κατεφρονήσαμεν ἀγαθότητος, εἰκότως ἡμᾶς ὠμοτάτῳ, καὶ

ordering that we be enslaved and left far from our own homeland. *All your works are true and your ways straight. All your judgments are true; you made truthful judgments in all you inflicted on us, even against the holy city of our fathers, Jerusalem, because it was in truth and justice that you inflicted all this on us for our sins* (vv. 27–28). All the words have the same sense, but he brought out the same meaning in different ways, praising God's righteous judgment and allowing no room for ingratitude.

Hence, after his reference to Jerusalem, calling it *holy*, and naming it *city of those fathers* who were chosen, he immediately went on to give the reason for the retribution. *You inflicted all this on us because of our sins, because we sinned and were wrong to depart from you* (vv. 28–29): it was not without reason that you handed over to the enemy the city you consecrated and allowed us to become captives; rather, it was *because we sinned and were wrong to depart from you.* The phrase *from you* is highlighted to give the sense, from you the maker and creator, the good Lord, nourisher, protector, freeing from the slavery of the Egyptians, dividing the sea, leading through the depths, flooding the dry rock | with pangs from blows,[84] providing all the other good things recorded. So *we were wrong to depart from you and sinned in everything*: we did not break this or that command, but all your commands. *We did not heed the commandments of your law, or keep them or discharge them, as you told us so that it would be good for us* (v. 30). Here, too, he brought out once more the great degree of his piety and wisdom: The observance of the laws and commandments, he is saying, provided nothing to the lawgiver, but to us were a source of abundance of good things; so this was the reason you imposed those laws, to supply us with an occasion of salvation.

Since we transgressed, therefore, *All that you inflicted on us and all you did to us you did by a true judgment* (v. 31): the punishment fits the crime. Then, to explain it, he goes on, *You gave us into the hands of lawless people, hostile, rebellious, and you handed us over to an unjust king, the most wicked in all the earth* (v. 32): since we did not serve you as our king, and instead spurned your goodness, you were right to oblige us to serve a king who is the most cruel, most harsh, and completely oblivious of justice, with subjects who are also in accord with the king's viciousness. Yet

1328

---

[84] Editor Schulze suggests that the text is corrupt in regard to this phrase.

ἀπηνεστάτῳ, καὶ οὐδαμῶς εἰδότι τὸ δίκαιον δουλεύειν ἠνάγκασας βασιλεῖ, ἔχοντι καὶ τοὺς ὑπηκόους τῇ βασιλικῇ πονηρίᾳ συμβαίνοντας. Ἀλλ'
ὅμως καὶ ἐν τοσούτοις ὄντες κακοῖς πάσης ἐστερήμεθα παρρησίας, καὶ
προσφέρειν σοι δέησιν ὑπὸ τῆς αἰσχύνης κωλυόμεθα· τοῦτο γὰρ σημαίνει
λέγων·

λγ'. «Καὶ νῦν οὐκ ἔστιν ἡμῖν ἀνοῖξαι τὸ στόμα, αἰσχύνη καὶ ὄνει-
δος ἐγενήθημεν τοῖς δούλοις σου, καὶ τοῖς σεβομένοις σε.» Ἐμφράττει,
φησίν, ἡμῶν τὸ στόμα τῆς παρανομίας τὸ πλῆθος· ἀλλ' ὅμως ἐπονείδιστοι, καὶ καταγέλαστοι, καὶ λίαν ἐπίχαρτοι τοῖς πολεμίοις γενόμενοι
ἡμεῖς, οἱ δοῦλοί σου προσαγορευόμενοι, ἱκετεύομέν σε, διὰ τὸ ἐπικείμενον ἡμῖν τῆς σῆς δεσποτείας ὄνομα δεῖξαι τοῖς ἐναντίοις τὴν σὴν ἰσχύν,
καὶ μὴ παντελῶς ἡμᾶς τῆς σῆς προμηθείας ἀλλοτριῶσαι.

λδ'. «Μὴ παραδῷς γὰρ ἡμᾶς, φησίν, εἰς τέλος διὰ τὸ ὄνομά σου,
καὶ τὴν διαθήκην σου μὴ ἀποστήσῃς, καὶ μὴ διασκεδάσῃς τὸ ἔλεός σου
ἀφ' ἡμῶν.» Τολμῶμεν δέ, φησί, ταῦτα λέγειν, πολλὰ ἐνέχυρα τῆς σῆς
ἀγαθότητος ἔχοντες· πρῶτον μὲν αὐτὸ τῆς σῆς Δεσποτείας τὸ ὄνομα·
ἔπειτα τὸν ἀμέτρητον ἔλεον, ᾧ κεχρημένος ἰθύνεις τὰ σύμπαντα· πρὸς
τούτοις, τὰς πρὸς τοὺς πατέρας ἡμῶν συνθήκας· ὑπέσχου γὰρ ἐκείνοις
περίβλεπτόν τε καὶ ἔνδοξον τὸ ἐκείνων γένος ποιήσειν. Εἶτα καὶ τῶν
ὀνομάτων τῶν πατέρων μέμνηται, τῇ μνήμῃ τῶν δικαίων τὸν ἀγαθὸν
1329 Δεσπότην εἰς ἔλεον ἐκκαλούμενος. |

λε', λς'. «Διὰ Ἀβραάμ, φησί, τὸν ἠγαπημένον ὑπὸ σοῦ, καὶ διὰ
Ἰσαὰκ τὸν δοῦλόν σου, καὶ Ἰσραὴλ τὸν ἅγιόν σου, οἷς ἐλάλησας αὐτοῖς
λέγων· Πληθυνῶ τὸ σπέρμα ὑμῶν ὡσεὶ τὰ ἄστρα τοῦ οὐρανοῦ, καὶ ὡς
τὴν ἄμμον τὴν παρὰ τὸ χεῖλος τῆς θαλάσσης.» Ταῦτα, φησίν, ἐκείνοις
ὑπέσχου, Δέσποτα, οὓς ἠγάπησάς τε καὶ ἀοιδίμους ἐποίησας, ὥστε τῇ
ψάμμῳ μὲν κατὰ τὸν ἀριθμὸν παραβάλλεσθαι τὸ γένος, τοῖς δὲ ἀστρά-
σι παραπλησίως εἶναι λαμπρόν τε καὶ ὑψηλόν, καὶ περιφανές. Εἶτα ἐκ
παραλλήλου ταῖς ἐπαγγελίαις τὰ πράγματα τίθησιν.

λζ'. «Ὅτι, Δέσποτα, φησὶν ἐσμικρύνθημεν παρὰ πάντα τὰ ἔθνη,
καὶ ἐσμεν ταπεινοὶ ἐν πάσῃ τῇ γῇ σήμερον.» Καὶ ἵνα μὴ ψευδῶς κατ-
ηγορήσῃ τῶν ὑποσχέσεων, εὐθὺς τὴν αἰτίαν ἐπήγαγε, λέγων· «Διὰ τὰς
ἁμαρτίας ἡμῶν.» Οὐ γὰρ σύ, φησί, Δέσποτα, τὰς ὑποσχέσεις ἐψεύσω,
ἀλλ' ἡμεῖς τὰς συνθήκας παρέβημεν, καὶ πολλοὶ ὄντες κατὰ τὴν ὑπόσχεσιν, καὶ ἀριθμοῦ κρείττους, διὰ τὰς ἁμαρτίας ἡμῶν ὀλιγώθημεν. Τοῦτο
γὰρ ἠνίξατο εἰρηκώς· «Ἐσμικρύνθημεν.» Οὐ γὰρ εἶπε, Σμικροί ἐσμεν,
καὶ ὀλίγοι παρὰ πάντα τὰ ἔθνη, ἀλλ', «Ἐσμικρύνθημεν,» τουτέστιν,
Ἐγενόμεθα μὲν ἀριθμοῦ κρείττους κατὰ τὴν σὴν ὑπόσχεσιν, παραβάντες
δέ σου τὰς ἐντολὰς ὀλίγοι ἀντὶ πολλῶν ἐγενόμεθα. Εἶτα ὑποδείκνυσι τῷ

despite being in such awful trouble, we have lost all forthrightness and are prevented by shame from offering a petition to you
(the meaning of the following words). *And now we cannot open our
mouth, we have become a shame and reproach to your servants and
those who reverence you* (v. 33):[85] the mass of lawlessness stops our
mouth; yet though we have become shameful, ridiculous, and an
object of mockery to the enemy, we who are called your servants
implore you by the name of your lordship imposed on us to show
your strength to the adversaries and not eliminate us completely
from your providence.

For your name's sake do not surrender us forever, do not relin-
quish your covenant, and do not snatch your mercy from us (v. 34):
we presume to say this because we have many pledges of your
goodness—firstly, the very name of your lordship; then, the im-
measurable mercy which you exercise in guiding all things; in
addition to this the treaties with our ancestors, promising them
to make their race illustrious and glorious. He next mentions as
well the ancestors' names, summoning the good Lord to mercy by
mention of those righteous ones. | *For the sake of Abraham your* 1329
*beloved, for the sake of Isaac your servant and Israel your holy one,
to whom you said, I shall multiply your offspring like the stars of the
sky and like the sand on the sea shore* (vv. 35–36): you promised this,
Lord, to those whom you guided and made famous so that the race
rivaled the grains of sand for number and became as bright, lofty,
and illustrious as the stars.

He next compares their present situation with the promises.
*Lord, we have become fewer than any other nation, and are lowly in
all the earth today* (v. 37). And lest he falsely find fault with the
promises, he immediately supplied the reason, *because of our sins*:
you did not utter false promises, Lord, it was we who broke the
agreements; many though we were in accord with the promise and
beyond counting, our numbers have dwindled because of our sins.
He implied this, in fact, by saying *We have become fewer*; he did
not say, We are few in comparison with all the nations, but *We
have become fewer*, that is, Whereas we were beyond counting in
accord with your promise, we broke your commandments and became few after being many. He then details to God the misfortune

---

[85] Other forms of the text, both those of Theodotion and the LXX, read,
"Shame and reproach have befallen your servants."

84   THEODORET : COMMENTARY ON DANIEL

Θεῷ τὴν κατέχουσαν συμφοράν, οὐχ ὡς ἀγνοοῦντα διδάσκων, ἀλλὰ τῇ διηγήσει τῶν λυπηρῶν εἰς φιλανθρωπίαν ἐκκαλούμενος.

λη΄. «Καὶ οὐκ ἔστι, φησίν, ἐν τῷ καιρῷ τούτῳ ἄρχων, καὶ προφήτης, καὶ ἡγούμενος.» Ἀπεστερήμεθα γάρ, φησί, βασιλείας, προφητείας, ἱερωσύνης, τῶν θείων σου καὶ μεγάλων δωρεῶν, δι' ὧν κυβερνώμενοι διετελοῦμεν. «Οὐδὲ ὁλοκαύτωσις, οὐδὲ θυσία, οὐδὲ προσφορά, οὐδὲ θυμίαμα.» Καὶ δεικνὺς τὴν αἰτίαν, δι' ἣν ἀδύνατον θῦσαι, ἀκολούθως ἐπήγαγεν· «Οὐδὲ τόπος τοῦ καρπῶσαι ἐνώπιόν σου, καὶ εὑρεῖν ἔλεον.» Ὁ γὰρ σὸς νόμος τὴν τῶν θυσιῶν λειτουργίαν ἑνὶ περιέγραψε τόπῳ, καὶ παρανομία σαφὴς τὸ ἐν ἑτέρῳ τόπῳ προσενεγκεῖν σοι θυσίαν. Τούτων ἀκούειν οὐκ ἐθέλουσιν οἱ Ἰουδαῖοι, ἀλλὰ τοὺς ὀφθαλμοὺς μύσαντες, καὶ τὰ ὦτα βύσαντες, πάντα τολμῶσι παρανόμως ἐπιτελεῖν. Οἱ δὲ ἅγιοι παῖδες οὗτοι, τοῦ νόμου τὸν σκοπὸν ἐπιστάμενοι, ἔλεγον μὴ εἶναι τόπον τοῦ καρπῶσαι ἐνώπιον αὐτοῦ, καὶ εὑρεῖν ἔλεον· Καὶ ἐπειδὴ τούτου, φησί, τυχεῖν ἀδύνατον, πόρρω τῆς ἱερᾶς ἐκείνης πόλεως ὄντας, εὑρήκαμεν τρόπον τινὰ θεραπείας, ὦ Δέσποτα.

λθ΄, μ΄. «Ἐν ψυχῇ γὰρ συντετριμμένῃ, καὶ πνεύματι ταπεινώσεως προσφέροντές σοι τὴν ἱκετείαν, προσδεχθῆναι αὐτὴν παρακαλοῦμεν. Ὡς ἐν ὁλοκαυτώμασι κριῶν καὶ ταύρων, καὶ ὡς ἐν μυριά|σιν ἀρνῶν πιόνων, οὕτω γενέσθω ἡ θυσία ἡμῶν ἐνώπιόν σου σήμερον, καὶ ἐκτελείσθω ὄπισθέν σου· ὅτι οὐκ ἔστιν αἰσχύνη τοῖς πεποιθόσιν ἐπὶ σοί.» Ἐπειδὴ γάρ, φησίν, ὁ σὸς νόμος ἐν παντί σοι τόπῳ προσφέρειν τὰς νενομισμένας θυσίας οὐ συγχωρεῖ, ἀντὶ κριῶν, καὶ ταύρων, καὶ ἀρνῶν τὸν ἀριθμὸν νικώντων, συντετριμμένην σοι καὶ τεταπεινωμένην καρδίαν προσφέρομεν, καὶ παρακαλοῦμεν γενέσθαι σοι ταῦτα πάσης θυσίας ἡδίω, ἐπειδὴ εἴωθας τοὺς πεποιθότας ἐπὶ σοὶ πάσης αἰσχύνης ἐλευθεροῦν. Ταῦτα δὲ οὐχ ἁπλῶς οὕτως εἴρηκεν ὁ ἅγιος οὗτος ἀνήρ, ἀλλ' ὑπὸ τοῦ προφήτου δεδιδαγμένος Δαβίδ, ὃς ἐν τῷ πεντηκοστῷ λέγει ψαλμῷ, ὅτι «Εἰ ἠθέλησας θυσίαν, ἔδωκα ἄν· ὁλοκαυτώματα οὐκ εὐδοκήσεις· θυσία τῷ Θεῷ πνεῦμα συντετριμμένον, καρδίαν συντετριμμένην καὶ τεταπεινωμένην ὁ Θεὸς οὐκ ἐξουδενώσει.» Καὶ πάλιν ἐκ προσώπου τοῦ Θεοῦ· «Μὴ φάγομαι κρέα ταύρων, ἢ αἷμα τράγων πίομαι; Θῦσον τῷ Θεῷ θυσίαν αἰνέσεως, καὶ ἀπόδος τῷ Ὑψίστῳ τὰς εὐχάς σου, καὶ ἐπικάλεσαί με ἐν ἡμέρᾳ θλίψεώς σου, καὶ ἐξελοῦμαί σε, καὶ δοξάσεις με.» Καὶ μετὰ βραχέα· «Θυσία αἰνέσεως δοξάσει με, καὶ ἐκεῖ ὁδός, ἐν ᾗ δείξω αὐτῷ τὸ σωτήριόν μου.» Ταῦτα δεδιδαγμένος ὁ θεῖος οὗτος ἀνήρ, τὴν συντετριμμένην καρδίαν ἀντὶ πάσης δεχθῆναι θυσίας ἱκέτευσεν. Εἶτα ἐπάγει·

μα΄. «Καὶ νῦν ἐξακολουθοῦμέν σοι ἐν ὅλῃ καρδίᾳ, καὶ φοβούμεθά σε, καὶ ζητοῦμεν τὸ πρόσωπόν σου, μὴ καταισχύνῃς ἡμᾶς.» Τὸ γὰρ

gripping them, not as though informing him in his ignorance but to summon him to lovingkindness by recounting the disasters. *At this time there is no ruler, prophet, or leader* (v. 38): we are deprived of kingship, prophecy, priesthood, your marvelous divine gifts by which we have constantly been guided.[86] *No burnt offering, sacrifice, offering, or incense.* And to bring out the reason why it was not possible to offer sacrifice, he logically went on, *No place to offer firstfruits in your presence and find mercy.* The law, you see, prescribed the ritual of sacrifices in one place, and offering sacrifice in another place was a blatant offense.

The Jews were unwilling to hear this; closing their eyes and blocking their ears, they continued to perform everything in contravention of the law. These holy young people, on the contrary, understood the purpose of the law and said there was no place to offer firstfruits in his presence and find mercy. Since it is impossible to attain this, he is saying, being at a distance from that holy city, we have found some way to worship, Lord. *With a contrite heart and a spirit of lowliness we offer supplication to you and implore that it be accepted. As though with burnt offerings of rams and bulls, and as though with ten thousands | of fat lambs, let our offering come* 1332 *before you today and let it be performed in accord with your wishes,[87] because there is no shame for those who trust in you* (vv. 39–40): since your law does not permit the prescribed sacrifices to be offered in every place, instead of rams, bulls, and lambs beyond counting we offer a contrite and humbled heart, and beg that it be more pleasing to you than any sacrifice, since you are in the habit of freeing from all shame those who trust in you. Now, this holy man did not speak this way of himself: he was schooled by the prophet David, who in the fifty-first psalm says, "If you had wanted sacrifice, I would have given it; you will not be pleased with burnt offerings. A contrite spirit is a sacrifice to God, a contrite and humbled heart God will not despise."[88] And again on God's part, "Surely I do not eat the flesh of bulls, or drink goats' blood? Sacrifice to God a sacrifice of praise, pay your vows to the Most High, call upon me in the day of your tribulation, and I shall rescue you and you will glorify me"; and shortly after, "A sacrifice of praise will glorify me,

[86] Cf. Hos 3:4.
[87] Of this phrase the translators' note to the NRSV observes, "Meaning of Gk uncertain."
[88] Ps 51:16–17.

πλῆθος τῶν συμφορῶν ἑτέρους ἡμᾶς ἀνθ' ἑτέρων εἰργάσατο, καὶ παραβάτας ὄντας τῶν σῶν ἐντολῶν, ἐν ὅλῃ σε καρδίᾳ καὶ φοβεῖσθαι καὶ ζητεῖν παρεσκεύασε. *Πρόσωπον δὲ Θεοῦ ἐνταῦθα τὴν εὐμένειαν ἐκάλεσε, καὶ τὴν τῆς ἐλευθερίας ἀπόδοσιν, καὶ τὴν τῆς κηδεμονίας ἀπόληψιν, ἧς ἀπολαύοντας δυνατὸν ἦν ὁρᾶν καὶ τὸν θεῖον νεών, καὶ τὰς ἐπιτελουμένας αὐτόθι λατρείας, δι' ὧν ἀσώματον ὄντα τὸν Θεὸν καὶ ἀόρατον ὁρᾶν ἐφαντάζοντο.* Ἐπειδὴ τοίνυν τοσαύτην ἡμῶν διὰ τῆς τιμωρίας εἰργάσω μεταβολήν,

μβ', μγ'. «Μὴ καταισχύνῃς ἡμᾶς, ἀλλὰ ποίησον μεθ' ἡμῶν κατὰ τὴν ἐπιείκειάν σου, καὶ κατὰ τὸ πλῆθος τοῦ ἐλέους σου. Καὶ ἐξελοῦ ἡμᾶς κατὰ τὰ θαυμάσιά σου, καὶ δὸς δόξαν τῷ ὀνόματί σου.» Διὰ ταῦτα, φησίν, οἴκτου ἡμᾶς καὶ φιλανθρωπίας ἀξίωσον· ἐλεεῖν τε γὰρ πέφυκας, καὶ μακροθυμίᾳ κεχρῆσθαι πρὸς ἅπαντας, σύνδρομόν τε ἔχεις τῇ βουλήσει τὴν δύναμιν· καὶ μαρτυρεῖ τὰ διηνεκῶς ὑπὸ σοῦ γενόμενα θαύματα. Τὰ γὰρ εἰς ἡμᾶς γενόμενα, καὶ τὸ σὸν ὄνομα ὑμνεῖσθαι παρασκευάσει, οὐχ ὑφ' ἡμῶν μόνον σωζομένων, ἀλλὰ καὶ ὑπὸ τῶν τὴν ἡμετέραν σωτηρίαν ὁρώντων.

«Δὸς δόξαν τοίνυν τῷ ὀνόματί σου, Κύριε. (μδ', με'.) Καὶ ἐντραπείησαν πάντες οἱ ἐνδεικνύ|μενοι τοῖς δούλοις σου κακά, καὶ καταισχυνθείησαν ἀπὸ πάσης δυναστείας, καὶ ἡ ἰσχὺς αὐτῶν συντριβείη. Γνώτωσαν, ὅτι σὺ Κύριος ὁ Θεὸς μόνος, καὶ ἔνδοξος ἐφ' ὅλην τὴν οἰκουμένην.» Ταύτης γὰρ εἰς ἡμᾶς γινομένης φιλανθρωπίας, καταλυθήσεται μὲν τῶν ἐναντίων τὸ θράσος, σβεσθήσεται δὲ αὐτῶν ἡ λύττα, καὶ φρόνημα αὐτῶν τὸ ὑψηλὸν συντριβήσεται, καὶ γνώσονταί σε μόνον εἶναι Κύριον καὶ Θεόν, ὑπὸ πάσης ἄξιον ὑμνεῖσθαι τῆς οἰκουμένης· καὶ οἱ νῦν πολλοὺς προσκυνοῦντες θεούς, τῶν μὲν οἰκείων θεῶν γνώσονται τὴν ἀσθένειαν, τὴν δὲ σὴν προσκυνήσουσι δύναμιν. Οἱ μὲν οὖν ἔνδον ἐν τῇ καμίνῳ χορεύοντες διετέλουν· οἱ δὲ τοῦ βασιλέως ὑπηρέται, καὶ τῶν ἁγίων κατήγοροι, οὐκ ἔληγον ὕλην τῇ φλογὶ χορηγοῦντες, καὶ κληματίδας, καὶ στυππίον, καὶ *νάφθαν*· εἶδος δὲ τοῦτό ἐστιν ἐν ἐκείνῃ τῇ χώρᾳ γινόμενον, ἐξάψαι τὴν φλόγα δυνάμενον. Τοσαύτη δὲ ἦν χορηγουμένη τῇ

1333

and there is the path in which I shall show him my salvation."[89]
Schooled in these sentiments, this divine man begged that a contrite heart be accepted in place of any sacrifice.

He then went on, *And now we follow you with all our heart,
we fear you and seek your face; do not put us to shame* (v. 41): the
great number of the misfortunes made us different from before,
and from being transgressors of your commandments they caused
us to fear and seek you with all our heart. By God's *face* here he referred to his benevolence, the restoration of freedom and regaining
his providence: for those who enjoyed it there was the possibility
of seeing both the divine temple and the rituals performed there,
in which they imagined they saw God, incorporeal and invisible
though he is. Since, then, you brought about such a change in us
by means of punishment, *Do not put us to shame; instead, deal with
us according to your mildness and according to the abundance of your
mercy. Deliver us according to your marvelous actions, and give glory
to your name* (vv. 42–43): for this reason regale us with compassion
and lovingkindness; it is natural for you to be merciful and show
longsuffering to all, and you have the power to second your wishes,
as the marvels constantly performed by you confirm. In fact, what
is done for us will also cause your name to be praised, not only by
us who are saved but also by those witnessing our salvation. *So
give glory to your name, Lord. Let all those who bring trouble on your
servants be confounded, | let them be frustrated in all their power, and   1333
let their strength be crushed. Let them know that you alone are Lord
God, glorious throughout the whole world* (vv. 43–45): when this lovingkindness is shown us, the audacity of the adversaries will be
defeated, their rage snuffed out, their lofty attitude crushed, and
they will know that you alone are Lord and God, worthy of being
praised by the whole world. Those who now worship many gods
will know the weakness of their own gods and will worship your
might.

While those inside the furnace, then, continued moving to
and fro, the king's ministers, being also the holy ones' accusers,
did not stop fueling the fire with branches, tow and naphtha,
a substance occurring in that country capable of lighting fires.
But the fuel fed to the fire was so copious that it spread out

[89] Ps 50:13–15, 23.

πυρᾷ τροφῇ, ὡς ἐπ' ἐννέα καὶ τεσσαράκοντα πήχεις διαχυθῆναι, καὶ τῶν Χαλδαίων ἐμπρῆσαι τοὺς πλησιάζοντας. Καὶ οἱ μὲν ἔξωθεν ἐξῆπτον τὴν φλόγα· θεῖος δὲ ἄγγελος ἐσκεδάννυ τὴν φλόγα, καὶ τὸ μέσον τῆς καμίνου τῶν ἀνθράκων ἐγύμνου, καὶ αὖράν τινα ψυχράν τε καὶ μετρίως ὑγράν, καὶ πολλὴν τοῖς ἁγίοις ἡδονὴν πραγματευομένην, ὠδίνειν τὸ πῦρ παρεσκεύαζε, καὶ ταύτην τοῖς τῶν ἁγίων ἐπαφιέναι σώμασιν.

ν'. «Ἐποίησε γάρ, φησί, τὸ μέσον τῆς καμίνου ὡς πνεῦμα δρόσου διασυρίζον, καὶ οὐχ ἥψατο αὐτῶν τὸ καθόλου τὸ πῦρ, καὶ οὐκ ἐλύπησεν αὐτούς, οὐδὲ παρηνώχλησεν αὐτοῖς.» Ἀλλὰ μηδεὶς ταῦτα ἀφορῶν σμικρυνέτω τοὺς τῶν ἁγίων ἀγῶνας, τῶν δὲ ἱερῶν ἐκείνων ἀναμιμνησκέσθω λόγων· «Ἔστιν ὁ Θεὸς ἐν οὐρανοῖς, ᾧ ἡμεῖς λατρεύομεν, δυνατὸς ἐξελέσθαι ἡμᾶς ἐκ τῆς καμίνου τῆς καιομένης, καὶ ἐκ τῶν χειρῶν σου, βασιλεῦ, ῥύσεται ἡμᾶς.» Καί, «Ἐὰν μή, γνωστὸν ἔστω σοι, βασιλεῦ, ὅτι τοῖς θεοῖς σου οὐ λατρεύομεν, καὶ τῇ εἰκόνι τῇ χρυσῇ, ἣ ἔστησας, οὐ προσκυνοῦμεν.» Ὥστε οἱ ἅγιοι παῖδες ἐκεῖνοι τῆς φλογὸς ἐκείνης κατεφρόνησαν, οὐ τοῦτο τὸ τέλος ὁρῶντες, ἀλλὰ θάνατον προσδεχόμενοι· ὁ δὲ ἀγωνοθέτης ἐβράβευσεν, ὡς ἠθέλησε, καὶ τούς τε ἀλιτηρίους ἐκείνους κατήσχυνε, καὶ τούτους ἀοιδίμους ἀπέφηνε. Ταύτης τοίνυν τῆς σωτηρίας ἀπολαύσαντες οἱ μακάριοι καὶ τρισμακάριοι παῖδες, καὶ πολλάκις τοῦτο, οὐκ ἔτι ἑνὶ τὸν Θεὸν ὑμνεῖν παρεχώρησαν, ἀλλ',

να'. «Ὡς ἐξ ἑνός, φησί, στόματος ὕμνουν καὶ ἐδόξαζον τὸν Θεόν, καὶ ηὐλόγουν ἐν τῇ καμίνῳ,» τὴν ἀρίστην αὐτῶν συμφωνίαν, καὶ θαυμαστὴν ὑμνῳδίαν, τῇ παρὰ τὴν εἰκόνα συμφωνίᾳ καὶ τοῖς | μουσικοῖς ἀντιτάξαντες ὀργάνοις, καὶ δεικνύντες, ὅσῳ τὸ μὴ προσκυνῆσαι τὴν εἰκόνα τοῦ προσκυνῆσαι λυσιτελέστερον. Ἄρχονται δὲ οὕτως τοῦ ὕμνου·

νβ'. «Εὐλογητὸς εἶ, Κύριε, ὁ Θεὸς τῶν πατέρων ἡμῶν, καὶ αἰνετὸς καὶ ὑπερυψούμενος εἰς τοὺς αἰῶνας· καὶ εὐλογημένον τὸ ὄνομα τῆς δόξης σου, τὸ ἅγιον, καὶ ὑπεραινετόν, καὶ ὑπερυψούμενον εἰς τοὺς αἰῶνας.» Ἔρωτός ἐστι θερμοτάτου καὶ ἀπληστοτάτου τὰ ῥήματα· τούτῳ γὰρ τετρωμένοι, ζητοῦσιν ὀνόματα τοῦ ὑμνουμένου τὴν ἀξίαν παραδηλῶσαι δυνάμενα, καὶ μὴ εὑρίσκοντες, ταῖς ὑπερθετικαῖς αὐτὰ προθέσεσιν ἐξυφαίνουσιν, «ὑπερυψούμενον» ὀνομάζοντες, καὶ «ὑπεραινετόν,» καὶ οὐκ αὐτὸν μόνον, ἀλλὰ καὶ τὸ ὄνομα τῆς δόξης αὐτοῦ. Καλῶς δὲ παντα-

forty-nine cubits and incinerated the astrologers close by.[90] While those outside fed the flames, an angel from God extinguished the flames, kept the middle of the furnace clear of burning coals, and caused the fire to produce a cool and moderately damp breeze that brought considerable relief to the holy ones and to direct it on to the saints' bodies. *It made the middle of the furnace,* the text says, *like a breath of dew whistling through it; the fire did not touch them at all or distress them or trouble them greatly* (v. 50). Let no one contemplating this, however, minimize the holy ones' trials; instead, let them recall those sacred words, "The God in heaven whom we serve is capable of rescuing us from the blazing furnace, and he will rescue us from your hands, O King," and "If not, let it be known to you, O King, that we will not serve your gods and worship the golden image that you set up."[91] The result was that those holy young people scorned that awful flame, not seeing this outcome but expecting death; the arbiter of the contest, however, awarded them the prize as he wished, and confounded the guilty while making the others illustrious.

On attaining this preservation, therefore, the blessed and thrice-blessed young people, as often happens, did not allow only one to sing God's praises, instead *as with one voice they praised and glorified God and blessed him in the furnace* (v. 51), producing their excellent harmony and remarkable hymn-singing in opposition to the harmony and musical instruments used for the statue, | and   1336 showing how much more advantageous was not adoring the statue than adoring it. They begin the hymn in this fashion, *Blessed are you, Lord, God of our ancestors, to be praised and highly exalted forever; and blessed is the holy name of your glory, to be highly praised and highly exalted forever* (v. 52). They are the words of a love that is most ardent and inexhaustible; stricken with it, they search for terms capable of conveying the dignity of the one to be praised, and not finding them they invent them by forming compounds, speaking of God in terms of *to be highly praised and highly exalted*— and not only him but also a term for his glory. Now, they do well

---

[90] Theodoret does not note any inconsistency between the mention of the death of those who threw the heroes into the fire in v. 22 and their still stoking the fire here (a fact that suggests to some modern commentators that the prose vv. 46–51 are a later insertion—though the king later knows of the angel they record).

[91] Vv. 17–18.

χοῦ «Κύριον καὶ Θεὸν τῶν πατέρων» ἀποκαλοῦσι, σφᾶς αὐτοὺς ἀναξίους εἶναι ταυτησὶ τῆς προσηγορίας ὁμολογοῦντες.

νγ'. «Εὐλογημένος εἶ ἐν τῷ ναῷ τῆς ἁγίας δόξης σου, καὶ ὑπεραινετός, καὶ ὑπερένδοξος εἰς τοὺς αἰῶνας.» Ἄληστον ἔχουσι τοῦ θείου νεὼ τὴν μνήμην, καὶ ἀκριβεῖς ὄντες τοῦ νόμου φύλακες, ἐννόμως προσεύχονται· ἀντὶ τοῦ· Εἰς ἐκεῖνον ἀποβλέποντες τὸν νεώ, ἔνθα σου ἡ δόξα ἐπιφαίνεσθαι εἰώθει, τοῦτόν σοι τὸν ὕμνον προσφέρομεν· εἰ γὰρ καὶ μυριάκις ἐμπέπρησται, τῆς σῆς ἁγιωσύνης μετέχει. Καὶ ἵνα μή τις ὑπολάβῃ περιγράφειν αὐτοὺς τόπῳ τὸν ἀσώματόν τε καὶ ἀπεριόριστον Θεόν, ἀναγκαίως ἐπάγουσιν·

νδ'. «Εὐλογητὸς εἶ ἐπὶ θρόνου τῆς βασιλείας σου, καὶ ὑπερυψούμενος εἰς τοὺς αἰῶνας.» Εἶτα δεικνύντες τίνα θρόνον καλοῦσιν, εὐθὺς ἐπιφέρουσιν·

νε'. «Εὐλογητὸς εἶ, ὁ βλέπων ἀβύσσους, καθήμενος ἐπὶ Χερουβὶμ, καὶ ὑπερύμνητος, καὶ ὑπερυψούμενος εἰς τοὺς αἰῶνας.» Καὶ ἐπειδὴ καὶ ὁ νεὼς ἐκεῖνος εἶχε τῶν Χερουβὶμ τὰς εἰκόνας ἐν τοῖς ἁγίοις τῶν ἁγίων, ὡς ἂν μηδεμία τοῖς ἀκούουσιν ἐντεῦθεν γένηται βλάβη, καὶ περιγεγράφθαι νομίσωσι τὸν Θεόν, θεραπεύουσι τὸν ἀκροατὴν, λέγοντες·

νϛ'. «Εὐλογητὸς εἶ ἐν τῷ στερεώματι τοῦ οὐρανοῦ, καὶ ὑπερύμνητος, καὶ ὑπερυψούμενος εἰς τοὺς αἰῶνας.» Πανταχοῦ γὰρ, φασίν, εἶ, καὶ τὰ σύμπαντα πληροῖς, καὶ πᾶσαν περιέχεις τὴν κτίσιν. Οὕτως ὑμνήσαντες καλοῦσιν ἅπασαν τὴν γενητὴν φύσιν εἰς κοινωνίαν τῆς ὑμνῳδίας, οὐ μόνον τὴν λογικὴν, ἀλλὰ καὶ τὴν ἄλογόν τε καὶ ἄψυχον.

νζ'. «Εὐλογεῖτε γὰρ, φασί, πάντα τὰ ἔργα Κυρίου, τὸν Κύριον, ὑμνεῖτε καὶ ὑπερυψοῦτε αὐτὸν εἰς πάντας τοὺς αἰῶνας.» Καὶ οὐκ ἀνέχονται τῆς κοινῆς κλήσεως μόνης, ἀλλὰ καὶ ἰδίᾳ ἕκαστον συγκαλοῦσιν, καὶ οὐ μόνον τὰ ὁρώμενα, ἀλλὰ καὶ τὴν ἀόρατον φύσιν. |

1337

νη'. «Εὐλογεῖτε γὰρ, φασίν, ἄγγελοι Κυρίου, τὸν Κύριον· ὑμνεῖτε καὶ ὑπερυψοῦτε αὐτὸν εἰς τοὺς αἰῶνας.» Καὶ ἵνα μὴ, καθ' ἕκαστον ἑρμηνεύων, εἰς μῆκος ἄπειρον ἐκτείνω τὸν λόγον, καλοῦσιν εἰς τὴν χορείαν, καὶ οὐρανόν, καὶ τὰ ὕδατα τὰ ὑπεράνω τῶν οὐρανῶν, καὶ τὰς δυνάμεις τὰς τὸν θεῖον θρόνον περιπολούσας. Καλοῦσι δὲ καὶ ἥλιον, καὶ σελήνην, καὶ τοὺς ἄλλους φωστῆρας· καὶ οὐ μόνον τὰ κατ' οὐρανόν, ἀλλὰ καὶ τὰ ἐν τῷ ἀέρι γινόμενα, ὄμβρον καὶ δρόσον, καὶ πνεύματα· εἶτα τὰς ἐναντίας ποιότητας, ψῦχος καὶ καῦμα· εἶτα φύσιν ὁμοῦ καὶ ἐνέργειαν, πῦρ καὶ καῦμα· τὸ μὲν γὰρ πῦρ φύσεως ὄνομα, τὸ δὲ καῦμα οὐκέτι οὐσία, ἀλλὰ πυρὸς ἐνέργεια. Καλοῦσι δὲ καὶ δρόσον, καὶ νιφετόν, καὶ πάγον, καὶ ψύχος, καὶ πάχνας, καὶ χιόνας, καὶ ἀστραπάς, καὶ νεφέλας, τὰ συγγενῆ καὶ ὁμόφυλα. Εἶτα νύκτας καὶ ἡμέρας, καὶ τὰ τούτων ποιητικά,

constantly to invoke *Lord and God of the ancestors*, admitting that they themselves are unworthy of this title.

Blessed are you in the temple of your holy glory, highly to be praised and highly glorious forever (v. 53). They hold an indelible memory of the divine temple, and being scrupulous observers of the law they pray according to the law in the sense, With eyes fixed on that temple where your glory is accustomed to manifest itself, we offer this hymn of praise: even if set on fire countless times, it shares in your holiness. And lest someone form the idea that they confined the incorporeal and uncircumscribed God in a place, they necessarily go on to say, *Blessed are you on the throne of your kingdom, highly to be exalted forever* (v. 54). Then to show what throne they refer to, they immediately add, *Blessed are you who gaze into depths, seated on the cherubim, highly to be praised and highly to be exalted forever* (v. 55). And since that temple had images of the cherubim in the holy of holies, lest any harm come to the listeners at this point and they think God is circumscribed, they offer assistance to the listener by saying, *Blessed are you in the firmament of heaven, highly to be praised and highly to be exalted forever* (v. 56): you are everywhere, they are saying, you fill all things, and you encompass all creation.

Having thus sung praise, they call all created nature to a share in hymn-singing, not only the rational but also the irrational and inanimate. *Bless the Lord, all you works of the Lord, sing praise and highly exalt him forever* (v. 57). They refrain from giving only a common summons, instead inviting each individually, not only visible things but also invisible nature. | *Bless the Lord, you angels of the Lord, sing praise and highly exalt him forever* (v. 58). To avoid protracting this treatment to unlimited length by commenting on each verse, they summon to the choir heaven, the waters above the heavens and the powers encircling the divine throne. They also summon sun and moon and the other lights; and not only things in heaven but also those in the sky: cloud and dew and winds; then the diverse qualities, cold and heat; then its nature and effect together, fire and heat, since *fire* is the term for a nature whereas *heat* is not a substance but the effect of fire. They summon also dew, snowstorm, ice, cold, frost, snowfall, lightning flashes, clouds, and things of that kind and nature. Then nights and days, and what they produce, light and darkness, some being names, others events: "God called the light day, and the dark

1337

φῶς καὶ σκότος· τὰ μὲν γὰρ ὀνόματα, τὰ δὲ πράγματα· «Ἐκάλεσε γὰρ, φησίν, ὁ Θεὸς τὸ φῶς ἡμέραν, καὶ τὸ σκότος ἐκάλεσε νύκτα.» Εἰ γὰρ καὶ σκιὰ τὸ σκότος ἐστί, καὶ οὐκ οὐσία, ἀλλὰ πρᾶγμά ἐστι συμβεβηκός, καὶ τῆς νυκτὸς ποιητικόν. Καὶ ἐπειδὴ δρόσου καὶ νιφετοῦ ἐμνημόνευσαν, ἀναγκαίως δεικνύουσι καὶ τὰς τούτων πηγάς· «Εὐλογεῖτε γὰρ, ἔλεγον, ἀστραπαὶ καὶ νεφέλαι·» αἱ μὲν τίκτουσαι, αἱ δὲ τὰς ὠδῖνας προμηνύουσαι. «Ἀστραπὰς γὰρ, φησὶν ὁ προφήτης, εἰς ὑετὸν ἐποίησεν.» Οὕτω μνημονεύσαντες τῶν κατ' οὐρανὸν καὶ ἀέρα, καὶ ἑκάστῳ ὑμνεῖν παρακελευσάμενοι, ἐπὶ τὴν κοινὴν μητέρα τὴν γῆν τοῦ ὕμνου μεταφέρουσι τὴν παρακέλευσιν, καί φασιν·

οδ'. «Εὐλογείτω ἡ γῆ τὸν Κύριον, ὑμνείτω καὶ ὑπερυψούτω αὐτὸν εἰς τοὺς αἰῶνας.» Εἶτα κατὰ διαίρεσιν·

οε'. «Εὐλογεῖτε, ὄρη καὶ βουνοί, τὸν Κύριον.» Ἔπειτα τὰς ταύτης ὠδῖνας·

ος'. «Εὐλογεῖτε, πάντα τὰ φυόμενα ἐν τῇ γῇ, τὸν Κύριον.» Εἶτα τὴν ἀρδείαν ἧς δέονται· «Εὐλογεῖτε, αἱ πηγαί, τὸν Κύριον.» Καὶ ἐπειδὴ τῆς κάτω μοίρας ἐστὶ καὶ ἡ θάλασσα, καὶ οἱ ποταμοί, ἀναγκαίως καὶ τούτων ἐποιήσαντο τὴν μνήμην· μνημονεύουσι δὲ καὶ τῶν τῆς θαλάττης τροφίμων.

οθ'. «Εὐλογεῖτε γὰρ, φησί, κήτη, καὶ πάντα τὰ κινούμενα ἐν τοῖς ὕδασι, τὸν Κύριον.» Μετὰ ταῦτα τὰ πετεινὰ καλοῦσι, καὶ τὰ θηρία, καὶ τὰ κτήνη, καὶ ἔσχατον ἁπάντων τῶν ἀνθρώπων τὴν φύσιν, τῆς κοσμογονίας τὴν τάξιν φυλάξαντες. Καὶ γὰρ ὁ μακάριος Μωσῆς, πρῶτα μὲν φῦναι τῷ θείῳ λόγῳ τὰ δένδρα συνέγραψεν, εἶτα τῶν νηκτῶν παραχθῆναι τὰ γένη, καὶ πρὸς τούτοις καὶ σὺν τούτοις τῶν ἀεροπόρων ὀρνίθων τὴν φύσιν, μετὰ δὲ ταῦτα θηρία καὶ κτήνη, τελευταῖον δὲ τὸν ἄνθρωπον. Καλέσαντες δὲ τῶν ἀνθρώπων τὴν φύσιν εἰς ὑμνῳδίαν, πάλιν κατὰ
| διαίρεσιν ὑμνεῖν παρεγγυῶσι τὸν Ποιητήν· καὶ πρώτους μὲν τῶν ἄλλων ἁπάντων τοὺς υἱοὺς Ἰσραὴλ τοῦτο ποιεῖν παρακελεύονται· καὶ τούτους δὲ πολλαχῶς διαιροῦσι, καὶ τάττουσι πρώτους τοὺς ἱερεῖς, ἅτε δὴ τὴν θείαν λειτουργίαν πεπιστευμένους. Εἶτα, ἵνα μὴ νομισθῶσι μόνοις τοῖς ἱερεῦσι περιγράφειν τὴν ὑμνῳδίαν, ἐπάγουσιν·

πε'. «Εὐλογεῖτε, δοῦλοι Κυρίου, τὸν Κύριον, ὑμνεῖτε καὶ ὑπερυψοῦτε εἰς πάντας τοὺς αἰῶνας·» μονονουχὶ λέγοντες, ὅτι δυνατὸν εὐνοϊκῶς δουλεύειν τῷ Δεσπότῃ καὶ τὸν ἱερωσύνης γεγυμνωμένον. Προκηρύττουσι καὶ τὴν ἀνάστασιν·

πς'. «Εὐλογεῖτε γὰρ, φασί, πνεύματα καὶ ψυχαὶ δικαίων, τὸν Κύριον·» τουτέστιν, αἱ πνευματικαὶ τῶν δικαίων ψυχαί, αἱ τῶν ἀνθρωπίνων παθῶν ὑπέρτεραι γενόμεναι, αἱ τοῦ Πνεύματος τὴν χάριν ὑποδεξάμεναι.

he called night,"[92] remember; you see, even if darkness is shadow and not substance, it is an event that happens, and produces night. And since they mentioned dew and snowstorm, they necessarily bring out also their source: *Bless, lightnings and clouds* (v. 73), some giving birth, others foretelling the birth; the inspired author says, remember, "He made lightnings for rain."[93]

Having thus made mention of the things in heaven and in the sky, and bidden each to sing praise, they transfer the invitation to praise to mother earth, saying, *Let the earth bless the Lord, sing praise and highly exalt him forever* (v. 74). Then individually, *Bless the Lord, mountains and hills* (v. 75). Then what it gives birth to, *Bless the Lord, all that grows in the ground* (v. 76). Then the watering it needs, *Bless the Lord, you springs* (v. 78). And since the sea and the rivers are from the lower part, they necessarily made mention of these as well; and they mention also what are nourished in the sea, *Bless the Lord, you sea monsters and all that move in the waters* (v. 79). After that they summon the birds, the wild beasts, the cattle, and last of all the human race, keeping the order of the creation of the world. Blessed Moses, remember, recorded first the emergence by the divine word of the trees, the production of the species that swim, and in addition to those and with those the classes of flying birds, and after them wild beasts and cattle, and finally the human being.

Now, in summoning human nature to hymn-singing, once again | they urge them individually to sing the praises of the cre- 1340 ator: first of all they bid the children of Israel do it, dividing them in many ways, putting the priests first as being entrusted with divine worship. Then, in case they be thought to confine the hymn-singing to the priests alone, they continue, *Bless the Lord, you servants of the Lord, praise and highly exalt him forever* (v. 85), as if to say that it is possible to serve the Lord devotedly even for the person who does not boast of priesthood. They also proclaim ahead of time the resurrection: *Bless the Lord, spirits and souls of the righteous* (v. 86), that is, the spiritual souls of the righteous, those who proved superior to human passions and have received the grace of the Spirit. Next also those possessing some forms of virtue: *Bless the Lord, all you who are holy and humble in heart* (v.

[92] Gen 1:5.
[93] Ps 135:7.

Ἔπειτα καὶ τοὺς ἀρετῆς εἴδη τινὰ κεκτημένους·

πζ'. «Εὐλογεῖτε, φασίν, ὅσιοι καὶ ταπεινοὶ τῇ καρδίᾳ, τὸν Κύριον.» Δυνατὸν γὰρ, φασίν, ἀδικίας ἀπηλλαγμένους, καὶ ταπεινῷ φρονήματι κεχρημένους, καὶ ἀρέσκειν Θεῷ καὶ τὸν ἁρμόττοντα ὕμνον προσφέρειν. Ταῦτα δὲ οὐκ ἀδολεσχίᾳ χρώμενοι κατέλεξαν ἅπαντα, ἀλλὰ πρῶτον μὲν τὸ περὶ τὸν Δεσπότην πυρσεύοντες φίλτρον, καὶ σφᾶς αὐτοὺς ἀναμιμνήσκοντες τῶν ἀρρήτων εὐεργεσιῶν, καὶ τῆς τῶν ἀνθρώπων ἔνεκεν ἐξ ἀρχῆς γενομένης δημιουργίας· διὰ γὰρ τούτων μηνύουσι τῶν λόγων, ὅτι Ὑμνοῦμέν σε καὶ ὑπερυψοῦμεν, ὅτι δι' ἀγγέλων ἡμᾶς εὐεργετεῖς, ὅτι οὐρανὸν ἡμῶν χάριν ἐδημιούργησας, ἡλίῳ δὲ τὴν ἡμέραν φωτίζεις, καὶ τῇ σελήνῃ τῆς νυκτὸς κεραννύεις τὸ ἀφεγγές, καὶ τοῦ χρόνου ἡμᾶς τὰ μέτρα διδάσκεις· ὑμνοῦμέν σε, ὅτι καὶ λειμῶνα ἡμῖν ἀστέρων βλαστῆσαι τὸν οὐρανὸν παρεσκεύασας, καὶ ἄνθεσιν ἀμαράντοις ἑστιᾷς ἡμῶν τὰς ὄψεις, καὶ τῆς νυκτὸς ἡμῖν διὰ τοῦ δρόμου τούτων παρέχεις τὰ μέτρα γινώσκειν. Καὶ τίς ἄν σε πρὸς ἀξίαν ὑμνήσειεν, ὁρῶν τῶν ὡρῶν τὰς μεταβολάς, τῶν τροπῶν τὰς ἀλλαγάς, καῦμα προσφόρως ἐν θέρει γινόμενον; εἶτα πνευμάτων αὔρας ἀναψυχούσας, ψῦχος ἐν χειμῶνι καὶ ὑετὸν ἐπιφερόμενον, καὶ ἕκαστον ῥυθμῷ καὶ τάξει προβαῖνον, ἀστραπὰς τὸν ὑετὸν μηνυούσας, νεφέλας τὸν ὑετὸν ὠδινούσας, ὄρη καὶ πεδία ληΐοις κομῶντα, καὶ ἄλσεσι, πηγὰς ὑπαναβλυζούσας, καὶ ἀρδείαν τοῖς φυτοῖς προσφερούσας, ποταμοὺς ἄπαυστα τρέχοντας, καὶ τοῦ δρόμου παῦλαν οὐ δεχομένους, θάλατταν ἐν μέσῳ κειμένην, φιλίας καὶ ὁμονοίας αἰτίαν, καὶ χωρίον κοινὸν τούτων κἀκείνων δεχόμενον τὰ συμβόλαια; Καὶ ἵνα μὴ καθ' ἕκαστον λέγω, πρῶτον μὲν τούτων ἁπάντων ἐμνημόνευσαν οἱ μακάριοι, τὴν οἰκείαν ἐπιδεικνύντες εὐγνωμοσύνην, καὶ θερμότερον ἐπιτελέσαι τὸν ὕμνον τῇ μνήμῃ τῶν εὐεργεσιῶν βουλόμενοι· ἔπειτα δέ, καὶ
1341 τοὺς Χαλδαίους | ἔξωθεν ὑπακούοντας παιδεῦσαι πειρώμενοι, ὅτι τὰ ὑπ' αὐτῶν προσκυνούμενα στοιχεῖα τοῦ Θεοῦ τῶν ὅλων [ἐστὶ] ποιήματα. Διὰ τοῦτο καὶ πυρὸς καὶ ὑδάτων. ἡλίου τε καὶ σελήνης, οὐρανοῦ τε καὶ γῆς ἐναργῶς μνημονεύουσι, πεῖσαι βουλόμενοι τοὺς ἀνοήτους, παύσασθαι μὲν τοῦ προσκυνεῖν τὰ ὁρώμενα, τὸν δὲ τούτων Δεσπότην ἐπιγνῶναι, καὶ τὴν πρέπουσαν αὐτῷ θεραπείαν προσενεγκεῖν. Εἰκὸς γὰρ ἦν τὸ μέγα θαῦμα θεωμένους, καὶ τοῦ πυρὸς τὴν ἧτταν ὁρῶντας, καὶ αὐτῶν δὲ καὶ τοῦ βασιλέως αὐτῶν αἰσχύνην, τῶν αἰχμαλώτων δὲ ἐκείνων παίδων τὴν σωτηρίαν τε καὶ παρρησίαν, δέξασθαι διὰ τῆς ὑμνῳδίας τὴν τῆς εὐσεβείας διδασκαλίαν. Οὕτως ὑμνήσαντες τελευταίως ἐπάγουσιν·

πη'. «Εὐλογεῖτε, Ἀνανία, Ἀζαρία, Μισαήλ, τὸν Κύριον, ὑμνεῖτε καὶ ὑπερυψοῦτε αὐτὸν εἰς τοὺς αἰῶνας.» Οὕτως ἑαυτοὺς ἐσχάτους ἡγοῦντο τῆς κτίσεως, καὶ πάντων ἀνθρώπων εὐτελεστάτους. Τοιοῦτος

87): it is possible for those freed from iniquity and exercising a humble attitude to please God and offer a suitable hymn of praise.

Now, far from wasting their time in listing all these, they are firstly enkindled with love for the Lord and remind themselves of his ineffable kindnesses and of creation, which occurred at the beginning for the sake of human beings. By these words, in fact, they declare, We praise and highly exalt you for bringing us kindnesses through angels, for creating heaven for our sake, illuminating the day with the sun and blending the darkness of the night with the moon, and teaching us the periods of time. We praise you for causing the sky to produce stars for us like a meadow, feeding our eyes on unfading blooms, and through their course providing us with knowledge of the stages of the night. Who could adequately sing your praises on seeing the changes of the seasons, the alterations of the solstices, heat offered at the right time in summer, then cooling breaths of wind, cold and rain brought in winter, each proceeding in rhythm and order, lightning announcing the rain, clouds producing the rain, mountains and plains covered in crops and groves, springs bubbling up and providing water for the plants, rivers flowing without ceasing and not coming to an end of their course, the sea positioned between land masses, responsible for friendship and harmony, a shared place for commerce between two parties?

Not to cite every detail, the blessed men first mentioned all these things as a demonstration of their gratitude and in their wish to compose a more ardent hymn by listing the benefits. Secondly, it was also an attempt to instruct the astrologers | listening out-   1341
side that the elements adored by them were created by the God of all—hence their explicit mention of fire and water, sun and moon, heaven and earth in their wish to convince the uncomprehending people to cease worshiping visible things, acknowledge their Lord and offer fitting adoration to him. You see, it was likely that on witnessing the great miracle and observing the vanquishing of the fire, the shaming of them and the king, and the preservation and forthrightness of those young captives, they would accept the instruction in godliness given in the hymn-singing.

After such a song of praise, they went on in conclusion, *Bless the Lord, Hananiah, Azariah, and Mishael, praise and highly exalt him forever* (v. 88). They thus considered themselves the least of creation and the most insignificant of all people. Blessed Paul

ἦν καὶ ὁ μακάριος Παῦλος, λέγων· «Ἐμοὶ τῷ ἐλαχιστοτέρῳ πάντων ἁγίων ἐδόθη ἡ χάρις αὕτη.» Καὶ ἀλλαχοῦ· «Χριστός, φησίν, ἦλθεν εἰς τὸν κόσμον ἁμαρτωλοὺς σῶσαι, ὧν πρῶτός εἰμι ἐγώ.» Καὶ τῶν μὲν ἁμαρτωλῶν πρῶτον ἑαυτὸν ὀνομάζει, τῶν δὲ ἁγίων ἔσχατον ἀποκαλεῖ· οὕτω καὶ οἱ μακάριοι οὗτοι ἐσχάτους ἑαυτοὺς παρακελεύονται ὑμνεῖν τὸν Κύριον, καὶ ὑπερυψοῦν αὐτὸν εἰς τοὺς αἰῶνας. Εἶτα διηγοῦνται τὸ θαῦμα· «Ὅτι ἐρρύσατο ἡμᾶς ἐξ ᾅδου, καὶ ἔσωσεν ἡμᾶς ἐκ χειρὸς θανάτου.» Ἀνθρωπίναις γὰρ ἀπηγορεύθημεν ψήφοις.

«Καὶ ἐρρύσατο ἡμᾶς ἐκ μέσου καιομένης φλογός· καὶ ἐκ μέσου πυρὸς ἐρρύσατο ἡμᾶς. (πθ'.) Ἐξομολογεῖσθε τοίνυν τῷ Κυρίῳ, ὅτι χρηστός, ὅτι εἰς τὸν αἰῶνα τὸ ἔλεος αὐτοῦ.» Τί γὰρ χρηστότερον, τί δὲ ἀγαθώτερον τοῦ τοσούτῳ ἐν τοῖς καθ' ἡμᾶς χρησαμένου ἐλέῳ; Καὶ τοσαύτην ἀρετὴν ἐπιδειξάμενοι, ἐλέῳ φασὶ τῆς σωτηρίας τετυχηκέναι. Εἶτα ἐπειδὴ μόνων τῶν υἱῶν Ἰσραὴλ ἐμνημόνευσαν ἄνω, καλοῦσι καὶ τοὺς ἐν τοῖς ἔθνεσιν εὐσεβοῦντας, καὶ τὸν Θεὸν θεραπεύειν ἐσπουδακότας.

ζ'. «Εὐλογεῖτε, πάντες οἱ σεβόμενοι τὸν Κύριον, τὸν Θεὸν τῶν θεῶν, ὑμνεῖτε καὶ ἐξομολογεῖσθε, ὅτι εἰς πάντας τοὺς αἰῶνας τὸ ἔλεος αὐτοῦ, καὶ εἰς τὸν αἰῶνα τῶν αἰώνων.» Καὶ τὸ ἄπειρον αὐτοῦ τῆς ἀγαθότητος δεῖξαι φιλονεικοῦντες, καὶ ἡττώμενοι, πολλάκις τὸ τῶν αἰώνων ἀναστρέφουσιν ὄνομα. Τοιοῦτος τῶν ἁγίων τούτων ὁ ὕμνος οὗτος καὶ τὸν θηριώδη καὶ ἀπηνῆ βασιλέα ἐκπλήξας, τῶν μὲν βασιλικῶν ἐξανέστησε θρόνων, δραμεῖν δὲ παρ' αὐτοὺς παρεσκεύασε, καὶ θεωρεῖ τέτταρας ἀντὶ τριῶν ἐν τῇ καμίνῳ χορεύοντας. |

«Καὶ λέγει τοῖς μεγιστᾶσιν αὐτοῦ· Οὐχὶ ἄνδρας τρεῖς ἐβάλομεν εἰς μέσον τοῦ πυρὸς πεπεδημένους; (ζβ'.) Καὶ ἰδοὺ ἐγὼ θεωρῶ ἄνδρας τέσσαρας λελυμένους, καὶ περιπατοῦντας ἐν μέσῳ τοῦ πυρός, καὶ διαφθορὰ οὐκ ἔστιν ἐν αὐτοῖς, καὶ ἡ ὅρασις τοῦ τετάρτου ὁμοία υἱῷ Θεοῦ.» Ὦ τῆς ἀρρήτου μακροθυμίας! Εἰκότως ἐβόων οἱ ἅγιοι παῖδες· «Ὅτι εἰς πάντας τοὺς αἰῶνας τὸ ἔλεος αὐτοῦ, καὶ εἰς τὸν αἰῶνα τῶν αἰώνων.» Ἰδοὺ γὰρ καὶ τοῦτον ὠμότητι τοσαύτῃ καὶ τύφῳ χρησάμενον, καὶ τὸ θεῖον σέβας ἁρπάσαι καὶ τοὺς θείους θεράποντας ὠμῶς καὶ θηριωδῶς κολάσαι πειραθέντα, πρὸς τὴν εὐσέβειαν ποδηγεῖ, καὶ τὴν οἰκείαν αὐτῷ θαυματουργίαν ὑποδείκνυσι, καὶ τὸν ἀποσταλέντα εἰς ἐπικουρίαν τῶν ἁγίων ἄγγελον ἐμφανῆ αὐτῷ ποιεῖ. Καὶ ἐκπλήττει μὲν αὐτόν, πρῶτον τῷ ἀριθμῷ, ἀντὶ τριῶν τέσσαρας ὑποδείξας· ἔπειτα τῇ λύσει τῶν δεσμῶν· λελυμένους γὰρ ἀντὶ δεδεμένων ἑώρα· ἔπειτα τῇ σωτηρίᾳ· «Διαφθορὰ

was also like that in saying, "To me, the least of all the saints, this grace was given," and elsewhere, "Christ came into the world to save sinners, of whom I am the foremost."[94] He names himself as the first of sinners, and he calls himself the least of the saints; likewise these blessed people invite themselves last to sing the Lord's praises and highly exalt him forever. Then they describe the marvel, *Because he rescued us from Hades and saved us from the hand of death*: we had despaired of any human intervention. *He rescued us from the midst of the blazing flame, and from the midst of the fire he rescued us. So confess to the Lord that he is good, that his mercy is forever* (vv. 88–89). After all, what could be better, what kinder than the one exercising such mercy in our predicament? In an expression of such wonderful virtue they admit that it was through mercy that they attained salvation. Next, since they had mentioned above only the children of Israel, they invite also godly people among the nations zealous in serving God. *Bless the God of gods, all you who reverence the Lord, praise and confess that his mercy is forever and ever and ever* (v. 90). In their efforts to bring out his unlimited goodness, which proved fruitless, they many times repeat the word *forever*.

This hymn of these holy people, being of this nature, astonished the cruel and harsh king: he rose from the royal throne, ran to them, and observed four instead of three moving to and fro in the furnace. | *He said to his noblemen, Did we not throw three men bound into the fire? Lo, I discern four men unbound walking about in the midst of the fire, no harm having come to them, and the fourth has the appearance of a son of God* (vv. 91–92). What indescribable 1344 longsuffering! The three young people were right to cry aloud, *His mercy is forever and ever and ever.* Even this man, guilty of such awful cruelty and conceit, attempting to arrogate to himself divine reverence and punish cruelly and savagely the divine servants, it brings to godliness, gives him a glimpse of characteristic wonderworking, and allows him a vision of an angel sent to the assistance of the holy ones. It also astonishes him, first by the number, giving a glimpse of four instead of three, then by the loosing of bonds (he saw them to be unbound instead of bound), then by the preserva-

---

94 Eph 3:8; 1 Tim 1:15. Theodoret does not take occasion from the use of the singers' Hebrew names at this point and their inviting themselves to sing after having done so at length to detect a further indication of the long hymn's being inserted; but he does sense an irregularity.

γὰρ, φησίν, οὐκ ἔστιν ἐν αὐτοῖς.» Ὅθεν ἐκπλαγείς, καὶ καταλύσας τὸν τῦφον, προσέρχεται·

λγ′. «Καί φησι· Σιδράχ, Μισάχ, καὶ Ἀβδεναγώ, οἱ δοῦλοι τοῦ Θεοῦ τοῦ ὑψίστου, ἐξέλθετε καὶ δεῦτε. Καὶ ἐξῆλθον Σιδράχ, Μισάχ καὶ Ἀβδεναγὼ ἐκ μέσου τοῦ πυρός.» Μεμάθηκεν ὁ μάταιος, ὁ λέγων· «Τίς ἐστι Θεός, ὃς ῥύσεται ὑμᾶς ἐκ τῶν χειρῶν μου;» ὅτι ἔστι Θεὸς ἄρρητον ἔχων δύναμιν, τῷ πυρὶ κελεύων ἐναντίαν ἐπιδείξασθαι τοῖς ἁγίοις ποιότητα. Ὃν γὰρ Θεὸν ἐκεῖνος οὐκ ἐνόμιζεν, ἔγνω ὅτι ἔστι Θεός, καὶ ὕψιστος Θεός. Ἐξελθόντων δὲ τῶν ἁγίων, θαυμάζουσι μὲν ἅπαντες σατράπαι, καὶ τοπάρχαι, καὶ στρατηγοί, θεωροῦντες ἀκήρατα διατηρηθέντα τῶν ἁγίων τὰ σώματα, καὶ τὰς τρίχας αὐτὰς οὐδεμίαν αἴσθησιν ἐκ τῆς φλογὸς δεξαμένας ἐκείνης· οὐ τὰς τρίχας δὲ μόνον, ἀλλὰ καὶ αὐτὴν τὴν ἐσθῆτα, καὶ τὰ ὑποδήματα ἀκέραια μείναντα, ὡς καὶ αὐτῆς ἀπηλλάχθαι τῆς ἀπὸ τοῦ πυρὸς ὀσμῆς. Εἶτα ὑμνεῖ ταῦτα θεασάμενος ὁ Ναβουχοδονόσορ, καὶ λέγει·

λε′. «Εὐλογητὸς ὁ Θεὸς τοῦ Σιδράχ, Μισάχ, καὶ Ἀβδεναγώ, ὃς ἀπέστειλε τὸν ἄγγελον αὐτοῦ, καὶ ἐρρύσατο τοὺς παῖδας αὐτοῦ, ὅτι ἐπεποίθεισαν ἐπ᾽ αὐτῷ, καὶ τὸ ῥῆμα τοῦ βασιλέως ἠλλοίωσαν, καὶ παρέδωκαν τὰ σώματα αὐτῶν, ὅπως μὴ λατρεύσωσι, μηδὲ προσκυνήσωσι παντὶ θεῷ ἑτέρῳ, ἀλλὰ τῷ Θεῷ αὐτῶν.» Ἀεὶ τῇ πείρᾳ παραλαμβάνων ὁ μάταιος τοῦ Θεοῦ τὴν δύναμιν, λήθῃ τὰ θαύματα παραδίδωσι. Τοῦτο καὶ ἐπὶ τοῦ θειοτάτου πεποίηκε Δανιήλ· ἀναστὰς γὰρ προσεκύνησεν αὐτῷ, καὶ μαναὰ καὶ εὐωδίαν προσενεχθῆναι αὐτῷ παρενεγγύησε. Καὶ νῦν δὲ ὡσαύτως θεασάμενος τῶν ἁγίων τούτων τὴν σωτηρίαν, ὑμνεῖ τὸν Θεόν, καὶ θαυμάζει τοὺς ἄνδρας, ὅτι ἠλλοίωσαν τὸ ῥῆμα τοῦ βασιλέως, καὶ προετίμησαν, φησίν, εὐσεβῆ θάνατον παρανόμου ζωῆς. |

λϛ′. «Καὶ νῦν, φησίν, ἰδοὺ ἐγὼ ἐκτίθημι δόγματα, ὅπως πᾶς λαός, φυλή, γλῶσσα, ἣ ἂν εἴπῃ βλασφημίαν κατὰ τοῦ Θεοῦ Σιδράχ, Μισάχ, καὶ Ἀβδεναγώ, εἰς ἀπώλειαν ἔσονται, καὶ οἱ οἶκοι αὐτῶν διαρπαγήσονται, καθότι οὐκ ἔστι Θεὸς ἕτερος, ὃς δυνήσεται ῥύσασθαι οὕτως.» Καὶ τῷ ὄντι τῇ πείρᾳ τοῦτο μεμάθηκεν· πολλῶν γὰρ καλουμένων θεῶν τὰ τεμένη καταλύσας, καὶ τὰ ταμεῖα συλήσας, βωμοὺς ἀνασπάσας, καὶ τοὺς ἱερωμένους αὐτῶν κατασφάξας, οὐδεμιᾶς θείας εὐεργεσίας ἐδέξατο πεῖραν· κατὰ δὲ τῶν τῷ Θεῷ ἀνακειμένων τῇ λύττῃ χρησάμενος, εἶδε τοῦ Θεοῦ καὶ τὴν ἄπειρον δύναμιν, καὶ τὴν μακροθυμίαν τὴν ἄρρητον· τοὺς

tion (*no harm having come to them*, he says).

Thus astonished and relieved of his conceit, he came near. *He said, Shadrach, Meshach, and Abednego, servants of God the Most High, come out and approach me. Shadrach, Meshach, and Abednego came out of the midst of the fire* (v. 93), The vain person who had said, *Who is the God who will rescue you from my hands?* had learned that he is the God who has unspeakable power, bidding the fire demonstrate to the holy ones an opposite quality; he knew that the one he did not believe to be God is God and Most High God.[95] Now, when the holy ones emerged, everyone— satraps, local officials and generals—were amazed to see the bodies of the holy ones preserved intact, not even their hair experiencing any harm from that awful flame. Not only their hair, but even their clothing and footwear remained untouched so as to be free of any smell of fire. Then, on perceiving this, Nebuchadnezzar sings praise in the words, *Blessed be the God of Shadrach, Meshach, and Abednego, who sent his angel and rescued his young people because they trusted in him, resisted the king's command, and surrendered their bodies to prevent their worshiping and bowing down to any other god than their God* (v. 95).

Despite his constant experience of God's power, that vain man consigned the miracles to oblivion. He had done the same thing in the case of the most divine Daniel as well, having risen, worshiped him, and ordered a grain offering and incense to be offered him. In this case, too, on perceiving the preservation of these holy ones, he sang God's praises and marveled at the men for resisting his command and preferring a pious death to a lawless life. | *And now, behold, I issue decrees: if any people, tribe,* 1345 *or language blasphemes against the God of Shadrah, Meshach, and Abednego, they will meet with destruction and their houses will be despoiled, because there is no other god who will succeed in rescuing them* (v. 96). He had learned this from actual experience: having destroyed the shrines of many so-called gods, plundered the precincts, overturned altars, and slain those consecrated to them, he had no experience of divine beneficence; but after venting his spleen against those dedicated to God, he saw both the unlimited

---

[95] Has the king been converted? Theodoret suggests as much, whereas modern commentators point out that the term Most High God (Hebrew *El Elyon*) is used by non-Israelites such as Melchizedek (Gen 14:19–20), Balaam (Num 24:16), and the king of Babylon (Isa 14:14).

μὲν γὰρ οἰκείους θεράποντας ἀκραιφνεῖς διεφύλαξεν, αὐτὸν δὲ τέως δίκας
τῆς μανίας οὐκ εἰσεπράξατο, ἐπιμείναντα δὲ τῇ δυσσεβείᾳ μετὰ βραχὺ
μετρίως ἐκόλασεν, εἶτα μετανοίᾳ χρησάμενον φιλανθρωπίας ἠξίωσεν.

ζ'. «Τότε δὲ ὅμως κατεύθυνε, φησίν, ὁ βασιλεὺς τὸν Σιδράχ,
Μισάχ, καὶ Ἀβδεναγώ, ἐν τῇ χώρᾳ Βαβυλῶνος, καὶ ηὔξησεν αὐτούς,
καὶ ἠξίωσεν αὐτοὺς ἡγεῖσθαι πάντων τῶν Ἰουδαίων τῶν ἐν τῇ βασιλείᾳ
αὐτοῦ.» Τοσαύτην ὁ Δεσπότης τῶν θεραπεύειν αὐτὸν ἐσπουδακότων
ποιεῖται προμήθειαν. Καὶ εἰκότως ἐβόων οἱ ἅγιοι παῖδες οὗτοι, ὅτι «Οὐκ
ἔστιν αἰσχύνη τοῖς πεποιθόσιν ἐπὶ σοί.» Καὶ ἡμεῖς τοίνυν ταύτην κτη-
σώμεθα τὴν ἐλπίδα, πάσης ὁμοῦ προτιμῶντες τῆς κτίσεως τὸν Ποιητήν
τε καὶ Κυβερνήτην· καὶ γενέσθωσαν ἡμῖν οἱ μακάριοι οὗτοι παῖδες ὠφελείας παράδειγμα, εὐσεβείας ἀρχέτυπον, ποδηγοὶ πρὸς Θεόν, καὶ τὰ ὑπὸ
τοῦ Θεοῦ τοῖς ἀξίοις χορηγούμενα· ὧν γένοιτο πάντας ἡμᾶς ἐπιτυχεῖν,
χάριτι καὶ φιλανθρωπίᾳ τοῦ Κυρίου ἡμῶν Ἰησοῦ Χριστοῦ, μεθ' οὗ τῷ
Πατρὶ δόξα, σὺν τῷ ἁγίῳ Πνεύματι, νῦν καὶ ἀεί, καὶ εἰς τοὺς αἰῶνας
τῶν αἰώνων. Ἀμήν.

ΤΟΜΟΣ Δ'

η'. «Ναβουχοδονόσορ ὁ βασιλεὺς πᾶσι τοῖς λαοῖς, φυλαῖς, γλώσσαις, τοῖς οἰκοῦσιν ἐν πάσῃ τῇ γῇ, εἰρήνη ὑμῖν πληθυνθείη.» Προὔργου
νομίζω, πρότερον τὴν ὑπόθεσιν τῆσδε τῆς ἐπιστολῆς καὶ τὴν | αἰτίαν
διεξελθεῖν, εἶθ' οὕτως τὴν ἑρμηνείαν ποιήσασθαι. Ὁ Ναβουχοδονόσορ
τῆς Ἀσίας ἁπάσης κεκρατηκώς, καὶ τὴν Αἴγυπτον δὲ ὑφ' ἑαυτὸν ποιησάμενος, καὶ Αἰθίοπας τοὺς πρὸς Αἴγυπτον χειρωσάμενος, ὠμῶς μὲν
λίαν καὶ ἀπηνῶς ἐχρήσατο τοῖς ὑπηκόοις, εἰς τοσαύτην δὲ ἤλασεν ἀλα-
ζονείαν, ὡς νομίζειν οὐ μόνον τῶν καλουμένων θεῶν, ἀλλὰ καὶ αὐτοῦ
τοῦ ὄντως Θεοῦ μείζων εἶναι καὶ δυνατώτερος. Τοῦτον δὲ αὐτοῦ τὸν
ἀπληστότατον τῦφον, οὐ μόνον ὁ θεσπέσιος διδάσκει Δανιήλ, ἀλλὰ καὶ
ὁ θειότατος Ἡσαΐας ὁ προφήτης, μᾶλλον δὲ αὐτὸς ὁ τῶν ὅλων Θεὸς
διὰ τοῦ προφήτου φθεγγόμενος οὕτως· «Οὐαὶ Ἀσσυρίοις, ἡ ῥάβδος τοῦ
θυμοῦ μου καὶ ὀργῆς μού ἐστιν ἐν ταῖς χερσὶν αὐτῶν· τὴν ὀργήν μου εἰς

1348

power of God and his ineffable longsuffering. After all, he kept his own servants safe, and for the time being did not call him to account for his insane rage—though shortly after he punished him moderately when he persisted in his impiety, and then accorded him lovingkindness when he turned to repentance.

The king nevertheless at that time appointed Shadrach, Meshach, and Abednego to positions in the land of Babylon, heaped honors on them, and granted them control of all the Jews in his kingdom (v. 97). The Lord exercises such providence in favor of those zealous in serving him. These holy young people were right to cry aloud, *No shame comes to those who trust in you.* May we, therefore, practice this hope, putting the creator and governor ahead of all his creation. And may these blessed young people prove an example of benefit, a paradigm of godliness, guides to lead us to God and to what is provided by God to the deserving. May this be the good fortune of us all, thanks to the grace and lovingkindness of our Lord Jesus Christ, to whom with the Father and the Holy Spirit be glory, now and forever, for ages of ages. Amen.

CHAPTER 4

King Nebuchadnezzar to all the peoples, tribes, languages, inhabitants of all the earth: may peace be granted you in abundance (v. 1). I think it worthwhile, firstly, to outline the theme of this letter and its contents, | and then interpret it in the following way.[96]   1348
Nebuchadnezzar was in control of the whole of Asia, had brought Egypt under his control, and had subjugated the Ethiopians living near Egypt. Nevertheless he treated his subjects very harshly and had reached such a state of arrogance as to think that he was greater and more powerful than not only the so-called gods but even the true God himself. This insatiable conceit of his not only the divinely inspired Daniel brings out but also the most divine prophet Isaiah—or, rather, the God of all himself speaking through the prophet in these terms, "Woe to you Assyrians, the rod of my anger and my rage is in their hands. I dispatch my rage against

---

[96] The chapter has structural oddities, beginning as a letter in the first person from the king, changing to third person in v. 19. The story, involving another dream interpreted by Daniel, also has a moral purpose, curbing Nebuchadnezzar's (Antiochus's) overweening pride.

ἔθνος ἄνομον ἀποστελῶ, καὶ ἐν τῷ ἐμῷ λαῷ συντάξω ποιῆσαι σκῦλα καὶ προνομήν, καὶ καταπατεῖν τὰς πόλεις, καὶ θεῖναι αὐτὰς εἰς κονιορτόν.» ῾Ο δὲ λέγει, τοιοῦτόν ἐστι· Θρήνων μέν εἰσιν ἄξιοι ᾿Ασσύριοι, μυρίων ὄντες ἐργάται κακῶν· ἀλλ᾽ ὅμως τούτοις διακόνοις εἰς τὰς κατὰ τῶν ἁμαρτωλῶν χρήσομαι τιμωρίας, καὶ οἷόν τινα ῥάβδον κολαστικὴν τούτους τοῖς παρανομοῦσιν ἐπάξω· οὐ τοῖς ἄλλοις δὲ μόνον ἀνθρώποις, ἀλλὰ καὶ τῷ προσαγορευομένῳ μου λαῷ. ᾿Επάξω δέ, διὰ τὴν πολλὴν αὐτοῦ ἀσέβειαν, καὶ παρανομίαν, καὶ τάς τε πόλεις αὐτῶν διὰ τούτων καθελῶ, καὶ τὰ ἐν ταῖς πόλεσι σκῦλα τούτων γενέσθαι παρασκευάσω. ᾿Εγὼ μὲν οὖν, οἷόν τινι δημίῳ τῷ ᾿Ασσυρίῳ χρώμενος, δίκας δι᾽ αὐτοῦ τοὺς παρανομοῦντας εἰσπράττομαι. «Αὐτὸς δέ, φησίν, οὐχ οὕτως ἐνεθυμήθη, καὶ τῇ ψυχῇ οὐχ οὕτως λελόγισται· ἀλλὰ ἀπαλλάξει ὁ νοῦς αὐτοῦ, καὶ τοῦ ἐξολοθρεῦσαι ἔθνη οὐκ ὀλίγα. Καὶ ἐὰν εἴπωσιν αὐτῷ· Σὺ μόνος εἶ ἄρχων, καὶ ἐρεῖ· Οὐκ ἔλαβον τὴν χώραν τὴν ἐπάνω Βαβυλῶνος, καὶ Χαλάνην, οὗ πύργος ᾠκοδομήθη, καὶ ἔλαβον ᾿Αραβίαν, καὶ Δαμασκόν, καὶ Σαμάρειαν; ῝Ον τρόπον ταύτας, καὶ πάσας τὰς χώρας λήψομαι.» Διὰ τούτων μὲν οὖν τὴν ἀλαζονείαν αὐτοῦ δήλην πεποίηκε. Εἶτα προαγορεύει τὰ καταληψόμενα τὴν ᾿Ιερουσαλὴμ κακά, ὑποδείκνυσι δὲ καὶ τὰς τῆς τιμωρίας αἰτίας· «᾿Ολολύξατε γάρ, φησί, τὰ γλυπτὰ ἐν ᾿Ιερουσαλήμ, καὶ ἐν Σαμαρείᾳ· ὃν τρόπον γὰρ ἐποίησα ἐν Σαμαρείᾳ καὶ τοῖς χειροποιήτοις αὐτῆς, οὕτω ποιήσω καὶ ἐν ᾿Ιερουσαλήμ, καὶ τοῖς εἰδώλοις αὐτῆς.» Μεμαθήκαμεν δέ, ὅτι τῆς ᾿Ιερουσαλὴμ Σενναχηρεὶμ ὁ τῶν ᾿Ασσυρίων οὐ περιεγένετο βασιλεύς, ὁ δὲ Ναβουχοδονόσορ εἰς Βαβυλῶνα τὰ βασίλεια μεταθείς, καὶ βασιλικὴν ἐκείνην ἀποφήνας πόλιν μετὰ τὴν τῆς Νινευῆ κατάλυσιν, ἐπεστράτευσε τῇ ᾿Ιουδαίᾳ, καὶ ἀνάστατον τὴν ᾿Ιερουσαλὴμ πεποιηκώς, τοὺς μὲν πλείστους τῶν οἰκητόρων ἀνεῖλε, τοὺς δὲ λοιποὺς ἐξανδραποδίσας αἰχμαλώτους ἀπήγαγεν· ὡς εἶναι δῆλον κἀντεῦθεν, ὡς 1349 μίαν οἶδεν ἡ θεία Γραφὴ τὴν ᾿Ασσυρίων | καὶ Βαβυλωνίων βασιλείαν· καὶ ἐκ τῶν ἐπαγομένων δὲ τοῦτο ῥάδιόν ἐστι καταμαθεῖν. «῎Εσται γάρ, φησίν, ὅταν συντελέσῃ Κύριος ποιῶν πάντα ἐν τῷ ὄρει Σιὼν καὶ ἐν

a lawless nation, and among my people I will arrange for them to rape and pillage, trample down cities, and reduce them to dust." Now, what he is saying is something like this:[97] Assyrians deserve lamentation, being productive of countless evils; yet I shall use them as ministers to punish sinners, and shall inflict them like a kind of punitive rod on the transgressors—and not only on the other people but also on those called my people. Now, I shall inflict them for its great impiety and lawlessness, destroy their cities through them, and cause the contents of the cities to be plundered. So by using the Assyrian like an executioner, I shall through him call the transgressors to account. "In his case, however," the text goes on, "the intention was not like this, the thoughts of his heart not like this. Instead, his mind feels free to destroy and wipe out not a few nations. If they say to him, You alone are in charge, he will reply, Did I not take the country above Babylon and Calno, where the tower was built? Did I not take Arabia, Damascus, and Samaria? In the way I took them I shall also take all the countries." In this, then, he made clear his arrogance. He then forecasts the troubles about to befall Jerusalem, and gives a glimpse also of the reasons for the retribution: "Bewail the statues in Jerusalem and in Samaria: in the way I treated Samaria and its artifacts, so shall I treat Jerusalem and its idols."

Now, we learned that Sennacherib king of the Assyrians did not prevail over Jerusalem.[98] Nebuchadnezzar transferred the capital to Babylon, made that the royal city after the destruction of Nineveh, invaded Judah, razed Jerusalem, slew most of the inhabitants, took the rest captive and led them off to slavery. So it is clear from this that the divine Scripture treats the Assyrian | 1349 and the Babylonian as the one kingdom, as is easy to discover from the following. "When the Lord has finished doing everything on

[97] To reinforce the story's point, Theodoret quotes the Lord speaking through Isaiah (10:5–16) about the use of (not Babylonians, but) Assyrians to discipline his own people, the first verse being problematic for all commentators, and so calling for a rough summary.

[98] We have seen that Theodoret (with others) does not distinguish clearly between Assyrian and Babylonian Empires. Here he is smoothing over the bloody transition of power from the failing Assyrian Empire (Esarhaddon and Ashurbanipal succeeding Sennacherib) to the Babylonian, first under Nabopolassar from 625, and then from 605 Nebuchadnezzar, who in fact did make Babylon the seat of the empire and attacked Judah three times from 598 to 582 (Theodoret thinking usually of the second invasion of 588).

Ἱερουσαλήμ, ἐπάξει Κύριος ἐπὶ τὸν νοῦν τὸν μέγαν τὸν ἄρχοντα τῶν Ἀσσυρίων, καὶ ἐπὶ τὸ ὕψος τῆς δόξης τῶν ὀφθαλμῶν αὐτοῦ.» Ἐτιμωρήσατο δὲ τὴν Ἱερουσαλὴμ ὁ Θεός, οὐ διὰ τοῦ Σενναχηρείμ, ὃς τῶν Ἀσσυρίων ἐβασίλευσεν, ἀλλὰ διὰ τοῦ Ναβουχοδονόσορ. Ὁ μὲν γὰρ, οὐ μόνον οὐκ ἐπόρθησε τὴν πόλιν, ἀλλὰ καὶ ἅπασαν ἀπολωλεκὼς τὴν στρατείαν, ἀπέδρα μόνος, καὶ οἴκοι τὴν σφαγὴν παρὰ τῶν υἱῶν ἐδέξατο· ὁ δὲ Ναβουχοδονόσορ καὶ τὴν πόλιν καθεῖλε, καὶ ἐνέπρησε τὸν θεῖον νεών, καὶ τὸν λαὸν ἀπήγαγε δορυάλωτον. Διδάσκει τοίνυν ἡμᾶς ἡ θεία Γραφή, ὅτι μετὰ τὸ συντελέσαι Κύριον ποιοῦντα πάντα ἐν τῷ ὄρει Σιὼν καὶ ἐν Ἱερουσαλήμ, ἃ ἠπείλησε λέγων· «Ὀλολύξατε, τὰ γλυπτὰ ἐν Ἱερουσαλήμ· ὃν τρόπον γὰρ ἐποίησα Σαμαρείᾳ καὶ τοῖς εἰδώλοις αὐτῆς, οὕτω ποιήσω καὶ τῇ Ἱερουσαλὴμ καὶ τοῖς χειροποιήτοις αὐτῆς,» ἐπάξει, φησί, Κύριος ἐπὶ τὸν νοῦν τὸν μέγαν, τὸν ἄρχοντα τῶν Ἀσσυρίων. Καὶ οὐ λέγει τῶν Βαβυλωνίων, ἀλλὰ τῶν Ἀσσυρίων· μία γὰρ τούτων κἀκείνων ἡ βασιλεία. Νοῦν δὲ μέγαν καλεῖ διὰ τὸ ὑψηλὸν καὶ ἀλαζονικὸν τῶν βουλευμάτων· διὸ καὶ εἰκότως ἐπάγει· «Καὶ ἐπὶ τὸ ὕψος τῆς δόξης τῶν ὀφθαλμῶν αὐτοῦ.» Καὶ οὐχ ἁπλῶς ἔφη, «τῆς δόξης αὐτοῦ,» ἀλλὰ «τῆς δόξης τῶν ὀφθαλμῶν αὐτοῦ·» τουτέστιν, ὃς ἄνθρωπος ὢν ὑψηλότατός τε καὶ μέγιστος εἶναι φαντάζεται. Εἶπε γάρ· «Ἐν τῇ ἰσχύϊ μου ποιήσω, καὶ ἐν τῇ σοφίᾳ τῆς συνέσεώς μου ἀφελῶ ὅρια ἐθνῶν, καὶ τὴν ἰσχὺν αὐτῶν προνομεύσω, καὶ σείσω πόλεις κατοικουμένας, καὶ τὴν οἰκουμένην ὅλην καταλήψομαι τῇ χειρί μου ὡς νοσσιάν, καὶ ὡς καταλελειμμένα ὠὰ ἀρῶ, καὶ οὐκ ἔσται ὃς διαφεύξηταί με, ἢ ἀντείπῃ μοι» Οὕτω γυμνώσας τῶν λογισμῶν τοῦ Ἀσσυρίου τὸν τῦφον, ἐλέγχει τῶν ἐνθυμημάτων τὸ μάταιον, καὶ διδάσκει, ὡς οὐδὲν ἂν τῶν ὑπ' αὐτοῦ γενομένων ἐγένετο, μὴ τοῦ Θεοῦ συγχωρήσαντος, καὶ βουληθέντος δίκας τῆς ἀσεβείας εἰσπράξασθαι τοὺς ταῦτα ὑπ' αὐτοῦ πεπονθότας. Οὗ χάριν εἰκότως ἐπάγει· «Μὴ δοξασθήσεται ἀξίνη ἄνευ τοῦ κόπτοντος ἐν αὐτῇ; ἢ ὑψωθήσεται πρίων ἄνευ τοῦ ἕλκοντος αὐτόν; Ὡσαύτως ἐάν τις ἄρῃ ῥάβδον ἢ ξύλον.» Καθάπερ, φησίν, ἀδύνατον, αὐτομάτως ἀξίνην, ἢ πρίονα, ἢ ῥάβδον κινηθῆναι· τηνικαῦτα γὰρ τούτων ἕκαστον ἐνεργεῖ, ἡνίκα ἄν τις τῇ χειρὶ χρησάμενος κινῆσαι ταῦτα θελήσειεν· οὕτω καὶ σύ, τῆς ἐμῆς παραχωρησάσης σοι προμηθείας, πεποίηκας ἃ πεποίηκας, διὰ τὴν τῶν πεπονθότων παρανομίαν. Μὴ τοίνυν νόμιζε, τῇ οἰκείᾳ σοφίᾳ καὶ δυνάμει ταῦτα κατωρθωκέναι. Εἰ δὲ οὐ βούλει ταῦτα σωφρόνως μαθεῖν, καὶ

Mount Sion and in Jerusalem, he will call to account the ruler of the Assyrians for his conceited attitude and for the loftiness of the glory of his eyes." Now, God punished Jerusalem, not through Sennacherib, who ruled the Assyrians, but through Nebuchadnezzar: whereas the former not only failed to sack the city but lost his whole army, took to his heels by himself, and met his death at home at the hands of his sons,[99] Nebuchadnezzar destroyed the city, burned down the divine temple, and took the people captive. The divine Scripture teaches us, therefore, that after the Lord has brought to completion all he threatened to do on Mount Sion and in Jerusalem in saying, "Bewail the statues in Jerusalem: in the way I treated Samaria and its artifacts, so shall I treat Jerusalem and its idols," he (the Lord, I mean) will call to account the ruler of the Assyrians for his conceited attitude. He does not say Babylonians, but "Assyrians": the kingdom of the one and the other is the same. Now, by "conceited attitude" he means the loftiness and arrogance of his plans; hence he rightly added, "and for the loftiness of the glory of his eyes," and not simply "glory" but "the glory of his eyes"—that is, despite being human, he imagined himself very lofty and important. He said, in fact, "I shall accomplish it with my strength, and with the wisdom of my understanding I shall cancel boundaries of nations and plunder their might, I shall shake populated cities and with my own hand take possession of the whole world like a bird's nest and do away with it like abandoned eggs, and there is no one who will escape or gainsay me."

Having thus laid bare the conceit of the Assyrian's thoughts, he censures the futility of his desires, and conveys the fact that nothing of what was done by him would happen without God's permitting it and wanting to call to account for impiety those who had suffered this from him. Hence he was right to add, "Surely an axe will not be glorified apart from the one wielding it? Or the saw exalted apart from the one pulling it? Likewise for anyone holding rod or staff." As it is impossible, he is saying, for axe or saw or rod to move of itself (each of these operating when someone chooses to move them by using their hand), so too you did what you did, when my providence allowed you, on account of the lawlessness of the victims. So do not think you achieved this by your own wisdom and power. If, however, you are not prepared to learn

99. Cf. 2 Kgs 19:35–37.

1352 τὴν ἀλαζονικὴν ὀφρὺν καταλῦσαι, τῇ πείρᾳ μαθήσῃ, ὅτι | ταῦθ' οὕτως
ἔχει. «Ἀποστελεῖ γὰρ Κύριος Σαβαὼθ εἰς τὴν σὴν τιμὴν ἀτιμίαν, καὶ
εἰς τὴν σὴν δόξαν πῦρ καιόμενον καυθήσεται.» Καὶ ἐν ἑτέρῳ δὲ χωρίῳ
πάλιν τοιαῦτά φησιν ὁ Θεὸς πρὸς τὸν προφήτην· «Καὶ λήψῃ τὸν θρῆνον
τοῦτον ἐπὶ τὸν βασιλέα Βαβυλῶνος, καὶ ἐρεῖς ἐν τῇ ἡμέρᾳ ἐκείνη· Πῶς
ἀναπέπαυται ὁ ἀπαιτῶν; καὶ ἀναπέπαυται ὁ ἐπισπουδαστής; Συνέτριψεν
ὁ Θεὸς τὸν ζυγὸν τῶν ἁμαρτωλῶν, τὸν ζυγὸν τῶν ἀρχόντων, πατάξας
ἔθνος θυμῷ, πληγῇ ἀνιάτῳ.» Εἶτα δείκνυσι τὴν τῆς οἰκουμένης εὐφρο-
σύνην· «Πᾶσα ἡ γῆ, φησί, μετ' εὐφροσύνης, καὶ τὰ ξύλα τοῦ Λιβάνου
εὐφρανθήσονται ἐπὶ σοί, καὶ ἡ κέδρος τοῦ Λιβάνου· ἀφ' οὗ κεκοίμησαι,
οὐκ ἀνέβη ὁ κόπτων ἡμᾶς.» Τροπικῶς δὲ ταῦτα λέγει· καὶ *κέδρους τοῦ
Λιβάνου* προσαγορεύει, ἢ τὸν Ἰσραὴλ ἐπίσημον ὄντα, καὶ ἔνδοξον, ἢ
τοὺς λαμπροὺς ἐν ἀξιώμασι, καὶ βασιλεύειν πεπιστευμένους. Καὶ μετὰ
βραχέα, κωμῳδῶν αὐτοῦ τὸν τῦφον, καὶ τὴν τῆς ἀλαζονείας διδάσκων
κατάλυσιν· «Πῶς ἐξέπεσε, φησίν, ἐκ τοῦ οὐρανοῦ ὁ Ἑωσφόρος, ὁ πρωῒ
ἀνατέλλων; συνετρίβη ἐπὶ τὴν γῆν ὁ ἀποστέλλων πρὸς πάντα τὰ ἔθνη;
Σὺ δὲ εἶπας ἐν τῇ διανοίᾳ σου· Εἰς τὸν οὐρανὸν ἀναβήσομαι, καὶ ἐπάνω
τῶν ἀστέρων θήσω τὸν θρόνον μου· καθιῶ ἐν ὄρει ὑψηλῷ, ἐπὶ τὰ ὄρη τὰ
ὑψηλὰ πρὸς βορρᾶν, ἀναβήσομαι ἐπάνω τῶν νεφελῶν, καὶ ἔσομαι ὅμοιος
τῷ Ὑψίστῳ.» Εἶτα δείκνυσι τῆς ἀνθρωπίνης εὐημερίας τὸ ἐπίκηρον·
«Σὺ δέ, φησίν, ὁ ταῦτα λογίσασθαι τετολμηκώς, εἰς ᾅδην καταβήσῃ, καὶ
εἰς τὰ θεμέλια τῆς γῆς. Οἱ ἰδόντες σε θαυμάσουσιν ἐπὶ σέ, καὶ ἐροῦσιν·
Οὗτος ὁ ἄνθρωπος, ὁ παροξύνων τὴν γῆν, ὁ σείων βασιλεῖς, ὁ θεὶς τὴν
γῆν ὅλην ἔρημον, καὶ τὰς πόλεις αὐτῆς καθεῖλε· τοὺς ἐν ἐπαγωγῇ οὐκ
ἠλέησε· πάντες οἱ βασιλεῖς τῶν ἐθνῶν ἐκοιμήθησαν ἐν τιμῇ, ἄνθρωπος
ἐν τῷ οἴκῳ αὐτοῦ· σὺ δὲ ῥιφήσῃ ἐν τοῖς ὄρεσιν, ὡς νεκρός, ἐβδελυγ-
μένος, μετὰ πολλῶν τεθνηκότων ἐκκεκεντημένων μαχαίρᾳ, καταβαινόν-
των εἰς ᾅδην.» Καὶ ἵνα μὴ πάσας τὰς περὶ αὐτοῦ προφητείας παραγα-
γὼν ἀποκνήσω τῷ μήκει, τούς τε νῦν ἀκούοντας, καὶ τοὺς εἰς ὕστερον

this lesson in a sensible fashion and put an end to your lofty arro-
gance, you will learn by experience that | this is the way things   1352
are: "The Lord Sabaoth will send dishonor upon your honor, and
a burning fire will be kindled upon your glory." And in another
place God says such things to the prophet,[100] "You will take up
this lament against the king of Babylon, and you will say on that
day, How has the importunate one fallen? How has the oppres-
sor fallen? God smashed the yoke of the sinners, the yoke of the
rulers, striking a nation with anger, with an incurable blow." Then
he brings out the joy of the world: "All the earth with gladness,
and the trees of Lebanon will rejoice over you, and the cedar of
Lebanon; since you have fallen asleep, no one has come up to chop
us down." Now, he says this figuratively, using the term "cedars
of Lebanon" either for Israel's fame and glory or for those of high
rank entrusted with reigning. And shortly after, to mock his conceit and bring out the collapse of his arrogance, he says, "How
it is fallen from heaven, the daystar that rises at dawn! Brought
crashing to the ground was the one who sent dispatches to all the
nations. You said to yourself, I shall ascend to heaven, I shall set
my throne above the stars of heaven, I shall sit on a high mountain facing the high mountains to the north, I shall rise above the
clouds, I shall be like the Most High." Then to emphasize the
impermanence of human prosperity, "Now, on the contrary, after presuming to entertain these thoughts, you will descend into
Hades and the foundations of the earth. Those seeing you will be
amazed at you and will say of you, This is the one who provokes
the earth, who shakes kings, renders the whole world desolate,
and destroys its cities, yet had no mercy on those in his train. All
the kings of the earth went to their rest in honor, each in his own
house, whereas you by contrast will be cast out on the mountains
like a loathsome corpse along with many dead people pierced with
a sword, going down into Hades."

Lest in citing all the prophecies of him I prove wearisome
through long-windedness, I shall, after referring the present lis-

[100] This time, in citing parts of Isa 14:4–19 to document his dossier further, Theodoret is closer to the mark, these verses against "the king of Babylon"
probably being a later insertion into the work of Isaiah of Jerusalem with either
Nebuchadnezzar or the later Nabonidus in mind.

τούτοις ἐντευξομένους εἰς ἐκεῖνα παραπέμψας, τοὺς γνῶναι τὸν τῦφον αὐτοῦ καὶ τὴν ὠμότητα βουλομένους, ἐπὶ τὸ προκείμενον ἐπανάξω τὸν λόγον. Τοῦτον τοίνυν ὁ τῶν ὅλων Θεὸς εἰς εὐσέβειαν ποδηγῆσαι θελήσας, πολλὰ πολλάκις σωτήρια προσενήνοχε φάρμακα, καὶ πρῶτον μὲν ἐν τῷ δευτέρῳ τῆς βασιλείας ἔτει, ὄναρ αὐτῷ τὴν εἰκόνα ἐκείνην ὑπέδειξεν, εἶτα τῇ λήθῃ τοῦ ἐνυπνίου εἰς χρείαν τοῦ προφήτου κατέστησεν· ἔπειτα διὰ τῆς ἑρμηνείας τὰς τῶν βασιλέων διαδοχὰς ἐδίδαξεν ἀκριβῶς, τῆς ἀν-
1353 θρωπίνης εὐημερίας ὑποδεικνὺς τὸ | βραχὺ καὶ ἐπίκηρον. Καὶ παραυτίκα μὲν ὠφέλειαν ἐδέξατο, καὶ τὸ ἄμετρον σέβας τῷ Δανιὴλ προσενήνοχεν· ὡς Θεῷ γὰρ λιβανωτὸν αὐτῷ καὶ σπονδὰς προσενεχθῆναι προσέταξεν. Ἀλλὰ πάλιν, οὐ πολλοῦ διελθόντος χρόνου, τὴν εἰκόνα ἐκείνην ἀνέστησε, καὶ ἅπαντας τοὺς ὑπηκόους προσκυνεῖν αὐτὴν κατηνάγκασε, καὶ τοὺς τὴν εὐσέβειαν προτετιμηκότας, τῇ ἀπλήστως τραφείσῃ πυρᾷ παραδέδωκεν. Ἀλλὰ πάλιν ὁ ἀγαθὸς Δεσπότης, μακροθυμίᾳ χρησάμενος, δίκας μὲν αὐτὸν τῆς τε ἀλαζονείας καὶ τῆς θηριωδίας οὐκ εἰσεπράξατο, τὴν δὲ θείαν αὐτῷ δύναμιν ὑποδείκνυσι, τοὺς εὔνους θεράποντας τῆς φλογὸς ἐκείνης ἐλευθερώσας. Πάλιν δὲ ὀλίγην ἐκεῖθεν ὠφέλειαν δεξάμενος, ὑμνεῖ μὲν τὸν τῶν ὅλων Θεόν, ἀπειλεῖ τε τὴν ἐσχάτην τιμωρίαν τοῖς βλάσφημόν τι κατ' αὐτοῦ φθεγγομένοις· ἀλλ' εὐθὺς καὶ παραυτίκα, καὶ ἐν αὐτῷ τῷ ἐνιαυτῷ, λήθῃ πάλιν τὴν μεγίστην ταύτην παραδοὺς θαυματουργίαν, ἐπιστρατεύει τοῖς Ἱεροσολύμοις, καὶ καθαιρεῖ μὲν τὰ τῆς πόλεως τείχη, πυρπολεῖ τε τὸν ἅγιον τοῦ Θεοῦ νεών, κατατολμᾷ δὲ τῶν τούτου ἀδύτων, καὶ πάντα συλήσας τὰ ἀναθήματα εἰς τὴν Βαβυλῶνα σὺν τοῖς αἰχμαλώτοις ἀπήνεγκεν. Ὅτι δὲ κατὰ τοῦτον ἐπεστράτευσε τὸν καιρόν, καὶ ὁ μακάριος ἡμᾶς διδάσκει Ἱερεμίας οὑτωσὶ λέγων· «Ὁ λόγος ὁ γενόμενος παρὰ Κυρίου πρὸς Ἱερεμίαν ἐν τῷ ἐνιαυτῷ τῷ δεκάτῳ Σεδεκίου βασιλέως Ἰούδα, οὗτος ἐνιαυτὸς ὀκτωκαιδέκατος τῷ Ναβουχοδονόσορ τῷ βασιλεῖ Βαβυλῶνος, καὶ δύναμις βασιλέως Βαβυλῶνος ἐχαράκωσεν ἐν Ἱερουσαλήμ.» Καὶ τῆς εἰκόνος δὲ τὸ διήγημα συγγράφων ὁ μακάριος Δανιὴλ τοῦτον τέθεικε τὸν χρόνον· «Ἔτους ὀκτωκαιδεκάτου Ναβουχοδονόσορ ὁ βασιλεὺς ἐποίησεν εἰκόνα χρυσῆν·» ὡς εἶναι δῆλον, ὅτι ἐν

teners and later readers[101] to them if they want to learn of his
conceit and cruelty, return to the matter in hand. The God of all,
then, in his wish to guide this man to godliness, frequently provided many salutary remedies: first, in the second year of his reign
he let him see in a dream that image; then, by his forgetting the
dream he brought him to need the prophet; next, through the interpretation he conveyed precisely the succession of kings, giving
him a glimpse of the brevity and impermanence of human pros-
perity. | At the outset he profited from the experience and offered   1353
excessive reverence to Daniel, ordering that incense and libations
be offered to him as to a god. In turn, however, before much time
had passed, he set up that statue and obliged all his subjects to worship it, and consigned to the fire that was fed unceasingly those
who set greater store by godliness. In turn, however, the good
Lord, who by exercising longsuffering did not call him to account
for his arrogance and ferocity, gave him a glimpse of divine power
by freeing his devoted servants from those awful flames. But in
turn he gained little benefit from it: while he sang the praises of
the God of all and threatened with the ultimate penalty those who
uttered blasphemy against him, right from the outset in that very
same year he consigned this wonderful miracle to oblivion. He advanced on Jerusalem, destroyed the city walls, set fire to the holy
temple of God, presumed to enter its precincts, seized all the offerings, and carried them off to Babylon along with the captives.
Now, the fact that he attacked at that time blessed Jeremiah also
informs us in these words, "The word that came from the Lord
to Jeremiah in the tenth year of Zedekiah king of Judah, which
was the eighteenth year of Nebuchadnezzar king of Babylon, when
the might of the king of Babylon besieged Jerusalem."[102] Blessed
Daniel in recording a description of the statue cited this date,
"In his eighteenth year King Nebuchadnezzar made a statue of

---

[101] There is an implication here that some of his flock in the 430s are hearing this commentary directly from their bishop, while later ages are left to read
the text (as with Theodoret's commentaries generally). Does the atypical pro-
lixity and unusually heavy scriptural documentation of the moral theme, as well
as this mention of "listeners," suggest that this material has been developed as
part of a homily and incorporated here for "later readers"?

[102] Jer 32:1–2 in reference to Nebuchadnezzar's second campaign in 588–
587.

ἀρχῇ τοῦ ἔτους ἀπήτησε τὴν τῆς εἰκόνος προσκύνησιν· εἶτα τὴν στρατιὰν προπέμψας ἠκολούθησε καὶ αὐτός, περιεγένετό τε τῆς Ἱερουσαλὴμ
ἑνδεκάτῳ μὲν ἔτει τῆς βασιλείας Σεδεκίου, ἐννεακαιδεκάτῳ δὲ τῆς ἑαυτοῦ βασιλείας. Ἐπειδὴ τοίνυν οὐδεμίαν οὐδαμόθεν ὁ δείλαιος ὠφέλειαν
ἐδέξατο, ἀγανακτήσας ὁ τῶν ὅλων Θεὸς δεδίττεται μὲν αὐτὸν πρότερον
δι' ἐνυπνίου, εἶτα διὰ τοῦ Δανιὴλ τὰ διὰ τοῦ ἐνυπνίου σημαινόμενα δῆλα ποιεῖ. Καὶ οὐδὲ οὕτως εὐθὺς ἐπάγει τὴν τιμωρίαν, ἀλλὰ προσφέρει
μὲν αὐτῷ συμβουλὴν καὶ παραίνεσιν διὰ τοῦ Δανιὴλ, ἐνιαυτόν τε ὅλον
μακροθυμεῖ τὴν μεταμέλειαν ἀναμένων. Ὡς δὲ οὐδεμίαν ἰατρείαν ἐκ τῆς
μακροθυμίας ἠθέλησε δρέψασθαι, ἃ ἠπείλησεν ἐπιφέρει κακά· τιμωρεῖταί
τε αὐτὸν οὐχ ἁπλῶς, ἀλλὰ τὸν ἀλαζόνα νοῦν ἐκεῖνον τὸν τὰ ὑπὲρ φύσιν ὀνειροπολήσαντα, φρενοβλαβείᾳ παίει καὶ παραπληξίᾳ. Εἶτα θηριώδη
1356   γενόμενον ἐξελαθῆναι παρα|σκευάζει, καὶ τὰς ἐρήμους οἰκεῖν ἐπὶ χρόνῳ
μακρῷ. Ἔπειτα αἴσθησιν παρασκευάζει αὐτὸν λαβεῖν τῶν κατεχόντων
δεινῶν· οὔτε γὰρ ἦν οἷόν τε αὐτὸν ὠφέλειαν δρέψασθαι ἀναισθήτως καὶ
ἀναλγήτως παντελῶς διακείμενον. Οὕτως ἀνανεύσας ἐκεῖνος, ἐπιγινώσκει μὲν τὰς ὀξυρρόπους τοῦ βίου μεταβολάς, θρηνεῖ δὲ καὶ ὀλοφύρεται
τὴν οἰκείαν ἀβελτηρίαν, ὁμολογεῖ τε τὴν τοῦ Θεοῦ βασιλείαν ἀδιάδοχον
εἶναι, εἰς ἅπαντας διαμένουσαν τοὺς αἰῶνας. Ταῦτα τῇ πείρᾳ διδαχθείς,
πάλιν διὰ τὴν ἄρρητον τοῦ Θεοῦ φιλανθρωπίαν εἰς τὴν οἰκείαν ἀπελήλυθε
βασιλείαν· ἀδικεῖν δὲ νομίσας ἅπαντας τοὺς ἀνθρώπους, εἰ κρύψειε Θεοῦ
τὴν προμήθειαν, δι' ἐπιστολῆς πᾶσι τοῖς κατὰ τὴν οἰκουμένην ὑπηκόοις
ἐξηγεῖται τήν τε προτέραν εὐημερίαν, καὶ συμβᾶσαν δυσκληρίαν· εἶτα τὴν
μεταμέλειαν, δι' ἧς τὸν Δεσπότην ἐξιλεώσατο. Ἡ μὲν οὖν τῆς ἐπιστολῆς ὑπόθεσις αὕτη· διὰ πλειόνων δὲ αὐτὴν ἐποιησάμην, καὶ τὸν τούτου
τῦφον ταῖς Γραφικαῖς μαρτυρίαις δεῖξαι βουληθείς, καὶ τοῦ Θεοῦ τῶν
ὅλων τὴν περὶ πάντας κηδεμονίαν δήλην ποιῆσαι θελήσας. Φέρε τοίνυν,
τῆς κατὰ μέρος ἑρμηνείας ἀρξώμεθα. «Ναβουχοδονόσορ ὁ βασιλεὺς πᾶσι τοῖς λαοῖς, φυλαῖς, γλώσσαις, τοῖς οἰκοῦσιν ἐν πάσῃ τῇ γῇ, εἰρήνη ὑμῖν

gold."[103] So it is clear that at the beginning of the year he required the worship of the statue, then sent the army and personally followed it, and conquered Jerusalem in the eleventh year of the reign of Zedekiah and the nineteenth year of his own reign.

Since the wretch gained no benefit from any event, therefore, the God of all was angered and put fear into him, firstly through a dream, and then by means of Daniel he made clear what was indicated by the dream. Instead of immediately bringing retribution on him for this, he offers him advice and counsel through Daniel, showing longsuffering for a whole year in expectation of repentance. But since he chose not to gain any cure from the longsuffering, he inflicted the troubles he had threatened; instead of punishing him straight out, he struck with insanity and dementia that arrogant mind that had dreamed of preternatural things.[104] Then when he became wildly enraged, he caused him to be driven out | and live in the desert for a long time. He next caused him to gain an appreciation of the fate that had befallen him; after all, it was impossible for one who lacked all sense and feeling to reap any benefit. Thus, after refusing to do so, that fellow acknowledged the rapid changes in his life, wept and wailed for his own stupidity, and confessed God's kingdom to be without succession, lasting for all ages. Learning this from experience, he once more through God's ineffable lovingkindness returned to his own kingdom. In the belief, however, that it would be an injustice to all people if he were to conceal God's providence, he recounted in a letter to all his subjects throughout the world his former prosperity and the misfortune that befell him, then the repentance by which he won the Lord over.

1356

While this is the theme of the letter, then, I developed it at length in my wish to bring out this man's conceit through the scriptural texts, and in my desire to make clear the care of the God of all for everyone. So come now, let us begin the commentary in detail. *King Nebuchadnezzar to all the peoples, tribes, languages, in-*

[103] Dan 3:1 Greek.

[104] Theodoret is unable to document these unexpected developments in Nebuchadnezzar's life for the simple reason that there is no historical evidence for them. The hypothesis that they are associated rather with the later Nabonidus is confirmed by the discovery at Qumran of a fragment of a *Prayer of Nabonidus* recounting such events, thus encouraging the idea that there was a cycle of Daniel stories in circulation among Jews at that late time.

πληθυνθείη.» Προσήκει τούτοις ἁρμόσαι τοῖς λόγοις τὴν προφητικὴν ἐκείνην φωνήν· «Ἀγαθόν μοι ὅτι ἐταπείνωσάς με, ὅπως ἂν μάθω τὰ δικαιώματά σου.» Τῇ πείρᾳ δὲ καὶ οὗτος διδαχθεὶς σωφρονεῖν, εὐσεβείας ἀπεφάνθη διδάσκαλος, καὶ τὰ οἰκεῖα πάθη φάρμακα πᾶσιν ἀνθρώποις προτίθησι, καὶ οὐ μόνον τοῖς ὑπηκόοις, ἀλλὰ καὶ τοῖς ἔξω τῆς βασιλείας ὑπάρχουσι. Καλῶς δὲ καὶ ἁρμοδίως τὴν προσηγορίαν ἐποιήσατο· «Εἰρήνη ὑμῖν πληθυνθείη·» τουτέστιν, ἀπείρατοι γένοισθε ὧν ἐπειράθην κακῶν, εἰρήνης ἀπολαύοντες διατελεῖτε. Εἶτα ἐπάγει·

μθ'. «Τὰ σημεῖα καὶ τὰ τέρατα, ἃ ἐποίησε μετ' ἐμοῦ ὁ Θεὸς ὁ ὕψιστος, ἤρεσεν ἐνώπιον ἐμοῦ ἀναγγεῖλαι ὑμῖν.» Τῶν θείων, φησί, θαυμάτων αὐτόπτης γενόμενος, νενόμικα δίκαιον κοινωνοὺς ὑμᾶς ἅπαντας τῆς τούτων θεωρίας λαβεῖν. Οὐκ ἔστι γὰρ τὰ τυχόντα, ἀλλὰ μεγάλα καὶ ἰσχυρά, καί !

ρ'. «Ὡς μεγάλα καὶ ἰσχυρά· ἡ βασιλεία αὐτοῦ βασιλεία αἰώνιος, καὶ ἡ ἐξουσία αὐτοῦ εἰς γενεὰν καὶ γενεάν.» Τὰ μὲν γὰρ ἀνθρώπινα, ὁποῖα ἂν ᾖ, τέλος ἔχει, καὶ τέλος ταχύ· μόνη δὲ διαρκὴς καὶ ἀσάλευτος ἡ τοῦ Θεοῦ βασιλεία. Οὕτω προδιδάξας τὴν τῶν πραγμάτων αἰτίαν, ἄρχεται τῆς κατ' αὐτὴν διηγήσεως.

ΚΕΦΑΛΑΙΟΝ Δ'

α'. «Ἐγὼ Ναβουχοδονόσορ εὐθηνῶν ἤμην ἐν τῷ οἴκῳ μου, καὶ εὐθαλῶν ἐπὶ τοῦ θρόνου μου, καὶ πίων ἐν τῷ λαῷ μου.» Τέθεικε δὲ τὴν ἑαυτοῦ προσηγορίαν οὐχ ἁπλῶς, ἀλλ' ἵνα τὸ ὄνομα μαρτυρήσῃ τοῖς λόγοις. Ἐπειδὴ γὰρ σφόδρα ἐπίσημος ἦν, ἅτε δὴ πάντων τῶν κατὰ τὴν Ἀσίαν, καὶ τὴν Αἴγυπτον, καὶ τὴν Αἰθιοπίαν, τὴν ἡγεμονίαν λαβών, προτέθεικεν αὐτοῦ τὴν προσηγορίαν, ἀρκοῦσαν εἰς μαρ|τυρίαν τῶν λεγομένων. Ἔφη δέ· Ἐν ἄκρᾳ οὖν εὐκληρίᾳ, καὶ μυρίοις ἀγαθοῖς περιρρεόμενος διετέλουν· ἐν τούτοις δὲ ὤν,

β'. «Ἐνύπνιον, φησίν, εἶδον, καὶ ἐφοβέρισέ με, καὶ ἐθαύμασα ἐπὶ τούτοις πᾶσι, καὶ ἐταράχθην ἐπὶ τῆς κοίτης μου, καὶ αἱ ὁράσεις τῆς κεφαλῆς μου συνετάραξάν με.» Ἐν τοσαύτῃ γὰρ ὑπάρχων εὐημερίᾳ, ὄναρ εἶδον λυπηρόν, καὶ ἐξεδειματώθην μὲν σφόδρα τῇ θεωρίᾳ τοῦ ἐνυπνίου, ἐταρασσόμην δὲ πλέον τὰ διὰ τούτου σημαινόμενα κατιδεῖν οὐ δυνάμενος· οὗ χάριν τοὺς ταῦτα δυναμένους ἑρμηνεύειν συνεκάλεσα.

δ', ε'. «Καὶ εἰσεπορεύοντο ἐπαοιδοί, μάγοι, Γαζαρηνοί, Χαλδαῖοι, καὶ τὸ ἐνύπνιον εἶπον ἐγὼ ἐνώπιον αὐτῶν, καὶ τὴν σύγκρισιν αὐτοῦ οὐκ ἐγνώρισάν μοι· ἕως οὗ ἕτερος εἰσῆλθεν ἐνώπιόν μου, Δανιὴλ, οὗ τὸ ὄνομα Βαλτάσαρ, κατὰ τὸ ὄνομα τοῦ Θεοῦ μου, ὃς Πνεῦμα Θεοῦ ἅγιον

habitants of all the earth: may peace be granted you in abundance (v.
1). There is need to relate to these words that inspired statement,
"It is good for me that you humbled me, so that I might learn your
ordinances."[105] Brought to his senses by experience, he too became a teacher of piety, citing his own sufferings as a remedy for
all people, not only his subjects but also those living outside the
kingdom. It was proper and appropriate for him to add the greeting, *May peace be granted you in abundance*, that is, may you not
experience the troubles I experienced, and may you continue to
enjoy peace.

He then goes on, *The signs and wonders that God the Most
High worked in my case I am pleased to report to you* (v. 2): being an
eyewitness of the divine marvels, I thought it right to make you
all sharers in the vision I had of them; after all, far from being
chance events, they were wonderful and mighty. *How wonderful
and mighty! His kingdom is an eternal kingdom, and his authority
from generation to generation* (v. 3): while human affairs, such as
they are, have an end, indeed a rapid end, God's kingdom alone
is lasting and unending.

Having thus conveyed in advance the content of the events,
he begins the account accordingly. *I, Nebuchadnezzar, was enjoying good fortune in my home, prospering on my throne and popular
with my people* (v. 4). It was not without purpose that he cited his
own name: it was to confirm his name in word; since he was very
famous as having control of everyone throughout Asia, Egypt, and
Ethiopia, he cited his name at the beginning as sufficient confir-
mation | of what was said. He meant, I was at the height of good   1357
fortune and surrounded continually with countless good things.
While enjoying them, *I had a dream, and it scared me, I was astonished at it all, my sleep was disturbed and the visions in my head
alarmed me* (v. 5): while enjoying such great prosperity, I had a distressing dream, and I was very frightened by the contents of the
dream, and was further disturbed by being unable to grasp what
was signified by it. Hence I summoned those capable of interpreting it. *In came magicians, soothsayers, enchanters, and astrologers,
and I told the dream in their presence, but they did not inform me
of its interpretation until another one came into my presence, Daniel,
with the name Belteshazzar according to the name of my God, having*

[105] Ps 119:71.

ἔχει ἐν αὐτῷ.» Οὐχ ἁπλῶς δὲ ταῦτα τέθεικεν, ἀλλὰ παράλληλα, ἵνα τῇ παρεξετάσει δήλην ἅπασι ποιήσῃ τὴν τοῦ προφήτου σοφίαν· διὸ καὶ τὰ ἔθνη καταλέγει τῶν σοφῶν Βαβυλῶνος, ἵνα δείξῃ τοὺς μὲν οὐδὲν ὅλως ἐπισταμένους, τὸν δὲ ὑπὸ τοῦ θείου Πνεύματος φωτιζόμενον. Καλεῖ δὲ αὐτὸν οὐκ ἀπὸ μόνης τῆς προσηγορίας, ἣν αὐτὸς ἐπιτέθεικεν, ἀλλὰ τὸ Ἑβραῖον προστίθησιν ὄνομα. «Δανιὴλ γάρ, φησίν, οὗ τὸ ὄνομα Βαλτάσαρ κατὰ τὸ ὄνομα τοῦ Θεοῦ μου.» Οὕτω γάρ, φησίν, αὐτὸν ἐξ ἀρχῆς ἐθαύμασα, ὡς τοῦ πάλαι ὑπ' ἐμοῦ προσκυνουμένου Θεοῦ ἐπιθεῖναι αὐτῷ τὴν προσηγορίαν. Καὶ τὴν αἰτίαν δεικνύς, «Ὃς Πνεῦμα Θεοῦ ἅγιον ἔχει ἐν ἑαυτῷ.» Καὶ τοῦτο δὲ ἐκ τῆς τοῦ προφήτου διδασκαλίας μεμαθήκαμεν. Πόθεν γὰρ ἑτέρωθεν ἐγνώκει τοῦ παναγίου Πνεύματος τὴν προσηγορίαν τοῖς κιβδήλοις εἰδώλοις προστετηκώς; «Καὶ τὸ ἐνύπνιον, φησίν, ἐνώπιον αὐτοῦ εἶπον.» Εἶπον δὲ οὕτως ἀρξάμενος·

ϛ', ζ'. «Βαλτάσαρ, ὁ ἄρχων τῶν ἐπαοιδῶν, ὃν ἐγὼ ἔγνων, ὅτι Πνεῦμα ἅγιον ἐν σοί, καὶ πᾶν μυστήριον οὐκ ἀδυνατεῖ σοι, ἄκουσον τὴν ὅρασιν τοῦ ἐνυπνίου, οὗ εἶδον, καὶ τὴν σύγκρισιν αὐτοῦ εἰπέ μοι. Καὶ αἱ ὁράσεις τῆς κεφαλῆς μου ἐπὶ τῆς κλίνης μου.» Τοὺς πολλοὺς τῶν ἀνθρώπων αἱ εὐημερίαι πολλάκις ἐπιλανθάνεσθαι τῶν εὐεργετησάντων παρασκευάζουσιν, αἱ δὲ χρεῖαι ἀνακαλοῦνται τῶν εὖ πεποιηκότων τὴν μνήμην. Καὶ ὑγιαίνων μέν τις τὸ σῶμα, τῆς τοῦ ἰατροῦ τέχνης οὐ λαμβάνει τὴν μνήμην· ἀρρωστίᾳ δὲ περιπεσών, ἀναμιμνήσκεται, ὡς καὶ ἤδη πρότερον τοῦτο παθὼν διὰ τοῦ δεῖνος τοῦ ἰατροῦ τῆς ὑγείας ἀπήλαυσεν· οὕτω καὶ ὁ Ναβουχοδονόσορ, ἡνίκα μὲν τοὺς ἁγίους ἐκείνους τῇ πυρᾷ παρεδίδου, τῆς τοῦ Δανιὴλ εὐεργεσίας οὐκ ἐμνημόνευσεν· ἐπειδὴ δὲ πάλιν εἶδεν ἐνύπνιον, | καὶ θόρυβον εἶχεν ἐν τῇ ψυχῇ, τῆς τοῦ Δανιὴλ ἀνεμνήσθη σοφίας, καὶ τῆς τοῦ προτέροι ἐνυπνίου ἀναμνήσεώς τε καὶ ἑρμηνείας. Διὸ καὶ Πνεῦμα Θεοῦ ἔχειν αὐτὸν λέγει, καὶ πᾶν μυστήριον ἑρμηνεύειν αὐτὸν ἱκανὸν εἶναι, καὶ παρακαλεῖ καὶ τοῦτο τὸ ἐνύπνιον, ἄδηλον ὄν, δῆλον αὐτῷ καταστῆσαι. Εἶτα λέγει τὸ ἐνύπνιον, καί φησιν·

1360

a holy spirit of God in him (vv. 7–8). He did not give these details casually: it was in parallel so as to make clear to everyone the
prophet's wisdom by comparison—hence his listing the national-
ities of the wise men of Babylon so as to highlight the fact that
whereas they understood absolutely nothing, he was illuminated
by the divine Spirit.[106] He not only refers to him by the name he
had given him, but adds the Hebrew name: *Daniel, with the name
Belteshazzar according to the name of my God.* In other words, he is
saying, I admired him from the beginning so much as to give him
the name of the god once worshiped by me.[107] And he brings out
the reason: *having a holy spirit of God in him.* We learned this from
information from the prophet: how else could he have known the
name of the Most Holy Spirit when in thrall to fraudulent idols?

I narrated the dream in his presence: I narrated it, beginning in
this fashion. *Belteshazzar leader of the magicians, I know the holy
spirit is in you, and no mystery is impossible for you. Listen to the
vision in the dream I had, and tell me its interpretation, and the visions in my head on my bed* (vv. 9–10). Good fortune often causes
the general run of people to forget their benefactors, whereas it
is necessity that recalls to mind those who have treated us well;
and while the person in good health does not keep in mind the
physician's competence, on falling ill they remember they had that
complaint before and returned to good health thanks to such and
such a physician. So too Nebuchadnezzar: when he consigned
those holy people to the fire, he did not remember Daniel's fa-
vor; but when he later had a dream | and felt alarm in his soul,   1360
he remembered Daniel's wisdom and his recall and interpretation
of the previous dream. Hence he said he had God's Spirit and
was capable of interpreting every mystery, and he requested him
to make clear to him this dream as well, obscure as it was.

---

[106] Theodoret is referring to the words Γαζαρηνοί, Χαλδαῖοι in his text
for enchanters and astrologers, both places (Gezer and Chaldea) having a reputation for astrology and fortune telling.

[107] Like Theodoret, the author thought that the Bel in the name Belteshazzar referred to the Babylonian god of that name, whereas the full name
represents a Babylonian form meaning "Guard his life!" which would normally
be preceded by a god's name, such as Marduk. While noting that Daniel is a
Hebrew name, Theodoret does not here reduce it to its elements, "My judge is
God" or "God has judged."

«'Εθεώρουν δένδρον ἐν μέσῳ τῆς γῆς. (η'.) Καὶ τὸ ὕψος αὐτοῦ ἔφθασεν ἕως τοῦ οὐρανοῦ, καὶ τὸ κῦτος αὐτοῦ εἰς τὰ πέρατα τῆς γῆς.» Διὰ δὲ τοῦ δένδρου αὐτὸν ἔφη σημαίνεσθαι ὁ μακάριος Δανιήλ, τὸ δὲ ὕψος λέγει φθάσαι ἕως τοῦ οὐρανοῦ, οὐ τὴν φύσιν τοῦ δένδρου σημαίνων, ἀλλὰ τοὺς λογισμοὺς καὶ τὰς φαντασίας. Διὸ καὶ ὁ Ἡσαΐας ἔλεγεν· «'Επάξει ὁ Θεὸς ἐπὶ τὸν νοῦν τὸν μέγαν, τὸν βασιλέα τῶν 'Ασσυρίων, καὶ ἐπὶ τὸ ὕψος τῆς δόξης τῶν ὀφθαλμῶν αὐτοῦ.» *Νοῦν δὲ μέγαν* αὐτὸν προσηγόρευσεν, ὡς μεγάλα φαντασθέντα, καὶ ὀνειροπολήσαντα, ἃ μετὰ βραχέα διηγήσατο· «Σὺ γὰρ εἶπας· 'Επάνω τῶν ἀστέρων θήσω τὸν θρόνον μου, καὶ ἔσομαι ὅμοιος τῷ Ὑψίστῳ.» Διὰ τοῦτο ὁρᾷ τὸ ὕψος τοῦ δένδρου ἐφθακὸς ἕως τοῦ οὐρανοῦ· ἐπειδὴ δὲ καί, ὡς ἔπος εἰπεῖν, πάσης τῆς οἰκουμένης ἐκράτησεν, ὁρᾷ τοῦ δένδρου τὸ κῦτος, τουτέστι, τὸν ὄγκον τοῦ εὔρους, ἐκταθὲν μέχρις αὐτῶν τῶν περάτων τῆς γῆς.

θ'. «Τὰ φύλλα αὐτοῦ, φησίν, ὡραῖα, καὶ ὁ καρπὸς αὐτοῦ πολύς.» Καλεῖ δὲ *φύλλα* μὲν τὴν ὁρωμένην εὐπρέπειαν, τὴν ἐν ἐσθῆτι, καὶ θρόνῳ, καὶ βασιλείοις, ἀσπιδηφόροις τε καὶ δορυφόροις, καὶ πεζαιτέροις· *καρπὸν* δὲ τὸν πανταχόθεν προσφερόμενον φόρον. Διὸ *πολὺν τὸν καρπόν, ἀλλ' οὐ καλόν,* ἔφη· οὐ γὰρ εἶχε τὸ δίκαιον. «Καὶ τροφὴ πάντων ἐν αὐτῷ.» Οἵ τε γὰρ γεωργοῦντες, διὰ τῆς αὐτοῦ κηδεμονίας εἰρήνης ἀπολαύοντες, τοὺς ἀπὸ τῆς γῆς καρποὺς ἐκομίζοντο· οἵ τε στρατευόμενοι, παρ' αὐτοῦ τὰ σιτηρέσια κομιζόμενοι, τὴν ἐν ὅπλοις ἐποιοῦντο ζωήν. «Ὑποκάτω αὐτοῦ, φησίν, κατεσκήνουν τὰ θηρία τὰ ἄγρια, καὶ ἐν τοῖς κλάδοις αὐτοῦ κατῴκει τὰ πετεινὰ τοῦ οὐρανοῦ, καὶ ἐξ αὐτοῦ ἐτρέφετο πᾶσα σάρξ.» Οἵ τε γὰρ θηριώδη βίον ζῶντες βάρβαροι, οἵ τε λογικώτεροι καὶ ἡμερώτεροι, καὶ ὀξεῖς καὶ πτηνοὶ τὴν διάνοιαν, ὑπὸ τὴν τούτου ἐξουσίαν βιοτεύοντες διετέλουν.

ι'. «'Εθεώρουν τοίνυν, φησίν, ἐν ὁράματι τῆς νυκτὸς ἐπὶ τῆς κοίτης μου, καὶ ἰδοὺ εἰρ καὶ ἅγιος ἀπ' οὐρανοῦ κατέβη.» *Εἶρ* καλεῖ τὸν ἐγρηγορότα· τοῦτο γὰρ ἑρμηνεύεται τῇ Ἑλλάδι φωνῇ. *Ἐγρηγορότα* δὲ καλεῖ τὸν ἄγγελον, ἵνα τούτου σημήνῃ τὸ ἀσώματον· ὁ γὰρ σῶμα περικείμενος ὕπνῳ δουλεύει· ὁ δὲ ὕπνου κρείττων σώματος ἐλεύθερος. Εἶδον

He then describes the dream as follows. *I had a vision of a tree in the middle of the earth, its top reaching to heaven and its trunk to the ends of the earth* (v. 10–11). By the tree blessed Daniel said he personally was depicted, and he said its height reached to heaven to suggest not the real tree but his thoughts and imaginings. Hence Isaiah also said, "God will call to account the ruler of the Assyrians for his conceited attitude and for the loftiness of the glory of his eyes,"[108] referring to his "conceited attitude" for his having lofty imaginings and dreams, which he described shortly afterwards, "You said, in fact, I shall set my throne above the stars, and shall be like the Most High."[109] This is the reason he sees the height of the tree reaching to heaven; but since, so to say, he even had control of the whole world, he sees the tree trunk—that is, the extent of its breadth—expanding as far as the ends of the earth. *Its foliage was charming, and its fruit abundant* (v. 12). By *foliage* he refers to the visible splendor in apparel, throne, palace, warriors bearing shields and javelins, and foot-soldiers, and by *fruit* to the tribute offered from all quarters—hence his saying *its fruit abundant* but not beautiful, there being no justice in it. *And there was food for all in it*: in one sense, the farmers took advantage of peace for tending it and reaped fruit from the earth, and in another, the soldiers gathered provisions from it and spent their life under arms. *The wild animals sheltered under it, the birds of heaven dwelt in its branches, and all flesh fed from it*: barbarians lived a wild life, whereas more reasonable and civilized people, rapid and uplifted in their thinking, continued to pass their life under his authority.

So I continued looking in the vision of the night on my bed and, lo, a holy eir descended from heaven (v. 13). By *eir* he refers to the watcher, the meaning in Greek. By watcher he means an angel,[110] thus bringing out its bodiless form: what is clad in a body is subject to sleeping, whereas what is rid of a body is superior to the

---

[108] Isa 10:12.

[109] Isa 14:14. For the true identity of these arrogant kings, see note 100 above.

[110] It is not that Theodoret goes behind his text to cite the Hebrew form *ʿir*: he finds it thus in Theodotion. This is the only use of the word in the Old Testament in reference to an angel, though it is (according to Alexander Di Lella, "Daniel," *NJBC*, 413) frequently so used in Jewish apocryphal works and at Qumran.

τοίνυν, φησίν, ἄγγελον, ἀσώματον ἔχοντα φύσιν, ὃς ἀπ' οὐρανοῦ κατέ-
1361 βη. |

ια΄. «Καὶ ἐφώνησεν ἐν ἰσχύϊ, καὶ οὕτως εἶπεν· Ἐκκόψατε τὸ δένδρον, καὶ ἐκτίλατε τοὺς κλάδους αὐτοῦ, καὶ ἐκτινάξατε τὰ φύλλα αὐτοῦ
καὶ διασκορπίσατε τὸν καρπὸν αὐτοῦ.» Καὶ βλέπει μὲν τὸν ἄγγελον ἀπ'
οὐρανοῦ καταβεβηκότα, ἵνα μάθῃ, ὡς αὐτὸς ὁ τῶν ὅλων Δεσπότης τὴν
κατ' αὐτοῦ ἀπόφασιν ἐποιήσατο. Διδάσκεται δὲ καὶ τίς ὁ δεδωκὼς αὐτῷ
τὴν βασιλείαν, καὶ ἀποτιθέμενος τὴν βασιλείαν· ὁρᾷ γὰρ τὸ μὲν δένδρον
ἐκτεμνόμενον, τοὺς δὲ κλάδους χωριζομένους, τουτέστι, τοὺς ὑπάρχους,
καὶ τοὺς στρατηγούς, καὶ σατράπας, καὶ τοὺς ἄλλην τινὰ ἡγεμονίαν
παρ' αὐτοῦ πεπιστευμένους· τὰ δὲ φύλλα ἐκτινασσόμενα ἣν περιεβέβλη-
το δόξαν δίκην φύλλων ἐκρέουσάν τε καὶ μαραινομένην· τὸν δὲ καρπὸν
διασκορπιζόμενον· τοῦ γὰρ βασιλέως ἐκείνη περιπεσόντος τῇ συμφορᾷ,
οἱ τὸν δασμὸν ἀπαιτοῦντες εἰς ἑαυτοὺς λοιπὸν ἀδεῶς τὸ κέρδος παρέ-
πεμπον. «Σαλευθήτω, φησί, τὰ θηρία ὑποκάτωθεν αὐτοῦ, καὶ τὰ ὄρνεα
ἀπὸ τῶν κλάδων αὐτοῦ.» Οἱ γὰρ παρὰ γνώμην δουλεύειν ἠναγκασμένοι,
ἀφορμὴν εὑρόντες τὴν τοῦ βασιλέως μεταβολήν, τοῦ ὑπακούειν ἀπέστησαν.

ιβ΄. «Πλὴν τὴν φυὴν τῶν ῥιζῶν αὐτοῦ ἐν τῇ γῇ ἐάσατε· καὶ ἐν
δεσμῷ, φησί, σιδηρῷ καὶ χαλκῷ, καὶ ἐν τῇ χλόῃ τῇ ἔξω, καὶ ἐν τῇ δρόσῳ τοῦ οὐρανοῦ αὐλισθήσεται.» Ὡς γὰρ φρενοβλαβείᾳ, καὶ παραπληξίᾳ,
καὶ φρενίτιδι νόσῳ περιπεσών, καὶ μεμηνώς, καὶ κορυβαντιῶν, καὶ κατὰ
πάντων λυττῶν, ἀναγκαίως δεσμὰ περιέκειτο· ἀλλ' ὅμως οὐδὲ ταῦτα ἦν
ἱκανὰ ἔνδον αὐτὸν κατέχειν· ἀλλὰ δραπετεύων ἐν ἐρήμοις διέτριβεν, ὑπαίθριος ταλαιπωρῶν, καὶ κτηνῶν δίκην τὴν πόαν σιτούμενος. Τοῦτο γὰρ
σημαίνει εἰρηκώς·

«Καὶ μετὰ τῶν θηρίων ἡ μερὶς αὐτοῦ· ἐν τῷ χόρτῳ τῆς γῆς ἡ καρδία αὐτοῦ· ἀπὸ τῶν ἀνθρώπων ἀλλοιωθήσεται. (ιγ΄.) Καὶ καρδία θηρίου
δοθήσεται αὐτῷ, καὶ ἑπτὰ καιροὶ ἀλλαγήσονται ἐπ' αὐτόν.» Καὶ τοῦτο
δὲ τὴν τοῦ Θεοῦ μακροθυμίαν δηλοῖ· χρόνῳ γὰρ βραχεῖ τὴν τιμωρίαν
περιορίζει, ἀναμένων τὴν ἀπὸ τῆς παιδείας τεχθησομένην μεταμέλειαν.
Εἶτα δείκνυσιν, ὡς ἀναντιρρήτως ἔσται τὰ εἰρημένα.

ιδ΄. «Διὰ συγκρίματος, φησίν, εἴρ ὁ λόγος, καὶ ῥῆμα ἁγίων τὸ
ἐπερώτημα.» Ἀψευδὴς, φησίν, ὁ λόγος· ἄγγελος γὰρ ἅγιος ὁ εἰρηκώς,
ἐγρηγορώς, ἀσώματος. Εἴρηται δὲ ταῦτα, φησί, καὶ γίνεται, οὐ μάτην,
ἀλλ' «Ἵνα γνῶσιν οἱ ζῶντες, ὅτι κυριεύει ὁ Ὕψιστος τῆς βασιλείας τῶν
ἀνθρώπων, καὶ ᾧ ἐὰν δόξῃ, δώσει αὐτήν, καὶ ἐξουθένημα ἀνθρώπου ἀναστήσει ἐπ' αὐτήν.» Ταῦτα, φησίν, ὁ ἄγγελος ἔφη, ὅτι τούτου χάριν τὰ

need for sleeping. So he means, I saw an angel, bodiless in nature, who descended from heaven. | *He cried aloud and spoke thus, Chop* 1361 *down the tree, and pluck off its branches, strip its foliage, and scatter its fruit* (v. 14). He looks to the angel descended from heaven to learn that the God of heaven personally delivered the verdict against him. He is also informed who it was who had given him the kingdom and is now laying it aside: note the tree cut down and the branches separated from it, meaning the prefects, generals, satraps, and those entrusted with other forms of authority by him; the stripped foliage, meaning the glory in which he had been invested falling and fading like leaves; and the fruit scattered, meaning that at the fall of the king in that misfortune those demanding tribute then had no qualms about directing the gain to themselves. *Let the wild beasts move from under it, and the birds from its branches*: those forced into slavery against their will took occasion from the change in the king's fortunes to cease obeying him.

But leave the stump of its roots in the ground, and with a band of iron and bronze, and in the grass outside, and it will lodge in the dew of heaven (v. 15): having fallen victim to madness, insanity, and mental disease, being deranged in a frenzy and raging against everyone, he had to be kept in chains, yet even these did not suffice to restrain him; he took to his heels and lived in the wilderness, suffering hardship in the open, and feeding on grass like cattle.[111] He suggested as much, in fact, by saying, *His lot with the wild beasts, his heart in the grass of the earth, he will be alienated from human beings. A wild beast's heart will be given him, and seven times will pass over him* (vv. 15–16). This indicates God's longsuffering: he will confine his punishment to a brief period, looking for a repentance that will be produced by his chastisement. He next brings out that the words are beyond dispute. *The word comes by a decree of the watchman, and the question is a statement of holy ones* (v. 17): the word is reliable, a holy angel the speaker, vigilant, incorporeal. It is not without purpose, he goes on, that it is said and comes to pass: *It is for the living to know that the Most High is lord of the kingdom of human beings, and he gives it to whomever he pleases, and what is despised by human beings he raises up over it*: this is what the

[111] Should Theodoret recall to his readers' attention the "holy stump" of Isa 6:13; 11:1 (though the LXX terminology differs there)?

κατὰ τὸ δένδρον γενήσεται, ἵνα διὰ τούτου μάθωσιν ἅπαντες, ἕνα εἶ-
1364   ναι | Θεὸν Δεσπότην καὶ βασιλέα, τοὺς ἐπὶ γῆς καθιστῶντα βασιλέας,
καὶ ἐγχειρίζοντα, ᾧ ἐὰν θέλῃ, τὴν βασιλείαν. Δεικνὺς γὰρ τὴν ἑαυτοῦ
ἐξουσίαν, καὶ τὸν εὐτελέστατον ἔστιν ὅτε, καὶ οὐδὲν εἶναι νομιζόμενον,
ἀποφαίνει βασιλέα, καὶ τοὺς ἐν τοῖς μεγίστοις ὄντας ἀξιώμασιν ὑπακούειν αὐτῷ παρασκευάζει. Οὕτω πληρώσας τὸ τοῦ ἐνυπνίου διήγημα,
φησὶ πρὸς τὸν Δανιήλ·

ιε΄. «Τοῦτο τὸ ἐνύπνιον εἶδον ἐγὼ Ναβουχοδονόσορ ὁ βασιλεύς·
καὶ σύ, Βαλτάσαρ, τὸ σύγκριμα εἰπὲ κατέναντι·» ἀντὶ τοῦ, ἀληθῶς καὶ
ἀκριβῶς· «ὅτι πάντες οἱ σοφοὶ τῆς βασιλείας μου οὐ δύνανται τὸ σύγκριμα αὐτοῦ δηλῶσαί μοι, σὺ δὲ δύνασαι.» Καὶ τὴν αἰτίαν δεικνύς, «Ὅτι,
φησί, Πνεῦμα Θεοῦ ἅγιον ἐν σοί.» Οἱ μὲν γὰρ ἀνθρωπίνοις κέχρηνται
λογισμοῖς, σὺ δὲ παρὰ Θεοῦ μανθάνεις τὰ κεκρυμμένα.

ις΄. «Τότε Δανιήλ, οὗ τὸ ὄνομα Βαλτάσαρ, ἀπηνεώθη ὡσεὶ ὥραν
μίαν, καὶ οἱ διαλογισμοὶ αὐτοῦ συνετάρασσον αὐτόν.» Ἔδει γὰρ δειχ-
θῆναι τὴν ἀνθρωπίνην ἀσθένειαν, καὶ τότε ἀναφανῆναι τὴν ἐμπνέουσαν
χάριν. «Ἀπεκρίθη τοίνυν ὁ βασιλεύς, καὶ εἶπε· Βαλτάσαρ, τὸ ἐνύπνιον
τοῦτο καὶ ἡ σύγκρισις αὐτοῦ μὴ κατασπευσάτω σε.» Εἶδε γὰρ αὐτὸν
θορυβούμενον, καὶ ἀναγκαίως ψυχαγωγεῖ, μαθεῖν ἐφιέμενος ὅπερ ἀγνοεῖ·
λέγει τοίνυν αὐτῷ· Μὴ σφόδρα ἐπείγου, ἀλλὰ κατὰ σχολὴν τὰ μηνυό-
μενα διὰ τοῦ ἐνυπνίου εὑρών, ταῦτά μοι δῆλα κατάστησον. «Ἀπεκρίθη
τοίνυν ὁ Βαλτάσαρ, καὶ εἶπε· Κύριέ μου βασιλεῦ, τὸ ἐνύπνιον τοῦτο τοῖς
μισοῦσί σε, καὶ ἡ σύγκρισις αὐτοῦ τοῖς ἐχθροῖς σου.» Σφόδρα σοφῶς καὶ
συνετῶς ἀπεύχεται μὲν αὐτῷ λυπηρὰ τοῦ προοιμίου ἀρξάμενος, σημαίνει
δὲ ὅμως τὴν ἀλήθειαν.

ιζ΄, ιη΄. «Τὸ δένδρον, φησί, τὸ μεγαλυνθὲν καὶ ἰσχυκός, οὗ τὸ ὕψος
ἔφθασεν εἰς τὸν οὐρανόν, καὶ τὸ κύτος αὐτοῦ εἰς πᾶσαν τὴν γῆν. Καὶ τὰ
φύλλα αὐτοῦ εὐθαλῆ, καὶ ὁ καρπὸς αὐτοῦ πολύς, καὶ τροφὴ πᾶσιν ἐν
αὐτῷ, ὑποκάτω αὐτοῦ κατῴκει τὰ θηρία τὰ ἄγρια, καὶ ἐν τοῖς κλάδοις
αὐτοῦ κατεσκήνουν τὰ ὄρνεα τοῦ οὐρανοῦ, σὺ εἶ, βασιλεῦ.» Ἄξιον δὲ
θαυμάσαι τοῦ Δανιὴλ τὴν σοφίαν· οὐ γὰρ ἁπλῶς εἶπε, Τὸ δένδρον τὸ
μέγα, ἀλλά, «Τὸ μεγαλυνθὲν καὶ τὸ ἰσχυκός·» τουτέστιν, Οὐκ ἄνωθεν
ἦσθα μέγας, ἀλλὰ κατὰ μέρος γεγένησαι, καὶ τὴν ἰσχὺν δὲ οὐκ ἐξ ὠδίνων
ἔσχες, ἀλλὰ κατὰ βραχὺ ταύτην προσέλαβες. Διὸ πάλιν ἐπάγει·

ιθ΄. «Ὅτι ἐμεγαλύνθης, καὶ ἴσχυσας, καὶ ἡ μεγαλωσύνη σου ἐμεγαλύνθη καὶ ἔφθασεν εἰς τὸν οὐρανόν, καὶ ἡ κυρεία σου εἰς τὰ πέρατα
τῆς γῆς.» Καὶ ταῦτα δὲ σφόδρα ἁρμοδίως καὶ προσφόρως οὐρανῷ καὶ
1365   γῇ προσήρμοσε· τὴν μὲν γὰρ κυρείαν εἶπεν ἐφθακέναι | εἰς τὰ πέρατα

angel means, that the fate of the tree will come to pass for this purpose, for everyone to know through this that there is one | God, 1364 Lord and King, who appoints kings on the earth and entrusts the kingdom to whomever he wishes. In fact, to bring out his own authority, he appoints as king the one who is at one time the most insignificant and thought to be of no value, and makes those of greatest rank obey him.

Having thus completed the account of the dream, he says to Daniel, *This is the dream I, King Nebuchadnezzar, saw; and you, Belteshazzar, give the interpretation openly* (v. 18), that is, truly and precisely, *Because all the wise men of my kingdom are unable to disclose to me its interpretation, whereas you can.* And to give the reason, *Because the holy spirit of God is in you*: whereas they have recourse to human reasoning, you learn hidden things from God. *Then Daniel, who had the name Belteshazzar, was dismayed for a moment, and his thoughts were in disarray* (v. 19). It was necessary, you see, for human weakness to be displayed, and at that point the charism of inspiration to be demonstrated. *So the king said in reply, Belteshazzar, Do not let the dream and its interpretation upset you.* He noticed him alarmed, you see, and necessarily encouraged him because he longed to learn what he did not know; so he says to him, There is no hurry, at your leisure find out what was conveyed in the dream, and make it clear to me.

So Belteshazzar said in reply, My lord king, may the dream be for those who hate you, and its interpretation for your enemies. It was very wise and intelligent of him to begin by deprecating any misfortunes for him and yet point out the truth. *The tree that had grown to great size and strength, with its height reaching to heaven and its trunk across the whole earth, its foliage luxuriant, its fruit abundant, nourishment in it for all, with wild beasts dwelling under it and the birds of heaven taking shelter in its branches—it is you, O King* (vv. 20–22). Daniel's wisdom is worth admiring: he did not say simply, The big tree, but Grown to great size and strength— in other words, Instead of being great from the beginning, you became great gradually, and instead of having strength from the outset, you gradually acquired it. Hence he goes further, *Because you have grown great and strong, your greatness has increased, you reach to heaven and your lordship to the ends of the earth.* It was very fitting and appropriate for him to relate these things to heaven and earth: he said his lordship had reached | the ends of the earth, 1365

τῆς γῆς, τουτέστι τὴν ἐξουσίαν· εἰς δὲ τὸν οὐρανὸν οὐκέτι τὴν κυρείαν, ἀλλὰ τὴν μεγαλωσύνην, τουτέστι, τὴν τοῦ λογισμοῦ φαντασίαν.

κ΄, κα΄. «Καὶ ὅτι εἶδεν, φησίν, ὁ βασιλεὺς εἶρ καὶ ἅγιον καταβαίνοντα ἐκ τοῦ οὐρανοῦ, καὶ εἶπεν· Ἐκτίλατε τὸ δένδρον, καὶ διαφθείρετε αὐτό· πλὴν τὴν φυὴν τῶν ῥιζῶν αὐτοῦ ἐν τῇ γῇ ἐάσατε, καὶ ἐν δεσμῷ σιδηρῷ καὶ χαλκῷ, καὶ ἐν τῇ χλόῃ τῇ ἔξω, καὶ ἐν τῇ δρόσῳ τοῦ οὐρανοῦ αὐλισθήσεται, καὶ μετὰ θηρίων ἀγρίων ἡ μερὶς αὐτοῦ, ἕως οὗ ἑπτὰ καιροὶ ἀλλοιωθῶσιν ἐπ' αὐτόν. Καὶ τοῦτο ἡ σύγκρισις αὐτοῦ, βασιλεῦ.» Καὶ ἀξιόπιστον ποιῶν τὸν λόγον, ἀναγκαίως ἐπήγαγε· «Καὶ σύγκριμα Ὑψίστου ἐστίν, ὃ ἔφθασεν ἐπὶ τὸν κύριόν μου τὸν βασιλέα.» Ἐντεῦθεν ἔστιν ἀκριβῶς καταμαθεῖν τῆς ἀποστολικῆς διδασκαλίας τὸ χρήσιμον. «Πᾶσα γάρ, φησί, ψυχὴ ἐξουσίαις ὑπερεχούσαις ὑποταττέσθω.» Καὶ γὰρ καὶ ὁ μακάριος Δανιὴλ κύριον αὐτὸν τὸν δυσσεβῆ βασιλέα καλεῖ, καὶ τῷ νόμῳ τῆς ἐξουσίας πειθόμενος, ταῖς πρεπούσαις προσηγορίαις κέχρηται, καὶ λυπηρὰν οὖσαν τοῦ ἐνυπνίου τὴν ἀλήθειαν ὑποδείκνυσιν.

κβ΄. «Ἐκδιώξουσι γάρ σε, φησίν, ἀπὸ τῶν ἀνθρώπων, καὶ μετὰ θηρίων ἀγρίων ἔσται ἡ κατοικία σου, καὶ χόρτον ὡς βοῦν ψωμιοῦσί σε, καὶ ἀπὸ τῆς δρόσου τοῦ οὐρανοῦ τὸ σῶμά σου βαφήσεται, καὶ ἑπτὰ καιροὶ ἀλλαγήσονται ἐπὶ σοί.» Ἑπτὰ δὲ καιροὺς οἱ μὲν ἔφασαν ἑπτὰ ἔτη, οἱ δὲ τρία καὶ ἥμισυ. Οὐ γὰρ εἰς τέσσαρας τροπὰς ἡ θεία Γραφὴ τὸν ἐνιαυτὸν διαιρεῖ, ἀλλ' εἰς δύο τὰς γενικωτάτας, χειμῶνα καὶ θέρος· ἑπτὰ οὖν τοιαῦτα τμήματα τρία καὶ ἥμισυ πληροῖ ἔτη· Τοσοῦτον δέ, φησίν, ἐν τῇ συμφορᾷ διατελέσεις χρόνον· «ἕως οὗ γνῷς, ὅτι κυριεύει ὁ Ὕψιστος τῆς βασιλείας τῶν ἀνθρώπων, καὶ ᾧ ἐὰν δόξῃ, δώσει αὐτήν.» Ἐπειδὴ γὰρ ὀνειροπολεῖς εἶναι θεός, μᾶλλον δὲ καὶ κρείττων Θεοῦ, ἀφαιρεῖταί σου Θεὸς καὶ τὸν ἀνθρώπινον λογισμόν, καὶ τοῖς θηρίοις σε ἐοικέναι ποιήσει, ἵνα τῇ πείρᾳ μάθῃς, τί μὲν ἄνθρωπος, τί δὲ Θεός, καὶ τί μὲν ἀνθρωπίνη εὐκληρία, τί δὲ θεία βασιλεία, καὶ ὅτι ταύτης τυχεῖν ἀδύνατον μὴ βουλομένου Θεοῦ.

κγ΄. «Καὶ ὅτι εἶπε, φησίν· Ἐάσατε τὴν φυὴν τῶν ῥιζῶν τοῦ δένδρου, ἡ βασιλεία σου σοὶ μενεῖ, ἀφ' ἧς ἂν γνῷς τὴν βασιλείαν τὴν οὐράνιον.» Ἀποστερηθεὶς γὰρ τῆς βασιλείας, κἀκεῖνα ὑπομείνας ἅπαντα, ἐπιγνώσῃ τῆς βασιλείας τὸν χορηγόν, εἶτα γνοὺς ἀπολήψῃ πάλιν τὴν

that is, his authority, whereas it was not yet his lordship that had reached to heaven but his imaginings.

Because the king saw, he went on, *an eir and holy one descending from heaven, and said, Cut down the tree and destroy it, but leave the stump of its roots in the ground, with a band of iron and bronze, in the grass outside, and it will lodge in the dew of heaven, and its lot is with the wild beasts until seven times pass over him. This is the interpretation, O King* (vv. 23–24). And to make his words more trustworthy, he of necessity went on, *It is a decree of the Most High that has come upon my lord the king.* At this point it is possible to learn the value of the apostolic teaching, "Let every person be subject to the governing authorities";[112] blessed Daniel, note, calls the impious king *lord*, and influenced by the norm of authority he adopts the appropriate titles, and he gives a glimpse of the truth of the dream, distressing though it is.

They will expel you from human company, your dwelling place will be with wild beasts, they will feed you grass like an ox, your body will be dipped in the dew of heaven, and seven times will pass over you (v. 25). Now, while some commentators claimed the *seven times* are seven years, others said three and a half. The divine Scripture, in fact, divides the year not into four seasons but into two more generic parts, winter and summer; so seven divisions of that kind amount to three and a half years.[113] You will spend such a length of time in misfortune, he says, *until you come to learn that the Most High has lordship over the kingdom of human beings and will give it to whomever he pleases*: since you dream of being God—or, rather, even better than God—God will take from you even human reason and will make you resemble the beasts so that you may learn from experience what is man and what is God, what is human fortune and what is divine kingship, and the fact that it is impossible to attain it unless God wishes.

And because he said, Leave the trunk of the roots of the tree, your kingdom will remain for you from the time you acknowledge the kingdom of heaven (v. 26): after being deprived of the kingdom and enduring all that, you will acknowledge the provider of kingship; then, when you know him, you will in turn regain your former au-

---

[112] Rom 13:1.

[113] Hippolytus offered the former interpretation (only), Guinot tells us (*L'Exégèse,* 716). The Qumran *Prayer of Nabonidus,* on the other hand, speaks of seven years of isolation for that king.

προτέραν ἐξουσίαν· ἵνα καὶ τῇ ἀφαιρέσει, καὶ τῇ ἀποδόσει, μάθῃς ἀκριβῶς, τίς ὁ τῶν ὅλων κυβερνήτης, τίς ὁ σοφῶς ἅπαντα ἰθύνων καὶ πρυτανεύων. Οὕτως εἰρηκὼς τὰ ἐσόμενα, παραίνεσιν εἰσφέρει καὶ συμβουλὴν ἀρίστην, καὶ φάρμακον προσφέρει συμβαῖνον τῷ τραύματι. |

κδ΄. «Διὰ τοῦτο γὰρ, φησί, βασιλεῦ, ἡ βουλή μου ἀρεσάτω σοι, καὶ τὰς ἁμαρτίας σου ἐν ἐλεημοσύναις λύτρωσαι, καὶ τὰς ἀδικίας σου ἐν οἰκτιρμοῖς πενήτων.» Δηλοῖ δὲ διὰ τούτων τὴν ἄπληστον ὠμότητα ἢ κατὰ τῶν ὑπηκόων ἐχρήσατο. Βούλει, φησί, φιλανθρωπίας ἀπολαῦσαι; ἐπίδειξαι ταύτην εἰς τοὺς τὴν αὐτὴν σοὶ φύσιν λαχόντας· οὕτω γὰρ πείσεις τὸν δικαστὴν σβέσαι τὴν ἀπειλὴν, καὶ καταλιπεῖν ἀτέλεστον. «Ἴσως γὰρ, φησίν, ἔσται μακροθυμία τοῖς παραπτώμασί σου.» Ὁ μὲν οὖν προφήτης ταύτην εἰσηγήσατο τὴν γνώμην· ὁ δὲ μείνας ἀτεράμων καὶ ἀκαμπὴς, ἐδέξατο τῆς παρανομίας τὰ ἐπίχειρα, καὶ ἅπερ ἤκουσεν ἀλγεινά, ταῦτα τοῖς ὀφθαλμοῖς ἐθεάσατο. Εἶτα καὶ σημαίνει τῆς θείας μακροθυμίας τὸν χρόνον· δυοκαίδεκα γὰρ διαδραμόντων μηνῶν, ἐδέξατο ἡ διὰ τῆς προρρήσεως ἀπειλὴ τῶν πραγμάτων τὸ τέλος. Καὶ τοσοῦτον χρόνον εἰς μεταμέλειαν εἰληφώς, κακῶς τὴν τῆς μεταμελείας ἀνάλωσε προθεσμίαν. Πρὸς ὃν ὁ μακάριος εἴποι ἂν Παῦλος εἰκότως· «Ἢ τοῦ πλούτου τῆς χρηστότητος αὐτοῦ, καὶ τῆς ἀνοχῆς, καὶ μακροθυμίας καταφρονεῖς, ἀγνοῶν, ὅτι τὸ χρηστὸν τοῦ Θεοῦ εἰς μετάνοιάν σε ἄγει; Κατὰ δὲ τὴν σκληρότητά σου καὶ ἀμετανόητον καρδίαν, θησαυρίζεις σεαυτῷ ὀργὴν ἐν ἡμέρᾳ ὀργῆς, καὶ ἀποκαλύψεως, καὶ δικαιοκρισίας τοῦ Θεοῦ, ὃς ἀποδώσει ἑκάστῳ κατὰ τὰ ἔργα αὐτοῦ· τοῖς μὲν καθ' ὑπομονὴν ἔργου ἀγαθοῦ δόξαν, καὶ τιμὴν, καὶ ἀφθαρσίαν ζητοῦσι, ζωὴν αἰώνιον· τοῖς δὲ ἐξ ἐριθείας, καὶ ἀπειθοῦσι μὲν τῇ ἀληθείᾳ, πειθομένοις δὲ τῇ ἀδικίᾳ, θυμὸς καὶ ὀργή· θλίψις καὶ στενοχωρία ἐπὶ πᾶσαν ψυχὴν ἀνθρώπου τοῦ κατεργαζομένου τὸ κακόν.» Ταῦτα γὰρ συνέβη καὶ τῷ Ναβουχοδονόσορ, τῇ τοῦ Θεοῦ μακροθυμίᾳ εἰς δέον οὐ χρησαμένῳ. Καὶ τούτου μάρτυς αὐτὸς οὑτωσὶ λέγων·

κς΄, κζ΄. «Καὶ μετὰ δώδεκα μῆνας, ἐν τῷ ναῷ τῆς βασιλείας αὐτοῦ ἐν Βαβυλῶνι περιπατῶν ἦν, καὶ ἐπὶ τῶν τειχῶν τῆς πόλεως μετὰ πάσης τῆς δόξης αὐτοῦ, καὶ ἐπὶ τῶν πύργων αὐτοῦ διεπορεύετο. Καὶ ἀπεκρίθη ὁ βασιλεὺς καὶ εἶπεν· Οὐκ αὕτη ἐστὶ Βαβυλὼν ἡ μεγάλη, ἣν ἐγὼ ᾠκοδόμησα εἰς οἶκον βασιλείας, ἐν κράτει τῆς ἰσχύος μου, εἰς τιμὴν τῆς δόξης μου;» Βλέπε τοῦ φρονήματος τὸν ὄγκον, βλέπε τὴν τῆς

thority, so that by removal and restoration you will learn precisely
who is the governor of everything, who it is who wisely guides and
orders everything. Having foretold the future in this way, he offers exhortation and excellent advice, and applies a remedy suited
to the wound. | *Hence, O King, may my advice be acceptable to you;*   1368
atone for your sins with almsgiving and for your iniquities with com-
passion for the poor (v. 27). In this he implies the insatiable cruelty
with which he treated his subjects. Do you wish, he asks, to receive
lovingkindness? Give evidence of it to those who share the same
nature as you, this being the way you will persuade the judge to
cancel his threat and leave it unfulfilled: *Perhaps there will be long-*
suffering for your failings.

While the prophet delivered this verdict, then, the other man
continued to be unfeeling and inexorable, and so he received the
wages of his lawlessness, and witnessed with his own eyes the sor-
rows of which he had heard. The text then conveys also the span of
divine longsuffering: after the passage of twelve months the threat
in the prophecy reached its factual conclusion. Though given such
a length of time to repent, he failed to meet the deadline for repentance; it would be of him that blessed Paul spoke, "Do you despise
the riches of his kindness, forbearance and longsuffering? Are you
unaware that the kindness of God leads you to repentance? In your
hard and impenitent heart, however, you are storing up wrath for
yourselves on the day of wrath, revelation and right judgment by
God, who will render to everyone according to each one's works—
eternal life to those who by perseverance in good works seek glory
and honor and immortality, while anger and wrath will come to
those who in self-seeking do not obey the truth but obey iniquity.
There will be tribulation and distress for every person guilty of
evildoing."[114]

These events, you see, happened also to Nebuchadnezzar for
not properly taking advantage of God's lovingkindness; he himself
testifies to it in what follows. *After twelve months he was walking in*
the temple of his kingdom in Babylon and traversing the walls of the
city and his towers in all his splendor. The king's response was as fol-
lows: Is not this mighty Babylon, which I personally built as the house
of the kingdom in the power of my strength for the honor of my glory?
(vv. 29–30) Note the pretentious attitude, note the excess of arro-

[114] Rom 2:4–9.

ἀλαζονείας ὑπερβολήν. Ἐγὼ γὰρ αὐτήν, φησί, βασιλικὴν πόλιν ἐποιησάμην βασίλεια καταστησάμενος ἐν αὐτῇ, εἰς τιμὴν τῆς δόξης μου·
ἐποίησα δὲ ταῦτα ἰσχὺν ἔχων μεγίστην, καὶ πάντων κεκρατηκώς. Ἀλλὰ
μὴν φρυαττόμενος καὶ βρενθυόμενος, τοιούτοις ἐχρήσατο τοῖς λόγοις· ὁ
1369   δὲ Δεσπότης Θεὸς παραυτίκα τὴν τιμωρίαν ἐπήγαγεν. |
     κη΄. «Ἔτι γάρ, φησί, τοῦ λόγου ὄντος ἐν τῷ στόματι τοῦ βασι-
λέως, φωνὴ ἀπ᾽ οὐρανοῦ ἐγένετο.» Ἐπειδὴ γὰρ εἰς τὸν οὐρανὸν ἀνελθεῖν
ὠνειροπόλησεν, ἐκεῖθεν δέχεται τὴν ἀπόφασιν· καὶ ἐπειδὴ οὐκ ἀπέχρησεν
αὐτῷ τὰ κάτω βασίλεια, ἀλλ᾽ ἅμα καὶ τῶν ἄνω μανικῶς ἐπεθύμησεν,
ἔρημος γίνεται καὶ τῶν κάτω· καὶ τὸν οὐρανὸν ἁρπάσαι θελήσας, καὶ
τῆς γῆς ἐξελαύνεται. «Φωνὴ τοίνυν ἦλθεν ἀπ᾽ οὐρανοῦ· Σοί, σοὶ λέγεται, Ναβουχοδονόσορ βασιλεῦ.» Ὁ δὲ τῆς ἀντωνυμίας διπλασιασμὸς οὐχ
ἁπλῶς πρόσκειται, ἀλλ᾽ εἰς ἔλεγχον ἐναργέστερον τοῦ πρὸς ὃν ταῦτα λέγεται. Καλεῖ δὲ αὐτὸν ἔτι βασιλέα, καὶ τὴν παροῦσαν ἔτι δόξαν, καὶ τὴν
ἐσομένην οὐκ εἰς μακρὰν ἀτιμίαν δεικνύς.
     «Ἡ βασιλεία σου, φησί, παρῆλθεν ἀπὸ σοῦ. (κθ΄.) Καὶ ἀπὸ τῶν
ἀνθρώπων σε ἐκδιώξουσι, καὶ μετὰ θηρίων ἀγρίων ἡ κατοικία σου καὶ
χόρτον ὡς βοῦν ψωμιοῦσί σε, καὶ ἑπτὰ καιροὶ ἀλλαγήσονται ἐπὶ σοί, ἕως
οὗ γνῷς, ὅτι κυριεύει ὁ Ὕψιστος τῆς βασιλείας τῶν ἀνθρώπων, καὶ ᾧ
ἐὰν δόξῃ, δώσει αὐτήν.» Εἶτα δεικνὺς τὴν τῆς τιμωρίας ὀξύτητα, καὶ
παραυτίκα, φησί, τῷ λόγῳ τὸ ἔργον ἐπηκολούθησεν.
     λ΄. «Αὐτῇ, φησί, τῇ ὥρᾳ συνετελέσθη ὁ λόγος ἐπὶ Ναβουχοδο-
νόσορ, καὶ ἀπὸ τῶν ἀνθρώπων ἐδιώχθη.» Ἐξεδιώχθη δὲ πρῶτον μὲν
δι᾽ αὐτὸ τὸ πάθος· μανίᾳ γὰρ παρεδόθη καὶ λύττῃ καὶ μυρία ἂν εἰργάσατο κακά, εἴπερ ἀδείας ἀπήλαυσεν· ἔπειτα δὲ καὶ διὰ τὴν ἀπέχθειαν,
ἣν περὶ αὐτὸν ἅπαντες ἔχοντες, ἡνίκα μὲν ἔρρωτο, ἐπειρῶντο λανθάνειν,
συμφορᾷ δὲ περιπεσόντι ἐπέθεντο, τῆς ὠμότητος αὐτὸν βδελυξάμενοι.
«Καὶ χόρτον ὡς βοῦς, φησίν, ἤσθιεν.» Ἴδιον γὰρ τῶν παραπαιόντων,
οὐ μόνον τὸ λέγειν καὶ πράττειν ἀλόγιστά τε καὶ ἄτακτα, ἀλλὰ καὶ τὸ
ἐσθίειν ἅπαντα τὰ προσπίπτοντα· τοῦτο δ᾽ ἄν τις ἴδοι καὶ νῦν τοὺς ὑπὸ
δαιμόνων ἐνοχλουμένους ποιοῦντας καὶ πάσχοντας. Οὐ μόνον δὲ ὡς βοῦς
ἤσθιε τὸν χόρτον, ἀλλὰ «Καὶ ἀπὸ τῆς δρόσου τοῦ οὐρανοῦ τὸ σῶμα αὐτοῦ ἐβάφη.» Ὑπαίθριος γὰρ ταλαιπωρῶν, καὶ γυμνῷ τῷ σώματι κρυμῷ
τε προσπαλαίων καὶ φλογμῷ, ἀναγκαίως ἑτέραν ἐδέξατο χρόαν. «Ἕως
οὗ αἱ τρίχες αὐτοῦ, ὡς λεόντων, ἐμεγαλύνθησαν, καὶ οἱ ὄνυχες αὐτοῦ,
ὡς ὀρνέων.» Μὴ ἀποκειρόμενος γὰρ συνήθως, μηδὲ ἀφαιρούμενος τῶν
ὀνύχων τὰ περιττά, ἀναγκαίως ἐν τοσούτῳ χρόνῳ τοιαύτας ἔσχηκε καὶ
τρίχας καὶ ὄνυχας. Διὰ δὲ τούτων ἁπάντων ἐσήμαινε τὸ ἀτημέλητον

gance. I myself built the royal city, he is saying, establishing the palace in it for the honor of my glory, and I did it with my mighty power, being also in control of everything. While he used such words in his unruly swaggering, however, the Lord God immediately brought retribution to bear. | *While the words were still in the* 1369 *king's mouth, a voice came from heaven* (v. 31): since he dreamed of going up to heaven, he received the verdict from there; and since he was not satisfied with the palace here below, and instead at the same time he insanely hankered after one on high, he was deprived of the one here below and in his wish to snatch heaven he was driven also from earth.

So *a voice came from heaven, To you, to you comes the verdict, King Nebuchadnezzar.* The repetition of the pronoun was not accidental: it was for clearer proof of the one to whom this was addressed. He refers to him as still king and his glory as still current so as to highlight the dishonor that would not be long in coming. *The kingdom has passed from you. They will hunt you from human company, your dwelling will be with the wild beasts, they will feed you grass like an ox, and seven times will pass over you until you acknowledge that the Most High has lordship of the kingdom of human beings, and will give it to whomever he pleases* (vv. 31–32).

Then, to bring out the rapidity of the retribution, the event followed immediately on the word. *At the same hour the sentence was fulfilled in Nebuchadnezzar's case. He was hunted from human company* (v. 33). He was hunted, firstly, on account of the ailment itself: he fell victim to insanity and frenzy, and would have committed countless evils if he had been left to himself; and, secondly, also on account of the hostility all felt for him when he was well, trying to escape his notice, but when a victim of misfortune they attacked him, loathing him for his cruelty. *He ate grass like an ox.* It is typical of deranged people not only to say and do what is irrational and disorderly, but also to eat everything they come upon; even today you could see people possessed by demons acting and suffering this way. Not only was he in the habit of eating grass like an ox, however: *his body was dipped in the dew of heaven:* suffering from exposure, and struggling in his naked body with frost and heat, he inevitably took on a different color. *Until his hair grew as long as lions' and his nails as long as birds':* not grooming himself in the usual way or cutting his nails, over time he inevitably had hair and nails like this. By all this it suggested his condition of neglect

αὐτὸν καὶ ἀκηδεμόνευτον εἶναι. Τῆς γὰρ θείας ἔρημος γενόμενος προμηθείας, οὐδὲ τῆς παρὰ τῶν οἰκείων ἐπιμελείας ἀπήλαυσεν, καὶ ταῦτα
γυναικὸς οὔσης, καὶ παίδων, καὶ συγγενῶν· ἀλλὰ θηρίου δίκην τοὺς ἀοι-
κήτους χώρους διετέλει περινοστῶν, τὴν τῶν ἀλόγων τροφὴν τῇ γαστρὶ
1372 παραπέμπων· ἐπειδὴ γὰρ, « Ἄνθρωπος ὢν | καὶ ἐν τιμῇ ὢν μεγίστῃ, οὐ
συνῆκεν, ἀλλὰ παρασυνεβλήθη τοῖς κτήνεσι τοῖς ἀνοήτοις, καὶ ὡμοιώ-
θη αὐτοῖς,» καὶ θηριώδει γνώμῃ κατὰ τῶν ὑπηκόων ἐκέχρητο, εἰκότως
καὶ μάλα δικαίως τὸν κτηνώδη καὶ θηριώδη βίον κατεδικάσθη. Ἀλλ' ὁ
φιλάνθρωπος Δεσπότης, λύσας τὴν τιμωρίαν, ὡς ἀγαθός, καὶ τῇ πείρᾳ
διδάξας, ὡς αὐτός ἐστι τῶν ἁπάντων Κύριος, πάλιν αὐτὸν ἐπανήγαγε,
καὶ τὴν βασιλείαν αὐτῷ τὴν προτέραν ἐπίστευσε.
    λα'. « Μετὰ γὰρ τέλος, φησί, τῶν ἡμερῶν, ἐγὼ Ναβουχοδονόσορ
τοὺς ὀφθαλμούς μου εἰς τὸν οὐρανὸν ἀνέλαβον.» Οὐχ ἁπλῶς δὲ προστέθεικε τὸ ἐγώ, ἀλλὰ διδάσκων ἅπαντας ἀνθρώπους, ὡς Ὁ τῇ ἀλαζονείᾳ
ἐκείνῃ χρησάμενος, ὁ εἰρηκώς· « Τίς ἐστιν ὁ Θεός, ὃς ἐξελεῖται ὑμᾶς ἐκ
τῶν χειρῶν μου;» ὁ ὀνειροπολήσας εἰς τὸν οὐρανὸν ἀναβῆναι, καὶ ἐπάνω
τῶν ἀστέρων θεῖναι τὸν θρόνον μου, ἐδιδάχθην τῇ πείρᾳ τὸ δέον, ἔμαθον διὰ τῆς τιμωρίας σωφρονεῖν, τὴν ἐμαυτοῦ δουλείαν ἐπέγνων. Διὸ καὶ
ἀνέλαβον τοὺς ὀφθαλμούς μου εἰς τὸν οὐρανόν, καὶ ἅμα τε τοῦτο ἐποίησα, «Καὶ αἱ φρένες μου ἐπεστράφησαν.» Ἀντὶ τοῦ, Τῆς παραφροσύνης
ἐλεύθερος ἐγενόμην, καὶ τὸν λογισμὸν ἐρρώσθην· παραυτίκα δὲ ὑγιῆ τὸν
νοῦν ἀπέλαβον. «Καὶ τῷ Ὑψίστῳ εὐλόγησα, καὶ τὸν ζῶντα εἰς τοὺς
αἰῶνας ᾔνεσα, ὅτι ἡ ἐξουσία αὐτοῦ ἐξουσία αἰώνιος, καὶ ἡ βασιλεία αὐτοῦ εἰς γενεὰν καὶ γενεάν.» Γνοὺς γὰρ τῇ πείρᾳ, τί μὲν ἄνθρωπος, τί δὲ
Θεός, τὸν μὲν Ὕψιστον καὶ ζῶντα προσαγορεύει, καὶ βασιλέα αἰώνιον
ἀποκαλεῖ, τὴν δὲ οἰκείαν εὐτέλειαν ἐπιγινώσκει. Διό φησι·
    λβ'. «Καὶ πάντες οἱ κατοικοῦντες τὴν γῆν εἰς οὐδὲν ἐλογίσθησαν.»
Μέχρι μὲν γὰρ τοῦ παρόντος ᾤμην εἶναι ἐμαυτὸν μέγιστόν τε καὶ ὑψ-
ηλότατον, νῦν δὲ ἔγνων σαφῶς, ὡς πᾶσα τῶν ἀνθρώπων ἡ φύσις Θεῷ
παραβαλλομένη οὐδέν ἐστι. Καὶ ζητήσας εὐτελείας προσηγορίαν, καὶ μὴ
εὑρὼν ἀξίαν, τὸ οὐδὲν τέθεικεν, ἔμφασιν ἔχον ἱκανὴν τοῦ σφαλεροῦ καὶ
εὐδιαλύτου τῆς φύσεως. Καὶ τὸν μὲν Θεὸν καὶ Ὕψιστον, καὶ Δεσπότην,
καὶ ζῶντα καὶ βασιλέα αἰώνιον ἀπεκάλεσεν, ἅπαντας δὲ ἀνθρώπους οὐδὲν προσηγόρευσεν. Οὕτω δὲ καὶ ὁ μακάριος Ἡσαΐας τοῖς εἰδώλοις τὴν
θείαν παραβάλλων φύσιν, τὸ τῶν ἀνθρώπων εἰς μέσον παρήγαγε γένος.

and carelessness: bereft of divine providence, he was not even a recipient of care from his own—wife, children, kith and kin; instead, like a wild animal he kept frequenting uninhabited places, filling his stomach with the food of brute beasts. In fact, since "though human | and enjoying great pomp, he had no sense, being comparable rather to irrational cattle, and being like them,"[115] and since he gave free rein to a wild manner toward his subjects, it was very right and proper that he should be condemned to the life of cattle and wild animals.

1372

The loving Lord, however, terminated the punishment in his goodness; after teaching him by experience that it is he who is the Lord of all, in turn he brought him back and entrusted his former kingdom to him. *At the end of that time,* the text goes on, *I, Nebuchadnezzar, lifted my eyes to heaven* (v. 34). He inserted the word *I*, not by accident, but to teach all people, I am the one who had shown that awful arrogance, who had said *Who is the god who will save you from my hands?* and who dreamed of ascending to heaven and putting my throne above the stars, and I was taught my proper place by experience, learned through punishment to come to my senses, and acknowledged my position as a slave. Hence I lifted up my eyes to heaven, and as soon as I did so, *my reason returned to me,* that is, I was rid of my derangement and came to my senses, and immediately I became of sound mind again.

I blessed the Most High and praised the one who lives forever, because his authority is an eternal authority, and his kingdom from generation to generation. Knowing from experience what man is, and what God is, on the one hand he gave him the name *Most High* and *living,* and called him eternal king, and on the other he acknowledged his own insignificance. Hence he says, *All the inhabitants of the earth were reckoned as nothing* (v. 35): up to the present I thought myself very great and elevated, whereas now I know clearly that all human nature is nothing compared to God. Having sought a term for insignificance and not found one suitable, he used *nothing,* which gives a sufficient clue to the instability and impermanence of nature; while calling God *Most High, Lord, living* and *eternal king,* he spoke of all human beings as *nothing.* In similar fashion also blessed Isaiah in comparing the divine nature with the idols focused on human nature: "If all the nations are

[115] Ps 49:12.

« Εἰ γὰρ πάντα τὰ ἔθνη, φησίν, ὡς σταγὼν ἀπὸ κάδου, καὶ ὡς ῥοπὴ ζυγοῦ ἐλογίσθησαν, καὶ ὡς σίελος λογισθήσονται· ὁ δὲ Λίβανος οὐχ ἱκανὸς εἰς καῦσιν, καὶ πάντα τὰ τετράποδα οὐχ ἱκανὰ εἰς ὁλοκάρπωσιν, καὶ πάντα τὰ ἔθνη εἰς οὐδέν εἰσι, καὶ εἰς οὐδὲν ἐλογίσθησαν αὐτῷ· τίνι ὁμοιώσετε Κύριον; καὶ τίνι ὁμοιώματι ὁμοιώσετε αὐτόν; » Τοσαύτην ὠφέλειαν ὁ Ναβουχοδονόσορ ἐκ τῶν συμφορῶν ἐδέξατο, ὅτι προφητικῶς

1373 περὶ Θεοῦ καὶ φρονεῖ καὶ φθέγγεται· καὶ ὡς ἐκ συμφωνίας | τινὸς ἀπὸ τῆς κτίσεως πᾶσαν τὴν ὑμνῳδίαν ὑφαίνει. « Πάντες, φησίν, οἱ κατοικοῦντες τὴν γῆν ὡς οὐδὲν ἐλογίσθησαν, καὶ κατὰ τὸ θέλημα αὐτοῦ ποιεῖ ἐν τῇ δυνάμει τοῦ οὐρανοῦ, καὶ ἐν τῇ κατοικίᾳ τῆς γῆς. » Καὶ αὕτη δὲ ἑτέρου προφήτου διδασκαλία. Ὁ γὰρ μακάριος Δαβὶδ λέγει· « Πάντα ὅσα ἠθέλησεν ὁ Κύριος, ἐποίησεν ἐν τῷ οὐρανῷ καὶ ἐν τῇ γῇ. » Τοῦτο καὶ οὗτος κηρύττει. « Ἃ γὰρ θέλει, φησί, καὶ ἐν τῇ δυνάμει τοῦ οὐρανοῦ, καὶ ἐν τῇ κατοικίᾳ τῆς γῆς, » πρυτανεύει καὶ δεσπόζει, οὐ μόνον τῆς γῆς, ἀλλὰ δὴ καὶ αὐτῶν τῶν οὐρανῶν. Εἶτα καὶ ἄμαχον δεικνὺς τῆς δυνάμεως· « Καὶ οὐκ ἔστι, φησίν, ὃς ἀντιστήσεται τῇ χειρὶ αὐτοῦ, καὶ ἐρεῖ αὐτῷ· Τί τοῦτο ἐποίησας; » Ἀνάγκη γὰρ στέργειν τὰ ὑπ᾽ αὐτοῦ γινόμενα, ἐάν τε θυμήρη, ἐάν τε ἀλγεινὰ ᾖ· τολμηρὸν γὰρ τὸ ἀντιτείνειν, καὶ αἰτιᾶσθαι τὰ ὑπ᾽ αὐτοῦ σοφῶς πρυτανευόμενα. Ταῦτα, φησί, γνοὺς καὶ ὁμολογήσας, καὶ τὸν Ὕψιστον δοξάσας, εἰς ἐμαυτὸν ἐπανῆλθον, καὶ τὴν προτέραν βασιλείαν μετ᾽ εὐσεβείας ἀπέλαβον.

λγ΄. « Αὐτῷ γὰρ τῷ καιρῷ αἱ φρένες μου ἐστράφησαν πρός με, καὶ εἰς τὴν τιμὴν τῆς βασιλείας μου ἦλθον, καὶ ἡ μορφή μου ἐπέστρεψεν ἐπ᾽ ἐμέ. » Αὐχμῶν γὰρ, ὡς εἰκός, καὶ ῥυπῶν, ἀποκειράμενος καὶ τὰ περιττὰ τῶν ὀνύχων ἀφελόμενος, καὶ τὸν ῥύπον ἀπονιψάμενος, καὶ τῆς θείας χάριτος ἀπολαύσας, ἐπεγνώσθη ὅτι ἄνθρωπος ἦν ἐκεῖνος, ὁ πρότερον τὴν μεγίστην διέπων βασιλείαν. « Καὶ οἱ τύραννοί μου, φησί, καὶ οἱ μεγιστᾶνές μου ἐπεζήτουν με. » Ἀποθέμενοι γὰρ κἀκεῖνοι τὸ μῖσος, διάθεσιν περὶ ἐμὲ καὶ φίλτρον ἔλαβον. « Καὶ ἐπὶ τὴν βασιλείαν μου ἐκραταιώθην, καὶ μεγαλωσύνη περισσοτέρα προσετέθη μοι. » Καὶ τοῦτο δὲ πάλιν εὐσεβείας γέμει τὸ ῥῆμα· οὐ γὰρ εἶπε, Μεγαλωσύνην περισσοτέραν ἐκτησάμην, ἀλλά, « Προσετέθη μοι, » τὸν χορηγὸν ὑποδεικνύς, καὶ τῶν ἀγαθῶν κηρύττων τὸν αἴτιον.

λδ΄. « Νῦν οὖν, φησίν, ἐγὼ Ναβουχοδονόσορ αἰνῶ, καὶ ὑψῶ, καὶ δοξάζω τὸν βασιλέα τοῦ οὐρανοῦ, ὅτι πάντα τὰ ἔργα αὐτοῦ ἀληθινά, καὶ αἱ τρίβοι αὐτοῦ κρίσεις, καὶ πάντας τοὺς πορευομένους ἐν ὑπερηφανίᾳ δύναται ταπεινῶσαι· » Λαβὼν γὰρ πεῖραν τῶν λυπηρῶν, εἶτα τούτων

like a drop from a bucket, and are accounted as a turn of the scale, and will be accounted as spittle, while Lebanon is not sufficient for burning, and all its animals not sufficient for a burnt offering, and all the nations are nothing, and were reckoned as nothing in comparison with him, to what will you liken the Lord? and with what analogy compare him?"[116]

This was the kind of benefit Nebuchadnezzar drew from the misfortunes, thinking and speaking of God in inspired mode; as though from some harmony | drawn from creation he composes   1373
his complete hymn of praise. *All the inhabitants of the earth were reckoned as nothing; he acts according to his will in the might of heaven and in the populace of earth.* This is also the teaching of another author: as blessed David said, "All that the Lord wished he did in heaven and on earth,"[117] so he too proclaims, *He acts according to his will in the might of heaven and in the populace of earth,* governing and controlling, not only earth but even the very heavens as well. Then, to bring out the invincibility of his power, *There is no one who will oppose his hand or say to him, Why did you do that?* One must accept gladly what is done by him, be it pleasing or distressing: resisting or criticizing what is wisely ordained by him is a rash endeavor.

After realizing and confessing this, and glorifying the Most High, he came to himself and resumed his former reign in a godly spirit. *At that time my reason returned to me, I returned to the position of my reign, and my condition was restored to me* (v. 36). Squalid and dirty, in all likelihood, unkempt and with nails grown long, he washed away the dirt, and thanks to divine grace he was recognized as the person who previously had administered the mighty kingdom. *My rulers and my nobility sought me out*: they put aside their hatred and adopted a friendly attitude to me. *I took control of the kingdom, and further greatness was added to me.* This remark also is redolent of godliness: he did not say, I acquired further greatness, but *it was added to me,* hinting at the source and proclaiming the one responsible for the good things. *So now I, Nebuchadnezzar, praise and exalt and glorify the king of heaven, because all his works are true, his ways are judgments, and he is able to bring low all who proceed haughtily* (v. 37): having had experience

---

[116] Isa 40:15–18.
[117] Ps 115:3.

ἀπαλλαγείς, αἰνῶ καὶ ὑμνῶ τὸν ταῦτά μοι κἀκεῖνα λυσιτελῶς ἐπαγαγόν-
τα, καὶ λίαν σοφῶς· καὶ οἶδα αὐτὸν οὐρανοῦ βασιλέα καὶ τῶν ἁπάντων
Δεσπότην, ἀληθείᾳ χρώμενον καὶ δικαίως ἅπαντα πρυτανεύοντα, καὶ
τοὺς ὑπερηφανίᾳ χρωμένους ταπεινῶσαι δυνάμενον. Μαθόντες τοίνυν,
ὅπως ὑπερηφανία καὶ τῦφος τοὺς χρωμένους λωβᾶται, καὶ ὡς ὁ τούτοις
χαίρων τρυγᾷ καρποὺς οὐκ ἀγαθούς, τὴν μητέρα τῶν ἀγαθῶν ταπει-
1376 νοφροσύνην κτησώ|μεθα· τοῦτο γὰρ καὶ ὁ Κύριος μακαρίζει τὸ κτῆμα,
ὡς πρόσοδον ἔχον τὴν βασιλείαν τῶν οὐρανῶν. «Μακάριοι γὰρ, φησίν,
οἱ πτωχοὶ τῷ πνεύματι, ὅτι αὐτῶν ἐστιν ἡ βασιλεία τῶν οὐρανῶν.»
Προτίθησι δὲ καὶ ἑαυτὸν ἀρχέτυπον τοῖς ὠφελεῖσθαι βουλομένοις, λέ-
γων· «Μάθετε ἀπ' ἐμοῦ, ὅτι πρᾶός εἰμι, καὶ ταπεινὸς τῇ καρδίᾳ.» Καὶ
δεικνύς, ἡλίκος τούτων ὁ καρπός, εὐθὺς ἐπήγαγε· «Καὶ εὑρήσετε ἀνά-
παυσιν ταῖς ψυχαῖς ὑμῶν.» Εἰ δὲ τῶν ἁπάντων ὁ Ποιητὴς καὶ Δεσπότης
ταπεινὸν ἑαυτὸν καλεῖ καὶ διὰ τῶν πραγμάτων δείκνυσι, ποίας ἑτέρας
συμβουλῆς δεῖται ἄνθρωπος, ὁ χοῦς, ὁ πηλός, ἡ βῶλος, ἡ σποδός, ἡ ματαιότης, τὸ ἄνθος, ὁ χόρτος; Ταῦτα γὰρ ἅπαντα ὑπὸ τῆς θείας Γραφῆς
προσαγορεύεται. Αἰσχυνθῶμεν τοίνυν τὴν τοῦ Δεσπότου μετριότητα, ὅς,
πλούσιος ὢν, δι' ἡμᾶς ἐπτώχευσεν, ἵνα ἡμεῖς τῇ ἐκείνου πτωχείᾳ πλου-
τήσωμεν, καὶ τῆς φύσεως τὸ θνητὸν καταμάθωμεν· καὶ τῆς παρούσης
εὐημερίας θεώμενοι τὸ ὀξύρροπον, μηδὲν μὲν ἀλαζονικὸν ἐπὶ τοῖς παροῦ-
σι φρονήσωμεν· γελάσωμεν δὲ μᾶλλον αὐτῶν τὸ εὔτρεπτον καὶ ἀβέβαιον,
καὶ ἐπιθυμῶμεν ἐκείνων ἐπιτυχεῖν τῶν ἀγαθῶν, ἃ διαρκῆ τὴν φύσιν καὶ
μόνιμον ἔχει· ὧν γένοιτο πάντας ἡμᾶς ἀπολαῦσαι, χάριτι καὶ φιλανθρωπίᾳ τοῦ Κυρίου ἡμῶν Ἰησοῦ Χριστοῦ, μεθ' οὗ τῷ Πατρὶ δόξα, σὺν τῷ
ἁγίῳ Πνεύματι, νῦν καὶ ἀεί, καὶ εἰς τοὺς αἰῶνας τῶν αἰώνων. Ἀμήν.

ΤΟΜΟΣ Ε΄ — ΚΕΦΑΛΑΙΟΝ Ε΄

Ναβουχοδονόσορ, Εὐϊλὰδ Μαροδὰχ, Βαλτάσαρ.
α΄. «Βαλτάσαρ ὁ βασιλεὺς ἐποίησε δεῖπνον μέγα τοῖς μεγιστᾶσιν αὐτοῦ.» Οὗτος υἱός μέν ἐστι τοῦ Ναβουχοδονόσορ, οὐκ εὐθὺς δὲ
αὐτὸν διεδέξατο· ὁ γὰρ Εὐϊλὰδ Μαροδὰχ ἀδελφὸς αὐτοῦ ὢν πρεσβύτε-

of misfortune, and then being rid of it, I sing the praises of the one who to my advantage brought upon me one condition and the other in his great wisdom. I know he is the king of heaven and Lord of all, acting in truth, governing everything justly, and capable of humbling those behaving haughtily.

Learning how arrogance and conceit bring harm on those so affected, therefore, and that the one who takes satisfaction in them reaps a harvest that is not good, let us acquire humility, the mother of good things. | This acquisition it is, after all, that the Lord 1376 blesses as winning the kingdom of heaven for its investor: "Blessed are the poor in spirit, for theirs is the kingdom of heaven." He also offers himself as a model to those willing to gain from it: "Learn from me that I am gentle and humble in heart"; and to bring out the fruit of this, he immediately went on to say, "And you will find rest for your souls."[118] Now, if the creator and Lord of all calls himself humble and proves it in his deeds, what further advice is needed for a human being who is dust, clay, soil, ashes, futility, flower, grass—all being names given us by the divine Scripture? Let us therefore be ashamed in the face of the Lord's modesty: though rich he became poor for our sake so that we might become rich through his poverty.[119] Let us learn the mortality of nature, and perceiving the brevity of happiness here below, let us come to no grandiose ideas about the present life—or, rather, let us mock its mutability and impermanence, and long to acquire those good things which are by nature lasting and abiding. May it be the good fortune of us all to attain this, thanks to the grace and lovingkindness of our Lord Jesus Christ, to whom with the Father and the Holy Spirit be glory, now and forever, for ages of ages. Amen.

CHAPTER 5

King Belshazzar made a great feast for his nobles (v. 1). This man was the son of Nebuchadnezzar, but did not directly succeed him: his brother Evil-merodach, being the older, came to the throne,[120]

---

[118] Matt 5:3; 11:29.

[119] 2 Cor 8:9.

[120] As noted above, Theodoret has a version of royal succession in Babylon that goes directly from Nebuchadnezzar's son Evil-merodach to Belshazzar (the same name given to Daniel), who is really the son of Nabonidus (Neriglissar

ρος ἐβασίλευσε, καὶ τοῦτο ἡ τῶν Βασιλειῶν ἡμᾶς ἱστορία διδάσκει, καὶ
ὁ μακάριος Ἱερεμίας ὁ προφήτης, οὑτωσὶ λέγων· «Καὶ ἐγένετο ἐν τῷ
τριακοστῷ καὶ ἑβδόμῳ ἔτει ἀπῳκισθέντος τοῦ Ἰωακεὶμ βασιλέως Ἰούδα, ἐν τῷ δωδεκάτῳ μηνί, καὶ ἐν τῇ τετράδι καὶ εἰκάδι τοῦ μηνός, ἔλαβεν
Εὐϊλὰδ Μαροδὰχ, βασιλεὺς Βαβυλῶνος, ἐν ᾧ ἐνιαυτῷ ἐβασίλευσε, τὴν
1377   κεφαλὴν Ἰωακεὶμ βασιλέως Ἰούδα, καὶ ἐξήγαγεν | αὐτὸν ἐξ οἴκου, οὗ
ἐφυλάττετο, καὶ ἐλάλησεν αὐτῷ χρηστά, καὶ ἔδωκεν αὐτῷ τὸν δίφρον ἐπάνω τῶν θρόνων τῶν βασιλέων τῶν μετ᾽ αὐτοῦ ἐν Βαβυλῶνι, καὶ ἤλλαξε
τὴν στολὴν τῆς φυλακῆς αὐτοῦ, καὶ ἤσθιε διαπαντὸς ἄρτον κατὰ πρόσωπον αὐτοῦ πάσας τὰς ἡμέρας ἃς ἔζησεν.» Ἰωακεὶμ δὲ οὗτός ἐστιν ὁ καὶ
Ἰεχωνίας· Ἰωακεὶμ γὰρ τὸν τούτου πατέρα, τὸν καὶ Ἐλιακεὶμ, ἐφ᾽ οὗ
ὁ μακάριος ἠχμαλωτεύθη Δανιήλ, ἐν τῇ Ἱερουσαλὴμ ἀνελὼν ὁ Ναβουχοδονόσορ, ἔρριψεν ἔξω τοῦ τείχους, ὡς ἡ θεία διδάσκει Γραφή. Μετὰ
τὸν Ναβουχοδονόσορ τοίνυν Εὐϊλὰδ Μαροδὰχ βασιλεύει· μετὰ δὲ τοῦτον
ὁ Βαλτάσαρ. Καταλέλοιπε δὲ τούτου τὴν μνήμην ὁ θειότατος Δανιήλ,
ἐπειδὴ οὐχ ἱστορίαν ἁπλῶς, ἀλλὰ προφητείαν συγγράφει· οὗ χάριν οὐδὲ
ἅπαντα τὰ ὑπὸ τοῦ Ναβουχοδονόσορ γεγενημένα συνέγραψεν, ἀλλ᾽ ἐκεῖνα μόνον, ὧν ἀναγκαία ἦν διὰ τὴν ὠφέλειαν ἡ μνήμη. Ἐπειδὴ τοίνυν
καὶ ἐπὶ τοῦ Βαλτάσαρ μέγιστον ἔδειξεν ὁ Θεὸς θαῦμα, καὶ ἱκανόν, οὐ
μόνον τοῖς τηνικάδε ἀνθρώποις, ἀλλὰ καὶ τοῖς ὕστερον ποτὲ γενομένοις,
εὐλάβειαν ἐνθεῖναι καὶ δέος, καὶ πρὸς εὐσέβειαν ποδηγῆσαι, οὐκ ᾠήθη
δίκαιον τοσαύτην εὐεργεσίαν κατακρύψαι σιγῇ, ὅσιον δὲ ποιεῖν νενόμικεν
ἀνάγραφον αὐτό, καὶ πᾶσιν ὑπόμνημα διδασκαλίας καταλιπεῖν. Διό φη-
σιν· «Βαλτάσαρ βασιλεὺς ἐποίησε δεῖπνον μέγα τοῖς μεγιστᾶσιν αὐτοῦ
χιλίοις, καὶ ἔναντι τῶν χιλίων ὁ οἶνος.» Τουτέστι, τοῖς χιλίοις ἀρκῶν,
πρὸς τὸν τοσοῦτον ἀριθμὸν ηὐτρεπισμένος.

β΄. «Πίνων δέ, φησίν, ὁ Βαλτάσαρ εἶπεν ἐν τῇ γεύσει τοῦ οἴνου,
τοῦ ἐνεγκεῖν τὰ σκεύη τὰ χρυσᾶ καὶ ἀργυρᾶ, ἃ ἐξήνεγκε Ναβουχοδο-

as the story of the Kings informs us, as also blessed Jeremiah in these words, "In the thirty-seventh year of the exile of King Jehoiachin of Judah, in the twelfth month, on the twenty-fourth day of the month, Evil-merodach king of Babylon in the year he came to the throne showed favor to King Jehoiachin of Judah, brought | him out of the house where he was under guard, spoke to him   1377 kindly, and gave him a seat above the thrones of the kings who were with him in Babylon. He changed out of his prison garb, and adopted the habit of eating his meals in his presence all the days he lived."[121] Now, this Jehoiachin is also Jeconiah; his father was Jehoiakim, also known as Eliakim, in whose time Daniel was enslaved, and who was killed in Jerusalem by Nebuchadnezzar, who cast him outside the walls, as the divine Scripture informs us.[122]

After Nebuchadnezzar, then, Evil-merodach ruled, and after him Belshazzar. The most divine Daniel, however, omitted mention of the former man, since he was composing not history pure and simple but prophecy—hence his not recording everything done by Nebuchadnezzar, either, but only those things of which mention was required with a view to bringing benefit. So since also in the time of Belshazzar God gave evidence of a wonderful miracle capable of instilling reverence and dread not only in the people of that time but also in those of any later time and of leading them to the true religion, he did not think it right to conceal in silence such a great act of kindness, judging it instead a holy thing to put it in writing and leave for everyone a record of the teaching.

Hence the text reads, *King Belshazzar made a great feast for a thousand of his nobles, and there was drinking in the presence of the nobles*, that is, enough for a thousand, prepared for such a large number. *In his drinking Belshazzar gave orders while tasting the wine for the gold and silver vessels to be brought in that his father*

and Labashi-marduk also omitted after Evil-merodach, as they are in the Bible) and never really king. The passage of a couple of decades covering these reigns in which Daniel is still a survivor also encourages collapsing them. The brotherly relationship mentioned here may have arisen from the possibility that Belshazzar's mother was the daughter of Nebuchadnezzar.

[121] Jer 52:31–33; cf. 2 Kgs 25:27–30.

[122] Cf. 2 Kgs 24:8–12. Theodoret outlined this account of succession in Judah at the beginning of his commentary on chapter 1 (the death of Jehoiakim thought rather to have been due to natural causes).

νόσορ, ὁ πατὴρ αὐτοῦ, ἐκ τοῦ ναοῦ τοῦ ἐν Ἱερουσαλήμ· καὶ ἔπινον ἐν αὐτοῖς ὁ βασιλεύς, καὶ οἱ μεγιστᾶνες αὐτοῦ, καὶ αἱ παράκοιτοι αὐτοῦ, καὶ αἱ παλλακαὶ αὐτοῦ.» Διδάσκει δὲ ἡμᾶς διὰ τούτων ὁ προφήτης, οὐ μόνον τὴν τῆς ἀσεβείας ὑπερβολήν, ἀλλὰ καὶ τὴν ἐκ τῆς ἀμετρίας τοῦ οἴνου γενομένην βλάβην. «Πίνων γάρ, φησίν, ὁ βασιλεὺς εἶπεν ἐν τῇ γεύσει τοῦ οἴνου, τοῦ ἐνεγκεῖν τὰ σκεύη τὰ χρυσᾶ καὶ τὰ ἀργυρᾶ.» Κατέχωσε γὰρ ἡ μέθη τὸν λογισμόν, καὶ ἡ ἀκρασία τὴν κατὰ τοῦ Θεοῦ μανίαν ἐγέννησε· καὶ τὰ ἀφιερωμένα τῇ τοῦ Θεοῦ θεραπείᾳ σκεύη, ἃ Ναβουχοδονόσορ, ὁ πατὴρ αὐτοῦ, ἔλαβε μέν, τοῦ Θεοῦ προδεδωκότος, ἐτίμησε δὲ ὡς ἐνόμισε, καὶ τῆς τῶν ἀνθρώπων ἠλευθέρωσε χρήσεως, τούτοις ὡς κοινοῖς οὗτος ἐτόλμησε χρήσασθαι· οὐ γὰρ εἶπε μόνον, ἀλλὰ καὶ τὸ ἔργον τοῖς λόγοις ἐπέθηκεν.

γ'. «Ἠνέχθησαν γάρ, φησί, τὰ σκεύη τὰ χρυσᾶ καὶ τὰ ἀργυρᾶ, ἃ ἐξήνεγκε Ναβουχοδονόσορ ἐκ τοῦ ναοῦ τοῦ Θεοῦ τοῦ ἐν Ἱερουσα-
1380 λήμ.» Καλῶς δὲ τὴν τῆς ἀτοπίας ἔδειξεν ὑπερβολήν, πρὸς τῷ ναῷ | καὶ τοῦ Θεοῦ μνημονεύσας, καὶ τοῦ ναοῦ δὲ δεικνὺς τὸ ἐπίσημον, τὴν τῆς Ἱερουσαλὴμ προσηγορίαν προσέθηκε. Ταῦτα γάρ, φησί, τὰ σκεύη οὐ τισὶ τῶν δοκούντων, καὶ ὄνομα μόνον ἐχόντων, ἀνέκειντο θεῶν, ἀλλ' αὐτῷ τῷ ἐπὶ πάντων Θεῷ, ὃς τήν τε Ἱερουσαλὴμ ἐξελέξατο, καὶ τὸν ἐν αὐτῇ νεὼν τῆς οἰκείας ἐπλήρωσε δόξης. Ἀλλὰ ταῦτα τὰ ἄψαυστα, καὶ τῷ Θεῷ τῶν ὅλων ἀνακείμενα, οὐχ ὡς δεομένῳ, ἀλλ' ὡς ἀποδεχομένῳ τῶν προσφερόντων τὸ εὔγνωμον, ὁ δυσσεβὴς βασιλεὺς εἰς μέσον ἐνεγκών, ἔπινεν ἐν αὐτοῖς· οὐ μόνον δὲ αὐτός, ἀλλὰ καὶ οἱ μεγιστᾶνες αὐτοῦ, καὶ αἱ παράκοιτοι αὐτοῦ, καὶ αἱ παλλακαὶ αὐτοῦ ἔπινον οἶνον· τουτέστι, μέθης ἐποίησεν ὄργανα τῆς θείας λειτουργίας τὰ ὄργανα, καὶ τὰς τῆς ἀκολασίας αὐτὸν ἐμφορούσας διὰ τούτων ἀπολαύειν τοῦ οἴνου προσέταξεν. Ἔπειτα τῆς ἀσεβείας τὸ ἔσχατον ὑποδεικνὺς ὁ προφήτης ἐπήγαγε·

δ'. «Καὶ ᾔνεσαν τοὺς θεοὺς τοὺς χρυσοῦς, καὶ ἀργυροῦς, καὶ χαλκοῦς, καὶ σιδηροῦς, καὶ ξυλίνους, καὶ λιθίνους.» Κραιπαλῶν γὰρ ὁ παμμίαρος, καὶ τοῖς θείοις σκεύεσιν ἐντρυφῶν, λήθην μὲν ἔσχε τοῦ τῶν ἁπάντων Δεσπότου, ὕμνοις δὲ τοὺς οὐκ ὄντας ἐγέραιρε θεούς, ἐξ ὕλης ἀψύχου πεποιημένους, καὶ οὐδὲ ἀπὸ τῆς τέχνης τὸ ἐνεργεῖν ἠρανισμένους· μόνην δὲ μορφὴν δεξαμένους ἐνεργείας ἐστερημένη. Ἀλλ' οὐκ ἠνέσχετο τῶν ὅλων ὁ Πρύτανις, τῇ μακροθυμίᾳ, καὶ τοὺς τηνικάδε ἀνθρώπους, καὶ τοὺς μετ' ἐκείνους λυμήνασθαι· παραυτίκα δὲ τὴν οἰκείαν δείκνυσιν δύναμιν.

ε'. «Ἐν αὐτῇ γάρ, φησί, τῇ ὥρᾳ ἐξῆλθον ἀστράγαλοι χειρὸς ἀν-

Nebuchadnezzar carried off from the temple in Jerusalem. The king, his nobles, his wives and his concubines drank from them (v. 2).[123] In this the prophet teaches us not only the extent of the impiety but also the harm coming from excess in drinking: *In his drinking the king gave orders while tasting the wine for the gold and silver vessels to be brought in.* In other words, intoxication confused his thinking, and intemperance gave rise to this insane action against God: the vessels consecrated to the worship of God, which his father Nebuchadnezzar had seized when God surrendered them, but had honored in the way he thought fit and had kept from human use, this man presumed to use like ordinary vessels, not only giving the order but giving effect to the order.

The gold and silver vessels were brought in that Nebuchadnezzar had taken from the temple of God in Jerusalem (v. 3). He did well to bring out the height of the impropriety by mentioning God in addition to the temple, | and adding the name *Jerusalem* to high-   1380
light the fame of the temple: These vessels were consecrated (it is saying), not just to what seem to be gods that possess the bare name, but actually to the God of all, who chose Jerusalem and filled its temple with his characteristic glory. Yet these vessels, not for human touch, consecrated to the God of all—not that he needed them, accepting rather the gratitude of the offerers—the impious king exposed to public view and drank with them. Not only he himself but also his nobles, his wives, and his concubines drank wine—in other words, he turned the instruments of divine worship into instruments of drunkenness, and bade those satisfying his lusts enjoy the wine in them. Then, to give a glimpse of the extreme degree of the impiety, the prophet went on, *They sang the praises of the gods of gold, silver, bronze, iron, wood, and stone* (v. 4). The utterly loathsome drunkard wallowed in the divine vessels and gave no thought to the Lord of all, celebrating in song false gods made of lifeless wood and devoid of even artificial movement, representing only a form without any mobility.

The one who governs all things, however, could not allow the people of the time and those coming later to be harmed by his longsuffering; and immediately he revealed his peculiar might. *At that very hour fingers emerged from a human hand and began to*

[123] Theodoret's text is at variance with all others and with what follows in reading the final verb in the indicative instead of reading a final clause.

θρώπου, καὶ ἔγραφον κατέναντι τῆς λαμπάδος, ἐπὶ τὸ κονίαμα τοῦ τοίχου τοῦ οἴκου τοῦ βασιλέως, καὶ ὁ βασιλεὺς ἐθεώρει τοὺς ἀστραγάλους τῆς χειρὸς τῆς γραφούσης.» Ἐπειδὴ γὰρ τὰ ἐνεργείας ἁπάσης ἐστερημένα ὕμνησεν εἴδωλα, καὶ τοῦ τῶν ἁπάντων Θεοῦ κατεφρόνησε, διδάσκει αὐτὸν ὁ τῶν ὅλων Δημιουργὸς τῆς θείας αὐτοῦ φύσεως τὸ ἀόρατον καὶ ἀσώματον. Μόνους γὰρ αὐτῷ δακτύλους ὑποδείκνυσι γράφοντας, παιδεύων αὐτόν, ὡς οὐδ' ἂν τούτους ἐθεάσατο, εἰ μὴ παρέσχεν αὐτὸς τῆς χρείας τὴν ἀφορμήν· μεγίστην δὲ καὶ οἱ σύσσιτοι ἐντεῦθεν ὠφέλειαν ἐλάμβανον, διδασκόμενοι τοῦ μὲν Θεοῦ πρὸς τῷ ἀσωμάτῳ καὶ ἀοράτῳ, τὸ δυνατόν· τῶν δὲ ὑπ' αὐτῶν ὑμνηθέντων θεῶν, πρὸς τῷ ὑλικῷ καὶ ἀψύχῳ, τὸ παντελῶς ἀδρανές τε καὶ ἀσθενές. Ὅτι δὲ πολὺ δέος ἅπασιν ἐνειργάσατο τοῦτο τὸ θαῦμα, ὁ προφήτης μεμαρτύρηκεν, οὕτως εἰπών·

ς'. «Τότε τοῦ βασιλέως ἡ μορφὴ ἠλλοιώθη, καὶ οἱ διαλογισμοὶ αὐτοῦ συνετάραξαν αὐτόν, καὶ οἱ σύνδεσμοι τῆς ὀσφύος αὐτοῦ διελύοντο, καὶ τὰ γόνατα αὐτοῦ τοῦτο τούτῳ συνεκρούοντο.» Εἰ δὲ δακτύλων 1381 γραφόντων θεωρία οὕτως ἐξεδειμάτωσε τὸν | τὴν μεγίστην διέποντα βασιλείαν, ὡς καὶ τῶν ἄρθρων τὰς ἁρμονίας ὑπὸ τοῦ δέους διαλυθῆναι, τρόμον τε καὶ κλόνον ὑπομεῖναι τὰ μέλη, τί οὐκ ἂν ὑπέμενεν ὁ θεομισής, πρηστῆρας ἢ κεραυνοὺς θεασάμενος, ἢ ἀγγέλους βλοσυρὸν βλέποντας, καὶ τῷ καινοπρεπεῖ τῶν σχημάτων δεδιττομένους. Τούτων γὰρ τὴν θέαν οὐδὲ ὁ μέγας Δανιὴλ ἀδεῶς ἐνεγκεῖν ἠδυνήθη. Ἀληθῶς, «Τί ὑπερηφανεύεται γῆ καὶ σποδός;» Τοσούτου τοίνυν δέους ἀναπλησθείς,

ζ'. «Ἐφώνησεν ἐν ἰσχύϊ τοῦ εἰσαγαγεῖν μάγους, Χαλδαίους, Γαζαρηνούς.» Ὁ γὰρ φόβος εἰργάζετο τὴν βοήν, καὶ τῆς ψυχῆς ὁ θόρυβος μαθεῖν κατήπειγε τὴν ἀπόφασιν. Εἶτα προτίθησιν ἆθλον τῷ τὴν γραφὴν ἀναγινώσκοντι καὶ τὴν ἑρμηνείαν ἐπάγοντι, ἐσθῆτα βασιλικὴν, καὶ χρυσοῦν περιδέρραιον, καὶ τὸ τὴν τρίτην τάξιν ἔχειν μετὰ τὸν βασιλέα. Ἀλλὰ τῶν μὲν μάγων καὶ Χαλδαίων τὸ ἄθεον ἐξηλέγχετο· εὑρεῖν γὰρ οὐκ ἴσχυον τὴν τῶν θείων γραμμάτων ἀνάγνωσιν, καὶ ταῦτα ἄθλου τοσούτου προκειμένου, καὶ λίαν αὐτοὺς προτρέποντος.

θ'. «Ὁ δὲ βασιλεὺς Βαλτάσαρ ἐταράχθη, καὶ ἡ μορφὴ αὐτοῦ ἠλλοιώθη ἐπ' αὐτῷ, καὶ οἱ μεγιστᾶνες αὐτοῦ συνεταράττοντο.» Ἐντεῦθεν δῆλον, ὅτι τῆς τῶν ἄλλων ὠφελείας προμηθούμενος ὁ Δεσπότης, οὐκ εὐθὺς τοῦ βασιλέως ἀφείλετο τὴν ζωήν· ἀλλὰ πρῶτον μὲν ὑπέδειξε τοῦ γράφοντος τοὺς δακτύλους. Τούτῳ δὲ καταπλήξας καὶ δέος ἐντεθεικώς,

write near the lampstand on the plaster of the wall of the king's house. The king saw the fingers of the hand that was writing (v. 5). Since, you see, he had sung the praises of the idols, deprived as they were of any power to move, and had scorned the God of all, the Lord of all gives him a lesson in his invisible and incorporeal nature by letting him see only fingers writing, the purpose being to instruct him that he would not even see them were it not that he personally had provided the occasion of need. His fellow diners also got great benefit from it through being given a lesson in God's power, in addition to his being incorporeal and invisible, by contrast with the gods celebrated by them, totally inactive and weak as they were, in addition to being wooden and lifeless.

The fact that this marvel instilled deep fear in everyone the prophet has confirmed, speaking in these terms, *At that point the king's face turned pale, his thoughts alarmed him, the sinews of his loins loosened, and his knees knocked together* (v. 6). Now, if the sight of fingers writing so terrified the | governor of the great kingdom that the coordination of his limbs failed through fear and his legs were affected by fear and trembling, what would this hater of God not have suffered on experiencing thunder and lightning, or angels of grim aspect instilling terror with the novelty of their appearance? Not even the mighty Daniel could bear the vision of these things unmoved. In truth, "Why will dust and ashes be proud?"[124] He was therefore struck with such terror that *he cried out in a loud voice to bring in soothsayers, astrologers, and fortune tellers* (v. 7), fear causing the cry and a panic-stricken soul pressing him to learn the meaning of the vision. He then offers to anyone reading the writing and supplying the interpretation a prize of royal apparel, a golden chain and occupying the third place after the king.

The godlessness of the soothsayers and astrologers was put to the test, for they were unable to unravel the text of the divine script, despite such a prize being on offer to urge them on. *King Belshazzar was alarmed, his face turned pale, and his nobles were alarmed with him* (v. 9). From this it is clear that the Lord was concerned for the welfare of the others and did not take the king's life on the spot, instead giving a glimpse of the writer's fingers. But having startled him by this and instilled fear, he caused the wise

1381

---

[124] Sir 10:9.

παρεσκεύασε μὲν κληθῆναι τοὺς σοφοὺς τῶν Χαλδαίων, ἐξήλεγξε δὲ αὐτῶν τὸ ψευδές τε καὶ ἀσθενές, ἐν χρείᾳ δὲ τῆς τοῦ Δανιὴλ σοφίας κατέστησεν, ἵνα διὰ τῆς τούτου γλώττης, καὶ τοῦτον ἐλέγξῃ, καὶ τοὺς ἄλλους
εὐεργετήσῃ, καὶ τούτων οὕτω γενομένων, τηνικαῦτα τὴν τιμωρίαν ἐπ-
αγάγῃ τῷ δυσσεβεῖ βασιλεῖ. Ταραττομένων τοίνυν καὶ τοῦ βασιλέως, καὶ
τῶν δαιτυμόνων,

    ι΄. « Ἡ βασίλισσα κατέναντι τῶν λόγων τοῦ βασιλέως, καὶ τῶν
μεγιστάνων αὐτοῦ, εἰς τὸν οἶκον τοῦ πότου εἰσῆλθε.» Τουτέστι, βου-
λευομένων αὐτῶν τί πρακτέον, καὶ ἄλλων ἄλλα εἰσηγουμένων, ἃ τὸ δέος
ἠνάγκαζεν, ἡ βασίλισσα εἰσελήλυθε. Δοκεῖ δέ μοι αὐτὴ μήτηρ αὐτοῦ εἶ-
ναι· αἱ γὰρ παράκοιτοι σὺν ταῖς παλλακίσι τοῦ δείπνου μετεῖχον· ἔπινον
γὰρ ἐν τοῖς σκεύεσι τοῖς χρυσοῖς καὶ ἀργυροῖς, αὐτὸς καὶ οἱ μεγιστᾶνες αὐτοῦ, καὶ αἱ παράκοιτοι αὐτοῦ, τουτέστιν, αἱ γαμεταὶ αὐτοῦ, καὶ αἱ
παλλακαὶ αὐτοῦ, αἱ οὐ κατὰ νόμον, ἀλλὰ δι᾽ ἀκολασίαν συνοῦσαι. Αὐτὴ
δὲ μετὰ τὸν θόρυβον εἰσελήλυθε, καὶ εἰκὸς ἦν ὡς γεγηρακυῖαν τῆς μέθης
ἐκείνης καὶ τῶν κορδακισμῶν, ἤγουν ὀρχησμῶν, τηνικαῦτα μὴ μετέχειν.
«Καὶ ἀπεκρίθη, φησίν, ἡ βασίλισσα, καὶ εἶπε· Βασιλεῦ, εἰς τοὺς αἰῶνας
1384 ζῆθι.» Τοῦτο δέ, ὡς ἔοικε, πρόσρησις ἦν τοῖς τότε | βασιλεῦσιν ὑπὸ τῶν
ἀρχομένων προσφερομένη. Καὶ μέχρι δὲ νῦν τὸ ἔθος τοῦτο κεκράτηκεν·
αἰωνίους γὰρ καλεῖν τινες τῶν ἀνοήτων καὶ τοὺς νῦν βασιλεῖς εἰώθασι,
καὶ ἐν ταῖς συγγραφαῖς δὲ τῶν συμβολαίων τοῦτό τινες προσγράφουσιν,
ἀμαθίᾳ μᾶλλον ἢ ἀσεβείᾳ δουλεύοντες. Φησὶ τοίνυν ἡ βασίλισσα· «Μὴ
ταραττέτωσάν σε οἱ λογισμοί σου, καὶ ἡ μορφή σου μὴ ἀλλοιούσθω.»
Εἶτα τὴν αἰτίαν ἐπάγει, δι᾽ ἣν ἐκβάλλει τὸ δέος·

    ια΄. « Ἔστιν ἔτι, φησίν, ἀνὴρ ἐν τῇ βασιλείᾳ σου, ἐν ᾧ Πνεῦμα
Θεοῦ ἅγιον ἐν αὐτῷ, καὶ ἐν ταῖς ἡμέραις τοῦ πατρός σου γρηγόρησις καὶ
σύνεσις εὑρέθη ἐν αὐτῷ.» Ἔστι δὲ καὶ ἐντεῦθεν κατανοῆσαι, ὡς μήτηρ
αὐτοῦ μᾶλλόν ἐστιν αὕτη· διὸ καὶ τὰ πάλαι γεγενημένα ὡς ἀγνοοῦντα
διδάσκει, καὶ τὸν μακάριον Δανιὴλ δῆλον αὐτῷ ποιεῖ, καὶ θείου Πνεύματος ἀνάπλεων εἶναι ὁμολογεῖ, καὶ αὐτοῖς τοῖς τοῦ Ναβουχοδονόσορ
κέχρηται λόγοις. Ταυτὰ γὰρ κἀκεῖνος ἔφη περὶ τοῦ Δανιήλ, προστέθεικε
δέ, ὅτι «Καὶ ἐν ταῖς ἡμέραις τοῦ πατρός σου γρηγόρησις καὶ σύνεσις
εὑρέθη ἐν αὐτῷ.» *Γρηγόρησιν* δὲ ἐκάλεσε τὴν τῆς ψυχῆς νῆψιν καὶ τὴν
σύνεσιν, τῶν κεκρυμμένων τὴν κατανόησιν, καὶ τῶν τοὺς πολλοὺς λανθα-
νόντων τὴν θεωρίαν. «Καὶ ὁ βασιλεύς, φησί, Ναβουχοδονόσορ ὁ πατήρ
σου ἄρχοντα ἐπαοιδῶν, μάγων, Χαλδαίων, Γαζαρηνῶν κατέστησεν αὐτόν.» Εἶτα καὶ τὴν αἰτίαν προστίθησιν·

men of the Chaldeans to be summoned, and showed up their falsity and weakness, while producing the need for Daniel's wisdom
so as through his tongue to accredit him and benefit the others,
and with this happening to inflict punishment at that stage on the
impious king. When the king and the guests were alarmed, then,
*Amidst the king's and his nobles' words the queen entered the ban-
queting hall* (v. 10), that is, with them pondering what should be
done, and various people making various suggestions under pressure of fear, the queen entered. Now, in my view, this lady was
his mother:[125] the wives were attending the banquet along with
the concubines, and drinking from the gold and silver vessels was
himself and his nobles, his wives—that is, his spouses—and his
concubines, partners of his not by law but in lust. Now, this lady
entered after the hubbub, and being old she probably was not a
party at that stage to the drunkenness and antics, or dancing, at
any rate. *In response the queen said, O King, live forever!* This was
probably an introduction offered at that time to | kings by their   1384
subjects; even to this day this custom prevails: some stupid people are in the habit of using the word eternal of the kings of today,
and in contracts some add it in writing under the influence of ignorance rather than impiety.

The queen said, therefore, *Do not let your thoughts disturb
you, or your face change color.* She then goes on to give the reason
to expel fear: *There is a man in your kingdom who has a holy spirit of
God in him, and in the days of your father alertness and understanding were found in him* (v. 11). Now, it is possible to understand from
this as well that she was rather his mother; hence she informs him
also of ancient happenings as though unfamiliar, acquainting him
with blessed Daniel, stating her belief that he was filled with a divine spirit, and using the actual words of Nebuchadnezzar, who
had said this of Daniel, remember.[126] She added, *In the days of
your father alertness and understanding were found in him.* Now,
by *alertness* she referred to vigilance of soul, and by *understanding* to a grasp of hidden things and an insight into what escaped
many. *Your father King Nebuchadnezzar,* she went on, *made him
chief of magicians, soothsayers, astrologers, and fortune tellers,* adding

[125] Were the book of Esther in the canon of Antioch (the Antiochenes
seem not to cite it directly), Theodoret could have found a close parallel in the
figure of Queen Vashti.
[126] Dan 4:6.

ιβ'. «Ὅτι πνεῦμα περισσὸν ἐν αὐτῷ.» Ἀντὶ τοῦ, Ὑπερβάλλουσαν
ἔχει τὴν τοῦ Πνεύματος χάριν. Ἔπειτα καταλέγει τῆς πνευματικῆς ἐνεργείας τὰ εἴδη. «Καὶ φρόνησις, φησί, καὶ σύνεσις, συγκρίνων ἐνύπνια,
καὶ ἀναγγέλλων κρατούμενα, καὶ λύων συνδέσμους, Δανιήλ.» Οὗτος γὰρ
θείου Πνεύματος δοχεῖον γενόμενος, σοφῶς μὲν ἅπαντα βουλεύεται, συνετῶς δὲ ἅπαντα φθέγγεται· τὰ δὲ τῶν ἐνυπνίων αἰνίγματα δῆλα ποιεῖ, καὶ
τὰ ἀσαφίᾳ τινὶ κεκρυμμένα τῆς ἀσαφίας ἐλευθεροῖ, καὶ οἷον ὑποδέσμους
τινὰς ὄντα καὶ σήμαντρα, καὶ ὡς ἐν ταμιείοις φρουρούμενα τῶν δεσμῶν
ἀπαλλάττων, διαλύει τε καὶ ἀνοίγνυσι, καὶ εἴσω τούτων τοὺς βουλομένους ποιεῖ· τοῦτο γὰρ σημαίνει τό· «Ἀναγγέλλων κρατούμενα καὶ λύων
συνδέσμους, Δανιήλ.» Τούτου, φησί, χάριν «Ὁ βασιλεὺς ἐπέθηκεν αὐτῷ ὄνομα Βαλτάσαρ.» Ἐπειδὴ γὰρ εἶδεν αὐτὸν ὑπὸ θείας φωτιζόμενον
ἐνεργείας, τῆς τοῦ Θεοῦ αὐτοῦ προσηγορίας ἠξίωσε. «Νῦν οὖν κληθήτω
Δανιήλ, καὶ τὴν σύγκρισιν αὐτοῦ ἀναγγελεῖ σοι.» Καὶ οὐ λέγει, Κληθήτω Βαλτάσαρ· τῇ γὰρ πείρᾳ μεμαθηκότες τοῦ προφήτου τὴν δύναμιν,
προτιμῶσι τῆς Χαλδαίας τὴν Ἑβραίαν προσηγορίαν· οὗ χάριν ἐφεξῆς
λοιπὸν αὐτὸν Δανιὴλ ὀνομάζουσι.

ιγ'. «Τότε γάρ, φησί, Δανιὴλ εἰσῆλθεν ἐνώπιον | τοῦ βασιλέως,
καὶ εἶπεν ὁ βασιλεὺς τῷ Δανιήλ· Σὺ εἶ Δανιὴλ ὁ ἀπὸ τῶν υἱῶν τῆς αἰχμαλωσίας τῆς Ἰουδαίας;» Ἔοικεν οὗτος ὑπὸ πολλῆς δυσσεβείας μετὰ
τὴν τοῦ πατρὸς τελευτὴν τὴν τοῦ Δανιὴλ συνουσίαν φυγών· διὸ παραυτίκα τῷ δέει καταπλαγείς, τοὺς μὲν μάγους καὶ τοὺς Χαλδαίους καλεῖ,
τοῦ δὲ προφήτου καὶ τὴν μνήμην τῆς διανοίας ἐξέβαλεν. Ἐπειδὴ δὲ ἡ
μήτηρ αὐτοῦ ἀνέμνησε τῶν ἐπὶ τοῦ πατρὸς γεγενημένων θαυμάτων, καὶ
κληθεὶς εἰσῆλθεν ὁ Δανιήλ, ἐπέγνω μὲν αὐτὸν παραυτίκα· οὐ γὰρ ἄν, εἴπερ ἠγνόησε, τοῦ γένους ἀνέμνησε, καὶ τὴν αἰχμαλωσίαν τῆς Ἰουδαίας
εἰς μέσον παρήγαγεν. Πυνθάνεται δὲ ὅμως, καί φησι· «Σὺ εἶ Δανιὴλ ὁ
ἀπὸ τῶν υἱῶν τῆς αἰχμαλωσίας τῆς Ἰουδαίας;» Καὶ μηδέπω συνομο-
λογήσαντος ἐκείνου·

ιδ'. «Ἤκουσα, φησί, περὶ σοῦ, ὅτι Πνεῦμα ἅγιον ἐν σοί, καὶ γρηγόρησις, καὶ σύνεσις, καὶ σοφία περισσὴ εὑρέθη ἐν σοί.» Ἁρμόττει καὶ
περὶ τούτου λέγεσθαι, ὃ περὶ τοῦ Ἰσραὴλ ἔλεγεν ὁ Προφήτης· «Ὅταν ἀπέκτεινεν αὐτούς, τότε ἐξεζήτουν αὐτόν.» Ἰδοὺ γὰρ καὶ τοῦτον τὸ
τῆς θείας δυνάμεως κατηνάγκασε δέος, τὸν ὄντα Θεὸν ἀντὶ τῶν οὐκ ὄντων ὀνομάζειν Θεόν, καὶ τοῦ ἁγίου Πνεύματος τὴν χάριν ὑμνεῖν, καὶ
κατηγορεῖν μὲν τῶν σοφῶν Βαβυλῶνος, ὡς τὴν θείαν οὐ δυνηθέντων

the reason, *because an extraordinary spirit was in him* (v. 12), that is, he has the surpassing grace of the Spirit.

She next lists the kinds of spiritual activity: *good sense, understanding, interpretation of dreams, reporting conundrums, solving problems, Daniel*: having become a receptacle of the divine Spirit, he gives wise advice on everything, makes intelligent utterances on everything, clarifies riddles in dreams, removes the obscurity from what is hidden in some obscurity, and by setting free what is held in bondage in secret recesses, as it were, he undoes and releases it like shackles and seals of a kind, admitting to it all who wish (the meaning of *reporting conundrums and solving problems, Daniel*). Hence she goes on, *The king gave him the name Belteshazzar*: since he saw he was enlightened by a divine impulse, he accorded him the name of his god. *So now let Daniel be summoned, and he will announce to you its interpretation.* She did not say, Let Belteshazzar be summoned: knowing from experience the prophet's powers, they preferred the Hebrew name to the Chaldean, hence calling him from then on by the name Daniel.

Then Daniel came into | the king's presence, and the king said 1385 *to Daniel, Are you Daniel, one of the children of the Jewish captivity?* (v. 13). He seems for reasons of deep impiety to have shunned the company of Daniel after the death of his father. Hence as soon as he was struck with fear, he summoned the soothsayers and the astrologers, while also expelling from his mind memory of the prophet; but when his mother reminded him of the miracles worked in the time of his father, and Daniel was summoned and came in, he recognized him at once. After all, had he not known him, he would not have recalled his nationality and brought to the fore the captivity of Judah. Nevertheless, he questions him in the words, *Are you Daniel, one of the Jewish captivity?* And while he had still to admit it, he said, *I have heard of you that a holy spirit is in you, and alertness, intelligence, and extraordinary wisdom were found in you* (v. 14). What the inspired author said of Israel is consistent also with what is said of this man, "When he killed them, they sought him out":[127] it was fear of the divine power, note, that forced him to give the name God to the true God in place of those not really gods, to praise the grace of the Holy Spirit, to accuse the wise men of Babylon of being unable to read the divine script,

[127] Ps 78:34.

γνῶναι γραφήν, παρακαλεῖν δὲ τὸν τοῦ Θεοῦ προφήτην δῆλα ποιῆσαι τὰ ἀγνοούμενα. Ὑπισχνεῖται δὲ αὐτῷ καὶ τὴν πορφυρίδα δώσειν, καὶ τὸν μανιάκην, καὶ τρίτην τάξιν τῆς βασιλείας. Ἀλλ' ὁ μακάριος Δανιήλ, γελάσας τοῦ δυσσεβοῦς τὰς βασιλικὰς ὑποσχέσεις, εἶπεν αὐτῷ· «Τὰ δόματά σου σοὶ ἔστω, καὶ τὴν δωρεὰν τῆς οἰκίας σου ἑτέρῳ δός· ἐγὼ δὲ γραφὴν ἀναγνώσομαι τῷ βασιλεῖ, καὶ τὴν σύγκρισιν γνωρίσω σοί, βασιλεῦ.» Ἀποστολικὴ τῷ ὄντι τῶν προφητῶν ἡ φωνή. Καὶ γὰρ ἐκείνους ὁ Κύριος κήρυκας ἀποστέλλων πᾶσιν ἀνθρώποις, παρεκελεύσατο, λέγων· «Δωρεὰν ἐλάβετε, δωρεὰν δότε.» Καὶ ὁ μακάριος οὗτος προφήτης ἔλεγε τῷ βασιλεῖ· «Τὰ δόματά σου σοὶ ἔστω, καὶ τὴν δωρεὰν τοῦ οἴκου σου ἑτέρῳ δός· ἐγὼ δὲ τὴν γραφὴν ἀναγνώσομαι τῷ βασιλεῖ, καὶ τὴν σύγκρισιν γνωρίσω σοι, βασιλεῦ.» Οὐ γὰρ ἔμαθον τὰ θεῖα πωλεῖν, οὐδὲ μισθὸν ἀνθρώπινον ὑπὲρ τῶν θείων μυστηρίων λαμβάνειν· προῖκα τοίνυν δέχου τῶν ἀγνοουμένων τὴν γνῶσιν.

ιη', ιθ'. «Ὁ Θεός, φησίν, ὁ ὕψιστος, τὴν βασιλείαν καὶ τὴν μεγαλωσύνην, καὶ τὴν τιμήν, καὶ τὴν δόξαν ἔδωκε Ναβουχοδονόσορ, τῷ πατρί σου. Καὶ ἀπὸ τῆς μεγαλωσύνης, ἧς ἔδωκεν αὐτῷ, πάντες λαοί, καὶ φυλαί, καὶ γλῶσσαι ἦσαν τρέμοντες αὐτόν, καὶ φοβούμενοι ἀπὸ προσώπου αὐτοῦ.» Μὴ νομίσῃς, φησίν, ὅτι τῇ οἰκείᾳ ῥώμῃ χρησάμενος ὁ σὸς πατὴρ ἄπασαν τὴν οἰκουμένην ὑπέταξε, καὶ τὰ | μυρία τῶν ἐθνῶν γένη γλώσσαις χρώμενα διαφόροις ὑπὸ μίαν ἐποιήσατο βασιλείαν. Ὁ γὰρ τῶν ὅλων Δεσπότης, τῶν ἁπάντων Ποιητής, ὁ σοφῶς ἅπαντα πρυτανεύων, αὐτῷ δέδωκε τὴν βασιλείαν, καὶ διὰ τὸν θεῖον ὅρον ὁ τοῦ πατρός σου φόβος τοῖς ὑπηκόοις ἐπέκειτο. «Καὶ οὓς ἐβούλετο αὐτὸς ὕψου, καὶ οὓς ἐβούλετο αὐτὸς ἐταπείνου.» Τοσαύτην, φησίν, ἔλαβε παρὰ τοῦ Θεοῦ τὴν ἐξουσίαν, ὡς δύνασθαι καὶ τοὺς ἐν ὕψει ὄντας ταπεινοὺς ἀποφαίνειν, καὶ τοὺς ἀφανεῖς λίαν καὶ εὐτελεῖς περιβλέπτους ποιεῖν.

κ'. «Καὶ ὅτε ὑψώθη ἡ καρδία αὐτοῦ, καὶ τὸ πνεῦμα αὐτοῦ ἐκραταιώθη τοῦ ὑπερηφανεύσασθαι, κατηνέχθη ἀπὸ θρόνου τῆς βασιλείας αὐτοῦ.» Ὥσπερ γάρ, φησίν, «αὐτὸς οὓς ἐβούλετο ὕψου, καὶ οὓς ἐβούλετο ἐταπείνου,» οὐ ψήφῳ πάντως δικαίᾳ τοῦτο ποιῶν· οὕτως ὁ τῶν ἁπάντων Βασιλεὺς καὶ Δεσπότης ἔδωκε μὲν ὡς ἠθέλησε, τῷ πατρί σου τὴν βασιλείαν, θεασάμενος δὲ αὐτὸν ἀμέτρῳ φρονήματι κεχρημένον, ἀλαζονικῶς τε καὶ τετυφωμένως τὴν βασιλείαν ἰθύνοντα, καὶ τῆς ὑπερηφανίας τὴν

1388

and to appeal to God's prophet to reveal the unknown. He also promises to give him the purple, the chain, and third place in the kingdom.

Blessed Daniel, however, replied to him in mockery of the royal promises of the impious man, *Keep your presents, and give the gift of your house to someone else. I shall read the script for the king, and inform you of its interpretation, O King* (v. 17). A truly New Testament reply from Old Testament authors: the Lord, remember, in sending those heralds to all people gave them the following directions, "You received without payment, give without payment."[128] And this blessed prophet said to the king, *Keep your presents, and give the gift of your house to someone else. I shall read the script to the king, and inform you of its interpretation, O King*: I am not in the habit of selling divine things, or of taking payment from human beings for the divine mysteries; so receive the knowledge of the unknown without charge. *God the Most High gave your father Nebuchadnezzar kingdom, magnificence, honor, and glory. On the basis of the glory he gave him, all people, tribes, and languages were in awe of him and trembled in his presence* (vv. 18–19): do not think it was by relying on his own strength that your father subjected the whole world and | brought under one kingdom the countless races of the nations speaking various tongues. It was, in fact, the Lord of all, maker of everything, wise governor of all things, who gave him the kingdom, and it was as a result of the divine decree that fear of your father possessed his subjects. *He elevated those he wanted, and humbled those he wanted*: he received such great authority from God as to be able to set those in an elevated position in a lowly one, and make those very obscure and insignificant famous.

When his heart was lifted up and his spirit gained strength to the point of becoming haughty, he was deposed from the throne of his kingdom (v. 20): just as *he elevated those he wanted, and humbled those he wanted*, doing so not altogether by a right decision, so the King and Lord of all gave your father the kingdom as he wanted, but on perceiving him giving vent to an overweening sense of his own importance, running the kingdom in an arrogant and con-

1388

---

[128] Matt 10:8—literally, "An ἀποστολικός reply from προφῆται," a frequent form of reference to New Testament and Old Testament authors, respectively.

νόσον δεξάμενον, καὶ τῶν βασιλικῶν αὐτὸν ἐστέρησε θρόνων, καὶ τὴν παρὰ πάντων αὐτῷ προσφερομένην τιμὴν ἀφείλετο. Οὐ μόνης δὲ αὐτὸν τῆς βασιλείας ἐγύμνωσε, ἀλλὰ καὶ τῶν κοινῶν συλλόγων ἐξήλασε, καὶ φρενοβλαβείᾳ καὶ λύττῃ παραδούς, ὄνοις ἀγρίοις καὶ θηρίοις συνδιάγειν παρεσκεύασεν. Ὧν γὰρ τὸ ἄγριον ἐμιμήσατο, τούτων τὸν βίον ἐδέξατο. Ἀναμιμνήσκει δὲ αὐτόν, ὅτι καὶ πόαν ἤσθιεν δίκην βοῶν, καὶ γυμνὸς περινοστῶν, καὶ ὑπαίθριος ταλαιπωρῶν, τὴν μὲν προτέραν τοῦ σώματος ἀπέβαλε χρόαν, ἑτέραν δὲ εἰσεδέξατο, ἣν ὁ κρυμός τε καὶ ὁ φλογμὸς ἀπειργάσατο. Καὶ ταῦτα πάντα, φησίν, ὑπέμεινεν, «Ἕως οὗ ἔγνω, ὅτι κυριεύει ὁ Ὕψιστος τῆς βασιλείας τῶν ἀνθρώπων, καὶ ᾧ ἐὰν δόξῃ δίδωσιν αὐτήν.» Ἀλλ' ἐκεῖνος μὲν τῇ πείρᾳ τὸ δέον μεμάθηκε, καὶ δι' αὐτῶν ἐδιδάχθη τῶν πραγμάτων, ὡς τῶν μὲν ἀνθρωπίνων βέβαιον οὐδέν, ὁ δὲ τῶν ἁπάντων Θεός, αἰώνιον ἔχων τὸ κράτος, ὡς θέλει κυβερνᾷ τὰ ἀνθρώπινα, καὶ οἷς ἂν ἐθελήσῃ τῆς βασιλείας ὀρέγει τὴν δωρεάν.

κβ΄. «Σὺ δέ, φησίν, ὁ υἱὸς αὐτοῦ Βαλτάσαρ, οὐκ ἐταπείνωσας τὴν καρδίαν σου κατενώπιον τοῦ Θεοῦ, οὐ ταῦτα πάντα ἔγνως;» Τοῖς γὰρ τοῦ σοῦ πατρὸς οὐκ ἐσωφρονίσθης κακοῖς, οὐδὲ μανθάνειν ἠθέλησας ἐξ ὧν ἐκεῖνος πέπονθεν, τοῦ Θεοῦ τὴν ἰσχύν.

κγ΄. «Ἀλλ' ἐπὶ τὸν Κύριον τοῦ οὐρανοῦ ὑψώθης.» Καλῶς διδάσκει τοὺς παρόντας, μὴ προσκυνεῖν τὰ ὁρώμενα, ἀλλὰ τὸν τούτων Δημιουργὸν καὶ Δεσπότην· καὶ κατὰ ταὐτὸν καὶ τοῦ βασιλέως διελέγχει τὸν τῦφον· καὶ διδάσκει, ὡς ὁ μέγιστος οὐρανὸς δημιουργὸν ἔχει τὸν ἀόρατον Θεόν. Σὺ δέ, φησίν, ὑψηλο|τέραν ἀπέφηνας τὴν καρδίαν σου, οὐ τοῦ οὐρανοῦ, ἀλλὰ τοῦ Θεοῦ τοῦ οὐρανοῦ, τοῦ Κυρίου πάσης κτίσεως. Οὐ γὰρ ἄν, εἰ μὴ τοσοῦτον τῦφον ἐνόσησας, τὰ σκεύη τοῦ οἴκου αὐτοῦ ἐνεχθῆναι προσέταξας. «Καὶ σὺ καὶ οἱ μεγιστάνές σου, καὶ αἱ παράκοιτοί σου, καὶ αἱ παλλακαί σου ἐπίνετε οἶνον ἐν αὐτοῖς·» τουτέστιν, εἰς οἰνοφλυγίαν καὶ μέθην ἀπεχρήσω τοῖς τῷ Θεῷ ἀνακειμένοις σκεύεσιν. Εἶτα τὴν τῆς ἀσεβείας ὑπερβολὴν τραγῳδῶν, «Καὶ τοὺς θεούς, φησί, τοὺς χρυσοῦς, καὶ ἀργυροῦς, καὶ χαλκοῦς, καὶ σιδηροῦς, καὶ ξυλίνους, καὶ λιθίνους ᾔνεσας.» Καὶ ἐπιμένων τῇ κωμῳδίᾳ· «Οἳ οὐ βλέπουσι, καὶ οὐκ ἀκούουσι, καὶ οὐ γινώσκουσι.» Καὶ μὴν ἠδύνασαι συνιδεῖν τὸ ἐκείνων ἀδρανές, ἔκ τε τῆς ὕλης, καὶ ἐκ τῆς ἐπικειμένης αὐτῇ τέχνης, καὶ πρὸς τούτοις ἐκ τῆς

1389

ceited manner, a victim of haughtiness, he deprived him of the royal throne and stripped him of the honor paid him by everyone. Instead of divesting him only of the kingdom, however, he drove him also from normal association, gave him over to insanity and derangement, and caused him to live with wild asses and savage beasts, taking on the life of the animals whose ferocity he had imitated. He reminds him that he also ate grass like oxen, roaming about naked, suffering exposure, losing the original color of his body and taking on a different one as a result of the cold and heat. He endured all this, he said, *until he learned that the Most High has lordship of the kingdom of human beings and awards it to whomever he pleases* (v. 21).

That man for his part learned his proper place by experience, and he was instructed by actual events that nothing human is stable, whereas the God of all has everlasting control, governs human affairs as he wishes, and offers the gift of kingship to whomever he wishes. *You, on the other hand*, he went on, *his son Belshazzar, by not humbling your heart before God, have not learned all this* (v. 22):[129] you were not brought to your senses by your father's troubles, nor were you prepared to learn God's power through what he suffered. *Instead, you have elevated yourself above the Lord of heaven* (v. 23). He did well to instruct those present to worship not visible things but their creator and Lord. At the same time he also convicts the king of conceit, and teaches him that the highest heaven has for its creator the unseen God. You, he is saying, | made your heart more elevated, not than heaven, but than the God of heaven, the Lord of all creation; if you were not guilty of such awful conceit, you would not have ordered the vessels of his house to be brought in. *You, your nobles, your wives, and your concubines drank wine from them*, that is, you used for drunkenness and intoxication the vessels consecrated to God.

Then, to mock the enormity of his impiety, he says, *You sang the praises of the gods of gold, silver, bronze, iron, wood, and stone*; and persisting in the mockery, *which do not see, do not hear, and do not know*: you were actually capable of realizing their inability to act on the basis of the material, the skill applied to it, and in addition

1389

---

[129] This part of the verse concludes with a question mark in Schulze's text, but not Theodoret's paraphrase (nor does the text of Theodotion, it seems, nor does the sense suggest it).

τῶν μορίων ἀναισθησίας· γνώσεως γὰρ, καὶ ὄψεως, καὶ ἀκοῆς ἐστέρην
ται, καὶ τῶν αἰσθήσεων οὐδὲ τὴν μίαν ἐνέργειαν ἔσχον, ἀλλὰ μόνα γυμνὰ
τὰ ἰνδάλματα. Σὲ δὲ οὐδὲ τοῦτο ἔπεισε συνιδεῖν τὸ δέον, ἀλλὰ τοὺς μὲν
θεοὺς ὠφελεῖν μὴ δυναμένους αἰνῶν διατελεῖς. «Τὸν δὲ Θεόν, οὗ ἡ πνοή
σου ἐν τῇ χειρὶ αὐτοῦ, καὶ πᾶσαι αἱ ὁδοί σου, αὐτὸν οὐκ ἐδόξασας.» Κα
λῶς δέ, καὶ μάλα σοφῶς ἐκ παραλλήλου τεθεικὼς τά τε εἴδωλα καὶ τὸν
τῶν ἁπάντων Θεόν, διὰ τὴν τῶν ἀκουόντων ὠφέλειαν, καὶ δείξας ἐκεῖνα
μήτε βλέποντα μήτε ἀκούοντα, οὐκ ἐπήγαγε περὶ τοῦ τῶν ὅλων Θεοῦ,
ὅτι βλέπει, καὶ ἀκούει, καὶ γινώσκει, ἀλλὰ τὸ μεῖζον ἁπάντων τέθεικεν,
ὅτι «Ἡ ζωή σου καὶ αἱ ὁδοί σου ἐν τῇ χειρὶ αὐτοῦ·» μεῖζον γάρ ἐστι
τοῦ ζῆν τὸ καὶ τοῖς ἄλλοις παρέχειν ζωήν, καὶ ἀφαιρεῖσθαι πάλιν αὐτὴν
ὅταν θέλῃ. Ἔδειξε τοίνυν, ὅτι τὰ μὲν εἴδωλα καὶ ζωῆς καὶ αἰσθήσεως
ἁπάσης ἐστέρηνται· ὁ δὲ τῶν ὅλων Δεσπότης Θεὸς πάσης τῆς ζωῆς
ἐστι χορηγός, καὶ ταύτην δίδωσί τε καὶ λαμβάνει, κυβερνῶν ὡς θέλει.
Ἀλλ' ὅμως, φησί, τοῦτον τὸν τοιοῦτον, τὸν τοσοῦτον, τὸν τῆς ζωῆς καὶ
τελευτῆς ἐξουσίαν ἔχοντα, τὸν βασιλέας χειροτονοῦντα καὶ καταλύοντα,
τοῦτον οὐ μόνον οὐχ ὑμνήσας, μᾶλλον δὲ καὶ ἐμπαροινῶν διατελεῖς, τοῖς
ἀφορισθεῖσιν αὐτῷ σκεύεσιν ἐντρυφῶν.

κδ΄. «Διὰ τοῦτο ἐκ προσώπου αὐτοῦ ἀπεστάλη ἀστράγαλος χει
ρός, καὶ τὴν γραφὴν ταύτην ἐνέταξεν.» Καὶ οὐκ εἶπεν, Αὐτὸς γέγραφεν,
ἀλλ', «Ἀπεστάλη ἐκ προσώπου αὐτοῦ ἀστράγαλος χειρός·» τουτέστι,
γραφῆναι προσέταξε, καὶ οὐδὲ ὅλον ἔδειξέ σοι τὸν γράψαντα, ἀλλ' ἐξ
ελέγξαι σου τὸν τῦφον ἐθελήσας, μόνοις σε δακτύλοις ἐξέπληξε, καὶ
τοσούτου δέους ἐνέπλησε. Μάθε δέ, φησί, καὶ αὐτὴν τὴν γραφὴν, καὶ
τῆς γραφῆς ἑρμηνείαν.

κε΄, κϛ΄. «Ἡ μὲν οὖν γραφή ἐστιν αὕτη· Μανή, Θεκὲλ, Φαρές· τὸ
1392   δὲ σύγκριμα τοῦ ῥήματος τοῦτο.» | Σύγκριμα δὲ τὴν ἑρμηνείαν καλεῖ.
«*Μανή·* ἐμέτρησεν ὁ Θεὸς τὴν βασιλείαν σου, καὶ ἐπλήρωσεν αὐτήν·»
τουτέστιν, εἶδέ σε τῆς βασιλείας ἀνάξιον, καὶ ταύτης γυμνὸν ἐδοκίμασεν
ἀποφῆναι.

κζ΄. «*Θεκέλ·* ἐστάθη ἐν ζυγῷ, καὶ ηὑρέθη ὑστεροῦσα.» Ἐδίδαξε
δὲ οὐκ ἐκεῖνον μόνον, ἀλλὰ καὶ ἡμᾶς διὰ τούτων ὁ προφήτης, ὡς οὐδὲν
ἀστάθμητον παρὰ τῷ Θεῷ, ἀλλὰ καὶ ὁ ἔλεος καὶ ἡ μακροθυμία μέτρῳ
τινὶ καὶ σταθμῷ τοῖς ἀνθρώποις παρέχεται. Ἐπειδὴ τοίνυν, φησί, ὑπερ
έβης τῆς φιλανθρωπίας τοὺς ὅρους, δέχου τὴν θείαν ἀπόφασιν.

κη΄. «*Φαρές·* διῃρέθη ἡ βασιλεία σου, καὶ ἐδόθη Μήδοις καὶ Πέρ

to this their limbs' lack of senses. After all, they were devoid of knowledge, sight, and hearing, with no single sense operating, being only bare images. Even this, however, did not persuade you to acknowledge your duty; instead, you persisted in singing the praises of gods incapable of any benefit. *By contrast, the God in whose hand is your very breath and all your ways you did not glorify.* Now, he did well and showed much wisdom in putting in parallel the idols and the God of all with a view to the benefit felt by the hearers; after emphasizing that the former neither see nor hear, instead of proceeding to say in regard to the God of all that he sees and hears and knows, he cited the more powerful fact of all, Your life and your ways are in his hand, since providing life to others and in turn removing it at will is more important than having life. He brought out, then, that while the idols are deprived of life and all sensation, the Lord God of all is the source of all life, and both gives it and takes it, governing as he wills. Nevertheless, he is saying, despite his being of this stature, so great, with power of life and death, appointing kings and removing them, you not only did not sing his praises, but rather even persisted in your drunken behavior, making fun of vessels dedicated to him.

This was the reason a finger of a hand was sent from his presence and put this writing in place (v. 24). He did not say, He wrote, but *a finger of a hand was sent from his presence*, that is, he gave orders for it to be written. He did not show you the whole of the person who wrote it, he is saying; instead, in his wish to convict you of conceit, he startled you with fingers alone, and filled you with an awful dread. Acquaint yourself with the text itself and the interpretation of the text. *This, then, is the text: Mane, Thekel, Phares, and this is the interpretation of the expression* (vv. 25–26). By *interpretation* | he refers to the meaning. *Mane: God has mea-* 1392 *sured your kingdom and brought it to an end*, that is, He has seen you are unworthy of kingship, and he decided to leave you bereft of it. *Thekel: he was weighed in the balance, and found wanting* (v. 27). In this the prophet taught not only him but also us the lesson that nothing goes unweighed by God; instead, mercy and longsuffering are shown to people according to a certain measure and weight. Since, then, he is saying, you exceeded the limit of lovingkindness, receive the divine sentence. *Phares: your kingdom has been divided,*

σαις.» Ἀναγκαῖον δὲ ζητῆσαι, τί δήποτε τὸν μὲν Ναβουχοδονόσορ παιδεύσας ὁ τῶν ὅλων Θεὸς πάλιν εἰς τὴν βασιλείαν ἐπανήγαγε, τοῦτον δὲ παραυτίκα καὶ τῆς βασιλείας ἐστέρησε, καὶ τῆς ζωῆς. Σκοποῦντες τοίνυν εὑρίσκομεν, πρῶτον μέν, ὅτι Ναβουχοδονόσορ ἕτερον ἀσεβείας τίσαντα δίκας οὐκ ἐθεάσατο, διὸ καὶ συγγνώμης αὐτὸν ἠξίωσεν ἡ δικαία τοῦ Θεοῦ ψῆφος· οὗτος δέ, τὴν μεγίστην τοῦ πατρὸς θεασάμενος τιμωρίαν, οὐδὲν ἐκεῖθεν ἀπώνατο. Εἰκότως τοίνυν ὁ δίκαιος κριτὴς ἐπ' ἐκείνου μὲν ῥητῷ χρόνῳ τὴν τιμωρίαν περιώρισε, τοῦτον δὲ οὐδεμιᾶς συγγνώμης ἠξίωσεν. Ἄλλως τε καὶ πάντα προορῶν ὁ Θεὸς τὰ ἐσόμενα, καὶ οὕτως αὐτὰ σαφῶς γινώσκων ὡς ἤδη γενόμενα, ἐκείνου μὲν προειδὼς τὴν μεταμέλειαν, οὕτω τὰ κατ' αὐτὸν ᾠκονόμησε, τούτου δὲ προγινώσκων τὴν μέχρι τέλους ἀσέβειαν, τῷ θανάτῳ καταλύει τῆς ἀσεβείας τὴν αὔξησιν. Εὐθὺς δὲ ἀκούσας Βαλτάσαρ τῶν ὑπὸ τοῦ Δανιὴλ ἑρμηνευθέντων, ἐκέλευσεν αὐτὸν τὸ προκείμενον ἆθλον λαβεῖν, τὴν πορφύραν, καὶ τὸν μανιάκην τὸν χρυσοῦν· εἶτα τοῦτον αὐτὸν διακοσμήσας τὸν τρόπον, τῇ τοῦ κήρυκος χρώμενος φωνῇ τοὺς ὑπηκόους ἐδίδασκεν, ὡς τρίτον αὐτὸν τῆς βασιλείας ἀπέφηνεν ἄρχοντα. Ἀλλ' οὐδὲν τούτων τὴν θείαν ἀπόφασιν ἔλυσεν.

λ'. «Ἐν αὐτῇ γάρ, φησί, τῇ νυκτὶ ἀνῃρέθη Βαλτάσαρ, ὁ βασιλεὺς Χαλδαίων.» Χαλδαῖον δὲ αὐτὸν ἐνταῦθα προσηγόρευσεν, ἵνα δείξῃ λοιπὸν τῆς Χαλδαϊκῆς βασιλείας τὸ τέλος. Ἀληθῶς «φοβερὸν τὸ ἐμπεσεῖν εἰς χεῖρας Θεοῦ ζῶντος,» κατὰ τὸν θεῖον Ἀπόστολον· φοβερόν, «τοῦ πλούτου τῆς χρηστότητος αὐτοῦ, καὶ τῆς ἀνοχῆς, καὶ μακροθυμίας καταφρονεῖν,» ἀλλὰ μὴ προσκυνεῖν καὶ θεραπεύειν εἰς δύναμιν. Τίς γὰρ σκληρὸς γενόμενος, ἤ φησιν ὁ προφήτης, ἐναντίον Κυρίου ὑπέμεινε;

and has been given to Medes and Persians (v. 28).¹³⁰

Now, it is necessary to enquire why on earth the God of all corrected Nebuchadnezzar and in turn restored him to his kingdom, but forthwith deprived this man of both kingdom and life. On consideration, then, we find, firstly, that Nebuchadnezzar had not observed another person paying the penalty for impiety, and hence God's just sentence granted him pardon, whereas this other man, though observing his father's heavy penalty, gained nothing from it. The just judge was therefore within his rights in confining punishment of the former to a specified time, whereas he granted the latter no pardon. In particular, God foresees all future events, and thus knows them clearly as if already in the past; so he knew ahead of time the repentance of the former, and arranged for his fate accordingly, whereas he knew ahead of time the latter's incorrigible impiety, and put a stop to the increase in impiety with death.

As soon as Belshazzar heard the interpretation by Daniel, he ordered that he receive the reward proposed, the purple and the gold chain. Then, after decking him out in this fashion, he used the proclamation of a herald to inform his subjects that he appointed him third ruler of the kingdom. None of this, however, mitigated the sentence. *On that very night*, the text says, *Belshazzar king of the Chaldeans was slain* (v. 30). He called him *Chaldean* here to emphasize that it was now the end of the Chaldean kingdom.

It is truly "a fearful thing to fall into the hands of the living God," according to the divine apostle, "to despise the riches of his kindness, forbearance and longsuffering," and not to worship and serve him to the extent of one's ability. I mean, what person with heart hardened, as the inspired author asks, could stand

¹³⁰ Even with his Syriac background, Theodoret makes no comment on the three forms he finds in Theodotion's text (they do not occur in the LXX, only the interpretation), or on the accuracy of Daniel's interpretation of them; instead, he moves at once to rationalize the difference in penalties suffered by Nebuchadnezzar and Belshazzar. Di Lella ("Daniel," 414) tells us that the three consonantal forms occurring in the Aramaic text Daniel apparently read first as monetary values, the mina, the shekel, the half mina, before interpreting them as verbs, "he counted/weighed/divided," and that the forms appearing in Greek as μανή and φαρές may in an older form of the conundrum have involved a pun on Medes and Persians, mention of whom Theodoret will not deal with at this point.

Τούτου χάριν καὶ ὁ μακάριος παρεγγυᾷ Δαβίδ· «Σήμερον ἐὰν τῆς φωνῆς αὐτοῦ ἀκούσητε, μὴ σκληρύνητε τὰς καρδίας ὑμῶν, ὡς ἐν τῷ παροργισμῷ.» Καὶ τοῦτο ἑρμηνεύων ὁ μακάριος παραινεῖ Παῦλος· «Βλέπετε, ἀδελφοί, μήποτε ἔσται ἔν τινι ὑμῶν καρδία πονηρὰ ἀπιστίας, ἐν τῷ ἀποστῆναι ἀπὸ Θεοῦ ζῶντος· ἀλλὰ παρακαλεῖτε ἑαυτοὺς καθ' ἑκάστην ἡμέραν, μέχρις ἂν οὗ τὸ σήμερον καλεῖται, ἵνα μὴ σκληρυνθῇ ἐξ ὑμῶν τις ἀπάτῃ τῆς ἁμαρτίας.» Οἶδε γὰρ πολλάκις ἡ ἁμαρτία ταῖς ἡδοναῖς ἡμᾶς καταθέλγουσα, καθάπερ ἐκεῖνον τὸν ἀνόητον βασιλέα διὰ τῆς μέθης, οὕτω σκληρύνειν ἡμῶν τὴν καρδίαν καὶ ἀντίτυπον ἀποφαίνειν, ὡς καὶ τῆς ἀσεβείας τὴν νόσον ῥᾳδίως εἰσδέχεσθαι. Φύγωμεν τοίνυν, παρακαλῶ, τοῦ διαβόλου τὴν ἐξαπάτην, καὶ τὴν ἐπίμονον ἀρετὴν τῆς ἡδονῇ βραχείᾳ κεχρημένης προτιμήσωμεν ἁμαρτίας, ἵνα τῆς μὲν τοῦ Βαλτάσαρ κοινωνίας ἀποφανθῶμεν ἀλλότριοι, τῆς δὲ τοῦ Δανιὴλ συμμορίας ἀπολαύσωμεν, ἐν Χριστῷ Ἰησοῦ τῷ Κυρίῳ ἡμῶν, μεθ' οὗ τῷ Πατρὶ δόξα, σὺν τῷ ἁγίῳ Πνεύματι, εἰς τοὺς αἰῶνας τῶν αἰώνων. Ἀμήν.

ΤΟΜΟΣ ΣΤ΄

Ναβουχοδονόσορ, Εὐιλὰδ Μαροδὰχ υἱὸς αὐτοῦ, Βαλτάσαρ ἀδελφὸς αὐτοῦ· Δαρεῖος Μῆδος, κατὰ Ἰώσηππον, υἱὸς τοῦ Ἀστυάγους, τοῦ δὲ Κύρου θεῖος πρὸς μητρός· ὁ δὲ Κῦρος Πέρσης· Ἕλληνες Κυαξάρην αὐτὸν προσκαλοῦσιν.

λα΄. «Καὶ Δαρεῖος ὁ Μῆδος παρέλαβε τὴν βασιλείαν ὢν ἐτῶν ἑξήκοντα δύο.» Ἡ μὲν τῶν Χαλδαίων βασιλεία τὸ τέλος ἔλαβε κατὰ τὴν θείαν πρόρρησιν· εἰς δὲ Μήδους μεταβέβηκεν ἡ τῆς οἰκουμένης ἡγεμονία. Οὕτω δὲ καὶ ὁ Δανιὴλ προηγόρευσε, καὶ τὸ Φαρὲς ἡρμήνευσε· «Διῃρέθη γάρ, φησίν, ἡ βασιλεία σου, καὶ ἐδόθη Μήδοις καὶ Πέρσαις.» Ἀλλὰ χρόνον ὀλίγον Δαρείου τοῦ Μήδου βασιλεύσαντος, Κῦρος, παραλαβὼν

in the presence of the Lord? Hence blessed David's exhortation, "If today you hear his voice, harden not your hearts as though in provocation." Interpreting this, blessed Paul exhorts us, "Take care, | brethren, that there be in you no wicked heart of unbelief to make you turn away from the living God. Rather, encourage one another every day, as long as it is called today, lest any of you be hardened by the deceitfulness of sin."[131] Sin, you see, often has the effect of enticing us with pleasure: like that senseless king in his drunkenness, so it can harden our heart and make it stubborn to such a degree that it even succumbs with ease to the ailment of impiety. Let us therefore shun, I beseech you, the devil's wiles and give preference to lasting virtue over sin that involves a brief delight, so that we may have no part in the lot of Belshazzar and share rather the company of Daniel, in Christ Jesus our Lord, to whom with the Father and the Holy Spirit be glory, for ages of ages. Amen.

1393

CHAPTER 6

Darius the Mede succeeded to the kingdom at the age of sixty-two. The kingdom of the Chaldeans came to an end according to the divine prophecy, and control of the world passed to the Medes. This is what Daniel also had prophesied in interpreting *Phares*, saying, *Your kingdom has been divided, and has been given to Medes and Persians.* Darius the Mede reigned for a short time,[132] however, and

---

[131] Heb 10:31; Rom 2:4; Ps 95:7–8; Heb 3:12–13. The opening verse of chapter 6 (in the Aramaic and in Theodotion) appears as 5:31 in modern versions.

[132] Theodoret now addresses the historical problems raised by the mention of the nonhistorical personage "Darius the Mede." Unwilling to admit that the author has fabricated this figure, Theodoret surveys (particularly biblical) statements about leaders of Medes and Persians, going back as far as Cyaxares king of the Medes in the seventh century and Astyages in the sixth (not father and son); the latter was grandfather of Cyrus, whose father Cambyses was Persian, and who toppled Astyages to become head of a combined Median-Persian Empire in 550. Theodoret is confused by the fictitious Darius in Dan 5:31, his being mentioned again in 6:28 as contemporary with "Cyrus the Persian," and the similarly erroneous statement he cites from Josephus, *Ant.* 10.248, of Darius and Cyrus working in concert. The result is that he has Darius I as son (not father) of Xerxes I (Ahasuerus), probably on the basis of 9:1—or is he thinking of Darius II son of Xerxes II (a mistake he appears to make in his work on the

τὴν ἀρχήν, εἰς Πέρσας αὐτὴν μετατίθησιν. Ἰώσηππος δὲ ὁ ἱστοριογράφος τὸν Δαρεῖον μὲν υἱὸν τοῦ Ἀστυάγους εἶναί φησι, τοῦ δὲ Κύρου θεῖον
πρὸς μητρός, τοὺς δὲ τῶν Ἑλλήνων συγγραφέας ἑτέρως αὐτοῦ τὸ ὄνομα τεθεικέναι· Κυαξάρην γὰρ αὐτὸν ἐκεῖνοι προσηγορεύκασι. Λέγει δέ,
ὅτι κατὰ ταὐτὸν ἐπιστρατεύσαντες τῇ Βαβυλῶνι Δαρεῖός τε καὶ Κῦρος,
ὁ τούτου ἀδελφιδοῦς, ἐκράτησαν τῆς πόλεως πολιορκίᾳ χρησάμενοι, καὶ
τὸν Βαλτάσαρ ἀνεῖλον κατ’ ἐκείνην τὴν νύκτα, καθ’ ἣν ἐν τῷ τοίχῳ τὰς
συλλαβὰς ἐκείνας γραφομένας ἐθεάσατο. Ἀλλ’ οὐκ ἐᾷ οὕτω πι|στεύειν
τὰ ὑπὸ τοῦ μακαρίου Δανιὴλ συγγεγραμμένα· διδάσκει δὲ ἡμᾶς ἐν τῷ
τέλει τοῦ κατὰ τὸν Δαρεῖον διηγήματος, ὅτι κατηύθυνε Δανιὴλ ἐν τῇ
βασιλείᾳ Δαρείου καὶ ἐν τῇ βασιλείᾳ Κύρου τοῦ Πέρσου, καὶ δείκνυσιν
ἑτέραν μὲν τοῦ Δαρείου βασιλείαν, ἑτέραν δὲ τοῦ Κύρου. Εἰ δὲ μία αὐτοῖς κατὰ τῆς Βαβυλῶνος ἐγεγόνει στρατεία, μία ἄρα ἦν καὶ ἡ βασιλεία·
νῦν δέ, ἄλλην μὲν ταύτην, ἄλλην δ’ ἐκείνην εἶναί φησι. Καὶ ἐν τῷ τέλει
δὲ τῆς προφητείας οὕτω φησὶν ὁ Δανιήλ· «Καὶ ὁ βασιλεὺς Ἀστυάγης
προσετέθη πρὸς τοὺς πατέρας αὐτοῦ, καὶ παρέλαβε τὴν βασιλείαν Κῦρος
ὁ Πέρσης.» Οὐ τοίνυν Δαρεῖος καὶ Κῦρος κατὰ ταὐτὸν βασιλεύσαντες,
τὸν Βαλτάσαρ ἀνεῖλον· ἀλλ’ ὁ μὲν Δαρεῖος ὁ Ἀσσουήρου πρότερον, ὕστερον δὲ Κῦρος ἐβασίλευσεν. Οὐδὲ ταῖς Ἑλληνικαῖς ἱστορίαις τὰ ὑπὸ τοῦ
Ἰωσήππου εἰρημένα συμβαίνει. Οὐδὲ γὰρ ἐν ἐκείναις ἔστιν εὑρεῖν, τὸν
Κυαξάρην τὸν τοῦ Ἀστυάγους υἱὸν αὐτὸν εἶναι τὸν Δαρεῖον, ὃν οὗτος ἔφη
σὺν τῷ Κύρῳ τὴν στρατείαν κατὰ τῆς Βαβυλῶνος ποιησάμενον· ὥστε
παντάπασιν ἀπίθανον εἶναι τὸν τοῦ Ἰωσήππου λόγον. Ἐγὼ δὲ τῇ θείᾳ
πειθόμενος Γραφῇ, τοῦ Ναβουχοδονόσορ εὑρίσκω τοῦτον θυγατριδοῦν·
τῷ γὰρ Ἱερεμίᾳ παρακελευσάμενος ὁ Θεὸς δεσμὰ ἑαυτῷ περιθεῖναι, καὶ
ταῦτα πέμψαι τοῖς πλησιοχώροις βασιλεῦσι, τῷ τῶν Ἰδουμαίων, καὶ
Μωαβιτῶν, καὶ Ἀμανιτῶν, Τυρίων τε καὶ Σιδωνίων, ταῦτα εἰπεῖν αὐτοῖς παρεγγύησεν· «Οὕτως εἶπε Κύριος ὁ Θεὸς Ἰσραήλ· Οὕτως ἐρεῖτε
πρὸς τοὺς κυρίους ὑμῶν· Ἐγὼ ἐποίησα τὴν γῆν ἐν τῇ ἰσχύϊ μου τῇ μεγάλῃ, καὶ τῷ βραχίονί μου τῷ ὑψηλῷ, καὶ δώσω αὐτήν, ᾧ ἂν δόξῃ ἐν
ὀφθαλμοῖς μου· ἔδωκα πᾶσαν τὴν γῆν τῷ βασιλεῖ Ναβουχοδονόσορ Βαβυλῶνος, δουλεύειν αὐτῷ, καὶ δουλεύσουσιν αὐτῷ πάντα τὰ ἔθνη, καὶ τῷ

Cyrus received the reins of government and transferred control to the Persians. Josephus the historian says that, while Darius was the son of Astyages and uncle of Cyrus, Greek writers give him a different name, calling him Cyaxares. He says that Darius and his nephew Cyrus advanced on Babylon together and gained control of it by besieging it, and they slew Belshazzar on the night he saw those syllables written on the wall. | 1396

What was recorded by blessed Daniel, however, does not allow us to accept this: he informs us at the end of the account of Darius that Daniel was prospering in the reign of Darius and in the reign of Cyrus the Persian, showing that the reign of Darius was different from that of Cyrus. If, on the other hand, there were one army that came against Babylon, surely there would have been one kingdom as well; but at this point he distinguishes between them. At the end of his work Daniel speaks in the following terms, "King Astyages was taken to his fathers, and Cyrus the Persian succeeded to the throne." [133] So Darius and Cyrus did not reign at the same time and kill Belshazzar; instead, Darius son of Ahasuerus ruled first, and Cyrus later. The statements by Josephus do not correspond to the Greek histories, either: it is not possible to find in them Cyaxares son of Astyages to be the same person as Darius, whom the other historian said conducted a campaign against Babylon along with Cyrus. The result is that the word of Josephus is completely incredible.

I for my part, on the contrary, put my trust in the divine Scripture, and find this man Darius to be the son of Nebuchadnezzar's daughter. In bidding Jeremiah put chains on, remember, and send them to the neighboring kings of the Idumeans, Moabites, Ammonites, Tyrians, and Sidonians, God told him to say this to them, "Thus says the Lord God of Israel, You will say this to your masters, I made the earth with my great strength and my outstretched arm, and shall give it to whoever is pleasing in my eyes. I have given the whole land to King Nebuchadnezzar of Babylon to serve him, and all the nations will serve him, his son and his son's

Twelve Prophets)?

[133] Dan 14:1 (beginning of the deuterocanonical story Bel and the Dragon, also from the Daniel cycle—factually correct in this case). The verse strangely appears at the conclusion of chapter 12 in Theodoret's text; see note there.

υἱῷ αὐτοῦ, καὶ τῷ υἱῷ τοῦ υἱοῦ αὐτοῦ, ἕως ἂν ἔλθῃ ὁ καιρὸς τῆς γῆς αὐτῶν.» Τοῦ τοίνυν Βαλτάσαρ υἱοῦ προσαγορευθέντος ὑπὸ τοῦ Δανιήλ, ζητητέον τὸν ἔκγονον. Εἰ δέ τις ἀντιλέγει, Μῆδον τὸν Δαρεῖον ὀνομάζεσθαι λέγων, μαθέτω ὡς οὐδὲν τοῦτο τῷ λόγῳ λυμαίνεται. Καὶ γὰρ ὁ Κῦρος θυγατριδοῦς ὢν τοῦ Ἀστυάγους, ὃς Μῆδος ἦν, καὶ Μήδων ἐβασίλευσε, Πέρσης ὀνομάζεται· ἐκ γὰρ τῆς πατρῴας συγγενείας φιλοῦσιν οἱ ἄνθρωποι τὰς ἐθνικὰς τιθέναι προσηγορίας. Εἰκὸς τοίνυν καὶ τὸν Δαρεῖον εἶναι μὲν Μήδου πατρός, Χαλδαίας δὲ μητρός, καλεῖσθαι δὲ τοῦτο ὅπερ ἦν ὁ πατήρ. Εἰ δ' οὐχ οὕτως ταῦτ' ἔχει, δειξάτωσαν οἱ βουλόμενοι τοῦ Ναβουχοδονόσορ τὸν ἔκγονον τῆς παππῴας βασιλείας κληρονομήσαντα, καὶ οὐδὲν περὶ τούτου ζυγομαχήσομεν. Ὅτι γὰρ παναληθὴς τοῦ μεγάλου Ἱερεμίου ἡ πρόρρησις, πᾶς τις εὖ φρονῶν ὁμολογήσειεν. Εἰ δέ τινι προΐσταται μὴ εἶναι θυγατριδοῦν τοῦ Ναβουχοδονόσορ τὸν Δαρεῖον,

1397 ἀλλ' υἱδοῦν, διὰ τὸ τὸν προφήτην εἰρηκέναι· «Δουλεύσουσιν αὐτῷ, | καὶ τῷ υἱῷ αὐτοῦ, καὶ τῷ υἱῷ τοῦ υἱοῦ αὐτοῦ·» μαθέτω τῆς θείας Γραφῆς τὸ ἰδίωμα· ἐξ ἀρρένων γὰρ γενεαλογεῖν εἰωθυῖα, καὶ τὸν ἔκγονον εἰπεῖν ἐθελήσασα, υἱὸν τοῦ υἱοῦ προσηγόρευσεν. Ἀλλ' ὅτι μὲν τοῦ υἱοῦ οὐκ ἔστιν υἱός, ὁ μακάριος Δανιὴλ μαρτυρεῖ, λέγων· «Δαρεῖος ὁ Μῆδος παρέλαβε τὴν βασιλείαν.» Ὅτι δὲ μέχρις ἐκγόνων παραπέμψει τὴν βασιλείαν ὁ Ναβουχοδονόσορ, ὁ θεῖος προεῖπεν Ἱερεμίας. Ἐξ ἑκατέρας τοίνυν προφητείας εὑρεῖν δυνατὸν τὸ ἀληθές· ἐκ μὲν τῆς Ἱερεμίου, ὅτι καὶ ὁ ἔκγονος τοῦ Ναβουχοδονόσορ τῆς βασιλείας ἀνθέξεται· ἐκ δὲ τῆς τοῦ μακαρίου Δανιήλ, ὅτι Βαλτάσαρ τοῦ υἱοῦ τοῦ Ναβουχοδονόσορ, τῇ θείᾳ ψήφῳ τελευτήσαντος, Δαρεῖος ὁ Μῆδος παρέλαβε τὴν βασιλείαν. Ἐντεῦθεν σκοπούμενοι, καὶ τὸ ἀψευδὲς τῶν προφητῶν ἐπιστάμενοι, εὑρίσκομεν τοῦτον Μῆδον μὲν ὄντα πατρόθεν, Χαλδαῖον δὲ ὄντα μητρόθεν, καὶ τοῦ Ναβουχοδονόσορ ἔκγονον. Ταῦτα μὲν οὖν ἡμεῖς ἑκατέρας προφητείας τὸ ἀληθὲς ζητήσαντες ηὕρομεν· ὡς δὲ φίλον ἑκάστῳ περὶ τούτου φρονείτω· οὐδεμία γὰρ ἐκ τῆς περὶ τὸ γένος ἀμφιβολίας γενήσεται βλάβη. Φέρε τοίνυν, τῆς κατὰ μέρος ἑρμηνείας ἁψώμεθα.

son until the time of their own land comes."¹³⁴ Since his son is
called Belshazzar by Daniel, then, we must inquire as to the grandson. If, however, you object to this with the claim that Darius is
called the Mede, be assured that this does not undermine the statement: Cyrus was the son of the daughter of Astyages, who was a
Mede and reigned over Medes, but he is called a Persian: people
like to assign nationality on the basis of paternal relationship. It
was therefore likely also that Darius was the son of a Median father and a Chaldean mother, and was called after his father. But if
this is not the case, let it be proved by those who want to that Nebuchadnezzar's grandson inherited the ancestral kingdom, and we
shall have no quarrel with that: everyone of good sense would admit that the great Jeremiah's prophecy is utterly true.

If, on the other hand, your preference is that Darius is not
the son of Nebuchadnezzar's daughter but of his son in view of
the prophet's saying, "They will serve him, | his son and his son's   1397
son," gain a familiarity with the idiom of the divine Scripture,
which is in the habit of developing a genealogy from the males, and
prefers to speak of a grandson by referring to him as son of the son.
The fact that he was not son of the son blessed Daniel confirms
by saying, "Darius the Mede succeeded to the kingdom;" and the
fact that Nebuchadnezzar passed the kingdom to his grandsons
the divine Jeremiah foretold. So it is possible to find the truth
on the basis of both inspired works, from Jeremiah the fact that
Nebuchadnezzar's grandson succeeded to the kingdom, and from
blessed Daniel the fact that on the death of Belshazzar, Nebuchadnezzar's son, as God decreed, Darius the Mede succeeded to the
kingdom. In consideration of this fact, and knowing the reliability of the inspired authors, we find this man to be a Mede on his
father's side, a Chaldean on his mother's side, and a grandson of
Nebuchadnezzar. This we found, then, by looking for the truth in
each of the inspired works; let each person take a position on it as
appeals to them: no harm will flow from uncertainty about race.

¹³⁴ Jer 27:4–7. Theodoret might admit that Josephus, too (whom he may
have accessed via Eusebius, Guinot believes [*L'Exégèse*, 748]), wishes to main-
tain the credibility of scriptural statement, suffering like him by taking it in
literalistic fashion, as Jeremiah is being misapplied here. The decision to recognize Darius as a grandson of Nebuchadnezzar is an "educated guess" by one
who has rated Evil-merodach and Belshazzar as his sons, now defunct.

ΚΕΦΑΛΑΙΟΝ ΣΤ'

Βασιλεύσας, φησίν, ὁ Δαρεῖος (α', β'.) «Ἔστησεν ἐπὶ τῆς βασιλείας αὐτοῦ σατράπας ἑκατὸν εἴκοσι, τοῦ εἶναι αὐτοὺς ἐν ὅλῃ τῇ βασιλείᾳ αὐτοῦ. Καὶ ἐπάνω αὐτῶν τακτικοὺς τρεῖς, καὶ ἦν Δανιὴλ εἷς ἐξ αὐτῶν, τοῦ ἀποδιδόναι αὐτοῖς τοὺς σατράπας λόγον, ὅπως ὁ βασιλεὺς μὴ ἐνοχλῆται.» Ἀληθῶς οὐδὲν ἀμβλύνειν δύναται τὴν εὐσέβειαν, ἀλλὰ τὰς οἰκείας πανταχοῦ ἀκτῖνας ἀφίησι, κἂν ἐν δούλῳ γένηται, κἂν ἐν αἰχμαλώτῳ, καὶ οὐδὲν ταύτης συσκιάσαι τὴν αἴγλην ἰσχύει, ἀλλὰ τὴν οἰκείαν ἀφίησιν ἀστραπήν. Καὶ τοῦτο πολλαχόθεν μὲν καὶ ἀλλαχόθεν ἔστιν ἰδεῖν, μάλιστα δὲ ἐκ τῶν κατὰ τὸν μακάριον Δανιήλ, ὃς δοῦλος καὶ δορυάλωτος γεγονώς, καὶ ξένην οἰκῶν, καὶ μεταξὺ βαρβάρων στρεφόμενος, διέλαμψε· ἐπὶ μὲν γὰρ τοῦ Ναβουχοδονόσορ προσεκυνήθη ὑπὸ τοῦ φοβερωτάτου βασιλέως. Διέπρεψε δὲ καὶ ἐπὶ τοῦ Βαλτάσαρ, περίβλεπτος δὲ ὡσαύτως ἦν καὶ ἐπὶ τοῦ Δαρείου· καὶ αἱ τῶν βασιλέων διαδοχαὶ μεταβολὴν αὐτῷ τῆς τιμῆς οὐκ εἰργάσαντο· ἀλλ' οἱ μὲν ἐσβέννυντο τῷ θανάτῳ, ὁ δὲ τὴν ἴσην ἐπὶ πάντων ἐκέκτητο λαμπηδόνα. Καὶ μὴν εἰώθασιν οἱ βασιλείαν ἤ τινα ἄλλην ἀρχὴν ἐγχειριζόμενοι, ἥκιστα θαρρεῖν τοῖς τῶν προτέρων οἰκειοτάτοις· οὗτος δὲ παρὰ πᾶσι τὴν αὐτὴν ἐκέκτητο παρρησίαν, καὶ τοῦ ἴσου γέρως ἐτύγχανε, τὴν αὐτήν τε ἡγεμονίαν ἐπιστεύετο· ὥσπερ ἀμέλει καὶ ἐπὶ τοῦ Δαρείου εἷς τῶν τριῶν ἐγένετο τακτικῶν. *Τακτικοὺς* δὲ ἡγοῦμαι προσαγορεύεσθαι τοὺς νῦν καλουμένους ὑπάρχους, σατράπας δὲ τοὺς τῶν ἐθνῶν ἡγεμόνας· ἀλλὰ καὶ τῶν τακτικῶν εἷς ὢν ὁ μακάριος Δανιήλ· |

1400

γ'. «Ὑπερενίκα, φησί, καὶ τοὺς τακτικούς, καὶ τοὺς σατράπας,» τοὺς τῶν ἐθνῶν ἡγεμόνας, κατέναντι, τουτέστιν ἐκ παραλλήλου, τιθέμενος, συγκρινόμενος καὶ παρεξεταζόμενος. Εἶτα λέγει τὴν αἰτίαν τῆς νίκης. «Ὅτι πνεῦμα, φησί, περισσὸν ἐν αὐτῷ·» τουτέστι, πολλῷ μείζονα καὶ πλείονα παρὰ τοῦ Θεοῦ τὴν χάριν ἐδέχετο. Μανθάνομεν δὲ ἐντεῦθεν, ὅτι καὶ τοῖς βιωτικὰς ἐγχειριζομένοις ἀρχάς, κἂν εὐσεβείας ὦσιν ἄμοιροι, δίδοταί τις θεόθεν χάρις σοφίας διὰ τὴν τῶν ἀρχομένων οἰκονομίαν. Καὶ τοῦτο ᾐνίξατο ὁ μακάριος Δανιήλ, εἰρηκώς· «Ὅτι πνεῦμα περισσὸν ἦν ἐν αὐτῷ,» τουτέστιν, ἀναλογοῦσαν τῇ εὐσεβείᾳ τὴν χάριν ἐδέδεκτο. Καὶ τοῦτο θεασάμενος, φησίν, «Ὁ βασιλεὺς κατέστησεν αὐτὸν ἐφ' ὅλης

So come now, let us begin a detailed commentary. After Darius came to the throne, the text says, *he set over his kingdom 120 satraps to be stationed throughout his whole kingdom. Over them were three supervisors, Daniel one of them, and to these the satraps were to give a report so that the king might not meet with any trouble* (vv. 1–2). Nothing, to be sure, can dull true religion: it spreads its rays everywhere, be it in slave or in captive; far from anything being capable of obscuring its splendor, it spreads its characteristic gleam. You can see this in many and varied places, but especially in the situations affecting blessed Daniel, who became slave and captive, inhabiting a foreign land, living among barbarians, and yet was illustrious; even under Nebuchadnezzar he was worshiped by the most fearsome king. He shone out also under Belshazzar, and was likewise conspicuous under Darius, succession in kings effecting no change in his esteem; rather, while they were snuffed out by death, he maintained equal prominence under them all. Normally, in fact, those entrusted with kingship or any other rule confide least in the people closest to their predecessors; but he enjoyed the same trust from all, receiving equal privileges and being entrusted with the same governance—hence, of course, his becoming one of the three supervisors under Darius. Now, by *supervisors* I think there is reference to what are now called viceroys,[135] and by *satraps* to the governors of the nations, Daniel being one of the supervisors. | 1400

He excelled the supervisors and the satraps (v. 3), the governors of the nations, the terms being cited in parallel for comparison and contrast. He then gives the reason for his excellence: *Because there was an extraordinary spirit in him*, that is, he had received from God a greater and more abundant grace. Now, from this we learn that to those also who are entrusted with conduct of earthly affairs, even if unsympathetic to religion, a grace of wisdom is given from God for their management of those they rule. Blessed Daniel implied as much in saying, *Because there was an extraordinary spirit in him*, that is, he had received the grace in keeping with his religious sentiments.[136] Perceiving this, *the king appointed him over*

---

[135] The term in his text is ταχτιχοί. Imperial organization in his time evidently reflected this structure, though history does not support its existence in Persian times.

[136] Comments like this by Theodoret are equivalent to his saying the work is autobiographical.

τῆς βασιλείας αὐτοῦ.» Συνιεὶς γὰρ, ὅτι θεοφιλὴς ὁ ἀνὴρ καὶ τῆς ἄνωθεν ἀπολαύων ῥοπῆς, πᾶσαν αὐτὸν ἐπέτρεψε τὴν βασιλείαν οἰκονομεῖν·
ἀλλὰ τὸ μέγεθος τῆς τιμῆς τὸν φθόνον ἠρέθισεν· «Οἱ δὲ τακτικοὶ καὶ
οἱ σατράπαι ἐζήτουν, φησί, πρόφασιν εὑρεῖν κατὰ τοῦ Δανιὴλ ἐκ τῆς
βασιλείας,» ἢ, ὥς τινα τῶν ἀντιγράφων ἔχει, «ἐκ πλαγίων τῆς βασι-
λείας·» τουτέστι, πάντα ἐπραγματεύοντο, εἰς τοὺς τῆς βασιλείας νόμους
πλημμελοῦντα αὐτὸν εὑρεῖν ἐφιέμενοι· ἀντὶ τοῦ, τὴν νῦν καλουμένην καθ-
οσίωσιν πλέξαι αὐτῷ βουλόμενοι. Ἀλλὰ διήμαρτον τοῦ σκοποῦ. «Πᾶσαν
γὰρ πρόφασιν, φησί, καὶ πᾶν παράπτωμα, καὶ ἀμπλάκημα οὐχ ηὗρον ἐν
αὐτῷ, ὅτι πιστὸς ἦν.» Καὶ τὴν μαρτυρίαν ταύτην ἔσχηκεν ὁ μακάριος
Δανιήλ, οὐ παρὰ τῶν ἀγαπώντων μόνον, ἀλλὰ καὶ παρὰ τῶν ἐπιβου-
λευόντων. «Τὴν γὰρ περὶ τὸν Θεὸν φυλάττων εὐσέβειαν, εὐνοίᾳ πολλῇ
καὶ περὶ τοὺς βασιλέας ἐκέχρητο. Ὡς δὲ μυρία τυρεύσαντες οὐχ ηὗρον
αὐτὸν εἰς τοὺς τῆς βασιλείας πλημμελοῦντα νόμους.»

ε΄. «Εἶπον, φησίν, οἱ τακτικοί· Οὐχ εὑρήσομεν κατὰ Δανιὴλ πρόφασιν, εἰ μὴ ἐν νομίμοις Θεοῦ αὐτοῦ.» Εἰδότες γὰρ αὐτοῦ τῆς εὐσεβείας
τὸ ἀκριβές, ἐκεῖ τὰ θήρατρα τῆς πονηρίας ἱστᾶσι.

ς΄ θ΄. «Καὶ προσίασι τῷ βασιλεῖ οἵ τε τακτικοὶ καὶ οἱ σατράπαι,
καὶ λέγουσιν αὐτῷ· Δαρεῖε βασιλεῦ, εἰς τοὺς αἰῶνας ζῆθι. Συνεβουλεύ-
σαντο πάντες οἱ ἐν τῇ βασιλείᾳ σου στρατηγοί, καὶ τοπάρχαι, ὕπατοι, καὶ
σατράπαι, τοῦ στῆσαι στάσει βασιλικῇ, καὶ ἐνισχῦσαι ὁρισμόν, ὅπως ὃς
ἐὰν αἰτήσῃ αἴτημα παρὰ παντὸς θεοῦ, ἢ ἀνθρώπου, ἕως ἡμερῶν τριάκοντα, ἀλλ᾽ ἢ παρὰ σοῦ, ἐμβληθήσεται εἰς τὸν λάκκον τῶν λεόντων.
Νῦν οὖν, βασιλεῦ, στῆσον τὸν ὁρισμόν, καὶ ἔκθες τὴν γραφήν, ὅπως
1401 μὴ ἀλλοιωθῇ τὸ δόγμα Μήδων καὶ Περσῶν, ὅπως ἂν | μὴ παραλλα-
γῇ κατέναντι τούτου. Τότε ὁ βασιλεὺς Δαρεῖος ἐπέταξε τὴν συγγραφὴν
καὶ τὸ δόγμα.» Οὐδὲν τοῦ φθόνου μιαρώτερον· οὗτος καὶ ἀσεβῆσαι τούτους ἠνάγκασε, καὶ δυσσεβὲς προθεῖναι πεποίηκε δόγμα, ἀπεῖργον τοὺς
βουλομένους εὐχὰς προσφέρειν Θεῷ. Οὐ γὰρ μόνον σφᾶς αὐτοὺς τοῦτο
ποιεῖν κωλύουσιν, ἀλλὰ καὶ τοὺς ἄλλους ἅπαντας τοὺς ὑπὸ τῆς βασιλείας
ὄντας. Καὶ ἵνα μὴ δῆλον γένηται τὸ κακούργημα, προστιθέασι τὸ μηδὲ

the whole of his kingdom: realizing that the man was beloved by God and enjoyed influence from on high, he entrusted him with the management of his whole kingdom. The greatness of the honor, however, gave rise to envy: *But the supervisors and the satraps studied how to find grounds against Daniel from the kingdom*, or, as some of the manuscripts have it, "from outreaches of the kingdom"[137]— that is, they left no stone unturned in their desire to find him infringing the laws of the kingdom, meaning, in their wish to incriminate him in what is now called treason.

But they failed in their purpose: *They found no grounds or any infringement or offense in him, because he was above reproach.* Blessed Daniel had the benefit of this testimony, not only from those who loved him, but also from those who schemed against him; while maintaining his devotion to God, he acquired also great support where the kings were concerned. Despite hatching countless stratagems, they did not find him transgressing the laws of the kingdom. *The supervisors said, We will not find any grounds against Daniel unless in connection with his own God's laws* (v. 5): knowing his religious scrupulosity, it was there they cast their wicked snares. *The supervisors and the satraps together approached the king and said to him, King Darius, live forever! All the generals, local officials, governors, and satraps in your kingdom are at one in advising you to determine by royal decree and institute an ordinance that if anyone makes a request of any god or man for thirty days except of you, they will be thrown into the den of lions. So now, O King, make the ordinance and publish the text so that the decree of the Medes and Persians may not be altered and | no change be made to contradict it.* 1401 *At that point King Darius gave orders for the notice and the decision* (vv. 6–9).

Nothing is more loathsome than envy: it pressured them into committing impiety, and caused an impious decree to be published forbidding those intent on offering prayers to God; they prevented not only themselves from doing it but also all others subject to royal control. And lest their malice be patent, they included the

[137] This vague phrase, which occurs in the Aramaic, appears in the Antioch text only, though apparently in various attempts to clarify it. In making this reference beyond his text, Theodoret is checking its accuracy as a translation for the first time since citing Symmachus on 1:4—a relatively low level of interest by him in the status of his text, understandable in a work where paleographical niceties are not of great urgency

παρὰ ἀνθρώπου αἰτῆσαί τι καὶ λαβεῖν ἐντὸς τῶν τριάκοντα ἡμερῶν· παρὰ μόνου δὲ τοῦ βασιλέως ἐν ἁπάσαις ταύταις ταῖς ἡμέραις ἐπαγγέλλειν τὴν χρείαν. Καὶ οὐ συνεῖδον οἱ τὸ ὀπτικὸν τῆς διανοίας τῷ φθόνῳ παραδεδωκότες, ὡς οὐ πάντα δύναται παρασχεῖν τοῖς αἰτοῦσιν ὁ βασιλεύς· οὔτε γὰρ ὑγείαν, οὔτε ζωήν, οὔτε τὸ γενέσθαι παίδων πατέρας, οὔτε ὑετῶν ἀφθονίαν, οὔτ᾽ ἄλλα πάντα, ἃ τὸν Θεὸν αἰτοῦντες λαμβάνομεν. Ἀλλὰ τὸ φρονεῖν ἀπολέσαντες ἀνατιθέασι τῷ βασιλεῖ τὰ τῷ Θεῷ προσήκοντα, πείθουσι δὲ καὶ τὸν ἀνόητον βασιλέα συμψηφίσασθαι καὶ κυρῶσαι τὰ δυσσεβῶς αἰτηθέντα. Ἀλλ᾽ ὁ μακάριος Δανιὴλ οὐδὲ βραχὺ τῶν δυσσεβῶν τούτων νόμων φροντίσας, «Εὐθὺς εἰς τὸν οἶκον αὐτοῦ, φησίν, εἰσελθών, τῶν θυρίδων ἀνεῳγμένων, ἐν τοῖς ὑπερῴοις αὐτοῦ, κατέναντι Ἱερουσαλὴμ τρεῖς καιροὺς τῆς ἡμέρας ἦν κάμπτων ἐπὶ τὰ γόνατα αὐτοῦ, καὶ προσευχόμενος, καὶ ἐξομολογούμενος ἐναντίον τοῦ Θεοῦ, καθὼς ἦν ποιῶν ἔμπροσθεν.» Ὅρα δὲ πόσα κατὰ ταὐτὸν ὁ λόγος ᾐνίξατο, τοῦ μακαρίου Δανιὴλ τὴν εὐσέβειαν καὶ τὴν ἀνδρείαν μηνύοντα. Πρῶτον μὲν γὰρ Δανιήλ, φησίν, ἡνίκα ἔγνω, ὅτι ἐνετάγη τὸ δόγμα, «Εἰσῆλθεν εἰς τὸν οἶκον αὐτοῦ,» τουτέστι, μαθὼν τὸν τεθέντα νόμον, καὶ σφόδρα καταφρονῶν, ἀντικρὺς ἐναντία δρῶν διετέλει· εἶτα καὶ ἕτερον τέθεικεν, ὃ σαφῶς αὐτοῦ τὴν ἀνδρείαν μηνύει· «Αἱ γὰρ θυρίδες, φησίν, ἀνεῳγμέναι.» Οὐ γὰρ κρύβδην, φησί, τὰς εὐχὰς ἐποιεῖτο, ἀλλὰ προφανῶς, καὶ πάντων ὁρώντων, οὐ φιλοτιμούμενος, ἀλλὰ τῆς δυσσεβείας τοῦ νόμου καταφρονῶν. Πρόσκειται δὲ καὶ ἕτερον, ταύτην αὐτοῦ τὴν ἀνδρείαν παραδηλοῦν· «Ἐν γὰρ τοῖς ὑπερῴοις αὐτοῦ.» Οὐ γὰρ ἐν ἐπιπέδῳ, ἀλλ᾽ ὡς ἐν περιωπῇ τινι προσέφερεν τῷ Θεῷ τὰς εὐχάς, κατάδηλος ὢν ἅπασι, τῷ τε ἐφ᾽ ὑψηλοῦ ἑστᾶναι, καὶ τῷ τὰς θυρίδας ἀναπεπταμένας ἔχειν. «Ηὔχετο δέ, φησί, κατέναντι Ἱερουσαλήμ·» τοῦτο δὲ οὐ μόνον τοὺς κατηγόρους παροξύνων ἐποίει, ἀλλὰ καὶ παλαιὸν νόμον πληρῶν. Ὁ γὰρ Σολομὼν τὸν νεὼν ἐκεῖνον δειμάμενος, καὶ τῶν ἐγκαινίων ἐπιτελῶν τὴν πανήγυριν, προσηύξατο μὲν τὴν θείαν χάριν ἐπικαλούμενος, καὶ ταύτης πλήρη γενέσθαι τὸν νεὼν ἱκετεύων. Πρὸς δὲ ἑτέροις πλείστοις καὶ τοῦτο προσέθηκε· «Καὶ ἔσται, φησίν, ἐὰν παραδῷς τὸν λαόν σου ἐνώπιον τῶν ἐχθρῶν αὐτῶν, καὶ αἰχμαλωτεύσουσιν αὐτὸν οἱ αἰχμαλωτίζοντες εἰς

γῆν μακράν, ἢ | ἐγγύς, καὶ ἐπιστρέψωσι καρδίας αὐτῶν ἐν τῇ γῇ οὗ μετηνέχθησαν ἐκεῖ, καὶ δεηθῶσί σου ἐν γῇ μετοικίας αὐτῶν, λέγοντες· Ἡμάρτομεν, ἠδικήσαμεν, ἠνομήσαμεν, καὶ ἐπιστρέψωσι πρὸς σὲ ἐν ὅλῃ καρδίᾳ αὐτῶν, καὶ ἐν ὅλῃ τῇ ψυχῇ αὐτῶν, ἐν τῇ γῇ τῶν ἐχθρῶν αὐτῶν οὗ μετήγαγες αὐτούς, καὶ προσεύξωνται πρὸς σὲ ὁδὸν γῆς αὐτῶν, ἧς δέδωκας τοῖς πατράσιν αὐτῶν, καὶ τῆς πόλεως, ἧς ἐξελέξω, καὶ τοῦ οἴκου, οὗ ᾠκοδόμησα τῷ ὀνόματί σου, καὶ εἰσακούσῃ ἐκ τοῦ οὐρανοῦ, ἐξ ἑτοίμου

veto on anyone's asking or receiving anything even from a man
inside thirty days, allowing only to the king a report of need in
all those days. In surrendering their mind's eye to envy, they did
not understand that the king could not supply everything to petitioners, like health, life, fathering children, abundance of rain, and
anything else that we receive when we ask it of God. Losing their
senses, however, they ascribed to the king what belongs to God,
and persuaded the foolish king to reach the same verdict and rat-
ify their impious request.

Blessed Daniel, however, gave no thought to these impious
laws even for a moment. *He went in to his house at once, with the
windows on its upper floor open opposite Jerusalem to pray on his knees
three times a day and make confession before God, just as he had done
in the past* (v. 10). Now, note how much this verse implied in a
few words in mentioning the piety and courage of blessed Daniel.
Firstly, when Daniel learned that the decision has been reached,
he went into his house—that is, when he got news of the passing
of the law, he had great scorn for it and continued openly doing
the opposite. It next mentions a further detail which reveals his
courage: the windows were open, it says—in other words, he said
his prayers, not in secret, but openly, with everyone watching, not
for vainglory but in scorn for the impiety of the law. A further detail is also given, indicating this courage of his, *on its upper floor*: he
offered prayers to God, not on the ground floor but in a prominent
place where he was obvious to everyone by being positioned on
high and having the windows open. He prayed *opposite Jerusalem*,
it says; he did this not only to provoke his accusers, but also to fulfill an ancient law: when Solomon built that famous temple and
celebrated the festival of consecration, he prayed a prayer of supplication for divine grace and implored that the temple be filled
with it, adding this in addition to other things, "If you surrender
your people to their foes, and they take them as captives to a land
distant or | near, and they have a change of heart in the land where   1404
they are transported, and pray to you in their exile in the words,
We sinned, we did wrong, we broke the law, and they turn back to
you with their whole heart and with their whole soul in the land of
their foes where you transferred them, and they pray to you toward
their land which you gave their ancestors, and the city which you
chose, and the house which I built to your name, may you hearken from heaven, forthwith from your dwelling place, and forgive

κατοικητηρίου σου, καὶ ἵλεως ἔσῃ ταῖς ἁμαρτίαις αὐτῶν αἷς ἥμαρτόν σοι, καὶ κατὰ πάντα τὰ ἀθετήματα αὐτῶν, ἃ ἠθέτησάν σε, καὶ δῴης αὐτοὺς εἰς οἰκτιρμοὺς ἐνώπιον τῶν αἰχμαλωτευσάντων αὐτούς.» Ταῦτα δὲ πεπαιδευμένος ὁ μακάριος Δανιήλ, κατέναντι Ἱερουσαλὴμ τετραμμένος τὴν προσευχὴν ἐποιεῖτο· οὐχ ἅπαξ δὲ τῆς ἡμέρας, ἀλλὰ καὶ τρὶς τοῦτο ποιῶν διετέλει. Καὶ τὸ σχῆμα δὲ τὴν τῆς διανοίας δείκνυσι συντριβήν. Κάμπτων γὰρ ἐπὶ τὰ γόνατα αὐτοῦ διετέλει τὴν ἐξομολόγησιν προσφέρων τῷ Θεῷ. Τούτων οὕτως γινομένων, οἱ τοῦ φθόνου δοχεῖα γενόμενοι γράφονται παρανομίας τὸν Δανιήλ, καὶ τὸν τεθέντα νόμον ἀναγινώσκουσι, καὶ τόν τε Δανιὴλ εἰσαγγέλλουσι, καὶ τὴν παράβασιν ἐξελέγχουσιν. Ὁ δὲ βασιλεὺς ἤλγησε μὲν τῆς γραφῆς ἀκούων, συνήγορος δὲ ἀντὶ κριτοῦ γενόμενος, ἀθῶον δεικνύναι τὸν Δανιὴλ ἐπειρᾶτο· τοῦτο γὰρ ἠνίξατο ἡ συγγραφὴ λέγουσα·

ιδ΄. «Τότε ὁ βασιλεύς, ὡς τὸ ῥῆμα ἤκουσε, πολὺ ἐλυπήθη ἐπ᾽ αὐτῷ, καὶ περὶ τοῦ Δανιὴλ ἠγωνίσατο τοῦ ἐξελέσθαι αὐτόν.» Ἀλλ᾽ οἱ κακοήθεις ἄνδρες ἐκεῖνοι, καὶ κακουργίᾳ συζῶντες, ἔγνωσαν τὸν τοῦ βασιλέως σκοπόν. Τοῦτο γὰρ σημαίνει τό, «Παρῃτήσαντο οἱ ἄνδρες ἐπὶ τὸν βασιλέα·» ἀντὶ τοῦ, συνῆκαν ὡς τῷ Δανιὴλ συναγωνίζεται. Εἶτα λέγουσι τῷ βασιλεῖ· «Γνῶθι, βασιλεῦ, ὅτι τὸ δόγμα Μήδοις καὶ Πέρσαις, τοῦ πάντα ὁρισμὸν καὶ στάσιν, ἣν ἐὰν ὁ βασιλεὺς στήσῃ, οὐ δεῖ παραλλάξαι.» Οὐκ εἶ, φασί, κύριος, ἃ νενομοθέτηκας ἀνατρέψαι· Μήδων γὰρ καὶ Περσῶν οἱ νόμοι παρακελεύονται, τοὺς τιθεμένους νόμους παρὰ πρώτου πληροῦσθαι τοῦ βασιλέως. Βιασθεὶς δὲ ὁ βασιλεὺς τῷ τε δῆθεν εὐλόγῳ τῶν λόγων καὶ τῷ πλήθει τῶν κατηγόρων, παραδίδωσι μὲν τοῖς λέουσι τὸν μακάριον Δανιήλ· ἐπεύχεται δὲ αὐτῷ σωτηρίαν λέγων· «Ὁ Θεὸς ᾧ λατρεύεις ἐνδελεχῶς, αὐτὸς ἐξελεῖταί σε.» Εὐσεβὲς τὸ ῥῆμα, καὶ τοῖς πρώτοις ἀσύμφωνον. Εἰ γὰρ τοσαύτην τῷ Θεῷ προσμαρτυρεῖς δύναμιν, πῶς ἐνομοθέτησας μηδένα τούτῳ εἰς τριάκοντα ἡμέρας προσεύξασθαι; Ἀλλ᾽ ἔοικεν ὁ Δαρεῖος χρηστὸς μὲν γεγενῆσθαι, καὶ τὸν τρόπον ἐπιεικής,

their sins by which they have sinned against you and all the transgressions they have committed against you, and show them pity
before their captors."¹³⁸ Instructed in this, Daniel faced Jerusalem
in praying, and not just once a day: he continued doing it even
three times. His posture also shows his contrite heart: he continued to offer his confession to God on bended knee.¹³⁹

While this was going on, those who had become receptacles
of envy indicted Daniel for lawless behavior, read out the law that
had been passed, denounced Daniel and accused him of breaking
it. The king was sorry to hear of the indictment, turned advo-
cate instead of judge, and tried to prove Daniel innocent, the text
suggesting as much by saying, *At that point the king, on hearing
the report, was very sorry for him, and on Daniel's behalf went to
pains to save him* (v. 14). But those malicious men were bent on
evil and divined the king's purpose (suggested by the clause *They
prevailed upon the king*, that is, They realized he was on Daniel's
side). Then they said to the king, *Be aware, O King, that it is the
ruling of the Medes and Persians that whatever ordinance and decree
the king makes cannot be altered* (v. 15): you do not have the authority to overturn what you have prescribed, the laws of Medes and
Persians ordering that the laws passed by the previous king be fulfilled.

Under pressure both from the compelling logic of the words
and from the number of the accusers, the king surrendered blessed
Daniel to the lions, on the one hand, and on the other he prayed
for his salvation in the words, *The God whom you serve with constancy will rescue you.* A pious remark, though inconsistent with
the preceding: if you lend confirmation to God's having such great
power, how is it you legislated that no one pray to him for thirty
days? Darius, however, gave the impression of being kindly, sim-

¹³⁸ Cf. 1 Kgs 8:46–50; 2 Chr 6:36–39—a lengthy piece of documentation
to make the point of praying while facing Jerusalem.
¹³⁹ Theodoret does not mention whether thrice-daily prayer was a Jewish
habit only (cf. Ps 55:17—reduced to twice-daily in his comment on that psalm),
or was practiced also in early Christianity, as the *Didache* (8.3) requires (see Jean
Paul Audet, *La Didachè: Instructions des apôtres* [EBib; Paris: Gabalda, 1958],
371). Likewise with kneeling to pray: while standing was normal for Jews before the post-exilic period, Ezra kneels at prayer (9:5), as do Jesus (Luke 22:41)
and Peter (Acts 9:40) in the New Testament—but not the Pharisee or even the
publican (Luke 18:11–13). Nonetheless, Theodoret has not let details of the text
escape him.

καὶ μᾶλλον εὐσεβεία προσέχων, ψοφοδεὴς δὲ ὅμως καὶ λίαν εὐεξαπάτητος. Οὐ γὰρ ἂν βασιλείαν διέπων, ἀντὶ τοῦ ἄγειν, ὑπὸ τῶν ἀρχομένων ἤγετο· φαίνεται δὲ καὶ σφόδρα θαυμάζων τὸν Δανιήλ· «Ὁ Θεὸς γὰρ, φησίν, | ᾧ λατρεύεις ἐνδελεχῶς,» δι᾽ ὃν, φησί, καὶ τῶν ἐμῶν κατεφρόνησας νόμων, καὶ διηνεκῆ τὴν θεραπείαν αὐτῷ προσφέρεις, ἀμείψεταί σε τῆς εὐσεβείας, καὶ τῶν κατεχόντων δεινῶν ἀπαλλάξειεν. Εἶτα καὶ θαρρῶν τῇ τοῦ Θεοῦ δυνάμει, καὶ τὰς τῶν κατηγόρων ὑφορώμενος ἐπιβουλάς, λίθῳ μὲν ἐμφράττει τοῦ λάκκου τὸ στόμα, τοῖς δὲ τοῦ δακτυλίου ἐκτυπώμασιν ἐπιτίθησι σήμαντρα, ἵνα μή τις ὑπ᾽ ἐκείνων περὶ τὸν Δανιὴλ γένηται κακουργία· ἐθάρρει γὰρ ὡς τοὺς λέοντας οὐκ ἐάσει τοῦ Δανιὴλ ὁ Θεὸς τὸ ἱερὸν αὐτοῦ καὶ ἅγιον λυμήνασθαι σῶμα Ταῦτα τοίνυν ποιήσας,

ιη΄. «Ἀπῆλθεν ὁ βασιλεὺς εἰς τὸν οἶκον αὐτοῦ, καὶ ἐκοιμήθη ἄδειπνος, καὶ ἐδέσματα οὐκ ἤνεγκαν αὐτῷ, καὶ ὁ ὕπνος ἀπέστη ἀπ᾽ αὐτοῦ.» Τούτων δὲ ἕκαστον καὶ φιλανθρωπίαν αὐτῷ καὶ δειλίαν προσμαρτυρεῖ. Φιλανθρωπίας μὲν γὰρ τὸ μήτε σιτίων ἐθελῆσαι μετασχεῖν, μήτε ὕπνον τοῖς βλεφάροις πως δέξασθαι, ἀλλ᾽ ἄγρυπνον διατελέσαι, ἀλγοῦντα ἐπὶ τῇ ἀδίκῳ τοῦ Δανιὴλ τιμωρίᾳ· δειλίας δέ, τὸ οὕτω διακείμενον μὴ ἀντιστῆναι τοῖς κατηγόροις, καὶ τῇ βασιλικῇ ἐξουσίᾳ καὶ δυνάμει χρησάμενον σῶσαι τὸν ἀδικούμενον. Οὕτω δὲ τὴν νύκτα διατελέσας,

ιθ΄. «Ὁ βασιλεὺς Δαρεῖος ἀνέστη τοπρωῒ ἐν τῷ φωτί.» Τουτέστιν, ἔτι σκότους ὄντος, περὶ τὸ λυκόφως, ὡς καὶ δεηθῆναι λαμπάδων· τὸ γὰρ ἐν τῷ φωτὶ τοῦτο παραδηλοῖ.

«Καὶ σπουδῇ ἦλθεν ἐπὶ τὸν λάκκον τῶν λεόντων (κ΄.) Καὶ ἐν τῷ ἐγγίζειν αὐτὸν τῷ λάκκῳ,» τουτέστι, μηδέπω παρ᾽ αὐτὸν γενόμενος, «τῷ Δανιὴλ ἐν φωνῇ ἰσχυρᾷ ἐβόησε, καὶ ἀπεκρίθη ὁ βασιλεύς, καὶ εἶπε τῷ Δανιήλ.» Μηδέπω γὰρ παρ᾽ αὐτὸν τὸν λάκκον γενόμενος, ὑπὸ θερμῆς διαθέσεως βοᾶν ἠναγκάζετο, καὶ τὸν Δανιὴλ καλεῖν, καὶ πυνθάνεσθαι, εἰ τῆς θείας ἀπολαύσας ῥοπῆς, κρείττων ἐφάνη τῆς τῶν λεόντων ὠμότητος. «Δανιὴλ γάρ, φησίν, ὁ δοῦλος τοῦ Θεοῦ τοῦ ζῶντος, ὁ Θεός σου, ᾧ λατρεύεις ἐνδελεχῶς, εἰ ἠδυνήθη ἐξελέσθαι σε ἀπὸ στόματος τῶν λεόντων;» Ἕκαστον δὲ τῶν εἰρημένων εὐλαβῆ δείκνυσι τὸν βασιλέα, καὶ διὰ τὴν εὐσέβειαν χαίροντα τῷ Δανιήλ. Πρῶτον μὲν γὰρ δοῦλον αὐτὸν οὐχ ἑαυτοῦ, ἀλλὰ τοῦ Θεοῦ προσαγορεύει· εἶτα ζῶντα τὸν τοῦ Δανιὴλ ὀνομάζει Θεόν· ἔπειτα τὴν εὐσέβειαν ἐπαινῶν, «Ὦ σύ, φησίν, λατρεύεις ἐνδελεχῶς,» τουτέστιν, ὁ μηδὲ διὰ τὴν τοῦ νόμου ἀνάγκην ταύτης κω-

ple in manner, rather inclined to piety, yet timid and very easily deceived, not so much administering the kingdom as being led by his subjects instead of leading them. He also seems a great admirer of Daniel, saying, *God, | whom you serve constantly*, on whose account you even scorn my laws and to whom you unceasingly offer worship, will reward you for your piety and free you from the pressing troubles. Then, with confidence in God's power and suspecting the schemes of the accusers, he shut the opening of the den with a stone and placed a seal on it with his signet ring to prevent any mischief on the part of those of Daniel's company, trusting that God would not allow the lions to harm the sacred and holy body of Daniel.

1405

Having done this, then, *The king went off to his house; he went to bed without dining, they brought him no food, and sleep deserted him* (v. 18). Each of these details testifies both to his humanity and to his cowardice: a mark of his humanity was his refusing to partake of food or let his eyes rest in sleep, instead staying awake in grief for the unjust punishment of Daniel; it was a mark of cowardice that he was not so affected as to gainsay the accusers and invoke his royal authority and power to save the wronged. After passing the night in this way, *King Darius rose early at daybreak* (v. 19), that is, while it was still dark, around dawn, so that there was even need of lamps (the meaning of *at daybreak*). *He went in haste to the lions' den. On approaching the den*—that is, while he still not there—*he cried out to Daniel in a loud voice* (vv. 19–20).[140] While not yet at the actual den, he was forced by the ardor of his disposition to cry out and call on Daniel, and enquire if by relying on divine grace he proved superior to the lions' ferocity. *Daniel, servant of the living God, was your God whom you serve with constancy able to rescue you from the lions' mouth?* Each of these phrases shows the religious spirit of the king, who complimented Daniel on his piety: firstly, he calls him not his own servant but God's; next, he calls Daniel's God *living*; then, in praise of his piety, *whom you serve with constancy*, that is, you were not prevented from worship un-

---

[140] The text is corrupt, but Migne's text hints at an interchange between the king and Daniel by including the words *"and the king replied and said to Daniel"* at the end of the line. Such an interchange neither appears in Theodotion nor respects the movement of thought as paraphrased by Theodoret. The Aramaic, however, does involve some repetition of verbs, and this may be the source of the confusion.

λυθεὶς τῆς θεραπείας. Τὸ δέ, «Εἰ ἠδυνήθη ἐξελέσθαι σε ἀπὸ στόματος τῶν λεόντων;» σημαίνει· Εἰ ἠβουλήθη κρείττονά σε τῶν λεόντων ἀποφῆναι; Οὐ γὰρ ἂν ἐκάλεσεν ἀδύνατον τὸν Θεόν, ὃν ζῶντα προσηγόρευσε. Τούτων ἀκούσας, ὁ Δανιὴλ ἀπεκρίνατο λέγων·

1408   κα΄. «Βασιλεῦ, εἰς τοὺς αἰῶνας ζῆθι,» Τὴν συνήθη | πρόσρησιν τῶν οἰκείων λόγων προτάττει, ἀντὶ τοῦ Γένοιτό σοι ἐπὶ πλεῖστον ζῆν. Καὶ γὰρ καὶ ἐπὶ τοῦ παρόντος, ὡς καὶ ἤδη προειρήκαμεν, αἰωνίους τοὺς βασιλέας ἐν τοῖς τῶν συμβολαίων γραμματείοις τινὲς προσαγορεύειν εἰώθασιν.

κβ΄. «Ὁ Θεός μου, φησίν, ἀπέστειλε τὸν ἄγγελον αὐτοῦ, καὶ ἐνέφραξε τὸ στόμα τῶν λεόντων, καὶ οὐκ ἐλυμήναντό με, ὅτι καὶ ἔναντι αὐτοῦ εὐθύτης καὶ δικαιοσύνη εὑρέθη μοι, καὶ ἐνώπιον δέ σου, βασιλεῦ, παράπτωμα οὐχ εὑρέθη ἐν ἐμοί.» Δίκαιος γὰρ ὢν, φησίν, ὁ Θεός, καὶ δικαίως ἅπαντα πρυτανεύων, θεασάμενος ὅτι τῶν δυσσεβῶν νόμων τὴν αὐτοῦ προτετίμηκα θεραπείαν, καὶ εἰς τὴν σὴν δὲ βασιλείαν οὐδὲν πώποτε πεπλημμέληκα, κρείττονά με τῆς τῶν λεόντων ἀπέφηνε λύμης, καὶ μᾶλλον εἰκόνας λεόντων ἢ λέοντας ἔδειξεν.

κγ΄. «Τότε ὁ βασιλεύς, φησί, πολὺ ἠγαθύνθη ἐπ᾽ αὐτῷ, καὶ τὸν Δανιὴλ εἶπεν ἀνενέγκαι ἐκ τοῦ λάκκου.» Περιχαρὴς γὰρ γενόμενος, καὶ θυμηδίας ἀνάπλεως, ἅτε δὴ καὶ τοῦ Θεοῦ τὴν δύναμιν γνούς, καὶ τοῦ ἀγαπωμένου τὴν σωτηρίαν μαθών, παραυτίκα αὐτὸν ἐκ τοῦ λάκκου ἀνενεχθῆναι προσέταξε. Εἶτα θεασάμενος αὐτὸν σῶον καὶ ἐρρωμένον, καὶ οὐδεμίαν ἐσχηκότα διαφθορὰν ἐκ τῆς τῶν λεόντων προσβολῆς, τοὺς τοῦ Δανιὴλ κατηγόρους προσέταξε τοῖς λέουσι σὺν τοῖς υἱέσι καὶ γυναιξὶ ῥιφῆναι. «Καὶ οὐκ ἔφθασαν, φησίν, εἰς τὸ ἔδαφος τοῦ λάκκου, ἕως οὗ ἐκυρίευσαν αὐτῶν οἱ λέοντες, καὶ πάντα τὰ ὀστᾶ αὐτῶν ἐλέπτυναν.» Καὶ τοῦτο γὰρ τῆς θείας ἔργον δικαιοσύνης τε καὶ σοφίας. Ἵνα γὰρ μὴ λέγωσιν, ὡς διὰ πλησμονὴν καὶ κόρον οἱ λέοντες ἀπείχοντο. τοῦ Δανιὴλ, καὶ σμικρύνωσι τῷ φθόνῳ τὸ γενόμενον θαῦμα, ἐμβληθέντες ἐμαρτύρησαν τῇ τῶν λεόντων ὠμότητι· ἐξήρπαζον γὰρ αὐτοὺς καταφερομένους οἱ λέοντες, καὶ μηδέπω τοὺς χαλωμένους εἰς γῆν ἐφικνουμένους ἐξ αὐτοῦ τοῦ ἀέρος λαμβάνοντες ἐποιοῦντο τροφήν. Δίκας μὲν οὖν ἀξίας δεδωκότες τὸ δίκαιον

der pressure of the law. The question *Was he able to rescue you from the lions' mouth?* means, Was it his will to render you proof against the lions? After all, he would not have referred to God as powerless after calling him *living.*

On hearing this, Daniel replied, *O King, live forever!* (v. 21). He prefixes | the customary salutation to his own words, meaning, May it be your good fortune to live long; even at present, as we remarked before, remember, some people are in the habit of calling kings eternal in commercial documents. *My God sent his angel and shut the lions' mouth, and they did me no harm, because before him I was found upright and righteous, and in your presence, O King, no fault was found in me* (v. 22): righteous as he is and governing all things righteously, God perceived that I put his worship ahead of the impious laws and never committed any offence against your kingship; so he made me proof against harm from the lions, and showed them to be images of lions rather than lions.

At this the king was very glad for him, and he gave orders to bring Daniel up from the den (v. 23): he was overjoyed and full of satisfaction in coming to know God's power, and learning of the safety of his loved one, and he immediately ordered him to be brought up from the den. Then, on seeing him safe and sound, and showing no ill effects of his encounter with the lions, he ordered Daniel's accusers to be thrown to the lions along with their children and wives. *They did not get as far as the bottom before the lions overpowered them and crushed all their bones to pieces* (v. 24). This was, in fact, an effect of divine righteousness and wisdom: to prevent their claiming that the lions shunned Daniel on account of overfeeding and satiety, and thus through envy belittling the miracle that occurred, they were tossed in and confirmed the lions' ferocity; the lions fell upon them when they thrown in, and made food of them as they fell before they had hit the ground by snatching them in midair. [141] In paying due penalty, therefore, they

[141] Unlike the incident of the three (young) men's survival and hymn-singing amidst the flames in chapter 3, on which Theodoret moralized as the story-teller hoped, in this case of Daniel's survival among the lions, which also figures in early Christian thought (cf. Heb 11:33) and iconography as a symbol of the resurrection of the body, he remarks briefly only on its miraculous character (fortunately not caviling at the number of victims for the lions, there being 125 guilty officials plus family members!). For him, as he says in closing the chapter and his fifth tome, Daniel is a martyr to fidelity to the true religion (though this

κηρύττουσι τοῦ Θεοῦ· οὕτω δὲ ῥᾷστα καταναλωθέντες ὑπὸ τῶν θηρίων
τὴν τοῦ Θεοῦ σοφίαν ὑποδεικνύουσι, καὶ διδάσκουσιν ἅπαντας, ὡς οὐχ
ὁ τῶν λεόντων κόρος, ἀλλ᾽ ὁ περὶ τὸν Θεὸν τοῦ Δανιὴλ πόθος, τῆς τῶν
λεόντων αὐτὸν λύμης ἀπέφηνε κρείττονα. Ταῦτα θεασάμενος,

κε΄. «Δαρεῖος ὁ βασιλεὺς ἔγραψε πᾶσι τοῖς λαοῖς, φυλαῖς, γλώσσαις, τοῖς οἰκοῦσιν ἐν πάσῃ τῇ γῇ.» Ἀνόσιον ἡγησάμενος τοσαύτην κρύψαι θαυματουργίαν, καὶ μὴ πάντας ἀνθρώπους κοινωνοὺς τῆς εὐσεβείας
λαβεῖν. Γράφει τοίνυν οὕτως· «Εἰρήνη ὑμῖν πληθυνθείη·» τουτέστι, Γένοιτο ὑμᾶς διαπαντὸς εἰρήνης ἀπολαύειν. Ἔοικε δὲ τοῦτο τῇ παρ᾽ ἡμῶν
γινομένῃ προσηγορίᾳ· καὶ γὰρ ἡμεῖς ἐπιστέλλοντες προγράφειν εἰώθα-
μεν τό· Ἐν Κυρίῳ | χαίρειν. Εἶτα διηγεῖται τὸ ἐπωφελὲς καὶ ἐπικερδὲς
διήγημα.

κς΄. «Ἐκ προσώπου μου ἐτέθη δόγμα ἐν πάσῃ ἀρχῇ τῆς βασιλείας
μου, εἶναι πάντας τρέμοντας καὶ φοβουμένους ἀπὸ προσώπου τοῦ Θεοῦ
Δανιήλ.» Βούλομαι, φησί, πάντας ἀνθρώπους τοὺς ὑπὸ τὴν ἐμὴν τελοῦν-
τας ἐξουσίαν, τὸν τοῦ Δανιὴλ προσκυνεῖν Θεόν, καὶ μὴ ἁπλῶς καὶ ὡς
ἔτυχεν, ἀλλὰ μετὰ δέους καὶ φρίκης προσφέρειν αὐτῷ τὴν προσκύνησιν.
Καὶ τὴν αἰτίαν ἐπάγει, καὶ φησιν· «Ὅτι αὐτός ἐστι Θεὸς ζῶν, καὶ μένων
εἰς τοὺς αἰῶνας.» Διαρκὴς γάρ ἐστι, καὶ τροπὴν οὐδεμίαν δεχόμενος, καὶ
ἀεὶ ὡσαύτως ἔχει, καὶ εἰς τοὺς αἰῶνας διαμένει. Τούτοις ἐπάγει· «Καὶ ἡ
βασιλεία αὐτοῦ οὐ διαφθαρήσεται, καὶ ἡ κυρεία αὐτοῦ ἕως τέλους. (κζ΄.)
Ἀντιλαμβάνεται, καὶ ῥύεται.» Εἰσαεὶ δέ, φησί, διαμένει, καὶ βασιλείαν
ἔχων ἀνώλεθρον, καὶ δεσποτείαν τέλος οὐ δεχομένην, ῥυομένην δὲ καὶ
λυτρουμένην τοὺς εἰς αὐτὸν πεπιστευκότας. «Καὶ σημεῖα δὲ ποιεῖ ἐν τῷ
οὐρανῷ καὶ ἐπὶ τῆς γῆς.» Ἔστι δὲ ἰδεῖν αὐτοῦ τὰς θαυματουργίας, τάς
τε ἐν τῷ οὐρανῷ γινομένας, καὶ τὰς ἐπὶ τῆς γῆς, δι᾽ ὧν τὴν ἑαυτοῦ
δείκνυσι δύναμιν. Ταύτην ἡμῖν καὶ ἐπὶ τοῦ παρόντος ὑπέδειξεν· «Ἐξεί-
λατο γάρ, φησί, τὸν Δανιὴλ ἐκ στόματος τῶν λεόντων,» καὶ τῶν λιμῷ
καὶ θυμῷ τεθηγμένων θηρίων ἀπέφηνε κρείττονα. Ἡ μὲν οὖν ἐπιστολὴ
ταῦτα τὴν οἰκουμένην δεδίδαχε. Τὸ δὲ τοῦ διηγήματος τέλος περιέχει,
ὅτι κατηύθυνε Δανιὴλ ἐν τῇ βασιλείᾳ Δαρείου καὶ ἐν τῇ βασιλείᾳ Κύρου
τοῦ Πέρσου· τουτέστιν, ἐν ἑκατέρᾳ βασιλείᾳ διαλάμπων διετέλεσε, καὶ
ἐν πᾶσι διαπρέπων. Ἡμᾶς δὲ προσήκει τῆς εὐσεβείας μεμαθηκότας τὴν
δύναμιν, ταύτην προαιρεῖσθαι, καὶ πάντων αὐτὴν προτιθέναι, καὶ μηδε-
μιᾷ περιστάσει παραχωρεῖν· ἀλλὰ κἂν ἅπαντες ἄνθρωποι κατὰ ταυτὸν
καθ᾽ ἡμῶν διὰ ταύτην στρατεύσωσι, δέχεσθαι προθύμως τὴν προσβολὴν
τῇ ταύτης δυνάμει θαρροῦντας. Οὕτω γὰρ καὶ τῶν μακαρίων ἀποστόλων

proclaim God's righteousness, while in thus being consumed in a
trice by the wild beasts they give a glimpse of God's wisdom and
teach everyone that it was not the lions' satiety but Daniel's desire
for God that rendered him proof against harm from the lions.

On perceiving this, *King Darius wrote to all the peoples, tribes,
language groups, inhabitants in all the land* (v. 25): considering it
unbecoming to conceal such marvelous wonder-working, and not
make everyone acquainted with the true religion, he therefore
writes in these terms: *May peace be multiplied for you*, that is, May
it be your good fortune to enjoy peace forever. This resembles the
greeting used by us: in our letter writing we are in the habit of be-
ginning, "Greetings in the Lord." | Then he gives a useful and 1409
beneficial account. *From my presence a decree has gone out in all
my royal command for everyone to be in fear and trembling before the
God of Daniel* (v. 26): I want everyone living under my authority to
worship the God of Daniel, not idly and casually, but to offer him
worship in fear and trembling. He also gives the reason, *Because he
is the living God, abiding forever*: he is sufficient of himself, undergoing no change, always the same, continuing forever. To this he
adds, *His kingdom will never be destroyed, and his lordship is forever.
He defends and rescues* (vv. 26–27): he abides forever, he has an in-
destructible kingdom and a lordship without end that rescues and
redeems those who believe in him. *He works signs in heaven and
on earth*: it is possible to see his wonder-working, both that which
happens in heaven and that on earth, through which he brings out
his power. Even in the present case he has given us a glimpse of
it: *He rescued Daniel from the mouth of the lions*, and rendered him
proof against the appetites of wild beasts whetted by hunger and
rage. While the letter conveyed this to the world, then, the conclusion of the story tells that *Daniel prospered in the reign of Darius
and in the reign of Cyrus the Persian* (v. 28),[142] that is, he continued
to be conspicuous and illustrious in everything in each reign.

It behooves us for our part, being acquainted with the power
of true religion, to opt for it, prefer it to anything else, and give
ground before no threat. Instead, even should everyone at the one
time bring forces to bear on us on its account, we should vigorously withstand the attack by relying on its might. This was the

thought does not lead him to see Antiochus IV in focus).
    [142] This is the reference, of course, which proves a problem for both Jose-
phus and Theodoret in trying to identify "Darius the Mede."

ὁ χορός, ἀπὸ πάσης, ὡς ἔπος εἰπεῖν, τῆς οἰκουμένης πολιορκούμενος, ἄμαχος μεμένηκε, καὶ τοὺς πολεμίους ὑπηκόους ἐποιήσατο. Οὕτως ὁ μακάριος Δανιήλ, ὑπὸ τοσούτων σατραπῶν καὶ τακτικῶν ἐπιβουλευόμενος, ἀμείνων ἀπεφάνθη τῶν πολεμούντων· καὶ ἡνίκα δὲ οἱ δυσμενεῖς νενικηκέναι ᾠήθησαν, τηνικαῦτα πανωλεθρίαν ὑπέμειναν. Τοιαῦτα τοίνυν ἔχοντες παραδείγματα, εἰλικρινῆ τὴν περὶ τὸν Θεὸν φυλάξωμεν εὔνοιαν, ἵνα τῆς παρ' αὐτοῦ ῥοπῆς διηνεκῶς ἀπολαύσωμεν· ἧς γένοιτο πάντας ἡμᾶς ἐπιτυχεῖν, χάριτι καὶ φιλανθρωπίᾳ τοῦ Κυρίου ἡμῶν Ἰησοῦ Χριστοῦ, μεθ' οὗ τῷ Πατρὶ ἡ δόξα, σὺν τῷ ἁγίῳ Πνεύματι, εἰς τοὺς αἰῶνας

1412   τῶν αἰώνων. Ἀμήν. |

ΤΟΜΟΣ Ζ΄ — ΚΕΦΑΛΑΙΟΝ Ζ΄

α΄. «Ἐν τῷ πρώτῳ ἔτει Βαλτάσαρ, τοῦ βασιλέως Χαλδαίων, Δανιὴλ ἐνύπνιον εἶδε, καὶ ἡ ὅρασις τῆς κεφαλῆς αὐτοῦ ἐπὶ τῆς κοίτης αὐτοῦ, καὶ τὸ ἐνύπνιον ἔγραψε.» Μέχρι μὲν τούτων τῶν λόγων ὁ μακάριος Δανιὴλ ἱστορικώτερον τὴν προφητείαν συνέγραψε. Πρῶτον μὲν γὰρ εὐθὺς ἀρξάμενος τὰ συμβεβηκότα αὐτοῖς δορυαλώτοις γεγενημένοις ἐδίδαξε· προσέθεικε δὲ καὶ ὅσης παρὰ τοῦ Θεοῦ τῶν ὅλων κηδεμονίας ἀπήλαυσαν. Ἔπειτα διηγήσατο, ἡλίκας ὁ Ναβουχοδονόσορ τῆς ὠμότητός τε καὶ ἀλαζονείας ἔδωκε δίκας· μετὰ ταῦτα οἵαν ὁ Βαλτάσαρ ἔτισε τιμωρίαν τῶν ἱερῶν καταφρονήσας σκευῶν. Τούτου δὲ θείᾳ πληγῇ καταλυθέντος, καὶ εἰς Μήδους τῆς βασιλείας μετατεθείσης, τὰ καθ' ἑαυτὸν καὶ τὸν Δαρεῖον συνέγραψε, διδάξας, ὅπως μὲν ἐκεῖνος περὶ αὐτὸν διετέθη, οἵας δὲ αὐτὸς ὑπομείνας ἐπιβουλὰς ὑπό τε τῶν στρατηγῶν καὶ τῶν σατραπῶν, τῆς θείας ἔτυχεν ἀντιλήψεως. Ταῦτα οἱονεὶ συγγραφικῶς διηγησάμενος, ἄρχεται λοιπὸν διδάσκειν, ἃς διὰ τῶν ἀποκαλύψεων ἐδιδάχθη προρρήσεις. Καὶ πρῶτον μὲν τίθησι τὴν τῶν τεττάρων θηρίων ἀποκάλυψιν, σφόδρα ἐοικυῖαν τῷ τοῦ Ναβουχοδονόσορ ἐνυπνίῳ. Καὶ γὰρ ἐκεῖνος ἐν εἰκόνι μιᾷ τέτταρας ἐθεάσατο ὕλας, καὶ οὗτος ἀπὸ θαλάττης μιᾶς τέτταρα ἀνιόντα θηρία. Ἀλλ' ἵνα μὴ δὶς τὰ αὐτὰ λέγειν ἀναγκασθῶμεν, τῆς κατὰ μέρος ἑρμηνείας ἀρξώμεθα· σαφέστερον γὰρ ἐκεῖθεν τοῦτο δειχ-

way, in fact, that the band of the blessed apostles, under siege by the whole world, you might say, remained invincible, and made subjects of the enemy. This was the way blessed Daniel, in the face of the schemes of so many satraps and supervisors, emerged superior to the enemy; and at the moment the adversaries appeared to have prevailed, then it was they suffered overthrow. With these examples, therefore, let us keep a sincere disposition toward God so as to enjoy grace from him constantly. May it be the good fortune of us all to attain it, thanks to the grace and lovingkindness of our Lord Jesus Christ, to whom with the Father and the Holy Spirit be glory, for ages of ages. Amen. | 1412

CHAPTER 7

In the first year of Belshazzar king of the Chaldeans, Daniel had a dream, and there was a vision in his head in bed. He wrote down the dream (v. 1). Up to these words blessed Daniel composed the prophecy with more accent on factual details. First, remember, at the very beginning he conveyed what happened to the actual captives, and he went on to mention the great degree of care they enjoyed from the God of all. Then he recounted the heavy penalty Nebuchadnezzar paid for his cruelty and arrogance, and later the kind of retribution Belshazzar suffered for showing disrespect for the sacred vessels. When he was destroyed by divine intervention, and the kingdom was transferred to the Medes, he recorded his fate and that of Darius, informing us how the latter felt about him and the kinds of schemes he suffered at the hands of the generals and satraps, but received divine support.

Having recounted those things as a historian, as it were, he now begins to convey the predictions he learned about through the revelations.[143] Firstly, he cites the revelation of the four wild beasts, very similar to the dream of Nebuchadnezzar: he saw in one image four materials, and this man sees four beasts coming up from the sea. Lest we are forced to tell the same things twice, however, let us begin the commentary in detail, this being the way for

[143] Daniel, Theodoret tells us, is about to change from a role of prophet-historian, συγγραφεύς, to prophet-visionary in receipt of revelations, ἀποκαλύψεις.

θήσεται. «Ἐν τῷ πρώτῳ ἔτει Βαλτάσαρ, βασιλέως Χαλδαίων, Δανιὴλ
ἐνύπνιον εἶδε, καὶ αἱ ὁράσεις τῆς κεφαλῆς αὐτοῦ ἐπὶ τῆς κοίτης αὐτοῦ.»
Τουτέστι, καθεύδων τήνδε τὴν ἀποκάλυψιν ἐθεάσατο· ἐπειδὴ γὰρ μέλλει
καὶ ἃ μεθ' ἡμέραν εἶδε συγγράφειν, εἰκότως ἡμᾶς διδάσκει, τίνα μὲν ὄναρ
εἶδε, τίνα δὲ ὕπαρ. «Καὶ τὸ ἐνύπνιον, φησίν, ἔγραψεν.» Οὐ γὰρ ἠνέσχετο
κρύψαι τὰ θεόθεν αὐτῷ δειχθέντα, ἀλλ' εἰς ὠφέλειαν ἁπάντων συνέγραψεν. «Ἀρχὴ λόγων αὐτοῦ. Καὶ ἀποκριθεὶς εἶπε.» Τουτέστιν, ἤρξατο τῆς
διηγήσεως οὕτως·

β', γ'. «Καὶ ἐγὼ Δανιὴλ ἐθεώρουν ἐν ὁράσει μου τῆς νυκτός,
καὶ ἰδοὺ οἱ τέσσαρες ἄνεμοι τοῦ οὐρανοῦ προσέβαλον εἰς τὴν θάλασσαν
τὴν μεγάλην. Καὶ τέσσαρα θηρία μεγάλα ἀνέβαινον ἐκ τῆς θαλάσσης,
1413 διαφέροντα ἀλλήλων.» Ὁ μὲν οὖν Ναβουχοδονό|σορ εἰκόνα βλέπει, δι-
δασκόμενος τῶν παρόντων πραγμάτων τὸ μάταιον, καὶ ὅτι σχήματα
μᾶλλόν εἰσιν, ἤ φησιν ὁ θεῖος Ἀπόστολος, ἀλλ' οὐ πράγματα· οὐδὲν γὰρ
αὐτῶν μόνιμον, οὐδὲ βέβαιον, ἀλλὰ πάντα διαρρεῖ καὶ φθείρεται καὶ μα-
ραίνεται· ὁ δὲ μακάριος Δανιὴλ θάλασσαν βλέπει, τοῦ παρόντος βίου τὰ
κύματα διδασκόμενος. Ἐπειδὴ γὰρ τὴν ξένην ἰδεῖν ἠναγκάζετο δορυάλω-
τος γενόμενος, ἀναγκαίως τοῦ βίου τὸν κλύδωνα καὶ χειμῶνα διδάσκεται.
Καὶ ὁ μὲν βασιλεύς, ὡς μέγα φρονῶν «ἐπὶ χρυσῷ καὶ ἀργύρῳ, καὶ χαλκῷ, καὶ σιδήρῳ,» διὰ τούτων λαμβάνει τὰ τῶν βασιλειῶν αἰνίγματα, καὶ
τὰς τῶν βασιλέων μανθάνει διαδοχάς, καὶ διδάσκεται μὴ μεγάλα φρονεῖν
ἐπὶ τῇ βασιλείᾳ ὀξύρροπον ἐχούσῃ μεταβολήν. Ὁ δὲ προφήτης, ἅτε δὴ
τῶν ὑλῶν ἐκείνων καταφρονῶν, «τέσσαρα θηρία» βλέπει, διδασκόμενος,
ὡς αἱ φοβεραὶ αὗται βασιλεῖαι, αἱ πάντας ἀνθρώπους δεδιττόμεναι, τέλος λήψονται καὶ αὗται, μία δὲ μόνη ἡ ἀτελεύτητος μένει βασιλεία, ἣν
τοῖς ἁγίοις ηὐτρέπισεν ὁ τῶν ἁγίων Θεός. Θάλατταν τοίνυν καλεῖ τὸν
βίον, ἅτε δὴ μυρίας ἔχοντα τρικυμίας, ἀνέμους δὲ ταύτῃ προσβάλλοντας,
τὰς τῶν πραγμάτων μεταβολάς. Καθάπερ γὰρ νότου μὲν πνέοντος ἐπὶ τὸ
ἀρκτῷον μέρος διατρέχει τὰ κύματα, βορέου δὲ κινοῦντος τὴν θάλασσαν,
πάλιν τὸ ῥόθιον ἐπὶ τὸ νότιον μέρος ὠθεῖται· οὕτως, ἡνίκα μὲν Ἀσσύ-
ριοι κατεῖχον τῆς οἰκουμένης τοὺς οἴακας, πρὸς ἑαυτοὺς ἅπαντας εἷλκον

it to be brought out more clearly.[144] *In the first year of Belshazzar king of the Chaldeans, Daniel had a dream, and there was a vision in his head in bed*, that is, he had this revelation while asleep: since he would record also what he saw during the day, he was right to inform us what he saw in a dream and what while awake. *He wrote down the dream*: he could not bring himself to conceal what had been revealed to him from God, instead recording it for the benefit of everyone.[145] *The beginning of his words. In reply he said*, that is, he began his account thus.

I, Daniel, saw in my vision at night the four winds of heaven falling upon the great sea. Four large beasts came up out of the sea, different from one another (vv. 2–3). For his part Nebuchadnezzar | gazed upon an image, drawing a lesson in the futility of things of this life and the fact that they are rather appearances, as the divine apostle says, not realities, there being nothing lasting or stable in them, everything fluid and failing and fading.[146] Daniel, on the other hand, is gazing at a sea, gaining a lesson in the billows of the present life: since he was a captive and obliged to see a foreign land, he was inevitably schooled in life's storm and tempest. For his part the king, taking pride in gold, silver, bronze, and iron, found in them figures of the kingdoms, learning of the succession of kings, and being taught not to boast of kingship that is subject to rapid change. The prophet, on the other hand, full of scorn for those materials, is gazing at *four beasts* and learning that these fearsome kingdoms, which instill terror in all people, will themselves also come to an end, whereas one single kingdom abides without end, which the God of the holy ones prepared for the holy ones.

So by *sea* he refers to life in its having many tidal waves and winds buffeting it, the changes in circumstance: just as the waves beat toward the north when the south wind blows, whereas the breakers are driven toward the south when the north wind stirs up the sea, so when the Assyrians held the world's tiller, they drew

1413

[144] Clarity and lack of repetition continue to be the virtues to which he aspires.

[145] Thus closes v. 1 in Theodotion's text and modern versions such as the NRSV. The Aramaic, however, proceeds to add two further introductory phrases, possibly later insertions, and these appear in Theodoret's text.

[146] Cf. 1 Cor 7:31. Though Theodoret has noted the change in genre (if not identifying it accurately) after chapter 6, he still sees Daniel as composer of a single continuous work, the visions in both parts being comparable.

τοὺς ὑπηκόους· μεταβάσης δὲ τῆς βασιλείας εἰς Πέρσας, μετέβη παραυτίκα καὶ τῶν ὑπηκόων πρὸς ἐκείνους ὁ δρόμος. Μακεδόνων δὲ πάλιν τὰ σκῆπτρα λαβόντων, ἀφέντες ἅπαντες ἐκείνους οἷς ὑπήκουον πρότερον, τούτοις προσέφερον τὸν συνήθη δασμόν. Ἐπειδὴ δὲ Ῥωμαῖοι τὸ κατὰ πάντων ἀνεδήσαντο κράτος, εἰς τὴν ἑσπέραν συντρέχουσιν ἅπαντες, Μακεδόνων οὐδένα ποιούμενοι λόγον· τοῖς γὰρ ὑπηκόοις καὶ αὐτοὶ συνηρίθμηνται. Εἰκότως τοίνυν τὰς τῶν πραγμάτων μεταβολὰς ἀνέμοις ἀπείκασεν, οἳ νῦν μὲν ὧδε, νῦν δὲ ἐκεῖσε τῆς θαλάττης ὠθοῦσι τὰ κύματα. Τούτου δὲ χάριν καὶ τῶν τεσσάρων ἐμνημόνευσεν ἀνέμων, ἐπειδὴ καὶ τέσσαρες γεγόνασι βασιλειῶν διαδοχαί. Διδάσκει δὲ ἡμᾶς, καὶ ὁποίαν πρὸς ἄλληλα εἶχε τὰ θηρία διαφοράν.

δ'. «Τὸ πρῶτον γάρ, φησίν, ὡσεὶ λέαινα, καὶ πτερὰ αὐτῇ ὡσεὶ ἀετοῦ· ἐθεώρουν ἕως οὗ ἐξετίλη τὰ πτερὰ αὐτῆς, καὶ ἐξήρθη ἀπὸ τῆς γῆς, καὶ ἐπὶ ποδῶν ἀνθρώπου ἐστάθη, καὶ καρδία ἀνθρώπου ἐδόθη αὐτῇ.» Τὴν Ἀσσυρίων βασιλείαν, εἴτ' οὖν Χαλδαίων, αὐτὴ γὰρ πρώτη τοῦ πλείστου τῆς οἰκουμένης ἐκράτησε, διὰ τῆς λεαίνης ᾐνίξατο· βασιλικὸν γὰρ τὸ ζῶον, καὶ «τὰ πτερὰ ἀετῷ ἐοικέναι» φησί· καὶ γὰρ τοῦτο τὸ ζῶον
1416 τῶν πτηνῶν ἁπάντων κρατεῖ. Ὥσπερ τοίνυν καὶ τῆς εἰκόνος ἐκείνης |
ὁ Ναβουχοδονόσορ τὴν κεφαλὴν ἔφη τεθεᾶσθαι χρυσῆν· ἑρμηνεύων δὲ ὁ θειότατος Δανιὴλ ἔφη· «Ἡ κεφαλὴ ἡ χρυσῆ σὺ εἶ, βασιλεῦ·» οὕτω κἀνταῦθα τῶν θηρίων τὸ κράτιστον ἐπὶ τῆς πρώτης τέθεικε βασιλείας, οὐκ ἰσχὺν αὐτῇ πλείονα προσμαρτυρῶν, ἀλλ' ὡς πρώτην τιμιωτέραν ἀποφαίνων. Ἀλλ' ὅμως εἶδεν, ὡς «ἐξετίλη αὐτῆς τὰ πτερά·» τουτέστι, γυμνὴ τῶν ὑπηκόων ἁπάντων ἐγένετο, καὶ τῆς προτέρας ἐστερήθη δυνάμεως. «Καὶ ἐξήρθη, φησί, ἀπὸ τῆς γῆς·» ἀντὶ τοῦ, βασιλεύειν ἐπαύσατο. «Καὶ ἐπὶ ποδῶν, φησίν, ἀνθρώπου ἐστάθη.» Ἴση, φησί, τοῖς ὑπηκόοις ἐγένετο. «Καὶ καρδία ἀνθρώπου ἐδόθη αὐτῇ.» Μεμάθηκε, φησί, διὰ τῆς

all the subject peoples to themselves. With the change in imperial power to the Persians, immediately the course of the subject peoples was also in their direction, and in turn when the Macedonians took the scepter, they all ignored those to whom they were previously subject and to whom they paid the customary tribute. But when Romans got control of everyone, they all betook themselves to the west, setting no store by Macedonians, who were themselves numbered among the subject peoples.[147] He was right, therefore, to compare the changes in circumstance to winds, which drive the waves of the sea in one direction at one time, and in another at another time. This is also the reason he mentioned four winds, since there were four changes in kingdoms as well. He informs us also of how the beasts differed from one another.

The first was like a lioness, and its wings were like those of an eagle. I kept watching until its wings were plucked off; it was lifted up from the earth, it was made to stand on the feet of a human being, and it was given a human heart (v. 4). By the lioness he hinted at the empire of the Assyrians, or Chaldeans, this being the first to gain control of the greater part of the world; it was a royal animal, and he says its wings resembled those of an eagle, this animal ruling all the birds. So just as | Nebuchadnezzar also said he had a vision of that image's golden head, and the most divine Daniel in interpreting it said, "The head of gold is you, O King,"[148] likewise here too he cited the strongest of the wild animals in reference to the first kingdom, not to confirm its greater strength, but to indicate its pride of place. Still, he observed that *its wings were plucked off*, that is, it was deprived of all its subjects and stripped of its former power. *It was lifted up from the earth*, that is, its reign ceased. *It was made to stand on the feet of a human being*: it was put on a level with its subjects. *It was given a human heart*: it learned by

1416

---

[147] As in his interpretation of Nebuchadnezzar's dream in chapter 2, Theodoret with his contemporaries takes the four empires to be the Babylonian ("Assyrian"), Medo-Persian, Greco-Seleucid ("Macedonian"), and Roman for what the author intended to be Babylonians, Medes, Persians, and Greeks. Here he has the additional encouragement of Rev 13:1–2, which uses the imagery of this chapter of the Roman Empire. What he is not tapping into is the imagery of the primeval watery abyss (and sea monsters) occurring in the Old Testament in Gen 1–2, Job, the Psalms, and Isaiah, not to mention ancient Eastern mythology generally.

[148] Dan 2:38.

πείρας ἀνθρώπινα φρονεῖν, καὶ μὴ ὑπερβαίνειν τῇ φαντασίᾳ τῆς διανοίας
τὰ μέτρα τῆς φύσεως· ἐπειδὴ γάρ, ἡνίκα τὰ τῆς βασιλείας κατεῖχον
πηδάλια, τύφον ἐνόσουν καὶ ἀλαζονείας ἀμετρίαν· διὸ καὶ ὁ μακάριος
Ἡσαΐας φησίν· «Ἐπάξει ὁ Θεὸς ἐπὶ τὸν νοῦν τὸν μέγαν τὸν ἄρχοντα
τῶν Ἀσσυρίων·» εἰκότως καὶ τὴν τῶν πραγμάτων μεταβολὴν τῇ πείρᾳ
μαθόντες καὶ τῆς εὐημερίας τὸ σφαλερόν, ἀνθρώπινα φρονοῦσι, καὶ ἑαυτοὺς γινώσκουσι, καὶ καρδίαν ἀνθρωπίνην ἐκτήσαντο. Οὕτω μὲν οὖν τὰ
περὶ τοῦ πρώτου διηγήσατο θηρίου. Ἐπάγει δέ·
ε΄. «Καὶ ἰδοὺ θηρίον ἕτερον ὅμοιον ἄρκτῳ, καὶ εἰς μέρος ἓν ἐστάθη, καὶ τρία πτερὰ ἐν τῷ στόματι αὐτῆς ἀναμέσον τῶν ὀδόντων αὐτῆς,
καὶ οὕτως ἔλεγον αὐτῇ· Ἀνάστα, φάγε σάρκας πολλάς.» Τὴν Περσικὴν
ἐνταῦθα βασιλείαν αἰνίττεται· ἄρκῳ δὲ αὐτὴν ἐοικέναι φησί, διὰ τὸ τῶν
τιμωριῶν ὠμὸν καὶ ἀπηνές. Βαρβάρων γὰρ ἁπάντων ὠμότεροι περὶ τὰς
τιμωρίας οἱ Πέρσαι, ἐκδοραῖς χρώμενοι, καὶ τῇ κατὰ μέρος τῶν μορίων
ἐκτομῇ μακρὰς τὰς κολάσεις μηχανώμενοι, καὶ πικρὸν κατασκευάζον-
τες τοῖς κολαζομένοις τὸν θάνατον. Διὰ τοῦτο, φησί, καὶ ἔλεγον αὐτῇ·
«Ἀνάστα, φάγε σάρκας πολλάς·» οὐκ ἐπιτρέποντες τοῦτο ποιεῖν, ἀλλὰ
προλέγοντες τὰ ἐσόμενα, καὶ τὸ ὠμὸν καὶ ἀνήμερον προσμαρτυροῦντες.
«Τρία δέ, φησί, πτερὰ ἐν τῷ στόματι αὐτῆς.» Τῶν τριῶν γὰρ τῆς οἰκουμένης τμημάτων ἐκράτησε, τοῦ ἑῴου, καὶ τοῦ βορείου, καὶ τοῦ νοτίου.
Κῦρος μὲν γάρ, ὁ πρῶτος Περσῶν βασιλεύσας, τὸ Ἑῷον ἅπαν μέχρι τοῦ
Ἑλλησπόντου ὑφ᾽ ἑαυτὸν ἐποιήσατο· Καμβύσης δὲ ὁ τούτου παῖς καὶ
τὴν Αἴγυπτον ἐχειρώσατο, καὶ Αἰθίοπας ὑπηκόους ἀπέφηνε· Δαρεῖος δὲ
ὁ τοῦ Ὑστάσπου, Σκυθῶν τῶν Νομάδων ἐκράτησεν, οἳ τὸ βόρειον ἔλα-
χον μέρος τῆς οἰκουμένης οἰκεῖν. Ξέρξης δὲ ὁ Δαρείου ἐπεχείρησε μὲν
καὶ τὴν Εὐρώπην τοῖς ὑπηκόοις συνάψαι· ναυμαχίᾳ δὲ ἡττηθεὶς Ἀθη-
ναίων, αἰσχρῶς ἀνέστρεψε, καὶ τὴν ἀπὸ τῆς ἀπληστίας τικτομένην ἔμαθε

experience to adopt human ways of thinking, and in the imaginings of its mind not to surpass the limits of nature; since at the time they held the reins of the empire they suffered from conceit and unbridled arrogance, and hence blessed Isaiah said, "God will punish the ruler of the Assyrians for his self-importance."[149] It was right that they should learn by experience the mutability of circumstances and the impermanence of prosperity, adopt human ways of thinking, know their own limitations, and acquire a human heart. This, then, is the account he gave of the first beast.[150]

He goes on, *Lo, another beast, like a bear, raised up on one part, three wings in its mouth amidst its teeth; they said this to it, Rise up, eat much flesh* (v. 5). Here he is referring to the Persian Empire, saying it was like a bear on account of the cruelty and harshness of its punishments. The Persians, in fact, were more cruel than anyone else in punishing, employing cudgels, devising protracted torture with the cutting of parts of limbs, and inflicting an excruciating death on the victims—hence their saying to it, *Rise up, eat much flesh*, not to urge it to do so, but foretelling future events and testifying to its cruelty and ferocity. *Three wings in its mouth*: it ruled three quarters of the world, east, north and south, Cyrus, the first to rule Persia, bringing under him all the east as far as the Hellespont, Cambyses his son seizing Egypt and bringing the Ethiopians into subjection, and Darius the son of Hystaspes in control of the nomadic Scythians, who were allotted the northern part of the world.[151] Xerxes son of Darius tried to link Europe with his subjects, but he was defeated in a naval battle with the Athenians, retreated in shame, and learned the harm that ensues

---

[149] Isa 10:12.

[150] The précis of vv. 4–5 given in Rev 13 suggests to some commentators that they originally read to give the lion the three tusks ("wings"—the only three Babylonian kings whom the Bible and Theodoret know), with its wings plucked (when "Darius the Mede" captured Babylon). The bear is that "Darius," its lifted paw ("part") suggesting not ferocity but the humane characteristics of the Medes—hence human stance and heart. Obviously, the text in its present condition does not offer a compelling interpretation; and Theodoret's gives the impression of conjecture, like that of his modern counterparts.

[151] When not struggling to accommodate "Darius the Mede" into his historical scenario, Theodoret shows he is familiar with the succession in the Persian Empire. In 2 Macc 12:11 the term "nomad" will be used (applied by Theodoret here to Scythians in the north) of Arabs around Jamnia (Yavneh) engaged in battle by the Jews under the leadership of Judas Maccabeus.

1417 βλάβην. Τούτου χάριν φησί· « Τρία πτερὰ ἐν τῷ στόματι αὐτῆς· » | ἔνια δὲ τῶν ἀντιγράφων πλευρὰ ἔχει· οὐδὲν δὲ διαφέρει. Εἴτε γὰρ τοῦτο, εἴτε ἐκεῖνο τεθείη, διδάσκει ὡς τὰ τρία τμήματα τῆς οἰκουμένης καρποῦται, καὶ τὸν πανταχόθεν ὑποδέχεται φόρον. Καλῶς δὲ καὶ τό, « ἐν τῷ στόματι αὐτῆς » προστέθεικεν, ἵνα δείξῃ τὴν παρὰ πάντων χορηγουμένην εἰσφοράν. Καὶ ἐπειδὴ οὐ παντάπασιν ἡ βασιλεία αὕτη κατελύθη, ἀλλὰ μοῖράν τινα τῆς προτέρας ἡγεμονίας διέμεινεν ἔχουσα, οὐκ ἔφη μὲν ὑπομεῖναι αὐτὴν ἅπερ ἡ πρὸ αὐτῆς πέπονθε τῶν πτερῶν στερηθεῖσα, « καὶ ἐπὶ ποδῶν ἀνθρώπου σταθεῖσα, καὶ καρδίαν ἀνθρώπου λαβοῦσα· » εἶπε δὲ αὐτὴν εἰς ἓν στῆναι μέρος. « Εἰς ἓν δέ, φησί, μέρος ἐστάθη, » τουτέστι, κρατήσασα τῶν τριῶν τῆς οἰκουμένης τμημάτων, ἀπεστερήθη μὲν τοῦ πλείστου, ἑνὸς δὲ μέρους τὴν ἡγεμονίαν κατέσχε. Κρατοῦσα γὰρ τῆς Ἀσίας πάλαι ἁπάσης, καὶ τῆς Λιβύης, ἀπεστερήθη μὲν τῆς Αἰγύπτου καὶ τῆς Αἰθιοπίας· οὐκέτι δὲ Παλαιστινῶν, καὶ Φοινίκων, καὶ Σύρων κρατεῖ· ἀφήρηται δὲ καὶ τῆς Ἀσίας τὴν ἡγεμονίαν, καὶ ὁ Εὔξεινος δὲ Πόντος ἔξω τῶν σκήπτρων γεγένηται· κρατεῖ δὲ μόνης Περσίδος, καὶ Μηδίας, καὶ Ἀσσυρίας, καὶ τῶν πλησιοχώρων ὀλίγων ἐθνῶν. Διὰ τοῦτό φησιν, ὅτι « Εἰς ἓν μέρος ἐστάθη. » Ταῦτα καὶ περὶ τοῦ δευτέρου διηγησάμενος θηρίου,

ς΄. « Ὀπίσω, φησί, τούτου ἐθεώρουν, καὶ ἰδοὺ θηρίον ἕτερον ὡσεὶ πάρδαλις, καὶ αὐτῇ πτερὰ τέσσαρα πετεινοῦ ὑπεράνω αὐτῆς, καὶ τέσσαρες κεφαλαὶ τῷ θηρίῳ, καὶ ἡ ἐξουσία ἐδόθη αὐτῇ. » Τὴν Μακεδονικὴν βασιλείαν διὰ τούτων αἰνίττεται· καὶ μάλα προσφόρως παρδάλει τὸν Ἀλέξανδρον ἀπείκασε, διὰ τὸ ταχὺ καὶ ὀξὺ καὶ ποικίλον. « Τέτταρα δὲ πτερὰ πετεινοῦ » ἔφη τὸ θηρίον ἐσχηκέναι, ἐπειδὴ πτηνοῦ δίκην ὁ Ἀλέξανδρος τὰ τέσσαρα τῆς οἰκουμένης διαδραμὼν τμήματα, πάντας ὑφ᾽ ἑαυτὸν ἐποιήσατο· διὰ δὲ « τῶν τεσσάρων κεφαλῶν » τὴν μετὰ τὸν Ἀλέξανδρον γενομένην ᾐνίξατο τῆς ἡγεμονίας διαίρεσιν. Τέσσαρες γὰρ ἀνθ᾽ ἑνὸς κατέστησαν βασιλεῖς· καὶ Πτολεμαῖος μὲν ὁ Λάγου τῶν κατ᾽ Αἴγυπτον ἐνεχειρίσθη τοὺς οἴακας· Σέλευκος δὲ τῶν πρὸς ἕω τὴν ἡγεμονίαν ἰθύνειν ἐπιστεύθη· Ἀντίγονος δὲ τῆς Ἀσίας ἐκράτησε· τῆς δὲ Μακεδονίας, ὡς μέν τινές φασιν, Ἀντίπατρος· ὡς δὲ ἕτεροι, Φίλιππος ὁ καὶ Ἀριδαῖος, αὐτοῦ Ἀλεξάνδρου ἀδελφός. Αἱ μὲν οὖν τέσσαρες κεφαλαὶ τὰς

from greed. Hence his saying, *three wings in its mouth*, | though   1417
some of the manuscripts have "sides," which makes no difference:
whether it is one or the other, it conveys the fact that it exploited
three parts of the world and received tribute from all quarters.[152]

He did well to add *in its mouth* to highlight the contribu-
tion being made by everyone. And since the kingdom was not
completely destroyed, instead continuing with part of its former
influence, he did not say it suffered what the former one suffered
in being deprived of its wings, being made to stand on the feet of a
human being and receiving a human heart. Instead, he said it rose
up on one side: *it was raised up on one part*, that is, in being in control of three sections of the world, it was deprived of the majority
but held power over one part. In other words, while formerly in
control of the whole of Asia and Libya, it was deprived of Egypt
and Ethiopia; it no longer controls Palestine, Phoenicia, and Syria,
and it has also lost control of Asia, and Pontus Euxine is beyond
its sway. It rules only Persia, Media, and Assyria, and a few neighboring nations. Hence he says, *It was raised up on one part*.[153]

After this description of the second beast, he goes on, *In the
wake of this I saw another beast like a leopard, with four wings of a
bird on its back; the beast had four heads, and authority was given it*
(v. 6). In this he is hinting at the Macedonian kingdom: it was very
appropriate for him to compare Alexander to a leopard on account
of its speed and rapidity and diverse colors. He said the beast had
four wings of a bird because like a bird Alexander traversed the
four quarters of the world and brought all under his control; and
by *four heads* he referred to the division of command, four kings
taking the place of one: Ptolemy son of Lagus was entrusted with
the helm of Egyptian affairs, to Seleucus was given government
of matters in the east, Antigonos had control of Asia, Antiponos
Macedonia in the view of some commentators, but according to
others Antipater, and still others Philip, also called Arrhideus,
Alexander's own brother.[154] While the *four heads* refer to the four

---

[152] At least Theodoret looks for guidance in this obscure description to
other forms of the text, ἀντίγραφα, before cutting the Gordian knot. There is no
value for his readers in his being tentative.

[153] Theodoret the political-geographer sketches the limits of the Persian
Empire in his time.

[154] With equal relish in backgrounding the text for his readers, and after
some research into his predecessors' views, Theodoret sketches out the divisions

μετὰ τὸν Ἀλέξανδρον τέσσαρας ἡγεμονίας αἰνίττονται, τὰ δὲ τέσσαρα
πτερὰ αὐτὴν τοῦ Ἀλεξάνδρου τὴν δυναστείαν τῶν τεττάρων τῆς οἰκουμένης περιγενομένην τμημάτων· ἐξουσίαν δὲ ἔφη δεδόσθαι τῷ θηρίῳ,
ἐπειδὴ καὶ ὧν οἱ πρὸ αὐτοῦ μὴ ἐκεκρατήκεισαν, οὗτος ἐδείχθη κρατῶν,
ἀλλ᾽ ὅμως καὶ ἡ πάντων περιγενομένη βασιλεία τέλος ἐδέξατο.

ζ΄. « Ὀπίσω γὰρ τούτου, φησίν, ἐθεώρουν ἐν ὁράματι τῆς νυκτός,
1420 καὶ ἰδοὺ θηρίον τέταρτον φοβε|ρὸν καὶ ἔκθαμβον περισσῶς, καὶ οἱ ὀδόν-
τες αὐτοῦ σιδηροῖ καὶ μεγάλοι, καὶ οἱ ὄνυχες αὐτοῦ χαλκοῖ ἤσθιον καὶ
ἐλέπτυνον, καὶ τὰ ἐπίλοιπα τοῖς ποσὶν αὐτοῦ συνεπάτει, καὶ αὐτὸ διέφερε περισσῶς παρὰ πάντα τὰ θηρία τὰ ἔμπροσθεν αὐτοῦ.» Τὸ τέταρτον
θηρίον τὴν Ῥωμαϊκὴν καλεῖ βασιλείαν· ὄνομα δὲ αὐτῷ οὐ τίθησιν, ἐπειδὴ ἐκ πλειόνων ἐθνῶν ἡ Ῥωμαίων συγκροτηθεῖσα πόλις τῆς οἰκουμένης
ἐκράτησε· πρῶτον μὲν βασιλευομένη, εἶτα ὁτὲ μὲν δημοκρατουμένη, ὁτὲ
δὲ ἀριστοκρατουμένη· ὕστερον δὲ εἰς τὴν προτέραν ἐπανελθοῦσα βασιλείαν. Φοβερὸν δὲ λέγει τὸ θηρίον καὶ ἔκθαμβον περισσῶς, ἐπειδὴ τῶν
ἄλλων ἁπασῶν βασιλειῶν δυνατωτέρα αὕτη ἡ βασιλεία γεγένηται, καὶ
ἐπὶ τῆς εἰκόνος δέ, τετάρτην ὕλην τὸν σίδηρον τέθεικε, καὶ ἐπήγαγεν.
Ὥσπερ τοίνυν ὁ σίδηρος λεπτύνει καὶ ἐκδαμάζει πάντα, οὕτω πάντα
λεπτυνεῖ καὶ ἐκδαμάσει. Καὶ ἐνταῦθα δέ φησιν· «Οἱ ὀδόντες τοῦ θηρίου
σιδηροῖ·» ὡς εἶναι δῆλον, ὅτι τὴν αὐτὴν κἀνταῦθα βασιλείαν αἰνίττεται. «Ἤσθιε, φησί, καὶ ἐλέπτυνε.» Καὶ τῷ ὄντι μείζους ἐπετέθησαν
ὑπὸ Ῥωμαίων τοῖς ὑπηκόοις οἱ φόροι. «Καὶ τὰ ἐπίλοιπα, φησί, τοῖς
ποσὶν αὐτοῦ συνεπάτει.» Πόδας δὲ τῆς βασιλείας τὴν στρατείαν αἰνίττεται, ὑφ᾽ ὧν οὐ σμικραὶ ζημίαι τοῖς τε τὰς πόλεις οἰκοῦσι καὶ τὰς χώρας
ἐπάγονται. «Καὶ αὐτὸ διέφερε περισσῶς παρὰ πάντα τὰ θηρία τὰ ἔμπροσθεν αὐτοῦ.» Δυνατωτέρα γὰρ καὶ περιφανεστέρα ἡ Ῥωμαίων βασιλεία
τῶν πρὸ αὐτῆς βασιλειῶν ἀπεφάνθη. «Καὶ κέρατα αὐτῷ, φησί, δέκα.»
Σημαίνει ἐνταῦθα, ὅτι περὶ τὸ τέλος τῆς βασιλείας δέκα κατὰ ταὐτὸν
ἀναστήσονται βασιλεῖς, ὧν οἱ μὲν ἔσονται δυνατοί, οἱ δὲ λίαν ἀσθενεῖς.
Τοῦτο γὰρ καὶ ἐν τῷ τῆς εἰκόνος ἐνυπνίῳ ἐδίδαξε· καὶ γὰρ ἐκεῖ «οἱ δάκτυλοι τῶν ποδῶν δέκα, καὶ οὗτοι μέρος μὲν εἶχον σιδήρου, μέρος δέ τι
ὀστράκου·» ἑρμηνεύων δὲ ὁ μακάριος ἔφη Δανιήλ, ὡς «Τῆς βασιλείας
μέρος μέν τι ἔσται ἰσχυρόν, μέρος δέ τι ἀσθενές.» Ὡς εἶναι δῆλον, ὅτι
τὰ αὐτὰ σημαίνει ἀμφότερα τὰ ἐνύπνια.

«Καὶ κέρατα αὐτῷ δέκα, φησί. (η΄.) Προσενόουν, φησί, τοῖς κέ-
ρασιν αὐτοῦ, καὶ ἰδοὺ κέρας ἕτερον μικρὸν θεωρητὸν ἀνέβαινεν ἐν μέσῳ

governments after Alexander, then, and the *four wings* the actual empire of Alexander that prevailed over the four quarters of the world, he said *authority was given* to the beast, since he proved to be in control of what his predecessors did not. Nevertheless, even the kingdom dominating everything came to an end.

In the wake of it I saw in a dream by night a fourth beast, | 1420 *fearsome and extremely terrifying; its huge teeth of iron and its claws of bronze kept eating and crushing and trampling on the remains with its feet, and it easily destroyed all the beasts before it* (v. 7). By the fourth beast he refers to the Roman Empire, but does not give it a name because the city of the Romans was composed of many nations and ruled the whole world. It was first under kings, then at one time the people, and at another the aristocracy, but later it reverted to being a kingdom as before. He calls the beast *fearsome and extremely terrifying* since this empire proved more powerful than all the other empires. In the image he described the fourth material as iron, adding that just as iron crushes and dominates everything, so it will crush and dominate everything, whereas in this text he says the beast's teeth were of iron; so it is clear that here he also refers to the same empire. *It kept eating and smashing*: the taxes imposed by the Romans on their subjects were actually heavier. Also, *it kept trampling on the remains with its feet*. By *feet* he refers to the empire's army, by which not insignificant losses were sustained by the inhabitants of the cities and territories. *It easily destroyed all the beasts before it*: the Roman Empire proved more powerful and notorious than the empires before it.

It had ten horns, the text says, indicating here that about the end of the empire ten kings will arise at the one time, some of whom will be strong, others very weak. This, in fact, he conveyed also in the dream of the image: there too "the ten toes on its feet were partly iron, partly clay," which blessed Daniel interpreted to mean, "Part of the kingdom will be strong and part weak."[155] Hence it is clear that both dreams indicate the same thing. *And it had ten horns. I was pondering its ten horns, when lo and behold another horn appeared, small but conspicuous, rising up in the middle of*

of Alexander's empire (the alternative nomination of Philip is found in Eusebius and Jerome). Modern commentators, on the other hand, see the Persian Empire in focus, the four heads being the four of its kings mentioned in the Bible: Cyrus, Xerxes, Artaxerxes, and "Darius the Persian" (Neh 12:22).

[155] Dan 2:42.

αὐτῶν, καὶ τρία ἔμπροσθεν αὐτοῦ ἐξερριζώθη ἀπὸ προσώπου αὐτοῦ· καὶ ἰδοὺ ὀφθαλμοὶ ὡσεὶ ὀφθαλμοὶ ἀνθρώπου ἐν τῷ κέρατι τούτῳ, καὶ στόμα λαλοῦν μεγάλα καὶ ἐποίει πόλεμον πρὸς τοὺς ἁγίους.» Ἐνταῦθα τὸν Ἀντίχριστον αἰνίττεται, μεταξὺ τῶν δέκα κεράτων ἀναφαινόμενον. Λέγει δὲ ὅτι καὶ τρία κέρατα ἐξερρίζωσε τῶν ἔμπροσθεν αὐτοῦ· αἰνίττεται δὲ ὅτι τρεῖς βασιλεῖς καταλύσει ἀπὸ τῶν δέκα κατὰ ταὐτὸν βασιλευόντων. *Μικρὸν δὲ αὐτὸ κέρας καλεῖ, ὡς ἀπὸ μικρᾶς φυλῆς τῶν Ἰουδαίων φυόμενον· θεωρητὸν δέ, ὡς ἐπίσημον μετὰ ταῦτα γινόμενον. Διὰ δὲ | τῶν ὀφθαλμῶν τὴν φρόνησιν καὶ πανουργίαν ᾐνίξατο, ᾗ χρώμενος ἐξαπατήσει πολλούς. Ἀλλὰ καὶ στόμα, φησί, λαλοῦν μεγάλα, τουτέστιν, ἀλαζονικὰ καὶ ὑπέρογκα.* Σαφῶς δὲ ἡμᾶς ὁ μακάριος Παῦλος τοῦτο διδάσκει, λέγων· «Μή τις ὑμᾶς ἐξαπατάτω κατὰ μηδένα τρόπον, ὅτι ἐὰν μὴ ἔλθῃ ἡ ἀποστασία πρῶτον, καὶ ἀποκαλυφθῇ ὁ ἄνθρωπος τῆς ἁμαρτίας ὁ υἱὸς τῆς ἀπωλείας, ὁ ἀντικείμενος, καὶ ὑπεραιρόμενος ὑπὲρ πάντα λεγόμενον Θεόν, ἢ σέβασμα, ὥστε καὶ εἰς τὸν ναὸν τοῦ Θεοῦ εἰσελθόντα καθίσαι, ἀποδεικνύοντα ἑαυτόν, ὅτι ἐστὶ Θεός.» Τοῦτο αἰνιττόμενος καὶ ὁ μακάριος ἔφη Δανιήλ· «Καὶ στόμα λαλοῦν μεγάλα, καὶ ἐποίει πόλεμον μετὰ τῶν ἁγίων.» Πάντα γὰρ, φησί, πραγματεύεται, κοινωνοὺς τῆς πονηρίας καὶ τῆς τιμωρίας ἅπαντας ἀνθρώπους λαβεῖν ἐφιέμενος. Ἀλλὰ ταῦτα ποιῶν, φησίν, οὐκ ἐπὶ πολὺ διαρκέσει, ἀλλ᾽ ὡς τάχιστα καταλυθήσεται.

θ΄, ι΄. «Ἐθεώρουν γὰρ, φησίν, ἕως ὅτου θρόνοι ἐτέθησαν, καὶ Παλαιὸς ἡμερῶν ἐκάθισε, καὶ τὸ ἔνδυμα αὐτοῦ ὡσεὶ χιὼν λευκόν, καὶ ἡ θρὶξ τῆς κεφαλῆς αὐτοῦ ὡσεὶ ἔριον καθαρόν· ὁ θρόνος αὐτοῦ φλὸξ πυρός, οἱ τροχοὶ αὐτοῦ πῦρ φλέγον. Ποταμὸς πύρινος εἷλκεν ἐκπορευόμενος ἔμπροσθεν αὐτοῦ, χίλιαι χιλιάδες ἐλειτούργουν αὐτῷ, καὶ μύριαι μυριάδες παρειστήκεισαν αὐτῷ κριτήριον ἐκάθισε, καὶ βίβλοι ἠνεῴχθησαν.» Ἐκεῖνα μέν, φησίν, ἅπαντα ἐτόλμα τὸ κέρας τὸ λαλοῦν τὰ μεγάλα καὶ ἀλαζονικὰ καὶ ὑπέρογκα, καὶ τοῖς ἁγίοις πολεμοῦν, ἕως ἐκάθισε τὸ κριτήριον. Προσήκει δὲ εἰδέναι, ὅτι ἀσώματος ὢν ὁ Θεός, ἁπλοῦς τε καὶ ἀσχημάτιστος,

them, and three of its former ones were uprooted to make room for it.
There were eyes on this horn like human eyes, and a mouth speaking
lofty words, and it made war on the holy ones (vv. 7–8). Here there
is reference to the antichrist appearing between the ten horns, the
meaning being that he uprooted three horns to make room for it,
and the reference being to the three kings he will destroy of the
ten ruling at the one time. Now, he calls the horn itself *little* as
springing up from the little tribe of the Jews, and *conspicuous* as
becoming famous afterwards; by | the *eyes* he suggested the clev-   1421
erness and trickery he employed in trampling many underfoot.
He also says *a mouth speaking lofty words*, that is, arrogant and
haughty; blessed Paul gives a wise lesson in this in saying, "Let
no one deceive you in any way, because unless the rebellion comes
first, and the sinful one[156] is revealed, the child of ruin, the adver-
sary who is lifted up over every so-called god or object of worship
so as to enter and take a seat in God's temple, presenting himself as God."[157] Hinting at this, blessed Daniel also said, *a mouth*
speaking lofty words, and it made war on the holy ones: it tries every
stratagem in its desire to make all human beings sharers in wickedness and retribution.

In doing this, however, he says, he will not last long but will
be destroyed as quickly as possible. *I kept looking until thrones were*
set in place, and an Ancient of Days took his seat, his clothing as white
as snow, and the hair of his head like pure wool. His throne was fiery
flame, and its wheels burning fire. A river of fire issued forth and
flowed before him, a thousand thousands served him, and ten thousand
times ten thousand attended on him. The court sat, and books were
opened (vv. 9–10). It was the horn *speaking lofty words*, arrogant
and haughty, that perpetrated all those things, even *making war on*
the holy ones until *the court sat*. Now, we should realize that God is

---

[156] Modern critical editions of the New Testament read "the lawless one"
(ὁ ἄνθρωπος τῆς ἀνομίας) rather than "the sinful (ἁμαρτίας) one." The application of the term "antichrist" to this figure is not found in the New Testament,
which uses "antichrist" to describe false teachers who already have appeared (1
John 2:18, 22; 4:3; 2 John 7).

[157] 2 Thess 2:3–4, an apocalyptic premonition of the coming of "the
lawless one" based on the historical figure of Antiochus IV and passages from
Daniel. Modern commentators would also see Antiochus in focus as the "little horn," the ten other horns being interpreted variously. Theodoret accepts
Antiochus as this horn in 8:9 for the reason that his (Hebrew) text there has a
different form for "little," appearing as "strong" in Greek.

περιγραφήν οὐδεμίαν δεχόμενος, ἀλλ' ἀπερίγραφον ἔχων τὴν φύσιν, σχηματίζει πολλάκις πρὸς τὸ χρήσιμον, ὡς ἐθέλει, τὰς ὀπτασίας. Καὶ ἔστιν ἰδεῖν ἑτέρως μὲν αὐτὸν ἐπιφαινόμενον τῷ Ἀβραάμ, ἑτέρως δὲ τῷ Μωσῇ, καὶ ἄλλως τῷ Ἡσαΐᾳ, καὶ τῷ Ἰεζεκιὴλ δὲ ὡσαύτως ἑτέραν ὄψιν ἐπέδειξεν. Ὅταν τοίνυν τὴν τῶν ἀποκαλύψεων ἴδῃς διαφοράν, μὴ πολύμορφον ὑπολάβῃς τὸ Θεῖον, ἄκουσον δὲ αὐτοῦ λέγοντος διὰ Ὡσηὲ τοῦ προφήτου· «Ἐγὼ ὁράσεις ἐπλήθυνα, καὶ ἐν χερσὶ προφητῶν ὡμοιώθην.» Ὡμοιώθην εἶπεν, οὐκ ὤφθην· ὡς γὰρ βούλεται, σχηματίζει τὰς ὄψεις. Ὥσπερ ἀμέλει καὶ ὁ μακάριος Ἰεζεκιὴλ θεασάμενος ἐξ ἠλέκτρου καὶ πυρὸς συγκείμενον τὸν ὀφθέντα, διηγησάμενος τὴν ἀποκάλυψιν ἐπήγαγε· «Τοῦτο ὁμοίωμα δόξης Κυρίου.» Καὶ οὔτε αὐτὸν ἔφη τεθεᾶσθαι τὸν Κύριον, οὔτε αὐτὴν τὴν τοῦ Κυρίου δόξαν, ἀλλὰ τὸ ὁμοίωμα τῆς δόξης Κυρίου. Καὶ ἐνταῦθα τοίνυν ὁ μακάριος Δανιήλ, διὰ μὲν τοῦ *Παλαιοῦ τῶν ἡμερῶν* διδάσκεται τὸ αἰώνιον· οὕτω γὰρ καί τινες τῶν ἑρμηνευτῶν νενοη|κότες, ἀντὶ τοῦ *Παλαιοῦ τῶν ἡμερῶν, ὁ Παλαιῶν τὰς ἡμέρας* τεθείκασιν. Ὁρᾷ τε καὶ *τῆς τριχὸς τὴν καθαρότητα,* καὶ τῶν ἐνδυμάτων τὴν λαμπρότητα, τὸ ἄμωμον πανταχόθεν καὶ ἅγιον, οὐ μόνον τῆς θείας φύσεως, ἀλλὰ καὶ τῶν περὶ αὐτὴν νοουμένων διδασκόμενος, τουτέστι δικαιοσύνης, προνοίας κηδεμονίας, κρίσεως. Ἐπειδὴ γὰρ εἶδεν «τὸ κέρας ἀλαζονικοῖς μὲν χρώμενον λόγοις,» τοῖς τε τοῦ Θεοῦ θεράπουσι μυρίας καττύον ἐπιβουλάς, διδάσκεται διὰ τῆς πανταχόθεν ἀστραπτούσης καθαρότητος, ὡς οὐ παρορῶντος τοῦ Θεοῦ ταῦτα τολμᾶται, ἀλλὰ διὰ τὴν ἄρρητον συγχωροῦντος οἰκονομίαν. Καὶ ἵνα μή τις πάλιν ὑπολάβῃ βούλεσθαι μὲν τὸν Θεόν, ἅτε δὴ ἀγαθὸν ὄντα, τοῖς ἁγίοις ἐπαμύνειν, μὴ δύνασθαι δέ, ὁρᾷ καὶ «τὸν θρόνον ἐκ φλογὸς κατεσκευασμένον, καὶ τοὺς τροχοὺς ὡσαύτως πυρὸς ἔχοντας φύσιν, καὶ ποταμὸν πυρὸς τὸν θρόνον ἕλκοντα, καὶ χιλίας μὲν χιλιάδας λειτουργούσας, μυρίας δὲ μυριάδας παρεστώσας.» Καὶ διὰ τούτων μὲν τὸ δυνατὸν διδάσκεται τοῦ Θεοῦ, δι' ἐκείνων δὲ τὸ ἀκήρατόν τε καὶ ἄμωμον· διὰ δὲ τῆς παλαιότητος τὸ αἰώνιόν τε καὶ σοφόν, καὶ ἥμερον. Τούτοις ἐπάγει· «Κριτήριον ἐκάθισε, καὶ βίβλοι ἠνεῴχθησαν·» ἀντὶ τοῦ, Κρίσεως

incorporeal, simple and without form, uncircumscribed; yet while being uncircumscribed in nature, he often takes visible forms for people's benefit. It is possible to see him making himself visible in one way to Abraham, in another to Moses, yet another to Isaiah, and likewise in a different form to Ezekiel. So when you see the difference in the revelations, instead of thinking the divinity has many forms, listen to him speaking through the prophet Hosea, "I multiplied visions, and adopted likenesses in the works of the inspired authors."[158] He said, *I adopted likenesses*, not I appeared: he presents himself under the forms he wishes. Likewise, of course, blessed Ezekiel had a vision of someone composed of amber and fire, and after describing the revelation he added, "It was a likeness of the glory of the Lord:"[159] he did not say he saw the Lord, or the Lord's glory itself—only the likeness of the Lord's glory.

And here blessed Daniel, therefore, in the phrase *Ancient of Days* conveys the eternal; some of the commentators, in fact, took it likewise | and rendered it "The one who makes days old."[160]   1424
He sees also the purity of the hair and the splendor of the clothing, and is instructed to recognize the complete innocence and holiness, not only of the divine nature but also of what it betokens, namely, righteousness, providence, care, judgment. That is to say, since he had seen the horn using arrogant words and hatching countless schemes against God's servants, he is taught through the purity beaming from all sides that far from God overlooking his committing these crimes, he is permitting them in his ineffable providence. And in case you should get the idea that God in his goodness wishes to assist his holy ones but is unable to do so, he sees also that the throne was made of flame, the wheels likewise having the nature of fire, a river of fire issuing from the throne, a thousand thousands serving, and ten thousand times ten thousand in attendance. Through the latter he conveys God's power, and through the former his freedom from blemish or fault, while through the antiquity his being eternal, wise, and gentle. From here he proceeded, *The court sat, and books were opened*, that is, he

[158] Hos 12:10.

[159] Ezek 1:27–28.

[160] Hippolytus for one, Guinot tells us (*L'Exégèse*, 716), used the phrase in that form (a verbal form of the adjective Παλαιός) in commentary on Daniel. It may, on the other hand, have been only an alternative version of the Aramaic to which Theodoret is referring.

λοιπὸν ἐδοκίμασεν εἶναι καιρόν, καὶ ἀνέπτυξε τῶν ἑκάστῳ πεπραγμένων τὴν μνήμην. Βίβλους γὰρ τὰς μνήμας καλεῖ. Εἰ δέ τις καὶ τὴν τοῦ Κυρίου ὑπόσχεσιν ἡγεῖται ταῦτα αἰνίττεσθαι, ἣν τοῖς ἀποστόλοις ἔδωκε· «Τεθήσονται, λέγων, δέκα καὶ δύο θρόνοι, καὶ καθεσθέντες κρινεῖτε τὰς δώδεκα φυλὰς τοῦ Ἰσραήλ,» οὐδὲν ἀπεικός· ἀψευδὴς γὰρ ἡ τῆς ἀληθείας ἐπαγγελία.

ια΄. «Ἐθεώρουν, φησί, τότε ἀπὸ φωνῆς τῶν λόγων τῶν μεγάλων, ὧν τὸ κέρας ἐκεῖνο ἐλάλει, θεωρῶν ἤμην ἕως ἀνῃρέθη τὸ θηρίον, καὶ ἀπώλετο, καὶ τὸ σῶμα αὐτοῦ ἐδόθη εἰς κατάκαυσιν πυρός.» Διὰ γὰρ τὴν τοῦ κέρατος ἐκείνου μανίαν, τοῦ κριτηρίου, φησί, γενομένου, κατελύθη καὶ ἡ τετάρτη βασιλεία, «καὶ τὸ σῶμα τοῦ θηρίου ἐδόθη εἰς κατάκαυσιν πυρός.» Προσήκει δὲ ἐπισημήνασθαι, ὅτι οὐχ ἁπλῶς, ἐδόθη τὸ θηρίον εἰς καῦσιν πυρός, ἀλλά, «τὸ σῶμα αὐτοῦ,» εἶπεν. Ἐπειδὴ γὰρ διὰ τοῦ θηρίου πᾶσαν τὴν βασιλείαν αἰνίττεται, ἐν δὲ τῇ βασιλείᾳ οἱ μὲν εἰσὶν εὐσεβείας τρόφιμοι, οἱ δὲ κακίας ἐργάται, καὶ τοὺς μὲν πνευματικούς, τοὺς δὲ σαρκικοὺς προσαγορεύειν εἰώθαμεν, τῇ θείᾳ Γραφῇ πειθόμενοι, εἰκότως οὐκ εἶπε τὸ θηρίον δοθῆναι εἰς καῦσιν πυρός, ἀλλὰ τοῦ θηρίου τὸ σῶμα, τουτέστι, τοὺς παχυτέρους, καὶ σαρκικούς, καὶ πνευματικὸν πεφρονηκότας οὐδέν.

ιβ΄. «Καὶ τῶν λοιπῶν δὲ θηρίων μετεστάθη ἡ ἀρχή, καὶ μακαριότης ζωῆς ἐδόθη αὐτοῖς ἕως | καιροῦ καὶ καιροῦ.» Τῶν γάρ, φησίν, ἄλλων θηρίων ἤδη ἐπέπαυτο ἡ ἀρχή, εἰ καὶ πολλῶν ἐτῶν περίοδον ἐν τῷ κρατεῖν καταναλωσάντων· φανερὸς γὰρ ἑκάστῳ εἰς τὸ βασιλεύειν ὡρίσθη καιρός. Τούτων δέ, φησίν, οὕτω γινομένων, καὶ τῶν μὲν ἄλλων βασιλειῶν ἤδη πρότερον παυσαμένων, τῶν δὲ τῆς τετάρτης βασιλείας τιμωρίας ἀξίων τῷ πυρὶ παραδοθέντων.

ιγ΄, ιδ΄. «Ἐθεώρουν, φησίν, ἐν ὁράματι τῆς νυκτός, καὶ ἰδοὺ μετὰ τῶν νεφελῶν τοῦ οὐρανοῦ, ὡς Υἱὸς ἀνθρώπου ἐρχόμενος ἦν, καὶ ἕως τοῦ Παλαιοῦ τῶν ἡμερῶν ἔφθασε, καὶ ἐνώπιον αὐτοῦ προσηνέχθη. Καὶ αὐτῷ ἐδόθη ἡ τιμή, καὶ ἡ ἀρχὴ καὶ ἡ βασιλεία· καὶ πάντες οἱ λαοί, φυλαί, γλῶσσαι, αὐτῷ δουλεύσουσιν· καὶ ἡ ἐξουσία αὐτοῦ ἐξουσία αἰώνιος, ἥτις

decided it was time for judgment, and opened the record of each person's doings (by *books* referring to records). If, on the other hand, you think there is reference to the Lord's promise to the apostles, "Twelve thrones will be placed, and you will take your seat and judge the twelve tribes of Israel,"[161] it would not be out of place, the promise of the reality being reliable.

At that stage I continued to look as a result of the lofty words which that horn was uttering. I kept watching until the beast was done away with and destroyed, and its body given over to be burned by fire (v. 11): on account of the frenzy of that horn, when the court was held, the fourth empire also was destroyed, *and its body given over to be burned by fire.* Now, it should be noted that it is not simply the beast that was given over to burning by fire, but *its body*: since by *the beast* he referred to the whole empire, and in the empire some people were attached to the true religion while others were evildoers, and with the prompting of the divine Scripture we normally call the former spiritual and the latter physical,[162] he was right not to say the beast was given over to burning by fire, but the beast's body, that is, the more material, fleshly part, uninterested in spiritual things. *And the rule of the remaining beasts was changed, and length*[163] *of life was given to them for | one moment and another* (v. 12): the rule of the other beasts was already to an end, even if they used up a span of many years in exercising control, a definite time being assigned to each for reigning.

When all this had happened, the other empires already having previously come to an end, and those in the fourth empire having been consigned to the fire as deserving retribution, *I saw in a vision of the night one like a Son of Man coming with the clouds of heaven. He proceeded to the Ancient of Days, and was presented to him. He was given honor and rule and kingship, and all peoples, tribes, and language groups will serve him; his authority is an eternal au-*

1425

---

[161] Matt 19:28 loosely cited. Theodoret is by now presuming, as do modern commentators, that we have moved from prophecy of earthly empires to a celestial last judgment—the reality, ἀλήθεια, as he says of it.

[162] Cf. 1 Cor 15:44. The distinction is another example of Antiochene precision in commenting on a text. In earlier commentary (cf. 2:45) Theodoret had given the impression that he saw the Roman Empire lasting well beyond his own time, even to the second coming, bringing blessings to its citizens.

[163] Reading μακρότης, "length," rather than Migne's μακαριότης ("beatitude").

οὐ παρελεύσεται, καὶ ἡ βασιλεία αὐτοῦ οὐ διαφθαρήσεται.» Ἀληθῶς εἰς καιρὸν εἴποι τις ἂν πρὸς Ἰουδαίους, ἃ πάλαι πρὸς αὐτοὺς ὁ προφήτης ἔλεγεν· «Ὄψις πόρνης ἐγένετό σοι, ἀπηναισχύντησας πρὸς πάντας.» Τί γὰρ τούτων σαφέστερον τῶν λόγων; εὐαγγελικῶς γὰρ τῷ ὄντι μᾶλλον καὶ ἀποστολικῶς, ἢ προφητικῶς καὶ αἰνιγματωδῶς, ταῦτα ὁ Προφήτης ἐκήρυξεν. Ὅπερ γὰρ ὁ Κύριος ἐν τοῖς Εὐαγγελίοις λέγει. «Ὄψεσθε τὸν Υἱὸν τοῦ ἀνθρώπου ἐρχόμενον ἐπὶ τῶν νεφελῶν τοῦ οὐρανοῦ μετὰ τῶν ἀγγέλων αὐτοῦ·» καὶ ὁ μακάριος Παῦλος· «Ὅτι ὁ Κύριος ἐν κελεύσματι, ἐν φωνῇ ἀρχαγγέλου, καὶ ἐν σάλπιγγι Θεοῦ καταβήσεται ἀπ' οὐρανοῦ, καὶ οἱ νεκροὶ ἐγερθήσονται ἄφθαρτοι, καὶ ἡμεῖς οἱ ζῶντες οἱ παραλειπόμενοι ἁρπαγησόμεθα ἐν νεφέλαις εἰς ἀπάντησιν τοῦ Κυρίου εἰς ἀέρα, καὶ οὕτω πάντοτε σὺν Κυρίῳ ἐσόμεθα·» τοῦτο σαφῶς ἡμᾶς ἐδίδαξεν ὁ μακάριος Δανιήλ, τὴν δευτέραν Σωτῆρος ἐπιφάνειαν προθεσπίζων, *Υἱὸν μὲν ἀνθρώπου σαφῶς ἀποκαλῶν, δι' ἣν ἀνέλαβε φύσιν· ἐρχόμενον δὲ ἐπὶ τῶν νεφελῶν, κατὰ τὴν οἰκείαν ὑπόσχεσιν, ἵνα δείξῃ τὴν ἐξουσίαν· λαμβάνοντα δὲ τὴν τιμήν, καὶ τὴν ἀρχήν, καὶ τὴν βασιλείαν παρὰ τοῦ Παλαιοῦ τῶν ἡμερῶν, ὡς ἄνθρωπον.* Τοῦτο γὰρ καὶ ἐν τῷ δευτέρῳ ψαλμῷ ἐκ προσώπου αὐτοῦ τοῦ Κυρίου ὁ μακάριος λέγει Δαβίδ· «Κύριος εἶπε πρός με· Υἱός μου εἶ σύ, ἐγὼ σήμερον γεγέννηκά σε· αἴτησαι παρ' ἐμοῦ, καὶ δώσω σοι ἔθνη τὴν κληρονομίαν σου, καὶ τὴν κατάσχεσίν σου τὰ πέρατα τῆς γῆς.» Τοῦτο δὲ καὶ ὁ μακάριος λέγει Δανιήλ· «Πάντες γὰρ, φησί, λαοί, φυλαί, γλῶσσαι αὐτῷ δουλεύσουσι.» Καὶ δεικνὺς τὸ ἀτελεύτητον τῆς βασιλείας, «Ἡ ἐξουσία αὐτοῦ, φησίν, ἐξουσία αἰώνιος, ἥτις οὐ παρελεύσεται, καὶ ἡ βασιλεία αὐτοῦ οὐ διαφθαρήσεται.» Οὕτως

thority that will not pass away, and his kingship will not be destroyed
(vv. 13–14). To be sure, it would be opportune for one to say to
Jews what the prophet said to them of old, "You have the face of a
whore, you have no shame in the presence of anyone."[164] I mean,
what could be clearer than these words? The prophet made this
proclamation really more in the manner of the Gospels and epistles than obscurely in the manner of Old Testament writings; as
the Lord says in the Gospels, "You will see the Son of Man coming on the clouds of heaven with his angels,"[165] and blessed Paul,
"Because the Lord with a word of command, with the cry of an
archangel, and with God's trumpet will descend from heaven, and
the dead will be raised imperishable, and we the living who are left
will be caught up in the clouds to a meeting with the Lord in the
air, and thus we shall always be with the Lord."[166] This is what
blessed Daniel clearly taught us, prophesying the second coming
of the Savior, clearly calling him *Son of Man* on account of the nature he had assumed, *coming on the clouds* in keeping with his own
promise to bring out his authority, and receiving as man *honor and
rule and kingship* from the Ancient of Days. This, in fact, blessed
David in the second psalm also says on the part of the Lord himself, "The Lord said to me, You are my son, today I have begotten
you; ask it of me and I shall give you nations for your inheritance,
and the ends of the earth as your possession."[167] This, too, blessed
Daniel says, *All peoples, tribes, language groups will serve him*; and
to bring out the unending character of the kingdom, *his authority
an eternal authority that will not pass away, and his kingship will not
be destroyed.*

---

[164] Jer 3:2.

[165] Matt 24:30.

[166] 1 Thess 4:16–17, with "the dead shall be raised imperishable" drawn
from 1 Cor 15:52. Both Matt 24 and 1 Thess 4 are eschatological passages
that find this apocalyptic locus grist to their mill without clarifying it. For
Theodoret, by contrast, they do serve to achieve such clarification of Old Testament (προφητικός) material that is by its nature obscure (αἰνιγματώδης) simply
by being New Testament material (εὐαγγελικός, ἀποστολικός). Modern ex-
egetes, predictably, are much more tentative in assessing the New Testament's
application of "Son of Man" to Jesus, John Meier referring to it as "the most
widely debated and confusing" of all the titles applied to Jesus in the New Testament (Meier, "Jesus," *NJBC*, 1324).

[167] Ps 2:7–8.

οὖν γράψας τὴν ἀποκάλυψιν, ἐπήγαγεν·

1428   ιε'. «῎Εφριξε τὸ πνεῦμά μου· ἐγὼ Δανιὴλ ἐν τῇ | ἕξει μου, καὶ αἱ ὁράσεις τῆς κεφαλῆς μου συνετάρασσόν με.» ῟Η τε γὰρ ὄψις, φησί, φρικώδης ἦν, καὶ ἡ ἄγνοια τῶν αἰνιγμάτων ἐκύκα μου τὴν διάνοιαν, καὶ θορύβων ἐπλήρου.

ις'. «Προσῆλθον τοίνυν τινὶ τῶν ἑστηκότων, καὶ τὴν ἀκρίβειαν ἐζήτουν παρ' αὐτοῦ περὶ πάντων τούτων.» Ἑστηκότας δὲ λέγει τὰς χιλίας χιλιάδας, καὶ μυρίας μυριάδας, δι' ὦν οὐκ ἀριθμὸν εἶπε ῥητόν, ἀλλὰ τοῦ ἀριθμοῦ κρεῖττον ἐδήλωσε πλῆθος τῶν τε λειτουργούντων, καὶ τῶν παρεστηκότων. Οἱ μὲν γὰρ τιμιώτεροι οὐχ εἱστήκεισαν μόνον, ἀλλὰ καὶ λειτουργεῖν ἐκελεύοντο· οἱ δὲ λοιποὶ τῇ μετὰ δέους στάσει τὴν δουλείαν ἐμήνυον. Καὶ καθάπερ ἐπὶ τῶν ἀνθρωπίνων δικαστηρίων, οἱ μὲν τῶν ὑπηκόων ἱστᾶσιν φοβερώτερον δεικνύντες τὸ δικαστήριον, οἱ δὲ ἐξίασί τε καὶ εἰσίασι τῷ δικαστῇ τὰς ἀποκρίσεις κομίζοντες· οὕτως ἐν τῷ φοβερωτάτῳ δικαστηρίῳ εἶδεν ὁ Δανιὴλ τὰς μὲν μυριάδας παρεστώσας, τὰς δὲ χιλίας χιλιάδας λειτουργεῖν ἐμπεπιστευμένας. Προσελθὼν τοίνυν, φησί, καὶ ἐρόμενος τίς τῆς ἀποκαλύψεως ἡ ἑρμηνεία, ἔμαθεν παρά τινος τῶν ἑστώτων τὴν ἀλήθειαν.

ιζ', ιη'. «῎Εφη γάρ μοι· Ταῦτα τὰ θηρία τὰ μεγάλα τὰ τέσσαρα, τέσσαρες βασιλεῖαι ἀναστήσονται ἐπὶ τῆς γῆς, αἳ ἀρθήσονται. Καὶ παραλήψονται τὴν βασιλείαν ἅγιοι Ὑψίστου, καὶ καθέξουσιν αὐτὴν ἕως αἰῶνος, καὶ ἕως αἰῶνος τῶν αἰώνων.» Προσέχειν ἀκριβῶς δεῖ, ὅτι κἀνταῦθα τέσσαρας εἶπε βασιλείας, καὶ ἐπὶ τῆς εἰκόνος τέσσαρας· καὶ μὴ νομίζειν τὸ ὄστρακον ἑτέραν εἶναι παρὰ τὸν σίδηρον βασιλείαν. Καὶ γὰρ ἐκεῖ «τὸ τέλος τῆς σιδηρᾶς βασιλείας ἀσθενέστερον» ἔφη, καὶ ἐνταῦθα ὡσαύτως «τρία κέρατα ἔφη ἐκριζωθῆναι ἀπὸ τῶν δέκα,» ὡς ἀσθενέστερον δηλονότι διακείμενα. Αὖται τοίνυν, φησίν, αἱ βασιλεῖαι διαλυθήσονται, καὶ ἡ ἀληθὴς καὶ ἀτελεύτητος βασιλεία τοῖς τοῦ Ὑψίστου ἁγίοις δοθήσεται. Ἐκείνην τοίνυν, φησί, ποθῶν. μηδὲν ἡγοῦ τοῦ παρόντος αἰῶνος τὰς βασιλείας οὐκ εἰς μακρὸν δεξομένας τὸ τέλος. Εἶτά φησιν·

ιθ'. «Ἐζήτουν ἀκριβῶς περὶ τοῦ θηρίου τοῦ τετάρτου, ὅτι ἦν διαφέρον παρὰ πᾶν θηρίον, καὶ φοβερὸν περισσῶς· οἱ ὀδόντες αὐτοῦ σιδηροῖ, καὶ οἱ ὄνυχες αὐτοῦ χαλκοῖ· ἤσθιεν, καὶ ἐλέπτυνεν, καὶ τὰ λοιπὰ τοῖς ποσὶν αὐτοῦ κατεπάτει.» Ἐπισημήνασθαι δεῖ, ὅτι τοὺς μὲν ὀδόντας σιδηροῦς λέγει, τοὺς δὲ ὄνυχας χαλκοῦς. Ἡ μὲν γὰρ Ῥωμαίων βασιλεία τὸν παρὰ πάντων δέχεται φόρον, διὸ τοὺς ὀδόντας ἔφη σιδηροῦς. Ἐπειδὴ δὲ καὶ ἐκ τῆς Μακεδονικῆς βασιλείας πολλοὶ εἰς τὴν ὁπλιτικὴν τελοῦσι στρατείαν, ὅπερ δέ εἰσι θηρίῳ ὄνυχες, τοῦτο βασιλεῖ στρατιῶται, εἰκό-

Having thus recorded the revelation, then, he went on, *My spirit was terrified, I Daniel, in | my state of mind, and the visions in my head disturbed me* (v. 15): the sight was terrifying, and my ignorance of the riddles confused my mind and filled it with alarm. *So I approached one of the attendants and enquired of him clarification of all these things* (v. 16). By *attendants* he refers to the *thousand thousands and ten thousand times ten thousand*, by which he did not mean a definite number but suggested a crowd beyond counting of those serving and attending: those of higher rank not only stood but also were also bidden to serve, while the rest betrayed their subjection by standing in fear. Just as in the case of human courts some of the defendants stand about betraying the fearsome character of the proceedings, while others go in and out bringing responses to the judge, so in the most fearsome court Daniel saw the ten thousands of attendants, and the thousand thousands entrusted with service.

Having made his entrance, then, and asked what was the interpretation of the revelation, he learned the truth from one of the attendants. *He said to me, As for these four huge beasts, four empires will arise on earth, but will be removed. Holy ones of the Most High will receive possession of the kingdom and possess it for an age and for an age of ages* (vv. 17–18). We should take careful note that he mentioned *four empires* here and four in the case of the image, and we should not think the clay one was a different empire from the iron one; there he said the end of the iron empire would be weaker, and here likewise he said three horns were rooted up from the ten, obviously being weaker in placement. These empires will be destroyed, then, he is saying, and the true and unending kingdom will be given to the holy ones of the Most High. Looking forward with longing to that one, then, he is saying, set no store by the kingdoms of the present age that before long will come to an end.

He then says, *I made careful enquiry as to the fourth beast, which was different from all the other beasts and exceedingly fearsome; its teeth were of iron and its claws of bronze, it kept eating and crushing, and trampling the others with its feet* (v. 19). It should be noted that he says its teeth were of iron and its claws of bronze: the Roman Empire receives taxes from everyone—hence his saying its teeth were of iron. And since also many in the Macedonian Empire served in the infantry, and soldiers are to a king what claws are to a beast, he was right to say its claws were of bronze, since he also

1428

τως ἔφη τοὺς ὄνυχας χαλκοῦς, ἐπειδὴ καὶ τὴν τρίτην βασιλείαν χαλκῆν
1429 προσηγόρευσεν. Ἐπυνθανόμην γὰρ, φησί, |

κʹ. «Καὶ περὶ τῶν κεράτων αὐτοῦ τῶν δέκα τῶν ἐν τῇ κεφαλῇ
αὐτοῦ, καὶ τοῦ τετάρτου· τοῦ ἀναβάντος καὶ ἐκτινάξαντος τῶν προτέρων τρία, καὶ τὸ κέρας ἐκεῖνο ᾧ οἱ ὀφθαλμοὶ αὐτοῦ καὶ στόμα λαλοῦν
μεγάλα, καὶ ἡ ὅρασις αὐτοῦ μείζων τῶν λοιπῶν.» Οὐ δεῖ δὲ θαυμάζειν,
εἰ ἄνω μὲν σμικρὸν ἔφη τὸ κέρας, ἐνταῦθα δὲ τὴν ὅρασιν αὐτοῦ *μείζονα*
τῶν λοιπῶν· προσήκει τοῖς λεγομένοις ἀκριβῶς. Ὅτε μὲν γὰρ φυόμενον
εἶδε τὸ κέρας, μικρὸν αὐτὸ προσηγόρευσεν, ὡς καὶ ἀπὸ σμικροῦ ἔθνους
ὁρώμενον τοῦ Ἰουδαίων, καὶ ἀφανῆ τέως τὴν βασιλείαν ἔχον· μετὰ δὲ τὸ
ἐκριζῶσαι τρία κέρατα τῶν πρὸ αὐτοῦ, εἰκότως τὴν ὅρασιν αὐτοῦ *μείζω*
τῶν λοιπῶν ἀποκαλεῖ. Ἐπιφέρει τοίνυν ἔτι πυνθανόμενος,

καʹ. «Τί δήποτε τὸ κέρας ἐκεῖνο ἐποίει πόλεμον μετὰ τῶν ἁγίων,
καὶ ἴσχυσε πρὸς αὐτούς;» Ἀντὶ τοῦ, ἐταπείνωσεν αὐτούς.

κβʹ. «Ἕως οὗ ἦλθεν ὁ Παλαιὸς τῶν ἡμερῶν, καὶ τὸ κρῖμα ἔδωκεν
ἁγίοις Ὑψίστου, καὶ ὁ καιρὸς ἔφθασε, καὶ τὴν βασιλείαν κατέσχον οἱ
ἅγιοι.» Ἱκέτευσα φησί, μαθεῖν, τίνα τὸ κέρας ἐκεῖνο αἰνίττεται, τύφῳ
μὲν χρώμενον, ἀλαζονικοὺς δὲ λόγους προσφέρον, ταπεινοῦν δὲ τὴν τῶν
ἁγίων συμμορίαν, ἕως ἂν ὁ Παλαιὸς τῶν ἡμερῶν τῇ μὲν δικαίᾳ χρήσηται
ψήφῳ, ἀποδῷ δὲ καὶ τοῖς ἁγίοις τὴν βασιλείαν, καὶ τὸ ἐκείνου καταλύσῃ
κράτος.

κγʹ. «Καὶ εἶπέ μοι, φησίν, οὕτως· Τὸ θηρίον τὸ τέταρτον βασιλεία
τετάρτη ἔσται ἐν τῇ γῇ, ἥτις ὑπερέξει πάσας τὰς βασιλείας, καὶ κατα-
φάγεται πᾶσαν τὴν γῆν, καὶ συμπατήσει αὐτήν, καὶ κατακόψει αὐτήν.»
Ταῦτα δὲ οἱ μὲν πάλαι δι' αἰνιγμάτων ἐμάνθανον· ἡμεῖς δὲ τῇ πείρᾳ
μεμαθήκαμεν· ὁρῶμεν γὰρ τῆς προρρήσεως τὴν ἔκβασιν, τῶν εἰσφορῶν
τὴν εἴσπραξιν, τὴν κρατοῦσαν τῶν πλειόνων πενίαν, καὶ τὰ ἄλλα καθ'
ἑκάστην ἡμέραν γινόμενα ὁρῶμεν.

κδʹ. «Καὶ τὰ δέκα κέρατα αὐτοῦ, φησί, δέκα βασιλεῖς ἀναστήσονται.» Ἐπισημήνασθαι δὲ χρὴ, ὅτι οὐκ εἶπεν αὐτοὺς ἀναστήσεσθαι ἕνα
καθ' ἕνα ἀλλήλους διαδεχομένους, ἀλλὰ κατὰ ταὐτὸν ἀναστήσεσθαι· καὶ
ὅτι ταῦθ' οὕτως ἔχει, τὰ ἐπαγόμενα μαρτυρεῖ. «Καὶ ὀπίσω γὰρ αὐτῶν,
φησίν, ἀναστήσεται βασιλεὺς ἕτερος, ὃς ὑπεροίσει κακοῖς πάντας τοὺς
ἔμπροσθεν, καὶ τρεῖς βασιλεῖς ταπεινώσει.» Εἰ δὲ μὴ κατὰ ταὐτὸν ἐβα-
σίλευον, ἀλλὰ καθ' ἕνα ἕκαστος τὸν πρὸ αὐτοῦ διαδεχόμενος, πῶς οὗτος
τρεῖς κατὰ ταὐτὸν τῶν πρὸ αὐτοῦ ταπεινώσει; Οὐκοῦν εὔδηλον, ὡς τοὺς
δέκα πρὸς τῷ τέλει κατὰ ταὐτὸν ἀναστήσεσθαι προλέγει· ἔσχατον δὲ τὸν
Ἀντίχριστον ἀνιστάμενον, καὶ τῆς βασιλείας ἀντιλαμβανόμενον, πολεμή-
1432 σειν μὲν αὐτοῖς φησι, τρεῖς δὲ ἐξ αὐτῶν κα|ταλύσειν· μὴ ἀρκούμενος δὲ

called the third empire bronze. I made enquiries, in fact, | *also of*   1429
the ten horns on its head, and the fourth one that arose and knocked
out the three in its place—that horn having also eyes, a mouth utter-
ing lofty words, and its appearance more daunting than the rest (v. 20).
We should not be surprised if above he said the horn was "little,"
but here its appearance was *more daunting than the rest.* There is
need to pay precise attention to what is said: when he saw the horn
springing up, he called it "little" as arising from the little nation
of Jews that at that stage had an obscure kingdom; but after it uprooted the three horns in its place, he was right to call its aspect
more daunting than the rest.

So he continues to make further enquiries, asking why on
earth *did that horn make war on the holy ones and prevail over*
them (v. 21)—that is, humble them—*until the Ancient of Days came*
and gave judgment in favor of the holy ones of the Most High, and
the time came for the holy ones to take possession of the kingdom (v.
22): I begged to learn what was the reference in that horn, which
was exercising conceit, uttering arrogant words, and humbling
the company of the holy ones until the Ancient of Days exercises
righteous judgment, restores the kingdom to the holy ones, and
destroys the power of the other.

He said to me as follows, As for the fourth beast, there will be a
fourth empire on the earth, which will conquer all the empires, consume
all the earth, trample it down, and cut it to pieces (v. 23). While people in olden times came to know this in riddles, we have learned it
by experience, witnessing the outcome of the prophecy, the impo-
sition of taxes, the poverty gripping most people, and all the other
things we observe happening every day. *As for the ten horns, ten*
kings will rise up (v. 24). Now, it ought be noted that he did not say
they would rise up by succeeding one another, but would rise up
at the one time; what follows confirms that this is the case. *In their*
wake another king will arise, who will surpass all who precede him in
causing troubles, and he will humble three kings. Unless they reigned
at the one time, however, and instead succeeded one another, how
would he humble three before him at the one time? It is therefore
obvious that he is foretelling that the ten will arise at the one time
toward the end, and the antichrist will arise as the last, get control
of the empire, wage war on them, and destroy three of them | but   1432
will not be content with the victory over human beings.

τῇ κατὰ τῶν ἀνθρώπων νίκῃ·

κε΄. «Καὶ λόγους, φησί, πρὸς τὸν Ὕψιστον λαλήσει, καὶ τοὺς ἁγίους Ὑψίστου παλαιώσει, καί,» ὡς ἔνια τῶν ἀντιγράφων ἔχει, «ταπεινώσει· καὶ ὑπονοήσει τοῦ ἀλλοιῶσαι καιροὺς καὶ νόμον.» Τοσαύτη γὰρ, φησί, λύσσῃ χρήσεται καὶ μανίᾳ, ὡς ἀλαζονικοὺς μὲν καὶ βλασφήμους λόγους ἀκοντίσαι κατὰ τοῦ ὑψίστου Θεοῦ, πᾶν δὲ εἶδος τιμωρίας τοῖς εὐνοϊκῶς αὐτῷ δουλεύουσι καὶ ἁγιωσύνης μετέχουσιν ἐπαγαγεῖν· ὑποτοπήσει δέ, ὡς καὶ παντάπασι καταλύσει τὴν κρατοῦσαν εὐσέβειαν, καὶ τὴν ἀρίστην αὐτῆς πολιτείαν ἀμείψει. Τοῦτο γὰρ ἠνίξατο εἰρηκώς· «Ὑπονοήσει τοῦ ἀλλοιῶσαι καιροὺς καὶ νόμον·» τουτέστι, τὴν κατ᾽ ἐκεῖνον τὸν καιρὸν κατέχουσαν πολιτείαν. Εἶτα ἐπάγει· «Καὶ δοθήσεται ἐν χειρὶ αὐτοῦ.» Τουτέστι, συγχωρήσει ἡ τοῦ Θεοῦ προμήθεια· καὶ δεικνὺς τῆς τῶν κακῶν ἐκείνων ἀωρίας τὸν χρόνον· «Οὐ γὰρ εἰς τέλος ἐπιλησθήσεται ὁ πτωχός, καὶ ἡ ὑπομονὴ τῶν πενήτων οὐκ ἀπολεῖται εἰς τὸν αἰῶνα·» εἰρηκώς· «Δοθήσεται ἐν χειρὶ αὐτοῦ,» ἐπήγαγεν· «Ἕως καιροῦ, καὶ καιρῶν, καὶ ἥμισυ καιροῦ.» Τοῦτο δὲ σαφέστερον ἐν τῷ τέλει τῆς προφητείας ἡμᾶς ἐδίδαξεν. «Ἀπὸ καιροῦ γὰρ, φησί, παραλλάξεως τοῦ ἐνδελεχισμοῦ, καὶ δοθῆναι βδέλυγμα ἐρημώσεως, ἡμέραι χίλιαι διακόσιαι ἐννενήκοντα.» Καιρὸν οὖν, καὶ καιρούς, καὶ ἥμισυ καιροῦ, τρία ἥμισυ ἔτη λέγει, ἃ τὸ κέρας ἐκεῖνο τὸ λαλοῦν μεγάλα κρατήσει.

κς΄. «Ἀλλὰ τὸ κριτήριον, φησίν, ἐκάθισε, καὶ τὴν ἀρχὴν αὐτοῦ μεταστήσουσι, τοῦ ἀφανίσαι καὶ τοῦ ἀπολέσαι ἕως τέλους.» Τοῦτο δὲ καὶ ὁ μακάριος ἡμᾶς σαφῶς ἐδίδαξε Παῦλος. Εἰρηκὼς γὰρ ἐκεῖνα ἃ προειρήκαμεν, προσέθηκε καὶ ταῦτα· «Μόνον ὁ κατέχων ἄρτι ἕως ἐκ μέσου γένηται, καὶ τότε ἀποκαλυφθήσεται ὁ ἄνομος, ὃν ὁ Κύριος Ἰησοῦς ἀναλώσει τῷ πνεύματι τοῦ στόματος αὐτοῦ, καὶ καταργήσει τῇ ἐπιφανείᾳ τῆς παρουσίας κατ᾽ ἐνέργειαν τοῦ Σατανᾶ ἐν πάσῃ δυνάμει, καὶ σημείοις, καὶ τέρασι ψεύδους, καὶ ἐν πάσῃ ἀπάτῃ τῆς ἀδικίας ἐν τοῖς ἀπολλυμένοις.» Ὁ δὲ λέγει τοιοῦτόν ἐστι· Δεῖ τὸ κατέχον ἄρτι ἐκ μέσου γενέσθαι. Σβεσθήσεται γὰρ ἡ κατέχουσα πλάνη, καὶ λήξει ἡ τῶν εἰδώλων ἐξαπάτη, καὶ τότε ἀποκαλυφθήσεται ὁ ἄνομος. Τοῦτο δὲ καὶ ὁ

He will speak words against the Most High, and will wear out (or, as some manuscripts have it, "humble") *the holy ones of the Most High, and will plan to change seasons and the law* (v. 25): he will give vent to such awful fury and frenzy as to hurl arrogant and blasphemous words at the Most High God, and pile every form of punishment on those loyally serving him and practicing holiness. He will imagine that he will totally overthrow the religion in force, and change its excellent way of life (implied by saying, *he will plan to change seasons and the law*, that is, the way of life prevailing at that time). He then goes on, *It will be given into his hand*, that is, God's providence will allow it. And to bring out the length of time for these untimely troubles—after all, "the poor will not be forgotten forever, and the perseverance of the needy will not be lost forever"[168]—he went on, after saying, *it will be given into his hand*, to say, *for a time, and times, and half a time.* He explained this to us more clearly at the end of the work, "From the time of the change in the regular usage and the permission for the abomination of desolation, 1,290 days."[169] So *a time, and times, and half a time* means three and a half years for that horn uttering lofty words to be in power.

But the court sat, and they will bring a change to his rule, removing and destroying it forever (v. 26). Blessed Paul informed us of this more clearly: after saying what we already mentioned, he proceeded to say this, "Only until the one holding him in check is removed, and then the lawless one will be revealed, whom the Lord Jesus will consume with the breath of his mouth, and will annihilate him with the manifestation of his coming in the working of Satan with all power, signs, works of falsehood, and every kind of wicked deception among those who are perishing."[170] Now, what he means is something like this: what is holding him in check for now must be removed; deceit is holding him in check and will be snuffed out, the deception of the idols will cease, and then the lawless one will be revealed. The Lord also said this in the sa-

---

[168] Ps 9:18.

[169] Dan 12:11, a figure supplied by a later editor aware that 1,150 days (three and a half years) did not cover all the persecution (just as a still later editor in 12:12 increased it to 1,335). Theodoret does not (at either place) seem to recognize this number of years as half of the perfect number (seven)—hence a period of evil.

[170] Cf. 2 Thess 2:7–10.

Κύριος ἐν τοῖς ἱεροῖς Εὐαγγελίοις ἔφη. «Κηρυχθήσεται γὰρ τὸ Εὐαγ-
γέλιον εἰς πάντα τὰ πέρατα τῆς γῆς εἰς μαρτύριον αὐτοῖς, καὶ τότε ἥξει
τὸ τέλος.» Ἐκεῖθεν τοῦτο μαθὼν ὁ μακάριος Παῦλος διδάσκει Θεσσα-
λονικέας, καὶ δι' ἐκείνων ἅπαντας τοὺς τῆς εὐσεβείας ἐραστάς, ὅτι Μὴ
1433 νομίσητε νῦν | φανήσεσθαι τὸν τῆς ἀληθείας ἐχθρόν· δεῖ γὰρ πρότερον
σβεσθῆναι τὴν κατέχουσαν τῶν εἰδώλων πλάνην, καὶ κρατυνθῆναι τῶν
Εὐαγγελίων τὸ κήρυγμα, εἶθ' οὕτως ἀποκαλυφθῆναι τὸν ἄνομον. Εἶτα
ὑποδείκνυσιν αὐτοῦ καὶ τὸν ὄλεθρον· «Ὃν ὁ Κύριος, φησίν, Ἰησοῦς ἀναλώσει τῷ πνεύματι τοῦ στόματος αὐτοῦ, καὶ καταργήσει τῇ ἐπιφανείᾳ
τῆς παρουσίας αὐτοῦ.» Ἔπειτα δείκνυσι καὶ τίνα τρόπον ἐπιφαίνεται·
«Οὗ ἐστι, φησίν, ἡ παρουσία κατ' ἐνέργειαν τοῦ Σατανᾶ.» Μιμήσε-
ται γὰρ ὁ διάβολος τοῦ Θεοῦ καὶ Σωτῆρος ἡμῶν τὴν ἐνανθρώπησιν·
καὶ καθάπερ ὁ Κύριος δι' ἀνθρωπείας φύσεως ἐπιφανείς, τὴν ἡμετέραν
ἐπραγματεύσατο σωτηρίαν· οὕτω καὶ ὁ διάβολος, ἄξιον ὄργανον τῆς ἑαυτοῦ πονηρίας λαβών, δι' αὐτοῦ τὴν οἰκείαν ἐνέργειαν ἐπιδείξεται, ψευδέσι
σημείοις καὶ τέρασι, καὶ φαντασίᾳ θαυμάτων, τοὺς ῥᾳθύμους τῶν ἀνθρώπων ἐξαπατῶν. Καὶ διδάσκων τί δήποτε ταῦτα συγχωρεῖ γενέσθαι
ὁ τῶν ὅλων Θεός, ἐπήγαγεν· «Ἀνθ' ὧν τὴν ἀγάπην τῆς ἀληθείας οὐκ
ἐδέξαντο εἰς τὸ σωθῆναι αὐτούς, καὶ διὰ τοῦτο πέμψει αὐτοῖς ὁ Θεὸς ἐνέργειαν πλάνης, εἰς τὸ πιστεῦσαι αὐτούς, τῷ ψεύδει, ἵνα κριθῶσι πάντες
οἱ μὴ πιστεύσαντες τῇ ἀληθείᾳ, ἀλλ' εὐδοκήσαντες τῇ ἀδικίᾳ.» Ταὐτὸ
δὲ τοῦτο καὶ ὁ Κύριος πρὸς Ἰουδαίους ἔφη· «Ἐγὼ ἦλθον ἐν τῷ ὀνόματι τοῦ Πατρός μου, καὶ οὐκ ἐδέξασθέ με· ἔρχεται ἄλλος ἐν τῷ ὀνόματι
τῷ ἰδίῳ, κἀκεῖνον λήψεσθε.» Ταῦτα δὲ διδάσκων ὁ ἄγγελος τῷ Δανιὴλ
ἔφη, ὅτι «Λόγους πρὸς τὸν Ὕψιστον λαλήσει, καὶ τοὺς ἁγίους Ὑψίστου παλαιώσει, καὶ ὑπονοήσει τοῦ ἀλλοιῶσαι καιροὺς καὶ νόμον· καὶ
δοθήσεται ἐν χειρὶ αὐτοῦ ἕως καιροῦ, καὶ καιρῶν, καὶ ἥμισυ καιροῦ· καὶ
τὸ κριτήριον ἐκάθισε, καὶ τὴν ἀρχὴν αὐτοῦ μεταστήσουσι, τοῦ ἀφανίσαι
καὶ τοῦ ἀπολέσαι ἕως τέλους.» Ὁρᾶτε πῶς τὰ αἰνιγματωδῶς ὑπὸ τοῦ
ἀγγέλου ἡρμηνευμένα σαφῶς ὁ μακάριος ἐδίδαξε Παῦλος. Καὶ ὁ Κύριος
δὲ τὰς κατὰ τῶν ἁγίων ἐπαναστάσεις προσημαίνων, ἔλεγεν· «Ἔσται
θλῖψις μεγάλη, οἵα οὐ γέγονεν ἀπ' ἀρχῆς κόσμου ἕως τοῦ νῦν, οὐδ' οὐ
μὴ γένηται· καὶ εἰ μὴ ἐκολοβώθησαν αἱ ἡμέραι ἐκεῖναι, οὐκ ἂν ἐσώθη

cred Gospels, "The Gospel will be proclaimed to the ends of the earth in testimony to them, and then the end will come."[171] From this blessed Paul learned what he teaches the Thessalonians, and through them all disciples of the true religion, Do not think | the enemy of truth will now appear; first of all the deceit of the idols that is holding him in check must be snuffed out, and the preaching of the Gospel disseminated, and only then will the lawless one be revealed.

He then also gives a glimpse of his overthrow, "Whom the Lord Jesus will consume with the breath of his mouth, and will annihilate him with the manifestation of his coming." He next brings out also the manner in which he comes, "His coming against Satan's operating": the devil will imitate the incarnation of our God and Savior, and just as the Lord came in a human nature and procured our salvation, so too the devil will take an instrument adapted to his own wickedness and with it give evidence of his special activity by deceiving indifferent people with false signs and portents and an appearance of miracles. To convey why on earth it is that the God of all permits these things to happen, he went on, "Because they refused to love the truth and so be saved, and hence God will send them a powerful delusion, leading them to believe what is false, so that all who have not believed the truth but took pleasure in unrighteousness will be condemned."[172]

The Lord also said the same thing to Jews, "I came in my Father's name, yet you did not receive me; another comes in his own name, and him you will receive."[173] Now, to convey this the angel said to Daniel, *He will utter words against the Most High, will wear out the holy ones of the Most High, and plan to change seasons and the law. It will be given to him for a time and times and half a time. The court sat, and they will bring a change to his rule, removing and destroying it forever.* See how what was interpreted vaguely by the angel blessed Paul conveyed clearly; and to suggest in advance the uprisings against the holy ones, the Lord also said, "There will be great tribulation such as has never occurred from the foundation of the world until now, nor will it occur. If those days had not been shortened, no one would be saved; but

---

[171] Matt 24:14, part of the Matthean eschatological discourse.
[172] 2 Thess 2:10–12.
[173] John 5:43.

1433

πᾶσα σάρξ· διὰ δὲ τοὺς ἐκλεκτοὺς κολοβωθήσονται αἱ ἡμέραι ἐκεῖναι.»
Εἶτα συμβουλεύσας τοῖς ἁγίοις αὐτοῦ μαθηταῖς, καὶ δι’ ἐκείνων πᾶσιν
ἀνθρώποις, μὴ ἐξαπατᾶσθαι τοῖς λέγουσιν ὧδε εἶναι ἢ ἐκεῖ τὸν Χριστόν,
οὐκέτι γὰρ κρύβδην καὶ λάθρα, ἀλλὰ ἀναφανδὸν μετὰ δόξης φανήσεται,
ἐπήγαγε· «Τότε ὄψονται τὸν Υἱὸν τοῦ ἀνθρώπου ἐρχόμενον ἐπὶ τῶν νεφελῶν τοῦ οὐρανοῦ, μετὰ δυνάμεως καὶ δόξης πολλῆς, καὶ ἀποστελεῖ
τοὺς ἀγγέλους αὐτοῦ μετὰ σάλπιγγος μεγάλης, καὶ ἐπισυνάξουσι τοὺς
ἐκλεκτοὺς αὐτοῦ ἐκ τῶν τεσσάρων ἀνέμων, ἀπ’ ἄκρων τῶν οὐρανῶν ἕως
ἄκρου αὐτῶν.» Ταῦτα καὶ τῷ Δανιὴλ προλέγων ὁ ἄγγελος ἐπήγαγεν οἷς
ἤδη εἶπε· |

1436

κζ′. «Καὶ ἡ βασιλεία, καὶ ἡ ἐξουσία, καὶ ἡ μεγαλωσύνη τῶν βασιλέων τῶν ὑποκάτω παντὸς τοῦ οὐρανοῦ ἐδόθη ἁγίοις Ὑψίστου· καὶ ἡ
βασιλεία αὐτοῦ βασιλεία αἰώνιος ; καὶ πᾶσαι αἱ ἀρχαὶ αὐτῷ δουλεύσουσι καὶ ὑπακούσονται· ἕως ὧδε τὸ πέρας τοῦ λόγου.» Τουτέστι, πάντων
τῶν τοῦ βίου πραγμάτων τοῦτο τὸ τέλος· τὸ παύσασθαι μὲν ἁπάσας
τῆς γῆς τὰς βασιλείας, δοθῆναι δὲ τοῖς τοῦ Ὑψίστου ἁγίοις τὴν αἰώνιον
βασιλείαν· βασιλεύοντας δὲ ὑπακούειν αὐτῷ καὶ δουλεύειν εὐνοϊκῶς· αἰώνιος γὰρ αὐτοῦ ἡ βασιλεία, καὶ τὸ τέλος οὐ δεχομένη. Τούτων ἀκούσας,
φησίν, ἐγὼ Δανιὴλ δέους ἐνεπλήσθην πολλοῦ, ὡς μήτε τοὺς λογισμοὺς
ἡσυχάζειν ἐν ἐμοί, ἀλλὰ κυκᾶσθαι, καὶ διηνεκῶς ταράττεσθαι, καὶ τὴν
μορφήν μου πολλὴν ἀλλοίωσιν ἐντεῦθεν δέξασθαι. Ἀλλ’ ὅμως οὐκ ἔκπυ-
στα πεποίηκα τὰ ὑποδειχθέντα μοι μυστήρια, ἀλλ’ ἐν τῇ καρδίᾳ τηρῶν
αὐτὰ διετέλουν. Ὁ μὲν οὖν μακάριος Δανιὴλ ταῦτα ἡμᾶς ἐδίδαξεν. Ἐγὼ
δὲ τῶν Ἰουδαίων κατηγορίαν ἐπὶ τοῦ παρόντος ἀφείς, θαυμάζω κομιδῇ
τῶν τῆς εὐσεβείας διδασκάλων τινὰς Μακεδονικὴν βασιλείαν τὸ τέταρτον θηρίον ἀποκαλέσαντας· ἔδει γὰρ αὐτοὺς συνιδεῖν, πρῶτον μέν, ὅτι
τὸ τρίτον θηρίον τέσσαρας εἶχε κεφαλάς, ὃ σαφῶς ἐδήλου τὴν γεγενημένην μετὰ τὴν τοῦ Ἀλεξάνδρου τελευτὴν τῆς βασιλείας εἰς τέσσαρα

for the sake of the elect those says will be shortened." Then, after advising his holy disciples, and through them all people, not
to be deceived by those claiming Christ is here or there, since he
will appear no longer in hiding or secretly but publicly in glory, he
went on, "Then they will see the Son of Man coming on the clouds
of heaven with power and great glory, and he will send his angels
with a loud trumpet blast, and they will gather his elect from the
four winds, from one end of heaven to the other."[174]

In foretelling this also to Daniel, the angel added to what he
had already said, | *The kingship, authority, and greatness of the em-*   1436
pires under the whole of heaven were given to the holy ones of the Most
High. His kingdom is an everlasting kingdom, and all governments
will serve and obey him. At this point the end of the report (vv. 27–
28). In other words, this is the end of all the affairs of this life, all
the empires of earth coming to a close and the eternal kingdom being given to the holy ones of the Most High, with those in charge
obeying and devotedly serving him, since his kingdom is eternal
and does not come to an end.

On hearing this, he goes on, I, Daniel, was filled with such
deep fear as to prevent my thoughts being at peace in me, instead being confused and constantly upset, my appearance thus
undergoing a great transformation. Nonetheless, far from bruiting abroad the mysteries revealed to me, I continued to keep them
to myself.

Whereas blessed Daniel conveyed them to us, then, leaving aside criticism of the Jews for the time being, I for my part
am quite surprised at some teachers of religion referring to the
Macedonian Empire as the fourth beast.[175] After all, they ought
to realize, firstly, that the third beast had four heads, which clearly
indicated the division of the empire into four parts that happened

[174] Matt 24:21–22, 25–27, 30–31.

[175] After his lengthy study of New Testament eschatological statements,
Theodoret hastens to close commentary on this chapter, but not before disposing of the view that the fourth beast represented not the Roman Empire, as he
preferred, but the Macedonian—an issue he had raised in comment on the image
in chapter 2. Here he has a Christian commentator in view, possibly Theodore,
of whom he will use this phrase "teacher of religion" in criticizing him in his
commentary on Mic 4:2. One question affecting this is whether Theodore did
in fact compose a treatment on "the four prophets," as his Syrian catalogers
maintained—a position challenged by J. M. Vosté on the grounds of silence in
Greek and conciliar sources. See the introduction (xxvii n. 53).

μέρη διαίρεσιν· ἔπειτα δὲ προσέχειν ἔδει, ὅτι καὶ τὸ τέταρτον θηρίον δέκα κατὰ ταὐτὸν κέρατα ἔσχεν, καὶ τὸ μικρὸν κέρας τρεῖς ἐκριζῶσαι τῶν
πρὸ αὐτοῦ· τέσσαρες δέ, ἀλλ' οὐ δέκα βασιλεῖς τὴν Ἀλεξάνδρου βασιλείαν διεδέξαντο. Καὶ ἵνα τὰ ἄλλα καταλιπὼν ἐπὶ τὸ τέλος ἔλθω, ἔδει
καὶ τοῦτο συνιδεῖν, ὅτι μετὰ τοῦ τετάρτου θηρίου τὴν ἀναίρεσιν τοῖς
ἁγίοις τοῦ Ὑψίστου τὴν βασιλείαν ἔφη δοθήσεσθαι. Διὸ καὶ τὸ κριτήριον ἐκάθισεν· οἱ δὲ ἅγιοι τοῦ Ὑψίστου οὐ μετὰ Ἀντίοχον τὸν Ἐπιφανῆ
τὴν βασιλείαν ἐδέξαντο. Εἰ δὲ καὶ ἰσχύν τινα ἔλαβον οἱ μακάριοι Μακκαβαῖοι, ἀλλ' οὐκ ἐπὶ πλεῖστον. Ὁ μὲν γὰρ Ἰούδας τρία ἐστρατήγησεν
ἔτη· ὁ δὲ Ἰωνάθαν ἐννέα καὶ δέκα· ὁ δὲ Σίμων ὀκτώ· καὶ οἱ ἄλλοι δέ,
ἵνα μὴ καθ' ἕκαστον διεξιών, μῆκος ἐργάσωμαι τῷ λόγῳ, ὀλίγον τινὰ
κρατοῦντες χρόνον, ἢ τῷ θανάτῳ ἐσβέννυντο, ἢ περιστάσεσί τισι ζῶντες
τῆς ἡγεμονίας ἐστέρηντο. Ἄλλως τε δὲ οὔτε πάντες ἅγιοι οὗτοι· ἔνιοι
γὰρ καὶ πονηροὶ ἐν αὐτοῖς γεγένηνται· ἵνα δὲ καὶ θῶμεν πάντας αὐτοὺς
ἁγίους εἶναι, τούτους Ἡρώδης καταλύσας ἁπάσης βασιλεὺς ἀνεδείχθη
τῆς Ἰουδαίας. Πῶς τοίνυν ἀληθὲς τὸ ὑπὸ τοῦ ἀγγέλου εἰρημένον, ὅτι
μετὰ τὴν τοῦ κέρατος ἐκείνου κατάλυσιν ἡ βασιλεία, καὶ ἡ ἐξουσία, καὶ
ἡ μεγαλωσύνη τῶν βασιλέων τῶν ὑποκάτω παντὸς τοῦ οὐρανοῦ, ἐδόθη
ἁγίοις Ὑψίστου, καὶ ἡ βασιλεία αὐτοῦ βασιλεία αἰώνιος; Τούτων γὰρ
1437   οὐδὲν ἁρμόττει τοῖς Μακκαβαίοις. Οὔτε | γὰρ βασιλείαν ἐπιστεύθησαν,
ἀλλὰ στρατηγοῦντες ἐνίκων, καὶ ταχὺ τέλος ἐδέξαντο. Λείπεται τοίνυν
τὴν Ῥωμαϊκὴν βασιλείαν νοεῖν τὸ τέταρτον θηρίον. Ἐν γὰρ τῷ ταύτης
τέλει, οἱ μὲν δέκα βασιλεῖς κατὰ ταὐτὸν ἀναστήσονται, ὁ δὲ πάσης πονηρίας δημιουργὸς καὶ διδάσκαλος ἔσχατος ἀναφανήσεται, ἐκεῖνα ποιῶν
τε καὶ πάσχων, ἃ ἐδιδάχθημεν. Μετὰ δὲ τὴν ἐκείνου κατάλυσιν, ἡ τοῦ
Θεοῦ καὶ Σωτῆρος ἡμῶν ἀναφανήσεται παρουσία, καὶ τὸ πάντων ἀνθρώπων γενήσεται κριτήριον, καὶ ἀνοιγήσονται μὲν αἱ βίβλοι, τῶν ἑκάστῳ
βεβιωμένων αἱ μνῆμαι. «Παραδοθήσεται δὲ πυρὶ τὸ τοῦ θηρίου σῶμα,» τουτέστιν, οἱ μὲν τῆς ψυχῆς ἀφελόμενοι τὸ κράτος, τῷ δὲ σώματι
τὴν ἐξουσίαν προσνείμαντες, καὶ σαρκικῷ φρονήματι διὰ βίου χρησάμενοι. Ἀποδώσει δὲ ὁ δίκαιος κριτὴς τοῖς ἁγίοις τὴν βασιλείαν, βοῶν·

after the death of Alexander. Secondly, they should take note also
that the fourth beast had ten horns at the one time, and the little
horn uprooted three of them to make room for it, whereas it was
four kings and not ten who succeeded to the empire of Alexander. And to pass over other matters and come to a conclusion,
there is need to realize also that after the destruction of the fourth
beast he said the kingdom would be given to the holy ones of the
Most High. And that is why the court sat; but the holy ones
of the Most High did not receive the kingdom after Antiochus
Epiphanes. Now, even if the blessed Maccabees obtained a degree
of power, it was not for long: Judas was in charge for three years,
Jonathan for nineteen, Simon for eight, and the rest—not to deal
with each one and protract the account—were in control for a short
time before being either snuffed out by death or deprived of command while by some circumstance still alive. In particular, not
even all of them were holy: some among them even proved evil; yet
even conceding that all of them were holy, Herod disposed of them
and was proclaimed king of the whole of Judea.[176] So how could
what was said by the angel be true, that after the destruction of that
horn *the kingship, authority, and greatness of the empires under the
whole of heaven were given to the holy ones of the Most High, and his
kingdom is an everlasting kingdom?* It is, in fact, not at all applica-
ble to the Maccabees: instead of being | entrusted with kingship,   1437
they led troops and conquered, and met a rapid end.

It follows, then, that the fourth beast is to be understood as
the Roman Empire: at its end the ten kings will rise up at the one
time, and the creator and teacher of all evil will ultimately appear,
doing and suffering the things of which we were informed. After
his destruction the coming of our God and Savior will be manifested, the judgment of all people will take place, and there will be
an opening of "the books," the record of each one's life. *The body
of the beast will be handed over to fire*, that is, those who have removed control from the soul and accorded authority to the body,
adopting a material attitude in their life. The just judge, on the

[176] The Maccabees are prime candidates for "the holy ones" in a Jewish
interpretation. Such a view brings Antiochus IV into focus as the "little horn,"
the villain whose assault on Jewish religion could have prompted final composition of the book to encourage the persecuted. Theodoret's view of prospective
prophecy does not allow for this; so he brings in Herod from a century later as
a ploy to disqualify the Maccabees.

«Δεῦτε, οἱ εὐλογημένοι τοῦ Πατρός μου, κληρονομήσατε τὴν ἡτοιμα-
σμένην ὑμῖν βασιλείαν πρὸ καταβολῆς κόσμου·» ἧς γένοιτο πάντας ἡμᾶς
ἐπιτυχεῖν, χάριτι καὶ φιλανθρωπίᾳ τοῦ Κυρίου ἡμῶν Ἰησοῦ Χριστοῦ,
μεθ' οὗ τῷ Πατρὶ δόξα, σὺν τῷ ἁγίῳ Πνεύματι, εἰς τοὺς αἰῶνας τῶν
αἰώνων. Ἀμήν.

ΤΟΜΟΣ Η' — ΚΕΦΑΛΑΙΟΝ Η'

α'. «Ἐν ἔτει τρίτῳ τῆς βασιλείας Βαλτάσαρ, ὅρασις ὤφθη πρός
με· ἐγὼ Δανιήλ, μετὰ τὴν ὀφθεῖσάν μοι τὴν ἀρχήν.» Ἔτι, φησί, τῆς τῶν
Χαλδαίων, εἴτ' οὖν Ἀσσυρίων κατεχούσης βασιλείας, ἑτέραν ἀποκάλυψιν
εἶδον μετ' ἐκείνην τὴν προτέραν· δηλοῖ δὲ καὶ ὁ χρόνος τὸ ταύτης νεώτε-
ρον· τὴν μὲν γὰρ προτέραν εἶδεν ἐν τῷ πρώτῳ ἔτει Βαλτάσαρ, βασιλέως
Χαλδαίων, ταύτην δὲ ἐν τῷ τρίτῳ. Σημαίνει δὲ τὸν χρόνον οὐ μάτην,
ἀλλὰ διδάσκων, ὡς πρὸ πολλοῦ χρόνου τοῦ γενέσθαι τὰ πράγματα τὴν
τούτων πρόγνωσιν παρὰ Θεοῦ τῶν ὅλων ἐδέξατο.

β'. «Καὶ εἶδον, φησίν, ἐν τῇ ὁράσει, καὶ ἐγένετο ἐν τῷ ἰδεῖν με,
καὶ ἤμην ἐν Σούσοις τῇ βάρει, ἥ ἐστιν ἐν χώρᾳ Αἰλάμ.» Τὰ Σοῦσα μη-
τρόπολις ἦν πάλαι Περσῶν. Ἐπειδὴ τοίνυν τὴν τῆς Περσικῆς βασιλείας
μανθάνει κατάλυσιν, ἀναγκαίως ἐν ἐκείνῃ τῇ πόλει δοκεῖ βλέπειν τὴν
ἀποκάλυψιν. «Καὶ εἶδον, φησίν, ἐν ὁράματι·» ἀντὶ τοῦ, Οὐκ ἐγρηγορώς, οὐδὲ μεθ' ἡμέραν ταῦτα ἐθεασάμην, ἀλλ' ὄναρ μοι ταῦτα ἔδειξεν ὁ
τῶν ὅλων Θεός. | «Καὶ ἤμην, φησίν, ἐπὶ τοῦ Οὐβάλ.» Παρὰ τὴν πύλην,
φησίν, ἐδόκουν ἑστάναι· οὕτω γὰρ τοῦτό τινες τῶν ἑρμηνευτῶν τεθείκα-
σι.

γ'. «Καὶ ᾖρα τοὺς ὀφθαλμούς μου καὶ ἰδοὺ κριὸς εἷς ἑστηκὼς ἐπὶ
τοῦ Οὐβάλ, καὶ αὐτῷ κέρατα ὑψηλά, καὶ τὸ ἓν ὑψηλότερον τοῦ ἑτέρου,
καὶ τὸ ὑψηλότερον ἀνέβαινεν ἐπ' ἐσχάτου.» Τὴν Περσικὴν βασιλείαν
κριῷ ἐοικυῖαν ὁρᾷ, ἅτε δὴ πλούτῳ κομῶσαν, καὶ πολλὴν περιουσίας
ἔχουσαν ἀφθονίαν. Δύο κέρατα ἐν τῷ κριῷ θεωρεῖ, ἐπειδὴ πρῶτος μὲν
αὐτῶν ἐβασίλευσε Κῦρος, μέχρι δὲ παίδων μόνον τὴν βασιλείαν παρέπεμ-
ψε· Καμβύσου γὰρ τοῦ υἱέως αὐτοῦ τελευτήσαντος, ὀλίγους μὲν μῆνας

other hand, will give the kingdom to the holy ones, crying aloud, "Come, you blessed of my Father, inherit the kingdom prepared for you before the foundation of the world."[177] May it be the good fortune of us all to attain this, thanks to the grace and lovingkindness of our Lord Jesus Christ, to whom with the Father and Holy Spirit be glory, for ages of ages. Amen.

CHAPTER 8

In the third year of the reign of Belshazzar a vision came to me; I, Daniel, after the vision I had at the beginning (v. 1): with the empire of the Chaldeans (or Assyrians, if you like) still in control, I had another revelation after the previous one. The timing suggests it was more recent than that one: he saw the previous one in the first year of Belshazzar king of the Chaldeans, this one in the third year. Now, it is not without purpose that he indicates the time: it is to inform us that long before these things happened, he received foreknowledge of them from the God of all. *I saw in the vision and it occurred as I saw it; I was in the fort in Susa, which is in the district of Elam* (v. 2). In olden times Susa was the capital of Persia. Since he is learning of the overthrow of the Persian Empire, therefore, it follows that he seems to be having the revelation in that city. *I saw in a vision* means, I was not awake nor did I see it during the day: the God of all showed it to me in a dream. | 1440

I was at the ubal: I seemed to be standing at the gate (some translators rendering it this way).[178] *I raised my eyes and, lo, a ram standing at the ubal, with long horns, one longer than the other, and the longer one was rising to the heights* (v. 3). He sees the Persian Empire in the form of a ram since it was flush with wealth and had a great abundance of resources. He perceived two horns on the ram because Cyrus was the first to reign over it and transmitted the empire only to his sons; when his son Cambyses died, soothsayers

[177] Matt 25:34.
[178] Theodoret has noted that the LXX, reading Hebrew *'abul*, gives a rendering "(city) gate," πύλη, unlike Theodotion's transliterated form of Hebrew *'ubal*, "river." Unaware of the significance of the different Hebrew forms, Theodoret adopts the latter but accepts the sense of the former. As a Syriac speaker, he was better off when the text was in Aramaic in the previous chapters.

οἱ μάγοι κατέσχον τὴν βασιλείαν· παρέλαβε δὲ αὐτὴν μικρὸν ὕστερον
Δαρεῖος ὁ Ὑστάσπου, ὃς μέχρις ἐκγόνων καὶ ἀπογόνων τὴν βασιλείαν
παρέπεμψεν, ἕως Δαρείου τοῦ τελευταίου, ὃν Ἀλέξανδρος ὁ Μακεδὼν
ἀνελὼν τὴν βασιλείαν παρέλαβε. Τὰ τοίνυν δύο γένη τῶν βασιλέων διὰ
τῶν δύο κεράτων σημαίνεται· καὶ ἄμφω μὲν ὑψηλὰ θεωρεῖ, ὑψηλότερον
δὲ τοῦ προτέρου τὸ δεύτερον. Ὡς γὰρ ἤδη προειρήκαμεν, πλείων ἐπὶ
Δαρείου καὶ Ξέρξου ἡ βασιλεία ἐγένετο. Ὁ μὲν γὰρ Κῦρος τόν τε Εὔ-
ξεινον Πόντον καὶ τὴν Ἀσίαν ἐχειρώσατο· Δαρεῖος δὲ καὶ Σκύθας τοὺς
Νομάδας τοῖς ὑπηκόοις συνέταξεν· ὁ δὲ Ξέρξης καὶ τῇ Εὐρώπῃ τῆς βασιλείας ἐπειράθη τὸν ζυγὸν ἐπιθεῖναι. Τούτου χάριν δύο κέρατα ἐν τῷ
κριῷ θεωρεῖ, ἀλλὰ τὸ μὲν πρότερον, τὸ δὲ δεύτερον, καὶ τὸ δεύτερον
ὑψηλότερον τοῦ προτέρου.

δ'. «Καὶ εἶδον, φησί, τὸν κριὸν κερατίζοντα κατὰ θάλασσαν, καὶ
βορρᾶν, καὶ νότον.» Τά τε γὰρ βόρεια, τά τε νότια, ὑπήκοα εἶχεν ἅπαντα, ὡσαύτως δὲ καὶ τὰ ἑσπέρια μέχρις αὐτῆς τῆς θαλάσσης· καὶ τῶν
νήσων δὲ τὰς πλείστας δουλεύειν ἠνάγκασεν. Αὐτίκα τοίνυν τῷ Ξέρξῃ
καὶ Κύπριοι, καὶ Ῥόδιοι, Σάμιοί τε καὶ Λέσβιοι, καὶ Χῖοι, καὶ αἱ Κυ-
κλάδες ἅπασαι συνεμάχουν τὴν κατὰ τῆς Ἑλλάδος στρατείαν ποιουμένῳ.
Τούτου ἕνεκεν «Εἶδεν τὸν κριὸν κερατίζοντα κατὰ θάλασσαν, καὶ βορρᾶν, καὶ νότον. Καὶ πάντα, φησί, τὰ θηρία οὐ στήσεται ἐνώπιον αὐτοῦ,
καὶ οὐκ ἦν ὁ ἐξαιρούμενος ἐκ τῆς χειρὸς αὐτοῦ, καὶ ἐποίησε κατὰ τὸ
θέλημα αὐτοῦ, καὶ ἐμεγαλύνθη.» Θηρία δὲ πάλιν τὰς ἄλλας βασιλείας
καλεῖ τὰς μερικάς, τὴν Σύρων, τὴν Κιλίκων, τὴν Ἀράβων, τὴν Αἰγυ-
πτίων· θηρία δὲ αὐτὰς ὀνομάζει, διὰ τὸ φοβερὰς εἶναι τοῖς ἀρχομένοις.
Οὐδεμία τοίνυν, φησί, βασιλεία ἀντιστῆναι ἠδύνατο ἐκείνῃ τῇ βασιλείᾳ
κερατιζούσῃ κατὰ νότον, καὶ βορρᾶν, καὶ θάλασσαν, οὔτε οἷός τε ἦν τις
ἀνθρώπων ἐκείνης τῆς δυναστείας ἐλεύθερον ἀποφῆναί τινα, ἀλλ' ἅπαν
τὸ δοκοῦν εἰς πέρας ἦγε.

ε'. «Καὶ ἐγώ, φησίν, ἤμην συνιών.» Ταῦτα, φησί, θεωρῶν ἐλογι-
ζόμην παρ' ἐμαυτῷ, τὰ διὰ τού|των σημαινόμενα εὑρεῖν ἐφιέμενος· ἐμοῦ
δὲ πυνθανομένου· «Ἰδοὺ τράγος αἰγῶν ἤρχετο ἀπὸ Λιβὸς ἐπὶ πρόσωπον
πάσης τῆς γῆς.» Τισὶ δὲ τῶν ἀντιγράφων πρόσκειται καὶ τοῦτο· «Καὶ
οὐκ ἦν ἁπτόμενος τῆς γῆς, καὶ τῷ τράγῳ ἐκείνῳ κέρας ἓν θεωρητὸν
ἀναμέσον τῶν ὀφθαλμῶν αὐτοῦ.» Τὴν Μακεδονικὴν ἐνταῦθα βασιλείαν
ἐσήμανεν τοῦ ἐνυπνίου τὸ αἴνιγμα· τράγον δὲ αὐτὴν ὠνόμασε διὰ τὸ ταχὺ
καὶ εὐκίνητον· τοῦ κριοῦ γὰρ ὀξύτερος ὁ τράγος. Ἀπὸ Λιβὸς δὲ αὐτὸν
ἐληλυθέναι ἔφη· ἐπειδὴ πρότερον Αἴγυπτον χειρωσάμενος, οὕτως εἰς τὴν

1441

held power for a few months, but shortly afterwards Darius son of Hystaspes, who passed the empire on to his offspring and theirs up to the last Darius, whose empire Alexander the Macedonian took over after slaying him. So by the two horns he means two races of kings, seeing both to be tall, but the second taller than the first: as we said before, the empire became more extensive under Darius and Xerxes, Cyrus subjugating Euxine Pontus and Asia, Darius making subjects of the Scythian Nomads, and Xerxes endeavoring to put the yoke of empire on Europe.[179] This is the reason he sees two horns on the ram, the first and the second, with the second longer than the first.

I saw the ram charging to the sea, the north and the south (v. 4): he held everything to north and south in subjection as also westward to the very sea, and he forced most of the islands to serve as well; the people from Cyprus, Rhodes, Samos, Lesbos, Chios, and the Cyclades all joined Xerxes in the campaign against Greece. Hence he said that he saw *the ram charging to the sea, the north and the south. All the beasts will fail to withstand it, none was rescued from its hand, it did as it wished and grew larger.* By *beasts* he refers again to the other kingdoms individually, Syria, Cilicia, Arabia, Egypt, calling them *beasts* on account of their being fearsome to those they ruled. So no kingdom, he is saying, could resist that empire charging to the north, south, and west, nor could any human being liberate anyone from that power. Yet for all its appearance it met its end.

I was grasping the meaning (v. 5): while beholding this I pondered within myself, longing to discover | what was meant by it.   1441 While I was wondering, *Lo, a goat was advancing from the southwest on the face of the whole earth,* to which some of the manuscripts add, "not touching the ground, and on that goat one horn was visible between its eyes."[180] The dream's riddle here suggested the Macedonian Empire, calling it a *goat* because of its speed and fleetness of foot, a goat being faster than a ram. He said it came from the southwest: since it had previously subjugated Egypt, it thus ad-

---

[179] The author in v. 20 has the interpreter explain to Daniel that the two horns are the kings of Media and Persia, namely, "Darius the Mede" and Cyrus. Here, on the other hand, the two horns represent the two blood lines among the Persian kings.

[180] Both Theodotion and the LXX seem to include the "addendum," as well as the Hebrew; perhaps the Antiochene text does not.

Περσῶν ἐλήλυθε χώραν. Ἐνίκησε μὲν γὰρ τὸν Δαρεῖον ἐν τῇ Κιλικίᾳ, ἀλλ' ἐκεῖθεν τὴν Συρίαν, καὶ Φοινίκην, καὶ Παλαιστίνην διαδραμών, καὶ τὰς μὲν τῶν πόλεων ὁμολογίᾳ λαβών, τὰς δὲ βίᾳ ἑλών, εἰς τὴν Αἴγυπτον ὥρμησεν· εἶτα κἀκείνην τὴν βασιλείαν παραλαβών, τὴν Περσίδα καταλαμβάνει, καὶ τὴν μεγίστην αὐτῶν καταλύει βασιλείαν. Ἐν δὲ κέρας θεωρητὸν, τουτέστιν, ἐπίσημον καὶ περίβλεπτον, αὐτὸν καλεῖ τὸν Ἀλέξανδρον· ἀναμέσον δὲ τῶν ὀφθαλμῶν τοῦ τράγου φῦναι λέγει τὸ κέρας, διὰ τὸ ἀγχίνουν, καὶ συνετόν, καὶ πυκνὸν τῶν τοῦ Ἀλεξάνδρου φρενῶν.

ϛ', ζ'. «Καὶ ἦλθε, φησίν, ὁ τράγος ἕως τοῦ κριοῦ τοῦ τὰ κέρατα ἔχοντος, ὃν εἶδον ἑστῶτα ἐπὶ τοῦ Οὐβάλ, καὶ ἔδραμε πρὸς αὐτὸν ἐν ὁρμῇ τῆς ἰσχύος αὐτοῦ. Καὶ εἶδον αὐτὸν φθάσαντα ἕως τοῦ κριοῦ, καὶ ἐξηγριώθη πρὸς αὐτόν, καὶ ἔπαισε τὸν κριόν, καὶ συνέτριψεν ἀμφότερα τὰ κέρατα αὐτοῦ, καὶ οὐκ ἦν ἰσχὺς τῷ κριῷ τοῦ στῆναι ἐνώπιον αὐτοῦ· καὶ ἔρριψεν αὐτὸν ἐπὶ τὴν γῆν, καὶ συνεπάτησεν αὐτόν, καὶ οὐκ ἦν ὁ ἐξαιρούμενος τὸν κριὸν ἐκ τῆς χειρὸς αὐτοῦ.» Πρώτοις μὲν γὰρ τοῖς ἐκείνου συμβαλὼν στρατηγοῖς ἐν τοῖς κατὰ τὴν Ἀσίαν τόποις, πᾶσαν αὐτῶν ἐκείνην ἀφείλατο τὴν ἀρχήν. Εἶτα τοῦ Δαρείου κατὰ τὴν Κιλικίαν μετὰ πολλῆς τῆς στρατείας ἀπαντήσαντος, ἑτέρα γίνεται συμπλοκή, καὶ τρέπεται μὲν ὁ Δαρεῖος εἰς φυγήν, πολλοὺς δὲ τῆς στρατείας καταναλώσας ὁ Ἀλέξανδρος ἔλαβεν αἰχμαλώτους τοῦ Δαρείου τὰς θυγατέρας. Εἶτα αὖθις μετὰ τὴν ἐξ Αἰγύπτου ἐπάνοδον, περὶ τὴν Βαβυλῶνα παραταξάμενος, αὐτόν τε τὸν Δαρεῖον ἀνεῖλε, καὶ τὴν Περσικὴν κατέλυσε βασιλείαν. Συντριβῆναι δὲ λέγει ἀμφότερα τὰ κέρατα αὐτοῦ, ἐπειδὴ καὶ Μῆδοι καὶ Πέρσαι κατὰ ταὐτὸν ὠνομάζοντο, Κύρου τοῦ πρώτου βασιλεύσαντος, Μήδου μὲν ὄντος μητρόθεν, Πέρσου δὲ πατρόθεν· καὶ ἐπειδὴ ὁ πρῶτος αὐτῶν βασιλεὺς ἄμφω ταύτας εἶχε τὰς προσηγορίας, ἀναγκαίως καὶ οἱ ἀρχόμενοι, καὶ Μήδους καὶ Πέρσας τοὺς αὐτοὺς ὠνόμαζον. Εἰς γὰρ μίαν ἀρχὴν ἄμφω συνῆλθον αἱ βασιλεῖαι. Καὶ οἱ ἔξω δὲ συγγραφεῖς τοὺς αὐτοὺς καὶ Πέρσας καὶ Μήδους ὀνομάζουσιν. Οὕτω δέ, φησί, τῶν τοῦ κριοῦ συντριβέντων κεράτων,

η'. «Ὁ τράγος τῶν αἰγῶν ἐμεγαλύνθη ἕως σφόδρα.» Τῆς γὰρ Περσικῆς, εἴτ' οὖν Μηδικῆς, καταλυθείσης βασιλείας, τὸ κατὰ πάντων 1444   ὁ Ἀλέ|ξανδρος ἀνεδέξατο κράτος· ἀλλὰ καὶ οὗτος ὀλίγον ἐπιβιώσας χρόνον, τοῦ βίου τὸ τέλος ἐδέξατο. Καὶ τοῦτο δὲ εἶδεν ὁ μακάριος Δανιήλ. Διό φησι· «Καὶ ἐν τῷ ἰσχῦσαι αὐτὸν συνετρίβη τὸ κέρας τὸ μέγα.» Μετὰ τὴν νίκην ἐκείνην τὴν μεγίστην, φησί, τὸ κοινὸν τῶν ἀνθρώπων ὁ Ἀλέξανδρος ἐδέξατο τέλος. «Καὶ ἀνέβη, φησί, τέσσαρα κέρατα ὑποκάτωθεν αὐτοῦ εἰς τοὺς τέσσαρας ἀνέμους τοῦ οὐρανοῦ.» Τέσσαρα δὲ κέρατα,

vanced into the land of the Persians, conquering Darius in Cilicia, and from there traversing Syria, Phoenicia, and Palestine, taking some of the cities by surrender, securing others by force. It then also gained possession of that empire, occupied the Persians, and destroyed the greater part of their power. By the *one horn visible*, in the sense of famous and illustrious, he refers to Alexander; he says the horn was growing between its eyes on account of the shrewdness, intelligence, and sagacity of Alexander's thinking.

The goat advanced on the ram with the horns, which I had seen standing by the ubal, and ran at it with the force of its power. I saw it reach the ram, become furious with it, strike the ram, smash both its horns, and the ram had no strength to stand in its way. It threw it to the ground, trampled on it, and there was no one to rescue it from its hand (vv. 6–7). He first engaged with the other's generals in the places in Asia and removed all their control. Then when Darius engaged him in Cilicia with all his army, another battle was joined, Darius was put to flight, and Alexander wiped out many of the army and took the daughters of Darius captive. After the return from Egypt he next drew up his army near Babylon, slew Darius, and destroyed the Persian kingdom. Now, it says both its horns were smashed because both Medes and Persians were referred to at the same time, Cyrus being the first to come to the throne, who was a Mede on his mother's side and Persian on his father's; and since as their first king he bore both names, consequently also those ruled by them called the same people both Medes and Persians, both empires being joined into one. Secular historians also call the same people both Medes and Persians.[181]

With the ram's horns smashed in this way, *the goat grew very big* (v. 8): once the Persian Empire (or Median, if you like) was destroyed, | Alexander succeeded to power over everyone; but after a short life he met his end. This is what blessed Daniel saw— hence his saying, *The big horn was smashed while it was powerful*: despite that great conquest Alexander met the common fate of humankind. *Four horns came up in its place toward the four winds of heaven.* By *four horns* he hints at the four kings who succeeded

1444

[181] Theodoret, with "Darius the Mede" having to be inserted into the picture, keeps insisting that the Persian Empire is really both Mede and Persian though a single empire because Cyrus had roots in both races (Cyrus's displacement of the Medes under Astyages in 550 not taken into account; cf. note 132). The author also sees the empire as one.

τοὺς τέσσαρας βασιλέας, τοὺς κατὰ ταὐτὸν τὸν Ἀλέξανδρον διαδεξαμένους αἰνίττεται. Πτολεμαῖος γὰρ ὁ Λάγου τῆς Αἰγύπτου τὴν ἡγεμονίαν παρέλαβε· Σέλευκος δὲ ὁ Νικάνωρ τὴν Βαβυλῶνα κατεῖχε, καὶ τὰ ἄλλα μέρη τὰ μέχρι Συρίας διήκοντα· Ἀντίγονος δὲ τῆς Ἀσίας ἐκράτει, τῆς δὲ Μακεδονίας Ἀντίπατρος· ὡς δέ τισι τῶν συγγραφέων δοκεῖ, Φίλιππος, ὃς καὶ Ἀριδαῖος, ὁ καὶ Ἀλεξάνδρου ἀδελφός. Ἐπισημήνασθαι δὲ δεῖ, ὅτι καὶ τὸ τρίτον θηρίον τέσσαρας κεφαλὰς ἔχον ἐθεάσατο, καὶ τὸν τράγον μετὰ τὴν τοῦ ἑνὸς κέρατος συντριβὴν τέσσαρα φύσαντα κέρατα· ὡς εἶναι δῆλον τὰ αὐτὰ καὶ διὰ τοῦ τράγου, καὶ διὰ τοῦ τρίτου θηρίου σημαίνεσθαι.

θ′. «Καὶ ἐκ τοῦ ἑνός, φησί, τῶν κεράτων ἐξῆλθε κέρας ἐν ἰσχυρόν.» Ἀντίοχον λέγει τὸν Ἐπιφανῆ, ὃς Ἀντιόχου τοῦ ἐπικαλουμένου Μεγάλου υἱὸς ἐγεγόνει. «Καὶ ἐμεγαλύνθη, φησί, περισσῶς πρὸς νότον, καὶ πρὸς ἀνατολήν, καὶ πρὸς Λίβα, καὶ πρὸς τὴν δύναμιν.» Δυνατός, φησί, γενόμενος περιεγένετο μὲν τοῦ τῆς Αἰγύπτου βασιλέως, ὑφ' ἑαυτὸν δὲ καὶ τὰ πρὸς ἔω κείμενα ἐποιήσατο ἔθνη· ἐπεστράτευσε δέ, φησί, καὶ τοῖς Ἰουδαίοις, καὶ τὴν ἁγίαν μητρόπολιν κατεστρέψατο· δύναμιν γὰρ αὐτὴν προσηγόρευσε, διὰ τὴν ἐπανθοῦσαν τῷ ναῷ τηνικαῦτα χάριν θείαν. Καὶ τοῦτο σαφέστερον ποιῶν ἐπήγαγε·

ι′. «Καὶ ἐμεγαλύνθη ἕως τῆς δυνάμεως τοῦ οὐρανοῦ, καὶ ἔπεσεν ἐπὶ τὴν γῆν ἀπὸ τῆς δυνάμεως, καὶ ἀπὸ τῶν ἀστέρων, καὶ συνεπάτησεν αὐτούς.» Ταῦτα σαφέστερον ἡμᾶς ἡ τῶν Μακκαβαίων βίβλος ἥ τε πρώτη καὶ ἡ δευτέρα διδάσκει, καὶ Ἰώσηππος δὲ ὁ ἱστοριογράφος ἀκριβῶς ταῦτα συνέγραψε, καὶ ἡμεῖς δὲ συντόμως τὰ κατ' αὐτὸν διηγησόμεθα. Τῶν ἐκ γένους ἀρχιερατικοῦ πρὸς τὸν τηνικαῦτα ἀρχιερέα τῶν Ἰουδαίων στασιασάντων, οἱ ταύτης τῆς ἀρχῆς ἐφιέμενοι, πρὸς τὸν Ἀντίοχον παραγενόμενοι, πείθουσιν αὐτὸν τὴν Ἰουδαϊκὴν πολιτείαν εἰς Ἑλληνικὴν

Alexander at the one time: Ptolemy son of Lagus took control of Egypt, Seleucus Nicanor got possession of Babylon and the other parts bordering on Syria, Antigonus was in charge of Asia, Antipater Macedonia—or, as some historians think, Philip, who is also called Arrhideus, brother of Alexander.[182] Now, it should be noted that the third of the beasts he saw had four heads, and after the smashing of the one horn the goat grew four horns; so it is obvious that the same things are conveyed by the goat and the third beast.[183]

Out of one of the horns emerged one strong horn (v. 9).[184] He means Antiochus Epiphanes, who was son of Antiochus called the Great. *It grew to great size toward the south, toward the east, toward the southwest, and toward the strength*: on becoming strong he prevailed over the king of Egypt, and subjected the nations lying toward the east. He campaigned also, he says, against the Jews and trampled on the holy capital (calling it *strength* on account of the divine grace blossoming in the temple at that time). To make this clearer he went on, *It grew as high as the host of heaven, and fell on the earth from the host and from the stars, and trampled on them* (v. 10). The first and second books of the Maccabees inform us of this more clearly, and the historian Josephus made a precise record of it, and we shall outline concisely the facts about him.[185] When the Jews of the high-priestly family rebelled against the high priest of the time, those anxious for the position went to Antiochus and persuaded him to change the Jewish way of life

---

[182] Eusebius and Jerome, Guinot informs us (*L'Exégèse*, 719), nominate Philip.

[183] Modern commentators, on the other hand, see the reference by the author in the third beast's four heads in 7:6 to the four Persian kings mentioned in the Bible.

[184] Whereas the Hebrew speaks of a "little" horn (a different form from the Aramaic form occurring in that phrase in 7:8), Theodotion and LXX say "strong." That difference accounts for Theodoret's nominating the antichrist as the little horn in 7:8 and equally definitely Antiochus here; the two are not identified.

[185] Theodoret proceeds to do so—give a typically "concise" account of the excesses of Antiochus, though without being prompted to concede that this tyrant prompted the composition of the work. He assures the reader his summary is based on 1 and 2 Maccabees and Josephus; he could also have been reading the more prolix accounts he found in Theodore's introduction to psalms such as Ps 44.

μεταβάλλειν, καὶ γυμνάσιον ἐν τῇ πόλει οἰκοδομῆσαι. Τούτων γενομέ-νων, οἱ μὲν εὐσεβεῖς ἐν θρήνοις ἦσαν, τὴν προφανῆ τῶν νόμων ὁρῶντες παράβασιν, ὁ δὲ λοιπὸς ὅμιλος ἀδεῶς τὸν θεῖον ἐπάτει νόμον, καὶ εἰς τὴν τῆς περιτομῆς ἐξύβριζον ἐντολήν. Σφοδροτέρας δὲ γενομένης τῆς στάσεως, ἀφικόμενος ὁ Ἀντίοχος πλείστους μὲν ἀνεῖλε τῶν | εὐσεβῶν, τετόλμηκε δὲ καὶ τῶν τοῦ ναοῦ ἀδύτων ἐπιβῆναι. Καὶ ἐπιβὰς πάντα ἐσ-ύλησε τὸν νεών, τούς τε θησαυροὺς σφετερισάμενος, καὶ τὰ ἀναθήματα ἅπαντα, ἐκπώματά τε καὶ φιάλας, καὶ κρατῆρας, καὶ τὴν χρυσῆν τράπε-ζαν, καὶ τὸ χρυσοῦν θυμιατήριον, καὶ τὰς ἐκ χρυσίου κατεσκευασμένας λυχνίας, καὶ πάντα ἁπαξαπλῶς τῆς θείας ἱερουργίας τὰ ὄργανα. Πρὸς δὲ τούτοις καὶ βωμὸν ἐν τῷ τοῦ Θεοῦ νεῷ ᾠκοδόμησε τῷ Διΐ, καὶ πᾶ-σαν δὲ τὴν πόλιν εἰδώλων ἐνέπλησε, καὶ πάντας θύειν ἠνάγκαζεν· αὐτὸς δὲ καὶ χοῖρον ἔθυσεν ἐν τῷ θείῳ βωμῷ, καὶ Διὸς Ὀλυμπίου τὸν νεὼν προσηγόρευσε. Ταῦτα ἅπαντα ὁ μακάριος προδιδάσκει Δανιήλ· ὁρᾷ γὰρ διὰ τοῦ *κέρατος* αὐτὸν τὸν Ἀντίοχον, ὅτι «ἐμεγαλύνθη ἕως τῆς δυνά-μεως τοῦ οὐρανοῦ,» ἀντὶ τοῦ, τῇ μανίᾳ κατ' αὐτοῦ τοῦ Θεοῦ τῶν ὅλων ἐχρήσατο, ᾧ καὶ ὁ λεὼς καὶ ὁ νεὼς ἀνέκειτο. «Καὶ ἔπεσεν ἐπὶ τὴν γῆν ἀπὸ τῆς δυνάμεως καὶ ἀπὸ τῶν ἀστέρων, καὶ συνεπάτησεν αὐτούς.» Πλεῖστοι γὰρ ἐκ τοῦ λαοῦ, τὸν τοῦ Θεοῦ παραβάντες νόμον, τῆς τῶν οὐρανίων ἐξέπεσον τάξεως, καὶ ὑπὸ τῆς τούτου κατεπατήθησαν τυραν-νίδος, σφᾶς αὐτοὺς καταλύσαντες. *Ἀστέρας* δὲ αὐτοὺς ὠνόμασε διὰ τὸ περιφανὲς καὶ λαμπρὸν τῆς εὐσεβείας. Αἰνίττεται δὲ καὶ τὴν πρὸς τὸν Ἀβραὰμ ὑπόσχεσιν· «Ποιήσω γάρ, φησί, τὸ σπέρμα σου, ὡς τοὺς ἀστέ-ρας τοῦ οὐρανοῦ.» Οὐκ ἠρκέσθη γάρ, φησί, τῷ συμπατῆσαι πολλοὺς τῶν καλουμένων *ἀστέρων,* ἀλλὰ καὶ

ια'. «Ἕως ἄρχοντος τῆς δυνάμεως ἡδρύνθη.» Τῇ γὰρ λύττῃ καὶ μανίᾳ κατ' αὐτοῦ τοῦ Θεοῦ καὶ βασιλέως ταυτησὶ τῆς δυνάμεως, τουτέ-στι, τοῦ ἁγίου λαοῦ, ἐχρήσατο· καὶ ταῦτα ποιῶν, φησί, διετέλει, «Ἕως οὗ ὁ ἀρχιστράτηγος ῥύσηται τὴν αἰχμαλωσίαν·» ἀντὶ τοῦ, μέχρις ἂν τῆς ἄνωθεν τύχωμεν ῥοπῆς, καὶ διὰ τοῦ ἐπιτεταγμένου ἀρχαγγέλου τὴν ἡμετέραν προστασίαν, τύχωμεν σωτηρίας. Εἶτα σαφέστερον τὰ ὑπὸ τοῦ Ἀντιόχου τολμηθησόμενα προδιδάσκεται. «Καὶ δι' αὐτόν, φησί, θυσία ἐταράχθη παραπτώματι.» Οὐ συνεχώρει γὰρ τὰς κατὰ νόμον θυσίας

to the Greek, and to build a gymnasium in the city. When this
happened, devout people were in mourning at seeing the blatant
violation of the laws, while the remaining throng had no qualms
about trampling on the divine law and treating with contempt the
commandment about circumcision. When the uprising became
more serious, Antiochus arrived and put to death most of the | 1445
devout, and he had the audacity even to enter the precincts of the
temple; after entering he sacked the whole temple, appropriating
to himself the treasures, all the offerings, cups and bowls and vessels, the golden table, the golden censer, the lamp-stands made of
gold, and in short all the instruments of divine worship. In addition to this he built in God's temple an altar to Zeus, filled the
whole city with idols and obliged everyone to sacrifice, while he
himself sacrificed a pig on the divine altar and named the temple
after Zeus of Olympus.

Blessed Daniel foretold all this: in the horn he sees Antiochus
in person *growing as high as the host of heaven*, that is, venting insane rage against the God of all, to whom both people and temple
were dedicated. *It fell on the earth from the host and from the stars,
and trampled on them*: most of the people by transgressing God's
law quickly fell away from heavenly things, and they were trampled down by this tyrant to their own destruction. He referred to
them as *stars* on account of the fame and splendor of their piety,
hinting also at the promise to Abraham, "I shall make your offspring like the stars of heaven."[186] He was not satisfied, in fact,
with trampling down many of those called *stars*: *It even exalted
itself to the level of the ruler of the host*, venting its frenzy and insane rage against God himself, king of this host—that is, the holy
people—and continuing to do so *until the leading general will rescue the captivity* (v. 11),[187] that is, until we receive support from
on high and attain salvation as a result of the archangel appointed
as our patron.

Then he foretells with greater clarity the audacity that would
be committed by Antiochus. *On account of him sacrifice was dis-
rupted by transgression*: he did not permit the sacrifices prescribed
by law to be made, requiring instead that they be performed in the

[186] Gen 22:17.
[187] The Hebrew and Greek differ in vv. 11–12, the NRSV admitting obscurity.

προσφέρεσθαι, ἀλλὰ τῷ Ἑλληνικῷ τρόπῳ ταύτας ἐπιτελεῖσθαι ἠνάγκαζεν. Εἶτα ἐπάγει· «Ὅτι καὶ ἐγενήθη, καὶ κατευοδώθη αὐτῷ.» Τέως γὰρ
οὐδὲν ἐμπόδισμα γέγονε κωλῦον αὐτοῦ τὴν λύτταν.

ιβ'. «Καὶ τὸ ἅγιον, φησίν, ἐρημωθήσεται, καὶ ἐδόθη, φησίν, ἐπὶ
τὴν θυσίαν ἁμαρτία, καὶ ἐρρίφη χαμαὶ ἡ δικαιοσύνη, καὶ ἐποίησε, καὶ
εὐοδώθη.» Μανίᾳ γὰρ καὶ τυραννίδι χρώμενος, μιᾶναι μὲν τετόλμηκε
τὸ θυσιαστήριον παρανόμῳ θυσίᾳ χρησάμενος, ἔρημον δὲ τοῦ κόσμου
τὸν θεῖον κατέστησε νεών, ἐπάτησε δὲ τῆς δικαιοσύνης τοὺς νόμους, τὸν
1448   ἄδικον | φόνον τοῖς εὐσεβέσιν ἐπαγαγών, καὶ τέως, φησίν, «εὐωδοῦτο»
ταῦτα ποιῶν. Εἶτα,

ιγ'. «Ἤκουσά τινος ἁγίου λαλοῦντος, καὶ εἶπεν εἷς ἅγιος τῷ φελμουνὶ τῷ λαλοῦντι· Ἕως πότε ἡ ὅρασις στήσεται, καὶ ἡ θυσία ἡ ἀρθεῖσα,
καὶ ἡ ἁμαρτία τῆς ἐρημώσεως ἡ δοθεῖσα, καὶ τὸ ἅγιον, καὶ ἡ δύναμις
συμπατηθήσεται;» Τὸ φελμουνὶ τὸν τινά σημαίνει τῇ Ἑλλάδι φωνῇ·
μαρτυρεῖ δὲ τούτοις καὶ ἡ Σύρων φωνὴ γειτνιάζουσα τῇ Ἑβραίᾳ. Φησὶ
τοίνυν ὁ μακάριος Δανιήλ, ὅτι «Ἤκουσά τινος ἁγίου ἕτερον ἅγιον ἐρω-
τῶντος.» Δῆλον δὲ ὅτι ἀγγέλους διαλεγομένους ὁρᾷ καὶ βουλομένους
μαθεῖν, πόσος ἐστὶν ὁ χρόνος τῆς τολμωμένης ἀσεβείας τε καὶ παρανομίας, τῆς τε τοῦ ναοῦ ἐρημίας, καὶ τῆς ἀθέσμου καὶ βδελυρᾶς θυσίας,
καὶ τῆς τοῦ λαοῦ καταδυναστείας.

ιδ'. «Καὶ εἶπεν αὐτῷ, φησίν· Ἕως ἑσπέρας καὶ πρωΐ, ἡμέραι
δισχίλιαι καὶ τριακόσιαι, καὶ καθαρισθήσεται τὸ ἅγιον.» Ἑσπέραν δὲ
ἐκάλεσε τὴν ἀρχὴν τῶν συμφορῶν, πρωΐ δὲ τὸ τέλος τῶν συμφορῶν· ἐπειδὴ νυκτὶ καὶ σκότῳ ἐῴκει τὰ λυπηρά. Ἀπὸ τοῦ νῦν, φησί, τῆς ἀρχῆς
τῶν κακῶν, ἕως τέλους τόσος τέ ἐστι χρόνος. Ψηφιζόμεναι δὲ αἱ ἡμέραι αὗται ποιοῦσιν ἐξ ἐτῶν ἀριθμόν, καὶ ἐξ μηνῶν, κατὰ τὴν Ἑβραίων
ψῆφον· τοσοῦτον γὰρ ἐκράτησε χρόνον τῶν Ἰουδαίων ἡ συμφορά.

ιε'. «Καὶ ἐγένετο, φησίν, ἐν τῷ ἰδεῖν με, ἐγὼ Δανιήλ, τὴν ὅρασιν, ἐζήτουν σύνεσιν.» Ταῦτα, φησί, θεασάμενος, συνεῖναι καὶ μαθεῖν

Greek manner. He then goes on, *Because it was done and things prospered for him*: for the time being no impediment proved a check on his frenzy. *The holy place will be devastated. Sin was offered up as a sacrifice, righteousness was brought to the ground, he had his way and prospered* (v. 12): venting his tyrannical frenzy, he had the audacity to defile the altar by performing lawless sacrifice; he left the divine temple bereft of ornament, and he trampled on the laws of righteousness, | inflicting unjust slaughter on devout people, and 1448 (the text says) for the time being *prospering* while doing so.

I heard a holy one speaking, and another holy one said to the one speaking, How long will the vision last, the sacrifice be abolished, the sin of devastation be offered up, and the holy place and the host be trampled down? (v. 13). The word *phelmouni* means "a person" in Greek; Syriac, which is close to Hebrew, also confirms this.[188] So blessed Daniel is saying, I heard one holy one asking another holy one. Clearly he is witnessing angels conversing and wanting to learn how long is the period of the offenses of impiety and lawlessness, the devastation of the temple, the illicit and loathsome sacrifice, and the oppression of the people. *He replied to him, From evening to morning 2,300 days, and the holy place will be purified* (v. 14). By *evening* he referred to the beginning of the calamities, and by *morning* to the end of the calamities, since night and darkness are figures of distress. From the present time, the beginning of the troubles, to the end, he is saying, the period is of that length. Calculated by the Hebrew system these days amount to six years and six months, this being the length of time the Jews' calamity was in force.[189]

When I, Daniel, had seen the vision, I looked for understanding of it (v. 15): having witnessed it, I wanted to understand and

[188] Theodoret finds this transliterated Hebrew form in his text of Theodotion (as in LXX) for "the one (speaking)." Syriac (his native tongue, which he rightly relates to Hebrew, being a dialect of Aramaic) enables him to identify it as an indefinite pronominal form. Not all Theodotion manuscripts include it. Their grasp of Hebrew, like Theodoret's, is not up to the challenge of recognizing in the Hebrew forms they render as "the sin of devastation" an intentional deformation of the Phoenician name for the Greek god Zeus Olympios.

[189] Not a significant figure, of course, since despite his claim to familiarity with Hebrew counting, Theodoret has it wrong, three and a half years being the true figure. But the significance of even that figure eluded him at its previous occurrence (7:25), we noted, as it will at 12:11.

ἀκριβῶς ἐβουλόμην τὰ διὰ τούτων σημαινόμενα τῶν αἰνιγμάτων. «Καὶ ἰδοὺ ἔστη ἐνώπιόν μου ὡς ὅρασις ἀνδρός.» Καὶ ἐδόκουν, φησίν, ἄνδρα θεωρεῖν.

ις΄. «Καὶ ἤκουσα φωνὴν ἀνδρὸς ἀναμέσον τοῦ Οὐβὰλ, καὶ ἐκάλεσε, καὶ εἶπε· Γαβριήλ, συνέτισον ἐκεῖνον τὴν ὅρασιν.» Ἤκουσα δὲ καὶ ἑτέρου τινὸς ἀνθρωπείᾳ χρωμένου φωνῇ, καὶ κελεύσαντος τὸν παρεστῶτά μοι, ὃν καὶ Γαβριὴλ ὠνόμασεν, ἑρμηνεῦσαί μοι τῆς ἀποκαλύψεως τὰ αἰνίγματα. Ἔστι δὲ καὶ ἐκ τῶν εἰρημένων τεκμήρασθαι, ὅτι ὁ κελεύσας ὁ Δεσπότης ἐστί.

ιζ΄. «Καὶ ἦλθε, φησί, καὶ ἔστη ἐχόμενα τῆς στάσεώς μου.» Παραυτίκα, φησί, προσταχθεὶς ἀφίκετο, καὶ πλησίον μου ἔστη. «Καὶ ἐν τῷ ἐλθεῖν αὐτὸν ἐθαμβήθην, καὶ πίπτω ἐπὶ πρόσωπόν μου.» Ἱκανὰ ταῦτα τὸν Εὐνομίου τῦφον ἐλέγξαι, ὃς αὐτὴν εἰδέναι τοῦ Θεοῦ τὴν οὐσίαν ἀλαζονεύεται. Εἰ γὰρ ἀγγέλων τὴν θεωρίαν, καὶ ταύτην μετρουμένην τῇ τοῦ θεωροῦντος δυνάμει, ὁ τοσοῦτος προφήτης οὐκ ἤνεγκε, τί δυσσεβέστερον ἢ βδελυττότερον τῶν αὐτὴν εἰδέναι τοῦ Θεοῦ τὴν οὐσίαν σεμνυνομένων; 1449 ἀλλ' ἐπὶ τὸ προκείμενον ἐπανέλθωμεν. «Καὶ εἶπε | πρός με· Σύνες, υἱὲ ἀνθρώπου· ἔτι γὰρ εἰς καιροῦ πέρας καὶ ὅρασις.» Μὴ νομίσῃς, φησίν, ἐπὶ τοῦ παρόντος ταῦτα πέρας λαμβάνειν· μετὰ πολὺν γὰρ ἐτῶν ἀριθμὸν ταῦτα γενήσεται. Πληρουμένου γὰρ τοῦ ὡρισμένου καιροῦ, τότε πέρας τούτων ἕκαστον λήψεται.

ιη΄, ιθ΄. «Καὶ ἐν τῷ λαλεῖν αὐτὸν μετ' ἐμοῦ πίπτω ἐπὶ πρόσωπόν μου ἐπὶ τὴν γῆν, καὶ ἥψατό μου, καὶ ἔστησέ με ἐπὶ τοὺς πόδας μου. Καὶ εἶπεν· Ἰδοὺ ἐγὼ γνωρίζω σοι τὰ ἐσόμενα ἐπ' ἐσχάτων τῆς ὀργῆς τοῖς υἱοῖς τοῦ λαοῦ σου· ἔτι γὰρ εἰς καιροῦ πέρας μένει.» Θεασάμενός με, φησίν, ὑπὸ τοῦ δέους καταπεσόντα πρῶτον ἀνώρθωσέ με, ἔπειτα ψυχαγωγεῖ γνωρίζων, ὡς τούτου χάριν ἀφίκετο, ἵνα μοι τὰ ἐσόμενα προμηνύσῃ ποθοῦντι, καὶ ὁποῖα διὰ τὴν τοῦ Θεοῦ πάλιν ὀργὴν καταλήψεταί μου τὸν λαόν. Ἔπειτα τὸ ἐπικείμενόν μοι δέος ἀφελέσθαι βουλόμενος, ἐμήνυσεν ὅτι μετὰ χρόνον ταῦτα γενήσεται· ἡρμήνευσε δέ μοι καὶ ὧν ἐθεασάμην ἕκαστον, εἰρηκώς·

κ΄. «Οὗτος ὁ κριός, ὃν εἶδες, ὁ ἔχων τὰ κέρατα, βασιλεὺς Μήδων καὶ Περσῶν.» Ἐπειδὴ γὰρ εὐθὺς τὴν Χαλδαϊκὴν, εἴτ' οὖν Ἀσσυρίων, βασιλείαν Δαρεῖος ὁ Μῆδος παρέλαβε, καὶ τότε Κῦρος ὁ Πέρσης μετα-

learn the precise meaning of what was signified by these riddles. *Lo, there stood before me something looking like a man*: I seemed to see a man. *I heard a man's voice in the middle of the ubal, calling out in these terms, Gabriel, make that person understand the vision* (v. 16): I heard someone else as well using a human voice and bidding the one standing near me, whom he called Gabriel, to interpret the riddle of the revelation to me. It is possible from what was said to come to the conclusion that the one giving the orders was the Lord. *He came and stood close to my position* (v. 17): as soon as he was bidden, he arrived and stood near me. *When he came, I was astonished and fell prostrate.* This is sufficient to convict Eunomius of conceit for his arrogant claim to know God's essence: if such a great prophet could not bear the sight of angels, despite its being adapted to the ability of the viewer, what could be more impious and abominable than those pretending to know the very essence of God?[190] Let us, however, return to the text before us. | *He said to me, Understand, mortal man, the vision is still for the end of time*: do not think that these things come to fulfillment in the present age; they will happen after a great number of years. When the set time has run its course, then each of them will reach its fulfillment.

As he was speaking, I fell prostrate on the ground. He took hold of me and set me on my feet, and said, Lo, I make known to you what is to happen to this people at the end of the wrath; it abides until the end of time (vv. 18–19): perceiving me prostrate with fear, he first set me upright, then consoled me by making known why he had come, to inform me in my anxiety of the future and what in turn would overtake my people as a result of God's wrath. Then, in his wish to allay the fear besetting me, he mentioned that this would happen after a time, and interpreted to me the meaning of each of the things I had seen, saying, *This ram you saw with two horns is the king of Medes and Persians* (v. 20). Since at first Darius the Mede took possession of the Chaldean (or, if you like, Assyrian) Empire,

[190] Eunomius, pupil of Aëtius of Antioch and later bishop of Cyzicus, was responsible with his teacher for a radical form of Arianism known as Anomoeism in the mid-fourth century. In this doctrine, "since God's essence was 'ingenerateness,' ἀγεννησία, and nothing more, it was completely comprehensible by men," Kelly tells us (*Early Christian Doctrines* [5th ed.; San Francisco: Harper & Row, 1978], 249). Here Theodoret quickly dismisses Eunomius; in later works he will bracket him with Arius and frequently castigate them for their subordinationist teachings.

τέθεικεν εἰς Πέρσας τὴν βασιλείαν, ὃς καὶ Μῆδος ἦν καὶ Πέρσης διὰ τὴν τῶν γενῶν ἐπιμιξίαν· ἀναγκαίως Περσῶν τοὺς Μήδους προτέθεικεν, καί φησιν, ὅτι «ὁ κριὸς βασιλεύς ἐστι Μήδων καὶ Περσῶν.» Ἄμφω γὰρ καὶ ὁ τελευταῖος Δαρεῖος ὁ Ἀρσάμου προσαγορευόμενος, ὃν ὁ Μακεδὼν Ἀλέξανδρος κατέλυσε, διεῖπε τὰς βασιλείας.

κα΄. «Καὶ ὁ τράγος, φησί, τῶν αἰγῶν βασιλεὺς Ἑλλήνων· καὶ τὸ κέρας τὸ μέγα, ὃ ἦν ἀναμέσον τῶν ὀφθαλμῶν αὐτοῦ, αὐτός ἐστιν ὁ βασιλεὺς ὁ πρῶτος.» Λέγει δὲ τὸν Ἀλέξανδρον.

κβ΄. «Καὶ ὅτι συνετρίβη, καὶ ἔστη τέσσαρα κέρατα ὑποκάτωθεν αὐτοῦ, τέσσαρες βασιλεῖς ἀναστήσονται ἀπὸ τοῦ ἔθνους αὐτοῦ, καὶ οὐκ ἐν τῇ ἰσχύϊ αὐτοῦ.» Μετὰ γάρ, φησί, τὴν ἐκείνου τελευτήν, ἡ ἐκείνου βασιλεία εἰς τέσσαρας διαιρεθήσεται βασιλείας· ἀλλὰ καὶ τέτταρες ὄντες οἱ βασιλεύοντες οὐ δυνήσονται κατορθοῦν; ἃ ἐκεῖνος κατώρθου, ἐλάττους δὲ πολλῷ τῆς ἐκείνου ῥώμης ὀφθήσονται.

κγ΄. «Καὶ ἐπ' ἐσχάτου δέ, φησί, τῆς βασιλείας αὐτῶν, πληρουμένων τῶν ἁμαρτιῶν αὐτῶν.» Ὅταν, φησίν, εἰς ἄκρον ἀσεβείας ἐλάσωσι, καὶ πέρα τῶν μέτρων τῆς ἐμῆς μακροθυμίας παρανομήσωσιν.

«Ἀναστήσεται βασιλεὺς ἀναιδὴς προσώπῳ, καὶ συνιῶν προβλήματα. (κδ΄.) Καὶ κραταιὰ ἡ ἰσχὺς αὐτοῦ, καὶ οὐκ ἐν τῇ ἰσχύϊ αὐτοῦ.» Τὴν πανουργίαν τοῦ Ἀντιόχου διὰ τούτων αἰνίττεται, καὶ πρὸς τῇ πανουργίᾳ, ἣν ἐκέκτητο δύναμιν. Εἶτα διδάσκων | ὡς ταῦτα ποιήσει, τοῦ Θεοῦ δηλονότι συγχωροῦντος, ἀναγκαίως ἐπήγαγε· «Καὶ οὐκ ἐν τῇ ἰσχύϊ αὐτοῦ.» Καὶ τῷ Ἀσσυρίῳ δέ φησιν ὁ Θεὸς διὰ Ἡσαΐου τοῦ προφήτου· «Μὴ δοξασθήσεται ἀξίνη ἄνευ τοῦ κόπτοντος ἐν αὐτῇ; ἢ ὑψωθήσεται πρίων ἄνευ τοῦ ἕλκοντος αὐτόν;» Οὕτω δὲ καὶ ἐνταῦθα, φησίν, ὅτι ταῦτα τολμήσει ὁ Ἀντίοχος, οὐχ ὡς δυνατός, ἀλλὰ τοῦ Θεοῦ συγχωροῦντος.

«Καὶ θαυμαστά, φησί, διαφθερεῖ, καὶ κατευθυνεῖ, καὶ ποιήσει, καὶ διαφθερεῖ ἰσχυρούς, καὶ λαὸν ἅγιον. (κε΄.) Καὶ ὁ ζυγὸς τοῦ κλοιοῦ αὐτοῦ κατευθυνεῖ.» Ἀντὶ τοῦ, οὐδὲν αὐτῷ ἐμποδὼν ἔσται, ἀλλ' ὅσα ἂν θελήσῃ ταῦτα ποιήσει. Περὶ τῶν τοιούτων ὁ μακάριος παραινεῖ Δαβίδ, λέγων· «Μὴ παραζήλου ἐν τῷ κατευοδουμένῳ ἐν τῇ ὁδῷ αὐτοῦ, ἐν ἀνθρώπῳ ποιοῦντι παρανομίαν.» Συμβαίνει γὰρ πολλάκις καὶ τοὺς δυσσεβείᾳ καὶ παρανομίᾳ συζῶντας εὐοδοῦσθαι λίαν παράνομα τολμῶντας. «Ὁ ζυγὸς οὖν, φησί, τοῦ κλοιοῦ αὐτοῦ κατευθυνεῖ,» ἀντὶ τοῦ, πάντα ἃ ἂν προστάξῃ τοῖς ὑπηκόοις, ἀναγκάσει ταῦτα πληροῦν. Εἶτα τὸ πανοῦργον αὐτοῦ καὶ ὕπουλον προλέγων· «Δόλος, φησίν, ἐν τῇ χειρὶ αὐτοῦ, καὶ ἐν καρδίᾳ αὐτοῦ μεγαλυνθήσεται, καὶ δόλῳ διαφθερεῖ πολλούς.» Ἐξ ἀρχῆς γὰρ γυμνάσιον ἐν Ἱεροσολύμοις οἰκοδομηθῆναι προσέταξεν, εἶτα χοιρείων

and subsequently Cyrus the Persian, who was both Mede and Persian by a mixture of races, transferred the empire to the Persians, he consequently put Medes ahead of Persians in saying, *the ram is king of Medes and Persians*; Darius, called son of Arsamos, was the last of them and managed both empires, and Alexander the Macedonian disposed of him. *The goat is the king of the Greeks, and the big horn which was between its eyes is the first king* (v. 21), referring to Alexander. *It was broken and four kings replaced it: four kings will arise from his nation, but not with his power* (v. 22): after his death his empire will be divided into four kingdoms, but though those reigning over them are four, they will not succeed in achieving what he achieved, but will be seen to be much inferior to his strength.

At the end of their reign, when their sins are complete (v. 23): when they reach the height of impiety and transgress beyond the limits of my longsuffering. *A king shameless in aspect will arise, skilled in intrigue, his power great, but not with his own power* (vv. 23–24). In this he implies the malice of Antiochus, and in addition to the malice the power he acquired. Then, to stress | that he will do   1452 this with God's obvious permission, he consequently went on, *But not with his own power*. To the Assyrian also God says through the prophet Isaiah, "Will the axe take pride without the one to cut with it? or the saw be exalted without the one drawing it?"[191] Likewise here too he says that Antiochus will show such audacity, not by being powerful, but with God's permission. *He will cause stupendous destruction; he will govern, exert himself, destroy the strong and a holy people, and the yoke of his stocks will prosper* (vv. 24–25), that is, nothing will be an obstacle to him; instead, he will do what he wishes. Of such people blessed David says in exhortation, "Do not vie with the one who prospers in his way, with the one who commits lawlessness":[192] it often happens that people living a godless and lawless life prosper considerably in their lawless pursuits. So *the yoke of his stocks will prosper* means, he will force his subjects to carry out all he bids them.

He next foretells his malice and pretence: *Guile in his hand, and in his heart he will be magnified, and by guile he will destroy many*. From the outset he gave orders for a gymnasium to be built

---

[191] Isa 10:15.
[192] Ps 37:7.

μεταλαμβάνειν κρεῶν· ὕστερον δὲ καὶ θύειν ἠνάγκαζεν· ἐκέχρητο δὲ καὶ κωτίλοις λόγοις, τοὺς εὐσεβεῖς ἐξαπατῆσαι πειρώμενος, καὶ βασιλικὰς δωρεὰς ὑπισχνεῖτο, παρανομοῦντας ἅπαντας ἰδεῖν ἐφιέμενος. Διὰ τοῦτό φησι· «Δόλος ἐν τῇ χειρὶ αὐτοῦ, καὶ ἐν καρδίᾳ αὐτοῦ μεγαλυνθήσεται.» Μέγιστον γὰρ ἑαυτὸν πάντων ἀνθρώπων ἡγήσατο, «καὶ δόλῳ διαφθερεῖ πολλούς,» οὓς ἂν ἐξαπατῆσαι ἰσχύσῃ. «Καὶ ἐπὶ ἀπωλείᾳ πολλῶν, φησί, σταθήσεται.» Ἀντὶ τοῦ, ἐνστάσει χρήσεται, ἕως ἂν ἴδῃ πολλοὺς τὴν οἰκείαν ἀπολλύντας σωτηρίαν. Μὴ ἀρκούμενος δὲ τῇ κατὰ τῶν ἀνθρώπων μανίᾳ, «Καὶ ἐπὶ ἄρχοντα, φησίν, ἀρχόντων στήσεται.» Τουτέστι, κατ' αὐτοῦ τοῦ Βασιλέως τῶν βασιλέων, καὶ κυριεύοντος τῶν κυριευόντων, τῇ λύττῃ χρήσεται, μιαίνειν ἐπιχειρῶν τὸν ἀνακείμενον αὐτῷ νεών. Καὶ δεικνὺς τὴν δοθεῖσαν αὐτῷ κατὰ τῶν Ἰουδαίων συγχώρησιν, «Καὶ ὡς ᾠά, φησίν, ἐν χειρὶ συντρίψει αὐτούς.» Οὕτω, φησί, μετὰ πολλῆς εὐκολίας ταῦτα πάντα ἐργάσεται, ὡς εἴ τις ᾠὰ τῇ χειρὶ συντρίψαι θελήσειεν. Αἰνίττεται δὲ ἐνταῦθα καὶ τὴν αὐτῶν τῶν Ἰουδαίων ῥαθυμίαν, καὶ ὅτι αὐτοὶ τῶν θείων ἀμελήσαντες κατελείφθησαν ὑπὸ τοῦ Θεοῦ, καὶ γυμνοὶ τῆς ἄνωθεν προνοίας ἐγένοντο. Τούτοις ἐπιφέρει·

κϛʹ. «Καὶ ἡ ὅρασις τῆς ἑσπέρας καὶ τῆς πρωΐας τῆς ῥηθείσης ἀληθής ἐστιν.» Ἀντὶ τοῦ, καὶ ὁ ὡρισμένος χρόνος ταῖς συμφοραῖς ἀναμφιβόλως ἐστὶν ἀληθής. Ἐπειδὴ δὲ πολύς ἐστιν ἐν τῷ μέσῳ χρόνος, | «Καὶ σὺ σφράγισον, φησί, τὴν ὅρασιν, ὅτι εἰς ἡμέρας πολλὰς ἔσται.» Ἀντὶ τοῦ, Ἀσαφῆ αὐτὴν τοῖς πολλοῖς κατάλιπε· σοὶ γὰρ ὡς ποθοῦντι ταῦτα δῆλα πρὸ τῶν πραγμάτων πεποίηκα.

κζʹ. «Καὶ ἐγώ, φησί, Δανιὴλ ἐκοιμήθην, καὶ ἐμαλακίσθην ἡμέρας, καὶ ἀνέστην, καὶ ἐποίουν τὰ ἔργα τοῦ βασιλέως, καὶ ἐθαύμαζον τὴν ὅρασιν, καὶ οὐκ ἦν ὁ συνιῶν.» Μαθὼν γὰρ τὰ καταληψόμενά μου τὸν λαὸν πάλιν κακά, οὕτως ἀνιαρῶς διετέθην, ὡς καὶ ἀρρωστίᾳ περιπεσεῖν· ἀλλ' ὅμως καὶ τοῦτον διακείμενος τὸν τρόπον, ᾠκονόμουν τὰ παρὰ τοῦ βασιλέως ἐγκεχειρισμένα μοι, μηδενὸς γινώσκοντος τὴν τῆς ἀρρωστίας αἰτίαν. Οὗτος ᾔδει καὶ μετὰ τοῦ μακαρίου Παύλου λέγειν· «Τίς ἀσθενεῖ, καὶ οὐκ ἀσθενῶ; τίς σκανδαλίζεται, καὶ οὐκ ἐγὼ πυροῦμαι;» Καὶ τό· «Κλαίειν μετὰ κλαιόντων, καὶ χαίρειν μετὰ χαιρόντων.» Καί· «Εἰ πάσχει ἓν μέλος, συμπάσχει πάντα τὰ μέλη.» Οὕτω διακείμενος, καὶ ταύτην ἔχων περὶ τοὺς συνδούλους φιλοστοργίαν, μαθὼν τὰς πολλαῖς ὕστερον γενεαῖς καταληψομένας τοὺς συνδούλους αὐτοῦ συμφοράς, θρηνῶν καὶ ὀλοφυρόμενος διετέλει· καὶ ταῦτα εἰδὼς ἀκριβῶς ὡς αὐτὸς

in Jerusalem, then for the eating of pork; later he obliged them to sacrifice. He indulged in fancy talk in an attempt to deceive devout people, and promised regal gifts in his longing to see everyone infringing the law—hence the verse *Guile in his hand, and in his heart he will be magnified*: he considered himself the greatest of all, *and by guile he will destroy many* whom he manages to deceive. *He will be bent on the ruin of many*, that is, he will adopt a plan for seeing many forfeit their own salvation. But not content with his insane rage against people, *He will take a stand against the leader of leaders*,[193] that is, he will vent his frenzy against the very King of kings and Lord of lords in an endeavor to defile the temple dedicated to him. And to bring out the license given him against the Jews, *And he will crush them in his hand like eggs*: he will do all this with great ease, like someone wanting to smash eggs in his hand. Here he is referring to the indifference of the Jews themselves, and the fact that by their own neglect of God's worship they were abandoned by God and deprived of providence from on high.

To this he adds, *The vision of the evening and the morning that has been told is true* (v. 26), that is, the time determined for the calamities is true beyond all doubt. But since there is a long interval in between, | *seal up the vision because it will be in many days* 1453 *time*, that is, leave it obscure for many people; I have made it clear to you in your longing before the event. *I, Daniel, was confined to bed and was unwell for days. I got up and carried out the king's business. I was amazed at the vision, and there was no one who understood it* (v. 27): on learning the troubles that would overtake the people in due course, I became so unwell as to fall a victim to illness. Yet despite being thus indisposed, I managed the work entrusted to me by the king, with no one aware of the cause of the sickness. He was in the habit of saying along with blessed Paul, "Who is weak, and I am not weak? Who is made to stumble, and I am not indignant?" and "Weeping with those who weep, rejoicing with those who rejoice," and "If one limb suffers, all the limbs suffer together."[194] This man felt the same way, and he had this affection for his fellow slaves; and on learning of the calamities to overtake his fellow slaves many generations later, he kept weeping and wailing. He

---

[193] This clause, occurring in the Hebrew, is not in the Greek versions beyond appearing in the Antiochene text.

[194] 2 Cor 11:29; Rom 12:15; 1 Cor 12:26.

πεῖραν τούτων οὐδεμίαν λήψεται, ἀλλὰ τῆς παρούσης ζωῆς οὐκ εἰς μακρὰν ἀπαλλαγήσεται. Ταύτην προσήκει καὶ ἡμᾶς περὶ τοὺς ὁμοφυεῖς τε
καὶ ὁμοδούλους τὴν ἀγάπην ἔχειν, καὶ τὸ αὐτὸ εἰς ἀλλήλους φρονεῖν, καὶ
τὴν περὶ ἄλληλα τῶν μελῶν μιμεῖσθαι συμπάθειαν· ἐπειδὴ μέλη μὲν ἀλλήλων κεκλήμεθα, σῶμα δὲ ἠξιώθημεν προσαγορευθῆναι Χριστοῦ. Αὐτῷ
ἡ δόξα εἰς τοὺς αἰῶνας τῶν αἰώνων. Ἀμήν.

ΤΟΜΟΣ Θ΄ — ΚΕΦΑΛΑΙΟΝ Θ΄

α, β΄. «Ἐν τῷ πρώτῳ ἔτει Δαρείου τοῦ υἱοῦ Ἀσσουήρου ἀπὸ τοῦ
σπέρματος τῶν Μήδων, ὃς ἐβασίλευσεν ἐπὶ τῆς βασιλείας τῶν Χαλδαίων·
ἐν ἔτει ἑνὶ τῆς βασιλείας αὐτοῦ, ἐγὼ Δανιὴλ συνῆκα ἐν ταῖς βίβλοις τὸν
ἀριθμὸν τῶν ἐτῶν, ὃς ἐγενήθη λόγος Κυρίου πρὸς Ἱερεμίαν τὸν προφή-
1456 την εἰς συμπλήρωσιν ἐρημώσεως Ἱερουσαλὴμ, ἑβδομήκοντα ἔτη.» | Καὶ
ἐντεῦθεν δῆλον, ὡς ἑτέρα μὲν ἡ Δαρείου τοῦ Ἀσσουήρου βασιλεία, ἑτέρα δὲ ἡ Κύρου τοῦ Πέρσου· συμφωνεῖ δὲ καὶ τοῖς πρώην εἰρημένοις τὰ
νῦν ἀναγνωσθέντα. Οὐχ ἁπλῶς γὰρ Μῆδον τὸν Δαρεῖον προσηγόρευσεν,
ἀλλ᾽ «ἀπὸ τοῦ σπέρματος τῶν Μήδων·» ὡς εἶναι δῆλον, ὅτι οὐχ ἑκατέρωθεν, πατρόθεν φημὶ καὶ μητρόθεν, Μῆδος οὗτος ἦν· ἐβασίλευσε δ᾽
ὅμως ἐπὶ τὴν βασιλείαν τῶν Χαλδαίων, θείᾳ πληγῇ τοῦ Βαλτάσαρ μετὰ
τὴν ἀσέβειαν νύκτωρ ἀναιρεθέντος. Δοκεῖ δέ μοι λίαν βραχὺν βεβασιλευ-
κέναι χρόνον οὗτος ὁ Δαρεῖος. Ὁ γὰρ μακάριος Δανιήλ, ὡς ἤδη λοιπὸν
πληρωθέντα τὸν τῆς αἰχμαλωσίας ὅρον ἰδών, καὶ τὸν τῶν ἑβδομήκοντα
ἐτῶν συλλογισάμενος ἀριθμόν, ὃν διὰ τοῦ προφήτου Ἱερεμίου προεῖπεν

had a precise knowledge that he personally would not experience those things but would instead be freed from the present life before long.

It behooves us, too, to have this love for kith and kin and for our fellow servants, to think in common with one another, and imitate the fellow feeling of limbs with one another, since we are called members of one another, and have been given the name of Christ's body.[195] To him be the glory for ages of ages. Amen.

CHAPTER 9

In the first year of Darius son of Ahasuerus, from the line of the Medes, who came to the throne of the Chaldeans, in the first year of his reign I, Daniel, understood from the books the number of years which the word of the Lord to Jeremiah the prophet said was required for the completion of the devastation of Jerusalem, seventy years (vv. 1–2). From this | it is clear that the empire of Darius son of Ahasuerus 1456 was different from that of Cyrus the Persian; what has now been read is consistent with what was said previously.[196] He did not, note, call Darius a Mede pure and simple, but *from the line of the Medes*; so it is clear he was not a Mede on both sides, that is, his father's and his mother's. Yet he reigned over the empire of the Chaldeans when Belshazzar was slain at night by divine intervention following on his act of impiety.[197]

Now, it seems to me that this Darius reigned for a very short time: blessed Daniel, having a vision of the end of the captivity as already arrived at by that time, and reckoning the number of years at seventy, which the God of all had foretold through the prophet

---

[195] Cf. Rom 12:5; 1 Cor 12:27.

[196] Again here, as with the beginning of the commentary on chapter 4, there is a suggestion of oral treatment of the text, in this case in the terms used, "reading out aloud what was said a day or two ago."

[197] Theodoret had been led into initial troubles with the chronology of the book by the mention of "Darius the Mede" at the beginning of chapter 6, where he spoke (probably on the basis of 9:1) of "Darius son of Ahasuerus." Not showing a realization of the symbolic value of seven or seventy, he is now concerned to go to further lengths to rationalize the chronology by comparison of Daniel's statement on the extent of the exile with Jeremiah, Zechariah, and the apocryphal 1 Esdras, a book that has also been influenced by Jeremiah, taking the figure seventy as factual, not symbolic.

ὁ τῶν ὅλων Θεός, τὴν ὑπὲρ τοῦ λαοῦ ἱκετηρίαν προσφέρειν ἄρχεται τῷ Δεσπότῃ. Ἐπληρώθη δὲ ὁ χρόνος ἐπὶ Κύρου τοῦ Περσῶν βασιλέως, ὡς ὁ μακάριος Ἔσδρας φησίν· εὐθὺς γὰρ ἐν ἀρχῇ τοῦ συγγράμματος, μετὰ τὰ προοίμια, ἐν συντόμῳ τῆς ἁλώσεως τῶν Ἱεροσολύμων μνημονεύσας, καὶ τοῦ τῆς πατρίδος ἀνδραποδισμοῦ, καὶ τῆς εἰς Βαβυλῶνα τῶν αἰχμαλώτων μετοικίας, ἐπήγαγε· «Καὶ ἦσαν παῖδες αὐτῷ καὶ τοῖς υἱοῖς αὐτοῦ, μέχρι τοῦ βασιλεῦσαι Πέρσας, εἰς πλήρωσιν τοῦ ῥήματος τοῦ Κυρίου ἐν στόματι Ἱερεμίου, ἕως τοῦ εὐδοκῆσαι τὴν γῆν τὰ Σάββατα αὐτῆς, πάντα χρόνον τῆς ἐρημώσεως αὐτῆς σαββατιεῖ εἰς συμπλήρωσιν ἐτῶν ἑβδομήκοντα βασιλεύοντος Κύρου Περσῶν ἔτους πρώτου, εἰς συντέλειαν ῥήματος Κυρίου ἐν στόματι Ἱερεμίου.» Λέγει δὲ καὶ ὁ θειότατος Ἱερεμίας οὕτως· «Ἰδοὺ ἐγὼ ἀποστέλλω, καὶ λήψομαι τὴν πατριὰν τοῦ βορρᾶ, τὸν Ναβουχοδονόσορ βασιλέα Βαβυλῶνος τὸν δοῦλόν μου, καὶ ἄξω αὐτὸν ἐπὶ τὴν γῆν ταύτην, καὶ ἐπὶ τοὺς κατοικοῦντας αὐτήν, καὶ ἐπὶ πάντα τὰ ἔθνη τὰ κύκλω αὐτῶν, καὶ ἐξερημώσω αὐτοὺς εἰς ἀφανισμόν, καὶ εἰς συριγμόν, καὶ εἰς ὀνειδισμὸν αἰώνιον, καὶ ἀφελῶ ἀπ᾿ αὐτῶν φωνὴν χαρᾶς, καὶ φωνὴν εὐφροσύνης, καὶ φωνὴν νυμφίου, καὶ φωνὴν νύμφης, ὀσμὴν μύρου, καὶ φῶς λύχνου, καὶ ἔσται ἡ γῆ αὐτῆς πᾶσα εἰς ἀφανισμόν, καὶ δουλεύσουσιν ἐν τοῖς ἔθνεσιν ἑβδομήκοντα ἔτη. Καὶ ἐν τῷ πληρωθῆναι τὰ ἑβδομήκοντα ἔτη, ἐκδικήσω ἐπὶ τὸν βασιλέα Βαβυλῶνος, καὶ ἐπὶ τὸ ἔθνος ἐκεῖνο, φησὶ Κύριος, τὰς ἀνομίας αὐτῶν, καὶ ἐπὶ γῆν Χαλδαίων, καὶ θήσομαι αὐτοὺς εἰς ἀφανισμὸν αἰώνιον.» Ὁ μὲν οὖν μακάριος Ἱερεμίας ἠνίξατο συμπληροῦσθαι τῆς αἰχμαλωσίας τὸν χρόνον ἐν τῇ καταλύσει τῆς Χαλδαϊκῆς βασιλείας· ὁ δὲ Ἔσδρας καὶ σαφέστερον τοῦτο πεποίηκε, τοῦ Κύρου ποιησάμενος μνήμην. Εὑρίσκομεν δὲ καὶ τὸν θειότατον Ζαχαρίαν ἑτέρως τοῦτον ἀριθμοῦντα τὸν χρόνον. Μετὰ γὰρ τὴν τοῦ Κύρου τελευτήν, καὶ Καμβύσου τοῦ υἱέως αὐτοῦ, 1457   τοῦ Δαρείου τοῦ Ὑστάσπου τὸ | Περσῶν ἀναδησαμένου κράτος, τοῦ

Jeremiah, begins to offer supplication to the Lord for the people. But the time expired with the reign of Cyrus king of the Persians, as blessed Esdras says: at the very beginning of the account after the introduction he mentions concisely the capture of Jerusalem, the enslavement of his country, and the deportation of the captives to Babylon, and he goes on, "And they were servants to him and to his sons until the Persians began to reign, in fulfillment of the word of the Lord by the mouth of Jeremiah, Until the land has enjoyed its Sabbaths, it shall keep Sabbath all the time of its desolation until the completion of seventy years. In the first year of the reign of Cyrus king of the Persians, so that the word of the Lord by the mouth of Jeremiah might be accomplished."[198] The most divine Jeremiah also speaks this way, "Lo, I am sending, and shall take the country of the north, my servant Nebuchadnezzar king of Babylon, and shall bring him against this land and against its inhabitants and against all the nations round about them. I shall utterly destroy them and make them an object of hissing and everlasting taunting. I shall remove from them a sound of joy, a sound of happiness, a sound of a bride, a sound of a bridegroom, fragrance of anointing and light of a lamp. The whole of its land will become a ruin, and they will be slaves among the nations for seventy years. On the completion of the seventy years I shall take vengeance on the king of Babylon and on that nation for their lawlessness, says the Lord, and on the land of the Chaldeans, and I shall reduce them to everlasting oblivion."[199]

While blessed Jeremiah, then, referred to the accomplishment of the time of the captivity with the destruction of the Chaldean Empire, Esdras put it even more clearly in making mention of Cyrus. Now, we find also the most divine Zechariah numbering these years differently: after the death of Cyrus and his son Cambyses, Darius the son of Hystaspes | gained control   1457

---

[198] 1 Esdras 1:57–2:1 (not citing Jeremiah precisely). This book, now regarded as apocryphal by most Christians (but found in the Greek and Slavonic Bibles), is probably the original LXX version of a different form of the Hebrew text of Ezra-Nehemiah, and was thought of as canonical by Fathers such as Theodoret. The name "Esdras" is, of course, the Greek form of the Hebrew name Ezra.

[199] Jer 25:9–12. The use of the number seventy for a long period without any specification of time (found also in extra-biblical literature) occurs elsewhere in the Old Testament, e.g., Judg 1:7, 1 Sam 6:19; Ps 90:10.

χρόνου μνημονεύσας ὁ προφήτης· «Τῇ τετράδι γὰρ, φησί, καὶ εἰκάδι τοῦ ἐνδεκάτου μηνός, οὗτός ἐστιν ὁ μὴν Σαβὰτ, ἐν τῷ δευτέρῳ ἔτει ἐπὶ Δαρείου, ἐγένετο λόγος Κυρίου πρὸς Ζαχαρίαν τὸν Βαραχίου, υἱοῦ Ἀδδώ, τὸν προφήτην.» Καὶ ἐπήγαγε μετὰ βραχέα· «Καὶ ἀπεκρίθη ὁ ἄγγελος Κυρίου, καὶ εἶπε· Κύριε παντοκράτωρ, ἕως τίνος οὐ μὴ ἐλεήσῃς τὴν Ἱερουσαλήμ, καὶ τὰς πόλεις Ἰούδα ἃς περιεῖδες; Τοῦτο ἑβδομηκοστὸν ἔτος.» Καί τινες μὲν τῶν ἀπιστίαν νοσούντων διαφωνεῖν τοὺς ἁγίους νομίζουσι προφήτας· οἱ δὲ τοῖς ἱεροῖς λόγοις ἐντεθραμμένοι, ὑπὸ τῆς θείας φωτιζόμενοι χάριτος, τὴν τῶν ἁγίων προφητῶν εὑρίσκουσι συμφωνίαν. Φέρε τοίνυν, ἐκείνης τῆς αἴγλης τυχεῖν ἱκετεύσαντες, δήλην αὐτὴν τοῖς ἀγνοοῦσι ποιήσωμεν. Τὸν μὲν οὖν χρόνον τῆς αἰχμαλωσίας συμφώνως τεθείκασιν ἅπαντες, ὅ τε θεῖος Ἱερεμίας, ὅ τε θεσπέσιος Ζαχαρίας, καὶ ὁ μακάριος Ἔσδρας· τὸν ἑβδομηκοντούτην γὰρ ἀριθμὸν τεθείκασιν ἅπαντες· οὐκ ἀπὸ τῶν αὐτῶν δὲ καιρῶν ἀριθμεῖν ἀρχόμενοι τοῦτον τὸν χρόνον, οἱ μὲν εἰς Κῦρον, οἱ δὲ εἰς Δαρεῖον, τοῦτον καταλήγειν ἔφασαν τὸν ἀριθμόν. Οἱ μὲν γὰρ περὶ τὸν μακάριον Ἱερεμίαν καὶ Ἔσδραν, ἀπὸ τῆς ἀρχῆς τῆς πρώτης αἰχμαλωσίας ἀριθμοῦντες, εἰκότως μέχρι Κύρου, τοῦ Περσῶν βασιλέως, τὰ ἑβδομήκοντα περιορίζουσιν ἔτη. Ὁ δὲ θειότατος Ζαχαρίας ἀπὸ τῆς τελευταίας πολιορκίας, ἐν ᾗ τὴν πανωλεθρίαν ὑπέμειναν, ἀριθμῶν, ἐπὶ Δαρείου τοῦ Περσῶν βασιλέως, τὸν τῶν ἑβδομήκοντα ἐτῶν ἀριθμὸν συμπληροῦσθαί φησι· καὶ γὰρ ἐπὶ τούτου τῷ ὄντι ὁ θεῖος ἀνῳκοδομήθη νεώς. Ἐπειδὴ γὰρ τρὶς ὁ λαὸς αἰχμάλωτος γέγονε, πρῶτον μὲν ἐπὶ Ἰωακείμ, τοῦ υἱοῦ Ἰωσίου βασιλέως Ἰούδα, τὸ δὲ δεύτερον ἐπὶ Ἰεχονίου, τοῦ υἱοῦ Ἰωακείμ, τὸ δὲ τρίτον ἐπὶ Σεδεκίου, τοῦ ἀδελφοῦ μὲν τοῦ Ἰωακείμ, θείου δὲ τοῦ Ἰεχονίου, ἀναγκαίως τρὶς καὶ τῆς ἐπανόδου τυγχάνουσι. Πρῶτον μὲν γὰρ ἀφίησιν αὐτοὺς Κῦρος ὁ Πέρσης, εἶτα Δαρεῖος ὁ υἱὸς Ὑστάσπου, ἔπειτα Ἀρταξέρξης ὁ Ξέρξου, ἡνίκα πρότερον μὲν τὸν Ἔσδραν, μετ' ἐκεῖνον δὲ τὸν Νεεμίαν ἀπέστειλεν, ὥστε τὰ τῆς Ἱερουσαλὴμ ἀνοικοδομῆσαι τείχη. Τῶν μὲν οὖν πρώτων αἰχμαλώτων γεγενημένων ὁ ἑβδομηκονταέτης πληροῦται χρόνος ἐπὶ Κύρου τοῦ Πέρσου· τῆς δὲ τοῦ ναοῦ ἐρημίας ὁ αὐτὸς οὗτος χρόνος λαμβάνει τέλος ἐν τῷ δευτέρῳ ἔτει Δαρείου τοῦ Ὑστάσπου, ὡς εἶναι

of Persia, the prophet mentioning the date, "On the twenty-fourth
day of the eleventh month, the month of Shebat, in the second year
of Darius the word of the Lord came to the prophet Zechariah son
of Berechiah, son of Iddo"; and he went on shortly after, "The angel of the Lord replied, Lord Almighty, how long will you have no
mercy on Jerusalem and the cities of Judah that you have scorned?
It is the seventieth year."[200]

While some commentators suffering from unbelief think the
holy prophets are at odds, those nourished on the sacred words and
enlightened by divine grace find consistency in the holy prophets.
So come now, asking to receive that ray of light, let us make
it clear to those unaware of it. Everyone—the divine Jeremiah,
the divinely inspired Zechariah, and the blessed Esdras—is in
agreement in citing the period of the captivity, all mentioning the
number seventy; but they do not all begin to calculate this period by using the same date, some claiming that this number closes
with Cyrus, some with Darius. Some including blessed Jeremiah
and Esdras calculate it from the beginning of the first captivity,
and logically close the seventy years with Cyrus king of the Persians. The most divine Zechariah, on the other hand, calculates
it from the final siege in which they suffered ruin, and he claims
the number of seventy years is completed under Darius king of the
Persians, the divine temple in actual fact being built under the latter. You see, since the people were made captive three times—the
first under Jehoiakim son of Josiah king of Judah, the second under Jeconiah, and the third under Zedekiah brother of Jehoiakim
and uncle of Jeconiah—consequently they were also granted return three times: Cyrus the Persian was the first to release them,
then Darius son of Hystaspes, and finally Artaxerxes son of Xerxes
when he sent first Ezra and after him Nehemiah to rebuild the
walls of Jerusalem. The period for those who were the first taken
captive, then, is completed under Cyrus the Persian, while this
same period of the devastation of the temple reaches its conclusion
in the second year of Darius son of Hystaspes. The result is that

[200] Zech 1:7, 12. In later commentary on that prophet, Theodoret will
have further problems getting the numbers to add up; he still feels numerical
accuracy (or "textual coherence," in Young's term [*Biblical Exegesis*, 176]) is an
element of prophecy. Only victims of "unbelief," he goes on to say, could question that verity—unaware he is creating a false problem. Antiochene exegesis
generally suffers badly from this inability to recognize apocalyptic.

προφητείαν ἑκατέραν, τὴν Ἱερεμίου τε καὶ Ζαχαρίου, ὡσαύτως δὲ καὶ τὴν τοῦ Ἔσδρα συγγραφήν, ἀψευδῆ τε καὶ ἀληθῆ. Τοῦτον, φησί, τὸν χρόνον ὁ μακάριος Δανιὴλ συνιείς, καὶ ἀριθμήσας, καὶ εὑρὼν πλησιάζοντα·

γʹ. «Ἔδωκα τὸ πρόσωπόν μου, φησί, πρὸς Κύριον τὸν Θεόν, τοῦ ἐκζητῆσαι προσευχὴν καὶ δέησιν ἐν νηστείαις, καὶ σάκκῳ καὶ σποδῷ.» Οὐ γάρ, φησίν, ἁπλῶς ἀνέμενον τὴν τῆς αἰχμαλωσίας ἀπαλλαγήν, ἀλλ᾽ ἱκετείαν τῷ Δεσπότῃ προσέφερον, τὴν ἐλευθερίαν τοῖς ὁμοφύλοις αἰτῶν. Κἂν γὰρ μυριάκις ὑπό|σχηται ἀγαθά, ἀναξίους δὲ ἡμᾶς αὐτοὺς τῆς δωρεᾶς καταστήσωμεν, ἐμπόδιον γινόμεθα τῇ θείᾳ φιλοτιμίᾳ. Τοῦτο δὲ καὶ δι᾽ Ἐζεκιὴλ τοῦ προφήτου φησὶν ὁ Θεός· «Πέρας λαλήσω ἐπὶ ἔθνος καὶ βασιλείαν, τοῦ ἀνοικοδομεῖν καὶ καταφυτεύειν, καὶ ἔσται, ἐὰν στραφὲν τὸ ἔθνος ἐκεῖνο ποιήσῃ πονηρά, οὐ μὴ ἐπαγάγω ἐπ᾽ αὐτὸ πάντα τὰ ἀγαθὰ ἃ ἐλάλησα.» Ταῦτα πεπαιδευμένος ὁ μακάριος Δανιήλ, «νηστείᾳ, καὶ σάκκῳ, καὶ σποδῷ,» τὴν προσευχὴν πτερώσας προσέφερεν τῷ Θεῷ.

δʹ. «Καὶ προσηυξάμην, φησί, πρὸς Κύριον τὸν Θεόν μου, καὶ ἐξωμολογησάμην, καὶ εἶπον· Κύριε ὁ Θεός, ὁ μέγας καὶ θαυμαστός, ὁ φυλάσσων τὴν διαθήκην καὶ τὸν ἔλεον τοῖς ἀγαπῶσί σε, καὶ φυλάττουσι τὰ προστάγματά σου.» Καλεῖ δὲ μέγαν καὶ θαυμαστόν, ὡς μεγάλα καὶ θαυμαστὰ ποιεῖν δυνάμενον. Ἀπὸ γὰρ τῶν ἐνεργειῶν οἱ θεῖοι ἄνδρες τὰς θείας προσηγορίας τιθέναι φιλοῦσι. «Φυλάττειν δὲ καὶ αὐτὸν ἔφη τὴν διαθήκην καὶ τὸν ἔλεον τοῖς ἀγαπῶσιν αὐτόν,» τῶν πρὸς Ἀβραάμ, καὶ Ἰσαάκ, καὶ Ἰακὼβ ἀναμιμνήσκων ἐπαγγελιῶν. Μετὰ πάσης δὲ ἀκριβείας εὐχόμενος, διδάσκει, ὅτι οὐχ ἁπλῶς φυλάττει, ἀλλὰ «τοῖς ἀγαπῶσιν αὐτόν, καὶ φυλάττουσι τὰς ἐντολὰς αὐτοῦ.»Εἰ γάρ τις, φησί, παραβῇ σου τὰ προστάγματα, ἀνάξιον ἑαυτὸν τῶν ὑποσχέσεών σου καθίστησι. Τοῦτο δὲ καὶ ἡμῖν συνέβη.

εʹ. «Ἡμάρτομεν γάρ, φησίν, ἠδικήσαμεν, ἠσεβήσαμεν καὶ ἐξεκλίναμεν ἀπὸ τῶν ἐντολῶν σου, καὶ ἀπὸ τῶν κριμάτων σου.» Σφόδρα δὲ προσφόρως ἐπὶ τοῦ Θεοῦ τὰς ἐντίμους ἐκείνας καὶ θαυμαστὰς τεθεικὼς προσηγορίας, τὰς ἐκ διαμέτρου ἐναντίας σφίσιν αὐτοῖς ἐπιτέθεικεν. Οὐκ ἠρκέσθη δὲ τῷ εἰπεῖν ἡμάρτομεν, ἀλλὰ καὶ τὸ «ἠδικήσαμεν καὶ ἠσεβήσαμεν» προσέθηκεν, ἀγνώμονες περὶ τὰς σὰς εὐεργεσίας γενόμενοι. Ἠσεβήσαμεν δέ, ἄλλους ἀντὶ σοῦ θεοὺς προελόμενοι, ἀψύχους, ἀναισθήτους, οὐδεμίαν κεκτημένους ἰσχύν. Εἶτα δεικνὺς τὴν διηνεκῶς εἰς αὐτοὺς

both prophecies, Jeremiah's and Zechariah's, as also the record of
Esdras, are true and reliable.

Blessed Daniel, the text says, understood this, did his calcu-
lations, and found the time approaching. *I turned to the Lord God
to seek an answer by prayer and supplication with fasting, sackcloth,
and ashes* (v. 3): I did not simply await freedom from captivity:
I offered entreaty to the Lord, seeking liberation for my fellows;
if he promises | good things even countless times, but we render   1460
ourselves unworthy of the gift, we prove an obstacle to the divine generosity. God says as much through Ezekiel the prophet
as well, "At length I shall promise a nation or kingdom to rebuild
and plant them, but if that nation turns away and does evil, I will
not bring upon it all the good things I promised."[201] Instructed
in these things, blessed Daniel gave wings to his prayer *with fasting, sackcloth, and ashes*, and offered it to God. *I prayed to the Lord
my God, and made confession in the words, Lord, great and wonderful
God, keeping covenant and mercy with those who love you and keep
your commandments* (v. 4).[202] He calls him *great and wonderful* for
his ability to do great and wonderful things. Godly men, after all,
are accustomed to apply divine names on the basis of benefits con-
ferred; he spoke of his *keeping covenant and mercy with those who
love him* in recalling the promises to Abraham, Isaac, and Jacob.
Being very precise in his prayer, he mentions that he does not keep
it with anyone, but with *those who love him and keep his commandments*: if someone transgresses your commands, he renders himself
unworthy of the promises.

This happened in our case, too. *We sinned, we transgressed, we
committed impiety and we turned from your commandments and your
judgments* (v. 5). Having very appropriately assigned those honorable and marvelous titles to God, he implied the direct opposite of
themselves. It was not sufficient for him to say *We sinned*; he went
on to say *We transgressed, we committed impiety*, being ungrateful
for your benefits, by the phrase *we committed impiety* meaning the
choice of other gods that were lifeless, with no senses or strength.

---

[201] The reference, in fact, is to Jer 18:9–10.

[202] It is thought that originally v. 4 was followed immediately by v. 21,
and that a scribe has inserted at this point an older prayer written in better
Hebrew—features of the text that would be lost on Theodoret, though he might
have noted that the prayer is a communal confession, not an individual request
for enlightenment.

γινομένην τοῦ Θεοῦ κηδεμονίαν, καὶ τὴν πολλὴν τοῦ λαοῦ ἀναλγησίαν, ἐπήγαγε·

ς'. «Καὶ οὐκ εἰσηκούσαμεν τῶν δούλων σου τῶν προφητῶν, οἳ ἐλάλουν ἐν τῷ ὀνόματί σου πρὸς τοὺς βασιλεῖς ἡμῶν, καὶ πρὸς τοὺς ἄρχοντας ἡμῶν, καὶ πρὸς τοὺς πατέρας ἡμῶν, καὶ πρὸς πάντα τὸν λαὸν τῆς γῆς.» Οὐ γὰρ ἐπαύσατό σου ἡ χάρις ἐποπτεύουσά τε ἡμᾶς, καὶ διὰ τῶν προφητῶν διαλεγομένη, ποτὲ μὲν βασιλεῦσι καὶ ἄρχουσι, ποτὲ δὲ ἱερεῦσι καὶ διδασκάλοις (τούτους γὰρ πατέρας ἐκάλεσε), πολλάκις δὲ καὶ παντὶ τῷ λαῷ· ἀλλὰ καὶ τούτων οὕτω γενομένων ἡμεῖς διετελέσαμεν ἀντιλέγοντες. Διὸ εἰκότως προστέθεικεν·

1461   ζ'. «Σοί, Κύριε, ἡ δικαιοσύνη, καὶ ἡμῖν ἡ αἰσχύνη | τοῦ προσώπου, ὡς ἡ ἡμέρα αὕτη, ἀνδρὶ Ἰούδα, καὶ τοῖς κατοικοῦσιν Ἱερουσαλήμ, καὶ παντὶ Ἰσραήλ, τοῖς ἐγγὺς καὶ τοῖς μακράν, ἐν πάσῃ τῇ γῇ, οὗ διέσπειρας αὐτοὺς ἐκεῖ ἐν ἀθετήσει αὐτῶν, ᾗ ἠθέτησάν σε, Κύριε.» Τὰ μὲν γὰρ, φησίν, ὑπὸ σοῦ γεγενημένα, Δέσποτα, τὴν σὴν κηρύττει δικαιοσύνην· ἡμεῖς δὲ διὰ τὴν πολλὴν ἡμῶν παρανομίαν ἐν αἰσχύνῃ γενόμενοι, τῆς ἰδίας ἀγνωμοσύνης κατηγοροῦμεν. Σοὶ μὲν γὰρ ἐκ τῆς ἡμετέρας ἀσεβείας οὐδεμία προσεγένετο βλάβη· ἡμεῖς δὲ τῶν σπερμάτων ἐδεξάμεθα τοὺς καρπούς, καὶ ἐλεεινῶς, ὅτι τῶν ὁμοφύλων κατηγορῶν, καὶ ἑαυτὸν τοῖς παραβάταις συνάπτει.

η'. «Ἡμῖν, φησίν, ἡ αἰσχύνη τοῦ προσώπου, καὶ τοῖς βασιλεῦσιν ἡμῶν, καὶ τοῖς ἄρχουσιν ἡμῶν, καὶ τοῖς πατράσιν ἡμῶν, οἵτινες ἡμάρτομέν σοι.» Ἱκανὸν δὲ τούτων ἕκαστον εἰς ἔλεον ἐπικάμψαι καὶ τὸν ὠμότατον, μήτιγε τὸν ἡμερώτατον καὶ φιλανθρωπότατον. Δείκνυσι γὰρ διὰ τῶν λόγων οὐ τοὺς εὐτελεῖς τοῦ λαοῦ καὶ ἀφανεῖς μόνους αἰσχύνης ἀναπλησθέντας, ἀλλὰ καὶ αὐτοὺς τοὺς βασιλέας, καὶ τοὺς ἄρχοντας, καὶ τοὺς ἱερέας· τούτους γὰρ πατέρας ὠνόμασε. Καὶ δεικνὺς τῆς τιμωρίας τὸ δίκαιον, προστέθεικεν· «Οἵτινες ἡμάρτομέν σοι.» Ἀλλ' ἡμεῖς μὲν ἀξίους ἐκομισάμεθα τῆς παρανομίας τοὺς καρπούς·

θ'. «Τοῦ Κυρίου δὲ Θεοῦ ἡμῶν οἱ οἰκτιρμοὶ καὶ ἱλασμοί.» Πρέπει γάρ σοι, ἡμέρῳ ὄντι καὶ φιλανθρώπῳ, ἐλέῳ καὶ οἴκτῳ περὶ ἡμᾶς χρήσασθαι. Καὶ ἐπιμένων τῇ τῆς παρανομίας κατηγορίᾳ (ἤκουσε γὰρ τοῦ Θεοῦ δι' ἑτέρου προφήτου λέγοντος· «Λέγε σὺ τὰς ἀνομίας σου πρῶτον, ἵνα δικαιωθῇς»), οἰκειοῦται τὴν τοῦ λαοῦ παρανομίαν, καὶ τὴν ταύτης ποιεῖται κατηγορίαν, τὸν θεῖον ἔλεον ἐπαγγέλλων.

ι'. «Ὅτι ἀπέστημεν, φησί, καὶ οὐκ εἰσηκούσαμεν τῆς φωνῆς Κυρίου τοῦ Θεοῦ ἡμῶν, πορεύεσθαι ἐν τοῖς νόμοις αὐτοῦ, οἷς ἔδωκε κατὰ πρόσωπον ἡμῶν ἐν χειρὶ τῶν δούλων αὐτοῦ τῶν προφητῶν.» Φωτιζόμενοι γάρ, φησίν, ὑπὸ τῶν προφητῶν, καὶ ποδηγούμενοι πρὸς τὸ δέον,

Then to bring out God's constant care for them and the people's great insensitivity, he went on, *We have not hearkened to your servants the prophets, who kept speaking in your name to our kings, to our rulers, to our fathers, and to the whole people of the land* (v. 6): your grace did not cease watching over us and speaking through the prophets, at one time to kings and rulers, at another to priests and teachers (referring to them as *fathers*), and on many occasions to the whole people. Yet even when this happened, we continued to contradict you.

Hence he was right to proceed, *With you, Lord, is righteousness, and with us shame | of countenance, as on this day, with a man* 1461 *of Judah, the inhabitants of Jerusalem and all Israel, near and far, in all the land where you scattered them because of the lawlessness they committed against you, Lord* (v. 7): what has been done by you, Lord, proclaims your righteousness, whereas we are ashamed of our great lawlessness and accuse our own ingratitude. While, in fact, no harm comes to you from our impiety, we reap the fruits of these seeds (spoken in pitiable fashion, because in accusing his fellows he also associates himself with the transgressors). *Shame of countenance affects us, our kings, our rulers, and our fathers in as far as we sinned against you* (v. 8). Any of these would suffice to move even the cruelest person to pity, not to mention the gentlest and most loving. He is showing in these words, you see, not only the lowly and insignificant members of the people to be affected by shame, but also the very kings, rulers, and priests, referring to them as *fathers*. And to bring out the justice of the retribution, he added *since we sinned against you*.

While we reaped fruit befitting our lawlessness, *to the Lord our God belong compassion and propitiation* (v. 9): it is proper to you in your gentleness and love to exercise mercy and compassion toward us. And persisting in the accusation of lawlessness (he heard God saying in another prophet, you see, "Tell your sins first so as to be justified"),²⁰³ he applies to himself the people's lawlessness and censures it, proclaiming divine mercy. *Because we were unfaithful and did not hearken to the voice of the Lord our God so as to walk by his laws which he brought to our notice through his servants the prophets* (v. 10): though enlightened by the prophets and guided in our duty, we kept resisting all the time.

²⁰³ Isa 43:26.

ἀντιλέγοντες πάντα τὸν χρόνον διετελέσαμεν.

ια΄. «Καὶ πᾶς Ἰσραὴλ παρέβησαν τὸν νόμον σου, καὶ ἐξέκλιναν τοῦ μὴ ἀκοῦσαι τῆς φωνῆς σου.» Εἰ γὰρ οἱ μὲν παρέβησαν, οἱ δὲ φύλακες ἀκριβεῖς τῶν σῶν νόμων ἐγένοντο, οὐκ ἂν τὴν συμφορὰν ὑπέμειναν ταύτην· ἐπειδὴ δὲ κοινὴ παρὰ πάντων ἡ παρανομία τετόλμηται, εἰκότως φησίν· «Ἐπῆλθεν ἐφ᾽ ἡμᾶς ἡ κατάρα, καὶ ὁ ὅρκος ὁ γεγραμμένος ἐν τῷ νόμῳ Μωσῆ δούλου τοῦ Θεοῦ, ὅτι ἡμάρτομεν αὐτῷ.» Ὅρκον δὲ καλεῖ τὸν ἐν τῷ Δευτερονομίῳ ὑπὸ τοῦ Θεοῦ γεγενημένον· «Ἀρῶ γὰρ, φησίν, εἰς τὸν οὐρανὸν τὴν χεῖρά μου, καὶ ὀμοῦμαι τῇ δεξιᾷ μου, καὶ | ἐρῶ· Ζῶ ἐγὼ εἰς τὸν αἰῶνα, ὅτι παροξυνῶ ὡς ἀστραπὴν τὴν μάχαιράν μου, καὶ ἀνθέξεται κρίματος ἡ χείρ μου, καὶ ἐκδικήσω, καὶ ἀνταποδώσω δίκην τοῖς ἐχθροῖς μου, καὶ τοῖς μισοῦσί με ἀνταποδώσω· μεθύσω τὰ βέλη μου ἀφ᾽ αἵματος, καὶ ἡ μάχαιρά μου φάγεται κρέα ἀφ᾽ αἵματος τραυματιῶν, καὶ αἰχμαλωσίας, ἀπὸ κεφαλῆς ἀρχόντων ἐθνῶν.» Καὶ μικρὸν πρὸ τούτων φησίν· «Εἶπον· Διασπερῶ αὐτούς, παύσω δὲ ἐξ ἀνθρώπων τὸ μνημόσυνον αὐτῶν.» Τὴν δὲ κατάραν, τὴν ὑπὸ τῶν ἓξ φυλῶν, τὴν ἐν τῷ ὄρει τῷ Γεβὰλ γεγενημένην λέγει. Ἐκεῖνος τοίνυν, φησίν, ὁ ὅρκος, καὶ ἡ κατάρα ἡ ἐν τῷ νόμῳ Μωσέως γεγενημένη, πέρας ἔλαβεν ἐφ᾽ ἡμῶν.

ιβ΄. «Καὶ ἔστησε τοὺς λόγους αὐτοῦ, οὓς ἐλάλησεν ἐφ᾽ ἡμᾶς, καὶ ἐπὶ τοὺς κριτὰς ἡμῶν, καὶ ὅσοι ἔκριναν ἡμᾶς, ἐπαγαγεῖν ἐφ᾽ ἡμᾶς κακὰ μεγάλα.» Καὶ δεικνὺς τὴν τῶν κακῶν ὑπερβολήν, «Οἶα, φησίν, οὐ γέγονεν ὑποκάτω παντὸς τοῦ οὐρανοῦ κατὰ τὰ γενόμενα ἐν Ἰερουσαλήμ.» Οὐ γὰρ εὑρίσκω, φησί, παράδειγμα τῶν ἡμετέρων κακῶν. Εἶτα διδάσκων τῆς θείας προρρήσεως τὸ ἀψευδές·

ιγ΄. «Καθώς, φησί, γέγραπται ἐν τῷ νόμῳ Μωσέως.» Καὶ τῆς τιμωρίας ἐμφαίνων τὸ δίκαιον, «Πάντα, φησί, τὰ κακὰ ἦλθεν ἐφ᾽ ἡμᾶς, καὶ οὐκ ἐδεήθημεν τοῦ προσώπου Κυρίου τοῦ Θεοῦ ἡμῶν, ἀποστρέψαι ἀπὸ τῶν ἀδικιῶν ἡμῶν, καὶ τοῦ συνιέναι ἐν πάσῃ ἀληθείᾳ σου, Κύριε.» Οὐδὲ γὰρ τῶν τοσούτων ἡμῖν καὶ τηλικούτων ἐπενεχθεισῶν συμφορῶν, μεταμελείᾳ χρήσασθαι ἠβουλήθημεν, καὶ παύσασθαι μὲν τῆς προτέρας παρανομίας, θεραπεῦσαι δέ σε τῇ φυλακῇ τῶν νόμων. Διό φησιν·

ιδ΄. «Ἐγρηγόρησε Κύριος ὁ Θεὸς ἡμῶν ἐπὶ τὴν κακίαν ἡμῶν, καὶ ἤγαγεν αὐτὴν ἐφ᾽ ἡμᾶς.» Ὥσπερ γάρ τινα ὕπνον τὴν μακροθυμίαν ἀποσεισάμενος, τὴν ἀξίαν τῶν πεπολιτευμένων ἡμῖν ἐπήγαγε τιμωρίαν· ὅτι Ἅγιος, φησί, Κύριος ὁ Θεὸς ἡμῶν ἐπὶ πᾶσαν τὴν ποίησιν αὐτοῦ ἣν ἐποίησε, διότι οὐκ εἰσηκούσαμεν τῆς φωνῆς αὐτοῦ. Αὐτὸς μὲν γάρ, φησίν, ἀθῶός ἐστι, καὶ οὐδεμιᾶς μέμψεως ἐφ᾽ οἷς ἐποίησεν ἄξιος· ἡμεῖς δὲ δυσσεβείᾳ καὶ πονηρίᾳ συζήσαντες τὴν τιμωρίαν ἐπεσπασάμεθα. Οὕτω

All Israel transgressed your law, and turned away from listen-
ing to your voice (v. 11): if some had transgressed while others
proved exact in observing your laws, they would not have suffered
this calamity; but since transgression was committed by everyone
in common, he was right to say, *The curse has come upon us, and*
the oath written in the law of God's servant Moses, because we have
sinned against him. By *oath* he refers to the one made in Deuteronomy by God, "I shall lift up my hand to heaven and swear by my
right hand, and say, | As I live forever, I shall whet my sword   1464
like a lightning flash, my hand will take hold of judgment, I shall
take vengeance on my foes and avenge myself on those who hate
me. I shall make my arrows drunk with blood, and my sword
will eat flesh from bloody wounds, from captivity and from the
head of princes of nations." And a little before this he said, "I
declared, I shall scatter them and cancel their memory from humankind."[204] By *curse* he means the one made by the six tribes on
Mount Ebal.[205] So he is saying, The oath and the curse contained
in the Law of Moses took effect with us.

He established his words that he spoke against us and against
our judges, and all of us they judged so as to bring on us awful troubles
(v. 12). And to bring out the great extent of the troubles, *What has*
not happened under the whole of heaven has happened in Jerusalem: I
find no parallel with our troubles. Then to bring out the reliability of the divine prophecy, *As is written in the law of Moses* (v. 13).
And to highlight the justice of the retribution, *All the troubles have*
come upon us, and we have not presented our case to the Lord our God
to turn away from our iniquities and to ponder all your truth, Lord:
despite so many awful calamities befalling us, we refused to have
recourse to repentance, put a stop to the former lawlessness, and
give attention to you by the observance of your laws. Hence he
says, *The Lord our God kept watch over our evil and brought it upon*
us (v. 14): just as though aroused from longsuffering as from some
sleep, he imposed on us retribution befitting our behavior. *The*
Lord our God is holy in doing all his doings, because we did not hear-
ken to his voice: whereas he is innocent and deserving of no blame
for what he has done, we drew punishment down upon ourselves

[204] Deut 32:40–42, 26.
[205] Cf. Deut 27:13. The ritual described in Deut 26:11–16, of blessing
and cursing on two mountains by two groups of six tribes, probably requires
further comment by Theodoret.

τῆς παρανομίας τὴν κατηγορίαν ποιησάμενος, ἱκετεύει λοιπὸν καὶ τὴν φιλανθρωπίαν αἰτεῖ.

ιε', ις'. «Καὶ νῦν, Κύριε ὁ Θεὸς ἡμῶν, ὃς ἐξήγαγες τὸν λαόν σου ἐκ γῆς Αἰγύπτου ἐν χειρὶ κραταιᾷ, καὶ ἐποίησας σεαυτῷ ὄνομα, ὡς ἡ ἡμέρα αὕτη, ἡμάρτομεν, ἠνομήσαμεν· Κύριε, ἐν πάσῃ ἐλεημοσύνῃ σου ἀποστραφήτω δὴ ὁ θυμός σου ἀπὸ τῆς πόλεώς σου Ἱερουσαλήμ, ὄρους ἁγίου σου.» Ἀναμιμνήσκει τῶν προτέρων εὐεργεσιῶν, τῇ εὐγνωμοσύνῃ
1465 | τῆς μνήμης τὸν ἔλεον ἐπισπώμενος, καί φησι· Ῥάδιόν σοι, Δέσποτα, τὴν ἐλευθερίαν ἡμῖν χαρίσασθαι· καὶ γὰρ ἤδη θαυματουργίαις μυρίαις, καὶ τιμωρίαις κατὰ τῶν Αἰγυπτίων χρησάμενος, τῆς πικρᾶς δουλείας ἐκείνης τὸν σὸν λαὸν ἠλευθέρωσας, ὡς εἰς ἅπαντας ἀνθρώπους τῶν γεγενημένων θαυμάτων τὴν φήμην δραμεῖν, καὶ τὴν σὴν δύναμιν ἅπασι γενέσθαι δήλην. Καὶ ἐπειδὴ ἡμεῖς ἡμάρτομεν, καὶ τῆς σῆς φιλανθρωπίας ἀναξίους ἡμᾶς αὐτοὺς ἀπεφήναμεν, τὴν σὴν πόλιν ἱκετεύομεν τῆς σῆς ἀξιωθῆναι φειδοῦς, καὶ τὸ ὄρος ἐκεῖνο, ὃ διὰ τῆς σῆς ἐπιφανείας ἅγιον ἀπέφηνας. Καὶ ἐπιμένων τῇ ὑπὲρ τῆς πόλεως ἱκετείᾳ, «Ὅτι ἐν ταῖς ἁμαρτίαις ἡμῶν, φησί, καὶ ταῖς ἀδικίαις ἡμῶν, καὶ τῶν πατέρων ἡμῶν, Ἱερουσαλὴμ καὶ ὁ λαός σου εἰς ὀνειδισμὸν ἐγένοντο ἐν πᾶσι τοῖς περικύκλῳ ἡμῶν.» Διὰ γὰρ τὰς ἡμετέρας παρανομίας, καὶ ἁμαρτίας τῶν πατέρων ἡμῶν, ἡμεῖς τε τοῖς ὁμόροις ἐπίχαρτοι γεγενήμεθα, καὶ ἡ πολυθρύλλητος καὶ ἀοίδιμος πόλις τὴν ἐρημίαν ὑπέμεινεν.

ιζ'. «Καὶ νῦν εἰσάκουσον, Κύριε ὁ Θεὸς ἡμῶν, τῆς προσευχῆς τοῦ δούλου σου, καὶ τῶν δεήσεων αὐτοῦ, καὶ ἐπίφανον τὸ πρόσωπόν σου ἐπὶ τὸ ἁγίασμά σου τὸ ἔρημον.» Δέξαι, φησί, τοῦ δούλου σου τὴν δέησιν, Δέσποτα, καὶ βλέπε τὴν ἐρήμωσιν τοῦ ἁγιασθέντος ὑπὸ σοῦ τόπου, καὶ τῆς σῆς αὐτὸν αὖθις πλήρωσον χάριτος. Καὶ ἐπειδὴ ἀνάξιος ἦν ὁ λαὸς τούτων τυχεῖν, σφόδρα ἁρμοδίως ἐπήγαγεν· «Ἕνεκέν σου, Κύριε.» Τὰ σαυτῷ, φησί, πρέποντα ποίησον, Δέσποτα, καὶ μὴ τὰς ἡμετέρας λογίσῃ παρανομίας, ἀλλὰ τὰς ἀεννάους τῆς σῆς φιλανθρωπίας πηγάς. Καὶ ἐπιμένων τῇ προσευχῇ·

ιη'. «Κλῖνον, φησίν, ὁ Θεός μου, τὸ οὖς σου, καὶ ἄκουσον· ἄνοιξον τοὺς ὀφθαλμούς σου, καὶ ἴδε τὸν ἀφανισμὸν ἡμῶν, καὶ τῆς πόλεώς σου.» Καὶ ἔτι πλεῖον προσοικειῶν αὐτῷ τὴν πόλιν ἔφη· «Ἐφ' ᾗ ἐπικέκληταί σου τὸ ὄνομα ἐν αὐτῇ.» Τὸ δέ, «Κλῖνον τὸ οὖς σου, καὶ ἄνοιξον τοὺς ὀφθαλμούς σου,» ἀντὶ τοῦ, Μὴ ἀποστραφῇς μου τὴν δέησιν, ἀλλὰ μετ' εὐμενείας ἄκουσόν μου τῆς προσευχῆς. Οἶδε γὰρ καὶ αὐτός, ὡς τὸ Θεῖον ἀσώματον, ἑτέρως δὲ ἄνθρωπος ὢν οὐκ οἶδε διαλεχθῆναι Θεῷ. Ἀλλ' ἐπειδὴ τῶν ἀνθρώπων ἕκαστος διὰ μὲν τῶν ὀφθαλμῶν ὁρᾷ, διὰ δὲ τῶν ὤτων ἀκούει, τέθεικε ταῦτα καὶ ἐπὶ τοῦ ἀσωμάτου Θεοῦ, τὰς

by living a life of impiety and wickedness.

Having thus delivered an accusation of their lawlessness, he now turns to supplication and begs for lovingkindness. *And now, Lord our God, who rescued your people from the land of Egypt with a mighty hand, and made your name renowned as to this day, we have sinned, we have done wrong. Lord, in all your mercy let your anger be turned away from the city of Jerusalem, your holy mountain* (vv. 15–16). He recalls the former benefits, | attracting mercy by 1465 the courtesy of recollection, meaning, It is easy for you, Lord, to grant us freedom: you have already been responsible for countless miracles and sanctions against the Egyptians, freeing your people from that harsh slavery, with the result that the report of the miracles worked has sped to all people and your power is obvious to all. Since we have sinned and rendered ourselves unworthy of your lovingkindness, we beg that your city be accorded your compassion, along with that mountain which you made holy by your coming. Continuing his supplication for the city, *Because through our sins and our iniquities and our fathers' Jerusalem and your people have become an object of ridicule among all our neighbors*: on account of our transgressions and our fathers' sins, we provided malicious joy to our neighbors, and the celebrated and famous city suffered devastation.

Hearken now, Lord our God, to the prayer of your servant and his request, and reveal your face to your devastated sanctuary (v. 17): accept the entreaty of your servant, Lord, and consider the devastation of the place sanctified by you, and once again fill it with your grace. And since the people were unworthy to receive this, it was very appropriate for him to add *for your sake, Lord*: do what befits you, Lord, and consider not our transgressions but the ever-flowing springs of your lovingkindness. Continuing the prayer, *Incline your ear, O my God, and hear; open your eyes and see our desolation and your city's* (v. 18). And to associate the city still more closely with him, he said, *which bears your name*. The phrase *Incline your ear and open your eyes* means, Do not turn away from my appeal: listen to my prayer with benevolence. He was aware, you see, that the divinity is incorporeal, but as a human being he did not know how to converse with God in any other way; since each person sees with his eyes and listens with his ears, he put it this way even in the case of the incorporeal God, referring by it to his actions.

ἐνεργείας οὕτω καλῶν. Τούτοις ἐπάγει· «Ὅτι οὐκ ἐν ταῖς δικαιοσύναις ἡμῶν ἡμεῖς ῥίπτομεν τὸν οἰκτιρμὸν ἡμῶν ἐνώπιόν σου, ἀλλ᾽ ἐπὶ τοὺς οἰκτιρμούς σου τοὺς πολλούς, Κύριε.» Οὐ γὰρ ταῖς δικαιοσύναις ἡμῶν, φησίν, θαρροῦντες τὴν σὴν αἰτοῦμεν φιλανθρωπίαν, ἀλλὰ τῷ σῷ πεποιθότες ἐλέῳ τολμῶμεν τὴν δέησιν.

ιθ΄. «Εἰσάκουσον οὖν, Κύριε, ἱλάσθητι, Κύριε, πρόσχες, Κύριε· μὴ χρονίσῃς ἕνεκέν σου, ὁ Θεός | μου.» Ἄξιον δὲ θαυμάσαι τῶν εἰρημένων τὴν τάξιν. Ἱκετεύει γὰρ τὸν Θεόν, πρῶτον μὲν ἀκοῦσαι τῆς προσευχῆς, καὶ μὴ ἀπώσασθαι τὴν ἱκετηρίαν· εἶτα ἀκούσαντα ἵλεων γενέσθαι, ἵλεων δὲ γενόμενον *προσέχειν* εὐμενῶς, δείξαντα δὲ τὴν οἰκείαν εὐμένειαν ποιῆσαι καὶ πληρῶσαι τὴν ἱκετείαν. Τούτοις ἐπήγαγε· *Μὴ χρονίσῃς,* ἀντὶ τοῦ, Μὴ ἀναβάλῃ τὴν δέησιν εἰς ἕτερον χρόνον, ἀλλ᾽ αὐτίκα τῆς ἐπιφανείας ἡμᾶς ἀξίωσον. Καὶ τῆς εὐχῆς δὲ τὸ τέλος τῆς τοῦ Δανιὴλ ταπεινοφροσύνης ἄξιον. «Ἕνεκέν σου, φησίν, ὁ Θεός μου.» Οὐδὲ γὰρ ἐγώ, φησίν, ἄξιος τοῦ ταύτην λαβεῖν τὴν χάριν· ἀλλ᾽ «Ὅτι τὸ ὄνομά σου ἐπικέκληται ἐπὶ τὴν πόλιν σου, καὶ ἐπὶ τὸν λαόν σου.» Οὕτως αἰτήσας, καὶ μετὰ τοσαύτης προθυμίας τὴν ὑπὲρ τῶν ὁμοφύλων ἱκετηρίαν προσενεγκών, καὶ ἀντιβολήσας μὴ χρονίσαι τὸν Θεόν, παραυτίκα τῆς θείας ἀποκρίσεως ἀπολαύει.

κ΄. «Ἔτι γάρ μου, φησί, λαλοῦντος, καὶ προσευχομένου, καὶ ἐξαγορεύοντος τὰς ἀνομίας μου, καὶ τὰς ἁμαρτίας τοῦ λαοῦ Ἰσραὴλ, καὶ ῥιπτοῦντος τὸν ἔλεόν μου ἐναντίον Κυρίου τοῦ Θεοῦ μου. Καὶ ἔτι μου λαλοῦντος ἐν τῇ προσευχῇ, καὶ ἰδοὺ ἀνὴρ Γαβριὴλ, ὃν εἶδον ἐν τῇ ὁράσει μου ἐν ἀρχῇ, πετόμενος.» Ταύτην, φησί, τὴν ἱκετείαν προσφέρων, καὶ τῆς κοινῆς ἡμῶν παρανομίας κατηγορῶν, μηδέπω πέρας ἐπιθεὶς τῇ προσευχῇ, ὁρῶ τὸν Γαβριὴλ πετόμενον, καὶ πρὸς ἐμὲ θέοντα· ἔγνων δὲ τίς ἐστιν, ἤδη πρότερον ὄναρ αὐτὸν θεασάμενος· καὶ τὴν προσηγορίαν δὲ αὐτοῦ ἔμαθον, ἀκούσας τηνικαῦτα τοῦ Δεσπότου καλέσαντος, καὶ προστάξαντος· Γαβριήλ, συνέτισον ἐκεῖνον τὴν ὅρασιν. Ἄνδρα δὲ αὐτὸν κέκληκεν ἀπὸ τῆς θέας τὴν προσηγορίαν τεθεικώς. Καὶ γὰρ ἐν ἐκείνῳ τῷ ἐνυπνίῳ φησίν· «Ἰδοὺ ἔστη ἐνώπιόν μου ὡς ὅρασις ἀνδρός.» Οὗ χάριν καὶ ἐνταῦθά φησιν· «Ἰδοὺ ὁ ἀνὴρ Γαβριήλ, ὃν εἶδον ἐν τῇ ὁράσει μου ἐν ἀρχῇ, πετόμενος.» *Πετᾶσθαι* δὲ καὶ αὐτὸν ἔφη ὀξέως διατέμνοντα τὸν ἀέρα, καὶ παρ᾽ αὐτὸν θέοντα θεασάμενος. «Καὶ ἥψατό μου ὡσεὶ ὥραν θυσίας ἑσπερινῆς.» Ἀντὶ τοῦ, κατὰ τὸν καιρὸν τῆς ἑσπερινῆς λατρείας, ἢ τοσοῦτον καιρόν, ὅσον ἡ ἑσπερινὴ κατέχει λατρεία.

He went on from here, *We do not direct our appeal for compassion in your sight on the basis of our righteous actions, but on your great compassion, Lord*: we do not beg your lovingkindness by relying on our righteous actions; rather, we presume to pray with trust in your mercy. *So hearken, Lord, be propitious, Lord, attend, Lord, for your sake, O my God, do not delay* (v. 19). It is worth admiring the sequence of what is said: | he implores God, first, to hear 1468 his prayer and not to reject his appeal; then, on hearing him, to be propitious; and on being propitious, to give heed with benevolence; and on showing his characteristic benevolence, to carry out and fulfill the request. To this he added, *Do not delay*, that is, Do not put off the request any longer, but immediately grant us your coming. The end of the prayer is in keeping with Daniel's humility, *For your own sake, O my God*: I am not worthy to receive this grace, but *because your city and your people are called by your name*.

Having thus made the request, offered the appeal for his fellows with such enthusiasm, and entreated God not to delay, he immediately receives the divine reply. *While I was still speaking, praying, confessing my iniquities and the sins of the people of Israel, and directing my appeal for compassion in the sight of the Lord my God—while I was still speaking in my prayer, lo, a man, Gabriel, whom I had seen in my vision in the beginning, came in flight* (vv. 20–21): while offering this appeal, criticizing our common lawlessness, and before having brought the prayer to a close, I saw Gabriel in flight hastening toward me. I knew who he was, having already seen him before in a dream, and I had learned his name, having heard it when the Lord called it and gave orders, "Gabriel, make him understand the vision."[206] Now, he spoke of him as *a man*, using the word he had derived from the vision: in that dream it was said, "Lo, there stood before me something looking like a man"; hence he says here *Lo, a man, Gabriel, whom I had seen in my vision in the beginning, came in flight*. He said he *came in flight* since he moved through the air at speed and hurried toward him. *He touched me as if at the hour of evening sacrifice*, that is, at the time of evening worship, or for as long a time as evening worship took.

[206] Theodoret is less concerned to account for the ragged edge of the insertion than to avoid any contradiction a reader might sense in Daniel's recognizing Gabriel and knowing his name. So he refers such a reader back to 8:16, where however it is felt Gabriel has been unnecessarily introduced when in the previous verse the figure had been called a human figure.

κβ', κγ'. «Καὶ ἐλάλησε μετ' ἐμοῦ, καὶ εἶπε· Δανιήλ, νῦν ἐξῆλθον συμβιβάσαι σε σύνεσιν. Ἐν ἀρχῇ τῆς δεήσεώς σου ἐξῆλθεν ὁ λόγος, καὶ ἐγὼ ἦλθον τοῦ ἀναγγεῖλαί σοι, ὅτι ἀνὴρ ἐπιθυμιῶν σὺ εἶ· καὶ ἐννοήθητι ἐν τῷ ῥήματι, καὶ σύνες ἐν τῇ ὀπτασίᾳ.» Εὐθύς, φησίν, ἡνίκα ἤρξω προσεύχεσθαι, δεξάμενος ὁ κοινὸς Δεσπότης τὴν ἱκετείαν, καὶ θεασάμενός σου τὴν ἀγαθὴν ἐπιθυμίαν, ἀπέστειλέ με διδάξαι σε τὰ ἐσόμενα. Σὺ δὲ ἀκριβῶς πρόσεχε τοῖς λεγομένοις· βαθύτερα γὰρ ἢ κατὰ ἄνθρωπον τὰ λεχθησόμενα. Τοῦτο γὰρ λέγει· Σύνες ἐν τῇ ὀπτασίᾳ· τουτέστιν, | αἰνιγματωδῶς ταῦτα λεχθήσεται, καὶ δεῖ σοι κατανοήσεως ἀκριβοῦς εἰς τὸ νοῆσαι ταῦτα. Αἰνιγματωδῶς δέ ἐστιν ὅτε τὰ θεῖα λέγεται καὶ γράφεται, ἵνα μὴ πᾶσιν ᾖ δῆλα τὰ τοῖς ἁγίοις ἀποκαλυπτόμενα· οὕτω γὰρ ἂν εὐκαταφρόνητα ἐγεγόνει ὁμοίως ὑπὸ πάντων γνωριζόμενα. Ἄνδρα δὲ αὐτὸν ἐπιθυμιῶν καλεῖ, ἢ ὡς νηστείᾳ καὶ κακουχίᾳ ἑαυτὸν ἐκδεδωκότα, καὶ ἀνδρείως κατὰ τῶν τοῦ σώματος ἐπιθυμιῶν ἀγωνιζόμενον, ἢ ὡς ἐπιθυμοῦντα γνῶναι, καὶ μαθεῖν ἐφιέμενον τὰ τῷ λαῷ συμβησόμενα, ἢ ὅτι ἐράσμιός ἐστι καὶ λίαν ἐπέραστος, τὰς τῆς ἀρετῆς μαρμαρυγὰς ἀφιείς. Οὕτω διεγείρας τὸν προφήτην ὁ θεῖος ἀρχάγγελος εἰς τὴν τῶν ῥηθησομένων κατανόησιν, τὴν διδασκαλίαν προσφέρει.

κδ'. «Ἑβδομήκοντα ἑβδομάδες συνετμήθησαν ἐπὶ τὸν λαόν σου, καὶ ἐπὶ τὴν πόλιν τὴν ἁγίαν σου, ἕως τοῦ παλαιωθῆναι τὸ παράπτωμα, καὶ τοῦ τελεσθῆναι ἁμαρτίαν, καὶ τοῦ σφραγίσαι ἁμαρτίαν, καὶ ἀπαλεῖψαι τὰς ἀνομίας, καὶ τοῦ ἐξιλάσασθαι ἀδικίαν, καὶ τοῦ ἀγαγεῖν δικαιοσύνην αἰώνιον, καὶ τοῦ σφραγίσαι ὅρασιν καὶ προφήτην, καὶ τοῦ χρῖσαι Ἅγιον ἁγίων.» Πρὸ τῶν ἄλλων ἁπάντων ἐπισημήνασθαι δεῖ, ὅτι τοῦ προφήτου ἐν τῇ προσευχῇ τῷ Θεῷ λέγοντος περί τε τοῦ λαοῦ καὶ τῆς Ἱερουσαλήμ· «Ὁ λαός σου, καὶ ἡ πόλις σου, καὶ τὸ ἅγιόν σου.» Ἀντιστρέφων ὁ Θεὸς λέγει τῷ Δανιήλ· «Ἑβδομήκοντα ἑβδομάδες συνετμήθησαν ἐπὶ τὸν λαόν σου, καὶ ἐπὶ τὴν πόλιν τὴν ἁγίαν σου·» ὥσπερ οὐκ ἀξιῶν τὸν λαὸν ἑαυτοῦ καλεῖν τὸν πάλαι αὐτοῦ ὠνομασμένον λαόν, οὔτε μὴν τὴν πόλιν τὴν ὡσαύτως αὐτοῦ πάλαι προσαγορευομένην. Τοῦτο δὲ καὶ ἐπὶ τοῦ μεγάλου πεποίηκε Μωσέως. Ἡνίκα γὰρ τὸν μόσχον τεκτηνάμενοι τὸ θεῖον αὐτῷ προσήνεγκαν σέβας, ἔφη πρὸς τὸν προφήτην ὁ Θεός· «Σπεῦσον, κατάβηθι τὸ τάχος ἐντεῦθεν· ἠνόμησε γὰρ ὁ λαός σου, οὓς ἐξήγαγες ἐξ Αἰγύπτου.» Φησὶ τοίνυν ὁ Θεὸς αὐτὸν διὰ τοῦ ἀρχαγγέλου, ὅτι τὴν δέησίν σου δεξάμενος, καὶ οἰκοδομηθῆναι τὴν Ἱερουσαλὴμ συγχωρήσω, καὶ τὸν λαόν σου τῆς ἐπανόδου τυχεῖν κελεύσω. Μετὰ δὲ

He spoke to me thus, Daniel, I have come at this time to impart understanding to you. At the beginning of your prayer a statement was issued, and I have come to tell you that you are a man of desires. Consider what is in the word and understand what is in the vision (vv. 22–23): as soon as you began to pray, the Lord of all accepted your supplication, perceived your laudable desire, and sent me to convey the future to you. For your part, give precise attention to what is said; what will be said is too profound for a human being (the meaning of *understand what is in the vision*), that is, what will be said is in riddles, | and requires of you precise attention for grasp- 1469 ing it. Now, riddles occur when divine realities are spoken and written, the purpose being to prevent what is revealed to the holy ones becoming clear to everyone; after all, familiarity breeds contempt. He refers to him as *a man of desires* in the sense either as one given to fasting and hardship in a noble struggle against the desires of the flesh, or as one desiring to know and longing to discover what would happen to the people, or because he is beloved and very desirable in emitting flashes of virtue.[207]

Having thus stimulated the prophet to a grasp of what would be said, he offers the instruction. *Seventy weeks have been determined for your people and for your holy city for the fault to grow old, the sin to be finished, the sin to be sealed, the iniquities to be wiped out, the wrong to be forgiven, to introduce eternal righteousness, to seal vision and prophet, and to anoint the holy of holies* (v. 24). It should be noted before everything else that the prophet in his prayer to God said of the people and Jerusalem *your people, your city, your sanctuary.* In reply God says to Daniel, *Seventy weeks have been determined for your people and for your holy city,* as though not according the name "his people" to the people formerly called "his," nor indeed the city likewise formerly named as "his." He did this also in the case of the great Moses: when they acquired the calf and paid it divine reverence, God said to the prophet, "Hurry, descend from here quickly, your people whom you led out of Egypt have sinned."[208] Accordingly God tells him through the archangel, I have accepted your request, and I shall allow Jerusalem to be rebuilt and bid your people to be granted re-

[207] This term becomes a sobriquet for "Daniel" (cf. 10:11, 23), Theodoret using it in his preface to his Psalms commentary, as also in the preface to this work.
[208] Exod 32:7.

τὴν τῆς Ἱερουσαλὴμ οἰκοδομίαν, διαρκέσουσιν ἐπὶ τετρακόσια καὶ ἐννενήκοντα ἔτη κατὰ νόμον πολιτευόμενοι· τοσοῦτον γὰρ αἱ ἑβδομήκοντα ἑβδομάδες ποιοῦσι χρόνον, ἡμέρας ἑκάστης εἰς ἐνιαυτὸν λαμβανομένης. Ἐπειδὴ γὰρ ἑβδομηκονταέτει χρόνῳ τὴν αἰχμαλωσίαν αὐτῶν περιώρισεν, ἑπτάκις εἰς ἑαυτὸν τοῦτον ἀνελίξας τὸν χρόνον τὴν κατὰ νόμον πολιτείαν περιορίζει. «Ἑβδομήκοντα ἑβδομάδες συνετμήθησαν,» ἀντὶ τοῦ, ἐδοκιμάσθησαν, καὶ ἐκρίθησαν· οὕτω γάρ τινες τῶν ἑρμηνευτῶν ἐκ-

1472 δεδώκασιν· «ἐπὶ τὸν λαόν σου, καὶ ἐπὶ τὴν πόλιν | σου τὴν ἁγίαν, ἕως τοῦ παλαιωθῆναι τὸ παράπτωμα, καὶ τοῦ τελεσθῆναι ἁμαρτίαν·» ἀντὶ τοῦ, ἕως ἂν αὐξηθῇ αὐτῶν τὸ δυσσεβὲς τόλμημα, καὶ τέλος λάβῃ ἡ ἁμαρτία. Λέγει δὲ ἁμαρτίαν τελειουμένην, καὶ παράπτωμα παλαιούμενον, εἴτ᾽ οὖν αὐξανόμενον, καὶ εἰς ἔσχατον ἀφικνούμενον, τὸν κατὰ τοῦ Κυρίου τολμηθέντα σταυρόν. Πρὸ μὲν γὰρ τούτου μυρία τετολμηκότες κακὰ ἔδοσαν μὲν δίκας, καὶ ἔτισαν τιμωρίας ὑπὲρ ὧν ἐπλημμέλησαν, ἀλλὰ πάλιν συγγνώμης ἀπολαύσαντες φιλανθρωπίας ἠξιώθησαν· μετὰ δὲ τὴν κατὰ τοῦ Δεσπότου μανίαν, καὶ τὸν τολμηθέντα σταυρόν, οὐδεμιᾶς ἔτυχον ἀνακλήσεως, ὡς αὐτὰ βοᾷ τὰ πράγματα· ἀλλὰ πλειόνων ἢ τεσσαράκοντα καὶ τετρακοσίων διαδραμόντων ἐτῶν σποράδες μεμενήκασι, καὶ τῆς οἰκουμένης μέτοικοι. Διὰ τοῦτό φησι τῷ μακαρίῳ Δανιὴλ ὁ ἅγιος ἀρχάγγελος· «Ἑβδομήκοντα ἑβδομάδες συνετμήθησαν ἐπὶ τὸν λαόν σου, καὶ ἐπὶ τὴν πόλιν τὴν ἁγίαν σου, ἕως τοῦ παλαιωθῆναι τὸ παράπτωμα, καὶ τοῦ τελεσθῆναι ἁμαρτίαν.» Καὶ ἐπειδὴ ἔμελλεν ὁ Δεσπότης Χριστὸς τοῖς εἰς αὐτὸν πιστεύουσι τῶν ἁμαρτημάτων δωρεῖσθαι τὴν ἄφεσιν, ὡς καὶ ὁ μακάριος Ἰωάννης ἐβόα, λέγων· «Ἴδε ὁ ἀμνὸς τοῦ Θεοῦ ὁ αἴρων τὴν ἁμαρτίαν τοῦ κόσμου,» εἰκότως ἐπήγαγε· «Καὶ τοῦ σφραγίσαι ἁμαρτίας, καὶ τοῦ ἀπαλεῖψαι ἀνομίας, καὶ τοῦ ἐξιλάσασθαι ἀδικίας.» Ἀπήλειψε μὲν γὰρ τὰς ἀνομίας τῶν εἰς αὐτὸν πεπιστευκότων, ἐξαλείψας τὸ καθ᾽ ἡμῶν χειρόγραφον, ᾗ φησιν ὁ μακάριος Παῦλος. Ἐσφράγισε δὲ τὰς ἁμαρτίας, παύσας μὲν τὴν κατὰ νόμον πολιτείαν, τὴν δὲ τοῦ Πνεύμα-

turn; but after the rebuilding of Jerusalem a further 490 years of living according to the law will be required. This, you see, is the extent of the *seventy weeks*, each day being taken as a year: since he had set a period of seventy years for their captivity, he set the period of living according to the law by multiplying that period by seven, saying *Seventy weeks have been determined*—that is, thought fit and decided (the version of some translators)[209]—*for your people and for your holy city | for the fault to grow old and the sin to be*   1472 *finished*—that is, for the impious crime to reach its peak and the sin to come to an end.

Now, he speaks of *sin finishing* and *fault growing old*, or reaching its peak and going to extremes, in reference to the crime of crucifixion of the Lord: before this they paid the penalty for committing countless crimes and were called to account for what they were guilty of, but in turn they were vouchsafed lovingkindness and enjoyed pardon. After their frenzy against the Lord and the crime of crucifixion, however, they were granted no recall, as the events themselves bruit abroad; instead, after the passage of more than 440 years they have continued to be the world's vagrants and migrants.[210] This is the reason the holy archangel says to blessed Daniel, *Seventy weeks have been determined for your people and your holy city for the fault to grow old and the sin finished.* Since Christ the Lord would grant the forgiveness of sins to those believing in him, as blessed John also cried aloud in the words, "Behold the lamb of God who takes away the sin the world,"[211] logically he proceeded, *for the sin to be sealed, the iniquities wiped out and the wrong forgiven.* In fact, he wiped out the iniquities of those believing in him by canceling the bill against us of which blessed Paul speaks.[212] He sealed the sins by bringing to an end the way of life

---

[209] Namely, the LXX in the latter case, χρίνειν the verb in question.

[210] Again, Theodoret would like the numbers to add up instead of being taken symbolically. His own figure of 440 years of these misfortunes could, in fact, be taken to suggest he is composing this work in the 440s, but a date a decade earlier is more likely. On the other hand, 440 years is the length of time from Jeremiah's prophecy of "seventy years" in 605 to the height of persecution by Antiochus IV, but this was no more likely to have been in Theodoret's mind (although he may have been aware of it as an alternative view).

[211] John 1:29. The battery of New Testament texts assembled here suggests the commentator is drawing on a well-rehearsed and well-documented treatise on Jesus as the fulfillment of Old Testament prophecy.

[212] Cf. Col 2:14.

τος δωρησάμενος χάριν, ὑφ' ἧς βοηθούμενοι περιγίνονται τῶν παθῶν οἱ πνευματικῶς πολιτευόμενοι. Οἷς προστέθεικε· «Καὶ τοῦ ἀγαγεῖν δικαιοσύνην αἰώνιον.» Δικαιοσύνη δὲ αἰώνιος κυρίως ἐστὶν αὐτὸς ὁ Δεσπότης Χριστός. Περὶ γὰρ αὐτοῦ φησιν ὁ μακάριος Παῦλος· «Ἐδόθη ἡμῖν σοφία ἀπὸ Θεοῦ, δικαιοσύνη τε καὶ ἁγιασμός, καὶ ἀπολύτρωσις.» Καὶ περὶ τοῦ Εὐαγγελίου δὲ Ῥωμαίοις ἐπιστέλλων ἔφη, ὅτι «Δικαιοσύνη Θεοῦ ἐν αὐτῷ ἀποκαλύπτεται.» Ἐπειδὴ δὲ φιλοτιμίᾳ χρησάμενος, καὶ τὴν πρόξενον τῆς αἰωνίου ζωῆς δικαιοσύνην τοῖς εἰς αὐτὸν πεπιστευκόσιν ἐχαρίσατο, ἣν καὶ αἰτεῖν προσευχομένοις παρεκελεύσατο· «Αἰτεῖτε, λέγων, τὴν βασιλείαν τοῦ Θεοῦ, καὶ τὴν δικαιοσύνην αὐτοῦ·» ἀναγκαίως εἶπεν ὁ ἅγιος Γαβριήλ· «Καὶ τοῦ ἀγαγεῖν δικαιοσύνην αἰώνιον.» Προστέθεικε δέ· «Καὶ τοῦ σφραγίσαι ὅρασιν καὶ προφήτην·» τουτέστι, τοῦ δοῦναι μὲν τέλος ἁπάσαις ταῖς προφητείαις· «Τέλος γὰρ νόμου Χριστὸς εἰς δικαιοσύνην παντὶ τῷ πιστεύοντι·» παῦσαι δὲ λοιπὸν τὴν προφητικὴν χάριν ἀπὸ τοῦ Ἰουδαίων ἔθνους. Εἰ γὰρ μὴ ἐπιφανεὶς ὁ Δεσπότης Χριστὸς πεποίηκέ τε καὶ πέπονθεν, ἅπερ οἱ προφῆται προεῖπον, οὐκ ἂν 1473 ἐδεί|χθη τῶν προφητῶν ἡ ἀλήθεια. Πληροῖ τοίνυν, καὶ οἱονεὶ σφραγίζει καὶ βεβαῖοι τὰ ὑπὸ τῶν προφητῶν προρρηθέντα, ποιῶν ἅπαντα καὶ πάσχων τὰ ὑπ' ἐκείνων χρησμῳδηθέντα. Τούτοις πάλιν προστέθεικε· «Καὶ τοῦ χρῖσαι Ἅγιον ἁγίων.» Τίς δὲ οὗτός ἐστιν ὁ τῶν ἁγίων Ἅγιος; εἰπάτωσαν Ἰουδαῖοι· εἰ δὲ ἀγνοοῦσι, παρ' ἡμῶν μαθέτωσαν, ὡς αὐτός ἐστιν ὁ Δεσπότης Χριστός, διὰ μὲν Ἡσαΐου προλέγων· «Πνεῦμα Κυρίου ἐπ' ἐμέ, οὗ εἵνεκεν ἔχρισέ με Κύριος.» Ὑπὸ δὲ τοῦ Δαβὶδ μαρτυρούμενος, ὅτι «Ἠγάπησε δικαιοσύνην, καὶ ἐμίσησεν ἀνομίαν, καὶ διὰ τοῦτο ἐχρίσθη ἐλαίῳ ἀγαλλιάσεως παρὰ τοὺς μετόχους αὐτοῦ.» Μαρτυρεῖ δὲ καὶ ὁ μακάριος Πέτρος, τῶν ἀποστόλων ὁ κορυφαῖος, λέγων· «Ἰησοῦν τὸν ἀπὸ Ναζαρέτ, ὡς ἔχρισεν αὐτὸν ὁ Θεὸς Πνεύματι ἁγίῳ καὶ δυνάμει, ὃς διῆλθεν εὐεργετῶν, καὶ ἰώμενος πάντας τοὺς καταδυναστευομένους ὑπὸ τοῦ διαβόλου, ὅτι ὁ Θεὸς ἦν μετ' αὐτοῦ.» Διδάσκεται τοίνυν ὁ μακάριος

according to the law, on the one hand, and on the other by granting the grace of the Spirit, with the help of which those living a spiritual way of life prevail over the passions.

Further to this, *and to introduce eternal righteousness*. Now, Christ the Lord is properly *eternal righteousness* in person: of him blessed Paul says, "Wisdom has been given us from God, righteousness and sanctification and redemption;" and in writing to the Romans he said of the gospel, "God's righteousness is revealed in it."[213] And since in a display of generosity he granted righteousness as the source of eternal life to those believing in him, and bade them ask for it in prayer, "Ask for the kingdom of God and his righteousness,"[214] consequently the holy Gabriel said, *for introducing eternal righteousness*. He went on, *for sealing vision and prophet*, that is, for bringing to fulfillment all prophecies, "Christ being the end of the law to the justification of every believer,"[215] and from now on withdrawing the charism of inspiration on the part of the nation of the Jews. After all, if Christ the Lord had not come, worked and suffered, the truth of the prophets would not have been demonstrated; | so he fulfills, and as it were *seals* and   1473 confirms, what was foretold by the prophets, doing and suffering everything foretold by them. He continues further in this vein, *and for anointing the holy of holies*. Now, what is this *holy of holies*? Let Jews tell us; but if they do not know, let them learn from us that it is Christ the Lord, who foretells in Isaiah, "The Spirit of the Lord is upon me, hence the Lord anointed me." Testimony is given to him by David to the effect that "he loved righteousness and hated iniquity, and hence he was anointed with the oil of gladness above his fellows."[216] Blessed Peter, head of the apostles, also gives testimony in the words, "Jesus of Nazareth, whom God anointed with the Holy Spirit and with power, and who went about doing good and healing all those under the power of the devil, because God was with him."[217]

---

[213] 1 Cor 1:30; Rom 1:17.

[214] Matt 6:33.

[215] Rom 10:4.

[216] Isa 61:1, cited in Luke 4:18; Ps 45:7. In Di Lella's view ("Daniel," 418), the anointing of a holy of holies almost certainly refers to the consecration by Judas Maccabeus of the restored holy of holies in the Jerusalem temple.

[217] Acts 10:38.

Δανιήλ ὁ προφήτης, ὅτι τετρακοσίων καὶ ἐννενήκοντα ἐτῶν χρόνον ἔδοξε παρασχεθῆναι τῇ Ἱερουσαλὴμ εἰς τὸ τῶν θείων συνήθως δωρεῶν ἀπολαύειν, ἕως ἂν ἐκεῖνο τὸ ἀνόσιον καὶ φρικῶδες τολμήσῃ τόλμημα, τὸν κατὰ τοῦ Σωτῆρός φημι σταυρόν, ὃς Ἅγιος ἁγίων ὀνομαζόμενος, ἅτε δὴ ἁγιωσύνης ὑπάρχων πηγή, χρίεται μὲν κατὰ τὸ ἀνθρώπειον τῷ ἁγίῳ Πνεύματι, σφραγίζει δὲ καὶ βεβαιοῖ τὰς παλαιὰς προφητείας, πληρῶν ἅπαντα τὰ ὑπ' ἐκείνων προηγορευμένα, ἄφεσιν δὲ ἁμαρτημάτων τοῖς εἰς αὐτὸν πεπιστευκόσι χαρίζεται. Εἶτα διδάσκει ὁ θεῖος ἀρχάγγελος, πόθεν ἄρξασθαι δεῖ τοῦ τῶν ἑβδομήκοντα ἑβδομάδων ἀριθμοῦ.

κε'. «Καὶ γνώσῃ, φησί, καὶ συνήσεις, ἀπὸ ἐξόδου λόγων τοῦ ἀποκριθῆναι, καὶ τοῦ οἰκοδομηθῆναι Ἱερουσαλήμ, ἕως Χριστοῦ ἡγουμένου, ἑβδομάδες ἑπτὰ καὶ ἑβδομάδες ἑξήκοντα δύο.» Τινὲς μὲν οὖν ὑπολαμβάνουσι τὴν ἐπὶ Κύρου γενομένην τῆς οἰκοδομίας ἀρχήν, ἀρχὴν εἶναι τοῦ τῶν ἑβδομάδων ἀριθμοῦ, τινὲς δὲ ἀπὸ ἕκτου ἔτους τῆς βασιλείας Δαρείου τοῦ Ὑστάσπου τοῦ ἀριθμοῦ ἄρχονται· τηνικαῦτα γὰρ τοῦ ναοῦ ἡ οἰκοδομὴ τέλος ἔλαβε τὸ προσῆκον, τῶν περιοίκων διὰ τὴν πρὸς Ἰουδαίους δυσμένειαν ἐμποδὼν τῇ οἰκοδομίᾳ ἐν τῷ μέσῳ χρόνῳ γεγενημένων, καὶ Καμβύσου δὲ τοῦ Κύρου υἱέως ὑπὸ τούτων ἐξαπατηθέντος καὶ τὴν οἰκοδομίαν κωλύσαντος. Ἀλλ' οὐδὲν τούτων ἔχει τὸ ἀληθές. Πρῶτον μὲν γὰρ πλειόνων ἐτῶν ἀριθμός, εἴ τις ἐντεῦθεν ἀριθμῆσαι θελήσειεν, εὑρεθήσεται· ἔπειτα οὐκ ἔστιν εὑρεῖν ἐπ' ἄλλου ἐξάλειψιν ἁμαρτημάτων γεγενημένην, καὶ ἄφεσιν ἀδικημάτων, καὶ δικαιοσύνης αἰωνίου δόσιν, καὶ πλήρωσιν τῶν προφητικῶν θεσπισμάτων, καὶ Ἁγίου ἁγίων χρίσιν, ἢ ἐπὶ μόνου τοῦ Δεσπότου Χριστοῦ. Εἰ δ' οὕτως ταῦτα ἔχει, καὶ συνομολογοῦσιν οἱ τὸν ἀριθμὸν τῶν ἑβδομάδων οὕτω ποιεῖσθαι κελεύοντες, κάτωθεν ἄνω τὰ τετρακόσια καὶ ἐννενήκοντα ἀριθμήτωσαν ἔτη. Εἰ γὰρ ἀπὸ τῆς ἐπιφανείας τῆς παρὰ τὸν Ἰορδάνην γεγενημένης, ὁπηνίκα τοῦ κηρύττειν τε καὶ διδάσκειν καὶ θαυματουργεῖν ὁ Σωτὴρ καὶ Κύριος ἡμῶν ἤρξατο, ἀρξάμενοι τοῦ ἀριθμεῖν ἐπὶ τὰ ἄνω χωρήσαιμεν, οὐ μόνον οὐ μέχρι Κύρου, ἀλλ' οὐδὲ ἕως Δαρείου τοῦτον εὑρήσομεν φθάνοντα τὸν

Blessed Daniel the prophet, accordingly, teaches that God decided that a period of 490 years should be allotted to Jerusalem to enjoy divine gifts as usual until it committed that sacrilegious and fearsome crime[218]—I mean, the crucifixion of the Savior, who is known as holy of holies for his being the fount of holiness, and who is anointed in his humanity by the Holy Spirit, and seals and confirms the ancient prophecies by fulfilling everything foretold by them, and grants forgiveness of sins to those who believe in him.

The divine archangel then explains at what point calculation of the seventy weeks should begin. *You will know and understand, from the issuing of the words about response and building of Jerusalem until an anointed leader, seven weeks and sixty-two weeks* (v. 25). Some commentators, then, suppose that the beginning of rebuilding that happened under Cyrus is the beginning of the number of weeks. Others, however, begin the count from the sixth year of the reign of Darius son of Hystaspes when the rebuilding of the temple came to its due end with the raising of obstacles to rebuilding halfway through by neighboring peoples on account of hostility to Jews, Cambyses son of Cyrus being hoodwinked by them and forbidding the rebuilding.[219] But neither of these is true: firstly, a greater number of years would be arrived at if you wanted to count from that point; next, it is not possible to find a cancellation of sins occurring in the case of anyone else, or forgiveness of wrongs, gift of eternal righteousness, fulfillment of prophetic oracles or anointing of a holy of holies other than Christ the Lord. | 1476

If this is so, however, and those who want the number of weeks to be calculated that way are in agreement, let the 490 years be calculated in reverse. You see, if we were to begin counting from the appearance of our Lord and Savior at the Jordan when he commenced preaching and teaching and wonder-working, and go backwards, we would find the number fails to reach Darius, let

---

[218] So the 490 years, in Theodoret's calculation, is from the rebuilding of Jerusalem (he claimed above) to the crucifixion—a period of grace until its termination with that terrible event. It is a plausible, if gratuitous and probably not original, interpretation—if the number is to be taken in terms of ἱστορία, not symbol, and the genre of apocalyptic not to be respected.

[219] Trying to make sense of the number of years accepted as factual, Theodoret here disqualifies the views of both Julius Africanus (Guinot, *L'Exégèse*, 720) and Eusebius, his frequent source for accessing predecessors.

ἀριθμόν, ἀλλὰ τῷ εἰκοστῷ ἔτει τῆς Ἀρταξέρξου τοῦ Ξέρξου βασιλείας συμπληρούμενον, καθ᾽ ὃν καιρὸν ὁ Νεεμίας, οἰνοχόος ὢν τοῦδε τοῦ βασιλέως, ζῆλον λαβών, καὶ τὸν Θεὸν ἀντιβολήσας, καὶ τῆς ἄνωθεν ἀπολαύσας ῥοπῆς, ἱκετεύει μὲν τὸν βασιλέα ἐπιτρέψαι αὐτῷ τὴν τῶν περιβόλων τῆς Ἱερουσαλὴμ οἰκοδομίαν, τυχὼν δὲ εὐμενοῦς τοῦ βασιλέως, καταλαμβάνει μὲν τὴν πατρίδα, σὺν πάσῃ δὲ προθυμίᾳ καὶ τὰ λείποντα τῷ θείῳ προστίθησι νεῷ· ἀνίστησι δὲ καὶ τὰ τῆς πόλεως τείχη, καὶ πύργοις πάντοθεν ὀχυρώσας ἐπιτίθησι τὰς πύλας, καὶ προτρέψας τοὺς ἱερέας, ἔρημον οὖσαν τῶν οἰκητόρων τὴν πόλιν, πλήρη τῶν ἐνοικούντων ποιεῖ. Τοῦτο καὶ ὁ θεῖος ἀρχάγγελος αἰνιττόμενος ἔφη· «Καὶ γνώσῃ, καὶ συνήσεις ἀπὸ ἐξόδου λόγων τοῦ ἀποκριθῆναι, καὶ ἀνοικοδομηθῆναι Ἱερουσαλήμ, ἕως Χριστοῦ ἡγουμένου, ἑβδομάδες ἑπτά, καὶ ἑβδομάδες ἑξήκοντα δύο. Καὶ ἐπιστρέψει, καὶ οἰκοδομηθήσεται πλατεῖα, καὶ περίτειχος, καὶ ἐκκαινωθήσονται οἱ καιροί.» Ἀρξάμενος γάρ, φησίν, ἀριθμεῖν ἀπὸ τῆς οἰκοδομίας τῆς πόλεως, ἀπολαβούσης μὲν τὰ οἰκεῖα τείχη, δεξαμένης δὲ πλῆθος τῶν οἰκητόρων, ὡς πλατεῖαν αὐτὴν γενέσθαι διὰ τὸ πλῆθος τῶν ἐνοικούντων, εὑρήσεις ἕως Χριστοῦ ἡγουμένου ἑβδομάδας ἑπτὰ καὶ ἑβδομάδας ἑξήκοντα δύο. Χριστὸν δὲ ἡγούμενον αὐτὸν πάλιν ὠνόμασεν, ὃν Ἅγιον ἁγίων ἐκάλεσεν, ὡς ὁ μακάριος Πέτρος ἐν Ἰουδαίοις ἔφη δημηγορῶν· «Τὸν δὲ ἀρχηγὸν τῆς ζωῆς ἀπεκτείνατε, ὃν ὁ Θεὸς ἤγειρεν ἐκ νεκρῶν, λύσας τοῦ θανάτου τὰς ὠδῖνας.» Ἡγούμενος δὲ ἡμῶν ἐστι κατὰ τὸ ἀνθρώπειον, ὡς πρωτότοκος πάσης κτίσεως, τῆς νέας δηλονότι· «Εἴ τις γάρ, φησίν, ἐν Χριστῷ, καινὴ κτίσις.» Καὶ ὡς πρωτότοκος ἐκ τῶν νεκρῶν, ἵνα γένηται, ᾗ φησιν ὁ Παῦλος, «ἐν πᾶσιν αὐτὸς

alone Cyrus, expiring in the twentieth year of the reign of Artaxerxes son of Xerxes.[220] It was the time when Nehemiah, cupbearer
of this king, filled with zeal, implored God and received grace
from on high; he besought the king to allow him to rebuild the
walls of Jerusalem, and finding favor with the king he returned to
his homeland, and with complete enthusiasm restored what was
lacking to the divine temple. He also rebuilt the city walls, fortified them with towers at all points, and inserted gates, instructing
the priests and making the city, which was bereft of inhabitants,
full of residents.[221]

In a reference to this the divine archangel also said, *You will
know and understand from the issuing of the words to respond and rebuild Jerusalem until an anointed leader seven weeks and sixty-two
weeks. It will return, its streets and walls will be rebuilt, and the times
will be renewed*: beginning the calculation from the rebuilding of
the city, which recovered its walls and received a great number of
inhabitants so as to become extended on account of the vast number of residents, you would find six weeks and sixty-two weeks up
to an *anointed leader*. Now, it gave Christ a second name as *leader*
after naming him *holy of holies*, as blessed Peter said in addressing
Jews, "You killed the author of life, but God raised him from the
dead, relieving the pains of death."[222] He is our leader in his humanity as "the firstborn of all creation"—that is, a new creation:
"If anyone is in Christ, there is a new creation"—and as firstborn
from the dead, so as to have, as Paul says, "first place in every-

---

[220] Is Theodoret arguing that if we take the 483 years ("seven weeks and
sixty-two weeks" of years) back from Jesus' baptism, we arrive at the twentieth
year of Artaxerxes (I), i.e., the year 446? This would be correct mathematically
if (omitting the error of about six years in our calendar introduced by Diony-
sius Exiguus in the sixth century) Jesus is thirty-two years of age at his baptism
(Luke 3:23 says "about thirty"). Or is this to fall into the same temptation to
take numbers at face value as Theodoret? In any case, modern versions divide
the text after "seven weeks," leaving the "sixty-two weeks" for the next stage of
the distribution of the original seventy weeks.

[221] Cf. Neh 2–4.

[222] A conflation of Acts 3:15 and 2:24. The Χριστός in the text of Dan
9:25 could be rendered "anointed leader" or "Christ the leader," Theodoret
opting for the latter to strengthen his reading of the numbers. Modern commentators, on the other hand, see a reference to Cyrus, or Zerubbabel, or the
high priest Joshua ben Jozadak, but (unlike Theodoret) they despair of getting
the numbers to add up.

πρωτεύων.» Τούτου χάριν αὐτὸν καὶ ὁ ἅγιος Γαβριὴλ Χριστὸν ἡγούμενον προσηγόρευσεν. Ἕως τοίνυν αὐτοῦ ἀπὸ τῆς οἰκοδομίας τῆς Ἱερουσαλήμ, «ἑβδομάδες ἑπτὰ καὶ ἑβδομάδες ἑξήκοντα δύο.» Ἵνα δὲ μὴ
μάτην ταῦτα ληρεῖν τινες ἡμᾶς ὑπολάβωσιν, φέρε καὶ αὐτῶν τῶν ἐτῶν
παραθήσωμεν τὸν ἀριθμόν. Οὐκοῦν ἀπὸ μὲν τοῦ εἰκοστοῦ ἔτους τῆς βασιλείας Ἀρταξέρξου τοῦ Ξέρξου, ἐφ' οὗ Νεεμίας εἰς τὴν Ἱερουσαλὴμ
1477   ἀφικόμενος ἀνεγεῖραι ἤρξατο τὰ τείχη | τῆς πόλεως, ἕως Δαρείου τοῦ
Ἀρσάμου, ὃν Ἀλέξανδρος ὁ Μακεδὼν ἀνελὼν τὴν τῶν Περσῶν κατέλυσε βασιλείαν, ἔτη ἐστὶ τέτταρα καὶ δέκα πρὸς τοῖς ἑκατόν· ἀπὸ δὲ ἕκτου
ἔτους Ἀλεξάνδρου, ἐν ᾧ Δαρεῖος ἀνηρέθη, ἕως Γαΐου Ἰουλίου Καίσαρος,
αὐτοκράτορος πρώτου Ῥωμαίων, ἔτη τὰ πάντα τῆς Μακεδόνων βασιλείας διακόσια ὀγδοήκοντα δύο· ἀπὸ δὲ τῆς ἀρχῆς Ἰουλίου Καίσαρος
ἕως πεντεκαιδεκάτου ἔτους Τιβερίου Καίσαρος, ἡνίκα Ἰωάννης ὁ Βα-
πτιστὴς ἦλθε παρὰ τὸν Ἰορδάνην κηρύσσων βάπτισμα μετανοίας, καὶ
βοῶν· «Ἴδε ὁ ἀμνὸς τοῦ Θεοῦ, ὁ αἴρων τὴν ἁμαρτίαν τοῦ κόσμου,»
ἔτη ἐστὶ ἑβδομήκοντα τρία. Ταῦτα ὁμοῦ συναγόμενα ποιεῖ ἐτῶν ἀριθμὸν
τετρακοσίων ἑξήκοντα καὶ ἐννέα· ταῦτα δὲ Ἑβραϊκὰ ἔτη ποιεῖ τετρακόσια ὀγδοήκοντα τρία· τοσαῦτα δὲ ποιοῦσιν αἱ ἑπτὰ καὶ ἑξήκοντα δύο
ἑβδομάδες. Εἰδέναι γὰρ χρή, ὡς Ἑβραῖοι, κατὰ τὸν τῆς σελήνης δρό-
μον ἀριθμοῦντες τὸν ἐνιαυτόν, ἕνδεκα ἡμέρας περιττὰς ἀποφαίνουσιν,
ἃς καὶ ἡμεῖς ἐμβολίμους καλοῦμεν· ὁ γὰρ τῆς σελήνης δρόμος ἐν εἴ-
κοσιν ἐννέα ἡμέραις καὶ ὥραις ἓξ συμπληροῦται. Οὕτω δὲ ἀριθμοῦντες
τριακοσίων καὶ πεντήκοντα καὶ τεσσάρων ἡμερῶν ποιοῦσι τὸν ἐνιαυτόν.
Ἐπειδὴ τοίνυν ὁ ἅγιος ἀρχάγγελος τῷ μακαρίῳ Δανιὴλ διαλεγόμενος ἀνδρὶ Ἑβραίῳ, καὶ διδάσκων αὐτὸν ἀριθμὸν τῶν ἐτῶν, τὸν συνήθη πάντως
ἔλεγεν ἀριθμόν, ἀναγκαίως προσθεῖναι δεῖ τὰ ἀπὸ τῶν ἐμβολίμων συν-

thing."[223] Hence holy Gabriel called him *Christ the leader*. To him from the rebuilding of Jerusalem, therefore, are *seven weeks and sixty-two weeks*.

Now, in case some people suspect we are talking stuff and nonsense, come now, let us cite the actual number of the years. From the twentieth year of the reign of Artaxerxes son of Xerxes, when Nehemiah arrived in Jerusalem and began to raise the walls | 1477 of the city, to Darius son of Arsamus, who was slain and the empire of the Persians overthrown by Alexander the Macedonian, is a 114 years.[224] From the sixth year of Alexander, when Darius was slain, to Gaius Julius Caesar, first emperor of the Romans, 282 years, including all the empire of the Macedonians. From the rule of Julius Caesar until the fifteenth year of Tiberius Caesar, when John the Baptist went to the Jordan preaching a baptism of repentance and crying aloud, "Behold the lamb of God, who takes away the sin of the world,"[225] seventy-three years. Altogether that makes 469, but in Hebrew years 483, which is the total of *seven weeks and sixty-two weeks*. One should be aware, you see, that Hebrew people calculate the year by the cycle of the moon, and thus dispense with an extra eleven days, which we call intercalary, the cycle of the moon being completed in twenty-nine days six hours. Calculating in this fashion they come up with a year of 354 days.[226] Since, then, the holy archangel, in speaking to blessed Daniel, a Hebrew man, and informing him of the number of the years, cited the number in quite usual fashion, the need consequently remains to add the years amassed from the intercalary days; when these are added,

[223] Col 1:5; 2 Cor 5:17; Col 1:18.

[224] That is, from 445 to 431. The next period of 282 years thus extends from 431 to Caesar's crossing the Rubicon in 49, tantamount in Theodoret's view to his becoming "first emperor of the Romans" (Augustus being called by him "second emperor" in comment on 2:45).

[225] John 1:29, the baptism of Jesus thus happening around CE 24 by this calculation (in contrast to the year 32 arrived at by using the "seventy weeks," as observed above in note 220).

[226] More important, the difference in *years* is fourteen and a half (5,313 days)—which bridges the gap between those 469 years (Artaxerxes to Jesus) and the 483 ("seven weeks and sixty-two weeks")—as long as the symbolic value of numbers is overlooked. (Theodoret, typically, acquaints his readers with the Jews' use in later times of a Babylonian system for their ecclesiastical calendar based on the cycle of the moon, an intercalary month thus being required every five years—as the "holy archangel" knew, of course, he adds.)

αγόμενα έτη· τούτων γὰρ προστιθεμένων, τὰ τρία καὶ ὀγδοήκοντα πρὸς τοῖς τετρακοσίοις εὑρεθήσεται έτη· τοσαῦτα δὲ συνάγουσιν αἱ ἑπτὰ καὶ ἑξήκοντα δύο ἑβδομάδες. Διεῖλε δὲ αὐτὰς οὐχ ἁπλῶς, ἀλλὰ πραγμάτων ἐνίων προσημαίνων μεταβολάς. Ἀπὸ γὰρ τῆς οἰκοδομίας τῆς Ἱερουσαλήμ, ἣ ἐγένετο ἐπὶ Νεεμίου καὶ Ἐσδρου, μέχρις Ὑρκανοῦ τοῦ τελευταίου ἐκ τῶν Ἀσαμοναίων ἀρχιερέως, ὃν ἀνεῖλεν Ἡρώδης, ὁ τῶν δύο καὶ ἑξήκοντα ἑβδομάδων ἀριθμὸς συμπληροῦται· ἀπὸ δὲ τῆς ἐκείνου σφαγῆς, μέχρι τῆς τοῦ Σωτῆρος ἡμῶν ἐπιφανείας, καὶ τῆς εἰς τὸν Ἰορδάνην ἀφίξεως, αἱ λοιπαὶ ἑπτὰ ἑβδομάδες τὸ τέλος λαμβάνουσιν. Ἐν δὲ τούτῳ τῷ χρόνῳ, μετὰ τὴν Ὑρκανοῦ, φημί, ἀναίρεσιν, μέχρι τῆς τοῦ Σωτῆρος ἡμῶν ἐπιφανείας, παρανόμως λοιπὸν οἱ ἀρχιερεῖς ἐγίνοντο. Τοῦ γὰρ νόμου κελεύοντος διὰ βίου τοὺς ἀρχιερέας ἱερατεύειν, καὶ μετὰ τὴν τελευτὴν τοὺς διαδόχους λαμβάνειν, Ἡρώδης, καὶ οἱ μετ' ἐκεῖνον Ῥωμαῖοι, ὠνητὰς τὰς ἀρχιερωσύνας ποιησάμενοι, συχνὰς αὐτῶν ἐποιοῦντο διαδοχάς· ἐνίους δὲ οὐδὲ ἐκ τοῦ ἱερατικοῦ γένους καταγομένους ἀρχιερέας προεχειρίζοντο. Καὶ τοῦτο διδάσκων Ἰώσηππος ὁ Ἑβραῖος συγγραφεὺς οὕτω φησί· «Τὴν βασιλείαν Ἡρώδης παρὰ Ῥωμαίων ἐγχειρισθείς, οὐκέτι τοὺς ἐκ τοῦ Ἀσαμωναίου γένους (οὗτοι δὲ ἦσαν οἱ καλούμενοι Μακκαβαῖοι) καθίστησιν ἀρχιερέας, ἀλλά τισιν ἀσή-
1480 μοις καὶ μόνον ἐξ Ἑβραίων οὖσι.» Καὶ | μετ' ὀλίγα πάλιν οὕτω φησίν· «Ἔπραξε δ' ὅμοια τῷ Ἡρώδῃ περὶ τῆς καταστάσεως τῶν Ἰουδαίων ἀρχιερέων Ἀρχέλαός τε ὁ παῖς αὐτοῦ, καὶ μετὰ τοῦτον οἱ Ῥωμαῖοι τὴν ἀρχὴν παρειληφότες.» Καὶ ἑτέρωθί φησι· «Βαλέριος δὲ Γράτος, Ῥωμαίων στρατηγός, παύσας ἱερατεύειν Ἄνανον, Ἰσμαὴλ ἀρχιερέα ἀποφαίνει τὸν τοῦ Φαβί· καὶ τοῦτον μετ' οὐ πολὺ μεταστήσας, Ἐλεάζαρον τὸν τοῦ Ἀνάνου τοῦ ἀρχιερέως υἱὸν ἀποδείκνυσιν ἀρχιερέα· ἐνιαυτοῦ δὲ διαγενομένου καὶ τόνδε παύσας, Σίμωνι τῷ Καθίμου τὴν ἀρχιερωσύνην παραδίδωσιν. Οὐ πλέον δὲ καὶ τῷδε ἐνιαυτοῦ τὴν τιμὴν ἔχοντι διεγένετο χρόνος, καὶ Ἰώσηππος, ὁ καὶ Καϊάφας, διάδοχος ἦν αὐτῷ.» Ταῦτα διδάσκων καὶ ὁ μακάριος Λουκᾶς φησιν· «Ἔτους πεντεκαιδεκάτου Τιβερίου Καίσαρος, ἐπὶ ἀρχιερέων Ἄννα καὶ Καϊάφα.»

you will find 483 years, a number equivalent to the *seven weeks and sixty-two weeks*.

Now, far from his making this division without purpose, it was to foretell the development in certain events: from the rebuilding of Jerusalem, which happened in the time of Nehemiah and Ezra, to Hyrcanus, the last high priest of the Hasmoneans, whom Herod slew, the number of *sixty-two weeks* is arrived at; and from his murder to the coming of our Savior and his arrival at the Jordan the remaining *seven weeks* reach their completion.[227] Now, in this period—after the killing of Hyrcanus, I mean, until the coming of our Savior—high priests were appointed illegally: though the law required that high priests serve for life and be succeeded only on their death, Herod and the Romans after him put the office of high priest up for sale and were responsible for a rapid succession, and appointed some as high priest who were not even from the priestly family. Relating this the Hebrew historian Josephus says, "On being appointed king by the Romans, Herod no longer installed as high priests those of the Hasmonean family, known as Maccabean, but some who were undistinguished, their only claim being Hebrew nationality"; and | shortly after he speaks in similar terms, "His son Archelaus imitated Herod in the appointment of high priests of the Jews, and as did also the Romans after him when they came to power"; and elsewhere, "Valerius Gratus, a Roman general, brought the priesthood of Annas to an end, and appointed as high priest Ishmael son of Phiabi; not long afterwards he replaced him and installed as high priest Eleazar son of Annas the high priest, and after the passage of a year he relieved him and handed the office of high priest to Simon son of Camith. He enjoyed the office for no more than a year when Joseph, also called Caiaphas, succeeded him."[228] Blessed Luke also informs us of this, "In the fifteenth year of Tiberius Caesar, when Annas and Caiaphas were high priests" (though we never heard of two high

1480

[227] Theodoret is now looking at the archangel's numbers from a third point of view, the high priests of the latter period, apparently arriving at a still different date for the baptism of Jesus, Hyrcanus II being killed by Herod the Great in 31.

[228] *Ant.* 20.247, 249, 18.33-35. Valerius Gratus was prefect in Judea immediately before Pontius Pilate.

Δύο δὲ κατὰ ταὐτὸν ἀρχιερέας κατὰ νόμον γεγενημένους οὐ μεμαθήκαμεν πώποτε. Ταῦτα προλέγων ὁ ἅγιος Γαβριήλ·

κϛ′. «Καὶ μετὰ τὰς ἑβδομάδας, φησί, τὰς ἑξήκοντα δύο, ἐξολοθρευθήσεται χρίσμα, καὶ κρῖμα οὐκ ἔστιν ἐν αὐτῷ.» Ὡς εἶναι δῆλον, ὅτι τὰς ἑξήκοντα δύο ἑβδομάδας προτέρας τέταχε, καὶ μετὰ ταύτας τὰς ἑπτά, ἐν αἷς, φησίν, ἐξολοθρευθήσεται χρίσμα, τουτέστιν, ἡ τοῖς ἀρχιερεῦσιν ἐπανθοῦσα χάρις. Καὶ ἐπειδὴ καὶ οἱ παρανόμως προχειριζόμενοι ἀρχιερεῖς ὠνομάζοντο, εἰκότως ἐπήγαγε· «Καὶ κρῖμα οὐκ ἔστιν ἐν αὐτῷ.» Εἰ γὰρ καὶ χρίονται, φησίν, ἀλλ᾽ οὐ κατὰ λόγον χρίονται, παρανόμως δὲ τοῦτο ποιεῖν τολμῶσι. Καὶ ἀνωτέρω δὲ δῆλον πεποίηκεν, ὡς τὰς ἑπτὰ ἑβδομάδας τελευταίας τέταχεν· «Ἕως γὰρ Χριστοῦ ἡγουμένου ἑβδομάδες ἑπτά, καὶ ἑβδομάδες ἑξήκοντα δύο.» Ἕως γὰρ τοῦ ἡγουμένου Χριστοῦ τὰς ἑπτὰ πολλαπλασιαζούσας ἑβδομάδας παρ᾽ αὐτὴν αὐτοῦ τὴν μνήμην τέθεικεν, ἵνα γνῶμεν ὡς ἀπὸ τοῦ Χριστοῦ καὶ ἐπὶ τὰ ἄνω ἀριθμεῖν βουλόμενοι, τὰς ἑπτὰ πρότερον ἑβδομάδας εὑρήσομεν, καὶ τότε τὰς ἑξήκοντα δύο. Καὶ τοῦτο σαφέστερον ποιῶν· «Ἐπιστρέψει, φησί, καὶ οἰκοδομηθήσεται πλατεῖα καὶ περίτειχος, καὶ ἐκκαινωθήσονται οἱ καιροί.» Τουτέστιν, ὁ πρὸ τῆς οἰκοδομίας χρόνος. «Καὶ μετὰ τὰς ἑβδομάδας, φησί, τὰς ἑξήκοντα δύο, ἐξολοθρευθήσεται χρίσμα.» Καὶ οὐκ εἶπε, μετὰ τὰς ἑπτά, ἀλλὰ μετὰ τὰς ἑξήκοντα δύο, μεθ᾽ ἅς εἰσιν αἱ ἑπτά, «ἐν αἷς ἐξολοθρευθήσεται χρίσμα, καὶ κρῖμα οὐκ ἔστιν ἐν αὐτῷ·» Ἡρώδου μὲν ἀλλοφύλου βασιλεύοντος· πατρόθεν γὰρ Ἀσκαλωνίτης ἦν, μητρόθεν δὲ Ἰδουμαῖος· τῶν δὲ καλουμένων ἀρχιερέων οὐ κατὰ νόμον χριομένων, ἀλλ᾽ ὑπὸ τῶν ἀλλοφύλων ἀρχόντων προχειριζομένων, Ἡρώδου τε καὶ 1481 Ἀρχελάου, καὶ τῶν Ῥωμαίων | στρατηγῶν. Εἶτα λέγει καὶ τὴν καταληψομένην πανωλεθρίαν τήν τε πόλιν, καὶ αὐτὴν ταύτην τὴν ἀλλόφυλον βασιλείαν, καὶ τὴν παράνομον ἀρχιερωσύνην, καί φησι· «Καὶ τὴν πόλιν καὶ τὸ ἅγιον διαφθερεῖ σὺν τῷ ἡγουμένῳ τῷ ἐρχομένῳ.» Καὶ γὰρ ἡ

priests serving together according to the law).[229]

Foretelling this the holy Gabriel says, *And after the sixty-two weeks, anointing will be destroyed, and judgment is not in him* (v. 26). So it is clear that he placed the sixty-two weeks first, and after them the seven in which *anointing will be abolished*, that is, the grace flourishing in the high priests.[230] And since those appointed illegally were called high priests, he was right to proceed, *And judgment is not in him*: if they are anointed, but not anointed in accordance with the law, they take it upon themselves to act illegally. Above he had made it clear that he placed the seven weeks last, *until an anointed leader seven weeks and sixty-two weeks*: the seven weeks until Christ the leader multiplied many times he put in his very memory for us to know that if we wish to calculate from Christ and go backwards, we shall find the seven weeks first and then the sixty-two. And to make it clearer, *It will return, its streets and walls will be rebuilt, and the times will be renewed*, that is, the period before the rebuilding. *And after the sixty-two weeks, the anointing will be destroyed.* He did not say after the seven but *after the sixty-two*, on which the seven follow, in which *the anointing will be destroyed, and there will be no judgment in him*, Herod being a foreign king, from Ashkelon on his father's side,[231] Idumean on his mother's, and the so-called high priests not anointed according to the law but appointed by the foreign rulers Herod, Archelaus, and the Roman | prefects.

1481

He then mentions the ruin which would overtake the city, this foreign kingdom itself, and the illegal high priesthood, saying, *And he will destroy the city and the holy place along with the leader who is to come*: the city will be overthrown, and the holy tem-

[229] Luke 3:1–2. Theodoret is right to query this coupling of Caiaphas and his father-in-law in the position; Joseph Fitzmyer remarks, "Since there was never more than one high priest at a time, the phrase raises a question again about either the accuracy of Luke's information or of his interpretations. On the other hand, it may have been customary to speak of an ex-high priest as such even when he was already out of office" (*The Gospel according to Luke I-IX* [AB 28; Garden City, N.Y.: Doubleday, 1981], 458).

[230] Theodoret's text gives a rendering of "anointing" for Hebrew "an anointed one," which seems to refer to the high priest Onias III murdered in 171. He proceeds to rationalize the text, which is at odds with the Hebrew.

[231] Herod the Great's father Antipater II was in fact Idumean.

πόλις, φησίν, ἀνάστατος γενήσεται, καὶ ὁ νεὼς ὁ ἅγιος παντελῆ κατάλυσιν δέξεται. Ταῦτα δὲ πείσεται ἡ πόλις σὺν τῷ ἡγουμένῳ τῷ ἐρχομένῳ, τουτέστι, τοῖς ἐρχομένοις παρανόμοις ἄρχουσιν. Ἡγούμενον γὰρ ἐρχόμενον τὴν ἀλλόφυλον βασιλείαν καὶ τὴν παράνομον ἀρχιερωσύνην ὠνόμασεν. Εἶτα διδάσκων, ὅτι πολλῷ χείρονα τῶν προτέρων ὑπομενοῦσι κακά, ἐπήγαγε· «Καὶ ἐκκοπήσονται ὡς ἐν κατακλυσμῷ·» τουτέστι, πανωλεθρίαν ὑπομενοῦσιν, οἵαν ὑπέμειναν οἱ πάλαι ἄνθρωποι τοῦ κατακλυσμοῦ τὴν γῆν πᾶσαν συγκαλύψαντος. Καὶ διδάσκων ὡς οὐδεμιᾶς ἀνακλήσεως ἢ ἀνέσεως τεύξονται, «Καὶ ἕως τέλους, φησί, πολέμου συντετμημένου ἀφανισμοῖς.» Ἀφανισμὸν γάρ, φησί, παντελῆ ὑπομενοῦσιν, οἷόν τινι κατακλυσμῷ τῷ πολέμῳ παραδοθέντες, καὶ εἰς τέλος τούτοις ὑποκλιθήσονται τοῖς κακοῖς, καὶ οὐδεμιᾶς πώποτε ἀνακλήσεως τεύξονται. Οὕτω τὰ περὶ τῆς Ἰουδαίων προθεσπίσας πανωλεθρίας, ἐπανέρχεται πάλιν εἰς τὸν τῶν ἑβδομήκοντα ἑβδομάδων ἀριθμόν, καὶ τὴν λείπουσαν ταῖς ἑξήκοντα ἐννέα προστίθησι, καί φησιν·

κζʹ. «Καὶ δυναμώσει διαθήκην πολλοῖς ἑβδομὰς μία, καὶ ἐν τῷ ἡμίσει τῆς ἑβδομάδος ἀρθήσεται θυσία καὶ σπονδή, καὶ ἐπὶ τὸ ἱερὸν βδέλυγμα τῆς ἐρημώσεως, καὶ ἕως συντελείας καιροῦ συντέλεια δοθήσεται ἐπὶ τὴν ἐρήμωσιν.» Τίνα μὲν οὖν ἔσται μετὰ τὰς ἑξήκοντα δύο ἑβδομάδας ἐν ταῖς ἑπτὰ ἑβδομάσι, προείρηκα, φησί· προσήκει δὲ μαθεῖν καὶ τὰ ἐν τῇ ἄλλῃ ἑβδομάδι γενησόμενα. Ἐν γὰρ ταύτῃ ἡ Καινὴ Διαθήκη δοθήσεται τοῖς πιστεύουσι, καὶ δυνάμεως ἁπάσης αὐτοὺς πληρώσει· «Μεσούσης δὲ ταύτης τῆς ἑβδομάδος, ἀρθήσεται θυσία καὶ σπονδή.» Παυθήσεται, φησίν, ἡ κατὰ νόμον θυσία, τῆς ἀληθοῦς προσφερομένης θυσίας τοῦ ἀμώμου ἀμνοῦ, τοῦ αἴροντος τὴν ἁμαρτίαν τοῦ κόσμου. Ταύτης γὰρ λοιπὸν προσενεχθείσης, τέλος ἐκείνη λήψεται. Οὗ χάριν, εὐθὺς τῆς θυσίας πληρωθείσης, καὶ τοῦ Σωτῆρος ἡμῶν ἀφέντος τὸ πνεῦμα, τὸ καταπέτασμα τοῦ ναοῦ ἐρράγη ἀπὸ ἄνωθεν ἕως κάτω, τὰ πάλαι ἀθεώρητα τοῖς πᾶσι ποιοῦν θεωρητά, καὶ τὰ ἄψαυστα καὶ ἄβατα ἀποφαίνων βατά. Ἐπειδὴ γὰρ τὸ καταπέτασμα διεῖργεν ἀπὸ τῶν ἁγίων τὰ Ἅγια τῶν ἁγίων ἔχοντα τὸ ἱλαστήριον, καὶ τὰ Χερουβὶμ, καὶ τὴν κιβωτόν, ῥαγὲν διόλου τὸ καταπέτασμα διὰ τῶν πραγμάτων ἔδειξεν, ὡς ἀπέστη τῶν ἔνδον ἡ παρεδρεύουσα χάρις, καὶ κοινὰ γέγονε τὰ πάλαι τῷ ἀρχιερεῖ μόνῳ βατά. Τοῦτο δὲ γέ|γονεν ὑπὲρ τοῦ κόσμου παντὸς τῆς θυσίας

ple will undergo complete destruction.[232] The city will suffer this *along with the leader who is to come,* that is, those illegal rulers who are to come; by *the leader who is to come* he referred to the foreign kingdom and illegal high priest. Then, to bring out that they will suffer far worse troubles than before, he went on, *They will be cut down as in a flood,* that is, they will meet with ruin such as people of old met with when the flood overwhelmed the whole earth.[233] And to bring out that they will be granted no recall or relief, *And to the end of war assigned with desolations:* they will meet with utter desolation, consigned to war as though to some flood, succumbing finally to these troubles and never gaining any recall.

Having thus made predictions of the Jews' ruin, he returns to the number of seventy weeks, supplying the one missing after the sixty-nine. *One week will confirm a covenant of one week for many people, and in half a week sacrifice and libation will cease; an abomination of desolation on the temple, and to the consummation of time a consummation will be given to the desolation* (v. 27): I have foretold what will occur in the seven weeks after the sixty-two weeks; but there is need to learn as well what will happen in the other week. In fact, the new covenant will be given to the believers in this week, and he will fill them with all power: *in the middle of this week sacrifice and libation will cease:* sacrifice according to the law will come to an end when the true sacrifice of the innocent lamb, who takes away the sin of the world, is offered; when it is finally offered, the other will cease. Hence, once the sacrifice was accomplished and our Savior sent the Spirit, "the veil of the temple was torn from top to bottom,"[234] causing the previously unseen realities to be visible to all, and making accessible what was untouchable and inaccessible. Since, you see, the veil separated from the holy ones the holy of holies that contained the mercy seat, the cherubim, and the ark, the complete tearing of the veil demonstrated in actual fact that grace, which had resided there, departed, and what was accessible only to the high priest became available to all. Now, this | happened with the offering of the sacrifice for the whole world.   1484

[232] The Greek obscures the author's reference to the plundering of Jerusalem by Antiochus IV.

[233] Gen 6–9.

[234] Matt 27:51. Unwilling to entertain as a possible scenario depicted by the author the desecration of the temple under Antiochus, Theodoret looks for portentous events at the crucifixion.

προσενεχθείσης. Εἰ δέ τις καὶ τὸν χρόνον καταμαθεῖν ἐθέλει, ἐκ τοῦ κατὰ Ἰωάννην Εὐαγγελίου μαθήσεται. Ὡς περὶ τὰ τρία ἔτη καὶ ἥμισυ κηρύξας ὁ Κύριος, καὶ τοὺς ἁγίους αὐτοῦ μαθητὰς τῇ διδασκαλίᾳ καὶ τοῖς θαύμασι βεβαιώσας, τότε τὸ πάθος ὑπέμεινε· μετὰ δὲ τὸν σταυρὸν καὶ τὸν θάνατον, καὶ τὴν ἀνάστασιν, καὶ τὴν εἰς οὐρανοὺς ἀνάβασιν, καὶ τὴν τοῦ ἁγίου Πνεύματος ἐπιφοίτησιν, τὸν λοιπὸν τῆς ἑβδομάδος χρόνον οἱ ἅγιοι ἀπόστολοι ἐν Ἱεροσολύμοις κηρύττοντές τε καὶ θαυματουργοῦντες, πολλάς τε ἀνθρώπων χιλιάδας εἰς τὴν εὐαγγελικὴν ποδηγήσαντες διδασκαλίαν, τῆς Νέας Διαθήκης ἠξίωσαν καὶ τῆς τοῦ παναγίου βαπτίσματος χάριτος τυχεῖν παρεσκεύασαν. Εἴτα τῶν κατὰ τὸν ἅγιον Στέφανον ὑπὸ τῶν Ἰουδαίων τολμηθέντων, διεσπάρησαν μὲν οἱ ἄλλοι κατὰ τὰς πόλεις τῆς Ἰουδαίας, οἱ δὲ θεῖοι ἀπόστολοι σμικρὸν ἐν Ἱεροσολύμοις διατρίψαντες χρόνον, εἰς τὴν Σαμάρειαν καὶ Καισάρειαν, Λύδδαν τε καὶ Ἰόππην περιιόντες, ἅπασιν ἀνθρώποις τὰ σωτήρια δόγματα προσφέρειν ἠπείγοντο. Τούτου χάριν ὁ θεῖος ἀρχάγγελος τῷ μακαρίῳ φησὶ Δανιήλ, ὅτι «Δυναμώσει διαθήκην πολλοῖς ἑβδομὰς μία,» τόν τε πρὸ τοῦ σταυροῦ τοῦ Κυρίου χρόνον, καὶ τὸν μετὰ τὴν ἀνάστασιν τοῦ Σωτῆρος τῶν ἁγίων ἀποστόλων ἐν Ἱεροσολύμοις διδασκαλίαν κατὰ ταὐτὸν συναγαγών. Εἴτα διαιρεῖ διχὰ τὴν ἑβδομάδα, καί φησι· «Καὶ ἐν τῷ ἡμίσει τῆς ἑβδομάδος ἀρθήσεται θυσία καὶ σπονδή.» Τῆς γὰρ ἀληθινῆς προσφερομένης θυσίας, τέλος λήψεται ἡ τοῦ νόμου σκιά. Καὶ ἐπὶ τούτοις φησίν· «Ἐπὶ τὸ ἱερὸν βδέλυγμα τῆς ἐρημώσεως» Διὰ ταύτην γάρ, φησί, τὴν θυσίαν οὐ μόνον ἐκείνη ἡ θυσία παυθήσεται, ἀλλὰ καὶ βδέλυγμα τῆς ἐρημώσεως ἐπὶ τὸ ἱερὸν δοθήσεται, τουτέστι, τὸ πάλαι σεπτὸν καὶ φρικῶδες ἔρημον ἀναφανήσεται. Σημεῖον δὲ τῆς ἐρημίας γενήσεται εἰκόνες τινὲς ἀπηγορευμέναι τῷ νόμῳ εἰς τοῦτον εἰσκομιζόμεναι. Τοῦτο δὲ πεποίηκε Πιλάτος νύκτωρ εἰς τὸν θεῖον νεὼν τὰς βασιλικὰς εἰσκομίσας εἰκόνας παρὰ τὸν θεῖον νόμον. Τοῦτο δὲ καὶ ὁ Κύριος ἐν τοῖς ἱεροῖς Εὐαγγελίοις τοῖς ἁγίοις αὐτοῦ

If you want to learn the time as well, you will find it in the Gospel according to John.[235] When the Lord had preached for about three and a half years, and had strengthened his holy disciples with teaching and miracles, he then underwent the passion. But after the crucifixion, death, resurrection, ascension into heaven, and coming of the Holy Spirit, the holy apostles spent the rest of the week preaching in Jerusalem, working wonders and guiding many thousands to the evangelical teaching, and they imparted the new covenant and caused them to enjoy the grace of all-holy baptism. Then, when the Jews took flagrant action against holy Stephen, while the others were scattered to the cities of Judea, the divine apostles stayed for a short time in Jerusalem, visiting Samaria and Caesarea, Lydda and Joppa, and they pressed on with proposing the saving doctrines to all people. This is the reason the divine archangel said to blessed Daniel, *One week will confirm a covenant for many people,* including as one both the period before the crucifixion of the Lord and that of the holy apostles teaching in Jerusalem after the resurrection.[236]

He next divides the week in two, saying, *And in half a week sacrifice and libation will cease*: with the offering of the true sacrifice the shadow of the law will come to an end. And further, *An abomination of desolation on the temple*: as a result of this sacrifice not only will the other sacrifice cease but as well *an abomination of desolation* will be inflicted on the temple—that is, that formerly venerable and fearsome place will be made desolate. A sign of the *desolation* will be the introduction into it of certain images forbidden by the law; Pilate was guilty of this by introducing into the divine temple by night the imperial images in violation of the law.[237] The Lord also in the sacred Gospels foretold to his holy

[235] Theodoret's choice of John's Gospel is interesting. Admittedly, John will look for significant events at the crucifixion, such as the piercing of Jesus' side, that may evoke memories of Daniel. As for Jesus' ministry lasting for about three and a half years, Theodoret is perhaps thinking of John's mention of three Passovers during the course of Jesus' ministry.

[236] Is Theodoret reduced to finding in the apostles' "week" of preaching in Jerusalem after the resurrection the "week" of v. 27? Modern commentators tend to see a reference to the years before the culmination of persecution by Antiochus, the "covenant" being the pact between him and renegade Jews.

[237] This story of Pilate's hybris on the occasion of entering on his period of office is recorded by both Josephus (*J.W.* 2.169–174; *Ant.* 18.55–59) and Eusebius (*Dem. ev.* 8.2.123; *Hist. eccl.* 2.6.3–4). Theodoret for his purposes prefers

προέλεγε μαθηταῖς· «Ὅταν ἴδητε τὸ βδέλυγμα τῆς ἐρημώσεως τὸ εἰρημένον διὰ Δανιὴλ τοῦ προφήτου, γινώσκετε, ὅτι ἤγγικεν ἡ ἐρήμωσις αὐτῆς. Τότε οἱ ἐν τῇ Ἰουδαίᾳ φευγέτωσαν εἰς τὰ ὄρη, καὶ ὁ ἐπὶ τοῦ δώματος μὴ καταβήτω ἆραί τι ἀπὸ τῆς οἰκίας αὐτοῦ.» Ταῦτα δὲ ἔλεγε σημαίνων τὸ τάχος τῆς καταληψομένης αὐτοὺς πανωλεθρίας. Καὶ μικρὸν δὲ πρὸ τούτων φησίν· «Ἱερουσαλήμ, Ἱερουσαλήμ, ἡ ἀποκτείνουσα τοὺς προφήτας, καὶ λιθοβολοῦσα τοὺς ἀπεσταλμένους πρὸς αὐτήν, ποσάκις ἠθέλησα ἐπισυναγαγεῖν τὰ τέκνα σου ὃν τρόπον ὄρνις ἐπισυνάγει τὰ νοσσία ἑαυτῆς ὑπὸ τὰς πτέρυγας, καὶ οὐκ ἠθελή|σατε. Διὰ τοῦτο λέγω ὑμῖν, ὅτι ἀφίεται ὁ οἶκος ὑμῶν ἔρημος.» Ταῦτα προλέγων ὁ ἅγιος Γαβριήλ, μετὰ τὸ προθεσπίσαι τῆς κατὰ τὸν νόμον λατρείας τὴν παῦλαν, ἐπήγαγε καὶ ἐπὶ τούτοις· «Ἐπὶ τὸ ἱερὸν βδέλυγμα τῆς ἐρημώσεως.» Καὶ ἵνα μὴ νομίσωσιν οἱ Ἰουδαῖοι πάλιν ἀπολήψεσθαι τὸν θεῖον νεὼν τὴν προτέραν εὐπρέπειάν τε καὶ δόξαν, ἀναγκαίως ἐπήγαγε· «Καὶ ἕως συντελείας καιροῦ συντέλεια δοθήσεται ἐπὶ τὴν ἐρήμωσιν.» Ἕως γάρ, φησί, τῆς τοῦ αἰῶνος συντελείας ἡ τῆς ἐρημώσεως συντέλεια μενεῖ, μεταβολὴν οὐ δεχομένη. Τοῦτο καὶ ὁ μακάριος ἔφη Δαβίδ· «Ἐν ὀργῇ συντελείας καὶ οὐ μὴ ὑπάρξουσι, καὶ γνώσονται ὅτι ὁ Θεὸς δεσπόζει τοῦ Ἰακὼβ, καὶ τῶν περάτων τῆς γῆς.» Γνώσονται δὲ ὅταν ἴδωσι τὸ σημεῖον τοῦ Υἱοῦ τοῦ ἀνθρώπου ἐν τῷ οὐρανῷ. Τότε γὰρ «κόψονται κατὰ φυλάς, τότε ὄψονται εἰς ὃν ἐξεκέντησαν.» Εἰ δ' οὐχ οὕτως ταῦτα ἔχει, ἐπειδὴ ὁ τῶν τετρακοσίων καὶ ἐννενήκοντα ἐτῶν διελήλυθεν ἀριθμός, καὶ ἕτερα δὲ πρὸς τούτοις πλέον ἢ τεσσαράκοντα καὶ τετρακόσια, δειξάτωσαν ἐπὶ τίνων ἔλαβε πέρας ἡ τοῦ ἀρχαγγέλου χρησμολογία. Ἐπὶ τῶν

disciples, "When you see the abomination of desolation mentioned in Daniel the prophet, realize that its desolation is at hand. Then is the time for those in Judea to flee to the mountains, and the one on the rooftop not to go down to take something from his house." He said this to highlight the rapidity of the disaster about to overtake them. And a little before this he says, "Jerusalem, Jerusalem, you who kill the prophets and stone those sent to it, how many times have I wanted to gather together your children in the way a bird gathers together its young under its wings, and you refused. | 1485 Hence I say to you, your house will be left desolate."238 Foretelling this, the holy Gabriel, after prophesying the end of the worship according to the law, went on further, *On the temple an abomination of desolation.*

In case the Jews should think the divine temple would recover its former splendor and glory, he consequently added, *And to the consummation of time a consummation will be given to the desolation*: until the end of the age the consummation of the desolation will continue, undergoing no change. Blessed David also said as much, "In fury of consummation, and they are not to survive, and they will know that God is lord of Jacob and of the bounds of the earth."239 They will know when they see the sign of the Son of Man in heaven: then they will mourn tribe by tribe, then they will look on him whom they have pierced.240 But if this is not the case, since the number of 490 years has passed, plus more than another 440,241 let them demonstrate in whose time the archangel's ora-

it to the desecration of the temple in 167 by Antiochus, the usual interpretation of "abomination of desolation" (see note 188 for the derivation of the term).

238 Matt 24:14–17; 23:37–38. The reader should note that Jesus declares Daniel to be a "prophet," which doubtless confirmed Daniel's place among the prophets for Theodoret.

239 Ps 59:13. In later commentary on the psalm Theodoret will take the verse to refer to such deplorable developments as the action of Gaius Caligula in erecting a statue of himself in the temple on becoming emperor in 37, Nero's commissioning Vespasian to pacify Judea, and the sacking of Jerusalem by Titus under Vespasian in 70.

240 Cf. Matt 24:30; John 19:37, citing Zech 12:10. Theodoret is accumulating New Testament documentation to build a case against the Jews (and modern commentators) in favor of Jesus' crucifixion as the fulfillment of Daniel's (prospective) prophecy.

241 If Theodoret is composing this work around 434, what *terminus a quo* (in the 540s B.C.E.) does he have in mind in compiling this total: the older

Μακκαβαίων; Ἀλλ' οὐκ ἔστι τετρακόσια καὶ ἐννενήκοντα ἔτη ἀπὸ Δαρείου μέχρις αὐτῶν, οὔτε μὴν ἀπὸ Κύρου τοῦ πρώτου Περσῶν βασι-
λεύσαντος· ἀπὸ γὰρ Κύρου μέχρις Ἀντιόχου τοῦ Ἐπιφανοῦς, ἐφ' οὗ οἱ
Μακκαβαῖοι ζηλώσαντες ἀντελάβοντο τῶν πραγμάτων, περὶ τὰ τριακό-
σια καὶ ἑβδομήκοντα καὶ δύο ἐστὶν ἔτη. Ἄλλως τε δέ, τίς τούτων Ἅγιος
ἁγίων κέκληται; Ἰούδας, ἢ Ἰωνάθαν, Σιμών, ἢ ὁ μετὰ τούτους; Καὶ
μὴν οὐδὲ Ἀβραὰμ ὁ πατριάρχης, οὐδὲ Μωσῆς ὁ νομοθέτης, οὐδὲ Ἠλίας
ὁ μέγιστος τῶν προφητῶν, Ἅγιος τῶν ἁγίων προσηγορεύθη πώποτε.
Οὐκοῦν καὶ ὁ χρόνος, καὶ αἱ προσηγορίαι τὴν τοῦ Κυρίου ἡμῶν Ἰησοῦ
Χριστοῦ σαφῶς ἡμῖν προεσήμαναν παρουσίαν, εἰς ὃν πεπιστευκότες, καὶ
τὴν δευτέραν αὐτοῦ παρουσίαν προσμένοντες, τῆς παρ' αὐτοῦ φιλανθρωπίας ἐν ἡμέρᾳ διαγνώσεως τυχεῖν ἱκετεύσωμεν· ἧς γένοιτο πάντας ἡμᾶς
ἐπιτυχεῖν, χάριτι καὶ φιλανθρωπίᾳ τοῦ Κυρίου ἡμῶν Ἰησοῦ Χριστοῦ,
μεθ' οὗ τῷ Πατρὶ δόξα, σὺν τῷ ἁγίῳ Πνεύματι, εἰς τοὺς αἰῶνας τῶν
1488   αἰώνων. Ἀμήν. |

ΤΟΜΟΣ Ι′ — ΚΕΦΑΛΑΙΟΝ Ι′

α′. «Ἐν ἔτει τρίτῳ Κύρου, τοῦ βασιλέως Περσῶν, λόγος ἀπεκαλύφθη τῷ Δανιήλ, οὗ τὸ ὄνομα ἐπεκλήθη Βαλτάσαρ.» Τισὶ δοκεῖ τὸν
χρόνον ἐσφάλθαι, καὶ ἀντὶ τοῦ ἐν ἔτει πρώτῳ, τρίτῳ θεῖναι τὸν ἐξ ἀρχῆς
τὸ βιβλίον γράψαντα· τούτου δὲ τεκμήριον, ἐκ τοῦ τὸν μακάριον εἰπεῖν
Δανιήλ, εὐθὺς μετὰ τὴν ἀρχὴν τῆς προφητείας· «Καὶ ἐγένετο Δανιὴλ
ἕως ἔτους ἑνὸς Κύρου τοῦ βασιλέως.» Εἰ γὰρ μέχρι τοῦ ἔτους μόνον
τοῦ πρώτου τῆς Κύρου βασιλείας διήρκεσε, φησίν, ὁ προφήτης, πῶς ἐν

cle was fulfilled. In the time of the Maccabees? There were not 490 years from Darius to them, nor from Cyrus, the first to rule over the Persians: from Cyrus to Antiochus Epiphanes, in whose time in their zeal the Maccabees took control of affairs, is about 372 years.[242] In particular, which of the latter was called *holy of holies*? Judas, or Jonathan, Simon, or the one after them? Actually, not even Abraham the patriarch, not even Moses the lawgiver, not even Elijah the greatest of the prophets was ever given the name holy of holies.

Both the timing, therefore, and the titles clearly foretell to us the coming of our Lord Jesus Christ. Believing in him and looking forward to his second coming, let us pray to receive lovingkindness from him on the day of decision. May it be the good fortune of us all to attain this, thanks to the grace and lovingkindness of our Lord Jesus Christ, to whom with the Father and the Holy Spirit be glory, for ages of ages. Amen.

CHAPTER 10

In the third year of Cyrus king of the Persians a word was revealed to Daniel, whose name was Belteshazzar (v. 1). Some think the date is wrong, and that the original scribe put "third" instead of "first" year. Evidence for this comes from blessed Daniel's saying right after the beginning of the work, "Daniel was there for one year of King Cyrus";[243] after all, if the prophet had lasted only to the first

Daniel's time in the court of "Darius son of Xerxes"?

[242] If Theodoret has in mind the response of the Maccabees to Antiochus's desecration of the temple in 167, it is a date 539 he is thinking of in Cyrus's reign. He is obviously aware of the alternative view that the book derives from the Maccabean period, but in his ignorance of the nature of apocalyptic he continues to insist the work is prospective prophecy.

[243] Dan 1:21. Theodoret is evidently claiming that some commentators blame a copyist (or "redacteur," in Guinot's term [*L'Exégèse*, 721]) for changing "first" (which he might have noted is found in the LXX) to "third" in the light of the earlier date. He chooses to call in question the obvious sense of the latter. Jerome (*Commentariorum in Danielem* [CCSL 75A; S. Hieronymi Presbyteri Opera pars 1, opera exegetica 5; Turnhout: Brepols, 1964], 88), on the other hand, simply observes that the contradiction offers a challenge to commentators, but Theodoret cannot leave it hanging, with biblical "coherence" in question. Taking the statement at face value, on the other hand, means that the year indicated is 536, which would be the seventieth, or perfect, year of Daniel's

τῷ τρίτῳ ἔτει τὴν ἀποκάλυψιν βλέπει ; Ἐγὼ δὲ ἡγοῦμαι οὐ ῥητὸν χρόνον
τὸ πρότερον σημάναι, οὐδὲ τῷ πρώτῳ ἔτει τῆς Κύρου βασιλείας τὴν τοῦ
μακαρίου Δανιὴλ περιορίσαι ζωήν. Οὐδὲ γὰρ εἶπεν, "Εως πρώτου ἔτους
Κύρου τοῦ βασιλέως, ἀλλ' «ἕως ἔτους ἑνός.» Βούλεται δέ, ὡς ἐμοί γε
δοκεῖ, διδάξαι τοὺς ἐντυγχάνοντας τῇ προφητικῇ συγγραφῇ, ὅτι δὴ καὶ
μέχρι Κύρου, τοῦ βασιλέως Περσῶν, διήρκεσεν, ὃς καὶ τῶν δορυαλώτων
Ἰουδαίων τοὺς βουλομένους ἐλευθέρους ἀποφήνας, προσέταξεν εἰς τὴν
ἐνεγκοῦσαν ἐπανελθεῖν, καὶ τὸν θεῖον ἀνεγεῖραι νεών. Τοῦτο δὲ σαφῶς
ἡμᾶς διδάσκει καὶ ὁ ἅγιος ἄγγελος τῷ Δανιὴλ μετὰ βραχέα διαλεγόμε-
νος· φησὶ γάρ· «Καὶ ἐγένετο ἐν ἔτει πρώτῳ Κύρου, ἔστην εἰς κράτος καὶ
ἰσχύν·» ἀντὶ τοῦ· Εὐθὺς τοῦ Κύρου βασιλεύσαντος, πάντα πραγματευόμενος διετέλουν, ὥστε τῆς αἰχμαλωσίας τὸν λαὸν ἀπαλλάξαι. Καὶ ἐν τῷ
τέλει δὲ τοῦ βιβλίου· Παρέλαβε, φησί, Κῦρος ὁ Πέρσης τὴν βασιλείαν,
καὶ ἦν Δανιὴλ συμβιωτὴς τοῦ βασιλέως, καὶ ἔνδοξος ὑπὲρ πάντας τοὺς
φίλους αὐτοῦ· ὥστε πάντοθεν δείκνυσθαι τοῦ τρίτου ἔτους τὸν ἀριθμόν.
«Ἐν τῷ τρίτῳ τοίνυν ἔτει τῆς Κύρου βασιλείας, ὁ λόγος ἀπεκαλύφθη
τῷ Δανιήλ, οὗ τὸ ὄνομα ἐπεκλήθη Βαλτάσαρ. Καὶ ἀληθινὸς ὁ λόγος, καὶ
δύναμις μεγάλη, καὶ σύνεσις ἐδόθη αὐτῷ ἐν τῇ ὀπτασίᾳ.» Εἰκότως δὲ
λόγον καὶ ὀπτασίαν καλεῖ· ἐθεάσατο μὲν γὰρ ἁγίους ἀγγέλους, ἤκουσε δὲ αὐτῶν διαλεγομένων καὶ μεμάθηκεν ἀκριβῶς τὰ ἐσόμενα. Λέγει
δὲ ἀληθῆ εἶναι τὸν λόγον, ὥστε ἀνενδοιάστως ἅπαντας τὰ ῥηθησόμενα
δέξασθαι.

β', γ'. «Ἐν ταῖς ἡμέραις ἐκείναις, ἐγὼ Δανιὴλ ἤμην πενθῶν τρεῖς
ἑβδομάδας ἡμερῶν. Ἄρτον ἐπι|θυμιῶν οὐκ ἔφαγον, καὶ κρέας καὶ οἶνος
οὐκ εἰσῆλθεν εἰς τὸ στόμα μου, καὶ ἄλειμμα οὐκ ἠλειψάμην, ἕως τριῶν
ἑβδομάδων ἡμερῶν.» Ἀναγκαῖον ζητῆσαι τὴν τοῦ πένθους αἰτίαν· ἀσαφῶς γὰρ αὐτὴν ἡ προφητεία διδάσκει. Πρῶτον μὲν γὰρ οὐδὲ ἐπέκειτό
τις ἀθυμίας ἀφορμή· ὅ τε γὰρ βασιλεὺς ἥμερός τε καὶ φιλάνθρωπος, καὶ
τὰ θεῖα τιμῶν, καὶ τοῦ Δανιὴλ τὴν φιλίαν περὶ πολλοῦ ποιούμενος, καὶ
ὅλος ὁ λαὸς εἰρήνης πολλῆς διὰ τὴν τοῦ βασιλέως ἀπήλαυεν ἠπιότη-
τα· μᾶλλον δέ, εἴ τις προσέχειν ἐθελήσειε τῇ τε τοῦ μακαρίου Ἰερεμίου
προφητείᾳ, καὶ τῇ τῶν Παραλειπομένων ἱστορίᾳ, καὶ τῇ τοῦ Ἔσδρα
συγγραφῇ, εὑρήσει τὸν Κῦρον ἐν τῷ πρώτῳ ἔτει τῆς βασιλείας, ἅπασι
τοῖς βουλομένοις τῶν Ἰουδαίων παρεγγυήσαντα τὴν ἐνεγκοῦσαν κατα-
λαβεῖν, καὶ τὸν θεῖον ἀνεγεῖραι νεών, ὥστε πανταχόθεν θυμηδίας ἔχειν
ἀφορμὰς τὸν προφήτην. Ἀλλὰ γὰρ εἴ τις ἀκριβῶς τούτων ἕκαστον ἐξε-

year of the reign of Cyrus, how would he have a revelation in the
third year? In my view, on the other hand, the first reference does
not specify a particular date, and it does not limit the life of blessed
Daniel to the first year of the reign of Cyrus. He did not say, in
fact, "until the first year of King Cyrus," but "for one year." Now,
his intention in my opinion is to inform those reading the inspired
work that he actually lasted until Cyrus king of the Persians, who
set free those of the Jewish captives who wished it, and bade them
return to their country and rebuild the divine temple. The holy
archangel also clearly informs us of this in talking to Daniel shortly
after, saying, "In the first year of Cyrus I rose to give power and
strength"—that is, As soon as Cyrus came to the throne, I kept doing everything to free the people from captivity. And at the end of
the book he says, "Cyrus the Persian took control of the kingdom,
and Daniel was his companion, enjoying a greater reputation than
all his friends."[244] Hence on all the evidence there is proof for the
number *the third year*.

In the third year of the reign of Cyrus, then, *a word was revealed to Daniel, whose name was Belteshazzar. The word was true,
and mighty power and understanding were given to him in the vision.*
He was right to speak of *word* and *vision*: he had seen holy angels,
heard them speaking and gained a precise knowledge of the future. He said the word was *true* so that everyone without question
would accept what would be said. *In those days I, Daniel, had been
grieving for three weeks of days. I had not eaten desirable food, | no*   1489
*meat or wine passed my lips, and I had not anointed myself for three
weeks of days* (vv. 2–3). There is need to enquire about the reason
for the grief, the text's information not being clear. Firstly, note,
no cause of depression was affecting him: the king was mild and
kind, respectful of divine things, appreciative of the friendship of
Daniel, and the people were enjoying deep peace as a result of the
king's kindness. Rather, if you were prepared to refer to the work
of blessed Jeremiah, the story of the Chronicles, and the history
of Esdras, you would find Cyrus in the first year of his reign urg-
ing all the Jews who wished to occupy their homeland and rebuild
the divine temple, the result being that the prophet had reason for
contentment on all scores. If, however, you were in fact to exam-

ministry since its beginning in 606. See note 256 below.
    [244] The first verse of Bel and the Dragon in Theodotion's version, but
occurring as the closing verse of Dan 12 in Theodoret's text.

τάσειεν, αὐτὰ ταῦτα εὑρήσει αἴτια τῆς τοῦ Δανιὴλ ἀχθηδόνος· τοῦ γὰρ
βασιλέως ἐπιτρέψαντος ἅπασι τοῖς ἐθέλουσι τὴν ἐλευθερίαν καὶ τὴν ἐπάνοδον, οἱ μὲν πλείους οἰκίας ἐν Βαβυλῶνι δειμάμενοι, καὶ τούτων τῷ
δεσμῷ κατεχόμενοι, τῆς ἐπανόδου καταφρονήσαντες, τὴν ξένην τῆς οἰκείας προείλοντο· μόνοι δὲ οἱ τῆς εὐσεβείας ἐρασταί, καὶ τῶν πατρῴων
νόμων φύλακες, τῶν ἐν Βαβυλῶνι κτημάτων καταφρονήσαντες, τὴν τῆς
πατρίδος ἐρημίαν καὶ αὐτῆς τῆς βασιλείας προὐτίμησαν. Τοῦτο τοίνυν
τῷ μακαρίῳ Δανιὴλ μέγιστον εἰργάσατο πένθος· τῆς τε γὰρ θείας ἐπαγγελίας τὸ ἀψευδὲς ὁρῶν, καὶ τοῦ βασιλέως τὸ ἥμερον καὶ φιλάνθρωπον,
καὶ τοῦ λαοῦ τὸ δυσπειθὲς καὶ δυσήνιον, σφόδρα τὴν ψυχὴν ἐτρύχετο,
καὶ πενθῶν καὶ θρηνῶν διετέλει. Ζητήσειεν δ᾽ ἄν τις εἰκότως, τί δήποτε
τῶν ἄλλων ἕνεκεν, ὡς ἐρραθυμηκότων καὶ τῆς ἐπανόδου καταπεφρονη-
κότων, θρηνῶν καὶ ὀλοφυρόμενος, αὐτὸς οὐκ ἐπανῆλθεν εἰς τὴν πατρίδα.
Εὑρήσει δὲ τὴν λύσιν, αὐτῆς τῆς αἰχμαλωσίας τὴν αἰτίαν σκοπούμενος.
Ὥσπερ γὰρ οὐ διὰ τὰς οἰκείας πλημμελείας εἴασεν αὐτὸν ὁ Θεὸς δορυάλωτον γενέσθαι, ἀλλὰ τῆς τοῦ λαοῦ προμηθούμενος ὠφελείας, καὶ
οἷόν τινα κηδεμόνα καὶ διδάσκαλον αὐτοῖς συμπέμπων· οὕτω καὶ ἐν τῷ
τῆς ἐπανόδου καιρῷ, τῶν πλειόνων τὴν οἴκησιν τὴν ἐν Βαβυλῶνι στερ-
ξάντων, πάλιν ὁ θεῖος προφήτης συνδιάγειν αὐτοῖς ἀναγκάζεται, ἵνα μὴ
ἔρημοι τῆς πνευματικῆς κηδεμονίας γενόμενοι εἰς ἀσέβειαν παντελῶς
ἐξωκείλωσι. Τούτου χάριν, καὶ βασιλέως τὴν εὐσέβειαν τιμῶντος τοῦ
τηνικάδε κρατοῦντος, καὶ πᾶσαν αὐτῷ θεραπείαν προσφέροντος, καὶ τῶν
ἄλλων προτιμῶντος ἁπάντων, οὐδεμίαν ὁ μακάριος Δανιὴλ λαμβάνει πα-
ραψυχήν, ἀλλ᾽ ἀνιᾷ καὶ λίαν αὐτὸν ἀλγύνει τοῦ λαοῦ τὸ δυσπειθές, καὶ ἡ
τῆς ἁγίας πόλεως λήθη. Οὗ χάριν καὶ τρεῖς ἑβδομάδας ἄσιτος διετέλεσεν·
«Ἄρτον γάρ, φησί, ἐπιθυμιῶν οὐκ ἔφαγον, καὶ κρέας καὶ οἶνος οὐκ εἰσῆλθεν εἰς τὸ στόμα μου, καὶ ἄλειμμα οὐκ ἠλειψάμην ἕως τριῶν ἡμερῶν
1492 | ἑβδομάδων.» Οὐδεμίαν γάρ, φησίν, ἐπιμέλειαν ἐν πάσαις ταύταις ταῖς
ἡμέραις τῷ σώματι προσενήνοχα, οὐκ ἀλοιφὴν ἔξωθεν, οὐ τροφὴν ἔνδο-
θεν. Καλῶς δὲ καὶ μάλα προσφόρως οὐκ ἐπὶ τῶν κρεῶν, ἀλλ᾽ ἐπὶ τοῦ
ἄρτου, τὸ τῶν ἐπιθυμιῶν προστέθεικεν. Ὁ γὰρ ἄρτος ἀναγκαία πάντων τροφή· κρεῶν γὰρ ἀπολαύουσιν οἱ εὐπορώτεροι, ἄρτου δὲ πρὸς τοῖς
εὐπορωτέροις καὶ οἱ πενέστεροι. Διὰ τοῦτο τὸν ἄρτον ἐπιθυμιῶν προσηγόρευσεν, ὡς καὶ κοινὴν ὄντα τροφήν, καὶ πάσης τροφῆς ἐρασμιώτατον.

ine each of these texts precisely, you would find these same factors responsible for Daniel's unease: with the king allowing freedom and return to everyone interested, some people who built bigger houses in Babylon were held in bondage by them and scorned the offer of return, preferring a foreign to a native home, while only religious devotees and observers of the ancestral laws, who scorned a stake in Babylon, preferred the desolation of their homeland even to the palace itself.

This it was, then, that caused blessed Daniel greatest grief: he saw the reliability of the divine promise, the king's mild and kindly manner, and the people's intractable and froward nature, and he was distressed in soul and kept grieving and mourning. You would be right, on the other hand, to enquire why on earth he was weeping and wailing for those others who were uninterested and scornful of returning, yet did not return to his homeland himself. Now, you would find the solution by considering the cause of the captivity itself. You see, just as it was not for his own failings that God allowed him to be taken prisoner, but out of concern for the people's benefit, sending him to accompany them like some carer and teacher, so too at the time of return, when most were happy with residence in Babylon, once more the divine prophet is obliged to share their life lest they be deprived of spiritual care and hurtle head over heels into godlessness. This is the reason why, with a king on the throne at the time who esteemed religion, provided him with every attention, and elevated him above everyone else, blessed Daniel takes no comfort, but is sore distressed and uneasy at the people's intractable attitude and forgetfulness of the holy city.

Hence he kept fasting even for three weeks: *I had not eaten desirable bread, no meat or wine passed my lips, and I had not anointed myself for three weeks of days*: | I paid my body no attention in all these days with anointing on the outside or food within. 1492 Now, it was right and proper for him to attach the word *desirable* not to *meat* but to *bread*: bread is essential nourishment for everyone, the more affluent treating themselves to meat whereas the needy have bread as well as the more affluent. This is the reason for his giving it the term *desirable bread*, since it was nourishment for everyone alike and more sought after than any other food.

δ'. «Καὶ ἐν ἡμέρᾳ εἰκάδι καὶ τετάρτῃ τοῦ μηνὸς τοῦ πρώτου, ἐν τῷ τρίτῳ ἔτει, ἐγὼ ἤμην ἐχόμενα τοῦ ποταμοῦ τοῦ μεγάλου, αὐτός ἐστι Τίγρις.» Ἐπισημήνασθαι δεῖ καὶ τὸν μῆνα, καὶ τὰς τῆς νηστείας ἡμέρας, εἰς ἔλεγχον τῆς Ἰουδαίων παρανομίας. Τῇ γὰρ τεσσαρεσκαιδεκάτῃ τοῦ πρώτου μηνὸς πρὸς ἑσπέραν τοῦ θείου νόμου προστάττοντος ἐπιτελεῖν τὸ Πάσχα, ὁ μακάριος Δανιὴλ μέχρι τῆς τετάρτης εἰκάδος ἄσιτος διετέλει. Εἰ δὲ εἴποιεν οἱ Ἰουδαῖοι, ὅτι ἄρτον ἐπιθυμιῶν οὐκ ἔφαγεν, ἅτε δὴ ἄρτους ἀζύμους ἐσθίων· πρῶτον μὲν τὴν οἰκείαν ἄνοιαν καὶ διὰ τούτων ἐλέγχουσιν· ἄρτος γὰρ καλεῖται καὶ ὁ ζυμίτης, καὶ ὁ ἄζυμος. Ἔπειτα δὲ τὰ ἐπαγόμενα ἀντικρὺς αὐτῶν ἐμφράττει τὸ ἀναίσχυντον στόμα. «Κρέας γὰρ, φησί, καὶ οἶνος οὐκ εἰσῆλθεν εἰς τὸ στόμα μου.» Εἰ δὲ κρεῶν οὐ μετέλαβε, πῶς τὸ Πάσχα ἐπετέλεσεν; Τὸ γὰρ Πάσχα οὐδὲν ἕτερον ἢ ἀμνὸς ἄρσην ἐνιαυσιαῖος, ἄμωμος, πρὸς ἑσπέραν θυόμενος καὶ ὀπτώμενος. Ὁ τοίνυν κρεῶν μὴ μεταλαβών, πῶς τὸ Πάσχα ἐπετέλει; Οὐκοῦν οὐκ ἐπετέλεσε τὸ Πάσχα τῷ νόμῳ πειθόμενος, ὃς διαρρήδην παρακελεύεται τὰς τρεῖς ἐπιτελεῖν ἑορτὰς εἰς τὸν τόπον, ὃν ἂν ἐκλέξηται Κύριος ὁ Θεός. Ἐναργῶς τοίνυν παρανομοῦσιν οἱ Ἰουδαῖοι ταύτας ἐν τῇ ξένῃ τολμῶντες ἐπιτελεῖν. Ἡμεῖς δὲ ἐπὶ τὸ προκείμενον ἐπανέλθωμεν. «Τῇ τετάρτῃ, φησί, καὶ εἰκάδι τοῦ πρώτου μηνός, ἐν τῷ τρίτῳ ἔτει, ἐγὼ ἤμην ἐχόμενα τοῦ ποταμοῦ τοῦ μεγάλου, αὐτός ἐστι Τίγρις.» Πάλιν καὶ ἐντεῦθεν διδασκόμεθα, ὡς οὐκ ἔσφαλται ὁ χρόνος· καὶ γὰρ ἐνταῦθα τῷ τρίτῳ ἔτει, ἀλλ' οὐ τῷ πρώτῳ ἔφη τὴν ὀπτασίαν ἑωρακέναι.

ε', ς'. «Καὶ ἦρα τοὺς ὀφθαλμούς μου, καὶ εἶδον, καὶ ἰδοὺ ἀνὴρ ἐνδεδυμένος βαδδεὶμ, καὶ ἡ ὀσφὺς αὐτοῦ περιεζωσμένη χρυσίῳ Ὠφάζ. Καὶ τὸ σῶμα αὐτοῦ ὡσεὶ Θαρσεῖς.» Βαδδεὶμ δὲ τῇ Ἑλλάδι φωνῇ τὰ βύσσινα σημαίνεται. Λέγει τοίνυν τὸ μὲν ἔνδυμα τοῦ ὀφθέντος βύσσινον τεθεᾶσθαι, τὴν δὲ ζώνην ἐκ χρυσίου Ὠφάζ, τουτέστι, χρυσίου λαμπροτάτου καὶ καθαρωτάτου· «τὸ δὲ σῶμα αὐτοῦ ὡσεὶ Θαρσεῖς·» ἀντὶ τοῦ, ἐῴκει τῷ δοκιμωτάτῳ χρυσίῳ ἐκ Θαρσεῖς φερομένῳ· καὶ γὰρ τῷ Σολομῶντι ἐκεῖθεν τὸ ἄπε|φθον ἐκομίζετο χρυσίον. «Καὶ τὸ πρόσωπον δὲ αὐτοῦ,

*On the twenty-fourth day of the first month in the third year, I
was by the great river, the Tigris* (v. 4).[245] Note should be taken both
of the month and of the days of fasting for proof of the Jews' lawlessness: while the divine law required Passover to be celebrated
on the evening of the fourteenth day of the first month,[246] blessed
Daniel continued his fasting until the twenty-fourth. Now, if the
Jews claim he did not eat *desirable bread* because he was eating unleavened bread, they firstly convict themselves even by this of their
own stupidity, both "leavened" and "unleavened" being referred
to as bread, after all. Next, what follows obviously shuts their
shameless mouth, *no meat or wine passed my lips*; but if he tasted
no meat, how did he celebrate Passover? Passover, remember, involves nothing other than a male lamb of one year, without flaw,
sacrificed and roasted toward evening. Since, therefore, he did not
eat meat, how was he celebrating Passover? So he could not have
been celebrating Passover in obedience to the law, which clearly
requires celebration of the three feast-days in the place which the
Lord God chose. Those Jews, therefore, who dared to observe the
days in a foreign land were breaking the law.

Let us, however, return to the theme. *On the twenty-first day
of the first month of the third year I was by the great river, the* Tigris.
We learn from this as well that the date is not wrong: he says he
had the vision in the *third year* and not in the first. *I raised my
eyes, and saw a man clothed in baddeim, with a belt of gold from Uphaz around his loins. His body was like tharsis* (vv. 5–6). In Greek
baddeim means fine linen; so he is saying that he noticed that the
clothing of the one he saw was of fine linen, and his belt of the
gold of Uphaz, that is, the purest and most resplendent gold.[247]
His body was like tharsis, that is, it resembled most precious gold
brought from Tharsis; Solomon, remember, brought refined gold
from there.[248] | *His face had the appearance of lightning*: beams like   1493

---

[245] The phrase "the first year" occurs only in Theodoret's text.

[246] Cf. Exod 12:1–9; we noted above Theodoret's knowledge of Jewish
ritual and institutions.

[247] Elements of the description are borrowed from similar visions in Ezek
1 and 9, where Hebrew *baddim* is also found. But Theodoret, who will treat of
Ezekiel in his next work, is not registering the similarities. Jer 10:9, on the other
hand, speaks of "silver from Tarshish and gold from Uphaz."

[248] 1 Kgs 10:22, e.g., does speak of Solomon bringing gold from Tharsis. Perhaps a more apposite citation might have been Ezek 1:16 in the vision

ὡς εἶδος ἀστραπῆς.» Αἴγλη, φησί, φωτοειδὴς ἐκ τοῦ προσώπου ἐφέρετο. «Καὶ οἱ ὀφθαλμοὶ αὐτοῦ ὡσεὶ λαμπάδες πυρός, καὶ οἱ βραχίονες αὐτοῦ καὶ τὰ σκέλη ὡς ὅρασις χαλκοῦ στίλβοντος, καὶ ἡ φωνὴ τῶν λόγων αὐτοῦ, ὡς φωνὴ ὄχλου.» Εἶχε δέ, φησί, καὶ τοὺς ὀφθαλμοὺς πῦρ ἀφιέντας, τοὺς δὲ βραχίονας τῷ καλλίστῳ χαλκῷ ἐοικότας· ἔδοξας δ' ἂν πλήθους ἀκούειν πολλοῦ διαλεγομένου ἀκούων.

ζ'. «Καὶ εἶδον ἐγὼ Δανιὴλ μόνος τὴν ὀπτασίαν, καὶ οἱ ἄνδρες οἱ μετ' ἐμοῦ οὐκ εἶδον τὴν ὀπτασίαν, ἀλλ' ἢ ἔκστασις μεγάλη ἐπέπεσεν ἐπ' αὐτούς, καὶ ἔφυγον ἐν φόβῳ.» Ἀλλ' ἴσως ἄν τις εἴποι· Καὶ τί δήποτε ἔφυγον, τὴν ὀπτασίαν μὴ θεασάμενοι; Ἀλλ' εἰκὸς τοῦτο πλέον αὐτοῖς ἀπεργάσασθαι τὸ δέος· μηδένα γὰρ θεώμενοι, καὶ φωνῆς μεγίστης ἀκούοντες, εἰκότως ἐκδειματωθέντες ἀπέδρασαν. Ἔκστασιν δὲ ἐνταῦθα καλεῖ οὐ τὴν δειλίαν μόνην, ἀλλὰ καὶ τὴν ἀορασίαν· ἔοικε δὲ ταῦτα τοῖς ἐπὶ τοῦ μακαρίου Παύλου γεγενημένοις κατὰ τὴν ὁδὸν τὴν πλησιάζουσαν τῇ Δαμασκῷ· καὶ γὰρ ἐκεῖ αὐτὸς εἶδε περιαστράψαν αὐτὸν φῶς· οἱ δὲ συνόντες ἐθεάσαντο μὲν οὐδέν, μόνης δὲ ἤκουσαν τῆς φωνῆς. Καὶ ἐνταῦθα τοίνυν ὡσαύτως φεύγουσιν οἱ συνόντες τῷ θείῳ προφήτῃ, μόνης ἀκούσαντες τῆς φωνῆς, μένει δὲ μόνος αὐτός.

η'. «Ἐγὼ γάρ, φησίν, ὑπελείφθην μόνος, καὶ εἶδον τὴν ὀπτασίαν τὴν μεγάλην ταύτην, καὶ οὐχ ὑπελείφθη ἐν ἐμοὶ ἰσχύς, καὶ ἡ δόξα μου μετεστράφη εἰς διαφθοράν, καὶ οὐκ ἐκράτησα ἰσχύος.» Τοσοῦτον γάρ μοι ἐνέπεσε δέος ἀπ' ἐκείνης τῆς θεωρίας, ὡς διαλυθῆναι μὲν τῶν ἄρθρων τὴν ἁρμονίαν, ἀμειφθῆναι δὲ τῆς τοῦ σώματος ἐπιφανείας τὸ χρῶμα, πάσης δὲ ἰσχύος ἔρημόν με γενέσθαι.

θ'. «Καὶ ἤκουσα, φησί, τὴν φωνὴν τῶν λόγων αὐτοῦ, καὶ ἐν τῷ ἀκοῦσαί με ἤμην κατανενυγμένος ἐπὶ πρόσωπόν μου, καὶ τὸ πρόσωπόν μου ἐπὶ τὴν γῆν.» Παραυτίκα γάρ, φησί, τῆς μεγίστης ἐκείνης ἀκούσας φωνῆς, ἔπεσα μὲν πρηνής· ἰδεῖν δὲ μὴ δυνάμενος τὴν φρικώδη θεωρίαν, εἰς τὴν γῆν μου τὸ πρόσωπον τέθεικα.

ι'. «Καὶ ἰδοὺ χεὶρ ἁπτομένη μου, καὶ ἤγειρέ με ἐπὶ τὰ γόνατά μου, καὶ ἐπὶ τὰ ἴχνη τῶν χειρῶν μου ἔστησέ με.» Οὕτω, φησί, διακείμενος ᾐσθανόμην οἷόν τινος χειρὸς ἁπτομένης μου, καὶ ἀνορθούσης· ἐγὼ δὲ τοῖς τε γόνασι καὶ ταῖς χερσὶ χρώμενος (διέλυσέ με γὰρ τὸ δέος), ἐπειρώμην ἀνίστασθαι.

ια'. «Ὁ δὲ εἶπε πρός με· Δανιήλ, ἀνὴρ ἐπιθυμιῶν, σύνες ἐν τοῖς λόγοις τούτοις, οἷς ἐγὼ λαλῶ πρὸς σέ, καὶ στῆθι ἐπὶ τῇ στάσει σου, ὅτι νῦν | ἀπεστάλην πρὸς σέ.» Πρόσεχε, φησίν, ἀκριβῶς τοῖς ὑπ' ἐμοῦ λεγομένοις, καὶ τὸ δέος ἀποθέμενος, μετὰ συνέσεως ἄκουε τῶν ῥηθησομένων·

light streamed from his face. *His eyes like burning lamps, his arms and legs like a glimpse of shining bronze, and the sound of his words like the sound of a multitude*: he had eyes that were emitting fire, and arms like the most beautiful bronze; you would think you were hearing a mighty crowd talking.

I, Daniel, alone had the vision; the men with me did not have the vision, though a great trance came upon them, and they fled in fear (v. 7). Perhaps you might ask, Why on earth did they flee, not having had the vision? This fact probably instilled greater fear into them: though seeing nothing, they heard a loud voice, and they ran off terrified.[249] Now, by *trance* here he refers not to fear alone but also to the invisibility; it was like what happened in the case of blessed Paul on the road near Damascus: there he saw a light flashing around him, whereas his companions saw nothing, hearing only the voice. So here likewise the companions of the divine prophet flee, hearing only the voice, and he remains alone. *I was left by myself, and had this marvelous vision; my strength left me, my appearance underwent a change, and I retained no strength* (v. 8): such fear came upon me from that vision that I lost the coordination of my limbs, my bodily complexion changed, and I was bereft of all strength. *I heard the sound of his words, and on hearing it I registered astonishment in my face, and my face was on the ground* (v. 9): as soon as I heard that loud voice, I fell prostrate; unable to bear the fearsome sight, I put my face to the ground.

And, lo, a hand touched me, raised me up to my knees and set me on the flat of my hands (v. 10): in this posture I felt something like a hand touching me and raising me up. For my part I was crawling on hands and knees, fear having loosed my joints, and I kept trying to get up. *He said to me, Daniel, man of desires, find understanding in these words I speak to you and stand up straight, because now | I have been sent to you* (v. 11): attend carefully to what is said   1496 by me, lay aside your fear, and listen with understanding to what will be told you: I have been sent to inform you of this; since you have proved superior to bodily desires, and have become a lover

episode, where as here Θαρσείς has the sense of "beryl"—a rare occurrence, admittedly.

[249] Not appreciating the apocalyptic character of the story, Theodoret feels the need to account for any unrealistic items, such as Daniel's knowing the archangel's name in the previous chapter. He finds confirmation of his surmise in Paul's incident on the road to Damascus in Acts 9:3–7.

ταῦτα γὰρ ἀπεστάλην διδάξαι σε· ἐπειδὴ τῶν μὲν τοῦ σώματος ἐπιθυμιῶν κρείττων ἐφάνης, ἐραστὴς δὲ ἐγένου τῶν θείων, καὶ φιλοστόργως δὲ περὶ τὸν λαὸν διακείμενος τὰ τούτῳ συμβησόμενα μαθεῖν ἐπεθύμησας. Καλεῖ δὲ αὐτὸν οὐ Βαλτάσαρ, ἀλλὰ Δανιήλ· τὸ μὲν γὰρ ἦν Χαλδαίων, τὸ δὲ Ἑβραίων ὄνομα· καὶ τὸ μὲν ὑπὸ εὐσεβῶν ἐτέθη, τὸ δὲ ὑπὸ δυσσεβῶν προσετέθη. Σημαίνει δὲ τὸ Δανιὴλ τῇ Ἑλλάδι φωνῇ κρίσιν Θεοῦ· ὡς εἶναι αὐτὸν καὶ φερώνυμον, καὶ δι' αὐτῶν κηρύττειν τῶν πραγμάτων, ὡς ὀρθῇ καὶ δικαίᾳ κρίσει χρώμενος ὁ Θεὸς τῆς προφητικῆς αὐτὸν ἠξίωσε χάριτος, καὶ τὰ πολλαῖς ὕστερον γενεαῖς ἐσόμενα δῆλα πεποίηκε. «Καὶ ἐν τῷ λαλῆσαι αὐτὸν πρός με τὸν λόγον, ἀνέστην ἔντρομος.» Ἤρκεσε μὲν γὰρ ὁ λόγος ἀναστῆσαί με, παντελῶς δὲ τὸ δέος οὐκ ἀπεθέμην.

ιβ'. «Καὶ εἶπε πρός με· Μὴ φοβοῦ, Δανιήλ, ὅτι ἀπὸ τῆς πρώτης ἡμέρας, ἧς ἔδωκας τὴν καρδίαν σου τοῦ συνιέναι καὶ κακωθῆναι ἐναντίον Κυρίου τοῦ Θεοῦ σου, ἠκούσθησαν οἱ λόγοι σου, καὶ ἐγὼ ἦλθον ἐν τοῖς λόγοις σου.» Ἐντεῦθεν διδασκόμεθα, ὅσον ἡμᾶς ἡ αὐθαίρετος ὀνίνησι κάκωσις. Καὶ γὰρ ὁ μακάριος Δανιὴλ κακώσας ἑαυτὸν τῇ αὐθαιρέτῳ νηστείᾳ, καὶ τὸν Κύριον ἐκζητήσας, παραυτίκα πέπεικεν, καὶ ὧν ἐπεπόθησεν ἔτυχεν. Τοῦτο γὰρ καὶ ὁ ὀφθεὶς αὐτῷ δῆλον ποιεῖ· «Ἀπὸ γὰρ τῆς πρώτης, φησίν, ἡμέρας, ἧς ἔδωκας τὴν καρδίαν σου συνιέναι καὶ κακωθῆναι ἐναντίον Κυρίου τοῦ Θεοῦ σου, ἠκούσθησαν οἱ λόγοι σου·» τεκμήριον δὲ τούτου μέγιστον ἔχεις τὴν ἐμὴν παρουσίαν. «Ἐγὼ γὰρ ἦλθον, φησίν, ἐν τοῖς λόγοις σου·» ἀντὶ τοῦ, Διὰ τοὺς λόγους σου, καὶ ἣν προσενήνοχας δέησιν.

ιγ'. «Καὶ ὁ ἄρχων, φησί, βασιλείας Περσῶν εἱστήκει ἐξ ἐναντίας μου, εἴκοσι καὶ μίαν ἡμέραν.» Ἐν αὐτῇ, φησί, τῇ πρώτῃ ἡμέρᾳ τῆς προσευχῆς σου δεχθείσης σου τῆς ἱκετείας, ἀπεστάλην πρὸς σέ· πάσας δὲ ταύτας τὰς ἡμέρας διεκώλυσέ μου τὴν πρὸς σὲ ἄφιξιν ὁ τῆς τῶν Περσῶν βασιλείας ἄρχων. «Καὶ ἰδοὺ Μιχαὴλ εἷς τῶν ἀρχόντων τῶν πρώτων ἦλθε βοηθῆσαί μοι, καὶ αὐτὸν κατέλιπον ἐκεῖ μετὰ τοῦ ἄρχοντος βασιλέως Περσῶν.» Ταῦτα σαφέστερον ἡμᾶς διδάσκει ὁ μακάριος Μωσῆς. «Ὅτε γάρ, φησί, διεμέρισεν ὁ Ὕψιστος ἔθνη, ὡς διέσπειρεν υἱοὺς Ἀδάμ, ἔστησεν ὅρια ἐθνῶν κατὰ ἀριθμὸν ἀγγέλων Θεοῦ.» Καὶ ὁ Κύριος ἐν τοῖς ἱεροῖς Εὐαγγελίοις φησὶ τοῖς ἀποστόλοις· «Ὁρᾶτε, μὴ καταφρονήσητε

of divine things, in your affection for the people you have desired to learn what will befall them.²⁵⁰ Now, he refers to him not as Belteshazzar but as Daniel, the former a Chaldean name, the latter a Hebrew one, the latter given by religious people, the former by the godless. *Daniel* in Greek means "judgment of God," and consequently in fidelity to his name he proclaimed in action that God exercised a right and proper judgment in vouchsafing him the charism of inspiration, and that he made clear what would happen generations later.

While he was addressing this remark to me, I stood up trembling: while his word was sufficient to raise me up, I did not completely lay aside my fear. *He said to me, Do not fear, Daniel: from the first day you gave your heart to understanding and humbling yourself before the Lord your God, your words were heard, and I have come in response to your words* (v. 12). From this we learn how great is the advantage to us of voluntary self-denial: blessed Daniel denied himself by voluntary fasting and sought the Lord, and he immediately won him over and gained what he desired. The one who appeared to him, in fact, made this clear to him in saying, *From the first day you gave your heart to understanding and denying yourself before the Lord your God, your words were heard*, and you have my coming as the clearest sign of this, for *I have come in response to your words*, that is, as a result of your words and the request you made.

The leader of the kingdom of the Persians opposed me for twenty-one days (v. 13): on the very first day of your prayer your petition was accepted, and I was sent to you; but for all these days the leader of the kingdom of the Persians prevented my reaching you. *And, lo, Michael, one of the chief leaders came to help me, and I left him there with the leader of the kingdom of the Persians*. Blessed Moses informs us of this more clearly, "When the Most High divided nations after dispersing the children of Adam, he set boundaries of nations according to the number of God's angels."²⁵¹ And the Lord says to the apostles in the sacred Gospels,

---

²⁵⁰ Cf. the interpretation Theodoret gave this sobriquet at its occurrence at 9:23 (occurring also at 10:19). Now for the first time he informs the reader of the meaning of the Hebrew name Daniel—though modern commentators prefer a rendering "my judge is God" or "God had judged."

²⁵¹ Deut 32:8 in this LXX form lent support to the idea in ancient Judaism that each nation had its guardian angel. Theodoret mentions also in other of his

ἑνὸς τῶν μικρῶν τούτων, ὅτι οἱ ἄγγελοι αὐτῶν καθ᾽ ἡμέραν ὁρῶσι τὸ πρόσωπον τοῦ Πατρός μου ἐν τοῖς οὐρανοῖς.» Καὶ ἄλλα δὲ πολλὰ τοιαῦτα ἐν τῇ θείᾳ Γραφῇ. Διδασκόμεθα τοίνυν ἐκ τούτων, | ὡς τῶν ἀγγέλων μὲν ἕκαστος τὴν ἑκάστου ἡμῶν ἐπιμέλειαν ἐγκεχείρισται, εἰς τὸ φρουρεῖν καὶ φυλάττειν, καὶ τῶν τοῦ πονηροῦ δαίμονος ἐπιβουλῶν ἀπαλλάττειν· οἱ δὲ ἀρχάγγελοι τὰς τῶν ἐθνῶν ἐπιστασίας ἐνεπιστεύθησαν, ὡς μακάριος ἐδίδαξε Μωσῆς. Συμφωνεῖ δὲ τούτοις καὶ ὁ μακάριος Δανιήλ· λέγει γὰρ καὶ αὐτὸς τῆς *βασιλείας Περσῶν ἄρχοντα·* καὶ πάλιν μετὰ βραχέα, *ἄρχοντα τῶν Ἑλλήνων,* καὶ τὸν Μιχαὴλ δὲ *ἄρχοντα τοῦ Ἰσραὴλ* ἀποκαλεῖ. Τούτων τοίνυν ἐντεῦθέν τε κἀκεῖθεν δήλων γεγενημένων, ζητητέον τί δήποτε ὁ τῆς Περσικῆς βασιλείας ἄρχων ἐναντιοῦσθαι ἐδόκει τῷ τὴν ὑπὲρ τοῦ λαοῦ ποιουμένῳ συνηγορίαν. Ὅτι μὲν γὰρ παθῶν ἐστι τῶν ἀγγέλων ἡ φύσις ἀμείνων, καὶ ἁγιωσύνης ἀνάπλεως, παντί που δῆλον. Ὅτι δὲ καὶ τοῖς θείοις νεύμασιν ἀνενδοιάστως ἕπονται, καὶ τοῦτο πανταχόθεν ἔστι καταμαθεῖν. Πῶς τοίνυν τῇ τῶν Ἰσραηλιτῶν κηδεμονίᾳ ἐναντιοῦσθαι ἐδόκει τῆς Περσῶν βασιλείας ὁ ἄρχων; Ἀλλὰ γὰρ εἴ τις ἀκριβῶς κατανοεῖν ἐθελήσειεν, εὑρήσει τῶν εἰρημένων τὸν νοῦν. Ὅ τε γὰρ *τῶν Περσῶν ἄρχων,* καὶ ὁ *τῶν Ἑλλήνων ἄρχων,* τουτέστιν, οἱ τὴν τούτων φυλακήν τε καὶ ἐπιμέλειαν ἐγκεχειρισμένοι, ἀναγκαίως, ἅτε δὴ φιλοστόργως περὶ τούτους διακείμενοι, ὧν τὴν κηδεμονίαν εἶχον, καὶ τοῦ Ἰσραὴλ δὲ τὴν παρανομίαν ὁρῶντες, ἐδυσχέραινον πλείονος αὐτοὺς βλέποντες ἀπολαύοντας προμηθείας. Οὐ γὰρ ᾔδεισαν τὸ μυστήριον τὸ ἀποκεκρυμμένον ἐν τῷ Θεῷ τῷ πάντα κτίσαντι. Μετὰ γὰρ τὴν τοῦ Σωτῆρος ἡμῶν ἐνανθρώπησιν, ὡς ὁ μακάριος ἔφη Παῦλος, ἐγνωρίσθη ταῖς ἀρχαῖς καὶ ταῖς ἐξουσίαις, διὰ τῆς Ἐκκλησίας ἡ πολυποίκιλος σοφία τοῦ Θεοῦ. Τοῦτο τοίνυν τὸ μυστήριον ἀγνοοῦντες, καὶ τὴν πολλὴν τοῦ Θεοῦ περὶ τὸν Ἰσραὴλ πρόνοιαν ὁρῶντες οἱ τῶν ἄλλων ἐθνῶν τὴν ἐπιμέλειαν πεπιστευμένοι, ἐδυσχέραινον θεώμενοι μάλιστα μετὰ νόμον, καὶ προφήτας, καὶ τοσαύτην διδασκαλίαν τε καὶ κηδεμονίαν, χεῖρον τῶν ὑπ᾽ αὐτῶν ποιμαινομένων διακειμένους, καὶ πλείοσιν ἐμπεφυρμένους κακοῖς. Τοῦτο καὶ ὁ τῷ μακαρίῳ Δανιὴλ ὀφθεὶς ἄγγελος ἔλεγε· «Καὶ ὁ ἄρχων βασι

"Be careful not to despise one of these little ones, because their angels each day look upon the face of my Father in heaven";[252] and there are many other similar statements in the divine Scripture. So we learn from this | that while each of the angels is entrusted   1497 with the care of each of us for guarding and protecting and ridding us of the wicked demon's wiles, the archangels were entrusted with the patronage of nations, as blessed Moses informs us. Now, blessed Daniel's words are consistent with this: he for his part also speaks of *leader of the kingdom of the Persians*, and in turn shortly after *leader of the Greeks*, and calls Michael *leader of Israel*.

So since this becomes clear from one source and another, the question must be asked why on earth the leader of the Persian kingdom seemed to be opposing the one responsible for advocacy of the people. After all, it is clear to anyone that angels by nature are proof against passions and full of holiness; and you can discover from every source that they respond to the divine wishes without question. How is it, then, that the leader of the kingdom of the Persians seemed to be opposing the care of the Israelites? If, however, you were interested in gaining a precise understanding, you would find the meaning of the words: the *leader of the Persians* and the *leader of the Greeks*, that is, those entrusted with their protection and care, consequent upon their being fond of those whom they cared for, observed the lawlessness of Israel and were displeased with seeing them enjoying greater care. After all, they did not know the mystery hidden in God the creator of all things; after the incarnation of our Savior, as blessed Paul says, "God's wisdom in its rich variety in the church was made known to the powers and authorities."[253] Unaware of this mystery, therefore, and observing God's great providence for Israel, those entrusted with the care of the other nations were displeased on seeing in them, especially despite law and prophets and so much teaching and care, a worse attitude than in those they were tending, and clinging to worse vices. The angel in his appearance to blessed Daniel also

works (e.g., his *Commentary on the Pauline Epistles*, on which see Robert C. Hill, trans., *Theodoret of Cyrus: Commentary on the Letters of St. Paul* [2 vols.; Brookline, Mass.: Holy Cross Orthodox Press, 2002]) the cult of the angels, especially Michael, in churches with which he was familiar, and the angels loom large at the beginning of his *Quaestiones on Genesis* (part of his *Quaestiones in Octateuchem*).

[252] Cf. Matt 18:10.
[253] Eph 3:9–10.

λείας Περσῶν εἰστήκει ἐξ ἐναντίας μου εἴκοσι καὶ μίαν ἡμέραν·» ἀντὶ τοῦ, Ταύτας ἁπάσας τὰς ἡμέρας πείθων αὐτὸν διετέλουν, ὡς δικαίως ταύτης οὗτοι ἀξιοῦνται τῆς προμηθείας· συνηγόρει δέ μοι καὶ ὁ Μιχαὴλ εἷς τῶν πρώτων ὑπάρχων ἀρχόντων. «Καὶ αὐτόν, φησί, κατέλιπον ἐκεῖ μετὰ τοῦ ἄρχοντος βασιλείας Περσῶν.»

ιδ'. «Καὶ ἦλθον συνετίσαι σε, ὅσα ἀπαντήσει τῷ λαῷ σου ἐπ' ἐσχάτων τῶν ἡμερῶν, ὅτι ἰδοὺ ἡ ὅρασις εἰς ἡμέρας.» Καὶ ἐμοῦ δέ, φησίν, ἀφικομένου πρὸς σὲ ἐπὶ τῷ σε προδιδάξαι τὰ μετ' οὐ πολὺν χρόνον συμβησόμενα τῷ λαῷ σου, ἐπέμεινεν ὁ Μιχαὴλ τῷ ἄρχοντι βασιλείας Περσῶν διαλεγόμενος. Καὶ οὐχ ἁπλῶς εἶπε τῷ ἄρχοντι Περ|σῶν, ἀλλὰ «τῷ ἄρχοντι βασιλείας Περσῶν,» ἀντὶ τοῦ, καὶ αὐτοῦ τοῦ βασιλέως Περσῶν ἄρχειν πεπιστευμένῳ.

ιε'. «Καὶ ἐν τῷ λαλῆσαι αὐτὸν μετ' ἐμοῦ κατὰ τοὺς λόγους τούτους, ἔδωκα τὸ πρόσωπόν μου εἰς τὴν γῆν, καὶ κατενύγην.» Ἀκούσας γάρ, ὅτι καὶ τῶν ἀγγέλων οἱ πρῶτοι δυσχεραίνουσι τὴν γινομένην εἰς τὸν λαὸν κηδεμονίαν, ἀθυμίας πάλιν ἀναπλησθεὶς συγκεκυφὼς εἰστήκειν, καὶ ἀναβλέπειν οὐ δυνάμενος.

ις', ιζ'. «Καὶ ἰδοὺ ὡς ὁμοίωσις Υἱοῦ ἀνθρώπου ἥψατο τῶν χειλέων μου, καὶ ἐλάλησα, καὶ εἶπον πρὸς τὸν ἑστῶτα ἐναντίον μου· Κύριε, ἐν τῇ ὁράσει σου ἐστράφη τὰ ἐντός μου ἐν ἐμοί, καὶ ἰδοὺ οὐκ ἔχω ἰσχύν. Καὶ πῶς δυνήσεται, Κύριε, ὁ παῖς σου λαλῆσαι μετὰ τοῦ Κυρίου μου τούτου; Καὶ ἐγὼ ἠσθένησα, καὶ ἀπὸ τοῦ νῦν οὐ στήσεται ἐν ἐμοὶ ἰσχύς, καὶ πνοὴ οὐχ ὑπελείφθη ἐν ἐμοί.» Θεασάμενός με, φησί, πάλιν ἀγωνίας ἀνάπλεων, οἷόν τινι ἀνθρωπείᾳ χειρὶ τῶν χειλέων μου ἁψάμενος, ἐνέθεικέ μοι διαλέξεως δύναμιν, καὶ εἶπον αὐτῷ, ὅτι Καὶ μόνη σου ἡ θεωρία δυνάμεως μὲν ἁπάσης ἔρημόν με κατέστησε, θορύβου τε καὶ ταραχῆς τὴν ψυχὴν ἀνέπλησε, καὶ τῆς προτέρας εὐταξίας τὸν λογισμὸν ἐγύμνωσεν. Τοσαύτην γὰρ ἀσθένειαν ἐκ τοῦ δέους ἐδεξάμην, ὡς μηδὲ συνήθως ἀναπνεῖν δύνασθαι τὸν ἀέρα· πῶς οὖν δυνήσομαι, ἢ συνιέναι τῶν ὑπὸ σοῦ λεγομένων, ἢ ἀπόκρισιν τὴν ἁρμόττουσαν ἀντιδοῦναι; Μηδεὶς δὲ νομιζέτω, τὸν ὀφθέντα αὐτὸν εἶναι τὸν Δεσπότην, ἐπειδὴ Κύριον αὐτὸν ὁ Δανιὴλ προσαγορεύει. Οὗτος γὰρ αὐτὸς ἐν τῷ τέλει τῆς ὀπτασίας· «Ἀνατείνας, φησίν, εἰς τὸν οὐρανὸν τὰς χεῖρας αὐτοῦ, ὤμοσεν ἐν τῷ ζῶντι Κυρίῳ,» τὴν δουλείαν εὐγνωμόνως ὁμολογῶν. Κύριον τοίνυν αὐτὸν ἀποκαλεῖ, οὐχ ὡς Θεόν, ἀλλὰ τιμὴν ἀπονέμων τὴν προσήκουσαν. Καὶ γὰρ ἡμεῖς τοῖς ἐντιμοτέροις τῶν ἀνθρώπων διαλεγόμενοι, τούτῳ κεχρῆσθαι εἰώθαμεν τῷ προσρήματι, ὥσπερ καὶ ὁ μακάριος Ἀβραὰμ τοὺς ἀγγέλους ὡς ἄνδρας θεασάμενος, καὶ ὡς ἀνδράσι διαλεγόμενος· «Δέομαι, Κύριε, εἶπεν, εἰ ἄρα ηὗρον χάριν ἐναντίον σου, μὴ παρέλθῃς τὸν

said as much, *The leader of the kingdom of the Persians opposed me for twenty-one days*, that is, I kept trying to convince him all that time that they rightly deserve this care, and Michael, one of the chief leaders, also supported me; *and I left him there with the leader of the kingdom of the Persians. And I have come to make you understand what will come upon your people at the end of the days because, lo, there is a vision for days* (vv. 13–14): while I came to you to inform you in advance of what will happen to your people before long, Michael kept talking with the leader of the kingdom of the Persians. He did not simply say, to the leader of the Persians, | 1500 but *to the leader of the kingdom of the Persians*, meaning, to the one entrusted with the actual king of the Persians.

While he was speaking to me in these terms, I lowered my face to the ground and was stupefied (v. 15): on hearing that the principal angels were displeased at the care given to the people, I was once more filled with unease and stood with head bent, incapable even of looking up. *And, lo, one in human form touched my lips. I addressed the one standing before me in the words, Lord, I was deeply moved by the sight of you; see, I have no strength. How will your servant, lord, be able to speak with my lord? I have grown weak, and from now on no strength will remain in me, no breath is left in me* (vv. 16–17): Seeing me once more filled with anxiety, he touched my lips with a human hand, as it were, and imparted to me the power of speech. I said, The very sight of you left me bereft of all power, filled my soul with alarm and panic, and deprived my thinking of its former logic. Such weakness did I experience from the fear as to deprive me even of the ability to breathe air in the usual way; so how shall I manage either to understand what is said by you or make an appropriate reply?

Now, let no one think that the one seen was the Lord from Daniel's calling him *lord*: he himself says at the end of the vision, "Raising his hands to heaven, he swore by the living Lord,"[254] dutifully confessing his condition as servant. So by *lord* he is not speaking of him as God, but paying him due respect; in speaking with people of more honorable status we normally use this title, as blessed Abraham did on seeing angels as men and addressing them as men, "I beg you, lord, if I have found favor in your sight, not to pass by your servant"; and blessed Rebekah said to the servant of

[254] Cf. 12:7.

παῖδά σου.» Καὶ ἡ μακαρία Ῥεβέκκα τῷ οἰκέτῃ τοῦ μακαρίου Ἀβρα-
άμ· «Πίε, φησί, κύριε, καὶ ταῖς καμήλοις σου ὑδρεύσομαι.» Οὐκοῦν καὶ
ἐνταῦθα τὸ Κύριος οὐ τὸν τῶν ὅλων σημαίνει Θεόν· καὶ τοῦτο σαφέστερον ἐκ τοῦ τέλους γνωρισόμεθα, τέως δὲ τῆς ἀκολουθίας ἐχώμεθα.

ιη', ιθ'. «Καὶ προσέθετο, φησί, καὶ ἥψατό μου ὡς ὅρασις ἀνθρώπου, καὶ ἐνίσχυσέ με, καὶ εἶπέ μοι· Μὴ φοβοῦ, ἀνὴρ ἐπιθυμιῶν, εἰρήνη
σοι, ἀνδρίζου, καὶ ἴσχυε.» Ἀντὶ τοῦ· Μηδὲν ἀγωνιάσῃς· οὐ γὰρ ἐπὶ λύ-
1501   μῃ σου παρεγενόμην, ἀλλ' ὥστε γνωρίσαι σοι, | ἃ μαθεῖν ἐπεθύμησας·
τὸ δέος τοίνυν ἀπορρίψας ἀνδρίζου, καὶ ἴσχυε. Καὶ τῷ λόγῳ τὸ ἔργον
ἐπηκολούθησε.

κ', κα'. «Καὶ ἐν τῷ λαλῆσαι, φησίν, αὐτὸν μετ' ἐμοῦ, ἐνίσχυσα,
καὶ εἶπον· Λαλείτω ὁ Κύριός μου, ὅτι ἐνίσχυσάς με. Καὶ εἶπεν· Εἰ οἶδας
τί ἦλθον πρὸς σέ; Καὶ νῦν ἐπιστρέψω τοῦ πολεμῆσαι μετὰ τοῦ ἄρχοντος Περσῶν· καὶ ἐγὼ ἐξεπορευόμην, καὶ ὁ ἄρχων τῶν Ἑλλήνων ἤρχετο.
Ἀλλ' ἢ ἀναγγελῶ σοι τὸ τεταγμένον ἐν Γραφῇ ἀληθείας, καὶ οὐκ ἔστιν
εἷς ἀντεχόμενος μετ' ἐμοῦ περὶ τούτων, ἀλλ' ἢ Μιχαὴλ ὁ ἄρχων ὑμῶν.»
Τί δήποτε γάρ, φησίν, ἕνα ἢ δύο λέγω, τόν τε Περσῶν ἄρχοντα, ἢ τῶν
Ἑλλήνων; Οὐδεὶς γὰρ τῶν ἐπουρανίων δυνάμεων βούλεταί τινος ἀγαθοῦ τὸν ὑμέτερον τυχεῖν λαόν, διὰ τὴν πολλὴν δηλονότι παρανομίαν, ἢ
μόνος Μιχαήλ, ὃς τὴν ὑμετέραν ἐνεχειρίσθη κηδεμονίαν. Τὸ δὲ πολεμῆσαι, ἀντὶ τοῦ, διαλεχθῆναι, καὶ πεῖσαι τέθεικεν, δεῖξαι βουλόμενος τήν
τε ἐκείνου δικαίαν κατὰ τοῦ λαοῦ ἀγανάκτησιν, καὶ τὴν αὐτοῦ περὶ τὸν
λαὸν εὔνοιαν. Εἰκὸς δὲ τὸν διαλεγόμενον εἶναι τὸν ἅγιον Γαβριήλ· οὗτος
γὰρ αὐτῷ καὶ ἤδη τὰς ἄλλας ἀποκαλύψεις ἡρμήνευσε.

ΚΕΦΑΛΑΙΟΝ ΙΑ'

α'. «Καὶ ἐγένετο, φησίν, ἐν ἔτει πρώτῳ Κύρου, ἔστην εἰς κράτος
καὶ ἰσχύν.» Εὐθύς, φησί, τοῦ Κύρου βασιλεύσαντος, καὶ τοῦ ὅρου τῆς
αἰχμαλωσίας συμπληρωθέντος, ἀνέστην ἕως οὗ τὴν ἄφεσιν τῷ λαῷ καὶ
τὴν ἐλευθερίαν ἐπραγματευσάμην.

β'. «Καὶ νῦν ἀναγγελῶ σοι ἀλήθειαν.» Λέγω δέ σοι μετὰ ἀληθείας
τὰ ἐσόμενα. «Ἰδοὺ ἔτι τρεῖς βασιλεῖς ἀναστήσονται ἐν τῇ Περσίδι.» Μετὰ Κῦρον ἐβασίλευσε Καμβύσης· τοῦτον οἱ Μάγοι διαδεξάμενοι, δέκα
μῆνας ἐβασίλευσαν· μετ' ἐκείνους Δαρεῖος ὁ Ὑστάσπου. «Καὶ ὁ τέταρ-

blessed Abraham, "Drink, lord, and I shall water your camels."²⁵⁵ So here, too, *lord* does not mean the God of all; we shall learn this more clearly from the conclusion, but for the time being let us keep to the sequence of the story.

A further one in human form came and touched me, strengthened me, and said to me, Do not fear, man of desires, peace be with you, be brave and strong (v. 18), that is, Do not be anxious: I have come, not to harm you, but to inform you | of what you desired 1501 to learn; so cast off your fear, be brave and strong. And action followed word: *When he spoke to me, I grew strong, and said, Let my lord speak, because you have strengthened me. He replied, Do you not know why I have come to you? I shall now return to fight against the leader of the Persians; I went off, and the leader of the Greeks came. But I shall announce to you what is set down in the book of truth; there is no one with me to resist them except Michael your leader* (vv. 19–21): why mention one or two, the leader of the Persians and of the Greeks? None of the heavenly powers wants your people to receive any good—the result of their lawlessness, clearly—except Michael alone, who has been entrusted with your care. He used *fight* in the sense of converse with and persuade, intending to bring out one person's justifiable annoyance with the people and the other's benevolence toward them. Now, the one talking was probably holy Gabriel, he being the one who had also previously interpreted the other revelations for him.²⁵⁶

CHAPTER I I

In the first year of Cyrus I rose to give power and strength (v. 1): as soon as Cyrus came to the throne, and the end of the captivity had been reached, I took my place until I had secured release and liberation for the people. *I shall now announce the truth to you* (v. 2): I am telling you in truth what will happen. *Lo, a further three kings will arise in Persia.* Cambyses was king after Cyrus; the soothsayers succeeded him and ruled for ten months, and after them

²⁵⁵ Gen 18:3; 24:46, where it is rather Abraham's servant whom Rebekah addresses.
²⁵⁶ The author of the book, in fact, makes a similar supposition, it is thought, by appending a chronological note that opens the next chapter (reading "Darius the Mede" in the Hebrew for "Cyrus" in the Greek versions).

τος, φησί, πλουτήσει πλοῦτον μέγαν παρὰ πάντας.» Τὸν Ξέρξην λέγει, τὸν τοῦ Δαρείου υἱόν. «Καὶ μετὰ τὸ κρατῆσαι αὐτὸν τοῦ πλούτου, ἐπαναστήσεται πάσαις ταῖς βασιλείαις τῶν Ἑλλήνων.» Τούτου καὶ οἱ ἔξω τοῦ καθ' ἡμᾶς λόγου ἱστοριογράφοι τε καὶ συγγραφεῖς, σοφισταί τε καὶ ῥήτορες μέμνηνται, καὶ διηγοῦνται αὐτοῦ τήν τε ὑπερήφανον στρατείαν, καὶ τὴν καταγέλαστον ἀναχώρησιν. Εἶτα μέχρις αὐτοῦ τὰ Περσικὰ ἐν κεφαλαίῳ διδάξας, καὶ τοὺς μετὰ τοῦτον βασιλεύσαντας, ὡς ἀσθενεστέρους γεγενημένους, καταλιπών, ἐπὶ τὸν Μακεδόνα τὸν λόγον μετήνεγκε, καί φησι·

γ', δ'. «Καὶ ἀναστήσεται βασιλεὺς δυνατός, καὶ κυριεύσει κυρείας πολλῆς, καὶ ποιήσει κατὰ τὸ θέλημα αὐτοῦ. Καὶ ἐὰν στῇ ἡ βασιλεία αὐτοῦ συντριβήσεται, καὶ διαιρεθήσεται εἰς τοὺς τέσσαρας ἀνέμους τοῦ οὐρανοῦ.» Τοῦ γὰρ Ἀλεξάνδρου, ὡς καὶ ἤδη προειρήκαμεν, τὴν ἁπάσης, ὡς ἔπος εἰπεῖν, τῆς οἰκουμένης ἀναδησαμένου βασιλείαν, εἶτα τὸ | κοινὸν τῶν ἀνθρώπων δεξαμένου τέλος, τετραχῆ ἡ βασιλεία διηρέθη, ὡς καὶ ἤδη πολλάκις εἰρήκαμεν, καὶ ἐνταῦθα δὲ πάλιν ὁ θεῖος ἀρχάγγελος οὕτως ἔφη· «Καὶ διαιρεθήσεται εἰς τοὺς τέσσαρας ἀνέμους τοῦ οὐρανοῦ, καὶ οὐκ εἰς τὰ ἔσχατα αὐτοῦ, οὐδὲ κατὰ τὴν κυρείαν αὐτοῦ, ἣν ἐκυρίευσεν.» Ὃ δὲ λέγει τοιοῦτόν ἐστιν· Ὁ Ἀλέξανδρος δώδεκα ἔτη τὰ πάντα βασιλεύσας, ἐν τοῖς ἓξ τοῖς τελευταίοις ἔτεσι, καὶ τὴν Περσῶν, καὶ τὴν τῶν Αἰγυπτίων κατέλυσε βασιλείαν, καὶ τὰ ἐν μέσῳ δὲ ἔθνη ἅπαντα ὑφ' ἑαυτὸν ἐποιήσατο. Λέγει τοίνυν, ὅτι οἱ μετ' αὐτὸν βασιλεύσοντες οὐδὲν ἐοικότες ὀφθήσονται τῷ Ἀλεξάνδρῳ, οὔτε κατὰ τὴν ῥώμην, οὔτε κατὰ τὴν ἐξουσίαν, ἣν ἐν τοῖς ἔτεσι τοῖς τελευταίοις ἐκτήσατο. Τοῦτο γὰρ λέγει· «Εἰς τὰ ἔσχατα αὐτοῦ, οὐδὲ κατὰ τὴν κυρείαν αὐτοῦ, ἣν ἐκυρίευσεν. Ὅτι ἐκτιλήσεται ἡ βασιλεία αὐτοῦ, καὶ δοθήσεται ἑτέροις ἐκτὸς τούτων.» Οὐ μόνον γάρ, φησίν, εἰς τούτους τέσσαρας διαιρεθήσεται, ἀλλὰ καὶ ἑτέροις χωρὶς τούτων δοθήσεται. Ἐπὶ γὰρ τούτων καὶ Ἀρσάκης ὁ Πέρσης πολέμῳ κρατήσας ἀνεδήσατο τὴν βασιλείαν, καὶ μέρος τι τῆς Περσικῆς ἀρχῆς ἀνεκτήσατο· ἐξ οὗ μέχρι τοῦ παρόντος οἱ Περσῶν βασιλεῖς Ἀρσακίδαι προσαγορεύονται, τῶν προτέρων οὐκ Ἀρσακιδῶν, ἀλλὰ Ἀχαιμενιδῶν ὀνομαζομένων. Καὶ Ῥωμαῖοι δέ, τῆς Μακεδονικῆς διαιρεθείσης βασιλείας, μείζονα ἔσχον τὴν ἰσχύν, ἀμέλει καὶ παρ' αὐτῶν

Darius son of Hystaspes. *The fourth will be much richer than all the others*—a reference to Xerxes, son of Darius. *After gaining control of the wealth, he will invade all the kingdoms of the Greeks.* Historians with a different purpose from ours, annalists, rhetoricians, and orators remember this man and recount his ambitious campaigning and ridiculous retreat.[257]

Having in summary form informed us of Persian affairs as far as this man, he passes over the kings reigning after him as proving weaker, and transfers his attention to the Macedonian as follows. *A powerful king will arise, and will rule with a strong rule and do what he wishes. When his kingdom comes to a standstill, it will be broken up and divided to the four winds of heaven* (vv. 3–4). After Alexander had acquired the whole world, so to say, as his kingdom, as I remarked before, and then | met the common end of human   1504 beings, the kingdom was divided into four, as we have already often remarked. Here, too, the divine archangel said in turn, *It will be divided into the four winds of heaven, and not to its extremities nor according to the rule with which it ruled.* What he means is something like this: Alexander ruled for twelve years in all, in the six last years overthrowing the kingdom of the Persians and the Egyptians, and bringing all the nations in the middle into subjection. So he means that those reigning after him would be seen as in no way similar to Alexander either in strength or in the authority he acquired in his last years. It says as much, in fact, *To its extremities nor according to the rule with which it ruled, because his kingdom will be plucked up and given to others besides these*: it will not only be divided into these four, but will also be given to others beyond them. In their time, in fact, Arsaces the Persian gained control of the empire in war and attached it to himself, and recovered part of the Persian rule; from then until the present day the Persian kings are called Arsacid, though the former ones were called not Arsacid but Achaemenid.[258] With the division of the Macedonian Empire,

---

[257] Theodoret makes a reasonable estimate of the identity of these kings, as he had referred to them in connection with the "wings" (Aramaic "tusks") of the beast in 7:5, though the Bible seems to know only of Cyrus, Ahasuerus (Xerxes), Artaxerxes, and "Darius the Persian" as Persian kings. He admits that his purpose in finding an historical basis for the prophecy is not that of secular historians.

[258] The Parthian king Mithridates I, also known by the dynastic name of Arsaces VI (171–138 B.C.E.), extended his rule over the whole Iranian plateau,

τούτων τῶν βασιλέων δασμὸν ἐκομίζοντο. Οὕτω τὴν διαίρεσιν προμη-
νύσας, τῶν μὲν δύο βασιλέων καταλιμπάνει τὴν μνήμην· οὔτε γὰρ ὁ τῆς
Ἀσίας, οὔτε ὁ τῆς Μακεδονίας, ἐπὶ πολὺν διήρκεσαν χρόνον· ἄλλως τε
δὲ οὔτε συνέβη τι λυπηρῶν διὰ τούτων Ἰουδαίοις. Μόνον οὖν τῶν δύο
μέμνηται, δι᾽ ὧν τῶν χαλεπῶν συμφορῶν ἐπειράθησαν Ἰουδαῖοι. Οὗτοι δέ εἰσιν, ὅ τε τῆς Αἰγύπτου βασιλεύς, καὶ ὁ τῶν πρὸς ἕω κειμένων
ἐθνῶν τὴν ἀρχὴν πεπιστευμένος· εἶχον δὲ τὰ βασίλεια ἔν τε Ἀντιοχείᾳ
καὶ Βαβυλῶνι. Προσήκει δὲ πρότερον ἡμᾶς τῶν ῥηθησομένων εἰπεῖν τὴν
ὑπόθεσιν, εἶθ᾽ οὕτως τῆς κατὰ μέρος ἑρμηνείας ἅψασθαι. Ὁ τράγος, ὃν
ὁ μακάριος εἶδε Δανιήλ, μετὰ τὴν συντριβὴν τοῦ ἑνὸς κέρατος, «τέσσαρα ἐβλάστησε κέρατα» τούτους αὐτοὺς τοὺς βασιλέας· «ἐκ τοῦ ἑνὸς
αὐτῶν ἕτερον ἔφυ κέρας,» ὃ τήν τε Αἴγυπτον σφόδρα κατεπολέμησε,
καὶ μυρίαις συμφοραῖς τὸ Ἰουδαίων περιέβαλεν ἔθνος· σημαίνεται δὲ διὰ
τούτου τοῦ κέρατος Ἀντίοχος ὁ Ἐπιφανής. Καὶ τὸ τέταρτον δὲ θηρίον
ὁ μακάριος εἶδε Δανιήλ, δέκα κέρατα ἐσχηκέναι, καὶ μεταξὺ τῶν κεράτων μικρὸν κέρας ἀνέβαινεν, ὀφθαλμοὺς ἔχον, καὶ στόμα λαλοῦν μεγάλα,
καὶ ἐποίει πόλεμον μετὰ τῶν ἁγίων. Πάλιν δὲ διὰ τούτων μανθάνομεν,
ὡς ἐν τῷ τέλει τῆς Ῥωμαϊκῆς βασιλείας δέκα κατ᾽ αὐτὸν ἀναστήσονται
βασιλεῖς, πολλὰ κατ᾽ ἀλλήλων ἐργαζόμενοι κακά, καὶ τὰς ἀλλήλων κατ-
αγωνιζόμενοι βασιλείας, ὃν τρόπον οἱ Μακεδόνες διετέλουν ποιοῦντες·
1505   καὶ | ὅτι τούτων οὕτω γινομένων, φανήσεται ὁ ἄνθρωπος τῆς ἁμαρτίας,
ὁ υἱὸς τῆς ἀπωλείας, τουτέστιν ὁ Ἀντίχριστος. Ἐπειδὴ τοίνυν ἔοικε τῆς
Ῥωμαίων βασιλείας τὰ τέλη τῇ διαιρέσει τῆς Μακεδονικῆς βασιλείας,
τὰ ὑπὸ τούτων κἀκείνων γενησόμενα κατὰ ταὐτὸν ὁ μακάριος διδάσκεται
Δανιήλ. Τινὰ μὲν γὰρ τῶν ῥηθησομένων τοῖς Μακεδόσιν ἁρμόττει, τινὰ
δὲ τοῖς ἐσομένοις δέκα κέρασι, καὶ τῷ μεταξὺ αὐτῶν βλαστήσαντι. Καὶ

the Romans became dominant, and of course they collected tribute from these same kings.

Having thus referred to the division, he omits mention of two
of the kings, neither one lasting long, the one of Asia and the one of
Macedonia, bringing no troubles to Jews, either. So he mentions
only the two who were the cause of Jews suffering harsh calamities, namely, the king of Egypt and the one entrusted with the rule
of the nations to the east, who had palaces in Antioch and Babylon.[259] Now, we should first state the theme of what is to be told
us, and then commence detailed commentary. The "goat" that
blessed Daniel saw after the smashing of the one horn produced
these same kings as four horns; from one of them another horn
grew, which made heavy attacks on Egypt and invested the Jewish
nation with countless calamities, the reference in this horn being
Antiochus Epiphanes.[260] The "fourth beast" that blessed Daniel
saw had ten horns, and between the horns a little horn sprang up,
with eyes and a mouth speaking lofty words, and it made war on
the holy ones. We learn from this in turn that at the end of the Roman Empire ten kings will arise at the one time, wreaking many
troubles on one another, the kingdoms contesting with one another in the way the Macedonians continued doing; and | when   1505
this happens, the sinful one will appear, the son of perdition, that
is, the antichrist.[261] Since the ends of the Roman Empire resemble
the division of the Macedonian Empire, blessed Daniel learns at
the one time of what will be done by the one and the other: some
of what will be said applies to the Macedonians, some to the ten
horns that are coming and to the one springing up between them.

leading to the unsuccessful action against him in 140 by the Median king
Demetrius recorded in 1 Macc 14:1–3. Cyrus, on the other hand, was from the
Achaemenid dynasty.

[259] Ptolemy I Soter (323–285) and Seleucus I Nicator (312–280), the latter at first a general of Ptolemy's, but later absorbing much of the territory of
Antigonus Cyclops, including Syria and Palestine. Hence the nomination by
modern commentators of Ptolemy and Seleucus as the two characters mentioned in 11:5, pace Theodoret.

[260] Antiochus IV Epiphanes (175–164) belonging to the Seleucid dynasty, as Theodoret explained in his commentary on chapter 8.

[261] Theodoret's own interpretation of the beasts in chapter 7, modern
commentators seeing the "divisions of the Macedonian Empire" rather than the
Romans in focus. He admits that his interpretation calls for some juggling of
references in the text.

ὅτι ταῦθ' οὕτως ἔχει, ἐξ αὐτῆς μαθησόμεθα τῆς προφητείας. Προσήκει τοίνυν ἡμᾶς μετὰ πάσης προσέχειν ἀκριβείας, καὶ διαιρεῖν προσφόρως τά τε τούτοις, τά τε ἐκείνοις ἁρμόττοντα. Ἔχομεν δὲ τούτου παράδειγμα τὴν εὐαγγελικὴν διδασκαλίαν. Καὶ γὰρ τοῦ Κυρίου τοῦ ναοῦ τοῦ ἐν Ἱεροσολύμοις εἰρηκότος τοῖς ἀποστόλοις· «Ἀμὴν, ἀμὴν λέγω ὑμῖν, οὐ μὴ μείνῃ ὧδε λίθος ἐπὶ λίθον, ὃς οὐ μὴ καταλυθῇ,» εἶτα ἐκείνων ἐρομένων· «Πότε ταῦτα ἔσται, καὶ τί τὸ σημεῖον τῆς σῆς παρουσίας;» Καὶ διπλῆν ἐρώτησιν προσαγαγόντων, ὁ Κύριος ἀναμὶξ ποιεῖται τὴν ἀπόκρισιν, κατὰ ταὐτὸν λέγων τά τε τοῖς Ἱεροσολύμοις συμβησόμενα, καὶ τὰ κατὰ τὸν τῆς συντελείας καιρὸν γενησόμενα. Οἱ δὲ τὰ θεῖα μεμυημένοι διαιροῦσιν εὐκρινῶς τά τε τούτοις, τά τε ἐκείνοις ἁρμόττοντα τοῖς καιροῖς. Τοῦτο τοιγαροῦν καὶ ἡμεῖς ἐνταῦθα μετὰ τῆς προσηκούσης ποιήσομεν ἀποδείξεως. Διδάξας τοίνυν τὸν μακάριον Δανιὴλ ὁ προσδιαλεγόμενος, ὅτι τετραχῇ διαιρεθήσεται ἡ βασιλεία, καὶ τοὺς δύο καταλιπών, τόν τε τῆς Μακεδονίας φημί, καὶ τὸν τῆς Ἀσίας, ἤτοι τοῦ Ἑλλησπόντου, ὡς καὶ πρὸς βραχὺν διαρκέσαντας χρόνον, καὶ Ἰουδαίους ἥκιστα λελυπηκότας, ἐπάγει·

ε΄. «Καὶ ἐνίσχυσεν ὁ βασιλεὺς τοῦ Νότου, καὶ ἀπὸ τῶν ἀρχόντων αὐτοῦ εἷς ἐνισχύσει ἐπ' αὐτόν, καὶ κυριεύσει κυρείαν πολλὴν ἐκτὸς ἐξουσίας αὐτοῦ.» Πτολεμαῖον δὲ λέγει τὸν Φιλοπάτορα, μὴ ἀρκεσθέντα τῇ τῆς Αἰγύπτου βασιλείᾳ, ἀλλὰ καὶ Φοινίκην, καὶ Σαμάρειαν, καὶ τὴν Ἰουδαίαν προσλαβόντα. Ἕνα δὲ ἀπὸ τῶν ἀρχόντων αὐτοῦ ἐνισχύοντα τὸν Σκοπᾶν λέγει, οὗ καὶ ὁ Ἰώσηππος ὁ Ἑβραῖος μέμνηται συγγραφεύς, ὃς ἄριστα στρατηγήσας, πολλὰ τῶν ἔξω τῆς τοῦ Πτολεμαίου βασιλείας τῷ Πτολεμαίῳ ὑπέταξε. Τοῦτο αἰνιττόμενος λέγει· «Καὶ κυριεύσει κυρείαν πολλὴν ἐκτὸς ἐξουσίας αὐτοῦ,» τουτέστι, κρατήσει ἐθνῶν πολλῶν ἔξω τῆς ἀφωρισμένης αὐτῷ ἐξουσίας ὄντων.

ς΄. «Καὶ μετὰ τὰ ἔτη αὐτοῦ συμμιγήσονται, καὶ θυγάτηρ τοῦ βασιλέως τοῦ Νότου εἰσελεύσεται πρὸς τὸν βασιλέα τοῦ Βορρᾶ, τοῦ ποιῆσαι συνθήκας μετ' αὐτοῦ.» Μετὰ τὴν τοῦ Φιλοπάτορος Πτολεμαίου τελευτὴν ἐβασίλευσε Πτολεμαῖος ὁ υἱὸς αὐτοῦ, ὁ Ἐπιφανὴς προσαγορευόμενος. Τοῦτο οὖν λέγει, ὅτι «Μετὰ τὰ ἔτη αὐτοῦ συμμιγήσονται·» καὶ διδάσκων, πῶς συμμιγήσονται· «Θυγάτηρ, φησί, τοῦ βασιλέως τοῦ Νότου

εἰσελεύσεται πρὸς τὸν βασιλέα | τοῦ βορρᾶ, τοῦ ποιῆσαι συνθήκας μετ'

That fact that this is so we shall learn from the prophecy itself.

We should therefore attend with complete precision, and assign appropriately some things to one group and some to the other. We have the evangelical teaching as a model in this with the Lord's saying to the apostles about the temple in Jerusalem, "Amen, amen, I say to you, no stone here will remain on another without being destroyed," and their then replying, "How will this be, and what will be the sign of your coming?" When they asked this double question, the Lord gave a twofold reply, saying at the one time what would befall Jerusalem and what would happen at the end-time. Initiates into divine realities, however, astutely distinguish between what applies to the former time and what applies to the latter.[262] We, too, in this case shall also act accordingly with the appropriate demonstration.

Having informed blessed Daniel, then, that the empire will be divided into four, and leaving two aside—namely, the kings of Macedonia and of Asia, or the Hellespont—as lasting only a short time and causing least harm to Jews, his interlocutor goes on, *The king of the south grew strong, and one of his leaders will grow stronger than he, and will rule with a greater rule than his* (v. 5). He is referring to Ptolemy Philopator,[263] who was not content with the kingdom of Egypt and took possession of Phoenicia, Samaria, and Judea. By the one of his leaders growing strong he refers to Scopas, mentioned also by Josephus the Hebrew historian,[264] who proved an excellent general and subjected to Ptolemy much of what lay beyond Ptolemy's kingdom (suggested by *he will rule with a greater rule than his*, that is, he will gain control of many nations beyond his assigned jurisdiction). *After his years they will be merged, and a daughter of the king of the south will come to the king of the north to make a treaty with him* (v. 6). After the death of Ptolemy Philopator his son Ptolemy, called Epiphanes, came to the throne, as the text says, *After his years they will be merged*, mentioning also how they would be merged: *A daughter of the king of the south will come to the king | of the north to make a treaty with him.* By *a king of* 1508

---

[262] Theodoret, probably aware that Matt 24 invokes material from Daniel in its apocalyptic message, maintains that Jesus is foretelling the Romans' destruction of Jerusalem, as "initiates into divine realities" would recognize, thus confirming his interpretation of these chapters.

[263] Ptolemy IV Philopator (221–203).

[264] *Ant.* 12.135, quoting Polybius, *Hist.* 16.39.1.

αὐτοῦ.» *Βασιλέα δὲ τοῦ βορρᾶ τὸν Ἀντίοχον λέγει, οὐ τὸν Ἐπιφανῆ, ἀλλὰ τὸν καλούμενον Μέγαν, τὸν τοῦ Ἐπιφανοῦς Ἀντιόχου πατέρα·* οὗτος γὰρ ἦν τοῖς Πτολεμαίοις ἐκείνοις ὁμόχρονος. «Καὶ οὐ κρατήσει ἰσχὺς βραχίονος, καὶ οὐ στήσεται τὸ σπέρμα αὐτοῦ, καὶ παραδοθήσεται αὕτη, καὶ οἱ φέροντες αὐτήν, καὶ ἡ νεᾶνις, καὶ ὁ κατισχύων αὐτὴν ἐν τοῖς καιροῖς» Ἀλλ᾽ ὁ μὲν γάμος, φησί, γενήσεται, οὐ μὴν ἐπὶ πολὺ διαρκέσει τὸ συνοικέσιον, ἀλλ᾽ ἀποδοθήσεται τῷ πεπομφότι αὐτὴν διὰ τῶν ἀγαγόντων αὐτήν, μετὰ τῶν προσενηνεγμένων αὐτῇ. Τοῦτο γὰρ λέγει· «Καὶ ὁ κατισχύων αὐτὴν ἐν τοῖς καιροῖς.» ὁ τὸν γάμον ἰσχυρὸν καὶ ποθεινὸν ἐργαζόμενος πλοῦτος.

ζ΄. «Καὶ ἀναστήσεται, φησί, ἐκ τοῦ ἄνθους ἐκ τῆς ῥίζης αὐτῆς ἐπὶ τῆς ἑτοιμασίας αὐτοῦ.» Ἀντὶ τοῦ, ἀποδοθήσεται μὲν τῷ γεγεννηκότι, παιδοποιήσει δὲ βασιλέα τῇ βασιλείᾳ τοῦ δεδωκότος ἐναντιωθησόμενον. «Καὶ ἥξει, φησί, πρὸς τὴν δύναμιν.» Δύναμιν δὲ καλεῖ τὴν Ἱερουσαλήμ, ὡς τῆς θείας χάριτος ἀπολαύουσαν, καὶ διὰ τῶν κατὰ καιρὸν γινομένων θαυμάτων τὴν θείαν ὑποδεικνύουσαν δύναμιν. Καὶ τοῦτο δὲ ἡμᾶς ἡ τρίτη τῶν Μακκαβαίων ἐδίδαξε βίβλος. Νενικηκὼς γὰρ παρ᾽ ἐλπίδα πᾶσαν Ἀντίοχον τὸν Μέγαν ὁ Πτολεμαῖος, ἀφίκετο μὲν εἰς τὰ Ἱεροσόλυμα, προσενήνοχε δὲ τῷ Θεῷ θυσίας πολυτελεῖς· πειραθεὶς δὲ τῶν ἀδύτων ἐπιβῆναι τοῦ ναοῦ, καὶ τοῖς ἱερεῦσι μεθ᾽ ἱκετείας ἀπείργουσιν, εἶξαι μὴ βουληθείς, μαστιγοῦται μὲν μάστιξιν ἀοράτοις· ἀπειλήσας δὲ τοῖς Ἰουδαίοις καταλαμβάνει τὴν Ἀλεξάνδρειαν, καὶ ποιεῖν ἐκεῖνα ἐπιχειρεῖ, ἃ ἡ ἱστορία διδάσκει. Τοῦτο καὶ ἡ προφητεία προλέγει. «Ἥξει, φησί, πρὸς τὴν δύναμιν, καὶ εἰσελεύσεται εἰς τὰ ὑποστηρίγματα τοῦ βασιλέως τοῦ Βορρᾶ, καὶ ποιήσει ἐν αὐτοῖς, καὶ κατισχύσει.» Ὑποστηρίγματα δὲ

the north he refers to Antiochus, not Epiphanes but the one called
Great, father of Antiochus Ephiphanes, a contemporary of those
Ptolemies.[265] *The strength of her arm will not prevail, her offspring
will not stand, and she will be surrendered along with her attendants,
her daughter and the one supporting her in those times*: there will be
a marriage, but they will not be together for long; instead, she will
be given back to the one sending her through those who brought
her, along with what was offered to her (the meaning of *the one supporting her in those times*, wealth being responsible for the strong
and desirable marriage).

*There will rise up from the flower out of her root for his prepara-
tion* (v. 7), that is, she will be given back to her parent, but will give
birth to a king who will oppose the kingdom of the one who gave
her. *He will come to the power.* By *power* he refers to Jerusalem as
enjoying divine grace and giving evidence of divine power in the
marvels happening opportunely. Now, the third book of the Maccabees informed us of this:[266] against all expectations Ptolemy
defeated Antiochus the Great, reached Jerusalem, and offered lav-
ish sacrifices to God; but on attempting to enter the precincts of
the temple, and refusing to yield to the priests, who resisted him
with remonstrances, he was scourged with invisible scourges. Uttering threats against the Jews, he returned to Alexandria, and set
about doing the things of which history informs us. This is what
the inspired text foretells, *He will come to the power and will enter the fortresses of the king of the north; he will take action in them*

---

[265] Having passed over a couple of generations of the Greek rulers so as
to bring the Romans into the picture, Theodoret has forfeited the likely scenario
of earlier events recounted in the following verses, summarized by Di Lella,
"Daniel," 419, as follows: "In ca. 250, Ptolemy II Philadelphus (285–246) gave
his daughter Bernice in marriage to Antiochus II Theos (261–246). But the latter's divorced wife Laodice eventually had not only Antiochus II Theos but also
Bernice and her infant son, with their Egyptian entourage, put to death. In
revenge for these crimes, Bernice's brother Ptolemy III Euergetes (246–221),
invaded Syria, put Laodice to death, defeated Laodice's son Seleucus II Call-
inicus (246–226), devastated the land, and carried off enormous booty to Egypt.
In 242–240, Seleucus II undertook a counteroffensive against Egypt but failed
miserably."

[266] 3 Macc 1–2, also cited (like 2 Esdras) as though canonical for
Theodoret, though today found in Greek and Slavonic Bibles only. He dis-
creetly forbears to repeat some of the far-fetched events recorded in later
chapters of the king's attempts to penalize the Alexandrian Jews.

καλεῖ τὰς τὸν φόρον αὐτῷ παρεχούσας πόλεις· οἷον γάρ πως στηρίζει καὶ ὑπερείδει τὴν βασιλείαν τὰ προσφερόμενα τέλη, δι' ὧν ἡ στρατιωτικὴ τρέφεται δύναμις.

η'. «Καί γε τοὺς θεοὺς αὐτῶν μετὰ τῶν χωνευτῶν αὐτῶν, πᾶν σκεῦος ἐπιθυμητὸν αὐτῶν, ἀργυρίου καὶ χρυσίου, μετ' αἰχμαλωσίας εἰσοίσει εἰς Αἴγυπτον, καὶ αὐτὸς στήσεται ὑπὲρ βασιλέα τοῦ Βορρᾶ.» Ἐν γὰρ τῇ πρώτῃ καὶ δευτέρᾳ συμπλοκῇ οἱ Πτολεμαῖοι νενικήκασιν, ὡς αἱ ἱστορίαι διδάσκουσιν. Λέγει δὲ καὶ Ἰώσηππος οὕτως· «Τοὺς γὰρ Ἰουδαίους ἐπ' Ἀντιόχου τοῦ μεγάλου βασιλεύοντος τῆς Ἀσίας, ἔτυχεν αὐτούς τε πολλὰ ταλαιπωρῆσαι, τῆς γῆς αὐτῶν κακουχουμένης, καὶ τοὺς τὴν Κοίλην Συρίαν νεμομένους. Πολεμοῦντος γὰρ αὐτοῦ πρὸς τὸν Φιλοπάτορα Πτολεμαῖον, καὶ πρὸς τὸν υἱὸν αὐτοῦ Πτο|λεμαῖον, ἐπικληθέντα δὲ Ἐπιφανῆ, κακοπαθεῖν συνέβαινεν αὐτοῖς, καὶ νικῶντος αὐτοῦ καὶ πταίοντος τὰ αὐτὰ πάσχειν.» Καὶ μετὰ βραχέα· «Νικήσας μέντοι, φησί, τὸν Πτολεμαῖον ὁ Ἀντίοχος, τὴν Ἰουδαίαν προσάγεται. Τελευτήσαντος δὲ τοῦ Φιλοπάτορος ὁ παῖς αὐτοῦ μεγάλην ἐξέπεμψε δύναμιν, καὶ στρατηγὸν τὸν Σκοπᾶν ἐπὶ τοὺς ἐν τῇ Κοίλῃ Συρίᾳ· ὃς πολλάς τε αὐτῶν πόλεις ἔλαβε, καὶ τὸ ἡμέτερον ἔθνος· πολεμούμενον γὰρ αὐτῷ προσέθετο. Μετ' οὐ πολὺ δὲ τὸν Σκοπᾶν ὁ Ἀντίοχος νικᾷ συμβαλὼν αὐτῷ πρὸς ταῖς πηγαῖς τοῦ Ἰορδάνου, καὶ πολλὴν αὐτοῦ τὴν στρατείαν διέφθειρεν· ὕστερον δέ, Ἀντιόχου χειρωσαμένου τὰς ἐν τῇ Κοίλῃ Συρίᾳ πόλεις, ἃς ὁ Σκοπᾶς κατεσχήκει, καὶ τὴν Σαμάρειαν, ἑκουσίως αὐτῷ προσέθεντο Ἰουδαῖοι, καὶ τῇ πόλει δεξάμενοι, πᾶσαν αὐτοῦ τῇ τε στρατείᾳ καὶ τοῖς ἐλέφασιν ἀφθονίαν παρέσχον, καὶ τοὺς ὑπὸ τοῦ Σκοπᾶ καταλειφθέντας ἐν τῇ ἄκρᾳ τῶν Ἱεροσολύμων φρουροὺς πολιορκοῦντι προθύμως συνεμάχησαν.» Καὶ ἵνα μὴ καὶ τὰ ἄλλα λέγων πέρα τοῦ μέτρου μηκύνω τὸ σύγγραμμα, εἰς ἐκεῖνα τὸν βουλόμενον παραπέμπω.

θ', ι'. «Καὶ εἰσελεύσεται, φησίν, εἰς τὴν βασιλείαν τοῦ βασιλέως τοῦ Νότου, καὶ ἀναστρέψει εἰς τὴν γῆν αὐτοῦ. Καὶ οἱ υἱοὶ αὐτοῦ συνάξουσιν ὄχλον δυνάμεων πολλῶν.» Υἱοὺς δὲ αὐτοῦ καλεῖ τὴν στρατείαν πεπιστευμένους, ὡς υἱοὺς ἀνθρώπων τοὺς ἀνθρώπους, καὶ υἱοὺς τῶν προφητῶν τοὺς προφήτας· ἰδίωμα γάρ ἐστι τῆς Ἑβραίων διαλέκτου.

and prevail, by *fortresses* referring to the cities providing him with tribute, this being the way the provision of taxes, through which military might is sustained, reinforces and supports the kingdom.

Even their gods along with their graven images, every precious vessel of theirs of silver and gold he will carry off to Egypt as booty, and he shall stand over the king of the north (v. 8). In the first and second encounter the Ptolemies were victorious, as history records. Josephus also says this: "When Antiochus the Great was ruling Asia, the Jews in fact suffered severe hardship, their country devastated, as well as the inhabitants of Coele Syria. In fact, when he was warring against Ptolemy Philopator and his son Ptolemy | called Epiphanes, their fate was to suffer difficulties, the same   1509 fate whether he won or lost." And shortly afterward, "When Antiochus defeated Ptolemy, he naturally occupied Judea. On the death of Philopator, his son sent a great force with Scopas as general against those in Coele Syria, taking many of their cities and our nation, which came under attack and was occupied by him. Not long afterwards Antiochus defeated Scopas after engaging him near the source of the Jordan, and destroyed much of his army. Later, when Antiochus had subjugated the cities in Palestine that Scopas had occupied and also Samaria, Jews willingly joined him, welcoming him into the city and providing abundant supplies to his army and elephants; and they enthusiastically helped the guards left by Scopas in the Jerusalem citadel when he mounted his siege." In case I prolong the account excessively by narrating other events as well, I refer an interested reader to them.[267]

He will enter the kingdom of the king of the north, and will return to his own land. His sons will assemble a mass of numerous forces (vv. 9–10), by *his sons* referring to those entrusted with military affairs, like "sons of men" for men, and "sons of the prophets" for prophets, this being an idiom of the Hebrew language.[268] *It will*

---

[267] A lengthy citation from Josephus (*Ant.* 12.129–130, 131–133), which does not bear closely on the text of Daniel. Theodoret thinks some of his readers may be able to access Josephus. His own major historical work comes later in his career.

[268] Theodoret's version of events in the Greek kingdoms does not envisage action by sons of a Ptolemy, so he takes refuge in a "Hebrew idiom." Had he not been so keen to get to the Romans, however, he might have thought of the sons of Seleucus II, by name Seleucus III Soter (226–223) and Antiochus III the Great (223–187). Ptolemy IV Philopator in 217 at the battle of Raphia

«Καὶ εἰσελεύσεται ἐρχόμενος, καὶ κατακλύζων.» Ἀντὶ τοῦ, ῥύμῃ φε-
ρόμενος, καὶ κατακλυσμοῦ δίκην ἅπαντα διαφθείρων. «Καὶ παρελεύσεται, καὶ καθιεῖται, καὶ συμπλακήσεται ἕως τῆς ἰσχύος αὐτοῦ.» Ἀντὶ
τοῦ, παντὶ σθένει χρώμενος ὁρμήσει μὲν κατὰ τῆς Αἰγύπτου, σπουδῇ δὲ
στρατοπεδεύσει, καὶ ἐν ἐκείνῃ τῇ χώρᾳ μεταθήσει τὸν πόλεμον. Τούτοις
ἐπάγει·

ια΄, ιβ΄. «Καὶ ἀγριανθήσεται ὁ βασιλεὺς τοῦ Νότου, καὶ ἐξελεύ-
σεται, καὶ πολεμήσει μετὰ τοῦ βασιλέως τοῦ Βορρᾶ, καὶ στήσει ὄχλον
πολύν, καὶ παραδοθήσεται ὄχλος ἐν χειρὶ αὐτοῦ. Καὶ λήψεται ὄχλον πολύν, καὶ ὑψωθήσεται ἡ καρδία αὐτοῦ, καὶ καταβαλεῖ μυριάδας, καὶ οὐκ
ἰσχύσει.» Τοῦ γὰρ βασιλέως τοῦ Νότου ἀντιπαραταττομένου μετὰ πλήθους πολλοῦ, περιγενήσεται, φησίν, ὁ Ἀντίοχος, καὶ λήψεται τὸν ὄχλον
ὑποχείριον, καὶ ὡς νενικηκὼς ὑπερηφανίᾳ χρήσεται, καὶ πολλὰς κατ-
ακοντίσει μυριάδας. Ἀλλ' ὅμως οὐ περιγενήσεται τῆς Αἰγύπτου, οὐδὲ
κρατήσει τῆς τοῦ Πτολεμαίου βασιλείας· οὗ χάριν δυσχεραίνων πάλιν,
φησίν·

ιγ΄. «Ἐπιστρέψει βασιλεὺς τοῦ Βορρᾶ, καὶ ἄξει ὄχλον πολὺν ὑπὲρ
τὸν πρότερον, καὶ εἰς τὸ τέλος τῶν καιρῶν, καὶ ἐπελεύσεται εἰσόδια
1512   ἐν δυνάμει μεγάλῃ καὶ ἐν ὑπάρξει πολλῇ.» Αὖθις γάρ, φησί, μείζω |
τῆς προτέρας συναγαγὼν στρατείαν ὁρμήσει κατὰ τῆς Αἰγύπτου, ποιήσει δὲ τοῦτο περὶ τὸ τέλος τῆς ἑαυτοῦ βασιλείας· τοῦτο γὰρ σημαίνει·
«Εἰς τὸ τέλος τῶν καιρῶν, καὶ ἐπελεύσεται εἰσόδια ἐν δυνάμει μεγάλῃ.» Ἐνταῦθα διπλασιασμός ἐστιν Ἑβραϊκός· ἠβουλήθη γὰρ εἰπεῖν, ὅτι
εἰσόδῳ μεγάλῃ χρήσεται. Ἰδίωμα δέ ἐστι καὶ Ἑβραίων, καὶ Σύρων· καὶ
οὗτοι γὰρ κἀκεῖνοι λέγειν εἰώθασιν· Εἰσερχόμενος εἰσελήλυθε, καὶ Ἐξ-
ερχόμενος ἐξελήλυθε, καὶ Ἐσθίων ἐσθίει, καὶ τὰ ἄλλα πάντα τὰ τοιαῦτα ὁμοίως. Πλείονι τοίνυν οἱ ἑρμηνευταὶ ἀκριβείᾳ χρώμενοι, καὶ τοῖς
Ἑβραίοις ἰδιώμασιν ἠκολούθησαν.

ιδ΄. «Καὶ ἐν τοῖς καιροῖς ἐκείνοις, φησί, πολλοὶ ἐπαναστήσονται
ἐπὶ βασιλέα τοῦ Νότου.» Οὕτω γὰρ Ἀντιόχου καταγωνισαμένου τὸν
Πτολεμαῖον, ὡς ἀσθενοῦς λοιπὸν καὶ οἱ πλησιόχωροι καταφρονήσουσι.
«Καὶ οἱ υἱοὶ τῶν λοιμῶν τοῦ λαοῦ σου ἐπαρθήσονται, τοῦ στῆσαι ὅρασιν,
καὶ ἐπαρθήσονται, καὶ ἀσθενήσουσι.» Πάλιν ἐνταῦθα υἱοὺς λοιμῶν τοὺς
λοιμοὺς προσηγόρευσεν· οἱ γὰρ πονηρίᾳ, φησί, καὶ μοχθηρίᾳ τρόπων συζῶντες, καὶ τὸ δυσσεβῶς ζῆν τῆς εὐσεβείας προαιρούμενοι, πειραθή-

come and go, inundating everything, that is, carried in a flood and destroying everything like an inundation. *It will pass through, settle down and engage with his strength,* that is, using all resources he will advance against Egypt, eagerly set camp, and move the war to another location. He continues in this vein, *The king of the south will be enraged and will sally forth, do battle with the king of the north, set up a mighty force, and the force will be delivered into his hand. He will capture the mighty force, his heart will be uplifted, he will overthrow countless numbers, and he will not prevail* (vv. 11–12): when the king of the south deploys a vast number, Antiochus will prevail, will take the force captive, as victor will show signs of arrogance, and slay countless numbers. Yet he will not get the better of Egypt, nor gain control of the kingdom of Ptolemy.

For this reason he will in turn be displeased. *The king of the north will return, will lead a force larger than before, and at the end of the times he will even penetrate with great might and much substance* (v. 13): he will again | assemble an army greater than before and   1512 advance on Egypt, doing so at the end of his reign (the meaning of *and at the end of the times he will even penetrate with great might and much substance*). It is a case here of Hebrew repetition: he meant that he will make a considerable advance; it is an idiom in Hebrew and Syriac, both peoples in the habit of saying, Entering he will enter, Leaving he left, Eating he eats, and similarly many other such phrases. Accordingly, the interpreters employed greater precision and followed the Hebrew idioms.[269]

In those times many will rebel against the king of the south (v. 14), Antiochus thus vying with Ptolemy, the result being that the neighboring peoples then also showed scorn for him in his weakness. *The children of pestilence among your people will be lifted up to confirm the vision, and they will be lifted up and will be weak.* Here again by *children of pestilence* he referred to pests: those with wicked and depraved habits, choosing to live a life of godlessness

defeated Antiochus III, who in turn defeated Ptolemy V Epiphanes in Palestine in 202–198.

[269] This time Theodoret does not invoke Hebrew parlance for the purposes of eisegesis, instead noting the duplication of adverbial phrases and verbal circumlocution (lit. "he will enter entrances"). It is a pattern that he is familiar with in Syriac and that can easily be verified in the Hebrew text in this case, and he congratulates "the interpreters" for their efforts to replicate it (though only Theodotion does so).

σονται διὰ τούτων τῶν βασιλέων τὴν νομικὴν καταλῦσαι λατρείαν, καὶ
οὐκ ἰσχύσουσιν· ἧττον γὰρ ὄντες ἀσεβεῖς οὗτοι θεραπεύοντες τὸ Ἰουδαῖον
διετέλεσαν ἔθνος.

ιε΄. «Καὶ εἰσελεύσεται, φησίν, ὁ βασιλεὺς Βορρᾶ, καὶ ἐκχεεῖ πρόσ-
χωμα, καὶ συλλήψεται πόλεις ὀχυράς.» Ἀντὶ τοῦ, πολιορκίᾳ, καὶ χώμα-
σι, καὶ μηχανήμασι χρήσεται. «Καὶ βραχίονες τοῦ βασιλέως τοῦ Νότου
οὐ στήσονται·» τουτέστι, πάσης δυνάμεως ἔρημος γενήσεται. «Καὶ ἀναστήσονται οἱ ἐκλεκτοὶ αὐτοῦ, καὶ οὐκ ἔσται ἰσχὺς τοῦ στῆναι.» Καὶ τοὺς
ἀριστέας δὲ αὐτοῦ συλλέγων ὀνήσει οὐδέν.

ις΄. «Καὶ ποιήσει ὁ εἰσπορευόμενος πρὸς αὐτὸν κατὰ τὸ θέλημα
αὐτοῦ, καὶ οὐκ ἔστιν ἑστὼς κατὰ πρόσωπον αὐτοῦ.» Ῥάδιον γάρ, φησί, λοιπὸν ἑκάστῳ καταφρονεῖν αὐτοῦ, τῷ μὴ δύνασθαι ἀνταγωνίζεσθαι,
καὶ τῶν ἐναντίων περιγενέσθαι. «Καὶ στήσεται ἐν τῇ γῇ τοῦ Σαβείρ.»
Ἔνια τῶν ἀντιγράφων, «ἐν τῇ γῇ τοῦ Σαβαεὶμ» ἔχει· τινὲς δὲ τῶν τὴν
Ἑβραίων φωνὴν εἰς τὴν Ἑλλάδα μεταβεβληκότων, γῆν θελήσεως τὴν
γῆν τοῦ Σαβεὶρ κεκλήκασι· σημαίνει δὲ τὴν τῆς ἐπαγγελίας γῆν, θελήσεως οὖσαν· καὶ τὸ ὄρος τὸ Σιών, ὃ ἠγάπησε καὶ εὐδόκησεν ὁ Θεὸς
κατοικεῖν ἐν αὐτῷ. Καὶ τὸ Σαβαεὶμ δὲ δυνάμεως ἑρμηνεύεται. Εἴτε γοῦν
γῇ εὐδοκίας, εἴτε γῇ δυνάμεως ἡ Ἰουδαία κέκληται (καὶ γὰρ καὶ ἄνω
δύναμιν αὐτὴν προσηγόρευσε, καὶ ἐνταῦθα Σαβαεὶμ εἴτ’ οὖν Σαβεὶρ),
εἰσελεύσεται, φησίν, ὁ βασιλεὺς τοῦ Βορρᾶ καὶ εἰς ταύτην τὴν γῆν. «Καὶ
1513   συντε|λεσθήσεται ἐν τῇ χειρὶ αὐτοῦ.» Τουτέστιν, εὐοδωθήσεται· οὕτω
γὰρ ἡμᾶς καὶ ὁ Ἰώσηππος διὰ τῆς ἱστορίας ἐδίδαξεν, ὅτι αὐτόματοι τὸν
Ἀντίοχον οἱ Ἰουδαῖοι δεξάμενοι σφόδρα ὑπ’ αὐτοῦ ἐτιμήθησαν.

ιζ΄. «Καὶ τάξει τὸ πρόσωπον αὐτοῦ, φησίν, εἰσελθεῖν ἐν ἰσχύϊ πάσης τῆς βασιλείας αὐτοῦ.» Ἐπιχειρήσει γὰρ ἅπασαν τοῦ βασιλέως τοῦ
Νότου σφετερίσασθαι τὴν βασιλείαν. «Καὶ εὐθεῖα, φησίν, ἅπαντα μετ’
αὐτοῦ ποιήσει.» Ἀποδώσει γὰρ αὐτῷ πάντα ὅσα ἥρπασεν. «Καὶ θυγατέρα τῶν γυναικῶν δώσει αὐτῷ τοῦ διαφθεῖραι αὐτήν, καὶ οὐ μὴ παρα-
μείνῃ, καὶ οὐκ αὐτῷ ἔσται.» Ὅπερ ἄνω ἀσαφῶς εἴρηκεν, τοῦτο ἐνταῦθα
σαφῶς· δώσει μὲν γὰρ αὐτῷ, φησί, γυναῖκα τὴν ἑαυτοῦ θυγατέρα, οὐκ

rather than piety, will try through these kings to overturn worship according to the law and will not succeed; the kings were less impious, and continued cultivating the Jewish nation. *The king of the north will come and construct siege works, and will take fortified cities* (v. 15), that is, he will use siege works and mounds and siege engines. *The arms of the king of the south will not endure*, that is, he will be bereft of all power. *His elite will not resist, and will have no strength to hold firm*: there will be no use assembling his champions.

The one invading in opposition to him will do what he wishes, and there will be no one to stand up to him (v. 16): with his inability to make a fight of it, it will be easy for anyone in future to scorn him and prevail over the adversaries. *He will make a stand in the land of Sabeir*. Some of the manuscripts have "in the land of Sabeim," while some of those turning the Hebrew term into Greek refer to the *land of Sabeir* as the "land of choice," the meaning being the land of promise, which is that of choice, and Mount Sion, which God loved and in which he was pleased to dwell. "Sabeim," on the other hand, means "power." In any case, whether Judea is called land of good pleasure or land of power (in fact, he called it *power* above, and here Sabeim or *Sabeir*), the king of the north will come into this land as well.[270] | *It will be completed by his hand*, that is,   1513 it will prosper in his ways, Josephus also in his account informing us likewise that the Jews spontaneously accepted Antiochus and were held in high esteem by him.[271]

He will set himself to enter with the force of his entire kingdom (v. 17): he will endeavor to make his own the entire kingdom of the king of the South. *He will put everything on a level footing with him*: he will return to him all he has seized. *He will give him a daughter of women to destroy her, but she will not stay, and will not be his.* What he said obscurely above he says clearly here: He will give him his

---

[270] Theodoret's response to an unfamiliar form in his text is typical. It is clearly a transliteration of a Hebrew form, and he notes it is represented differently in other manuscripts. Checking a version of the LXX, he finds a Greek rendering θέλησις (correctly translating the Hebrew *sebiy*, "choice"). Aware, however, that another text (that of Symmachus, in fact, Jerome tells us) offers "power," he boldly—without reference to the Hebrew—claims the meaning is "power," whereas this probably derives from a different Hebrew form *saba'*, neither Hebrew form occurring in v. 7, as he insists.

[271] *Ant.* 12.133–153.

εἰς μακρὰν δὲ αὕτη ἀποδοθήσεται τῷ δεδωκότι, καὶ τὸ συνοικέσιον διαλυθήσεται. Οὕτω δέ, φησί, διαθεὶς τὴν Αἴγυπτον,

ιη΄. «Ἐπιστρέψει τὸ πρόσωπον αὐτοῦ εἰς τὰς νήσους, καὶ συλλήψεται πολλάς, καὶ καταπαύσει ἄρχοντας ὀνειδισμοῦ αὐτοῦ· πλὴν ὁ ὀνειδισμὸς αὐτοῦ ἐπιστρέψει αὐτῷ.» Πολλὰς γὰρ τῶν νήσων ὑφ᾽ ἑαυτὸν ποιησάμενος, καὶ τοὺς ἐκείνων ἐθνάρχας τοῦ ἄρχειν παύσας, καταγελάστους ἐποίησεν. Ἀλλὰ τούτου, φησί, τοῦ ὀνειδισμοῦ καὶ αὐτὸς ἀπολαύσει. Ῥωμαῖοι γὰρ ἐν Θερμοπύλαις αὐτὸν καταγωνισάμενοι, καὶ τῆς πολλῆς αὐτὸν θρασύτητος παύσαντες, δασμὸν αὐτῷ χιλίων ταλάντων ἐπέθεσαν, καὶ τοῦτον φέρειν καθ᾽ ἕκαστον ἐνιαυτὸν κατηνάγκασαν, καὶ τὸν υἱὸν δὲ αὐτοῦ Ἀντίοχον τὸν ἐπικληθέντα Ἐπιφανῆ ὅμηρα λαβόντες ἐν τῇ Ῥώμῃ ἐφρούρουν. Καὶ τοῦτο ἡμᾶς ἡ πρώτη τῶν Μακκαβαίων διδάσκει· εἰρηκὼς γὰρ ὁ συγγραφεὺς περὶ τῶν τὴν Ἀλεξάνδρου δεξαμένων βασιλείαν, ἐπήγαγε· «Καὶ ἐξῆλθεν ἀπ᾽ αὐτῶν ῥίζα ἁμαρτωλός, Ἀντίοχος ὁ Ἐπιφανής, υἱὸς Ἀντιόχου τοῦ βασιλέως, ὃς ἦν ὅμηρα ἐν Ῥώμῃ. Τοῦτο προσημαίνων τῷ Δανιὴλ ὁ προσδιαλεγόμενος αὐτῷ ἔφη· «Πλὴν ὁ ὀνειδισμὸς αὐτοῦ ἐπιστρέψει αὐτῷ.» Τούτοις ἐπάγει·

ιθ΄. «Καὶ ἐπιστρέψει τὸ πρόσωπον αὐτοῦ, εἰς τὸ κατισχῦσαι τῆς γῆς αὐτοῦ.» Ταῦτα, φησίν, ἐν ταῖς νήσοις διαπραξάμενος, εἰς τὴν οἰκείαν ἐπανήξει βασιλείαν.

«Καὶ ἀσθενήσει, καὶ πεσεῖται, καὶ οὐχ εὑρεθήσεται. (κ΄.) Καὶ ἀναστήσεται ἐκ τῆς ῥίζης αὐτοῦ φυτὸν βασιλείας, καὶ ἐπὶ τὴν ἑτοιμασίαν αὐτοῦ παραβιβάζων.» Ἀντίοχον λέγει τὸν Ἐπιφανῆ, ὃς ἀποδρὰς ἀπὸ τῆς Ῥώμης, Σέλευκον τὸν ἀδελφὸν αὐτοῦ διεδέξατο. Ἀντίοχον γὰρ τὸν μέγαν Σέλευκος ὁ καλούμενος Φιλοπάτωρ διεδέξατο, υἱὸς αὐτοῦ ὤν· τοῦ δὲ Σελεύκου τελευτήσαντος, Ἀντίοχος ὁ Ἐπιφανὴς παραλαμβάνει τὴν βασιλείαν. Περὶ τούτου φησίν· «Ἀναστήσεται ἐκ τῆς ῥίζης αὐτοῦ φυτὸν βασιλείας, καὶ ἐπὶ τὴν ἑτοιμασίαν αὐτοῦ παραβιβάζων·» τουτέστι, τὴν 1516 τοῦ πατρὸς δυναστείαν μιμού|μενος, καὶ ἱκανὸς ὢν τὴν ἑτοιμασθεῖσαν ὑπ᾽ ἐκείνου κατασχεῖν βασιλείαν. Τοῦτο παραδηλῶν ἐπήγαγε· «Καὶ πράσσων δόξαν βασιλείας·» ἀντὶ τοῦ, ὑπεράγαν τῷ δραστηρίῳ χρώμενος. «Καὶ ἐν ταῖς ἡμέραις ἐκείναις συντριβήσονται, καὶ οὐκ ἐν προσώποις,

own daughter as his wife, but before long she will be returned to the giver, and the union will be dissolved.[272] Having treated Egypt in this fashion, he says, *He will set himself in the direction of the islands, and will capture many and bring to an end the rulers of his mockery; but his mockery will return to him* (v. 18): after bringing many of the islands into subjection, and ending the rule of their princes, he made them objects of ridicule. But he, too, will experience this mockery: Romans engaged him at Thermopylae, put an end to his audacity, imposed on him a tribute of a thousand talents, forced him to pay it every year, took his son Antiochus surnamed Epiphanes as a hostage and held him in Rome.[273] The first book of the Maccabees also informs us of this: after writing of those who inherited the kingdom of Alexander, the chronicler went on, "From them issued forth a sinful root, Antiochus Epiphanes, son of King Antiochus, who had been a hostage in Rome."[274] To foreshadow this to Daniel, the one speaking to him said *But he will bring his mockery back on him.*

He goes on in the same vein, *He will set himself to prevail over his land* (v. 19): after conducting these operations in the islands, he will return to his own kingdom. *He will be weak and will fall, and will not be found. There shall rise up from his root a plant of empire, making the transfer for his preparation* (vv. 19–20). It refers to Antiochus Epiphanes, who on return from Rome succeeded his brother Seleucus; Seleucus, called Philopator, was the successor of Antiochus the Great, being his son, and at his death Antiochus Epiphanes took over the kingdom. In reference to him the text says *There shall rise up from his root a plant of empire, making the transfer for his preparation,* that is, imitating the rule of his father | and capable of gaining possession of the kingdom prepared by him. To suggest as much he went on, *and bringing about the glory of kingship,* that is, exercising extreme vigor. *In those days they will*

1516

[272] A reference to the marriage of Cleopatra, daughter of Antiochus III, to Ptolemy V.

[273] Though Antiochus III was in fact defeated by the Romans at Thermopylae, mention of "the islands" suggests rather his subsequent defeat by the Roman consul L. Cornelius Scipio at Magnesia in western Asia Minor in 190.

[274] 1 Macc 1:10. Theodoret does not remark on the similarity in phrasing to Dan 11:20 on which he will immediately give his commentary; 1 Maccabees would seem to have been composed some decades after the date of composition of Daniel.

οὐδὲ ἐν πολέμοις.» Ἱκανὸς γάρ, φησίν, ἔσται καὶ μόνη τῇ φήμῃ ἀμαχητὶ καὶ ἀναιμωτὶ καταπλῆξαι πάντας, καὶ ἑαυτῷ ὑποτάξαι.

κα΄. «Καὶ στήσεται ἐπὶ τὴν ἑτοιμασίαν αὐτοῦ.» Τοσαύτη δέ, φησί, χρήσεται δυναστείᾳ, ὡς καὶ ἄνευ συμπλοκῆς κρατῆσαι τῆς πατρόθεν εἰς αὐτὸν παραπεμφθείσης βασιλείας. «Ἐξουδενώθη, καὶ οὐκ ἐδόθη ἐπ᾽ αὐτὸν δόξα βασιλείας.» Καὶ μήν, φησίν, οὐκ ἦν ἐπίδοξος, βασιλεὺς ὢν, ἀλλ᾽ εὐτελής τις ἐδόκει ἐν τῇ Ῥώμῃ φρουρούμενος. «Καὶ ἐπανήξει ἐπ᾽ εὐθηνίᾳ, καὶ κατισχύσει βασιλείας ἐν ὀλισθήμασι.» Ἀλλ᾽ ὅμως, φησί, καὶ λίαν ὢν ἐξουθενημένος, μετὰ πολλῆς ἥξει περιουσίας καὶ πλείστης δυνάμεως, καὶ κρατήσει τῆς βασιλείας δόλῳ συνεργῷ, καὶ ἐξαπάτῃ μᾶλλον χρώμενος. Τοῦτο δὲ καὶ ἐν τῇ δευτέρᾳ ὀπτασίᾳ ὁ μακάριος ἐθεάσατο Δανιὴλ, καὶ ἤκουσε τοῦ ἁγίου Γαβριὴλ, λέγοντος· «Δόλος ἐν τῇ χειρὶ αὐτοῦ, καὶ ἐν καρδίᾳ αὐτοῦ μεγαλυνθήσεται· καὶ διαφθερεῖ πολλούς, καὶ ἐπὶ ἀπωλείᾳ πολλῶν στήσεται. Καὶ ἐνταῦθα ὡσαύτως· «Κατισχύσει γάρ, φησί, βασιλείας ἐν ὀλισθήμασι.»

κβ΄. «Καὶ βραχίονες τοῦ κατακλύζοντος κατακλυσθήσονται ἀπὸ προσώπου αὐτοῦ, καὶ συντριβήσονται.» Πάλιν δὲ ἐνταῦθα τὴν τῶν Αἰγυπτίων ᾐνίξατο βασιλείαν, ὅτι κἀκεῖνοι οἱ τὰ μεγάλα δυνάμενοι, καὶ δίκην κατακλυσμοῦ τοὺς ἀνθισταμένους διαφθείροντες, καὶ ἀφανεῖς καὶ φρούδους ἀποφαίνοντες, καὶ οὗτοι ὑπ᾽ αὐτοῦ κατακλυσθήσονται, καὶ συντριβήσονται, οὐχ οὗτοι δὲ μόνοι, ἀλλά, «Καί γε ἡγούμενος διαθήκης.»

κγ΄. «Καὶ ἀπὸ τῶν συμμίξεων πρὸς αὐτὸν ποιήσει δόλον.» Ἐνταῦθα προσημαίνει τὴν γενομένην ἐπανάστασιν Ὀνίᾳ τῷ ἀρχιερεῖ ὑπὸ Ἰησοῦ τοῦ καὶ Ἰάσωνος, καὶ Ὀνίου τοῦ Μενελάου· τούτων γὰρ πρότερον μὲν ὁ Ἰάσων, πρὸς τὸν Ἀντίοχον δραμών, τὸν οἰκεῖον ἀδελφὸν τῆς ἀρχιερωσύνης ἐξέβαλεν· ὁ δὲ Μενέλαος, δῶρα καὶ χρυσίον ἀποσταλεὶς κομίσαι τῷ Ἀντιόχῳ, εἰς ἑαυτὸν πάλιν τὴν ἀρχιερωσύνην μεταθείς, ἐξήλασε τὸν Ἰάσωνα. Ἐντεῦθεν αἱ δειναὶ καὶ χαλεπαὶ συμφοραὶ τὸ Ἰουδαίων κατέλαβον ἔθνος, Ταῦτα ὁ μακάριος προδιδασκόμενος Δανιὴλ, ἀκούει, ὅτι «Βραχίονες τοῦ κατακλύζοντος κατακλυσθήσονται ἀπ᾽ αὐτοῦ.» Λέγει δὲ Πτολεμαῖον τὸν Φιλομήτορα· οὗτος γὰρ Πτολεμαῖον τὸν Ἐπιφανῆ

be broken, and not personally or in battle: he will prove capable of terrorizing everyone and subjecting them to himself by his reputation alone and without bloodshed.

And he will stand in his preparation (v. 21): he will apply such force as even without engagement to gain control of the kingdom transmitted to him from his father. *He was despised, and glory of kingship was not given to him*: though being king, he was not in fact glorious, seeming instead to be an insignificant figure because under guard in Rome. *But he will return with prosperity, and will gain control of kingship by underhand ways*: though an object of extreme scorn, he will come in great affluence and immense power and will lay hold of kingship, thanks to guile and the use of deceit instead. Now, blessed Daniel beheld this also in the second vision, and heard the holy Gabriel saying, "Guile in his hand, and in his heart he will be magnified, he will destroy many and will be bent on the ruin of many;"[275] here likewise *He will gain control of kingship in underhand ways. The right arm of the inundator will be inundated before his face, and will be crushed* (v. 22). Here again he hinted at the empire of the Egyptians, that though they too were very powerful, destroying their adversaries like an inundation, and rendering them totally undone, they themselves would be subject to an inundation from him and would be crushed—and not they alone but *the prince of the covenant as well*.

In the wake of associations with him he will employ trickery (v. 23). Here he suggests in advance the revolt against the high priest Onias by Joshua, also called Jason, and by Onias son of Menelaus. The former, Jason, had recourse to Antiochus and expelled his own brother from the high priesthood, while Menelaus, who had been sent to bring gifts and gold to Antiochus, transferred the high priesthood in turn to himself, and drove out Jason.[276] From this ensued woes and severe misfortunes for the nation of Jews. Informed of this in advance, blessed Daniel hears that *the right arm of the assailant will be assailed before him*, a reference to Ptolemy Philometor, who succeeded Ptolemy Epiphanes.[277] Proceeding in

---

[275] Cf. Dan 8:25.

[276] Still insisting that the author of Daniel is conveying future events "in advance," Theodoret sees a reference to the deposition and death of the high priest Onias at the hands of Jason and ("the son of"?) Menelaus, recorded—retrospectively—in 2 Macc 4.

[277] Antiochus defeated Ptolemy VI Philometor in 169.

διεδέξατο. Τούτοις ἐπήγαγε· «Καί γε ἡγούμενος διαθήκης.» Λέγει γὰρ τὸν ἀρχιερέα τὸν εὐσεβῆ, τὸν τοῦ Ἰάσωνος ἀδελφόν, καὶ προδιδάσκει, ὅτι κἀκεῖνον τοῦ ἀρχιερατεύειν παύσει. Εἶτα διδάσκει τὸν τρόπον· «Καὶ 1517 ἀπὸ τῶν συμμίξεων πρὸς αὐτὸν ποιήσει δόλον.» | Χρήσεται γάρ, φησί, διακόνοις τοῖς τὸ αὐτὸ γένος ἔχειν σεμνυνομένοις, καὶ δόλῳ συνεργῷ χρώμενος μυρία δεινὰ εἰς τὸ ἔθνος ἐργάσεται. «Ἀναβήσεται δὲ καὶ ὑπερισχύσει αὐτοῦ ἐν ὀλίγῳ ἔθνει.» Ἐξαπατήσας γὰρ τοὺς τὰ Ἱεροσόλυμα οἰκοῦντας, ὡς μετ' εἰρήνης εἰσιέναι μέλλων, πρῶτον μὲν ἐπιβῆναι τῶν ἀδύτων ἐτόλμησε τοῦ θείου νεώ, ἔπειτα ἅπαντα τὸν ἐπικείμενον κόσμον ἀφελών, καὶ τὰ ἀφιερωμένα τῇ θείᾳ λειτουργίᾳ σκεύη, οὕτως ἐξελήλυθεν. Αὖθις δὲ πάλιν ἐπιστρατεύσας τῇ πόλει, ὀκτὼ μὲν μυριάδας ἀνθρώπων κατέσφαξε, καὶ οὐδὲ τούτοις ἀρκεσθείς, τοὺς ἑαυτοῦ στρατηγοὺς ἀποστείλας, ἑτέρους πάλιν μυρίους φόνους εἰργάσατο. Ταῦτα προσημαίνων φησί·

«Καὶ ὑπερισχύσει αὐτοῦ ἐν ὀλίγῳ ἔθνει. (κδ΄.) Καὶ ἐν εὐθηνίᾳ, καὶ ἐν πίοσι χώραις ἥξει.» Οὔτε γὰρ δι' ἀπορίαν, φησί, μετ' ὀλίγων ἀφίξεται, ἀλλὰ διὰ τὴν τοῦ φρονήματος ἀλαζονείαν· ἔστι γὰρ αὐτῷ καὶ εὐθηνία καὶ ἀπόλαυσις μυρίων ἐθνῶν πιόνων, καὶ φόρον πολὺν χορηγούντων. «Καὶ ποιήσει ἃ οὐκ ἐποίησαν οἱ πατέρες αὐτοῦ καὶ οἱ πατέρες τῶν πατέρων αὐτοῦ· προνομὴν καὶ ὕπαρξιν, καὶ σκῦλα αὐτοῖς διασκορπιεῖ.» Πάντων γὰρ αὐτοῦ τῶν πατέρων, καὶ τῶν προγόνων ἁπάντων τὸ Ἰουδαίων ἔθνος τετιμηκότων, τἀναντία οὗτος πάντα ἐργάσεται, ἀναιρῶν καὶ ληϊζόμενος, καὶ ἐξανδραποδιζόμενος, καὶ τοῖς συστρατευομένοις τὰ τούτων δωρούμενος. «Καὶ ἐπ' Αἴγυπτον, φησί, λογιεῖται λογισμοὺς αὐτοῦ, καὶ ἕως καιροῦ.» Ἀντὶ τοῦ, οὐκ ἐπὶ πολὺ κρατήσει.

κε΄. «Καὶ ἐξεγερθήσεται ἡ ἰσχὺς αὐτοῦ καὶ καρδία αὐτοῦ ἐπὶ βασιλέα τοῦ Νότου, ἐν δυνάμει μεγάλῃ.» Ταύτην αὐτοῦ τὴν κατὰ τῆς Αἰγύπτου ἔφοδον, καὶ ἡ πρώτη τῶν Μακκαβαίων διδάσκει ἱστορία. «Εἰσῆλθε γάρ, φησίν, Ἀντίοχος εἰς Αἴγυπτον ἐν ὄχλῳ βαρεῖ, καὶ ἐν ἅρμασι καὶ ἐλέφασι, καὶ ἱππεῦσι, καὶ ἐν στόλῳ μεγάλῳ, καὶ συνεστήσατο πόλεμον πρὸς Πτολεμαῖον βασιλέα Αἰγύπτου, καὶ ἐνετράπη Πτολεμαῖος ἀπὸ προσώπου αὐτοῦ, καὶ ἔφυγε, καὶ ἔπεσαν τραυματίαι πολλοί, καὶ κατελάβοντο τὰς πόλεις τὰς ὀχυρὰς ἐν γῇ Αἰγύπτου, καὶ ἔλαβον τὰ σκῦλα τῆς, Αἰγύπτου.» Καὶ ταῦτα προδιδασκόμενος ὁ μακάριος Δανιὴλ ἤκουσε. «Καὶ ὁ βασιλεὺς τοῦ Νότου συνάψει πόλεμον πρὸς αὐτόν, ἐν δυνάμει μεγάλῃ καὶ ἰσχυρᾷ σφόδρα, καὶ οὐ στήσεται, ὅτι λογιοῦνται ἐπ' αὐτὸν λογισμούς.» Ἀντὶ τοῦ, πολλαῖς καὶ παντοδαπαῖς ἐνέδραις χρήσονται κατ' αὐτοῦ.

this vein, he said *the prince of the covenant as well*, meaning the pious high priest, brother of Jason, and conveying in advance that he would deprive the latter of the priesthood. He next mentions the way: *In the wake of associations with him he will employ trickery,* | that is, he will use as ministers those who glory in being of the 1517 same race, and by the exercise of trickery he will bring countless troubles on the nation.

He will rise up and prevail over him with a small nation: after deceiving the inhabitants of Jerusalem with the expressed intention of entering in peace, he first presumed to intrude into the precincts of the divine temple, then to remove everything adorning it and the vessels consecrated to divine worship, and so made his departure. At another time he advanced on the city and slaughtered eighty thousand people; not content even with that, he sent his generals and caused the death of countless others. To suggest as much in advance, he said, *He will prevail over him with a small nation. And he will come in prosperity and in rich districts* (vv. 23–24): it is not through insufficient resources that he comes with a few, but as a result of an arrogant attitude; he enjoys prosperity and access to countless rich nations supplying him with generous tribute. *He will do what his fathers and the fathers of his fathers did not do, he will scatter booty and resources and spoils on them*: whereas all his ancestors and all his predecessors showed respect for the nation of Jews, he did quite the opposite, carrying them off, plundering and enslaving them, and bestowing their possessions on his troops. *He will direct his plans against Egypt, if only for a time*, that is, he will not rule for long.

His strength and his heart will be aroused against the king of the south with great power (v. 25). This assault of his on Egypt the first account of the Maccabees also reports. "Antiochus entered Egypt with a strong force, with chariots, elephants, and cavalry, and with a large expedition. He did battle with Ptolemy king of Egypt, and routed Ptolemy before him; he fled, and many were wounded and fell. They occupied the fortified cities in the land of Egypt, and took spoils of Egypt."[278] Blessed Daniel was informed of this in advance on hearing *The king of the south will engage him in battle, with great and exceedingly strong forces, and will not stand firm, because they will direct plans against* him, that is, they will exercise

[278] 1 Macc 1:17–19.

κς'. «Καὶ φάγονται, φησί, τὰ δέοντα αὐτοῦ.» Τουτέστι, κατα-
ναλώσουσιν αὐτοῦ πᾶσαν τὴν πρόσοδον, καὶ τὸν τελούμενον αὐτῷ φόρον
1520 ληϊζόμενοι εἰς ἑαυτοὺς μεταθήσονται. «Καὶ συντρίψουσιν αὐ|τόν, καὶ δυ-
νάμεις αὐτοῦ καταλύσει, καὶ πεσοῦντα· τραυματίαι πολλοί.» Οὐκ αὐτὸν
γὰρ μόνον, ἀλλὰ καὶ τὴν στρατείαν αὐτοῦ δίκην κατακλυσμοῦ διαφθερεῖ,
καὶ πολὺν ἐργάσεται φόνον.
κζ'. «Καὶ ἀμφότεροι, φησίν, οἱ βασιλεῖς, αἱ καρδίαι αὐτῶν ἐπὶ
πονηρίαν, καὶ ἐπὶ τραπέζῃ μιᾷ ψευδῆ λαλήσουσι, καὶ οὐ κατευθυνεῖ.»
Ῥωμαῖοι γὰρ, ὡς Ἰώσηππος ἡμᾶς ὁ ἱστοριογράφος διδάσκει, ταύτην
αὐτοῦ μαθόντες τὴν στρατείαν, παρενεγγύησαν ἀποστῆναι τῆς Αἰγύπτου·
ὅθεν σπεισάμενος, φησίν, εἰρήνην, καὶ τραπέζης ἐκοινώνησε τῷ Πτολεμαίῳ. Τὸ δὲ ὕπουλον τῆς φιλίας διδάσκων ὁ τῷ Δανιὴλ προσδιαλεγόμενος, «Καὶ ἀμφότεροι, φησίν, οἱ βασιλεῖς, αἱ καρδίαι αὐτῶν ἐπὶ πονηρίαν,
καὶ ἐπὶ τραπέζῃ μιᾷ ψευδῆ λαλήσουσι, καὶ οὐ κατευθυνεῖ.» Ἀντὶ τοῦ,
οὐ βεβαία ἔσται ἡ εἰρήνη. «Ὅτι ἔτι πέρας ἔσται εἰς καιρόν.» Τουτέστιν, αὖθις γὰρ, τοῦ καιροῦ τούτου διαδραμόντος, συμπλακήσονται καὶ
παρατάξονται.
κη'. «Καὶ ἐπιστρέψει, φησίν, εἰς τὴν γῆν αὐτοῦ ἐν ὑπάρξει πολλῇ.» Ἀλλ' ὅμως τότε, φησίν, μετὰ πολλοῦ πλούτου, καὶ πολλῆς περιουσίας, εἰς τὴν οἰκείαν ἐπαναστρέψει βασιλείαν. «Καὶ ἡ καρδία αὐτοῦ ἐπὶ
διαθήκην ἁγίαν.» Μίαν δὲ λοιπὸν σχήσει σπουδὴν, ὥστε καταλῦσαι τὸν
ὑπὸ τοῦ Θεοῦ τοῖς Ἰουδαίοις δεδομένον νόμον. Ταῦτα δὲ βουλευσάμενος,
καὶ εἰς πέρας ἄξει τὰ βουλεύματα. «Καὶ ποιήσει γὰρ, φησί, καὶ ἐπιστρέψει εἰς τὴν γῆν αὐτοῦ.» Καὶ τοῦτο δὲ ἡ τῶν Μακκαβαίων βίβλος, καὶ
ἡ Ἰωσήππου ἱστορία διδάσκει.
κθ'. «Καὶ εἰς τὸν καιρὸν αὐτοῦ ἐπιστρέψει, καὶ ἥξει ἐν τῷ Νό-
τῳ, καὶ οὐκ ἔσται ὡς ἡ πρώτη καὶ ἡ ἐσχάτη» Ἀντὶ τοῦ, οὐχ ὁμοίως
νικήσει καὶ ἰσχύσει, ἀλλ' ἡττηθεὶς ἐπανήξει. Τὸ δὲ εἰς καιρὸν αὐτοῦ τὸν
ἐπιτήδειον τῷ πολέμῳ σημαίνει καιρόν.
λ'. «Καὶ εἰσελεύσονται εἰς αὐτὸν οἱ εἰσπορευόμενοι Κίτιοι, καὶ
ταπεινωθήσονται.» Παραλαβὼν γὰρ πολλοὺς Κυπρίους, καὶ ἑτέρους νη-
σιώτας (τὸ γὰρ Κίτιον μέχρι τῆς σήμερον πόλισμά ἐστι τῆς Κύπρου),
ὁρμήσει μὲν κατὰ τῆς Αἰγύπτου, ἡττηθεὶς δὲ καὶ ταπεινωθεὶς ἐπανήξει.
«Καὶ ἐπιστρέψει, φησί, καὶ θυμωθήσεται ἐπὶ διαθήκην ἁγίαν.» Πάντα

many and varied wiles against him. *And they will consume his necessities* (v. 25–26), that is, they will dispose of all his revenue, and seizing tribute meant for him they will transfer it to themselves. | *They will crush him, and he will destroy his forces, and many will be wounded and fall*: he will destroy like a deluge not only him but also his army, and will cause great slaughter. 1520

Both kings, their hearts intent on wickedness, will tell falsehoods at the one table, and it will not succeed (v. 27). Romans, as the historian Josephus informs us, learned of his campaign and ensured that he would leave Egypt;[279] on this basis he made peace and shared Ptolemy's table. But the one speaking in advance to Daniel brings out the shallowness of the friendship in saying *Both kings, their hearts intent on wickedness, will tell falsehoods at the one table, and it will not succeed*, that is, the peace will not be lasting. *Because in time it will still come to an end*, that is once more, when this moment passes, they will deploy forces and engage. *He will return to his own land with great resources* (v. 28): nevertheless at that time he will go back to his own kingdom with great wealth and many possessions. *His heart against the holy covenant*: from that time he will have a single resolve, to undo the law given by God to the Jews. Being so resolved, he will also put his intentions into effect: *He will do this and will return to his own land*. Both the book of the Maccabees and the account of Josephus report this.

At the right time for him he will return, and he will come in the south, and the last will not be like the first (v. 29), that is, he will not conquer and prevail in similar fashion, but will return defeated. *The right time for him* means the time suitable for war. *The advancing Kittim will come forward to him, and will be humbled* (v. 30): assembling many Cypriots and other islanders (even to this day Kition is the city of Cyprus), he will make a raid on Egypt but will be defeated and go back humbled.[280] *He will retreat and will direct*

[279] *Ant.* 12.242–244.
[280] It is thought the text refers to the second Egyptian campaign of Antiochus, when he defeated Ptolemy VII Euergetes II in 168 but was forced to leave Egypt by the Romans. Theodoret is correct in speaking of the (original) application of Hebrew *Kittim* to Cypriots, though it was later applied to other Mediterranean peoples (Macedonians in 1 Macc 1:1), including the Romans, as here. Theodoret's knowledge of geography is a factor in his continuing to think of Cyprus, though a less likely option in the context; he would be unaware of the use of the term by the Dead Sea community for the Romans (see, e.g., the

γὰρ, φησί, τὸν θυμόν, τὸν διὰ τὴν ἧτταν αὐτῷ προσγινόμενον, κατὰ τῆς
ἁγίας διαθήκης ἐμέσει. Καὶ δεικνὺς τὸ ἔργον, «Καὶ ποιήσει,» φησί. Ἐν
γὰρ τῇ δευτέρᾳ παρουσίᾳ τόν τε πολὺν ἐργάσεται φόνον, καὶ τῶν δια-
φυγόντων τὸν ἀνδραποδισμόν. «Καὶ ἐπιστρέψει, καὶ συνήσει ἐπὶ τοὺς
καταλιπόντας διαθήκην ἁγίαν.» Πᾶσαν, φησί, ποιήσεται πρόνοιαν τῶν
παρανομησάντων, καὶ τὸ μὲν Ἰουδαΐζειν ἀρνηθέντων, τὸ δὲ Ἑλληνίζειν
ἀσπασαμένων.

λα΄. «Καὶ βραχίονες ἐξ αὐτοῦ ἀναστήσονται, καὶ βεβηλώσουσι
1521 τὸ ἁγίασμα τῆς δυναστείας, καὶ με|ταστήσουσι τὸν ἐνδελεχισμόν, καὶ
δώσουσιν εἰς αὐτὸν βδέλυγμα ἠφανισμένον.» Βραχίονας καλεῖ, ὡς καὶ
ἤδη προειρήκαμεν, τοὺς ὑπουργοῦντας αὐτῷ στρατηγούς, ἅτε δὴ δίκην
βραχιόνων τά τε τοῦ βασιλέως πληροῦντας προστάγματα. Πέμψει τοιγαροῦν, φησί, τινὰς τὸ μὲν ἁγίασμα τῆς δυναστείας βεβηλοῦντας, ἀντὶ
τοῦ, τῷ Θεῷ τῷ παντοδυνάμῳ ἀνακείμενον νεών· βωμὸν δὲ εἰδωλικὸν
ἔνδον ἀναστήσοντας· τοῦτο γὰρ καλεῖ βδέλυγμα ἠφανισμένον. Διδάσκει
δὲ ἡμᾶς τοῦτο καὶ ἡ δευτέρα τῶν Μακκαβαίων· φησὶ γὰρ οὕτως· «Περὶ
δὲ τὸν καιρὸν τοῦτον, τὴν δευτέραν ἔφοδον ὁ Ἀντίοχος εἰς τὴν Αἴγυπτον
ἐστείλατο.» Εἶτα ἐν μέσῳ ὁ συγγραφεύς τινα περὶ τῆς τῶν νόθων ἀρχιε-
ρέων φιλονεικίας εἰρηκώς, ἐπήγαγε· «Προσπεσόντων δὲ τῷ βασιλεῖ, περὶ τῶν γεγονότων ὑπέλαβεν ἀποστατεῖν τὴν Ἰουδαίαν· Ὅθεν ἀναστρέψας
ἐξ Αἰγύπτου τεθηριωμένος τὴν ψυχήν, ἔλαβε τὴν πόλιν δορυάλωτον, καὶ
ἐκέλευσε τοῖς στρατιώταις κόπτειν ἀφειδῶς τοὺς ἐμπίπτοντας.» Εἶτα
διηγησάμενος, ὡς κατὰ πάσης ἡλικίας ὁ φόνος ἐχώρει, καὶ ὀκτὼ μυριάδες νεκρῶν ἠριθμήθησαν, πάλιν μετὰ βραχέα φησίν· «Ἀπεχθῆ δὲ πρὸς
τοὺς Ἰουδαίους διάθεσιν ἔχων ὁ Ἀντίοχος, ἔπεμψε μυσάρχην Ἀπολ-
λώνιον μετὰ στρατεύματος δισμυρίων πρὸς τοῖς δισχιλίοις, προστάξας
τοὺς ἐν ἡλικίᾳ πάσῃ πάντας κατασφάξαι.» Καὶ μετὰ βραχέα πάλιν φη-
σί· «Μετ᾽ οὐ πολὺν δὲ χρόνον ἀπέστειλεν ὁ βασιλεὺς γέροντα Ἀθηναῖον,
ἀναγκάζειν τοὺς Ἰουδαίους μεταβαίνειν ἀπὸ τῶν πατρίων νόμων, καὶ
τοῖς τοῦ Θεοῦ νόμοις μὴ πολιτεύεσθαι, μολῦναι δὲ καὶ τὸν ἐν Ἱερουσαλὴμ νεών, καὶ προσονομάσαι Διὸς Ὀλυμπίου.» Ταῦτα προαγορεύων
ὁ τῷ μακαρίῳ Δανιὴλ προσδιαλεγόμενος ἔφη· «Καὶ βραχίονες ἐξ αὐτοῦ ἀναστήσονται, καὶ βεβηλώσουσι τὸ ἁγίασμα τῆς δυναστείας, καὶ
μεταστήσουσι τὸν ἐνδελεχισμόν·» τουτέστι, τὴν καθ᾽ ἡμέραν τῷ Θεῷ
προσφερομένην λατρείαν. «Καὶ δώσουσιν εἰς αὐτὸν βδέλυγμα ἠφανισμέ-

his rage on the holy covenant: all the anger ensuing from his defeat he will vent on the holy covenant. And to bring out its effect, *He will do it*: at his second coming he will cause much slaughter and the enslavement of the fugitives. *He will retreat, and will pay heed to those who have forsaken the holy covenant*: he will exercise complete care of transgressors and those who have rejected the way of Judaism, instead embracing the way of Hellenism.

Arms of his will rise up, defile the sanctuary of power, | *inter-*   1521
rupt the regular ritual, and give to it a desolate abomination (v. 31). By *arms*, as we have already remarked,[281] he refers to the generals acting in his stead for the reason that they fulfill the king's commands like arms. So he is saying that he will dispatch some men to defile the *sanctuary of power*, that is, the temple consecrated to God Almighty and erect within an altar for idols (referring to it as *desolate abomination*). Now, the second book of Maccabees informs us of this as follows: "About this time Antiochus launched his second invasion of Egypt." Then, after inserting something to do with the rivalry between the illegitimate high priests, it went on, "When this came to the ears of the king, he presumed from what had occurred that Judea was in revolt. Hence he left Egypt with his spirit enraged and took the city captive, ordering his soldiers to cut down mercilessly those they met." After next recounting that the slaughter affected every age and the number of the dead reached eighty thousand, it shortly afterward went on to say, "Being very hostile to the Jews, Antiochus dispatched a hateful leader Apollonius with an army of twenty-two thousand, bidding him kill everyone of mature age." And shortly thereafter it says, "Not long afterward the king sent an Athenian elder to force the Jews to forsake the ancestral laws and not live by the laws of God, but rather to defile the temple in Jerusalem and give it the name of Olympian Zeus."[282]

The one speaking to blessed Daniel foretell this to him in the words, *Arms of his will rise up, defile the sanctuary of power, and interrupt the regular ritual*—that is, the worship daily offered

---

War Scroll, *Pesher Habakkuk* (esp. II, 12-IV, 14), and Geza Vermes, trans., *The Complete Dead Sea Scrolls* [New York: Penguin, 1998], 59–60).

[281] The usage, where "arms" is capable of a corporeal or a metaphorical sense, occurred already in vv. 6, 15, 22 (see note there), at none of which occurrences did Theodoret offer this explanation.

[282] 2 Macc 5:1, 11–12, 14; 6:1–2.

νον· » τὸν βωμόν, ὃν τῷ Διῒ ἀνέστησεν ὁ δυσσεβὴς βασιλεύς, καὶ χοῖρον ἐπ' αὐτοῦ προσενήνοχε.

λβ'. «Καὶ τοὺς ἀνομοῦντας, φησί, διαθήκην ἀπάξουσιν ἐν ὀλισθήμασι.» Τοὺς γὰρ παρανομίᾳ συζῶντας προφανῶς δυσσεβεῖν παρασκευάσουσι τοῖς ἀπατηλοῖς χρώμενοι λόγοις. «Καὶ λαός, γινώσκοντες Θεὸν αὐτῶν, κατισχύσουσι καὶ ποιήσουσι.» Τοὺς περὶ τὸν μακάριον Ματταθίαν ἐνταῦθα αἰνίττεται, ὃς πρῶτος τοῖς τοῦ Ἀντιόχου δόγμασιν ἀντιστάς, καὶ σὺν τοῖς υἱέσι τὴν ἔρημον καταλαβών, μετ' ὀλίγων στρατευόμενος τοὺς ἐκείνου κατηγωνίσατο στρατηγούς.

λγ'. «Καὶ οἱ συνετοὶ λαοῦ, φησί, συνήσουσιν εἰς πολλά.» Οἱ γὰρ εἰς δέον τῇ παρὰ τοῦ Θεοῦ χορηγηθείσῃ γνώσει χρώμενοι, σφόδρα τῶν ἐκείνου κατα|φρονήσουσι νόμων, καὶ τὴν ὑπὲρ τοῦ θείου νόμου τελευτὴν τῆς μετ' ἀσεβείας ζωῆς προτιμήσουσι. Καὶ τοῦτο σημαίνων ἐπήγαγε· «Καὶ ἀσθενήσουσιν ἐν ρομφαίᾳ, καὶ ἐν φλογί, καὶ ἐν αἰχμαλωσίᾳ καὶ ἐν διαρπαγῇ ἡμερῶν αὐτῶν.» Διαφόροις γὰρ καὶ παντοδαποῖς κολαστηρίοις ὁ δυσσεβὴς χρώμενος καταπλήττειν ἐπειρᾶτο τοὺς εὐσεβεῖς, ἄωρον αὐτοῖς ἐπιφέρων θάνατον, καὶ οἱονεὶ τὰς ὑπολοίπους αὐτῶν διαρπάζων ἡμέρας. Εἶτα τὰ ὑπὸ τοῦ μακαρίου Ματταθίου, καὶ τῶν υἱέων αὐτοῦ ἐσόμενα προλέγει·

λδ'. «Καὶ ἐν τῷ ἀσθενῆσαι αὐτοὺς βοηθήσονται βοήθειαν μικράν.» Τῆς γὰρ θείας χάριτος ἀπολαύσουσι, καὶ τέως τῶν πολεμούντων περιγενήσονται· οὐ μὴν εἰρήνης καὶ πολέμων ἀπαλλαγῆς ἐν ταῖς τούτων ἀπολαύσουσιν ἡμέραις. Διὸ *βοήθειαν μικρὰν* τὰς γενομένας ἐν μέσῳ τῶν πολέμων ἀνακωχὰς προσηγόρευσε. «Καὶ προστεθήσονται, φησί, πρὸς αὐτοὺς πολλοὶ ἐν ὀλισθήμασι.» Ταύτην γάρ, φησί, τὴν ἀνδραγαθίαν ὁρῶντες, καὶ τῶν ὀλισθησάντων πολλοὶ καὶ τὴν εὐσέβειαν ἀρνηθέντων, μεταμελείᾳ χρησάμενοι, πρὸς αὐτοὺς δραμοῦνται

λε'. «Καὶ ἀπὸ τῶν συνιέντων, φησίν, ἀσθενήσουσι πολλοί.» Καὶ τῶν εὐσεβεῖν δοκούντων εἰς τοὐναντίον τραπήσονται. «Τοῦ πυρῶσαι, φησίν, ἐν αὐτοῖς, καὶ τοῦ ἐκλέξασθαι, καὶ ἐκλευκᾶναι ἕως καιροῦ πέρας· διότι ἔτι εἰς καιρόν.» Οὐδὲ ταῦτα, φησί, βλάψει τοὺς ἐσομένους ἀνθρώπους· διδαχθήσονται γὰρ ἐντεῦθεν τοῖς προτέροις μὴ θαρρεῖν κατορθώμασιν, ἀλλ' ἀεὶ δεδοικέναι καὶ τρέμειν, κατὰ τὴν τοῦ μακαρίου Παύλου παραίνεσιν· «Ὁ δοκῶν γάρ, φησίν, ἑστάναι, βλεπέτω μὴ πέσῃ.» Αἱ γὰρ τῶν καιρῶν μεταβολαὶ οἱονεὶ πυροῦσι, καὶ δοκιμάζουσι, καὶ ἀποκρίνουσι τοῦ δοκίμου τὸ κίβδηλον· οὐ μὴν δὲ ἀλλὰ καὶ ἐκλευκαίνουσιν οἱονεὶ ἔριον, καὶ δοκιμάζουσιν, εἴτε φυσικήν, εἴτε ἐπείσακτον ἔχει τὴν χροιάν, καὶ εἴτε ὅλον διόλου ἐμπεφυκὸς τὸ χρῶμα, εἴτε τῇ ἐπιφανείᾳ ἐπικείμενον μόνῃ. Ταῦτα μέν, φησί, κατὰ τὸν παρόντα βίον μερικῶς γίνεται· ἐν

to God—*and transform to a desolate abomination* the altar that the impious king erected to Zeus and on which he offered a pig. *By underhand means they will seduce those violating the covenant* (v. 32): by the use of deceptive words they will cause those guilty of transgression to be brazenly unfaithful. *People who acknowledge their God will take courage and live up to it.* He is referring here to those in the company of blessed Mattathias, who was the first to resist the decrees of Antiochus, and who with his sons occupied the wilderness and together with a few others went on the attack and opposed his generals. *The wise members of the people will bring understanding to many things* (v. 33): those who properly use the knowledge supplied them by God will utterly despise that fellow's laws, | and will prefer death for the divine law to a life of godless- 1524 ness. To suggest as much, he went on, *They will fall to the sword, to flames, captivity, and robbery of their very life*: the impious one employed all kinds of different punishments in an attempt to move the godly, inflicting on them untimely death and as it were robbing them of the remainder of their life.

He then forecasts what would be done by blessed Mattathias and his sons. *In their weakness they will receive some little help* (v. 34): they will receive divine grace, and for a time will prevail over their attackers, though they will not actually enjoy peace and relief from wars in their time. Hence he called the truce occurring in the middle of the wars *some little help. Many who have lapsed will be joined to their number*: observing this courage of theirs, many who have lapsed and denied their religion will undergo repentance and come to join them. *Many of the wise will fail* (v. 35): some of those who appear to be pious will take the opposite course. *So that they may be purified, chosen, and cleansed until the end of time, for it is not yet time*: this will not harm people yet to be; they will be instructed by this not to rely on former virtuous actions, but to be always in fear and trembling, according to the exhortation of blessed Paul, "If you seem to stand firm, be careful not to fall."[283] The changes in the situation, you see, will as it were purify, test, and separate the dross from the true; they will have the same effect as the whitening of wool and testing whether its color is natural or artificial, whether the shade is innate throughout or applied to the surface alone. Although this happens to some extent in the present

[283] 1 Cor 10:12.

δὲ τῷ μέλλοντι χρόνῳ ἡ καθόλου τῶν ἀνθρώπων ἐξέτασις ἔσται. Ταῦτα περὶ Ἀντιόχου τοῦ Ἐπιφανοῦς εἰρηκώς, μεταβαίνει λοιπὸν ἀπὸ τῆς εἰκόνος ἐπὶ τὸ ἀρχέτυπον· ἀρχέτυπον δὲ τοῦ Ἀντιόχου ὁ ἀντίχριστος, καὶ τοῦ Ἀντιχρίστου εἰκὼν ὁ Ἀντίοχος. Ὥσπερ γὰρ ἐκεῖνος ἀσεβεῖν ἠνάγκαζεν Ἰουδαίους, καὶ πολιτεύεσθαι παρανόμως· οὕτως ὁ ἄνθρωπος τῆς ἁμαρτίας, ὁ υἱὸς τῆς ἀπωλείας, ὁ ὑπεραιρόμενος καὶ ὑπερυψούμενος ὑπὲρ πάντα λεγόμενον Θεὸν ἢ σέβασμα, ᾗ φησιν ὁ μακάριος Παῦλος, ὥστε αὐτὸν καὶ εἰς τὸν ναὸν τοῦ Θεοῦ εἰσελθόντα καθίσαι, ἀποδεικνύοντα ἑαυτόν, ὅτι ἔστι Θεός, ἐν πᾶσι σημείοις καὶ τέρασι ψεύδους· οὕτως οὗτος
1525 πάντα εἰς ἀπάτην τῶν εὐσε|βῶν διαπράξεται, νῦν μὲν ταῖς ἀπατηλαῖς θαυματουργίαις ἐξαπατᾶν καὶ φενακίζειν πειρώμενος, νῦν δὲ τῇ δυναστείᾳ χρώμενος, καὶ πᾶν εἶδος τιμωρίας ἐπιφέρων τοῖς τῆς εὐσεβείας τροφίμοις. Εἰ δέ τις ἀκολουθίαν τῆς προφητείας ἐπιζητῶν μὴ πιστεύει ταῦθ' οὕτως ἔχειν, εἰς νοῦν τὴν εὐαγγελικὴν διδασκαλίαν λαβέτω· καὶ γὰρ ἐκεῖ κατὰ ταυτὸν ὁ Κύριος τὰ περὶ τῆς κοινῆς συντελείας προλέγει, καὶ τὰ περὶ τῆς συντελείας τῆς Ἱερουσαλήμ· εἰρηκὼς γάρ· «Προσεύχεσθε ἵνα μὴ γένηται ἡ φυγὴ ὑμῶν χειμῶνος, μηδὲ ἐν Σαββάτῳ» (τοῦτο δὲ Ἰουδαίοις μόνοις ἁρμόττει)· εὐθὺς ἐπήγαγεν· «Ἔσται γὰρ θλίψις μεγάλη, οἵα οὐ γέγονεν ἀπ' ἀρχῆς κόσμου ἕως τοῦ νῦν, οὐδὲ μὴ γενήσεται· καὶ εἰ μὴ ἐκολοβώθησαν αἱ ἡμέραι ἐκεῖναι, οὐκ ἂν ἐσώθη πᾶσα σάρξ· διὰ δὲ τοὺς ἐκλεκτοὺς κολοβωθήσονται αἱ ἡμέραι ἐκεῖναι.» Καὶ δεικνὺς ὡς οὐδὲν τούτων Ἰουδαίοις προσήκει, ἐπήγαγεν· «Τότε ἐάν τις ὑμῖν εἴπῃ· Ἰδού, ὧδε ὁ Χριστός, ἢ ἐκεῖ, μὴ πιστεύσητε.» Καὶ προειρηκὼς περὶ τῶν ψευδοχρίστων ὀλίγα, ἐπάγει· «Ὥσπερ γὰρ ἡ ἀστραπὴ ἐξέρχεται ἀπὸ ἀνατολῶν καὶ φαίνεται ἕως δυσμῶν, οὕτως ἔσται καὶ ἡ παρουσία τοῦ Υἱοῦ τοῦ ἀνθρώπου.» Καὶ τὰ ἄλλα δὲ πάντα ὁμοίως, ἵνα μὴ καθ' ἕκαστον λέγω. Ἐντεῦθεν τοίνυν ποδηγούμενοι, καὶ τὴν προφητείαν νοήσομεν, μεταβᾶσαν μὲν ἀπὸ τοῦ Ἀντιόχου ἐπὶ τὸν Ἀντίχριστον, ὡς ἀπὸ εἰκόνος ἐπὶ ἀρχέτυπον, σαφῶς δὲ ἡμᾶς τὰ κατ' ἐκεῖνον προδιδάσκουσαν.

λς'. «Ποιήσει γάρ, φησί, κατὰ τὸ θέλημα αὐτοῦ ὁ βασιλεύς, καὶ ὑψωθήσεται, καὶ μεγαλυνθήσεται, ἐπὶ πάντα Θεόν, καὶ ἐπὶ τὸν Θεὸν τῶν θεῶν, καὶ λαλήσει ὑπέρογκα, καὶ κατευθυνεῖ.» Ἀντὶ τοῦ, εὐοδωθήσεται,

life, he is saying, in the time to come there will be a complete testing of people.

After these remarks in reference to Antiochus Epiphanes, he
then moves from the image to the archetype, the archetype in the
case of Antiochus being the antichrist, and the antichrist's image
Antiochus. In other words, just as he forced Jews to commit impiety and live a lawless life, so the sinful one, the son of destruction,
the one lifted up and exalted above every so-called god or object
of worship, as blessed Paul says, so that he enters and takes his
seat in God's temple, presenting himself as God, with all signs and
false portents[284]—in this way he will do everything to deceive the
godly, | at one time endeavoring to delude and cheat by deceptive   1525
wonder-working, at another by the use of force and application of
every kind of punishment to the devotees of piety. If, on the other
hand, on the basis of following the sequence of the work you do
not believe this to be the case, take account of the Gospel teaching: there the Lord at the one time foretells the details of the end
of everything and the details of the end of Jerusalem. After saying, remember, "Pray that your flight not be in winter or on the
Sabbath" (something applicable to Jews alone), he went on, "For
there will be great tribulation such as has not occurred from the
beginning of the world up until now, nor will occur. If those days
had not been shortened, no human being would be saved; but on
account of the elect those days will be shortened." And to bring
out that nothing of this applies to Jews, he went on, "If at that
time someone says to you, Look, here is the Christ, or there he is,
do not believe them." And after making some predictions about
false messiahs, he goes on, "As the lightning comes out of the east
and shines as far as the west, so too will the coming of the Son of
Man be"[285]—and, without my being exhaustive, many other similar statements.

Guided by this, then, let us also understand the work as moving from Antiochus to the antichrist, as from image to archetype,
on the one hand, and on the other giving us clear information in
advance about the former. *The king will do as he pleases, he will
be exalted and magnified over every god and over the God of gods,
he will give voice to inflated ideas and will prosper* (v. 36), that is,

[284] 2 Thess 2:3–4, 9.
[285] Matt 24:20–27.

ἀλλ' οὐκ εἰς τέλος. «Μέχρι γὰρ τοῦ συντελεσθῆναι τὴν ὀργήν.» Ἕως ἂν σφόδρα, φησί, τὴν θείαν ὀργὴν ἐκκαύσῃ, καὶ ταύτην ἐπισπάσηται. Ὀργὴν δὲ τὴν τιμωρίαν καλεῖ· ἀπαθὲς γὰρ τὸ Θεῖον. «Εἰς γὰρ συντέλειαν, φησί, καὶ σπουδὴν γίνεται.» Καὶ γὰρ οὗτος, φησί, προγινώσκων τὸ ἑαυτοῦ τέλος, πολλῇ χρήσεται σπουδῇ εἰς ἀσέβειαν ἅπαντας ἐκκαλούμενος, καὶ πολλοὺς κοινωνοὺς τῆς τιμωρίας λαβεῖν βουλόμενος. Τὰ δὲ ἐπαγόμενα σαφέστερον ἐλέγχει τὴν ἄνοιαν τῶν οἰομένων περὶ Ἀντιόχου ταῦτα εἰρῆσθαι. Φησὶ γάρ·

λζ'. «Καὶ ἐπὶ πάντας θεοὺς τῶν πατέρων αὐτοῦ οὐ συνήσει.» Εὑρίσκομεν δὲ τὸν Ἀντίοχον εἰδωλικῶν βωμῶν τήν τε Ἱερουσαλὴμ καὶ πᾶσαν τὴν Ἰουδαίαν ἐμπλήσαντα, καὶ ἐν τῷ ναῷ τοῦ Θεοῦ τῷ Διὶ θύσαντα, καὶ Διὸς μὲν Ὀλυμπίου τὸν ἐν Ἱεροσολύμοις νεὼν προσαγορεύσαντα, Διὸς δὲ Ξενίου τὸν ἐν τῷ Γαριζείν. Πῶς τοίνυν ὁ οὕτως δεισιδαίμων, ὁ οὕτως εἰδωλολάτρης, «ἐπὶ θεοὺς τῶν πατέρων αὐτοῦ οὐ συνήσει;»
1528 Πάντα γὰρ τοὐναντίον ὁ Ἀντίο|χος ποιῶν διετέλει· τοὺς πατρῴους γὰρ σέβων θεούς, τὸν ὑπὸ τῶν Ἰουδαίων προσκυνούμενον ἠρνεῖτο Θεόν. Οὐδαμῶς τοίνυν τῷ Ἀντιόχῳ ταῦτα ἁρμόττει· ἀλλ' αὐτῷ τῷ ἀρχετύπῳ τοῦ Ἀντιόχου, οὗ εἰκὼν καὶ τύπος ὁ Ἀντίοχος γεγονώς, νικῆσαι εἰς ἀσέβειαν ἅπαντας τοὺς πρὸ αὐτοῦ γενομένους βασιλέας ἐφιλονείκησε. Περὶ τοῦ Ἀντιχρίστου τοίνυν λέγει, ὅτι «Ἐπὶ πάντας θεοὺς πατέρων αὐτοῦ οὐ συνήσει. Καὶ ἐπὶ ἐπιθυμίαν γυναικῶν, καὶ ἐπὶ πάντα Θεὸν οὐ συνήσει.» Καὶ τοῦτο δὲ ἀντικρὺς ἐναντίον τοῖς τοῦ Ἀντιόχου ἐπιτηδεύμασιν. Οὗτος γὰρ οὐδὲ ταῖς γάμου νόμῳ συνημμέναις μόναις ἠρκεῖτο, ἐξ ὧν Ἀντίοχόν τε τὸν Εὐπάτορα καὶ Ἀλέξανδρον ἐπαιδοποίησεν, ἀλλὰ καὶ παλλακίσιν ἀκολάστοις ἐμίγνυτο. Τῆς δὲ μιᾶς καὶ ἡ δευτέρα τῶν Μακκαβαίων μνημονεύει, καί φησιν ὁ συγγραφεὺς οὕτως· «Συνέβη δὲ Ταρσεῖς καὶ Μαλλεώτας στασιάζειν, διὰ τὸ Ἀντιοχίδι τῇ παλλακῇ τοῦ βασιλέως ἐν δωρεᾷ δεδόσθαι.» Ὁ τοίνυν τοσαύτῃ δουλεύων ἀκολασίᾳ, ὡς πόλεις τοιαύτας καὶ τηλικαύτας ἑταιρικῷ δωρήσασθαι γυναίῳ, πῶς ἐπὶ ἐπιθυμίαν γυναικῶν οὐ συνήσει; Οὐκοῦν καὶ ἐντεῦθεν σαφῶς ἁμαρτάνοντες ἐξελέγχονται οἱ εἰς Ἀντίοχον ταῦτα λαμβάνειν ἐπιχειροῦντες. Ἡμεῖς δὲ ἐπανέλθωμεν ὅθεν ἐξήλθομεν. «Καὶ ἐπὶ ἐπιθυμίαν γυναικῶν, φησίν, καὶ ἐπὶ πάντα Θεὸν οὐ συνήσει, ὅτι ἐπὶ πάντας μεγαλυνθήσεται.»

he will enjoy success, but not finally: *until the wrath is fulfilled,* that is, until he inflames divine wrath and brings it on himself. By *wrath* he refers to retribution, the divinity not being subject to passion. *For it reaches completion and zeal:*[286] aware in advance of his own end, he will exercise great zeal in summoning everyone to impiety, wanting to have many sharers in the retribution. What follows provides a clearer refutation of the folly of those who think this is said in reference to Antiochus: *He will not understand about all his ancestors' gods* (v. 37). We find, by contrast, Antiochus filling Jerusalem and all Judea with altars for the idols, sacrificing to Zeus in God's temple, calling the temple in Jerusalem after Olympian Zeus and the one on Mount Gerizim after Zeus Xenios. So how could it be that one so superstitious, so devoted to worship of the idols, *will not understand about his ancestors' gods?* Antiochus, in fact, kept doing the opposite in all respects: | while   1528 reverencing his ancestral gods he denied the God worshiped by the Jews. This is therefore applicable in no way to Antiochus but to the actual archetype of Antiochus, of whom Antiochus was image and type, striving to surpass all his predecessors in impiety. It is of the antichrist, therefore, that he says *he will not understand about his ancestral gods, about the desire of women and about every god.* This, too, is clearly contrary to Antiochus's practices: far from being content with lawfully wedded wives, by whom he had his sons Antiochus Eupator and Alexander, he also had relations with lascivious concubines. The second book of the Maccabees refers to one of these, the chronicler speaking in these terms: "It happened that the people of Tarsus and Mallus revolted because their city had been given as a present to Antiochis, the king's concubine."[287] How could it be, then, that one in thrall to such extreme lasciviousness as to bestow such great cities on a courtesan *will not understand the desire of women?* In this case, too, those who attempt to take this in reference to Antiochus are therefore clearly proven to be wide of the mark.

For our part, however, let us resume where we left off. *He will not pay heed to the desire of women and to every god, because*

[286] The phrase "and zeal" in Theodoret's text is unsupported.

[287] 2 Macc 4:30. Theodoret's logic here is not helped by his not detecting in the phrase in his Greek version, "the desire of women," a reference to the god Tammuz-Adonis (given its proper name in Ezek 8:14; cf. Theodoret's comment there).

Ἀντὶ τοῦ, οἰήσεται πάντων εἶναι μέγιστος.

λη΄. «Καὶ Θεὸν Μαωζεὶμ ἐπὶ τόπου αὐτοῦ δοξάσει, καὶ Θεὸν ὃν οὐκ ἔγνωσαν οἱ πατέρες αὐτοῦ δοξάσει ἐν ἀργυρίῳ, καὶ χρυσίῳ, καὶ ἐν λίθῳ τιμίῳ, καὶ ἐν ἐπιθυμήμασι.» Τῶν γὰρ πατέρων αὐτοῦ πάντων τὴν οἰκείαν φύσιν ἐγνωκότων, καὶ τὸν ἐπὶ πάντων Θεὸν σφᾶς αὐτοὺς ὀνομάσαι μὴ τετολμηκότων, οὗτος Θεὸν ἰσχυρὸν καὶ δυνατὸν (τοῦτο γὰρ σημαίνει τὸ Μαωζεὶμ) ἑαυτὸν προσαγορεύει. Τὸ γὰρ, ἐπὶ τόπῳ αὐτοῦ, ἀντὶ τοῦ ἑαυτὸν τέθεικε.

λθ΄. «Καὶ ποιήσει τοῖς ὀχυρώμασι τῶν καταφυγῶν μετὰ Θεοῦ ἀλλοτρίου, ὃν ἐγνώρισε, καὶ πληθυνεῖ δόξαν, καὶ ὑποτάξει αὐτοῖς πολλούς, καὶ γῆν διελεῖ ἐν δώροις.» Ἀναστήσει γὰρ, φησίν, ἑαυτῷ ναούς, καὶ ἀργύρῳ, καὶ χρυσῷ, καὶ λίθοις τιμίοις αὐτοὺς καλλωπίσει, καὶ ὑποτάξει αὐτοῖς πολλούς, τοὺς ἐξαπατωμένους δηλονότι τοῖς τέρασιν, ἢ ταῖς κολάσεσιν χαυνουμένους. Ἀλλὰ καὶ «γῆν διελεῖ ἐν δώροις·» τοῖς γὰρ ὑπηκόοις καὶ ἀσεβεῖν αἱρουμένοις, καὶ γῆν δωρήσεται πλείστην.

μ΄. «Καὶ ἐν καιροῦ πέρατι, φησί, συγκερατισθήσεται μετ' αὐτοῦ βασιλεὺς Νότου, καὶ συναχθήσεται ἐπ' αὐτὸν βασιλεὺς τοῦ Βορρᾶ ἐν ἅρμασι, καὶ | ἐν ἱππεῦσι, καὶ ἐν ναυσὶ πολλαῖς, καὶ εἰσελεύσεται εἰς τὴν γῆν ἐν ταῖς κατακλύσεσι, καὶ συντρίψει.» Πολλάκις εἴπομεν, ὅτι τοῦ τετάρτου θηρίου τὰ δέκα κέρατα τὰ κατ' αὐτὸν φανέντα, δέκα βασιλέας σημαίνει ἐν τῷ τέλει τῆς Ῥωμαϊκῆς βασιλείας κατὰ ταυτὸν βασιλεύσοντας. Ἐκ τούτων τοίνυν πάλιν ὁ τοῦ *Νότου* βασιλεὺς πολεμήσει τούτῳ, ὃς τοῦ *Βορρᾶ* καλεῖται *βασιλεύς*. «Ἀπὸ βορρᾶ γὰρ, φησίν, ἐκκαυθήσεται τὰ κακὰ ἐπὶ πάντας τοὺς κατοικοῦντας τὴν γῆν.» Καὶ Ἀντίοχος δὲ, ὃς τούτου τύπος ἐτύγχανε, τοῦ *Βορρᾶ βασιλεὺς* ὠνομάζετο. Τοῦ τοίνυν βασιλέως τοῦ Νότου συμπλακέντος αὐτῷ, μετὰ πλήθους οὗτος καὶ ὀχυρωμάτων ἐγγείων τε καὶ θαλαττίων, καὶ ἐπιστρατεύσει αὐτῷ, καὶ τὴν νίκην ἀναδήσεται. Τούτους δὲ τοὺς πολεμίους, καὶ ἐν τοῖς ἱεροῖς Εὐαγγελίοις προεῖπεν ὁ Κύριος· «Ἐγερθήσεται γὰρ ἔθνος ἐπὶ ἔθνος, καὶ βασιλεία ἐπὶ βασιλείαν, καὶ ἔσονται λιμοί, καὶ λοιμοί, καὶ σεισμοὶ κατὰ τόπους· ταῦτα δὲ πάντα ἀρχαὶ ὠδίνων.» Ἔχοντες τοίνυν τῇ προφητείᾳ

he will be magnified over them all, that is, he will think himself the greatest of all. *In his place he will glorify the god Maozeim, and a god his ancestors did not know he will glorify with silver and gold, precious stones and desirable things* (v. 38): whereas all his ancestors acknowledged their natural limitations, and did not presume to name themselves as god over all things, he gives himself the title God mighty and strong (the sense of *Maozeim*)—hence his putting *in his place,* meaning himself.[288] *He will deal with fortresses of fugitives with a foreign god of whom he knew; he will magnify glory, subject many to them, and divide up the land as gifts* (v. 39): he will erect temples to himself, adorn them with silver, gold, and precious stones, and subject many to them—namely, those deceived by the portents or suborned by punishments. He will also *divide up the land as gifts*: he will bestow a great deal of the land on those subjects who opted for godlessness.

At the end of the time the king of the south will engage him in battle, and the king of the north will mass his forces against him with chariots, | horsemen, and many ships, and he will enter the land with deluges and will crush them (v. 40). We have often remarked that | 1529 the ten horns of the fourth beast which emerge against him refer to ten kings at the end of the Roman Empire who will reign at the same time. Of these in turn, then, *the king of the south* will make war on the one who is called *king of the north*; Scripture says, remember, "From the north, troubles will flare up against all the inhabitants of the land."[289] Now, Antiochus, who proved to be a type of this man, was given the name *king of the north*; so when the king of the south engaged him, he attacked him with vast numbers and military equipment on land and sea, and won the day. The Lord in the sacred Gospels also foretold these enemies, "Nation will rise up against nation, kingdom against kingdom, and there will be famine, pestilence, and earthquakes in various places; all this is the beginning of the birth-pangs."[290] So with the Lord's

[288] The Greek versions simply transliterate the Hebrew for "(god) of fortresses," a probable reference to the Roman god Jupiter Capitolinus, equivalent to Olympian Zeus. Unaware of this, Theodoret rationalizes, encouraged by the connotation of divinity in the name Epiphanes.

[289] Jer 1:14, a verse on which there is no remark in Theodoret's *Commentary on Jeremiah* (at least in the form we have it). The "north" in question in Jeremiah is more likely Babylon.

[290] Matt 24:7.

τῇδε τὴν Δεσποτικὴν πρόρρησιν συμφωνοῦσαν, νοήσομεν τὰ προκείμενα. «Καὶ παρελεύσεται,» φησί.

μα'. «Καὶ εἰσελεύσεται εἰς τὴν γῆν τοῦ Σαβείρ.» Πάλιν διὰ τοῦ Σαβεὶρ τὰ Ἱεροσόλυμα παρεδήλωσε. «Καὶ πολλοὶ ἀσθενήσουσι.» Δηλονότι οἱ ἐξαπατώμενοι, ἢ τῷ μεγέθει τῶν τιμωριῶν χαυνούμενοι. «Καὶ οὗτοι διασωθήσονται ἐκ χειρὸς αὐτοῦ, Ἐδὼμ καὶ Μωὰβ, καὶ ἀρχὴ υἱῶν Ἀμμών.» Οὐδὲ ταῦτα δὲ ἁρμόττει τῷ Ἀντιόχῳ· καὶ γὰρ τούτους καταστρεψάμενος, ἡγεμόνας αὐτοῖς κατέστησεν, ὧν εἷς ἦν ὁ Τιμόθεος, Ἀμμανιτῶν ἡγούμενος. Ἐπὶ δὲ τούτου τοῦ δυσσεβοῦς εἰκὸς τούτους διαφυγεῖν, ἅτε δὴ μηδὲ σπουδαίως εὐσεβοῦντας· τοῖς γὰρ σπουδαίοις πάντως ὁ δυσσεβὴς ἐπιστρατεύει. Εἰ δὲ καὶ τροπικῶς ταῦτα δεῖ νοῆσαι τὰ ὀνόματα, Ἐδὼμ ἑρμηνεύεται ὁ πυρρός· τούτου χάριν καὶ ὁ Ἡσαῦ Ἐδὼμ προσηγορεύθη, ὡς τοῦ ἑψήματος τοῦ φακοῦ ἐρυθροῦ ὄντος ἐπιθυμήσας, καὶ τὸ αἷμα δὲ ἐρυθρὸν ἔχει τὸ εἶδος. Οἱ τοίνυν τοῦ Δεσποτικοῦ αἵματος ἀξιούμενοι, καὶ ἀξίως τῆς δωρεᾶς ταύτης πολιτευόμενοι, ἐπανθοῦσαν αὐτοῖς ἔχουσι τὴν τοῦ Δεσποτικοῦ αἵματος χάριν· καὶ Μωὰβ δὲ προσαγορεύεται ὁ ἐκ τοῦ πατρὸς γεννηθείς. Οὕτω γὰρ ἡ πρεσβυτέρα τοῦ Λὼτ θυγάτηρ ἐκ τοῦ πατρὸς συλλαβοῦσα, εἶτα τεκοῦσα, προσηγόρευσε τὸν τεχθέντα. Οἱ τοίνυν υἱοὶ Θεοῦ προσαγορευόμενοι, «οἳ οὐκ ἐξ αἱμάτων, οὐδὲ ἐκ θελήματος ἀνδρός, οὐδὲ ἐκ θελήματος σαρκός, ἀλλ' ἐκ Θεοῦ ἐγεννήθησαν,» εἰκότως Μωὰβ ὀνομάζονται. Καὶ ὁ Ἀμμὰν δὲ τὸν υἱὸν τοῦ γένους σημαίνει· τοῦτο γὰρ ἡ θεία διδάσκει Γραφή. Λέγει γὰρ ὁ μακάριος Παῦλος ἐν Ἀθηναίοις δημηγορῶν· «Γένος οὖν ὑπάρχοντες τοῦ Θεοῦ, οὐκ ὀφείλομεν νομίζειν, | χρυσίῳ, ἢ ἀργύρῳ, ἢ λίθῳ, χαράγματι τέχνης καὶ ἐνθυμήσεως ἀνθρώπων τὸ Θεῖον εἶναι ὅμοιον.» Καὶ αὐτὸς δὲ ὁ Θεός, γένος αὐτοῦ τοὺς ἁγίους ἐκάλεσε· «Ποτίσαι γάρ, φησί, τὸ γένος μου τὸ ἐκλεκτόν, ὃ περιεποιησάμην τὰς ἀρετάς μου διηγεῖσθαι.»

prophecy corresponding to this prophecy, we shall be able to understand the verses before us.

He will pass through, he goes on. *He will enter the land of Sabeir* (v. 41), once again by *Sabeir* referring to Jerusalem.[291] *And many will fail*—namely, those deceived or influenced by the magnitude of the punishments. *These shall be saved from his hand, Edom, Moab, and the main part of the children of Ammon.* This does not apply to Antiochus, either: after vanquishing them, he set leaders over them, one of whom was Timothy, leader of the Ammonites. Now, under this impious fellow it is likely that those people escaped on the grounds of not being zealous in their religious practice; the impious fellow, remember, directed his attack totally against the zealous. If, on the other hand, these names ought be taken also in a figurative manner, *Edom* means the red one—hence Esau was called Edom for his longing for a dish of red lentils; blood is red in appearance, too, so those thought worthy of the Lord's blood, and living a life worthy of this gift, have the grace of the Lord's blood flourishing within them.[292] *Moab* means the one born of the father: Lot's older daughter conceived of her father, then gave birth and gave the name to the child; so God's children are referred to as "those born not of blood, or of the will of a man, or of the will of the flesh, but of God," and hence are properly called Moab.[293] *Ammon* means the son of the people, as the divine Scripture teaches: preaching in Athens blessed Paul said, "Since we are God's people, we ought not think | the deity is like   1532 gold, silver or stone, an image formed by the skill and imagination of human beings."[294] And God himself referred to the saints as his people, "To give a drink to my chosen people, the people I

[291] Cf. note 270. What seems a reference to a successful campaign of Antiochus in Egypt is otherwise unknown, so Theodoret feels justified in making some creative commentary and allegorical and sacramental interpretation.

[292] Since the historical reference in these verses is not obvious, Theodoret thinks he may (*pace* Diodore) venture into allegorical interpretation on the basis of popular etymology, citing Gen 25:25 in reference to Esau's coloring (as he does in his commentary also on Isa 63:1 and Song 3:6), and go further into eucharistic overtones.

[293] Theodoret thinks that the popular etymology involved in the Gen 19:37–38 account of the naming of Lot's daughters' sons is confirmed by John 1:13.

[294] Acts 17:29.

Οὐδὲν οὖν ἀπεικός, καὶ τοὺς τῆς θείας συγγενείας διὰ τῆς θείας χάριτος ἠξιωμένους Ἀμμὰν ὀνομάζεσθαι. Εἰ μὲν οὖν τροπικῶς βούλει νοῆσαι τὰ ὀνόματα, οὕτω νοήσεις. Εἰ δὲ ἱστορικῶς, ὡς ἤδη προειρήκαμεν, ὅτι τούτων καταφρονήσει, ὡς τῶν μὲν πλειόνων ἀσεβείᾳ συζώντων, αὐτῶν δὲ τῶν ὀλίγων τῶν ἐν αὐτοῖς εὐσεβῶν οὐ θερμῶς περὶ τὰ θεῖα διακειμένων.

μβ΄, μγ΄. «Καὶ ἐκτενεῖ, φησί, τὴν χεῖρα αὐτοῦ ἐπὶ τὴν γῆν Αἰγύπτου, καὶ ἡ γῆ Αἰγύπτου οὐκ ἔσται εἰς σωτηρίαν. Καὶ κυριεύσει ἐν τοῖς ἀποκρύφοις τοῦ χρυσίου καὶ τοῦ ἀργυρίου, καὶ ἐν πᾶσιν ἐπιθυμητοῖς Αἰγύπτου, καὶ Λιβύων, καὶ Αἰθιόπων, καὶ ἐν τοῖς ὀχυρώμασιν αὐτῶν.» Καὶ ταῦτα δὲ ἥκιστα ἁρμόττει τῷ Ἀντιόχῳ· οὔτε γὰρ Λιβύης, οὔτε Αἰθιοπίας ἐκράτησεν, οὔτε δὲ αὐτῆς τῆς Αἰγύπτου. Προσταχθεὶς γὰρ ὑπὸ Ῥωμαίων ἀνέστρεψεν· ὥστε ἐντεῦθεν σημαίνεσθαι τὰ τρία κέρατα, ἃ τὸ μικρὸν κέρας ἀνέτρεψεν. Καὶ γὰρ ἐνταῦθα τρία ἔθνη μέγιστα, Αἴγυπτον, καὶ Αἰθιοπίαν, καὶ Λιβύην, ὑπὸ τριῶν, ὡς εἰκός, βασιλέων κατεχόμενα καταλύσει οὗτος, καὶ ὑφ᾽ ἑαυτὸν ποιήσεται.

μδ΄. «Καὶ ἀκοαί, καὶ σπουδαὶ ταράξουσιν αὐτὸν ἐξ ἀνατολῶν, καὶ ἀπὸ βορρᾶ, καὶ ἥξει ἐν θυμῷ πολλῷ, τοῦ ἀναθεματίσαι καὶ ἀφανίσαι πολλούς.» Οὐδὲ τοῦτο τῷ Ἀντιόχῳ ἁρμόττει· ἐκεῖνον γὰρ οὐ φῆμαι διαταράξασαι τῆς Αἰγύπτου ἀπέστησαν, ἀλλὰ τὸ δόγμα Ῥωμαίων, ἀπὸ τῆς Ἑσπέρας, οὐκ ἀπὸ τῆς Ἕω πεμφθέν. Περὶ δὲ τούτου φησίν, ὅτι λαβὼν τὴν Αἴγυπτον, καὶ τὴν Λιβύην, καὶ τὴν Αἰθιοπίαν, καὶ ὑφ᾽ ἑαυτὸν ποιησάμενος, ὑπὸ φήμης τινὸς ταραχθεὶς ἀναστρέψει, καὶ ἥξει ἐν θυμῷ πολλῷ, «τοῦ ἀναθεματίσαι καὶ τοῦ ἀφανίσαι πολλούς.» Ταυτὸν δὲ λέγει δι᾽ ἀμφοτέρων· ἀφανίσαι γάρ ἐστι τὸ τῆς εὐσεβείας γυμνῶσαι, καὶ τὸ ἀναθεματίσαι, τὸ ἀλλότριον ἐκείνης ἀποφῆναι.

με΄. «Καὶ πήξει, φησί, τὴν σκηνὴν αὐτοῦ ἐν Ἀπαδανῷ, ἀναμέσον, φησί, τῶν θαλασσῶν, εἰς ὄρος Σαβεὶρ ἅγιον.» Οὐδὲ τοῦτο δὲ εὑρίσκομεν ὑπὸ Ἀντιόχου γεγενημένον. Ἐπεὶ εἰπάτωσαν, τίς ὁ τόπος οὗτος, ἐν ᾧ τὴν σκηνὴν αὐτοῦ κατέπηξεν ὁ Ἀντίοχος, ἀνὰ μέσον τῶν δύο θαλασσῶν διακείμενος; Ἀλλ᾽ οὐχ ἕξουσι δεῖξαι. Οὐκοῦν τούτων οὐδὲν οὐδέπω πέρας εἴληφεν, ἀλλὰ γενήσεται ταῦτα πάντα ὑπὸ τοῦ κοινοῦ τῶν ἀνθρώπων ἀλάστορος. Σαβεὶρ δὲ πάλιν τὴν τῷ Θεῷ ἀνακειμένην καλεῖ γῆν·

formed to proclaim my marvels;"²⁹⁵ it is not unlikely, therefore, that he gave the name Ammon to those thought worthy of divine kinship by divine grace. If, then, you wish to take the names in a figurative fashion, take them that way; if, on the other hand, in historical fashion, as we have already said, the meaning is that he will scorn them on the grounds that most lived lives of impiety, while few of them, though religious, were not ardent in their attitude to divine things.

He will stretch out his hand over the land of Egypt, and the land of Egypt will have no escape. He will gain control of the treasuries of gold and silver, of all desirable things of Egypt, Libya, and Ethiopia, and of all their fortresses (vv. 42–43). This least of all is applicable to Antiochus: he did not gain power over Libya, or Ethiopia, or Egypt itself; under orders from the Romans he turned back. So here there is reference to the three horns which the little horn overturned: three mighty nations, Egypt, Ethiopia, and Libya, probably under the control of three kings, he will overthrow and make subject to him. *Reports and concerns from the east and the north will alarm him, and he will come with great anger to curse and deprive many* (v. 44). This does not apply to Antiochus, either: it was not alarming reports that drove him from Egypt, but the Roman decree issuing from the west, not the east. In regard to this it says that he would take Egypt, Libya, and Ethiopia, make them subject to him, be alarmed by some report, turn back and come with great anger to curse and deprive many. Both terms give this meaning: *deprive* is to strip them of their piety, and *curse* is to declare them foreign to it.

He will pitch his tent in Apadanos between the seas on the holy mount of Sabeir (v. 45). We do not find this happening under Antiochus, either; otherwise, let them tell us what is this place where Antiochus pitched his tent situated between the two seas.²⁹⁶ But they will not be able to show us. None of these things, therefore, has been fulfilled; instead, they will all happen under humankind's common enemy. Now, by *Sabeir* once again he refers to the land

²⁹⁵ Isa 43:20.
²⁹⁶ The author's vagueness in locating the death of the villain Theodoret exploits to his advantage to disqualify Antiochus (who in fact died in Persia in 164) and substitute the antichrist. Unaware that the Hebrew text is employing a rare Old Persian word for "palace," he hazards a guess about the Ἀπαδανός in his text.

1533 Ἀπαδανὸν δὲ τόπον τινὰ οὕτως ὠνομασμένον, οὐ πόρρω | τῶν Ἱεροσολύμων διακείμενον· ἐκεῖ γὰρ δέξεται τὸν ὄλεθρον. «Ἥξει γὰρ, φησίν, ἕως μέρους αὐτοῦ, καὶ οὐκ ἔστιν ὁ ῥυόμενος αὐτόν.» Ἐκεῖνος γὰρ ὁ τοιαῦτα καὶ τοσαῦτα τετολμηκώς, καὶ τοσούτῳ φρονήματι χρησάμενος, ἐξαίφνης δέξεται τὴν τιμωρίαν, οὐδενὸς αὐτὸν δυναμένου ταύτης ἐλευθερῶσαι. Τοῦτο δὲ καὶ ὁ μακάριος σαφῶς λέγει Παῦλος· «Ὃν ὁ Κύριος, φησίν, ἀναλώσει τῷ λόγῳ τοῦ στόματος αὐτοῦ.» Καί· «Τῷ Πνεύματι διὰ χειλέων ἀνελεῖ τὸν ἀσεβῆ.»

ΚΕΦΑΛΑΙΟΝ ΙΒ'

α'. «Καὶ ἐν τῷ καιρῷ, φησίν, ἐκείνῳ ἀναστήσεται Μιχαὴλ ὁ ἄρχων ὁ μέγας, ὁ ἐφεστηκὼς τοῖς υἱοῖς τοῦ λαοῦ σου.» Ὁ γὰρ, φησί, τὴν ὑμετέραν κηδεμονίαν πεπιστευμένος ἀρχάγγελος, εἰς ἐπικουρίαν τῶν τηνικαῦτα πολεμουμένων ἀναστήσεται. Καὶ τοῦτο δὲ δι' ἑτέρας ἑρμηνείας δῆλον τοῖς ἀγνοοῦσι γενήσεται· διὰ γὰρ Μαλαχίου τοῦ προφήτου φησὶν ὁ Θεὸς πρὸς τοὺς Ἰουδαίους· «Ἰδοὺ ἐγὼ ἀποστελῶ ὑμῖν Ἠλίαν τὸν Θεσβίτην, πρὶν ἐλθεῖν τὴν ἡμέραν Κυρίου, τὴν μεγάλην καὶ ἐπιφανῆ, ὃς ἀποκαταστήσει καρδίαν πατρὸς πρὸς υἱόν, καὶ καρδίαν ἀνθρώπου πρὸς τὸν πλησίον αὐτοῦ, μὴ ἐλθὼν πατάξω τὴν γῆν ἄρδην.» Διδάσκει δὲ ἡμᾶς ὅτι, τοῦ Ἀντιχρίστου ἐκεῖνα τολμῶντος, φανήσεται ὁ μέγας Ἠλίας, κηρύττων Ἰουδαίοις τὴν τοῦ Κυρίου παρουσίαν, καὶ πολλοὺς ἐπιστρέψει· τοῦτο γὰρ λέγει τό, «Ἀποκαταστήσει καρδίαν πατρὸς πρὸς υἱόν,» τουτέστι, τοῖς ἐξ ἐθνῶν πεπιστευκόσι τοὺς Ἰουδαίους· τούτους γὰρ ἐκάλεσε πατέρας, ὡς πρεσβυτέρους κατὰ τὴν γνῶσιν. Διὰ τοῦτο οὐκ εἶπεν· Ἀποκαταστήσει καρδίαν υἱοῦ πρὸς πατέρα· ἀλλά, «Καρδίαν πατρὸς πρὸς υἱόν·» τὸν γὰρ Ἰουδαῖον πιστεύσαντα συνάψει τῇ Ἐκκλησίᾳ· καὶ ἐπειδὴ κατὰ μὲν τὴν γνῶσιν ὁ Ἰουδαῖος πρεσβύτερος, μία δὲ καὶ τούτων κἀκείνων ἡ φύσις, εἰκότως ἐπήγαγε· «Καὶ καρδίαν ἀνθρώπου πρὸς τὸν πλησίον αὐτοῦ,» διδάσκων, ὅτι μία μὲν τούτων κἀκείνων ἡ φύσις, ἡ δὲ θεογνωσία Ἰουδαίοις πρότερον ἐδόθη. Ἀπιστήσαντες δέ, ἔσχατοι ἀπεδείχθησαν· πιστεύσαντες δὲ διὰ τῶν τοῦ μεγάλου Ἠλιοῦ κηρυγμάτων,

dedicated to God, and by *Apadanos* to some place so-called, situated not far | from Jerusalem where he will come to grief. *He* 1533 *will meet with his fate, and there will be no one to rescue him*: that one who was responsible for so many awful exploits and exercising such an attitude will suddenly meet with retribution, with no one able to save him from it. This is what blessed Paul also clearly says, "The one whom the Lord will consume with the word of his mouth," and "He will destroy the godless one with breath through his lips."[297]

CHAPTER 12

At that time there will arise Michael the great leader, the one set over the children of your people (v. 1): the archangel entrusted with your care will rise up for assistance to those then under attack. This will also be made clear to the ignorant in another commentary: in the prophet Malachi God says to the Jews, "Lo, I shall send you Elijah the Tishbite before the arrival of the great and splendid day of the Lord, who will turn a father's heart to his child and people's heart to their neighbor lest I come and strike the land utterly."[298] His message to us is that when the antichrist commits these crimes, the mighty Elijah will appear, proclaiming to Jews the coming of the Lord, and will convert many (the meaning of "He will turn a father's heart to his child", that is, the Jews to the believers from nations, referring to the former as "fathers," being older in knowledge). Hence he did not say, He will turn a child's heart to his father, but "a father's heart to his child:" he will attach to the church the Jew who has come to faith. And since the Jew is older in knowledge, whereas the nature of both groups is the same, he went on, "and people's heart to their neighbor" to bring out that while the nature of both groups is the same, knowledge of God was given to Jews first. They proved disobedient, however, and were put last; but they found faith through the preaching of

[297] Cf. 2 Thess 2:8; Isa 11:4.
[298] Mal 4:5–6. The reason for quoting this reference to Elijah in one of the Twelve Prophets (he seems to be saying his commentary on them is "forthcoming," as it was his next work but one) may be, as it was in commenting on that place in Malachi, to qualify the Jews' monopoly on these eminent figures; non-Jewish members of the church also have a claim.

καὶ τοῖς τὴν πεμφθεῖσαν αὐτοῖς σωτηρίαν ἁρπάσασι συναφθέντες ἔθνεσιν, εἰς μίαν τελέσουσιν Ἐκκλησίαν. Τοῦτο καὶ ἐνταῦθα αἰνίττεται, ὅτι τούτων γινομένων ὑπὸ τοῦ Ἀντιχρίστου, ὁ ἅγιος Μιχαὴλ ὁ ἀρχάγγελος πάντα πραγματεύσεται, ὥστε τὸν Ἠλίαν ἀφικέσθαι καὶ προμηνῦσαι τοῦ Δεσπότου τὴν παρουσίαν, ἵνα τῆς σωτηρίας τύχωσιν οἱ τηνικαῦτα Ἰουδαῖοι. Εἶτα διηγούμενος τὴν ὑπερβολὴν τῶν κακῶν, ὧν ὁ δυσσεβὴς ἐκεῖνος διαπράξεται, φησί· «Καὶ ἔσται καιρὸς θλίψεως, οἵα οὐ γέγονεν ἀφ᾽ οὗ γέγονε τὸ ἔθνος ἐπὶ τῆς γῆς, καὶ ἕως τοῦ καιροῦ ἐκείνου.» Τοῦτο δὲ καὶ ὁ Κύριος ἐν τοῖς ἱεροῖς Εὐαγγελίοις ἔφη. «Ἔσται γάρ,

1536 φησί, θλῖψις, οἵα οὐ γέγονεν ἀπ᾽ ἀρχῆς αἰῶνος, οὐδὲ μὴ γένηται· καὶ | εἰ μὴ ἐκολοβώθησαν αἱ ἡμέραι ἐκεῖναι, οὐκ ἂν ἐσώθη πᾶσα σάρξ· διὰ δὲ τοὺς ἐκλεκτούς μου κολοβώσω τὰς ἡμέρας ἐκείνας.» Συμφωνεῖ τοίνυν τὰ προφητικὰ τοῖς εὐαγγελικοῖς θεσπίσμασι. Τούτοις ἐπάγει· «Καὶ ἐν τῷ καιρῷ ἐκείνῳ σωθήσεται ὁ λαός σου πᾶς ὁ εὑρεθεὶς γεγραμμένος ἐν τῇ βίβλῳ.» Ἀντὶ τοῦ, οἱ τῆς σωτηρίας ἄξιοι, οἱ τῷ κηρύγματι τοῦ Ἠλία ὑπακουσόμενοι, οὓς ἄνωθεν καὶ ἐξ ἀρχῆς προγινώσκει· τὴν γὰρ τοῦ Θεοῦ γνῶσιν βίβλον ὠνόμασε.

β΄. «Καὶ πολλοί, φησί, τῶν καθευδόντων ἐν γῆς χώματι ἐξεγερθήσονται, οὗτοι εἰς ζωὴν αἰώνιον, καὶ οὗτοι εἰς ὀνειδισμὸν καὶ εἰς αἰσχύνην αἰώνιον.» Εἰπάτωσαν οἱ τῷ Ἀντιόχῳ ταῦτα προσαρμόττειν ἐπιχειροῦντες, τίνες ἀνέστησαν ἐπ᾽ ἐκείνου, καὶ οἱ μὲν ζωῆς ἐτύγχανον αἰωνίου, οἱ δὲ ὀνειδισμὸν καὶ αἰσχύνην αἰώνιον ἐκαρπώσαντο. Εἰ δὲ τοὺς Μακκαβαίους εἴποιεν διὰ τούτων δηλοῦσθαι ἐκ τῶν σπηλαίων ἐξιόντας, μείζονα ὀφλήσουσι γέλωτα· εὑρεθήσονται γὰρ οἱ αὐτοὶ καὶ εὐσεβείας ἐρασταί, καὶ ἀσεβείας ἐργάται· ἡ γὰρ προφητεία φησί· «Πολλοὶ τῶν καθευδόντων ἐν γῆς χώματι ἐξεγερθήσονται, οὗτοι εἰς ζωὴν αἰώνιον, καὶ οὗτοι εἰς ὀνειδισμὸν καὶ αἰσχύνην αἰώνιον.» Ὥστε εἰ εἰς τοὺς Μακκαβαίοις ταῦτα λάβοιεν, αὐτοὺς τοὺς Μακκαβαίους φήσουσι καὶ πονηροὺς καὶ ἀγαθούς, ἢ τινὰς μὲν ἐξ αὐτῶν ἀγαθούς, τινὰς δὲ κακούς. Ἀλλ᾽ οὐδὲ τοῦτο ἔστιν εὑρεῖν· εὐσεβὴς γὰρ ἅπασα αὐτῶν ἡ συμμορία. Οὔτε δὲ ἡ ζωὴ ἡ αἰώνιος κατὰ τὸν παρόντα βίον αὐτοῖς ἁρμόττει· ἅπαντες γὰρ ἀναιρεθέντες ὑπεξῆλθον τοῦ βίου. Οὐκοῦν τοὺς γραώδεις μύθους ἐκείνους καταλιπόντες, τὴν κοινὴν ἐντεῦθεν τῶν τετελευτηκότων μανθάνωμεν ἀνάστασιν, καὶ τὴν

the mighty Elijah and were joined to the nations, who had grasped the salvation sent to them, and will form one church.

He suggests as much here, too, that when this is done by the antichrist, the holy Archangel Michael will do everything to ensure that Elijah comes and foretells the Lord's coming so that the Jews of that time will attain salvation. Then, to describe the extraordinary degree of the troubles which that impious one will bring about, he says, *There will be a time of tribulation such as has not happened since the nation came on earth until that time.* The Lord also said this in the sacred Gospels, "There will be tribulation such as has not happened from the beginning of the world, nor will it happen; | if those days had not been shortened, no human being would be saved; but for the sake of my elect I shall shorten those days."[299] So the prophetic statements are consistent with the Gospel predictions. He continues in this vein, *At that time all your people who are found recorded in the book will be saved*, namely, those worthy of salvation, who will hearken to Elijah's preaching, and whom he foreknows from the first and the very beginning (calling God's knowledge a *book*).

Many of those asleep in the dust of the earth will awaken, some to everlasting life and some to reproach and everlasting shame (v. 2). Let those endeavoring to apply this to Antiochus tell us who were resurrected in his time, some attaining everlasting life and some being rewarded with reproach and everlasting shame. If, on the other hand, they were to claim the Maccabees are indicated by this on the grounds of their leaving the caves, they would earn louder mockery since these will be found to be both lovers of piety and agents of impiety. The prophecy says, note, *Many of those asleep in the dust of the earth will awaken, some to everlasting life and some to reproach and everlasting shame.* And so if they were to take this to apply to the Maccabees, they would claim the Maccabees are both wicked and good, or some of them good and some evil. But it is not possible to establish this, either: the whole company of them is pious. Nor does eternal life apply to them in this world: all were slain and left this world.[300] Let us therefore abandon those old wives' tales and discover in this text the common resurrection of the de-

1536

[299] Matt 24:21–22.
[300] Likewise in discussing the reference in "the holy ones" in 7:27, Theodoret is ambiguous as to the claim of the Maccabees, denying that all of them were holy and then conceding that all were holy but still do not qualify.

μετὰ τὴν ἀνάστασιν γινομένην διάκρισιν· οἱ μὲν γὰρ αὐτῶν ζωῆς αἰωνίου κληρονομήσουσιν, οἱ δὲ καταγέλαστοι καὶ ἐπονείδιστοι εἰς αἰῶνα γενήσονται. Πολλοὶ δέ, ἀντὶ τοῦ πάντες ἔφη. Καὶ γὰρ ὁ μακάριος Παῦλος, ἀντὶ τοῦ πάντες, οἱ πολλοὶ τέθεικε, λέγων· «Εἰ γὰρ τῷ τοῦ ἑνὸς παραπτώματι οἱ πολλοὶ ἀπέθανον, πολλῷ μᾶλλον ἡ χάρις τοῦ Θεοῦ, καὶ ἡ δωρεὰ ἐν χάριτι τῇ τοῦ ἑνὸς ἀνθρώπου Ἰησοῦ Χριστοῦ εἰς τοὺς πολλοὺς ἐπερίσσευσε.»

γ΄. «Καὶ οἱ συνιέντες, φησίν, ἐκλάμψουσιν, ὡς ἡ λαμπρότης τοῦ στερεώματος.»Καὶ ὁ Κύριος δὲ ἐν τοῖς ἱεροῖς Εὐαγγελίοις φησί·«Τότε ἐκλάμψουσιν οἱ δίκαιοι, ὡς ὁ ἥλιος.» «Καὶ ἀπὸ τῶν δικαίων τῶν πολλῶν, ὡς οἱ ἀστέρες εἰς τοὺς αἰῶνας, καὶ ἔτι.» Οἱ μὲν γὰρ δοκιμώτατοι καὶ ἔκκριτο, τῇ τε τοῦ στερεώματος λαμπρότητι καὶ αὐτῷ τῷ ἡλιακῷ παρεικασθήσονται φωτί· οἱ δὲ τούτων ἐλάττους (τοῦτο γὰρ ἐσήμαινε διὰ τοῦ πολλῶν), τὰς τῶν ἀστέρων λαμπηδόνας μιμήσονται, δι' αἰῶνος ταύτην ἀφιέντες τὴν αἴγλην. Οὕτω δὴ καὶ ὁ μακάριος Παῦλος τῶν | εὐσεβῶν διεῖλε τὰ τάγματα. «Ἄλλη γὰρ, φησί, δόξα ἡλίου, καὶ ἄλλη δόξα σελήνης, καὶ ἄλλη δόξα ἀστέρων· ἀστὴρ γὰρ ἀστέρος διαφέρει ἐν δόξῃ.» Ταῦτα εἰπὼν ὁ τῷ Δανιὴλ προσδιαλεγόμενος, ἐπήγαγε·

δ΄. «Καὶ σύ, Δανιήλ, ἔμφραξον τοὺς λόγους, καὶ σφράγισον τὸ βιβλίον ἕως καιροῦ συντελείας, ἕως διδαχθῶσι πολλοί, καὶ πληθυνθῇ ἡ γνῶσις.» Ἐπίθες, φησί, τῷ βιβλίῳ τὰς τῆς ἀσαφείας σφραγίδας, καὶ μὴ δῆλα ἅπασι καταστήσῃς, ἕως ἂν πληθυνθῇ ἡ γνῶσις, καὶ πληρωθῇ ἡ σύμπασα γῆ τοῦ γνῶναι τὸν Κύριον, ὡς ὕδωρ πολὺ κατακαλύψαι θαλάσσας, κατὰ τὴν προφητείαν. Ταύτας ἡ τοῦ θείου Πνεύματος χάρις μετὰ τὴν τοῦ Σωτῆρος ἡμῶν ἐπιφάνειαν ἀφελοῦσα τὰς σφραγίδας, σαφῆ τὰ ἀσαφῆ πεποίηκε τοῖς πιστεύουσι.

ε΄, ς΄. «Καὶ εἶδον, φησίν, ἐγὼ Δανιήλ, καὶ ἰδοὺ δύο ἕτεροι εἱστήκεισαν, εἰς ἐντεῦθεν τοῦ ποταμοῦ, καὶ εἰς ἐντεῦθεν. Καὶ εἶπον τῷ ἀνδρὶ τῷ ἐνδεδυμένῳ τὸ βαδδίμ, ὃς ἦν ἐπάνω τοῦ ὕδατος τοῦ ποταμοῦ· Ἕως πότε τὸ πέρας ὧν εἴρηκας τῶν θαυμασίων, καὶ ὁ καθαρισμὸς τούτων;» Ἐγὼ μὲν γὰρ, φησίν, εἱστήκειν σιγῶν, καὶ ἐρωτᾶν μὴ τολμῶν, δύο δὲ ἕτεροι ταῖς ὄχθαις ἑκατέρωθεν ἐφεστῶτες τοῦ ποταμοῦ, ἤροντο τὸν τὴν βυσσίνην περιβεβλημένον ἐσθῆτα, τῇ τε τοῦ ὕδατος ἐποχούμενον ἐπιφα-

parted and the judgment conducted after the resurrection: some of them will inherit eternal life, others will be objects of ridicule and reproach forever. Now, by *many* he meant everyone: blessed Paul used "many" in the sense of everyone when saying, "If many died through one person's fall, much more did the grace of God and the free gift abound for many in the grace of one person Jesus Christ."[301]

Those with understanding will shine like the brightness of the firmament (v. 3). The Lord in the sacred Gospels also says, "The righteous will then shine like the sun."[302] *And some of the many righteous ones like the stars forever and ever:* those approved and chosen will be comparable with the brightness of the firmament and the light of the sun itself, while some who are inferior to them (an implication of the term *many*) will resemble the beams of the stars, emitting this ray forever. Blessed Paul likewise also | differ-   1537
entiated between the ranks of the pious, "The sun's glory is of one kind, the moon's glory of another, the stars' glory of another, star differing from star in glory."[303]

After saying this, Daniel's interlocutor went on, *For your part, Daniel, keep the words closed up and seal the book until the time of consummation, until many are taught and knowledge is increased* (v. 4): put seals of obscurity on the book, and ensure it is not clear to everyone, until knowledge is increased and the whole land filled with knowing the Lord, like deep water covering seas, as in the prophecy.[304] The grace of the divine Spirit removed these seals after the coming of our Savior, and made clear to the believers what was obscure.

And I, Daniel, looked and, lo, two others stood there, one on this bank of the river and the other on the other bank. They said to the man clothed in linen, who was upstream, How long for the wonders you have spoken of and for their purification? (vv. 5–6) I stood by silently, he is saying, not daring to ask a question; but two others standing on either side of the river asked the person clad in fine linen moving on the surface of the water, For how long a time will

[301] Rom 5:15.
[302] Matt 13:43.
[303] 1 Cor 15:41.
[304] Cf. Isa 11:9. Theodoret does not observe that the work originally concluded here, and that to this stylized ending further material has been added by a different writer.

νεία· Πόσον καθέξει χρόνον τὰ φοβερὰ ταῦτα καὶ φρίκης γέμοντα ; καὶ
πότε ἡ τούτων ἀπαλλαγὴ γενήσεται ;

ζ'. «Καὶ ἤκουσα τοῦ ἀνδρὸς τοῦ ἐνδεδυμένου τὸ βαδδὶμ, ὃς ἦν
ἐπάνω τοῦ ὕδατος τοῦ ποταμοῦ, καὶ ὕψωσε τὴν δεξιὰν αὐτοῦ, καὶ τὴν
ἀριστερὰν αὐτοῦ εἰς τὸν οὐρανόν, καὶ ὤμοσεν ἐν τῷ ζῶντι εἰς τὸν αἰῶνα, ὅτι εἰς καιρόν, καὶ καιρούς, καὶ ἥμισυ καιροῦ.» Ἐντεῦθεν ἀκριβῶς
μεμαθήκαμεν, ὅτι ὁ τότε διαλεγόμενος οὐκ αὐτὸς ἦν ὁ Δεσπότης. Ὁ
γὰρ Δεσπότης, ἐπεὶ κατ᾽ οὐδενὸς μείζονος ἄλλου εἶχεν ὀμόσαι, ἥ φησιν
ὁ θεῖος Ἀπόστολος, καθ᾽ ἑαυτοῦ ὤμοσε, λέγων· «Ζῶ ἐγώ, λέγει Κύριος.» Καὶ ὁ μακάριος δὲ Μωσῆς δείκνυσιν αὐτὸν λέγοντα· «Ἀρῶ εἰς
τὸν οὐρανὸν τὴν χεῖρά μου, καὶ ὀμοῦμαι τῇ δεξιᾷ μου, καὶ ἐρῶ· Ζῶ ἐγὼ
εἰς τὸν αἰῶνα.» Οὗτος δὲ εἷς ὢν τῶν ὑποκειμένων καὶ εὐνοϊκῶς περὶ
τὸν Δεσπότην διακειμένων, ἐξέτεινε μὲν εἰς τὸν οὐρανὸν ἄμφω τὰ χεῖ-
ρε, ὤμοσε δὲ ἐν τῷ ζῶντι εἰς τὸν αἰῶνα. Χεῖρας δὲ λέγει αὐτὸν ἔχειν ὁ
Δανιὴλ τοῦτο θεασάμενος. Ἀσώματον δ᾽ ὅμως ἴσμεν τῶν ἀγγέλων τὴν
φύσιν· σχηματίζουσι δὲ τὰς ὄψεις πρὸς τὸ χρήσιμον τῶν ὁρώντων· καὶ
πολλάκις μὲν ἡμερώτερον φαίνονται, συγκαταβάσει πλείονι χρώμενοι,
πολλάκις δὲ φοβερώτερον, σπουδαιοτέρους τοὺς ὁρῶντας ἐργαζόμενοι.

1540 «Ὤμοσε τοίνυν ἐν τῷ ζῶντι εἰς τὸν αἰῶνα, ὅτι εἰς καιρόν, καὶ καιρούς,
καὶ ἥμισυ καιροῦ.» | Σημαίνει δὲ τρία καὶ ἥμισυ ἔτη. Τοῦτο δὲ καὶ ἐπὶ
τοῦ κέρατος τοῦ ποιοῦντος πόλεμον μετὰ τῶν ἁγίων, ὃ μετὰ τὰ δέκα
βλαστήσει κέρατα ἐν τῷ τέλει τῆς Ῥωμαϊκῆς βασιλείας, ὁ ἅγιος ἔφη
Γαβριήλ. Εἰρηκὼς γάρ· «Τρεῖς βασιλεῖς ταπεινώσει, καὶ λόγους πρὸς
τὸν Ὕψιστον λαλήσει, καὶ τοὺς ἁγίους Ὑψίστου παλαιώσει·» ἐπήγα-
γε· «Καὶ δοθήσεται ἐν χειρὶ αὐτοῦ ἕως καιροῦ, καὶ καιρῶν, καὶ ἥμισυ
καιροῦ.» Τρία δὲ ταῦτα καὶ ἥμισυ ἔτη. *Τὸν καιρὸν* γὰρ ἐνιαυτὸν προσηγόρευσε, καὶ τοῦτο ἐκ τῶν μετὰ ταῦτα σαφέστερον μαθησόμεθα· «Ὅτι
εἰς καιρόν, φησί, καὶ καιρούς, καὶ ἥμισυ καιροῦ. Ἐν τῷ συντελεσθῆναι
διασκορπισμὸν λαοῦ ἡγιασμένου γνώσονται ἅγιον, καὶ συντελεσθήσονται ταῦτα πάντα.» Τρία γάρ, φησί, καὶ ἥμισυ ἔτη ὁ τοῦ ἡγιασμένου
λαοῦ κρατήσει διασκορπισμός, καὶ συντελεσθήσονται ταῦτα πάντα. Εἶτα γνώσονται τὸν ἅγιον. Τὸν μέγαν Ἠλίαν ἐνταῦθα αἰνίττεται· περὶ γὰρ

these fearsome things that are full of terror be in force? when will come relief from them? *I heard the man clad in linen who was upstream; he lifted his right hand and his left hand to heaven, and swore by the one who lives forever that it would be for a time, and times, and half a time* (v. 7). From this we gain precise knowledge that the one speaking at that time was not the Lord: the Lord, since he had no one else to swear by, as the divine apostle says, swore by himself, "As I live, says the Lord;" and blessed Moses shows him saying, "I will lift up my hand to heaven and swear by my right hand and say, As I live forever."[305] This person, on the contrary, being one of those subject and well-disposed to the Lord, stretched out both his hands to heaven *and swore by the one who lives forever*. Now, Daniel, who witnessed this, says he had hands, whereas we know angels are by nature incorporeal, presenting a visible appearance for the benefit of the viewers; often, as an exercise of greater considerateness,[306] they give the appearance of gentleness, often of inspiring fear to make the onlookers more zealous.

He swore by the one who lives forever, then, *that it would be for a time, and times, and half a time.* | It means three and a half years;   1540 the holy Gabriel said this was also the case with the horn waging war on the holy ones that would spring up after the ten horns at the end of the Roman Empire. After saying, remember, "He will humble three kings, he will speak words against the Most High, and will wear out the holy ones," he went on, "It will be given into his hand for a time, and times, and half a time."[307] This amounts to three and a half years: he called a year a *time*, as we shall learn more clearly from what comes next: *A time, and times, and half a time. When the scattering of the sanctified people comes to an end, they will know the holy one, and all this will come to an end*, in other words, the scattering of the sanctified people will last three and a half years, and all this will come to an end. Then they will know *the holy one*, a reference to mighty Elijah: when mighty Elijah ap-

---

[305] Heb 6:13–14; Deut 32:40 LXX.

[306] Theodoret does not often employ the term συγκατάβασις, which appears often on the lips of Chrysostom when speaking of divine considerateness manifested particularly in the Scriptures. See Robert C. Hill, "On Looking Again at *Synkatabasis*," *Prudentia* 13 (1981): 3–11.

[307] Dan 7:24–25. There, no more than here, did Theodoret note that this figure, being half the perfect number seven, denotes incompleteness, imperfection.

τὰ τέλη τῆς ἐκείνου δυναστείας ἀναφανεὶς ὁ μέγας Ἠλίας, τὴν δευτέραν τοῦ Σωτῆρος ἡμῶν ἐπιφάνειαν προκηρύξει. Τούτοις ἐπάγει ὁ μακάριος Δανιήλ·

η′. «Καὶ ἐγὼ ἤκουσα, καὶ οὐ συνῆκα, καὶ εἶπον· Κύριε, τί τὰ ἔσχατα τούτων;» Μὴ συνιείς, φησί, τὸ εἰρημένον περὶ τοῦ χρόνου, ἠναγκάσθην ἔρεσθαι, σαφέστερον μαθεῖν ἐφιέμενος· ἐπόθουν δὲ καὶ τὰ μετὰ ταῦτα ἐσόμενα διδαχθῆναι. Ὁ δὲ

θ′, ι′. «Ἔφη πρός με· Δεῦρο, Δανιήλ, ὅτι ἐμπεφραγμένοι καὶ ἐσφραγισμένοι οἱ λόγοι ἕως καιροῦ πέρατος. Ἕως ἐκλεγῶσι, καὶ ἐκλευκανθῶσι, καὶ πυρωθῶσιν οἱ πολλοί, καὶ ἀνομήσουσιν οἱ ἄνομοι, καὶ οὐ συνήσουσι πάντες ἀσεβεῖς, καὶ οἱ νοήμονες νοήσουσιν.» Οὐ μάτην, φησίν, ἀσαφέστερα ταῦτα εἴρηκα, καὶ οἱονεὶ σφραγίδας τοῖς λόγοις τὴν ἀσάφειαν ἐπέθηκα. Οὐδὲ γὰρ δεῖ πᾶσιν ἁπλῶς προσκεῖσθαι τὰ θεῖα, ἀλλ᾽ οἱ μὲν νοήμονες διὰ τῆς ἄνωθεν αὐτοῖς χορηγουμένης γνώσεως συνήσουσιν· οἱ δὲ ἀνομίᾳ καὶ δυσσεβείᾳ συζῶντες, οὐδὲν τῶν ἐγκειμένων νοῆσαι δυνήσονται· ὅταν δὲ ἔλθῃ τὰ πράγματα, σαφῶς τὰς περὶ τούτων μαθήσονται προφητείας. Τότε καὶ ἀποκριθήσονται τῶν δικαίων οἱ τῆς πονηρίας ἐργάται· πάντα γὰρ ἡ πύρωσις δοκιμάσει. Τοῦτο καὶ ὁ μακάριος ἔφη Παῦλος· «Ἑκάστου γάρ, φησί, τὸ ἔργον φανερὸν γενήσεται· ἡ γὰρ ἡμέρα δηλώσει, ὅτι ἐν πυρὶ ἀποκαλύπτεται, καὶ ἑκάστου τὸ ἔργον ὁποῖόν ἐστι τὸ πῦρ δοκιμάσει.» Πάλιν δὲ περὶ τοῦ μὴ δεῖν ἅπασιν ἁπλῶς προτιθέναι τὰ θεῖα, ὁ Κύριος ἐν τοῖς ἱεροῖς Εὐαγγελίοις φησί· «Μὴ δῶτε τὰ ἅγια τοῖς κυσί, μηδὲ τοὺς μαργαρίτας ὑμῶν ῥίψητε ἔμπροσθεν τῶν χοίρων.» Τὸν δὲ μακάριον Δανιὴλ ἅγιον ὄντα, καὶ εὔνουν τοῦ Δεσπότου θεράποντα, ὁ θεῖος ἄγγελος διδάσκει τῆς τοῦ Ἀντιχρίστου τυραννίδος

1541 τὸν χρόνον, καί φησιν· |

ια′. «Ἀπὸ καιροῦ παραλλάξεως τοῦ ἐνδελεχισμοῦ, καὶ δοθῆναι βδέλυγμα ἐρημώσεως, ἡμέραι χίλιαι διακόσιαι ἐννενήκοντα.» Ἐπειδὴ γὰρ εἰρηκὼς «εἰς καιρόν, καὶ καιρούς, καὶ ἥμισυ καιροῦ,» Εἶδε μὴ νενοηκότα τὸν μακάριον Δανιήλ, ἀναλύσας εἰς ἡμέρας τὸν χρόνον, δῆλον αὐτῷ τὸ ἀγνοούμενον πεποίηκε, τοῖς δὲ ἄλλοις καὶ οὕτως ἀσαφῆ τὸν λόγον κατέλιπε. Βδέλυγμα δὲ ἐρημώσεως αὐτὸν καλεῖ τὸν Ἀντίχριστον· ἐναλλαγὴν δὲ τοῦ ἐνδελεχισμοῦ, τῆς ἐκκλησιαστικῆς λειτουργίας τὴν τάξιν, ὑπὸ τῆς ἐκείνου μανίας καὶ λύττης σκεδαννυμένην τε καὶ παυομένην. Τούτοις ἐπιφέρει ὁ θεῖος ἄγγελος·

ιβ′. «Μακάριος ὁ ὑπομένων, καὶ φθάσας εἰς ἡμέρας χιλίας τριακοσίας τριάκοντα πέντε.» Αἰνίττεταί τε καὶ παραδηλοῖ ὡς, τούτου τὴν

pears about the end of that person's reign, he will proclaim our Savior's second coming.

Blessed Daniel continues in the same vein. *I heard and did not understand, and I said, Lord, what will be the outcome of these things?* (v. 8) Not understanding what was said about the time, I was forced to ask in my longing to learn more clearly. I desired also to be informed of what would happen after that. *He replied to me, Go your way, Daniel, because the words are closed up and sealed until the end of time. Until many are chosen, cleansed and purified, the lawless will break the law, all the godless will fail to understand, and the wise will have wisdom* (vv. 9–10): it was not without purpose that I said this obscurely and have imposed obscurity on the words like seals, nor should divine things be presented to everyone indiscriminately. Rather, the wise will grasp them, thanks to the knowledge supplied them from on high, whereas those guilty of lawlessness and impiety will be unable to grasp any of the contents. When the events come to pass, however, they will gain a clear understanding of the prophecies about them; then, too, evildoers will be separated from the righteous, the furnace testing everything. This is what blessed Paul also said, "Each one's work will become visible, for the day will disclose it, because it will be made manifest by fire, and the fire will test what sort of work each has done." Further, the Lord in the sacred Gospels speaks of the need not to present divine things to everyone indiscriminately: "Do not give holy things to dogs, nor cast your pearls before swine."[308]

Blessed Daniel being a holy and devout servant of the Lord, the holy angel informs him of the time of the tyranny of the antichrist in the words, | *From the time of the alteration in the daily ritual and the occurrence of the abomination of desolation, 1,290 days* (v. 11). Since he had said *a time, and times, and half a time,* and had seen that blessed Daniel did not understand, he clarified it for him in his ignorance by transposing the time into days while still leaving the statement obscure for the others. By *abomination of desolation* he refers to the antichrist, and by *alteration in the daily ritual* the program of congregational worship interrupted and brought to an end by that person's insane frenzy. The divine angel continues in this vein: *Blessed the one who perseveres and attains the 1,335 days* (v. 12). He suggests and indicates that when

[308] 1 Cor 3:13; Matt 7:6.

θεήλατον δεξαμένου πληγήν, ἐπιμενεῖ μὲν ὁ μέγας Ἠλίας κηρύττων τὰς ὑπολοίπους πέντε καὶ τεσσαράκοντα, φανήσεται δὲ ὁ Δεσπότης ἐπὶ τῶν νεφελῶν τοῦ οὐρανοῦ ἐρχόμενος, καὶ στεφανώσει τοὺς ἄσυλον τῆς ὑπομονῆς τὸ κτῆμα φυλάξαντας. Τοῦτο δὲ καὶ ὁ Κύριος ἐν τοῖς ἱεροῖς Εὐαγγελίοις φησίν· «Ὁ δὲ ὑπομείνας εἰς τέλος, οὗτος σωθήσεται.» Καὶ ἐντεῦθεν δὲ ἔστι μαθεῖν ἀκριβῶς, ὡς οὐδὲν τούτων ἁρμόττει τῷ Ἀντιόχῳ. Ἐπ’ ἐκείνου μὲν γὰρ δισχιλίας τριακοσίας ἡμέρας ἔφη, ἐπὶ δὲ τοῦ Ἀντιχρίστου χιλίας διακοσίας ἐννενήκοντα κρατήσειν τὴν συμφοράν· ὥστε καὶ τοῦ χρόνου τὴν διαφορὰν μαρτυρεῖν τῇ τῶν προσώπων καὶ τῶν πραγμάτων διαφορᾷ.

ιγ΄. «Καὶ σύ, φησί, δεῦρο καὶ ἀναπαύου.» Καιρός, φησίν, τοῦ δέξασθαί σε τοῦ βίου τὸ τέλος. «Ἔτι γὰρ ἡμέραι εἰς ἀναπλήρωσιν συντελείας.» Οὐκ ὀλίγος γὰρ, φησίν, ἔτι χρόνος ὑπολέλειπται τῇ τοῦ παρόντος βίου συστάσει. Καὶ ἐνταῦθα δὲ σαφῶς ἡμᾶς ἐδίδαξε τὴν συντέλειαν, καὶ ὅτι ἐν ἐκείνῃ τὰ προειρημένα γενήσεται. «Καὶ ἀναπαύσῃ καὶ ἀναστήσῃ εἰς τὸν καιρόν σου (ἀλλ’ ὀρθότερον τό, κλῆρόν σου, ὡς ἐκ τῶν ἑξῆς δῆλον), εἰς συντέλειαν ἡμερῶν.» Νῦν μὲν γὰρ, φησί, σὲ προσήκει τὸ κοινὸν δέξασθαι τέλος· ἀναστήσῃ δέ, καὶ οὐχ ἁπλῶς ἀναστήσῃ, ἀλλ’ εἰς τὸν κλῆρόν σου, τουτέστι, μετὰ τῆς τῶν ὁμοτρόπων συμμορίας. Καὶ δεικνύς, πότε, ἐπήγαγεν· «Εἰς συντέλειαν ἡμερῶν.» Οὕτω σαφῶς ἡμᾶς ὁ θεῖος ἀρχάγγελος διὰ τοῦ μακαρίου καὶ τρισμακαρίου Δανιὴλ ἐδίδαξε τὴν ἀνάστασιν. Οὕτω πληρώσας τὴν ἀποκάλυψιν ἐπήγαγεν ὁ προφήτης·

ιδ΄. «Καὶ ὁ βασιλεὺς Ἀστυάγης προσετέθη πρὸς τοὺς πατέρας αὐτοῦ, καὶ παρέλαβε Κῦρος ὁ Πέρσης τὴν βασιλείαν αὐτοῦ, καὶ ἦν Δανιὴλ συμβιωτὴς τοῦ βασιλέως, καὶ ἔνδοξος ὑπὲρ πάντας τοὺς φίλους αὐτοῦ.» Ὁ δὲ Ἀστυάγης τοῦ Κύρου μητροπάτωρ· ἐκείνου δὲ τελευτήσαντος, καὶ Κυαξάρου τοῦ υἱέως αὐτοῦ οἰκονομῆσαι τὴν βασιλείαν οὐ δυ|νηθέντος, ὁ Κῦρος τὴν τῶν Ἀσσυρίων καὶ Χαλδαίων καταλύσας βασιλείαν, τὸ Μήδων κράτος εἰς Πέρσας μετατέθεικε. «Σύσσιτος δέ, φησίν,

this person sustains a heaven-sent blow, mighty Elijah will continue preaching for the remaining forty-five days, when the Lord
will appear, coming in the clouds of heaven, and will crown those
preserving intact the possession of endurance. The Lord also says
this in the sacred Gospels, "The one who perseveres to the end
will be saved."[309] It is also possible from this to gain a precise realization that none of these things applies to Antiochus: it said the
calamity would last 2,300 days under him, but under the antichrist
1,290; so the difference in time confirms the difference in persons
and events.[310]

As for you, go your way and be at rest (v. 13): it is time for you
to meet your end. *There are still days for the completion of the end*:
no little time still remains of the period of the present life. Here he
clearly informed us of the end, and that what was foretold would
at that time come to pass. *You will rest and rise up for your time* (or
more properly *your inheritance*, as is clear from what follows)[311]
to the end of days: you must now undergo the end common to all;
but *you will rise*—and not simply rise but *for your inheritance*, that
is, in the company of likeminded people. And to explain when, he
went on, *to the end of days*. This is the way the divine archangel
through blessed and thrice-blessed Daniel gave us clear teaching
about the resurrection.

Having thus completed the revelation, the prophet continued, *King Astyages was laid to rest with his ancestors, and Cyrus the
Persian succeeded to his empire. Daniel was the king's companion, of
higher rank than all his friends* (v. 14). Astyages was the maternal
grandfather of Cyrus; on his death, with his son Cyaxares inca-
pable of managing the empire, | Cyrus destroyed the empire of the   1544
Assyrians and Chaldeans, and transferred the power of the Medes
to the Persians.[312] Now, he was the king's table companion and fa-

---

[309] Matt 10:22.

[310] Theodoret, who has had trouble following the numerical time references in chapters 7 and 8, is now quite confused, unable to recognize additions
by two later editors in vv. 11–12 to extend arbitrarily the time of persecution
once it became clear that 1,150 days (three and a half years) did not suffice.

[311] Theodoret appears to be correcting a slip by a copyist who put καιρόν
for κλῆρον.

[312] Theodoret's text contains what is (unbeknown to him, evidently) the
opening verse of the deuterocanonical story of Bel and the Dragon, also involving Daniel, again in Theodotion's version from a Semitic original, though the

ἦν τοῦ βασιλέως,» καὶ σύνοικος, καὶ πάντων αὐτοῦ τῶν συνήθων προτεταγμένος. Ταύτην γὰρ ἔχων τὴν παρρησίαν, καὶ τὰ εἰς αὐτὸν ὑπὸ τοῦ Θεοῦ διὰ τοῦ προφήτου Ἡσαΐου προρρηθέντα ὑπέδειξε, καὶ τὴν ἄφεσιν τοῦ λαοῦ ποιήσασθαι παρεσκεύασεν. Ἡμεῖς μὲν οὖν ταῦτα ἐκ τῆς θείας τοῦ Δανιὴλ μεμαθήκαμεν προφητείας. Ἰουδαίους δὲ θρηνεῖν δίκαιον ἔξω τοῦ προφητικοῦ καταλόγου τάττειν τὸν θεῖον τοῦτον προφήτην τολμῶντας, καὶ ταῦτα τῇ πείρᾳ μεμαθηκότας τῆς προφητείας τὸ ἀληθές. Ἀλλὰ γὰρ εὔδηλον, ὡς οἱ νῦν ταῖς ἄλλαις ἀσεβείαις καὶ ταύτην προστεθείκασι τὴν βλασφημίαν, τῆς τοῦ Σωτῆρος ἡμῶν ἐπιφανείας τὴν προφανῆ μαρτυρίαν ἀρνήσει τῇ τῆς προφητείας συσκιάζειν ἐπιχειροῦντες· ἀλλ᾽ οὐδὲν αὐτοῖς πλέον ὑπάρξει ταύτην ἀρνουμένοις τὴν προφητείαν· οἵ τε γὰρ ἄλλοι προφῆται μαρτυροῦσι, καὶ αὐτὰ βοᾷ τὰ πράγματα τὰς περὶ αὐτοῦ προρρήσεις ἁρπάζοντα. Ὅτι δὲ οἱ πάλαι Ἰουδαῖοι τὸν μακάριον Δανιὴλ μέγιστον ἀπεκάλουν προφήτην, μάρτυς ἀξιόχρεως Ἰώσηππος ὁ Ἑβραῖος, τὸ μὲν Χριστιανικὸν οὐ δεξάμενος κήρυγμα, τὴν δὲ ἀλήθειαν κρύπτειν οὐκ ἀνεχόμενος. Οὗτος ἐν τῷ δεκάτῳ τῆς Ἰουδαϊκῆς Ἀρχαιολογίας, πολλὰ μὲν καὶ ἕτερα περὶ τοῦ μακαρίου εἴρηκε Δανιήλ, προστίθησι δὲ καὶ ταῦτα· «Ἅπαντα γὰρ αὐτῷ, φησίν, παραδόξως, ὡς ἑνί τινι τῶν μεγίστων ἐχαρίσθη προφητῶν, καὶ παρὰ τὸν τῆς ζωῆς χρόνον τιμή τε καὶ δόξα, ἡ παρὰ τῶν βασιλέων καὶ τοῦ πλήθους· τελευτήσας δὲ μνήμην αἰώνιον ἔχει. Τὰ γὰρ βιβλία, ὅσα δὴ συγγραψάμενος κατέλιπεν, ἀναγινώσκεται παρ᾽ ἡμῖν ἔτι καὶ νῦν, καὶ πεπιστεύκαμεν ἐξ αὐτῶν, ὅτι Δανιὴλ ὡμίλει τῷ Θεῷ. Οὐ γὰρ τὰ μέλλοντα μόνον προφητεύων διετέλει, καθάπερ καὶ οἱ ἄλλοι προφῆται, ἀλλὰ καὶ τὸν καιρὸν ὥρισεν εἰς ὃν ταῦτα ἀποβήσεται.» Καὶ μετὰ βραχέα δέ, «Ἀπὸ δὲ τοῦ τέλους, φησί, τῶν προρρήσεων ἀληθείας πίστιν καὶ δόξαν θειότητος παρὰ τοῖς ὄχλοις ἀποφέρεται.» Καὶ ἐφεξῆς δὲ μυρία τοιαῦτα περὶ αὐτοῦ λέγει. Ὡσαύτως δὲ καὶ ἐν τῇ δωδεκάτῃ τῆς Ἀρχαιολογίας πάλιν οὕτω φησί· «Τὴν δὲ ἐρήμωσιν τοῦ ναοῦ συνέβη γενέσθαι κατὰ τὴν τοῦ Δανιήλου προφητείαν, πρὸ τετρακοσίων καὶ ὀκτὼ γενομένην ἐτῶν· ἔδειξε γὰρ ὅτι Μακεδόνες

miliar, the text says, and was ranked above all his acquaintances; enjoying this favor, he gave a glimpse of what had been prophesied of him by God through the prophet Isaiah and was responsible for the people's release being effected.

While we have come to this realization from the divine prophecy of Daniel, then, it is right for Jews to lament, having presumed to place this divine prophet outside the prophetic corpus, despite learning by experience the truth of the prophecy. After all, it is obvious that Jews of today add to their other impious acts the blasphemy of endeavoring by the denial of the prophecy to obscure the unambiguous testimony to the coming of our Savior. They stand to gain no further advantage from denying this prophecy: the other prophets confirm it, and the events themselves cry aloud that they correspond to the prophecies about him. Now, to the fact that the Jews of old used to call blessed Daniel the greatest prophet the Hebrew Josephus is a notable witness, who, while not accepting the Christian message, could not bring himself to conceal the truth. In the tenth book of the *Jewish Antiquities*, after saying many things about Daniel, he goes on to say this: "Everything was accorded him in surprising fashion as one of the greatest prophets, including esteem and glory for the length of his life by kings and populace. Now that he is dead, he has an immortal reputation: all the books that he wrote and left behind are read by us even now, and from them we have the belief that Daniel conversed with God. After all, he not only continued to prophesy the future like the other prophets but also specified the time when it would come to pass." And shortly after, "On the basis of the outcome of the prophecies he gains with the masses confidence in their accuracy and the impression of a divine quality"; and he continues saying countless other such things of him.[313] Likewise also in the twelfth book of the *Antiquities* he expresses himself in turn thus: "The devastation of the temple happened in accordance with the prophecy of Daniel, which was made 408 years before;

rest of the story and the further one of Susanna do not appear in his Bible, it would seem. Again, as in having to deal with the legendary "Darius the Mede" at the opening of chapter 6 (see note 132 there), he confuses the historical Cyaxares, king of the Medes in the seventh century and destroyer of Assyria, with this legendary figure.

[313] *Ant.* 10.266–268.

καταλύσουσιν αὐτόν.» Καὶ ταῦτα μὲν ὁ Ἰώσηππος τῷ προφήτῃ προσμαρτυρεῖ. Ἰουδαῖοι δέ, πᾶσαν ἀναισχυντίαν νοσοῦντες, οὐδὲ τοὺς ἑαυτῶν αἰσχύνονται διδασκάλους. Ἀλλ᾽ ἡμεῖς, παρακαλῶ, ὡς παρὰ Θεοῦ προφήτου τὴν τῶν μελλόντων δεξάμενοι πρόγνωσιν, εὐτρεπεῖς ἡμᾶς αὐτοὺς
1545   εἰς | ἐκείνην τὴν φοβερὰν καταστήσωμεν ἡμέραν, ἵνα μὴ εἰς αἰσχύνην αἰώνιον, ἀλλ᾽ εἰς ζωὴν ἀναστῶμεν αἰώνιον· ἧς γένοιτο πάντας ἡμᾶς ἐπιτυχεῖν, χάριτι καὶ φιλανθρωπίᾳ τοῦ Κυρίου ἡμῶν· Ἰησοῦ Χριστοῦ, μεθ᾽ οὗ τῷ Πατρὶ δόξα, σὺν τῷ ἁγίῳ Πνεύματι, νῦν καὶ ἀεί, καὶ εἰς τοὺς αἰῶνας τῶν αἰώνων. Ἀμήν.

he brought out that Macedonians would destroy it."[314] Whereas Josephus gives this additional witness to the prophet, Jews by contrast, afflicted with utter shamelessness, have no respect even for their own teachers.

Let us for our part, on the other hand, I beseech you, accept the foreknowledge of the future as from God's prophet and make ourselves ready for | that fearsome day, so that we may rise, not to   1545 everlasting shame, but to everlasting life. May it be the good fortune of us all to attain this, thanks to the grace and lovingkindness of our Lord Jesus Christ, to whom with the Father and the Holy Spirit be glory, now and forever, for ages of ages. Amen.[315]

[314] *Ant.* 12.322.
[315] Thus the commentary concludes, without the usual peroration craving the readers' indulgence for any shortcomings on the author's part, and perhaps expressing thanks for divine grace.

Select Bibliography

Audet, Jean Paul. *La Didachè: Instructions des apôtres.* EBib. Paris: Gabalda, 1958.

Azéma, Yvan, trans. *Théodoret de Cyr, Correspondance.* 4 vols. SC 40, 98, 111, 429. Paris: Cerf, 1955–1998.

Bardy, Gustave. "Interprétation chez les pères." *DBSup* 4:569–91.

Bouyer, Louis. *The Spirituality of the New Testament and the Fathers.* Translated by Mary Perkins Ryan. New York: Desclee, 1963.

Canivet, Pierre. *Histoire d'une entreprise apologétique au ve siècle.* Paris: Bloud & Gay, 1957.

Crouzel, Henri. *Origen.* Translated by A. S. Worrell. San Francisco: Harper & Row, 1989.

Daley, Brian E. "Apocalypticism in Early Christian Theology." Pages 3–47 in vol. 2 of *The Encyclopedia of Apocalypticism.* Edited by Bernard McGinn, John J. Collins, and Stephen J. Stein. 3 vols. New York: Continuum, 1998.

Di Lella, Alexander. A. "Daniel." Pages 406–20 in *NJBC.* Englewood Cliffs, N.J.: Prentice Hall, 1990.

Eissfeldt, Otto. *The Old Testament: An Introduction.* Translated by Peter R. Ackroyd. Oxford: Blackwell, 1965.

Fernández Marcos, Natalio. *The Septuagint in Context: Introduction to the Greek Versions of the Bible.* Translated by Wilfred G. E. Watson. Leiden: Brill, 2001.

Fitzmyer, Joseph A. *The Gospel according to Luke I–IX.* AB 28. Garden City, N.Y.: Doubleday, 1981.

Goldingay, John E. *Daniel.* WBC 40. Dallas: Word, 1989.

Guinot, Jean-Nöel. *L'Exégèse de Théodoret de Cyr.* ThH 100. Paris: Beauchesne, 1995.

———. "Theodoret von Kyros." *TRE* 33:250–54.

———, trans. *Théodoret de Cyr: Commentaire sur Isaïe.* 3 vols. SC 276, 295, 315. Paris: Cerf, 1980–1984.

Henry, René, ed., *Photius: Bibliothèque.* 9 vols. Paris: Belles Lettres, 1959–1991.

Hill, Robert C. "Chrysostom on the Obscurity of the Old Testament." *OCP* 67 (2001): 371–83.

———. "On Looking Again at *Synkatabasis.*" *Prudentia* 13 (1981): 3–11.

———. "A Pelagian Commentator on the Psalms?" *ITQ* 63 (1998): 263–71.

———. "Psalm 41 (42): A Classic Text for Antiochene Spirituality." *ITQ* 68 (2003): 25–33.

———. *Reading the Old Testament in Antioch*. BAC 5. Leiden: Brill, 2005.

———, trans. *St. John Chrysostom: Old Testament Homilies*. 3 vols. Brookline, Mass.: Holy Cross Orthodox Press, 2003.

———, trans. *Theodoret of Cyrus: Commentary on the Letters of St. Paul*. 2 vols. Brookline, Mass.: Holy Cross Orthodox Press, 2002.

———, trans. *Theodoret of Cyrus: Commentary on the Psalms*. 2 vols. FC 101–102. Washington: Catholic University of America Press, 2000–2001.

———, trans. *Theodoret of Cyrus: Commentary on the Song of Songs*. Early Christian Studies 2. Brisbane: Australian Catholic University, 2001.

Jellicoe, Sidney. *The Septuagint and Modern Study*. Oxford: Clarendon, 1968.

Jerome. *Commentariorum in Danielem*. CCSL 75A. S. Hieronymi Presbyteri Opera pars 1, opera exegetica 5. Turnhout: Brepols, 1964

Kahle, Paul. *The Cairo Geniza*. 2nd ed. Oxford: Blackwell, 1959.

Kerrigan, Alexander. *St. Cyril of Alexandria: Interpreter of the Old Testament*. AnBib 2. Rome: Pontifical Biblical Institute, 1952.

Kelly, John N. D. *Early Christian Doctrines*. 5th ed. San Francisco: Harper & Row, 1978.

———. *Golden Mouth: The Story of John Chrysostom: Ascetic, Preacher, Bishop*. Ithaca, N.Y.: Cornell University Press, 1995.

———. *Jerome: His Life, Writings, and Controversies*. London: Duckworth, 1975.

Meier, John P. "Jesus." Pages 1316–28 in *NJBC*. Englewoods Cliffs, N.J.: Prentice Hall, 1990.

Pusey, Philip E., ed. *Sancti Patris Nostri Cyrilli Archiepiscopi Alexandrini in XII Prophetas*. 2 vols. Sancti patris nostri Cyrilli archiepiscopi Alexandrini 1–2. Oxford: Clarendon, 1868. Repr., Brussels: Culture et Civilisation, 1965.

Quasten, Johannes. *Patrology*. 3 vols. Westminster, Md.: Newman, 1950–1960.

Rad, Gerhard von. *Old Testament Theology*. Translated by D. M. G. Stalker. 2 vols. Edinburgh: Oliver & Boyd, 1962–1965.

Schäublin, Christoph. *Untersuchungen zu Methode und Herkunft der antiochenischen Exegese*. Theophaneia: Beiträge zur Religions- und Kirchengeschichte des Altertums 23. Köln: Hanstein, 1974.

Vermes, Geza, trans. *The Complete Dead Sea Scrolls*. New York: Penguin, 1998.

Vosté, Jacques M. "La Chronologie de l'activité littéraire de Théodore de Mopsueste." *RB* 34 (1925): 54–81.

Young, Frances M. *Biblical Exegesis and the Formation of Christian Culture*. Cambridge: Cambridge University Press, 1997.

———. *From Nicaea to Chalcedon: A Guide to the Literature and Its Background*. Philadelphia: Fortress, 1983.

Zincone, Sergio, ed. *Omelie sull'oscurità delle profezie*. Verba Seniorum NS 12. Rome: Edizioni Studium, 1998.

General Index

Index of Biblical Citations

Index of Modern Authors

CPSIA information can be obtained
at www.ICGtesting.com
Printed in the USA
FSOW01n0140160516
20516FS